Ethnic and Racial Composition of Selected Religions, 2002

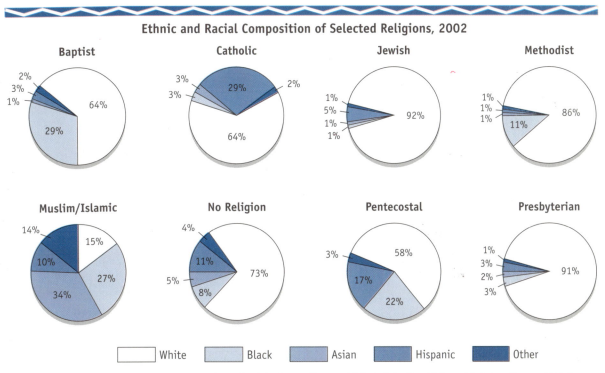

Baptist
- 64%
- 29%
- 1%
- 3%
- 2%

Catholic
- 64%
- 29%
- 3%
- 3%
- 2%

Jewish
- 92%
- 5%
- 1%
- 1%
- 1%

Methodist
- 86%
- 11%
- 1%
- 1%
- 1%

Muslim/Islamic
- 15%
- 27%
- 34%
- 10%
- 14%

No Religion
- 73%
- 8%
- 5%
- 11%
- 4%

Pentecostal
- 58%
- 22%
- 17%
- 3%

Presbyterian
- 91%
- 3%
- 2%
- 3%
- 1%

Legend: White | Black | Asian | Hispanic | Other

Source: Adapted from Egan Mayer, Barry A. Kosmin, and Aniela Keysar, "Race and Ethnic Make-Up of Selected Religious Groups, 2001," *American Religious Identification Survey 2001*, Graduate Center of the City University of New York.

Percent of Undocumented Migrants in U.S. Labor Force: 2005

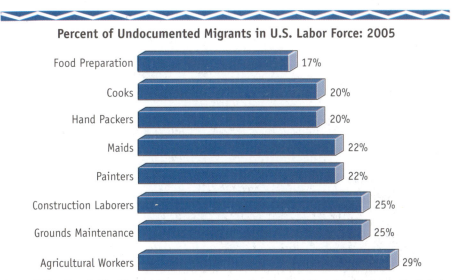

Occupation	Percent
Food Preparation	17%
Cooks	20%
Hand Packers	20%
Maids	22%
Painters	22%
Construction Laborers	25%
Grounds Maintenance	25%
Agricultural Workers	29%

Source: Jeffrey Passel, "The Size and Characteristics of the Unauthorized Migrant Population in the United States," *Pew Hispanic Center Research Report* 61 (2006).

D0162689

Strangers to These Shores

Race and Ethnic Relations in the United States

Ninth Edition

Vincent N. Parrillo
William Paterson University

PEARSON

Boston   New York   San Francisco
Mexico City   Montreal   Toronto   London   Madrid   Munich   Paris
Hong Kong   Singapore   Tokyo   Cape Town   Sydney

Editor-in-Chief: Karen Hanson
Senior Series Editor: Jeff Lasser
Editorial Assistant: Lauren Houlihan
Senior Marketing Manager: Kelly May
Production Supervisor: Beth Houston
Editorial Production Supervisor: NKGraphics/Black Dot Group
Composition and Prepress Buyer: Linda Cox
Manufacturing Buyer: Debbie Rossi
Electronic Composition: NKGraphics
Photo Researcher: Poyee Oster
Cover Administrator: Elena Sidorova

For related titles and support materials, visit our online catalog at www.ablongman.com

Between the time Website information is gathered and then published, it is not unusual for some sites to have closed. Also, the transcription of URLs can result in unintended typographical errors. The publisher would appreciate notification where these errors occur so that they may be corrected in subsequent editions.

ISBN-13: 978-0-205-58557-1   ISBN-10: 0-205-58557-4

Library of Congress Cataloging-in-Publication Data

Parrillo, Vincent N.
    Strangers to these shores : race and ethnic relations in the United States /
Vincent N. Parrillo.—9th ed.
      p. cm.
    Includes bibliographical references and index.
    ISBN-13: 978-0-205-58557-1 (alk.paper)
    ISBN-10: 0-205-58557-4 (alk. paper)
    1. United States—Race relations.   2. United States—Ethnic relations.   I. Title.
E184.A1P33 2009
305.800973—dc22   2008003457

Printed in the United States of America
10 9 8 7 6 5 4 3 2 1   12 11 10 09 08

Credits continue on page 648, which constitutes a continuation of the copyright page.

*To my Italian American father
and my Irish/German American mother*

Brief Contents

Contents

PART 2   European Americans   125

PART 3   Visible Minorities   **209**

PART 4   Other Minorities   **425**

PART **5**   **Contemporary Patterns and Issues**   537

Foreword

*S*trangers to These Shores is a book about diversity in a national community. The geneticists, demographers, social scientists, and ethicists tell us that a diversified population has a better chance than a homogeneous one of adapting to a changing environment. Benjamin Elijah Mays, an esteemed educator and former president of Morehouse College, has declared that no one is strong enough, wise enough, or rich enough to go it alone. And psychologist Howard Gardner has discovered that there are multiple intelligences distributed among human beings and that no single person is extraordinarily smart in all of them. These statements indicate the need for diversity in an effectively functioning society.

Vincent N. Parrillo has presented in this book sketches of the way of life of a variety of minority groups in the United States. A careful analysis of these groups reveals that each makes a unique contribution to the society at large based on the common wisdom of its members. The author dedicates *Strangers to These Shores* to his Italian American father and his Irish/German American mother. Thus, it may be said that this comprehensive volume and the excellent analysis found herein are manifestations of the beneficial effects of diversity in the human heritage of the author.

A common word used in the assessment of this book by several sociologists is *comprehensive*. It has been called a "comprehensive review," a "comprehensive examination," and a "comprehensive treatment" of majority–minority relations in the United States. We are invited to read in the pages that follow the story of a resilient society that is struggling to achieve unity out of diversity and, at the same time, guarantee the right to be different. Truly, there is an increasingly rich diversity among the people in the United States notwithstanding their difficulty in adapting to it.

The multiple cultural groups in this nation come together, conflict with each other, and eventually work out consensus or some other form of adaptation. This book makes available valuable information about the way of life of groups other than our own. It beckons us to participate (if not personally then vicariously) in the customs of these groups.

Robert Park, who taught sociology at the University of Chicago (a predominantly white institution) and Fisk University (a predominantly black institution) several decades ago, described people who understand the way of life of many different kinds of groups as having a wider horizon, keener intelligence, and a more rational point of view. If this is the kind of insight we would like to have, we should stay the course with this book as if it were our magic carpet that will carry us immediately into the unknown culture of many minority groups in this nation. And it will help us become better acquainted with them.

That *Strangers to These Shores* deals with groups rather than individuals is an important feature of this text. It trumps the tendency in this society to focus on individuals only. We forget that the *Brown v. Board of Education of Topeka*

Supreme Court decision that declared segregated public education unconstitutional in the United States was concerned about groups and categories of people as well as individuals. The court decision mentioned "children of the minority," "the plaintiffs," "school authorities," and "white children." This fact suggests that we are not likely to solve the social problems of our time unless our solutions are applicable to groups as well as individuals. Thus, learning about the specific needs and responsibilities of majority and minority groups today may lead us as a nation to a better understanding of how these groups may interact in the future for the public good as we strive to develop a more perfect union.

Of special value in this book are the sociological concepts and theories in Part 1 that are helpful in interpreting and understanding how and why strangers to these shores have adapted to the customs of this country the way they have. Three sociological theories central to an understanding of minority-group adaptations are functionalist, interactionist, and conflict theories. Professor Parrillo has made a major contribution to the study of intergroup relations by using conflict theory to enhance our understanding of race relations, ethnic relations, religious-group relations, and gender relations in a pluralistic society. He tells us that conflict theorists see disequilibrium and change as the norm and, therefore, explore how inequalities generate intergroup antagonisms.

To universalize the discussion on intergroup relations for all kinds of people, Part 4 of this book introduces us to religious minorities, gender issues (especially experienced by women), gay and lesbian people, population groups with disabilities and the elderly also known as senior citizens. This analysis shows how inequality, exploitation, and oppression have hindered people from full access to opportunities of this society because of the groups with which they are affiliated.

Inclusion of groups mentioned above demonstrates that all of us in some stage of our life-course are likely to experience minority or subdominant status in the community power structure because of the group or groups with which we identify. Learning about all sorts of people and their circumstances enhances our emotional intelligence by increasing our empathy for others.

The data in this book indicate that the United States is becoming increasingly a pluralistic nation of all sorts and kinds of minority groups. This trend eventually may include all white people since population projections by the U.S. Census Bureau reported in this book indicate that by the year 2050 people of color and white people will nearly achieve parity in the size of their populations. If these projections are accurate, all of us need to learn how to make a positive adaptation to minority status and understand better how to make the symbiotic relationships between majority and minority groups in our diversified society helpful to everyone and harmful to no one. There is no need to be fearful about trends in demographic data and changing power relationships among groups reported in this book, if during the intervening years all people in majority as well as minority groups are treated in loving, just, and respectful ways.

Charles V. Willie
Graduate School of Education, Harvard University

Preface

$\mathcal{R}$ace and ethnic relations is an exciting, challenging, and dynamic field of study. It touches all of us, directly and indirectly in many ways, and it does so on personal, regional, national, even global levels. Each generation thinks it lives through a unique situation, as shaped by the times or the "peculiarities" of a group's characteristics. In truth, each generation is part of a larger process that includes behavioral patterns inherited from past generations, who also thought their situation was unique.

Intergroup relations change continually, through alternating periods of quiet and turmoil, of entry of new groups of immigrants or refugees, and of problems sporadically arising between native-born racial or ethnic groups within the country. Often we can best understand these changes within the context of discernible, recurring patterns that are influenced by economic, political, psychological, and sociological factors. This is partly what C. Wright Mills meant when he spoke of the intricate connection between the patterns of individual lives and the larger historical context of society, a concept we discuss in Chapter 1.

To understand both the interpersonal dynamics and the larger context of changing intergroup relations—particularly the reality of historical repetitions of behavior—we must use social science theory, research, and analysis. Moreover, we can only truly appreciate a diverse society like the United States, as well as the broader applications of social science, by examining many groups, rather than focusing only on a few groups (as most other college texts that focus on this subject do).

I am gratified by the continued widespread adoptions of *Strangers to These Shores* and the favorable response from colleagues and students throughout the United States, Canada, and Europe. Their helpful comments and suggestions have been incorporated into this ninth edition to make an even better book.

The Organization of This Book

The first four chapters present a conceptual and theoretical overview of the subject area, giving students a basis for examining the experiences of the different minority groups discussed in subsequent chapters. Major sociological perspectives (functionalist, conflict, and interactionist), as well as some middle-range theories, are applied throughout the book, though overall its treatment of topics remains eclectic. Instructors can either follow this approach or emphasize their own theoretical viewpoint, since the book's structure allows for varying applications.

Following a presentation of some introductory concepts in the first chapter—particularly that of the stranger as a social phenomenon and the concept of the Dillingham Flaw—the first group of chapters examines differences in culture, reality perceptions, social class, and power as reasons for intergroup conflict. They also look at the dominant group's varying expectations about how minorities

xvii

should "fit" into its society. Chapters 1 and 2 include coverage of some middle-range conflict and interactionist theories. Chapter 3 explores the dimensions and interrelationships of prejudice and discrimination, and Chapter 4 covers the dominant–minority response patterns so common across different groups and time periods.

Chapters 5 through 14 offer the reader insights into the experiences of a wide array of minority groups. In-depth studies of the cultural orientations and degree of assimilation of each group are not possible, because the intent is to provide a broad comparative scope rather than extensive coverage of only a few groups. Not every racial and ethnic group is discussed, though more than fifty are included to illustrate the diversity of U.S. society. For a more comprehensive examination of any subject or group discussed in this book, the reader should consult the sources listed in the chapter notes and the suggested readings.

Chapter 15 returns to holistic sociological concepts in discussing ethnic consciousness; ethnicity as a social process; current racial and ethnic issues, fears, and reactions; and the various indicators of U.S. diversity in the 21st century.

Special Features of the Text

As in the past, this edition of the book incorporates several features to enhance understanding of the topics. A sociohistorical perspective opens each chapter to the study of specific groups. Preceding a retrospective summary at the end of each chapter is a sociological analysis of the groups' experiences using the functionalist, conflict, and interactionist perspectives. Tables, graphics, and text on social indicators provide clear insights into the socioeconomic status of contemporary minority groups. Most chapters include boxed firsthand accounts by immigrants of their experiences, International Scene boxes with critical thinking questions, boxed summaries of text highlights, and extensive photo, map, and line-art illustrations. Review questions and an annotated bibliography appear at the end of each chapter, along with a list of key terms. At the end of the book, the reader will find an accessible glossary and an appendix giving immigration statistics for the period 1820–2006. I also encourage readers to visit the book's Website at *www.pearsonhighered.com/mysockit* through the access code (packaged free of charge with each book on instructor's request). Here you will find animated maps, links, exercises, and newly released data that all relate directly to each chapter.

What's New in the Ninth Edition

This new edition reflects a number of changes:

First, and most important, is the continuance of our policy to provide a thorough updating to supply the most recent data and information throughout the book and the inclusion of the most current and relevant studies not only in sociology but in many other related fields as well.

Second, this book—often imitated by competitors—has always been the most comprehensive in the field and the leader in including new areas of study, and we continue that proud tradition. For example, in this edition you will find:

- A unique new section on minority-minority relations, with particular emphasis on black–brown relations (Chapter 4);

- A new chapter (Chapter 14) on gays, the elderly, and people with disabilities that not only examines all three groups but also uniquely includes components that illustrate their intersection with race and ethnicity;
- Application of labeling theory to its effect on self-esteem as it relates to the minority pattern of negative self image (Chapter 4);
- Additional insights into the use of diversity training in the corporate world and the military, drawing from the author's own experiences in conducting such programs (Chapter 3);
- A new International Scene box on minority segregation and defiance in France (Chapter 14);
- New key terms such as *macrosocial theories* and *microsocial theories* (Chapter 1); *labeling theory* (Chapter 4); *minority–minority relations* (Chapter 4); *slavery reparations* (Chapter 10); and *1.5 generation* (Chapter 15);
- New profile of the Southern Ute as an economically successful tribe (Chapter 7);
- New section on Muslim Americans confronting discrimination in the post-9/11 era (Chapter 12);
- A new Ethnic Experience box on the double marginality experienced in growing up an Italian American homosexual (Chapter 14);
- A new Minority Experience box on deaf people meeting the challenge of using communications technology (Chapter 14);
- A new Ethnic Experience box on experiencing family transnationalism as a new young immigrant (Chapter 15);
- A new International Scene box on multiculturalism in France (Chapter 15).

Other changes and additions include:

- An update in all chapters of the latest socioeconomic profiles of all racial and ethnic groups not only as text matter, but with maps, charts, tables, and graphics;
- An expanded discussion on the social construction of race and on the distinctions between race and ethnicity (Chapter 1);
- An expanded discussion on the distinction between the Dillingham Flaw and the Thomas Theorem (Chapter 2);
- A repositioning of the three theories of minority integration from Chapter 2 to Chapter 4 to create greater cohesiveness on the theme of intergroup relations;
- An expanded discussion on diversity training programs to include the research on their effectiveness (Chapter 3);
- A renaming of Chapter 4 to "Intergroup Relations" to recognize its inclusion on minority–minority relations as well as dominant–minority relations;
- An expanded discussion on the split-labor-market concept (Chapter 4);
- An expanded discussion about casinos on reservations (Chapter 7);
- Expanded discussion on Asian Indian occupation patterning (Chapter 9);
- Expanded discussion on Iraqi refugees and on Iranian and Iraqi American group identity in the current political climate (Chapter 9);
- Inclusion of arguments for and against slavery reparations (Chapter 10);
- Commentary about racism in the aftermath of Hurricane Katrina (Chapter 10);
- Contrast of the Haitian and Jamaican American communities (Chapter 10);
- Expanded discussion on the Turkish American experience (Chapter 9);

- Commentary on the current socioeconomic status of U.S. Catholics (Chapter 12);
- Expanded discussion of the "hot button" issues of immigration, illegal aliens, and language retention, bolstered by the latest research, data, and public opinion polls (Chapter 15);
- Expanded discussion on interracial dating and marriages (Chapter 15).

Supplementary Materials

For Instructors:

- *Instructor's Manual and Test Bank.* This manual contains learning objectives, chapter summaries, key terms and concepts, suggestions for class activities and media materials, and over 1,500 test questions (multiple choice, true/false, fill-in, short anwer, and essay).
- *Computerized Test Bank.* The printed Test Bank is also available through Allyn & Bacon's computerized testing system, TestGen EQ. This fully networkable test-generating software is available on a multiplatform CD-ROM for Windows and Macintosh. The user-friendly interface allows you to view, edit, and add questions, transfer questions to tests, and print tests in a variety of fonts. Search and sort features allow you to locate questions quickly and to arrange them in whatever order you prefer.
- *PowerPoint Presentation.* These PowerPoint slides feature lecture outlines for every chapter and corresponding artwork from the text.

For Students:

- *Research Navigator.* This research database is available free to students when the text is packaged with the Reseach Navigator Guide for Sociology. Searchable by keyword, it gives students access to thousands of full-text articles from scholarly social science journals and popular magazines and newspapers included in the ContentSelect Research Datebase, as well as a one-year archive of *New York Times* articles.
- *MySocKit.* This electronic supplement offers book-specific learning objectives, chapter summaries, flashcards, and practice tests as well as video clips and activities to aid student learning and comprehension. Also included in MySocKit are Research Navigator and weblinks giving you access to powerful and reliable research material.

Acknowledgments

Many people helped in the writing of this book. A number of students completed exceptional immigrant tape projects; excerpts of their projects appear in Chapters 5 through 14: Eunice Adjei, Bruce Bisciotti, Doris Brown, Michael Carosone, Hermione Cox, Milly Gottlieb, Daniel Kazan, Doreen LaGuardia, David Lenox, Sarah Martinez, Chairath Phaladiganon, Terrence Royful, Michelle Schwartz, Geri Squire, Luba Tkatchov, Leo Uebelein, and Yu-Jie Zeng. Their contributions bring a very human touch to the study of minority peoples.

I would like to thank the following reviewers for their helpful suggestions for this edition: Caron Cates, Sam Houston State University; Mark Hardt, MSU-Billings; James Rodgers, Hawkeye Community College; Regina Silletti,

Owens Community College; Glenn Sims, Glendale Community College; Jeanne Marie Velickovic, San Joaquin Delta College; LaSheila Yates, Southern Illinois University-Carbondale.

I also want to acknowledge my deep appreciation to colleagues who reviewed previous editions and offered useful comments. For the eighth edition: Mark Maier, Chapman University; Russell Hamby, Coker College; David Pilgrim, Ferris State University; Michael P. Perez, California State University-Fullerton; Mary Anne O'Neill, Rollins College; Larry D. Robinson, West Virginia University-Parker; Margo Ramlal-Nankoe, Ithaca College; Christopher Paul Lehman, St. Cloud State Univesity; Kathleen H. Sparrow, University of Lousiana-Lafayette; Furjen Deng, Sam Houston State University.

For the seventh edition: Charles W. Jarrett, Ohio University Southern Campus; Joanne Ardovini-Brooker, Sam Houston State University; Mark Weigand, Metropolitan State College of Denver; Jean Raniseski, Alvin Community College; C. Alison Newby, New Mexico State University.

For the sixth edition: Scott Burcham, University of Memphis; Thomas Shey, Chapman University; and Daniel Rosenbaum, Detroit College of Business.

For the fifth edition: Barbara Candales, Tunxis Community College; Roosevelt Langley, Lakewood Community College; Rick Sheffield, Kenyon College; Gaye Bourne, Central Ohio Technical College; Linda Green, Normandale College; Jeffrey Chin, LeMoyne College; Ron J. Hammond, Utah Valley State College; Kooros Mahmoudi, Northern Arizona University.

For the fourth edition: Racine Butler, East Los Angeles College; Bernardo M. Ferdman, State University of New York-Albany; Garfield A. Jackson, Columbus State Community College; and John P. Myers, Glassboro State College.

For the third edition: Anthony J. Cortese, Colorado State University; Terry Jones, California State University-Hayward; R. Paul Maiden, University of Maryland; Cynthia Rolling, Edgewood College; and Earl Smith, Washington State University.

For the second edition: Margaret Brooks-Terry, Baldwin-Wallace College; Juan L. Gonzalez, Jr., California State University-Hayward; Kathleen M. Handy, Louisiana State University-Shreveport; Maurice Jackson, University of California-Riverside; Christopher Jay Johnson, Northeast Louisiana University; Michael C. LeMay, Frostburg State College; Marios Stephanides, Spalding University; W. Austin Van Pelt, Arapahoe Community College; and Bruce B. Williams, Vanderbilt University.

For the first edition: Nijole V. Benokraitis, University of Baltimore; Phyllis L. Fleming, University of Minnesota-Twin Cities; George Gross, Northern Michigan University; Patrick H. McNamara, University of New Mexico; William H. Martineau, College of William and Mary; Chad Richardson, Pan American University; and Marios Stephanides, Spalding College.

I have also had the good fortune to work with a team at Allyn & Bacon whose competence, cooperation, and dedication have made the production of this edition a most satisfying project. My special thanks go to Jeff Lasser, Series Editor, for signing the project, helping get the work underway, and offering valuable input on the book's features and content. Production Supervisor Beth Houston was an important and helpful liaison in providing me with needed information and materials. Rebecca Dodson of the Black Dot Group proved herself the consummate professional in guiding the book through production and an early publication date. Carla Breidenbach was an excellent copyeditor and provided helpful suggestions that I deeply appreciate. I also thank all the other members of the Allyn & Bacon team for their collective efforts in developing, publishing, and distributing this book.

I am especially grateful to my friend and colleague Charles V. Willie for writing the foreword to this and the previous edition. My thanks also go to other friends and colleagues: Rubén Rumbaut for writing the forewords to the sixth and seventh editions; Peter I. Rose for those in the fourth and fifth editions; and the late Stanford M. Lyman for those in the second and third editions, as well as for his guidance in the development of the first edition.

Finally, I want to acknowledge my gratitude to my wife, Beth, for her support and to my children, Chrysti, Cara, Beverley, and Elizabeth, and grandchildren Jennifer and John, for the joy they bring to my life.

Vincent N. Parrillo
William Paterson University
Wayne, New Jersey 07470
E-mail: *parrillov@wpunj.edu*

About the Author

Born and raised in Paterson, New Jersey, Vincent N. Parrillo experienced multiculturalism early as the son of a second-generation Italian American father and Irish/German American mother. He grew up in an ethnically diverse neighborhood, developing friendships and teenage romances with second- and third-generation Dutch, German, Italian, and Polish Americans. As he grew older, he developed other friendships that frequently crossed racial and religious lines.

Professor Parrillo came to the field of sociology after first completing a bachelor's degree in business management and a master's degree in English. After teaching high school English and then serving as a college administrator, he took his first sociology course when he began doctoral studies at Rutgers University. Inspired by a discipline that scientifically investigates social issues, he changed his major and completed his degree in sociology.

Leaving his administrative post but staying at William Paterson University, Prof. Parrillo has since taught sociology for more than 30 years. He has lectured throughout the United States, Canada, and Europe and has regularly conducted diversity leadership programs for the military and large corporations. His keynote address at a bilingual educators' conference was published in *Vital Speeches of the Day,* which normally contains only speeches by national political leaders and heads of corporations and organizations.

Prof. Parrillo was a Fulbright Scholar in the Czech Republic and Scholar-in-Residence at the University of Pisa. He was the keynote speaker at international conferences in Belgium, Canada, Denmark, Germany, Italy, Poland, and Sweden. He has met with government leaders, nongovernment agency leaders, law enforcement officials, and educators in more than a dozen countries as a consultant on immigration policy, hate crimes, and multicultural education. He has done on-air interviews with *Radio Free Europe* and *Voice of America,* appeared on national Canadian television, and been interviewed by numerous Canadian and European reporters.

Prof. Parrillo's ventures into U.S. media include writing, narrating, and producing two PBS award-winning documentaries, *Ellis Island: Gateway to America* and *Smokestacks and Steeples: A Portrait of Paterson.* Contacted by reporters across the nation for his views on race and ethnic relations, he has been quoted in dozens of newspapers, including the *Chicago Sun-Times, Cincinnati Inquirer, Houston Chronicle, Hartford Courant, Omaha World-Herald, Orlando Sentinel,* and *Virginian Pilot.* He has appeared on numerous U.S. radio and television programs.

Prof. Parrillo is also the author of *Understanding Race and Ethnic Relations,* third edition (Allyn & Bacon), *Contemporary Social Problems,* sixth edition (Allyn & Bacon), *Cities and Urban Life,* fourth edition (with John Macionis), *Diversity in America,* third edition, and *Rethinking Today's Minorities.* His articles and book reviews have appeared in journals such as *The Social Science Journal, Sociological Forum, Social Forces, Journal of Comparative Family*

Studies, Journal of American Ethnic History, and the *Encyclopedia of American Immigration.* He is General Editor of the *Encyclopedia of Social Problems* for Sage Publications. Several of his books and articles have been translated into other languages, including Chinese, Czech, Danish, German, Italian, Japanese, Polish, Romanian, and Swedish.

An active participant in various capacities throughout the years in the American Sociological Association and Eastern Sociological Society, Prof. Parrillo has been listed in *Who's Who in International Education, Outstanding Educators of America, American Men and Women of Science,* and *Who's Who in the East.* In 2004, he received the Award for Excellence in Scholarship from William Paterson University. In March 2005, the Eastern Sociological Society named him its Robin M. Williams, Jr. Distinguished Lecturer for 2005–2006, and elected him as its vice president for 2008–2009.

PART 1

Sociological Framework

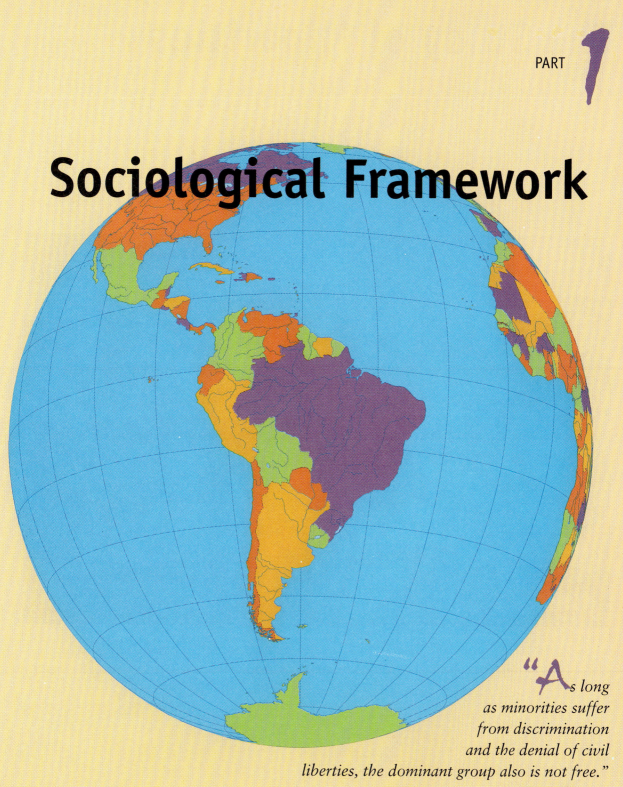

PART

"*As long
as minorities suffer
from discrimination
and the denial of civil
liberties, the dominant group also is not free.*"
Louis Wirth, 1945

The Study of Minorities

We pride ourselves on being a nation of immigrants. Many still call the United States a great melting pot where people of all races, religions, and nationalities come to be free and to improve their lives. Certainly, a great number of immigrants offer living testimony to that ideal; their enthusiasm for their adopted country is evident in countless interviews, some of which you will read in this book. As college students, regardless of how recently or long ago your family immigrated to the United States, most of you also provide evidence of the American Dream of freedom of choice, economic opportunity, and upward mobility.

Yet beneath the Fourth of July speeches, the nation's absorption of diverse peoples over the years, and the numerous success stories lies a disquieting truth. Native-born Americans have not always welcomed newcomers with open arms; indeed, they have often responded with overt acts of discrimination, ranging from avoidance to violence and murder. The dominant group's treatment of native-born blacks and Native Americans disturbingly illustrates the persistence of subjugation and entrenched inequality. Today, we continue to face serious problems in attitudes toward and treatment of Native Americans on reservations, poor blacks in urban ghettos, large concentrations of recent Asian and Hispanic immigrants, and Arab and Muslim Americans struggling to gain acceptance. For some, the American Dream becomes a reality; for others, blocked opportunities create an American nightmare.

Interethnic tensions and hostilities within a nation's borders are a worldwide phenomenon dating from thousands of years ago to the present. In the past few years, we have witnessed the horror of terrorist killings in Afghanistan, Indonesia, Iraq, the Philippines, Spain, Turkey, and the United States, to mention just a few. Religious factions in India, the Middle East, and Northern Ireland still harbor such animosity toward one another that violence continues to erupt sporadically. Since 2003, over 200,000 people have died in Darfur, a vast region in the west of Sudan. In the 1990s, the Orthodox Christian Serbs killed or expelled Bosnia Muslims in the name of "ethnic cleansing;" Serbs killed or expelled ethnic Albanians from Kosovo, prompting military action by NATO; and tribal warfare between the Hutu and Tutsi in Rwanda led to the massacre of hundreds of thousands. In the 1980s, a bloody war

3

raged among the Hausa, Ibo, and Yoruba tribes of Nigeria, and Saddam Hussein's regime killed hundreds of Kurds with poison gas in Iraq. A few years earlier, appalling bloodbaths among Kampucheans (Cambodians), Chinese, Laotians, and Vietnamese horrified the world. Elsewhere, other minorities, such as West Indians in Britain, Algerians in France, Turks in Germany, Roma (Gypsies) in the Czech Republic, and Palestinians in Israel, have encountered prejudice, discrimination, and occasional physical attacks. Within any society, groupings of people by race, religion, tribe, culture, or lifestyle can generate prejudices, tensions, and sporadic outbursts of violence.

Individuals of the dominant group usually absolve themselves of blame for a minority group's low status and problems, ascribing these instead to specific flaws they perceive within the group itself (e.g., slowness in learning the main language of the country or supposed lack of an accepted work ethic). Sociologists, however, note distinct patterns of interaction among different groups that transcend national boundaries, specific periods, or group idiosyncrasies. Opinions may vary as to the causes of these patterns of behavior, but a consensus does exist about their presence.

THE STRANGER AS A SOCIAL PHENOMENON

To understand intergroup relations, we must recognize that differences among various peoples cause each group to look on other groups as strangers. Among isolated peoples, the arrival of a stranger has always been a momentous occasion, often eliciting strong emotional responses. Reactions might range from warm hospitality to conciliatory or protective ceremonies to hostile acts. In an urbanized and mobile society, the stranger still evokes similar responses. From the Tiwi of northern Australia, who consistently killed intruders, to the nativists of any country or time, who continually strive to keep out "undesirable elements," the underlying premise is the same: The outsiders are not good enough to share the land and resources with the "chosen people" already there.

Similarity and Attraction

At least since Aristotle commented, "We like those who resemble us, and are engaged in the same pursuits," social observers have been aware of the similarity–attraction relationship.[1] Numerous studies have explored the extent to which a person likes others because of similar attitudes, values, beliefs, social status, or physical appearance. Examining the development of attraction among people who are initially strangers to one another, an impressive number of these studies have found a positive relationship between the similarity of two people and their liking for each other. Most significantly, the findings show that people's perception of similarity between themselves is a more powerful determinant than actual similarity.[2] Cross-cultural studies also support this conclusion.[3] Considerable evidence exists showing greater human receptivity to strangers who are perceived as similar than to those who are perceived as different.

Social Distance

One excellent technique for evaluating how perceptions of similarity attract closer interaction patterns consists of ranking **social distance.** Devised by Emory Bogardus in 1926, this measurement device has been used repeatedly over the years.[4] In five comparable studies spanning 50 years, researchers obtained responses from college students aged 18 to 35, about 10 percent of whom were black. The students selected the degree of social closeness or distance personally acceptable to members of a particular group.

These five national surveys measured the students' preferences among 30 groups, most of them Europeans but also including American Indians, Canadians, black Americans, and six Asian groups (Asian Indians, Chinese, Filipinos, Japanese, Japanese Americans, and Koreans). Some fluctuation occurred over the 50-year span of these surveys, most notably blacks moving upward from near the bottom to the middle. Generally, the distribution showed white Americans, Canadians, and northern and western Europeans in the top third, with southern, central, and eastern Europeans in the middle third, and racial minorities in the bottom third.

With a few exceptions, the relative consistent positioning of response patterns illustrated the similarity–attraction relationship. Italians moved up steadily, becoming the first group not from northwestern Europe to break into the top 10. The leap upward by blacks was even more dramatic, from near the bottom to the midpoint. International politics or war usually caused groups to drop: Germans, Italians, and Japanese in 1946 and Russians after 1946 (the era of the Cold War, McCarthyism, and the Vietnam War).[5] However, the political changes that Russia underwent in the 1990s enabled Russians to rise to 14th place in a smaller 1993 study.[6]

In 2001, I updated the list of groups and conducted a larger national study.[7] I eliminated mostly homogenized groups (e.g., Armenians, Czechs, Finns, Norwegians, Scots, and Swedes) and added various Asian, Hispanic, and West

With women and/or people of color now constituting three-fourths of new workers entering the U.S. labor force, such diversity poses challenges to managers and employees alike. Cultural and gender differences usually affect social distances among workers, which in turn could impact on employee morale, motivation, and teamwork.

Indian groups. In this new national study, conducted in the six weeks following the terrorist attacks of 9/11, the available choices were the same as in previous studies.

1. Would accept marrying into my family (1 point)
2. Would accept as a personal friend in my social circle (2 points)
3. Would accept as a neighbor on my street (3 points)
4. Would work in the same office (4 points)
5. Would only have as speaking acquaintances (5 points)
6. Would only have as visitors to my country (6 points)
7. Would bar from entering my country (7 points)

As expected, nonethnic whites remained in the top position as the most accepted, with other top 10 slots filled by Canadians, British, Irish, French, Germans, and Dutch, essentially continuing a 70-year pattern. What is particularly striking about the new listing, however, is the dramatic rise of African Americans. By ranking ninth, they broke the racial barrier in entering the top sector and placing ahead of other white ethnic groups. The rise of Italians into the second position (ahead of the previously dominating English, Canadians, and French) and the movement of Greeks into the seventh position were other significant changes. However, only one-hundredth of a point separated a group from the next ranked group in positions 13 through 25. Therefore, in the middle part of the list in Table 1.1, the exact placement of a group in relation to those near it should not be given much importance because these rankings may be the result of sampling variability and close scores.

Although this analysis is not directly comparable with the last previous study in 1977 (see results in Table 1.1) because of changes in the list of groups, some comparisons are still possible and the findings are encouraging in many ways. The spread in social distance—despite (1) increased diversity in society, (2) a revised list reflecting that demographic reality, and (3) increased diversity among respondents—continues to shrink. The 2001 overall mean score of 1.44 is significantly lower than the 1977 overall mean score of 1.93, as is the spread in social distance of 0.87 compared to 1.38. Despite the removal of more assimilated groups and the addition of less assimilated groups to the list, the downward trend in both indicators of social distance continued. These results suggest a growing level of acceptance of diverse groups among college students, even though many are recent arrivals, racial minorities, and/or from non-Western lands.

Remarkably, despite media reports of sporadic instances in the September 11, 2001, aftermath of group blame and hate crimes against those identified (sometimes erroneously) as Arabs or Muslims, that mindset did not extend to most respondents in this survey. Although relegating Muslims and Arabs to the bottom, respondents nevertheless gave them lower (i.e., more socially acceptable) mean scores than those received by 17 of the 30 groups in the 1977 study. Their distinction, between the ethnicity of the terrorists and others who were Arabs and/or Muslims, resulted in much lower scores than given to past low-ranked groups, which is indeed an impressive finding.

The ranking of Muslims and Arabs in the last two places is hardly surprising as a repercussion of the terrorist attacks, but how do we explain their comparatively low social distance nonetheless? Perhaps the answer is the same as for the strong findings for African Americans and other groups as well. This study may well bear witness to a "unity syndrome," the coalescing of various groups against a common enemy who attacked us. Only time will tell how lasting this new spirit

TABLE 1.1 U.S. Social Distance Changes, 1977 and 2001

1977		2001	
1. Americans (U.S. white)	1.25	1. Americans (U.S. white)	1.07
2. English	1.39	2. Italians	1.15
3. Canadians	1.42	3. Canadians	1.20
4. French	1.58	4. British	1.23
5. Italians	1.65	5. Irish	1.24
6. Swedish	1.68	6. French	1.28
7. Irish	1.69	7. Greeks	1.32
8. Hollanders	1.83	8. Germans	1.33
9. Scots	1.83	9. African Americans	1.34
10. Indians (American)	1.84	10. Dutch	1.35
11. Germans	1.87	11. Jews	1.38
12. Norwegians	1.93	12. Indians (American)	1.40
13. Spanish	1.98	13. Africans	1.43
14. Finns	2.00	14. Polish	1.44
15. Jews	2.01	15. Other Hispanic/Latino	1.45
16. Greeks	2.02	16. Filipino	1.46
17. Negroes	2.03	17. Chinese	1.47
18. Poles	2.11	18. Puerto Ricans	1.48
19. Mexican Americans	2.17	19. Jamaicans	1.49
20. Japanese Americans	2.18	20. Russians	1.50
21. Armenians	2.20	21. Dominicans	1.51
22. Czechs	2.23	22. Japanese	1.52
23. Chinese	2.29	23. Cubans	1.53
24. Filipinos	2.31	24. Koreans	1.54
25. Japanese	2.38	25. Mexicans	1.55
26. Mexicans	2.40	26. Indians (from India)	1.60
27. Turks	2.55	27. Haitians	1.63
28. Indians (from India)	2.55	28. Vietnamese	1.69
29. Russians	2.57	29. Muslims	1.88
30. Koreans	2.63	30. Arabs	1.94
Arithmetic mean of 44,640 racial reactions:	1.93	Arithmetic mean of 126,053 racial reactions:	1.44
Spread in distance:	1.38	Spread in distance:	0.87

Source: Carolyn A. Owen, Howard C. Eisner, and Thomas R. McFaul, "A Half-Century of Social Distance Research: National Replication of the Bogardus Studies," *Sociology and Social Research* 66 (October 1981): 89; Vincent N. Parrillo and Christopher Donoghue, "Updating the Bogardus Social Distance Studies: A New National Study," *The Social Science Journal* 42 (2005).

is, both in the bottom ranking of Muslims and Arabs and in the low social distance scores for all groups. This study captures social acceptance of groups only at a given moment in time. It is neither conclusive nor yet indicative of new patterns. Future social distance studies incorporating the new groups will ideally give a clearer picture of how tolerant Americans are in their ever-growing multiracial, multicultural society.

Sometimes the social distance maintained between minority groups is greater than that preserved between each minority and the dominant group.

For example, a 1989 study of 708 Anglos, 249 blacks, and 256 Mexican Americans in Texas found blacks and Mexican Americans more accepting of Anglos than of each other. However, higher-status members (those having more education and higher incomes) and youths of all three groups were generally more accepting of contact with the outgroup minority than were lower-status group members.[8]

Social distance affects many types of choices and actions, one of which is living with diverse others, whether on a college campus or in a neighborhood. A 2005 study found that, despite a public university's efforts, no reduction of social distance regarding roommates or dating occurred as its students progressed toward degree completion. White students showed greater social distance with blacks than with Hispanics, although cross-racial friendships did reduce the level of social distance.[9] Another 2005 study of the Toronto metropolitan area found that understanding social distance among groups proved more helpful in understanding residential segregation than just examining broad racial and pan-ethnic classifications.[10] Using simulation analyses, Mark Fossett (2006) reported that the persistence of segregation in recent decades results from a combination of discrimination, social distance, and status dynamics.[11]

Perceptions

By definition, the stranger is not only an outsider, but also someone different and personally unknown. People perceive strangers primarily through **categoric knowing**—the classification of others on the basis of limited information obtained visually and perhaps verbally.[12] People make judgments and generalizations on the basis of scanty information, confusing an individual's characteristics with typical group-member characteristics. For instance, if a visiting Swede asks for tea rather than coffee, the host may incorrectly conclude that all Swedes dislike coffee.

Native-born Americans have in the past perceived immigrants—first-generation Americans of different racial and ethnic groups—to be a particular kind of stranger: one who intended to stay. Eventually, the presence of immigrants became less of a novelty; then fear, suspicion, and distrust often replaced the natives' initial curiosity. The strangers remained strangers as each group sought its own kind for personal interaction.

The role of a stranger can be analyzed regardless of the particular period in history. Georg Simmel (1858–1918) theorized that strangers represent both *nearness,* because they are physically close, and *remoteness,* because they react differently to the immediate situation and have different values and ways of doing things.[13] The stranger is both inside and outside: physically present and participating but also outside the situation as a result of being from another place.

The natives perceive the stranger in an abstract, typified way, and so the individual becomes the *totality,* or stereotype, of the group. As someone unknown or unfamiliar, as someone not understood, the stranger is seen only in generalized terms, as a representative member of a "different" group. Of interest to Simmel was how the numbers of strangers influence the dynamics of intergroup relations.

In contrast, the stranger perceives the natives in concrete, individual terms. Simmel suggested that strangers have a higher degree of objectivity about the natives because the strangers' geographic mobility reflects mobility in their minds as well. The stranger is free from indigenous habit, piety, and precedent. Furthermore, because strangers do not participate fully in society, they have a certain mental detachment, causing them to see things more objectively.

Interactions

Simmel approached the role of the stranger through an analysis of the formal structures of life. In contrast, Alfred Schutz—himself an immigrant to the United States—analyzed the stranger as lacking "intersubjective understanding."[14] By this he meant that people from the same social world mutually "know" the language (including slang), customs, beliefs, symbols, and everyday behavior patterns that the stranger usually does not.

For the native, then, every social situation is a coming together not only of roles and identities but also of shared realities—the intersubjective structure of consciousness. What is taken for granted by the native is problematic to the stranger. In a familiar world, people live through the day by responding to the daily routine without questions or reflection. To strangers, however, every situation is new and is therefore experienced as a crisis (see The International Scene box).

Strangers experience a "lack of historicity"—a lack of the shared memory of those with whom they live. Human beings who interact together over a period of time "grow old together"; strangers, however, are "young," being newcomers, and they experience at least an approximation of the freshness of childhood. They

The International Scene

Enhancing German Interaction with Americans

DS International, an organization that runs exchange programs, distributed a pamphlet, "An Information Guide for Germans on American Culture," to Germans working as interns in U.S. companies. The pamphlet was based on previous German interns' experiences and on their interviews with other colleagues; its intent was to provide insights into U.S. culture to ease German interactions with Americans. Here are some examples:

- Americans say "Hello" or "How are you?" when they see each other. "How are you?" is like "Hello." A long answer is not expected; just answer, "Thank you, fine. How are you?"
- Using deodorant is a must.
- American women usually shave their legs and under their arms. Women who don't like to do this should consider wearing clothes that cover these areas.
- Expect to be treated like all other Americans. You won't receive special treatment because you are a German. Try not to talk with other Germans in German if Americans are around; this could make them feel uncomfortable.
- Please consider the differences in verbal communication styles between Americans and Germans. The typical German speaking style sounds abrupt and rude to

Americans. Keep this in mind when talking to Americans.
- Be polite. Use words like "please" and "thank you." It is better to use these too often than not enough. Also, be conscious of your voice and the expression on your face. Your voice should be friendly, and you should wear a smile. Don't be confused by the friendliness and easygoing, nonexcitable nature of the people. They are deliberate, think independently, and do things their own way. Americans are proud of their independence.
- Keep yourself out of any discussions at work about race, sex, religion, or politics. Be open-minded; don't make judgments based on past experiences in Germany.
- Be aware that there are a lot of different cultures in the United States. There are also many different churches, which mean a great deal to their members. Don't be quick to judge these cultures; this could hurt people's feelings.
- Do it the American way, and try to intermingle with the Americans. Think positive.

Critical Thinking Question: What guidelines for overcoming ethnocentrism should Americans follow when traveling to or working in other countries?

are aware of things that go unnoticed by the natives, such as the natives' customs, social institutions, appearance, and lifestyle. Also existing within the natives' taken-for-granted world are social constructions of race and ethnicity that, to the stranger, are new realities. Race as a social construct can be illustrated by the case of Barack Obama. To many whites, he is a black man. With a longstanding rigid racial classification system in the United States of white or nonwhite, perhaps this perception is understandable. Obama, however, has a black Kenyan father and a white American mother, so he is actually biracial. This, however, has led many blacks to question if he is "black enough" to be their "authentic" representative.[15] Within the racial divide, both blacks and whites are often strangers to each other, perceiving reality through different social constructs.

Sometimes the stranger may be made the comical butt of jokes because of unfamiliarity with the everyday routine of life in the new setting. In time, however, strangers take on the natives' perspective; the strangers' consciousness decreases because the freshness of their perceptions is lost. At the same time, the natives' **abstract typifications** about the strangers become more concrete through social interaction. As Schutz said, "The vacant frames become occupied by vivid experiences." As acculturation takes place, the native begins to view the stranger more concretely, and the stranger becomes less questioning about daily activities. Use of the term *naturalized citizen* takes on a curious connotation when examined from this perspective because it implies that people are in some way odd or unnatural until they have acquired the characteristics of the natives.

As its title suggests, this book is about the many strangers who came—and are still coming—to the United States in search of a better life. Through an examination of sociological theory and the experiences of many racial and ethnic groups, the story of how the stranger perceives the society and is received by it continually will be retold. The adjustment from stranger to neighbor may be viewed as movement along a continuum; however, this continuum is not frictionless, and assimilation is not inevitable. Rather, it is the process of social interaction among different groups of people.

Before we look at the main sociological perspectives, let us clarify three terms used extensively in this book. **Migration** is the general term that refers to the movement of people into and out of a specified area, which could either be within a country or from one country to another. Examples are the migration of people from one continent to another or the migration of U.S. blacks from the South to the North. **Emigration** is a narrower term that refers to the movement of people *out of* a country to settle in another, while **immigration** refers to the movement of people *into* a new country to become permanent residents. So we could speak, for example, of the *emigration* of people from Peru and their *immigration* into the United States. To the sending country, they are emigrants, whereas to the receiving country, they are immigrants.

MINORITY GROUPS

Although the term *group* is commonly used to refer collectively to a distinct or definable racial or ethnic people, it is a problematic word. In its sociological usage, **group** usually connotes a small, closely interacting set of persons. The term *minorities* sometimes refers to aggregates of millions of persons—clearly a size even larger than a **secondary group,** which consists of people who interact on an impersonal or limited emotional basis for some practical or specific purpose. Nonetheless, groups and group identity are important components of race and ethnic relations, and, with the preceding caveat in mind, I will use the term *group* throughout this book when referring to racial and ethnic groupings.

Development of a Definition

Sociologists use the term **minority group** not to designate a group's numerical representation but to indicate its relative power and status in a society. The term was first used in the World War I peace treaties to protect approximately 22 million of 110 million people in east central Europe, but it was most frequently used as a description of biological features or national traits. Donald Young in 1932 thus observed that Americans make distinctions among people according to race and national origin.[16]

Louis Wirth expanded Young's original conception of minority groups to include the consequences of those distinctions: group consciousness and differential treatment.[17] Wirth's contribution marked two important turning points in sociological inquiry. First, by broadening the definition of *minority group* to encompass any physical or cultural trait instead of only race or national origin, Wirth enlarged the range of variables to include the aged, people with disabilities, members of various religions or sects, and groups with unconventional lifestyles. Second, his emphasis on the social consequences of minority status leads to a focus on prejudice, discrimination, and oppression. Not everyone agrees with this approach. Richard Schermerhorn, for example, notes that this "victimological"

This joyful event—a Hindu parade in Schuylkill, Pennsylvania—illustrates how certain characteristics help define a minority group. Easily identifiable by their facial features and distinctive clothing, these Asian Indians share their sense of peoplehood through a cultural celebration of their religion and through social interaction.

approach does not adequately explain the similarities and differences among groups or analyze relationships between majority and minority groups.[18]

A third attempt to define minority groups rests on examining relationships between groups in terms of each group's position in the social hierarchy.[19] This approach stresses a group's social power, which may vary from one country to another, as, for example, does that of the Jews in Russia and in Israel. The emphasis on stratification instead of population size explains situations in which a relatively small group subjugates a larger number of people (e.g., the European colonization of African and Asian populations).

Minority-Group Characteristics

As social scientists reached some consensus on a definition of minority groups, anthropologists Charles Wagley and Marvin Harris identified five characteristics shared by minorities worldwide:

1. The group receives unequal treatment as a group.
2. The group is easily identifiable because of distinguishing physical or cultural characteristics that are held in low esteem.
3. The group feels a sense of group identity, that each of them shares something in common with other members.
4. Membership in the minority group has **ascribed status:** one is born into it.
5. Group members practice **endogamy:** they tend to marry within their group, either by choice or by necessity, because of their social isolation.[20]

In our discussion of racial and ethnic minorities, these five features provide helpful guidelines. However, we should also understand that the last two characteristics do not apply to certain other types of minority groups: Women obviously do not fit the last category (causing some controversy over whether or not they are a minority group) nor necessarily do the aged or people with disabilities. One is not born old, and people with disabilities are not always born that way.

Because our discussion of various minority groups rests on their subordination to a more powerful, although not necessarily larger group, we will use the term **dominant group** when referring to a minority group's relationships with the rest of society. Another consideration is that a person may be a member of both dominant and minority groups in different categories. For example, an American Roman Catholic who is white belongs to a prominent religious minority group but also is a member of the racially dominant group.

RACIAL AND ETHNIC GROUPS

Race is a categorization in which a large number of people sharing visible biological characteristics regard themselves or are regarded by others as a single group on that basis. Race may seem at first glance an easy way to group people, but it is not. The more than 6 billion humans inhabiting this planet exhibit a wide range of physical differences in body build, hair texture, facial features, and skin color. Centuries of migration, conquest, intermarriage, and evolutionary physical adaptation to the environment have caused these varieties. Anthropologists have attempted racial categorizations ranging from three to more than a hundred.

Some, such as Ashley Montagu, even argue that only one race exists—the human race.[21] Just as anthropologists apply different interpretations to biological groupings, so do most people. It is by examining these social interpretations that sociologists attempt to analyze and explain racial prejudice.

The social construction of race varies by culture and in history. The United States, for example has had a rigid racial classification ("white" and "nonwhite"), unlike Latin America, which acknowledges various gradations of race, reflecting the multiracial heritage of the people. U.S. purists have even subscribed to the "one-drop theory," that someone with even a tiny portion of nonwhite ancestry should be classified as black. However, it's not just outsider classification. Sometimes people will identify themselves as, say, black or Native American, when their DNA reveals a higher percentage of a different race. Racial classifications are thus often arbitrary, with individuals or society placing undue emphasis on race. Indeed, some geneticists argue that race is a meaningless concept, that far more genetic variation exists within races than between them, and that many racial traits overlap without distinct boundaries.[22] Furthermore, with more than 3 million people of mixed racial parentage living in the United States, many social scientists have called for the "deconstruction of race," arguing against the artificial boundaries that promote racial prejudice.[23]

Racism may be defined as linking the biological conditions of a human organism with alleged sociocultural capabilities and behavior to assert the superiority of one race. When people believe that one race is superior to another because of economic advantages or specific achievements, racist thinking prevails. The subordinate group experiences prejudice and discrimination, which the dominant group justifies by reference to such invidious perceptions. In this book, we will discuss how not only blacks but also Native Americans, Asians, Hispanics, and even white southern Europeans have encountered hostility because of social categorizations of their abilities based simply on their physical appearance.

Although I discuss racism more fully in Chapters 6 and 10, I should note that racism is a human invention, a good example of the social construction of reality. It slowly evolved out of efforts to sort humans into distinctive categories based on skin color and facial features. These developments included philosophers such as Immanuel Kant (1724–1804) offering biological distinctions of the "races of mankind" and 19th-century social Darwinists seeing human society as a "survival of the fittest" in which the naturally superior will win out. Physical anthropologists saw these groups distinguished by physical characteristics as falling into a hierarchy, with white Europeans (like themselves) at the top and blacks at the bottom, as rationalized by their dark color, their supposedly primitive culture, and especially because Europeans then knew of blacks as slaves. It was in this pseudoscientific context that racism emerged as an ideology. Although most modern scientists and social scientists have debunked the "scientific" claims of racism, as later discussed, racist ideologies still attract many followers.[24]

While *race* deals with visible physical characteristics, **ethnicity** goes beyond a simple racial similarity to encompass shared cultural traits and/or national origin. People may be of the same race but different in language and cultural practices, such as Africans, Haitians, and Jamaicans. Conversely, people may be of different races but still be members of the same ethnic group, such as Hispanics. The complexities of categorizing social groups by ethnicity don't stop there. People may be members of the same race and large ethnic group (such as the Belgians) but speak different languages (Dutch, French, or German) and so also may be members of different subcultural ethnic groups. Moreover, if we add the element of social class, we will find even more differences with even these subcultural ethnic groups.

Religion is another determinant of ethnic group composition. Sometimes religion and national origin seem like dual attributes of ethnicity, such as Irish and Italian Catholics (although not all Irish or Italians are Catholic). Sometimes, too, what appear to be these dual attributes—Arab Muslims, for example—are not so; for example, the majority of Arabs in the United States are Christians, with one-third of the total Arab American population being Catholic.[25] Religion most commonly links with other elements of ethnicity—national origin, culture, language—among immigrant groups. Even here, though, we should refrain from generalizing about all members of any national origin group (or any racial group) because of the extensive differences within such groups.

The word *race* often is incorrectly used as a social rather than a biological concept. Thus, the British and Japanese often are classified as races, as are Hindus, Latins, Aryans, Gypsies, Arabs, Basques, and Jews.[26] Many people— even sociologists, anthropologists, and psychologists—use *race* in a general sense that includes racial and ethnic groups, thereby giving the term both a biological and a social meaning. In recent decades, *ethnic group* has been used more frequently to include the three elements of race, religion, and national origin.[27] Such varied use of these terms results in endless confusion, for racial distinctions are socially defined categories based on physical distinctions. Some groups, such as African Americans, were once defined on racial grounds but emerged as ethnocultural groups. Various ethnic groups often get lumped together in much broader racial categories; for example, Asians and Native Americans.

In this book, the word *race* refers to the common social distinctions made on the basis of physical appearance. The term *ethnic group* refers only to social groupings that the dominant group considers unique because of religious, linguistic, or cultural characteristics. We will use both terms in discussing groups whose racial and ethnic characteristics overlap.

ETHNOCENTRISM

Understanding the concept of the stranger is important to understanding **ethnocentrism**—a "view of things in which one's own group is the center of everything, and all others are scaled and rated with reference to it."[28] *Ethnocentrism* thus refers to people's tendency to identify with their own ethnic or national group as a means of fulfilling their needs for group belongingness and security. (The word derives from two Greek words: *ethnos* ["nation"] and *kentron* ["center"].) As a result of ethnocentrism, people usually view their own cultural values as somehow more real and, therefore, superior to those of other groups, and so they prefer their own way of doing things. Unfortunately for human relations, such ethnocentric thought often negatively affects attitudes toward, and emotions about, those perceived as different.

Fortunately, social scientists are making increasing numbers of people aware of a more enlightened and positive alternative to ethnocentrism: **cultural relativism** in which beliefs and behavior are evaluated in the context of that culture. The more widespread this perspective becomes known and applied, the more there will be intergroup understanding and mutual acceptance.

Sociologists define an **ingroup** as a group to which individuals belong and feel loyal; thus, everyone—whether a member of a majority group or a minority group—is part of some ingroup. An **outgroup** consists of all people who are not members of one's ingroup. Studying majority groups as ingroups helps us understand their reactions to strangers of another race or culture entering their society. Conversely, considering minority groups as ingroups enables us to understand their efforts to maintain their ethnic identity and solidarity in the midst of the dominant culture.

From European social psychologists comes one of the more promising explanations for ingroup favoritism. **Social identity theory** holds that ingroup members almost automatically think of their group as better than outgroups because doing so enhances their own social status or social identity and thus raises the value of their personal identity or self-image.[29]

Ample evidence exists about people from past civilizations who regarded other cultures as inferior, incorrect, or immoral. This assumption that *we* are better than *they* generally results in outgroups becoming objects of ridicule, contempt, or hatred. Such attitudes may lead to stereotyping, prejudice, discrimination, and even violence. What actually occurs depends on many factors, including structural and economic conditions; these factors will be discussed in subsequent chapters.

Despite its ethnocentric beliefs, the ingroup does not always view the outgroup as inferior. In numerous documented cases, groups have retained their values and standards while recognizing the superiority of another group in specific areas.[30] Moreover, countless people reject their own ingroup by becoming "voluntary exiles, expatriates, outgroup emulators, social climbers, renegades, and traitors."[31] An outgroup may become a positive **reference group**—that is, it may serve as an exemplary model—if members of the ingroup perceive it as having a conspicuous advantage over their own group in terms of survival or adaptation to the environment, success in warfare, a stronger political structure, greater wealth, or higher occupational status.[32]

Ethnocentrism is thus an important factor in determining minority-group status in society; but, because of many variations in intergroup relations, it alone cannot explain the causes of prejudice. For example, majority-group members may view minority groups with suspicion, but not all minority groups become the targets of extreme prejudice and discrimination.

Some social-conflict theorists argue that when the ingroup perceives the outgroup as a serious threat competing for scarce resources, the ingroup reacts with increased solidarity and ethnocentrism and exhibits prejudice, discrimination, and hostility toward the outgroup.[33] According to this view, the degree of this hostility depends on several economic and geographic considerations. It would thus appear that ethnocentrism leads to negative consequences when the ingroup feels threatened. One counterargument to this view is that ethnocentric attitudes—thinking that because others are different, they are thus a threat—initially *caused* the problem. The primary difficulty with this approach, however, is that it does not explain variations in the frequency, type, or intensity of intergroup conflict from one society to the next or between different immigrant groups and the ingroup.

In the United States

Often, an ethnocentric attitude is not deliberate but rather an outgrowth of growing up and living within a familiar environment. Even so, if recognized for the bias it is, ethnocentrism can be overcome. Consider, for example, that Americans have labeled their major league baseball championship games a *World Series*, although until recently not even Canadian teams were included in an otherwise exclusively U.S. professional sports program. *American* is another word we use—even in this book—to identify ourselves to the exclusion of people in other parts of North and South America. The Organization of American States (OAS), which consists of countries in both North and Latin America, should remind us that others are equally entitled to call themselves Americans.

At one point in this country's history, many state and national leaders identified their expansionist goals as Manifest Destiny, as if divine providence had ordained specific boundaries for the United States. Indeed, many members of the clergy over the years preached fiery sermons regarding God's special plans for this country, and all presidents have invoked the deity in their inaugural addresses for special assistance to this country.

In Other Times and Lands

Throughout history, people of many cultures have demonstrated an ethnocentric view of the world. For example, British Victorians, believing their way of life superior to all others, concluded they were obliged to carry the "white man's burden" of cultural and intellectual superiority in colonizing and "civilizing" the non-Western world. Yet 2,000 years earlier, the Romans had thought natives of Britain were an especially inferior people, as indicated in this excerpt from a letter written by the orator Cicero to his friend Atticus: "Do not obtain your slaves from Britain because they are so stupid and so utterly incapable of being taught that they are not fit to form a part of the household of Athens."

The Greeks, whose civilization predated the Roman Empire, considered all those around them—Persians, Egyptians, Macedonians, and others—distinctly inferior and called them barbarians. (*Barbarikos*, a Greek word, described those who did not speak Greek as making noises that sounded like "bar-bar.")

Religious chauvinism blended with ethnocentrism in the Middle Ages when the Crusaders, spurred on by their beliefs, considered it their duty to free the Holy Land from the control of the "infidels." They traveled a great distance by land and sea, taking with them horses, armor, and armaments, to wrest control from the native inhabitants because those "infidels" had the audacity to follow the teachings of Muhammad rather than Jesus. On their journey across Europe, the Crusaders slaughtered Jews (whom they falsely labeled "Christ-killers"), regardless of whether they were men, women, or children, all in the name of the Prince of Peace. The Crusaders saw both Muslims and Jews not only as inferior peoples but also as enemies.

In the following passage, Brewton Berry offers several other examples of ethnocentric thinking in past times:

> Some writers have attributed the superiority of their people to favorable geographical influences, but others incline to a biological explanation. The Roman, Vitruvius, maintained that those who live in southern climates have the keener intelligence, due to the rarity of the atmosphere, whereas "northern

nations, being enveloped in a dense atmosphere, and chilled by moisture from the obstructing air, have a sluggish intelligence." . . . Ibn Khaldun argued that the Arabians were the superior people, because their country, although in a warm zone, was surrounded by water, which exerted a cooling effect. Bodin, in the sixteenth century, found an astrological explanation for ethnic group differences. The planets, he thought, exerted their combined and best influence upon that section of the globe occupied by France, and the French, accordingly, were destined by nature to be the masters of the world. Needless to say, Ibn Khaldun was an Arab, and Bodin a Frenchman. The Italian, Sergi, regarded the Mediterranean peoples as the true bearers of civilization and insisted that Germans and Asiatics only destroy what the Mediterraneans create. In like manner, the superiority of Nordics, Alpines, Teutons, Aryans, and others has been asserted by those who were members of each of these groups, or thought they were.[34]

Anthropologists examining the cultures of other peoples have identified countless instances of ethnocentric attitudes. One frequent practice has been in geographic reference and mapmaking. For example, some commercially prepared Australian world maps depicted that continent at the center in relation to the rest of the world (see Figure 1.1).

FIGURE 1.1

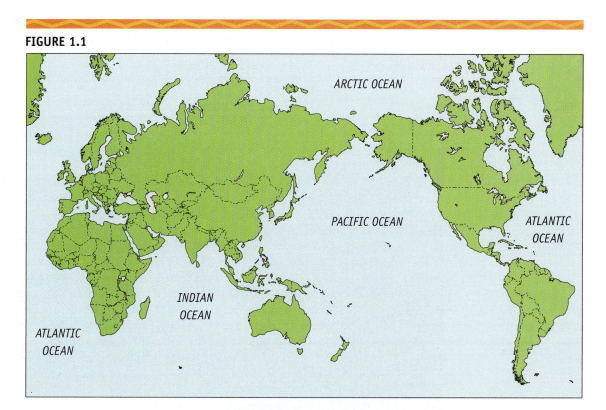

Unlike most U.S. maps of the world showing the American continents on the left side, this map—a common one in many Asian countries—puts the Americas on the right. The effect is to place these countries (such as Japan) in the center and not the edge, thus emphasizing the Pacific Rim rather than the Atlantic. Such repositioning is a form of ethnocentrism, shaping perceptions of the rest of the world.

There is nothing unusual about this type of thinking: the Chinese, who called their country the Middle Kingdom, were convinced that China was the center of the world, and similar beliefs were held by other nations—and are still held. The British drew the Prime Meridian of longitude to run through Greenwich, near London. Europeans drew maps of the world with Europe at the center, Americans with the New World at the center.[35]

But beyond providing a group-centered approach to living, ethnocentrism is of utmost significance in understanding motivation, attitudes, and behavior when members of racially or ethnically distinct groups interact, for it often helps explain misunderstandings, prejudice, and discrimination.

Eurocentrism and Afrocentrism

In recent years, many scholars and minority leaders have criticized the underrepresentation of non-European curriculum materials in the schools and colleges, calling this approach Eurocentric. **Eurocentrism** is a variation of ethnocentrism in which the content, emphasis, or both in history, literature, and other humanities primarily, if not exclusively, concern Western culture. Critics argue that this focus, ranging from the ancient civilizations of Greece and Rome to the writings of Shakespeare, Dickens, and other English poets and authors, ignores the accomplishments and importance of other peoples.

One counterforce to Eurocentrism is **Afrocentrism,** a viewpoint emphasizing African culture and its influence on Western civilization and the behavior of American blacks. In its moderate form, Afrocentrism is an effort to counterbalance Eurocentrism and the suppression of the African influence in American

This teacher stands among her students at the New Concept Development Center, a storefront school on Chicago's South Side. It offers an Afrocentric curriculum, with African themes infused in all subjects—English, history, math, science, and the arts. Advocates say such schools enhance educational achievement, motivation, and self-esteem.

culture by teaching African heritage as well.[36] In its bolder form, Afrocentrism becomes another variation of ethnocentrism. For example, a New York professor of African American studies, Leon Jeffries, became embroiled in controversy when he asserted the superiority of African "sun people" over European "ice people." Others who argue that Western civilization merely reflects the black African influence on Egyptian civilization find critics who charge them with excessively distorting history.[37]

For most advocates of pluralism, however, ethnocentrism in any form produces erroneous views. What is needed is a balanced approach that is inclusive, not exclusive, of the cultures, civilizations, and contributions of all peoples, both in the school curriculum and in our thinking.

OBJECTIVITY

When we are talking about people, usually those who differ from us, we commonly offer our own assumptions and opinions more readily than when we are discussing some other topic, such as astronomy or biology. But if we are to undertake a sociological study of ethnicity, we must question our assumptions and opinions—everything we have always believed without question. How can we scientifically investigate a problem if we have already reached a conclusion?

Sociologists investigate many aspects of society and social behavior—including the study of minority groups, race, class, and gender—through the **scientific method.** This involves repeated objective observation, precise measurement, careful description, the formulation and testing of hypotheses based on the best possible explanations, and the gathering of additional information about the questions that followed from those hypotheses so that ultimately theories may be proposed as explanatory systems. Although sociologists attempt to examine group relationships objectively, it is impossible to exclude their own subjectivity altogether. All human beings have **values**—socially shared conceptions of what is good, desirable, and proper or bad, undesirable, and improper. Because we are human, we cannot be completely objective, since these values influence our orientations, actions, reactions, and interpretations. For example, selecting intergroup relations as an area of interest and concern, emphasizing the sociological perspective of this subject, and organizing the material in this book thematically all represent value judgments regarding priorities.

In fact, **value neutrality** may be impossible to attain; we are all members of groups, and others have influenced our perceptions and experiences. It is nevertheless important to try conscientiously to maintain an open mind and examine this subject as objectively as possible. You must be aware of your own strong feelings about these matters and be willing to examine new concepts, even if they challenge previously held beliefs. To study this subject properly, you should attempt to be a stranger in your familiar world. Look at everything as if you were seeing it for the first time, trying to understand how and why it is, rather than just taking it for granted. In addition, you should recognize that all of us are members of groups; consequently, the debate about and study of intergroup relations is itself part of what we are studying. As part of an ingroup, we find all other outgroup members unlike our reference group; for this reason, our judgments about these "outsiders" are not as fully informed as the ones we make about known "insiders."

Trying to be *objective* about race and ethnic relations presents a strong challenge. People tend to use selective perception, accepting only information that agrees with their values or interpreting data in a way that confirms their attitudes about other groups. Many variables in life influence people's subjectivity about minority relations. Some views may be based on personal or emotional considerations or even on false premises. Sometimes, however, reasonable and responsible people disagree on the matter in an unemotional way. Whatever the situation, the study of minority-group relations poses a challenge for objective examination.

The subject of race and ethnic relations is complex and touches our lives in many ways. As members of the groups we are studying, all readers of this book come to this subject with preconceived notions. Because many individuals have a strong tendency to tune out disagreeable information, you must make a continual effort to remain open-minded and receptive to new data.

THE DILLINGHAM FLAW

Part of the problem with complaints about today's foreign-born presence in the United States lies in the critics' mistaken belief that they are reaching their judgments objectively. In comparing the supposedly nonassimilating newcomers to past immigrants, many detractors fall victim to a fallacy of thinking known as the **Dillingham Flaw.**[38]

Senator William P. Dillingham chaired a congressional commission on immigration that conducted extensive hearings between 1907 and 1911 on the massive immigration then occurring. In issuing its 41-volume report, the commission erred in its interpretation of the data by using simplistic categories and unfair comparisons of past and present immigrants and by ignoring three important factors: (1) differences of technological evolution in the immigrants' countries of origin; (2) the longer interval during which past immigrants had time to acculturate; and (3) changed structural conditions in the United States wrought by industrialization and urbanization.[39]

The *Dillingham Flaw* thus refers to any inaccurate comparison based on simplistic categorizations and anachronistic judgments. This occurs any time we apply modern classifications or sensibilities to an earlier time, when either they did not exist or, if they did, they had a different form or meaning. To avoid the Dillingham Flaw, we must resist the temptation to use modern perceptions to explain a past that contemporaneous people viewed quite differently.

Here is an illustration of this concept. Anyone who criticizes today's immigrants as being slower to Americanize, learn English, and become a cohesive part of U.S. society than did past immigrants is overlooking the reality of the past. Previous immigrant groups went through the same gradual acculturation process and encountered the same complaints. Ethnic groups that are now held up as role models and as studies in contrast to today's immigrants were themselves once the objects of scorn and condemnation.

To understand what is happening today, we need to view the present in a larger context—from a sociohistorical perspective. That is in part the approach taken in this book. By understanding past patterns in intergroup relations, we will better comprehend what is occurring in our times, and we will avoid becoming judgmental perpetrators of the Dillingham Flaw.

"Looking Backward"

"They desire to ban the newest arrivals at the bridge over which they and theirs arrived." Five wealthy men—from left to right, an Englishman, a German Jew, an Irishman, a German, and a Scandinavian—prevent the new immigrants from coming ashore and enjoying the same privileges they now enjoy. The shadows of the five wealthy men are representations of their social status before immigration. The Englishman's shadow is a stableman, the German Jew's is a notions peddler, and the others' are peasant farm workers. (This cartoon by Joseph Keppler appeared in *Puck* on January 11, 1893.)

PERSONAL TROUBLES AND PUBLIC ISSUES

Both ethnocentrism and subjectivity are commonplace in problems involving intergroup relations. In *The Sociological Imagination*, C. Wright Mills explained that an intricate connection exists between the patterns of individual lives and the larger historical context of society. Ordinary people do not realize this, however, and so view their personal troubles as private matters. Their awareness is limited to their "immediate relations with others" and "the social setting that is directly open to personal experience and to some extent [their] willful activity."[40] Personal troubles occur when individuals believe their values are threatened.

However, said Mills, what we experience in diverse and distinct social settings is often traceable to structural changes and institutional contradictions. The individual's local environment merely reflects the public issues of the larger social structure of social and historical life. An issue is a public matter concerning segments of the public who believe that one of their cherished values is being threatened.

To illustrate: If a handful of undocumented aliens is smuggled into the United States and placed in a sweatshop in virtual slavery, that is their personal trouble, and we look for a resolution of that particular problem. However, if large-scale smuggling of undocumented aliens into the country occurs, resulting in an underground economy of illegal sweatshops in many locales (as indeed happens), we need "to consider the economic and political institutions of the society, not just the personal situation and character of a scatter of individuals."[41]

Similarly, if a few urban African American or Hispanic American youths drop out of school, the personal problems leading to their quitting and the means by which they secure economic stability in their lives become the focus of our attention. On the other hand, if their dropout rate in most U.S. cities is consistently far greater than the national average (and it is), we must examine the economic, educational, and political issues that confront our urban institutions. These are larger issues, and we cannot resolve them by improving motivation, discipline, and opportunities for a few individuals.

Throughout this book, and particularly in the next chapter, we will examine this interplay of culture and social structure, ethnicity and social class. What often passes for assigned or assumed group characteristics—or for individual character flaws or troubles—needs to be understood within the larger context of public issues involving the social structure and interaction patterns.

Mills also said, "All sociology worthy of the name is 'historical' sociology."[42] Agreeing with that point, I will place all groups we study within a sociohistorical perspective so we can understand both historical and contemporary social structures that affect intergroup relations.

THE DYNAMICS OF INTERGROUP RELATIONS

The study of intergroup relations is both fascinating and challenging because relationships continually change. The patterns of relating may change for many reasons: industrialization, urbanization, shifts in migration patterns, social movements, upward or downward economic trends, and so on. However, sometimes the changing relationships also reflect changing attitudes, as, for example, in the interaction between whites and Native Americans. Whites continually changed the emphasis: exploitation, extermination, isolation, segregation, paternalism, forced assimilation, and more recently, tolerance for pluralism and restoration of certain (but not all) Native American ways. Similarly, African Americans, Asian Americans, Jews, Catholics, and other minority groups have all had varying relations with the host society.

Some recent world events also illustrate changing dominant-group orientations toward minority groups. The large migrations of diverse peoples into Belgium, Denmark, France, Germany, Italy, the Netherlands, Sweden, and the United Kingdom triggered a backlash in each of those countries. Strict new laws enacted in most of these nations in the 1990s resulted in a marked increase in deportations. **Ethnoviolence**—hostile behavior against people solely because of their race, religion, ethnicity, or sexual orientation—has also flared up, particularly in Germany and Italy, where neo-Nazi youths assaulted foreigners and firebombed their residences.

Elsewhere, intergroup relations fluctuate, as between Hindus and Muslims in India, Muslims and Christians in Lebanon, Arabs and Jews in the Middle East, Catholics and Protestants in Northern Ireland, and others. All go through varying periods of tumult and calm in their dealings with one another.

The field of race and ethnic relations has many theoreticians and investigators examining changing events and migration patterns. Each year, a vast outpouring of information from papers presented at meetings and from articles, books, and other sources adds to our knowledge. New insights, new concepts, and new interpretations of old knowledge inundate the interested observer. What both the sociologist and the student must attempt to understand, therefore, is not a fixed and static phenomenon but a dynamic, ever-changing one, about which more is being learned all the time.

SOCIOLOGICAL PERSPECTIVES

Sociology is the study of human relationships and patterns of behavior. Through scientific investigation, sociologists seek to determine the social forces that influence behavior as well as to identify recurring patterns that help them better understand that behavior.

Using historical documents, reports, surveys, ethnographies, journalistic materials, and direct observation, sociologists systematically gather empirical evidence about such intergroup relations. The sociologist then analyzes these data in an effort to discover and describe the causes, functions, relationships, meanings, and consequences of intergroup harmony or tension. Ascertaining reasons for the beginning, continuance, intensification, or alleviation of readily observable patterns of behavior among different peoples is complex and difficult, and not all sociologists concur when interpreting the data. Different theories, ideas, concepts, and even ideologies and prejudices may influence a sociologist's conclusions, too.

Disagreement among sociologists is no more unusual than in other areas of scientific investigation, such as physics debates about the creation of the universe, psychiatric debates on what constitutes a mental disorder, or genetic and social science debates over whether heredity or environment is more important in shaping behavior. Nonetheless, differing sociological theories play an important role in the focus of analysis and conclusions. In sociological investigation, three major perspectives shape analysis of the study of minorities: functional theory, conflict theory, and interactionist theory. The first two are **macrosocial theories,** in that they focus on society itself, while the third one is a **microsocial theory,** since it examines only one aspect within society. All three have a contribution to make, for each acts as a different lens that provides a distinct focus on the subject. In this book, each will thus serve as a basis for sociological analysis at the end of every chapter.

Functional Theory

Proponents of **functional theory** emphasize that the various parts of society have functions, or positive effects, that promote solidarity and maintain the stability of the whole. Sometimes called the *structural-functional paradigm* or model, it represents the core tradition of sociology, inspired by the writings of Auguste Comte (1798–1857), Herbert Spencer (1820–1903), and Émile Durkheim (1858–1917) in Europe, and developed further in the United States by Talcott Parsons (1902–1979) and Robert Merton (1910–2003).

This perspective emphasizes that society is a structure of beliefs and traditional ways of doing things. A society contains values (competition, honesty, success), **status positions** (occupational, class structure, gender roles), and institutions (family, education, religion, economics, and governance). Each of these parts plays a role in keeping the society going, although few people actually realize all the various functions of their society. Thus, functionalists organize their sociological analyses through identifying these many structures of society and investigating how well or poorly their functions operate.

Some components of the social structure have **manifest functions** (obvious and intended results), but they often have **latent functions** (hidden and unexpected results). For example, the obvious functions of the tourist visa program are to attract foreign visitors to build goodwill and to stimulate local economies at places they visit, thereby increasing the gross domestic product (GDP). One unintended result is thousands of visitors not returning after their visas expire and remaining here as illegal aliens.

Functionalists maintain that all the elements of a society should function together to maintain order and stability. Under ideal conditions, a society would be in a state of balance, with all its parts interacting harmoniously. Problems arise when parts of the social system become dysfunctional, upsetting the society's equilibrium. This system disorganization can occur for many reasons, but the most frequent cause is rapid social change. Changes in one part of the system necessitate compensatory adjustments elsewhere, but these usually do not occur fast enough, resulting in tensions and conflict.

Functionalists view dysfunctions as temporary maladjustments to an otherwise interdependent and relatively harmonious society. Because this perspective focuses on societal stability, the key issue in this analysis of social disorganization is whether to restore the equilibrium to its predisturbance state or to seek a new and different equilibrium. For example, how do we overcome the problem of undocumented aliens? Do we expel them to eliminate their exploitation, their alleged depression of regional wage scales, and their high costs to taxpayers in the form of health, education, and welfare benefits? Or do we grant them amnesty, help them enter the economic mainstream, and seal our borders against further undocumented entries? Whatever the solution—and these two suggestions do not exhaust the possibilities—functionalists emphasize that all problems regarding minorities can be resolved through adjustments to the social system that restore it to a state of equilibrium. Instead of major changes in the society, they prefer smaller corrections in the already functioning society.

Critics argue that this theoretical viewpoint focuses on order and stability and thus ignores the inequalities of gender, race, and social class that often generate tension and conflict. Those who see structural-functionalism as too conservative often favor the conflict perspective.

Conflict Theory

Proponents of **conflict theory,** influenced by Karl Marx's socioeconomic view of an elite exploiting the masses, see society as being continually engaged in a series of disagreements, tensions, and clashes as different groups compete for limited resources. They argue that social structure fails to promote the society as a whole, as evidenced by existing social patterns benefiting some people while depriving others.

Rejecting the functionalist model of societal parts that usually work harmoniously, conflict theorists see disequilibrium and change as the norm. They examine the ongoing conflict between the dominant and subordinate groups in society—such as between whites and people of color, men and women, or native born and foreign born. Regardless of the category studied, say conflict analysts, the pattern is usually that of those with power seeking to protect their privileges and those lower on the socioeconomic level struggling to gain a greater share than they have.

Conflict theorists focus on the inequalities that generate racial and ethnic antagonisms between groups. To explain why discrimination persists, they ask this question: Who benefits? Those already in power—employers and holders of wealth and property—exploit the powerless, seeking additional profits at the expense of unassimilated minorities. Because lower wages allow higher profits, ethnic discrimination serves the interests of investors and owners by weakening workers' bargaining power.

By putting economics into perspective, Marxist analysis offers penetrating insight into intergroup relations, but John Solomos and Les Back argue that this methodology does not provide a substantial explanation for contemporary racism and problems associated with it.[43] Conflict theorists counter that racism has much to do with maintaining power and controlling resources. Racism is an **ideology**—a set of generalized beliefs used to explain and justify the interests of those who hold them.

In this sense, **false consciousness**—holding attitudes that do not accurately reflect the objective facts of the situation—exists, and it impels workers to adopt attitudes that run counter to their own real interests. If workers believe that the economic gains by workers of other groups would adversely affect their own living standards, they will not support actions to end discriminatory practices. If workers struggling to improve their situation believe other groups entrenched in better job positions are holding them back, they will view their own gains as possible only at the expense of the better established groups. In both cases, the wealthy and powerful benefit by pitting exploited workers of different racial and ethnic groups against each other, causing each to have strong negative feelings about the other. This distorted view foments conflict and occasional outbursts of violence between groups, preventing workers from recognizing their common bond of joint oppression and uniting to overcome it.[44]

Critics contend that this theoretical viewpoint focuses too much on inequality and thus ignores the achieved unity of a society through the social cement of shared values and mutual interdependence among its members. Those who see conflict theory as too radical often favor the functionalist perspective. Still other critics reject both of these macrosocial theories as too broad and favor instead an entirely different approach, as explained in the next section.

Interactionist Theory

A third theoretical approach, **interactionist theory**, examines the microsocial world of personal interaction patterns in everyday life (e.g., social distance when talking, individual use of commonly understood terms) rather than the macrosocial aspects of social institutions and their harmony or conflict. **Symbolic interaction**—the shared symbols and definitions people use when communicating with one another—provides the focus for understanding how individuals create and interpret the life situations they experience. Symbols—our spoken language, expressions, body language, tone of voice, appearance, and images of television and other mass media—are what constitute our social worlds.[45] By means of these symbols, we communicate, create impressions, and develop understandings of the surrounding world. Symbolic interaction theories are useful in understanding race and ethnic relations because they assume that minority groups are responsive and creative rather than passive.[46]

Essential to this perspective, according to Peter L. Berger and Thomas Luckmann, is how people define their reality through a process they called the **social construction of reality.**[47] Individuals create a background against which to understand their separate actions and interactions with others. Taken-for-granted routines emerge on the basis of shared expectations. Participants see this socially constructed world as legitimate by virtue of its "objective" existence. In other words, people create cultural products: material artifacts, social institutions, ideologies, and so on (externalization). Over time, they lose awareness of having created their own social and cultural environment (objectification), and subsequently, they learn these supposedly objective facts of reality through the socialization process (internalization).

The interactionist perspective can be particularly helpful in understanding some of the false perceptions that occur in dominant–minority relations. As we will discuss shortly, racism is a good example of the social construction of reality. Another dimension of this viewpoint lies in misunderstandings between different groups rather than the shared understandings of members of the same group. One example is the oft-heard complaint that today's immigrants don't want to learn English or assimilate. Those who so believe offer as evidence the presence of foreign-language media programs or signs in stores and other public places, or they cite overheard conversations in languages other than English and/or differences in dress, or they point to residential ethnic clusters where "non-American" customs and practices, along with language, seemingly perpetuate nonassimilation. Critics often link such complaints with a comparison to previous immigrants, typically European, who were not like this and who chose to assimilate rather than remain apart from the rest of society.

In reality, these **nativists** (people who advocate a policy of protecting the interests of native inhabitants against those of immigrants) fail to realize that they are simply witnessing a new version of a common pattern among all immigrants who come to the United States. They create in their minds a reality about the newcomers' subculture as permanent instead of temporary, whereas their positive role model of past immigrant groups assimilating was actually seen by other nativists back then as also not assimilating, for the same reasons cited today. Interactionists would thus examine this reality that people create, the meaning they attach to that subjective reality, and how it affects their interactions with one another.

Critics complain that this focus on everyday interactions neglects the important roles played by culture and social structure, and the critical elements of class, gender, and race. Interactionists say they do not ignore the macroelements of society but that, by definition, a society is a structure in which people interact, and why and how they do that needs investigation and explanation.

Perhaps it would be most helpful if you viewed all three theoretical perspectives as different camera lenses looking at the same reality. Whether a wide-angle lens (a macrosocial view) or a telephoto lens (a microsocial view), each has something to reveal, and together they offer a more complete understanding of society. Table 1.2 summarizes the three sociological perspectives just discussed.

TABLE 1.2   Sociological Perspectives

	Functionalist	Conflict	Interactionist
Emphasis	Macrosocial View	Macrosocial View	Microsocial View
View of Society	Focus on a cooperative social system of interrelated parts that is relatively stable	Focus on society as continually engaged in a series of disagreements, tensions, and clashes	Focus on the microsocial world of personal interaction patterns in everyday life
Interaction Processes	Societal elements function together to maintain order, stability, and equilibrium.	Conflict is inevitable since there is always a societal elite and an oppressed group.	Shared symbols and definitions provide the basis for interpreting life experiences.
Interaction Results	Societal dysfunctions result from temporary disorganization or maladjustment.	Disequilibrium and change are the norm because of societal inequalities.	An internalized social construction of reality makes it seem to be objective fact.
Reason for Problems	Rapid social change is the most frequent cause of loss of societal equilibrium.	False consciousness allows the ruling elite to maintain power and benefit from exploitation.	Shared expectations and understandings, or their absence, explain intergroup relations.
How to Improve Society	Necessary adjustments will restore the social system to equilibrium.	Group struggle against oppression is necessary to effect social change.	Better intercultural awareness will improve interaction patterns.

RETROSPECT

Human beings follow certain patterns when responding to strangers. Their perceptions of newcomers reflect categoric knowing; if they perceive that the newcomers are similar, people are more receptive to their presence. What makes interaction with strangers difficult is the varying perceptions of each to the other, occasioned by a lack of shared understandings and perceptions of reality.

By definition, minority groups—regardless of their size—receive unequal treatment, possess identifying physical or cultural characteristics held in low esteem, are conscious of their shared ascribed status, and tend to practice endogamy. Racial groups are biologically similar groups, and ethnic groups are groups that share a learned cultural heritage. Intergroup relations are dynamic and continually changing.

Ethnocentrism—the tendency to identify with one's own group—is a universal human condition that contributes to potential problems in relating to outgroups. Examples of ethnocentric thinking and actions can be found in all countries throughout history. Eurocentrism and Afrocentrism are views emphasizing one culture or civilization over others.

The study of minorities presents a difficult challenge because our value orientations and life experiences can impair our objectivity. Even trained sociologists, being human, encounter difficulty in maintaining value neutrality. Indeed, some people argue that sociologists should take sides and not attempt a sterile approach to the subject. The Dillingham Flaw—using an inaccurate comparison based on simplistic categorizations and anachronistic judgments—seriously undermines the scientific worth of supposedly objective evaluations. Both ethnocentrism and subjectivity are commonplace in problems involving intergroup relations. Clearer understanding occurs by examining the larger context of how so-called personal troubles connect with public issues.

In sociological investigation of minorities, three perspectives shape analysis. Functional theory stresses the orderly interdependence of a society and the adjustments needed to restore equilibrium when dysfunctions occur. Conflict theory emphasizes the tensions and conflicts that result from exploitation and competition for limited resources. Interactionist theory concentrates on everyday interaction patterns operating within a socially constructed perception of reality.

KEY TERMS

Abstract typifications	False consciousness	Outgroup
Afrocentrism	Functional theory	Race
Ascribed status	Group	Racism
Categoric knowing	Ideology	Reference group
Conflict theory	Immigration	Scientific method
Cultural relativism	Ingroup	Secondary group
Dillingham Flaw	Interactionist theory	Social construction of
Dominant group	Latent functions	reality
Emigration	Macrosocial theories	Social distance
Endogamy	Manifest functions	Social identity theory
Ethnicity	Microsocial theory	Status positions
Ethnocentrism	Migration	Symbolic interaction
Ethnoviolence	Minority group	Value neutrality
Eurocentrism	Nativists	Values

DISCUSSION QUESTIONS

1. How are the social distance studies helpful to our understanding of intergroup relations?

2. How does the similarity-attraction concept help us to understand intergroup relations?

3. What is ethnocentrism? Why is it important in relations between dominant and minority groups?

4. Why is objective study of racial and ethnic minorities difficult?

5. Explain the Dillingham Flaw, and offer some examples.

6. How does a minority group differ from an ethnic group? How does a race differ from an ethnic group?

7. What are the focal points of the functional, conflict, and interactionist theories?

SUGGESTED READINGS

Asante, Molefi K. *The Afrocentric Idea,* rev. ed. Philadelphia: Temple University Press, 1998. Presents the provocative thesis that African culture permeates Western civilization and the behavior of black Americans.

Berger, Peter L., and Thomas Luckmann. *The Social Construction of Reality,* new ed. New York: Penguin Books, 1991. Highly influential work discussing how people define their reality and interact on the basis of shared expectations; still popular and available.

Gilroy, Paul. *Against Race: Imagining Political Culture beyond the Color Line.* Cambridge, MA: Harvard University Press, 2001. A provocative book that is both factual and utopian in its premise that humanity should not be divided into groups based on skin color.

Mills, C. Wright. *The Sociological Imagination,* reprint ed. New York: Oxford University Press, 2000. A classic book on understanding the links between apparently private problems of the individual and important social issues.

Parrillo, Vincent N. *Diversity in America,* 3rd ed. Thousand Oaks, CA: Pine Forge Press, 2008. Explains the Dillingham Flaw and examines multiculturalism throughout the nation's history.

Schutz, Alfred. "The Stranger," *American Sociological Review* 69 (May 1944): 449–507. Early, influential essay that is still highly pertinent today, explaining the interaction problems of a stranger.

Simmel, Georg. "The Stranger," In Kurt H. Wolff (ed.), *The Sociology of Georg Simmel,* 4th ed. New York: Free Press, 1969. Classic analysis of the role of the stranger made through an analysis of the formal structures of life.

Waters, Mary. *Ethnic Options: Choosing Identity in America.* Berkeley: University of California Press, 1990. Informative discussion of the role ethnicity plays in the pluralistic society of the United States and the evolution of group-identity politics.

MySocKit

Additional resources for this chapter can be found in MySocKit. If you have a subscription to MySocKit, go to www.mysockit.com to study, review, and go beyond the book to learn more about race and ethnic relations.

Culture and Social Structure

Understanding what makes people receptive to some, but not all, strangers requires knowledge of how culture and social structure affect perceptions and response patterns. Culture provides the guidelines for people's interpretations of situations they encounter and for the responses they consider appropriate. **Social structure**—the organized patterns of behavior among the basic components of a social system—establishes relatively predictable social relationships among the different peoples in a society. The distinctions and interplay between culture and social structure are important to the assimilation process as well. For example, cultural orientations of both minority and dominant groups shape expectations about how a minority group should fit into the society.

This chapter first examines the various aspects of culture that affect dominant–minority relations. We then discuss the significance of social class within the social structure. Next, we'll look at cultural differentiation and structural differentiation as bases for conflict, followed by an examination of varying cultural expectations about minority integration.

THE CONCEPT OF CULTURE

Human beings create their own social worlds and evolve further within them. Adapting to the environment, to new knowledge, and to technology, we learn a way of life within our society. We invent and share rules and patterns of behavior that shape our lives and the way we experience the world about us. The shared products of society that we call *culture*, whether material or nonmaterial, make social life possible and give our lives meaning. **Material culture** consists of all physical objects created by members of a society and the meanings/significance attached to them (e.g., cars, cell phones, DVDs, iPods, high-top sneakers, or clothing). **Nonmaterial culture** consists of abstract human creations and their meanings/significance in life (such as beliefs, customs, ideas, languages, norms, social institutions, and values). **Culture**, then, consists of physical or material objects as well as the nonmaterial attitudes, beliefs, customs,

31

TABLE 2.1 Basic U.S. Values

Within the diverse U.S. society of racial, ethnic, and religious groups, each with a distinctive set of values, exists a common core of values. Sociologist Robin Williams, after decades of study, identified 15 value orientations—the foundation of American beliefs, behaviors, definitions of social goals, and life expectations. Some are contradictory—freedom and individualism but external conformity; democracy and equality but racism and group superiority; nationalism but individualism—and these may spark divisions among people. Although other societies may subscribe to many of these values as well, this particular combination of values—virtually present from the nation's founding— have had and continue to have enormous impact in shaping U.S. society.

1. **Achievement and success.** Competition-oriented, our society places much value on gaining power, prestige, and wealth.

2. **Activity and work.** We firmly believe that everyone should work, and we condemn as lazy those who do not work.

3. **Moral orientation.** We tend to moralize, seeing the world in absolutes of right and wrong.

4. **Humanitarian mores.** Through charitable and crisis aid, we lean toward helping the less fortunate and the underdog.

5. **Efficiency and practicality.** We try to solve problems by the quickest, least costly means.

6. **Progress.** We think technology can solve all problems, and we hold an optimistic outlook toward the future.

7. **Material comfort.** We share the American Dream of a high standard of living and owning many material goods.

8. **Equality.** We believe in the abstract ideal of equality, relating to one another informally as equals.

9. **Freedom.** We cherish individual freedom from domination by others.

10. **External conformity.** Despite our professed belief in individualism, we tend to join, conform, and go along; and we are suspicious of those who do not.

11. **Science and rationality.** We believe that through science we can gain mastery over our environment and secure a better lifestyle.

12. **Nationalism.** We think the American way of life is the best and distrust "un-American" behavior.

13. **Democracy.** We believe that everyone has the right of political participation, that our government is highly democratic.

14. **Individualism.** We emphasize personal rights and responsibilities, giving the individual priority over the group.

15. **Racism and group superiority themes.** Through our attitudes and actions, we favor some racial, religious, and ethnic groups over others.

Source: Robin M. Williams Jr., *American Society: A Sociological Interpretation*, 3rd ed. (New York: Knopf, 1970).

lifestyles, and values shared by members of a society and transmitted to the next generation.

These cultural attributes provide a sense of peoplehood and common bonds through which members of a society can relate (Table 2.1). Most sociologists therefore emphasize the impact of culture in shaping behavior.[1] Through language and other forms of symbolic interaction, the members of a society learn the thought and behavior patterns that constitute their commonality as a people.[2] In this sense, culture is the social cement that binds a society together.

Shared cultural norms encourage solidarity and orient the behavior of members of the ingroup. **Norms** are a culture's rules of conduct—internalized by the members—embodying the society's fundamental expectations. Through norms, ingroup members (majority or minority) know how to react toward the acts of outgroup members that surprise, shock, or annoy them or in any way go against their shared expectations. Anything contrary to this "normal" state is seen as negative or deviant. When minority-group members "act uppity" or "don't know their place," majority-group members often get upset and sometimes act out their anger. Violations of norms usually trigger strong reactions because they appear to threaten the social fabric of a community or society. Eventually, most minority groups adapt their distinctive cultural traits to those of the host society through a process called **acculturation.** Intragroup variations remain, though, because ethnic-group members use different reference groups as role models.

An important component of intragroup cultural variations, seldom a part of the acculturation process, is religion. Indeed, not only does religion have strong links to the immigrant experience in the United States, as well as to African American slavery and pacification efforts toward Native Americans, but it also has many other connections to prejudice and social conflict. As subsequent chapters detail, the Catholic and Jewish faiths of past European immigrants provoked many manifestations (some quite violent and vicious) of Protestant nativism. Similarly, recent immigrants who are believers of such religions as Hinduism, Islam, Rastafarianism, or Santería often experience prejudice and conflict because of their faith, as have the Amish, Mormons, Quakers, and many others in the United States in past years. Religious conflict is a sad reality in many parts of the world—the Balkans, India, the Middle East, and Northern Ireland, to mention just a few.

Professional sports are another part of culture that provides an area for the study of prejudice and racism. Long excluded from major league sports, people of color now are prominent participants in baseball, basketball, boxing, football, and track. In fact, African Americans (13 percent of the population) account for 68 percent of National Football League (NFL) players and 73 percent of National

New York Mets General Manager Omar Minaya, born in the Dominican Republic, and Team Manager Willie Randolph, a former player and coach for the New York Yankees, are a rarity in Major League Baseball, where both African and Hispanic Americans are underrepresented in upper management.

Basketball Association (NBA) players. African Americans are underrepresented in Major League Baseball (MLB) with 8 percent, while Hispanics—barely represented in football and basketball—comprise 29 percent of all MLB players in 2006.[3] Nevertheless, the vast majority of owners, managers, and head coaches in all sports are white; and, in some sports (such as football), one's race and position on the field are closely linked. Whites dominate in offensive slots and blacks in defensive positions, and whites are more likely to play leadership roles on both sides of the line. Still, many blacks and Hispanics, and an increasing number of Asians, excel in athletics, serving as a source of racial and/or ethnic pride for many of their fellow group members.

U.S. colleges continued to provide the fewest opportunities for people of color at the top management level. In 2005, African Americans made up only 5.5 percent, 3.8 percent, and 1.9 percent, respectively, of athletic directors in Divisions I, II, and III. Women athletic directors comprised 7.8 percent, 18.7 percent, and 27.3 percent, respectively, in Divisions I, II, and III, the highest ever totals in all three divisions. The percentage of African Americans coaching in Divisions I, II, and III combined reached all time highs in men's basketball (25.2 percent) and football (3.2 percent).[4] While the progress is encouraging, the data also reveal that college and professional sports still need to do more to overcome embedded cultural biases.

The Reality Construct

Our perception of reality is related to our culture: Through our culture, we learn how to perceive the world about us. Cultural definitions help us interpret the sensory stimuli from our environment and tell us how to respond to them. Thus, "culture is something that intervenes between the human organism and its environment to produce actions."[5] It is the screen through which we "see," and we cannot get rid of it (Figure 2.1).

Language and Other Symbols. Culture is learned behavior, acquired chiefly through verbal communication, or language. A word is nothing more than a sym-

FIGURE 2.1   Cultural Reality

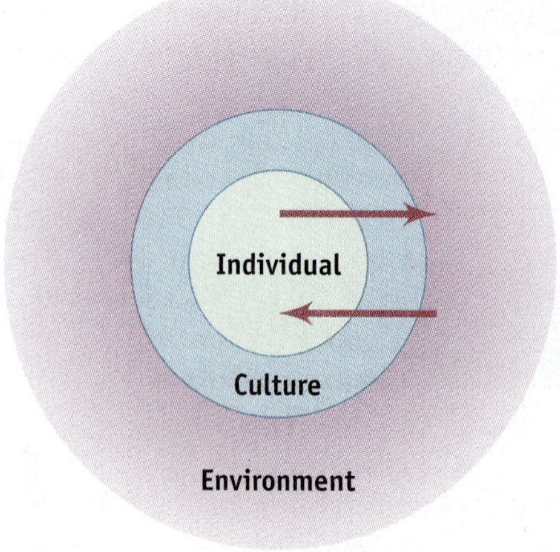

Each **Individual** observes the world through **Sense Perceptions**, which are evaluated in terms of **Culture** — values, attitudes, customs, and beliefs.

bol—something that stands for something else. Whether it is tangible (*chair*) or intangible (*honesty*), the word represents a mental concept that is based on empirical reality. Words reflect culture, however, and one word may have different meanings in different cultures. If you are *carrying the torch* in England, you are holding a flashlight, not yearning for a lost love; if you could use a *lift,* you want an elevator, not a ride or a boost to your spirits. Because words symbolically interpret the world to us, the **linguistic relativity** of language may connote both intended and unintended prejudicial meanings. For example, *black* is the symbol for darkness (in the sense of lightlessness) or evil, and *white* symbolizes cleanliness or goodness; and a society may subtly (or not so subtly) transfer these meanings to black and white people.

Walter Lippmann, a prominent political columnist, once remarked, "First we look, then we name, and only then do we see." He meant that until we learn the symbols of our world, we cannot understand the world. A popular pastime in the early 1950s, called "Droodles," illustrates Lippmann's point. The object was to interpret drawings such as those in Figure 2.2. Many people were unable to see the meaning of the drawings until it was explained. They looked but did not see until they knew the "names." Can you guess what these drawings depict before looking up this endnote?[6]

Interpreting symbols is not merely an amusing game; it is significant in real life. Human beings do not respond to stimuli but to their definitions of those stimuli as mediated by their culture.[7] The definition of beauty is one example. Beyond the realm of personal taste, definitions of beauty have cultural variations. For instance, in different times and places, societies have based their appraisal of a woman's beauty on her having distended lips, scar markings, tattoos, or beauty marks or on how plump or thin she was.

Nonverbal communication—or body language—is highly important, too. Body movements, gestures, physical proximity, facial expressions (there are between 100 and 136 facial expressions, each of which conveys a distinct meaning[8]), and **paralinguistic signals** (sounds but not words, such as a sigh, a kiss-puckering sound, or the *m-m-m* sound of tasting something good) all convey information to the observer-listener. Body language is important in intergroup relations, too, whether in conversation, interaction, or perception. Body language may support or belie one's words; it may suggest friendliness, aloofness, or deference.

Although some forms of body language are fairly universal (e.g., most facial expressions), many cultural variations exist in body language itself and in the interpretation of its meanings. Body movements such as posture, bearing, and gait

FIGURE 2.2   "Droodles"

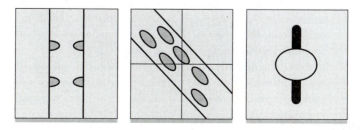

vary from culture to culture. The degree of formality in a person's environment (both past and present) and other cultural factors influence such forms of non-verbal communication. Consider the different meanings one could attach to a student's being unwilling to look directly into the eyes of a teacher. The teacher may assume that this behavior reflects embarrassment, guilt, shyness, inattention, or even disrespect. Yet if the student is Asian or Hispanic, such demeanor is a mark of respect. The symbol's definition, in this case the teacher's interpretation of what the student's body language means, determines the meaning the observer ascribes to it.

A person who is foreign to a culture must learn both its language and the rest of its symbol system, as the members born into that culture did through socialization. Certain gestures may be signs of friendliness in one culture but obscene or vengeful symbols in another. For example, in the United States, placing thumb and forefinger in a circle with the other fingers upraised indicates that everything is fine, but in Japan, this sign refers to money, and in Greece, it is an insulting anal expression.[9] Kisses, tears, dances, emblems, silence, open displays of emotions, and thousands of other symbols can and often do have divergent meanings in different cultures. Symbols, including language, help an ingroup construct a reality that may be unknown to or altogether different for an outgroup. Members of one group may then select, reject, ignore, or distort their sensory input regarding the other group because of cultural definitions.

The Thomas Theorem.   William I. Thomas once observed that, if people define situations as real, those situations become real in their consequences.[10] His statement, known as the **Thomas theorem**, relates directly to the *Dillingham Flaw* discussed in the first chapter. Whereas Thomas emphasized how definitions lead to actions that produce consequences to conform to the original, ill-founded definition, the Dillingham Flaw suggests the misguided thought process that may result in that definition in the first place.

The Thomas theorem is thus further testimony to the truth of reality constructs: Human beings respond to their definitions of stimuli rather than to the stimuli themselves. People often associate images (e.g., "yellow peril," "Indian menace," or "illegal aliens") with specific minority groups. They then behave according to the meaning they assign to the situation, and the consequences of their behavior serve to reaffirm the meaning; the definition becomes a self-fulfilling prophecy. For example, when whites define blacks as inferior and then offer them fewer opportunities because of that alleged inferiority, blacks are disadvantaged, which in turn supports the initial definition.

Several variables contribute to the initial definition, but culture is one of the most important of these. Culture establishes the framework through which an individual perceives others, classifies them into groups, and assigns certain general characteristics to them. Because ethnocentrism leads people to consider their way of life as the best and most natural, their culturally defined perceptions of others often lead to suspicion and differential treatment of other groups. In effect, each group constructs myths about other groups and supports those myths through ingroup solidarity and outgroup hostility. As each group's attitudes and actions toward other groups continue, the **vicious-circle phenomenon** plays out.[11] In such instances, people create a culturally determined world of reality, and their actions reinforce their beliefs. Social interaction or social change may counteract such situations, however, leading to their redefinition.

Gregory Razran conducted a study illustrating how cultural definitions can influence perception.[12] Twice within a two-month interval, he showed the same set of 30 pictures of unknown young women to the same group of 100 male college students and 50 noncollege men. Using a five-point scale, the subjects rated each woman's beauty, character, intelligence, ambition, and general likeableness. At the first presentation, the pictures had no ethnic identification, but at the second presentation, they were labeled with Irish, Italian, Jewish, and old American (English) surnames. All women were rated equally on the first presentation, but when the names were given, the ratings changed. The "Jewish" women received higher ratings in ambition and intelligence. Both "Jewish" and "Italian" women suffered a large decline in general likeableness and a slight decline in beauty and character evaluations. This study is one of many illustrating how cultural definitions affect judgments about others.

Through **cultural transmission,** each generation transmits its culture to the next generation, which learns those cultural definitions at an early age. This fact is dramatically expressed in the Rodgers and Hammerstein musical *South Pacific.* The tragic subplot is the touching romance between Lieutenant Cable and the young Tonkinese woman Liat. Although Cable and Liat are deeply in love, Cable's friends remind him that the couple's life would not be the same in the United States. Their differences in race and culture would work against a happy marriage for them, as would his own acceptance in Philadelphia high society. Miserable because of the choice his cultural values force him to make, he sings "Carefully Taught," a poignant song about how prejudice is taught to children:

> You've got to be taught to hate and fear,
> You've got to be taught from year to year.
> It's got to be drummed in your dear little ear,
> You've got to be carefully taught.
>
> You've got to be taught to be afraid,
> Of people whose eyes are oddly made,
> Of people whose skin is a different shade.
> You've got to be carefully taught.
>
> You've got to be taught before it's too late,
> Before you are six or seven or eight,
> To hate all the people your relatives hate.
> You've got to be carefully taught.
> You've got to be carefully taught.[13]

These lyrics reinforce the reality construct discussed earlier and illustrated in Figure 2.1. From family, friends, school, mass media, and all other sources of informational input, we learn our values, attitudes, and beliefs. Some of our learning reflects the prejudices of others, which we may incorporate in our own attitudes and actions.

CULTURAL CHANGE

Culture continually changes. Discoveries, inventions, technological advances, innovations, and natural disasters alter the customs, values, attitudes, and beliefs of a society. This section focuses on two common processes of cultural change:

cultural diffusion within a whole society and changes within a particular subculture of that society.

Cultural Diffusion

Paradoxically, although the members of a dominant culture wish to keep their society untainted by contact with foreign elements, cultures are inevitably influenced by other cultures—a phenomenon termed **cultural diffusion**. Ideas, inventions, and practices spread from one culture to another, albeit at different rates of diffusion. Negative attitudes and a large distance between groups can pose formidable barriers, and sometimes cultural diffusion occurs only under temporarily favorable conditions. Sometimes ideas are modified or reinterpreted before being accepted, such as when some native Latin American tribes of the early 20th century showed a fondness for automobile tires: They used them to make sandals, for they neither owned nor drove cars.[14]

Borrowed Elements. U.S. anthropologist Ralph Linton calculated that any given culture contains about 90 percent borrowed elements. To demonstrate both the enormity and the subtlety of cultural diffusion, he offered a classic portrait of the "100 percent American" male:

> Our solid American citizen awakens in a bed built on a pattern which originated in the Near East but which was modified in Northern Europe before it was transmitted to America. He throws back covers made from cotton, domesticated in India, or linen, domesticated in the Near East, or wool, from sheep, also domesticated in the Near East, or silk, the use of which was discovered in China. All of these materials have been spun or woven by processes invented in the Near East. He slips into his moccasins, invented by the Indians of the Eastern woodlands, and goes to the bathroom, whose fixtures are a mixture of European and American inventions, both of recent date. He takes off his pajamas, a garment invented in India, and washes with soap, invented by the ancient Gauls. He then shaves, a masochistic rite which seems to have been derived from either Sumer or ancient Egypt.
>
> Returning to the bedroom, he removes his clothes from a chair of southern European type and proceeds to dress. He puts on garments whose form originally derived from the skin clothing of the nomads of the Asiatic steppes, puts on shoes made from skins tanned by a process invented in ancient Egypt and cut to a pattern derived from the classical civilizations of the Mediterranean, and ties around his neck a strip of bright-colored cloth which is a vestigial survival of the shoulder shawls worn by the seventeenth-century Croatians. Before going out for breakfast he glances through the window, made of glass invented in Egypt, and if it is raining puts on overshoes made of rubber discovered by the Central American Indians and takes an umbrella, invented in southeastern Asia. Upon his head he puts a hat made of felt, a material invented in the Asiatic steppes.
>
> On his way to breakfast he stops to buy a paper, paying for it with coins, an ancient Lydian invention. At the restaurant a whole new series of borrowed elements confronts him. His plate is made of a form of pottery invented in China. His knife is of steel, an alloy first made in southern India, his fork a medieval Italian invention, and his spoon a derivative of a Roman original. He begins breakfast with an orange, from the eastern Mediterranean, a cantaloupe from Persia, or perhaps a piece of African watermelon. With this he has coffee, an Abyssinian plant, with cream and sugar. Both the domestication of cows and the idea of milking them originated in the Near East, while sugar was first made in

India. After his fruit and first coffee, he goes on to waffles, cakes made by a Scandinavian technique from wheat domesticated in Asia Minor. Over these he pours maple syrup, invented by the Indians of the Eastern woodlands. As a side dish he may have the egg of a species of bird domesticated in Indo-China, or thin strips of the flesh of an animal domesticated in Eastern Asia which have been salted and smoked by a process developed in northern Europe.

When our friend has finished eating he settles back to smoke, an American Indian habit, consuming a plant domesticated in Brazil in either a pipe, derived from the Indians of Virginia, or a cigarette, derived from Mexico. If he is hardy enough he may even attempt a cigar, transmitted to us from the Antilles by way of Spain. While smoking he reads the news of the day, imprinted in characters invented by the ancient Semites upon a material invented in China by a process invented in Germany. As he absorbs the accounts of foreign troubles he will, if he is a good conservative citizen, thank a Hebrew deity in an Indo-European language that he is 100 percent American.*

Cultural diffusion is also an important element in ethnic relations within our pluralistic society. It can take many forms, including widened food preferences such as tacos or burritos or the use within U.S. corporations of such Japanese management techniques as employee participation in setting work goals. Whatever the form, cultural diffusion is an ongoing process that influences various aspects of our culture and sometimes alters our views of the cultures of other peoples.

Cultural Contact. Culture can also undergo change through people of different cultures coming into contact with one another. Because people tend to take their own culture for granted, it operates at a subconscious level in forming their expectations. When people's assumptions are jolted through contact with an unfamiliar culture that supports different expectations, they often experience **culture shock,** characterized by feelings of disorientation and anxiety and a sense of being threatened.

Culture shock does not always occur. When people of two different cultures interact, many possible patterns can emerge. The two groups may peacefully coexist, with gradual cultural diffusion occurring. History offers some excellent examples of connections between migrations and innovations, wherein geographic conditions and native attitudes determined the extent to which a group resisted cultural innovations, despite invasions, settlements, or missionary work. The persistent pastoralism of Bedouin tribes and the long-sustained resistance to industrialization of Native Americans are two examples.[15] Stanley Lieberson, however, suggests that power alone determines the outcome, causing one group to become dominant and the other subservient.[16] If the subordinate group proves to be the nonmigratory group, the changes to its social organization can be devastating. No longer possessing the flexibility and autonomy it once enjoyed, it may suffer material deprivation and find its institutions undermined.

If the migratory group finds itself in the subordinate position, it must adapt to its new environment to survive. Most commonly, the minority group draws from its familiar world as it attempts to cope with the prevailing conditions. Group members form a subculture with unique behavior and interests—neither

*Ralph Linton, *The Study of Man* (1936), pp. 326–327. Reprinted by permission of Prentice-Hall, Inc., Upper Saddle River, NJ.

those of the larger society nor those of their old culture. For example, both Catholicism and Judaism have undergone significant changes in form and expression since taking root in the United States. U.S. ethnic subcultures typically blend elements of homeland and dominant U.S. cultures once group members adapt to their new environment.

Subcultures

Usually, immigrants follow a pattern of **chain migration,** settling in an area already containing family, friends, or compatriots who located there earlier. An ethnic community evolves, providing an emotional support system to these strangers in a strange land as they strive to forge a better life for themselves. Part of this process of cultural insulation among others like themselves is the re-creation in miniature of the world they left behind. Thus, **parallel social institutions**—their own clubs, organizations, newspapers, stores, churches, and schools duplicating those of the host society—appear, creating cohesiveness within the minority subculture, whether it is an immigrant or native-born grouping.

As **ethnic subcultures** among immigrants in the United States evolve in response to conditions within the host society, the immigrants sometimes develop a group consciousness unknown in their old countries. Many first-generation Americans possess a village orientation toward their homeland rather than a national identity. They may speak different dialects, feud with

Ethnic neighborhoods, particularly their commercial streets, have always been one of the most vivid displays, even to the most casual observer, of the presence of an immigrant subculture, such as this Pakistani neighborhood on Coney Island Avenue in Brooklyn, New York's Flatbush section.

other regions, and have different values, but their common experience in the United States causes them to coalesce into a national grouping. One example is Italian Americans, who initially identified with their cities of origin: Calabria, Palermo, Naples, Genoa, Salerno, and so on. Within a generation, many came to view themselves as Italians, partly because the host society classified them as such.

Yet even as a newly arrived group forges its community and subculture, a process called **ethnogenesis** occurs.[17] Shaped partly by the core culture in selectively absorbing some elements and modifying others, the group also retains, modifies, or drops elements from its cultural heritage as it adapts to its new country. The result is a distinctive new ethnic group unlike others in the host country, dominant or minority, but also somewhat different from the people who still live in the group's homeland. Thus, first-generation German Americans, for example, differ from other ethnic groups and from native-born U.S. citizens, but they also possess cultural traits and values that distinguish them from nonmigrating Germans.

Convergent Subcultures. Some ethnic subcultures are **convergent subcultures;** that is, they tend toward assimilation with the dominant society. Although recognizable by residential clustering and adherence to the language, dress, and cultural norms of their native land, these ethnic groups nonetheless eventually assimilate. As the years pass—possibly across several generations—the distinctions between the dominant culture and the convergent subculture gradually lessen. Eventually, this form of subculture becomes completely integrated into the dominant culture.

Because the subculture is undergoing change, its members may experience problems of **marginality**—living under stress in two cultures simultaneously. The older generation may seek to preserve its traditions and heritage, whereas the younger generation may be impatient to achieve full acceptance within the dominant society. Because of the impetus toward assimilation, time obviously favors the younger generation. The Dutch, German, and Irish subcultures are examples of once-prevalent ethnic subcultures that are barely visible today; Italian, Polish, and Slovak subcultures have also begun to converge more fully. These nationality groups still exhibit ethnic pride in many ways; but, for the most part, they are no longer set apart by place of residence or subcultural behavior. Because of their multigenerational length of residence, these nationality groups are less likely to live in clustered housing arrangements or to display behavior patterns such as conflict, deviance, or endogamy to any greater degree than the rest of the majority group.

Persistent Subcultures. Not all subcultures assimilate. Some do not even desire to do so, and others, particularly nonwhite groups, face difficulties in assimilating. These unassimilated subcultures are known as **persistent subcultures.** Some adhere as much as possible to their own way of life, resisting absorption into the dominant culture. Religious groups such as the Amish, some Hutterites, and Hasidic Jews reject modernity and insist on maintaining their traditional ways of life; they may represent the purest form of a persistent subculture in U.S. society. Other ethnic groups adopt a few aspects of the dominant culture but adamantly preserve their own way of life; examples are most Native Americans who live on reservations and many *Hispanos* (Spanish Americans) in the

Southwest. Chinatowns also support preservation of the Chinese way of life in many ways.

A minority group's insistence on the right to be different has not usually been well received among dominant-group members. This clash of wills sometimes leads to conflict; at the very least, it invites stereotyping and prejudice on both sides (see The International Scene box).

The International Scene

Attempts to Eliminate a Persistent Subculture

The world's 25 million Kurds are an ethnic group with their own language. They live mostly in the bordering lands of Iran, Iraq, Syria, and Turkey—a region known as Kurdistan, or "Land of the Kurds." After World War I, this territory was partitioned among Turkey, Syria, and Iraq. Once a nomadic people who followed the seasonal migrations of their sheep and goat herds, the Kurds were thus compelled to abandon their traditional ways for village life and settled farming.

A mostly Sunni Muslim people living in the Kurdistan region, the Kurds remain a persistent subculture, whereas those living in urban areas are at least nominally assimilated. Marriages are typically endogamous, with a strong extended family network. The Kurds were once a tribal people under the firm leadership of a sheikh or an aga; however, that aspect of societal life is now felt (in a much smaller degree) only in the villages.

In 1924, the Turkish government engaged in cultural repression by renaming Kurds "Mountain Turks," outlawing their language, and forbidding their wearing the distinctive Kurdish costume in or near major cities. The government also encouraged many Kurds to migrate to the urbanized portion of western Turkey to dilute their population concentration. Uprisings in 1925, 1927–1930, and 1937–1938 were crushed; hundreds of thousands of Kurds were killed or expelled from the area.

Saddam Hussein's killing of thousands of Iraqi Kurds in 1988 with chemical weapons brought these relatively unknown people to the attention of Western cultures. Then came the Kurds' dramatic flight from Hussein's military forces in the spring of 1991 across snow-clad mountains. Encouraged by the United Nation (UN) coalition's Gulf War victory, the Kurds had risen against the repressive Baghdad regime, only to have Hussein's remaining forces drive them out. Iran let 1 million refugees cross its border to safety, but Turkey closed its border. trapping about 500,000 Kurds in the mountains under harsh weather conditions. After two months, the coalition enticed the Kurds back into an area of Iraq designated as a "safe haven."

In Turkey, where the government has long attempted to suppress Kurdish culture, fighting erupted between government forces and the Kurds in the mid-1980s, mainly in southeastern Turkey. By 2000, 15 years after fighting began, more than 23,000 people had been killed, an estimated 3,000 Kurdish villages wiped off the map, and about 2 million refugees forced to relocate. Reforms passed in 2002 and 2003 to facilitate Turkish entrance in the European Union included ending bans on private education in the Kurdish language and on giving children Kurdish names, as well as ending martial law in that region.

Iraqi Kurdish forces aided the U.S.-led invasion of Iraq in 2003, joining with U.S. and British forces to seize the traditionally Kurdish cities of Kirkuk and Mosul. In 2005, Kurds held more than one-fourth of elected seats in the new Iraqi National Assembly. Today, Iraqi progressives see federalism—in which Kurds have local self-rule but also participate in the national government with other Iraqi nationalities—as a key element in building a unified, independent nation. Turkey—where half of all Kurds live and where they constitute 19 percent of the total population—is strongly opposed to any independence for the Kurds.

With Kurds themselves divided between assimilationist and nationalist goals, with instability the current norm in Iraq, and with Turkey's current stance against additional Kurdish gains, the Kurds continue to face an uncertain future.

Critical Thinking Questions: What other persistent subcultures have faced harsh repressive actions? Are there common reasons for these government-endorsed actions?

Source: Partly based on Susan Webb, "New Stage in Iraq's Struggle vs. Occupation," *People's Weekly World Newspaper* at www.pww. org/article/articleview/5313/1/142/ [June 17, 2007]; Sabrina Tavernise, "Turkey Rattles Its Sabers at Militant Kurds in Iraq," *New York Times* (June 7, 2007), p. A1.

Just as convergent subcultures illustrate assimilation, persistent subcultures illustrate pluralism. We will examine these two forms of minority integration shortly.

STRUCTURAL CONDITIONS

Relations between dominant and minority groups are influenced as much by structural conditions as by differences in culture. The nature of the social structure influences not only the distribution of power resources (economic, political, and social), but also the accessibility of those resources to groups who seek upward mobility. An expanding economy and an open social system create increased opportunities for minority-group members, thereby reducing the likelihood that tensions will arise. In contrast, a stagnant or contracting economy thwarts many efforts to improve status and antagonizes those who feel most threatened by another group's competition for scarce resources. Such a situation may serve as a breeding ground for conflicts among minority groups even more than between majority and minority groups because the group next highest on the socioeconomic ladder may perceive a threat from below more quickly and react negatively.

The state of the economy is only one important structural factor influencing the opportunities for upward mobility. Another is the degree of change between a minority group's old society and the new one. A traditional or agrarian society typically has a much more stable social structure than a society undergoing transformation through industrialization. The latter society offers dramatic changes in opportunities and lifestyles, not all of them for the better. A migrating minority group's compatibility with the social structure of the new land depends on the degree of similarity between the new country's structural conditions and those of its homeland. A person who leaves an agrarian society for an industrial one is poorly prepared to enter any but the lowest social stratum in a low-paying position. Opportunities for upward mobility may exist, however, if the new land's economy is growing rapidly. In this sense, the structural conditions in the United States from 1880 to 1920 were better for unskilled immigrants than are conditions today. Low-skill jobs are less plentiful today, and an unskilled worker's desire to support a family through hard work may not be matched by the opportunity to do so.

Meanwhile, technological advances have made the world smaller. Rapid transportation and communications (radio, television, telephone, computers, the Internet, fax machines, and e-mail) permit stronger ties to other parts of the world than in the past.[18] Accessibility to their homeland, friends, or relatives may make people less interested in becoming fully assimilated in a new land. Befriending strangers in the new country becomes less necessary. In addition, people's greater knowledge of the world, the rising social consciousness of a society, and structural opportunities for mobility all help to create a more hospitable environment for minority-group members.

STRATIFICATION

Social stratification is the hierarchical classification of the members of society based on the unequal distribution of resources, power, and prestige. The word *resources* refers to such factors as income, property, and borrowing capacity. *Power,* usually reflected by the stratified layers, represents the ability to influence or control others. *Prestige* relates to status and is either *ascribed* (based on age, sex, race, or family background) or *achieved* (based on individual accomplishments).

The process of stratification may moderate or exacerbate any strains or conflicts between groups, depending on the form that the stratification takes. The form can range from rigid and explicit to flexible and subtle—from the overt rigidity of slavery, caste, and forced labor to implicit class distinctions and discrimination based on race or ethnic group. Whether racial and ethnic groups face insurmountable barriers or minor obstacles in achieving upward mobility depends on the form of stratification. The more rigid the stratification, the more likely is the emergence of racial, religious, or other ideologies justifying the existing arrangements—as happened with the rise of racism during slavery in the United States.

The form of stratification affects how groups within the various strata of society view one another. Some people confuse structural differentiation with cultural differentiation. For example, they may believe that a group's low socioeconomic status is due to its values and attitudes rather than to such structural conditions as racism, economic stagnation, and high urban unemployment. The form of stratification is an important determinant of the potential for intergroup conflict. In the United States, both the possibility of upward mobility and structural obstacles to that possibility have existed. When the disparity between the perception of the American Dream and the reality of the difficulty of achieving it grows too great, the possibility of conflict increases.

SOCIAL CLASS

Social class is one categorization sociologists use to designate people's place in the stratification hierarchy; people in a particular social class have a similar level of income, amount of property, degree of power, status, and type of lifestyle. Many factors help determine a person's social class, including the individual's membership in particular racial, religious, and status groups. Although no clearly defined boundaries exist between class groupings in the United States, people have a tendency to cluster together according to certain socioeconomic similarities. The concept or image of social-class reality results from sociopsychological distinctions people make about one another on the basis of such variables as where they live and what they own, as well as to interactions that occur because of those distinctions.

In the 1930s, W. Lloyd Warner headed a classic study of social-class differentiation in the United States.[19] Using the **reputational method**—asking people how they thought others compared to them—Warner found a well-formulated class system in place. In Newburyport, Massachusetts, a small town of about 17,000 that he called "Yankee City," Warner identified six classes: upper-upper, lower-upper, upper-middle, lower-middle, upper-lower, and lower-lower.

Although Warner reached several faulty conclusions because he failed to take a sociohistorical approach, as Stephan Thernstrom points out, some of his findings have validity as to our focus here.[20] When Warner and his associates examined the distribution of ethnic groups among the various classes, certain factors emerged. First, a significant relationship existed between an ethnic group's length of residence and class status; the more recent arrivals tended to be in the lower classes. In addition, an ethnic group tended to be less assimilated and less upwardly mobile if its population in the community was relatively large, if its homeland was close (such as in the case of immigrant French Canadians), if its members had a sojourner rather than a permanent-settler orientation, and if limited opportunities for advancement existed in the community.[21]

Social class becomes important in intergroup relations because it provides a basis for expectations. As Alan Kerckhoff states, social class provides a particular setting for the interplay between the formative experiences of a child, others' expectations of the child, and what kind of adult the child becomes.[22] Beyond this significant aspect, social class also serves as a point of reference in others' responses and in one's self-perception. As a result, social class helps to shape an individual's world of reality and influences group interactions. Attitudes and behavior formed within a social-class framework are not immutable; however; they can change if circumstances change.

Class Consciousness

Just how important are the ethnic factors that Warner and others reported in shaping an awareness of social class? The significance of ethnic factors depends on numerous variables, including economic conditions, mobility patterns, and prevailing attitudes. John Leggett found that class consciousness depends on the ethnic factor: The lower a group's ethnic status in the society, the higher the level of class consciousness.[23] Other studies have shown that working-class ethnic groups tend to view their class as hostile to, and under the political control of, the higher-status classes.[24]

Because ethnic minorities are disproportionately represented among the lower classes and because middle-class values dominate in the United States, it seems reasonable to conclude that at least some of the attitudes of each group result from people's value judgments about social class. That is to say, the dominant group's criticism and stereotyping of the minority group probably rest in part on class distinctions.

Social-class status plays an important role in determining a minority group's adjustment to and acceptance by society. For example, because the first waves of Cuban (1960s) and Vietnamese (1970s) refugees who arrived in the United States possessed the education and occupational experience of the middle class, they succeeded in overcoming early native concerns and did not encounter the same degree of negativism as had earlier groups. In contrast, when unskilled and often illiterate peasants enter the lower-class positions in U.S. society, many U.S. citizens belittle, avoid, and discriminate against them because of their supposedly inferior ways. Frequently, these attitudes and actions reflect an awareness of class differences as well as cultural differences. Because the dominant group usually occupies a higher stratum in the social-class hierarchy, differences in social-class values and lifestyles—in addition to ethnic cultural differences—can be sources of friction.

Ethnicity and Social Class

Differences in stratification among various groups cannot be explained by a single cause, although many observers have tried to do so. For example, in his influential book *The Ethnic Myth*, Stephen Steinberg stressed the importance of social structure and minimized cultural factors.[25] For him, the success of Jews in the United States resulted more from their occupational skills in the urbanized country than from their values. Conversely, Thomas Sowell wrote in *Ethnic America* that the compatibility of a group's cultural characteristics with those of the dominant culture determines the level of a group's economic success.[26] Actually, structural and cultural elements intertwine. Emphasizing only social structure ignores such important cultural variables as values about education. Emphasizing only culture can lead to blaming people who do not succeed.

Colin Greer criticized those who overemphasize ethnic-centered analyses and ignore the larger question of class:

> This kind of ethnic reductionism forces us to accept as predetermined what society defines as truth. Only through ethnicity can identity be securely achieved. The result is that ethnic questions which could, in fact, further our understanding of the relationship of individuals to social structures are always raised in a way that serves to reconcile us to a common heritage of miserable inequities. Instead of realizing that the lack of a well-defined stratification structure, linked to a legitimated aristocratic tradition, led Americans to employ the language of ethnic pluralism in exchange for direct divisions by social class, we continue to ignore the real factors of class in our society. . . . What we must ultimately talk about is class. The cues of felt ethnicity turn out to be the recognizable characteristics of class position in this society: to feel black, Irish, Italian, Jewish has meant to learn to live in accommodation with that part of your heritage that is compatible with the needs and opportunities in America upon arrival and soon thereafter.[27]

In 1964, 10 years before Greer's observations, Milton Gordon first suggested that dominant–minority relations be examined within the larger context of the social structure.[28] This proposition marked an important turning point in racial and ethnic studies.[29] Although he believed that all groups would eventually become assimilated, Gordon offered an explanation of the present pluralistic society. His central thesis was that four factors, or social categories, play a part in forming subsocieties within the nation: ethnicity (by which Gordon also meant race), social class, rural or urban residence, and regionalism.[30] These factors unite in various combinations to create a number of **ethclasses**—subsocieties resulting from the intersection of stratifications of race and ethnic group with stratifications of social class. Additional determinants are the rural or urban setting and the particular region of the country in which a group lives. Examples of ethclasses are lower-middle-class white Catholics in a northeastern city, lower-class black Baptists in the rural South, and upper-class white Jews in a western urban area.

Numerous studies support the concept that race and ethnicity, together with social class, are important in social structures and intergroup conflicts.[31] For example, social scientists such as Thomas Pettigrew and Charles Willie argue that recognizing the intersection of race and class is a key element in understanding the continued existence of black poverty.[32] Not only do ethclass groupings exist, but people tend to interact within them for their intimate primary relationships. To the extent that this is true, multiple allegiances and conflicts are inevitable. According to this view, both cultural and structural pluralism currently exist; numerous groups presently coexist in separate subsocieties based on social class and cultural distinctions. Even people whose families have been in the United States for several generations are affiliated with, and participate in, subsocieties. Nonetheless, Gordon views assimilation as a linear process in which even **structural assimilation** (the large-scale entrance of minorities into mainstream social organization and institutions) will eventually occur.

Blaming the Poor or Society?

In 1932, E. Franklin Frazier formulated his conception of a disorganized and pathological lower-class culture. This thesis served as the inspiration for the controversial **culture-of-poverty** viewpoint that emerged in the 1960s.[33] The writings of two men—Daniel P. Moynihan and Oscar Lewis—sparked an intense debate that continues to resonate today. In his 1965 government report, "The Negro Family: The Case for National Action," Moynihan used Frazier's observations as a springboard for arguing that a "tangle of pathology" so pervaded the black community that it perpetuated a cycle of poverty and deprivation that only outside (government) intervention could overcome.[34]

Family Disintegration. Moynihan argued that family deterioration was a core cause of the problems of high unemployment, welfare dependency, illegitimacy, low achievement, juvenile delinquency, and adult crime:

> At the heart of the deterioration of the fabric of Negro society is the deterioration of the Negro family. It is the fundamental source of weakness of the Negro community at the present time. . . . The white family has achieved a high degree of stability and is maintaining that stability. By contrast, the family structure of the lower class Negroes is highly unstable, and in many urban centers is approaching complete breakdown.[35]

Moynihan described black males as occupying an unstable place in the economy, which prevented them from functioning as strong fathers and husbands. This environment, he said, served as a breeding ground for a continuing vicious circle: The women often not only raised the children but also earned the family income. Consequently, the children grew up in a poorly supervised, unstable environment; they often performed poorly or dropped out of school; they could secure only low-paying jobs—and so the cycle began anew.[36] The Moynihan Report called for federal action to create, among other things, jobs for black, male heads of household in the inner city:

> At the center of the tangle of pathology is the weakness of the family structure. Once or twice removed, it will be found to be the principal source of most of the aberrant, inadequate, or anti-social behavior that did not establish but now serves to perpetuate the cycle of poverty and deprivation. . . .
>
> What then is the problem? We feel that the answer is clear enough. Three centuries of injustice have brought about deep-seated structural distortions in the life of the Negro American. At this point, the present tangle of pathology is capable of perpetuating itself without assistance from the white world. The cycle can be broken only if these distortions are set right.[37]

In 1990, Moynihan reaffirmed his view that a link existed between specific cultural values and deteriorating conditions in lower-class black family life. Citing further social deterioration since the 1960s, he noted in particular the startling rise in out-of-wedlock births from 3 percent of white births and 24 percent of black births in 1963 to 16 percent and 63 percent, respectively, in 1987.[38] These distressing statistics led Moynihan to repeat a statement from his 1965 report:

> From the wild Irish slums of the nineteenth-century Eastern seaboard, to the riot-torn suburbs of Los Angeles, there is one unmistakable lesson in American history: a community that allows a large number of young men to grow up in broken families, dominated by women, never acquiring a stable relationship to male authority, never acquiring any set of rational expectations about the future—that community

asks for and gets chaos. Crime, violence, unrest, disorder—most particularly the furious, unrestrained lashing out at the whole social structure—that is not only to be expected; it is very near to inevitable.[39]

Perpetuation of Poverty. Moynihan's position shares the same premises as Oscar Lewis's theory about a subculture of poverty, detailed in *The Children of Sanchez* (1961) and *La Vida* (1966):[40]

> The culture of poverty, however, is not only an adaptation to a set of objective conditions of the larger society. Once it comes into existence it tends to perpetuate itself from generation to generation because of its effect on the children. By the time slum children are age six or seven they have usually absorbed the basic values and attitudes of their subculture and are not psychologically geared to take full advantage of changing conditions or increased opportunities which may occur in their lifetime.[41]

Politically, Lewis was a leftist, and he did not blame the poor as some critics misinterpreted. Rather, he emphasized the institutionalized tenacity of their poverty, arguing that the system damaged them.[42] Edward Banfield, a conservative, recast Lewis's position to assert that poverty continues because of subcultural patterns. Whereas Lewis held that the mechanics of capitalist production for profit caused poverty, Banfield found its cause in the folkways of its victims. Banfield argued that good jobs, good housing, tripled welfare payments, new schools, quality education, and armies of police officers would not stop the problem. He added,

> If, however, the lower classes were to disappear—if, say, their members were overnight to acquire the attitudes, motivations, and habits of the working class—the most serious and intractable problems of the city would all disappear. . . . The lower-class forms

This single, homeless mother of four children works as an administrative assistant for a high-tech company in California, but the family lives in a church-supported shelter because of her limited income. Living in a homeless shelter not only can be stressful on both the children and mother, but also may lead to multi-generational poverty.

of all problems are at bottom a single problem: the existence of an outlook and style of life which is radically present-oriented and which therefore attaches no value to work, sacrifice, self-improvement, or service to family, friends, or community.[43]

Another form of the "blame game" occurs during the political wrangling that goes on whenever welfare measures are considered. For example, when Congress passed the welfare reform act in 1996, its title was the Personal Responsibility and Work Opportunity Act, a not-too-subtle implication that the poor must change their ways if they want to escape poverty. The act's key provisions were a time limit on welfare payments and a requirement that welfare recipients, after two years, must work. No doubt some lazy people preferred living off a government handout than working, but that was only an extremely small percentage of the welfare recipients. Then, as now, the heavy majority of those living in poverty *do* work, but their limited education and job skills restrict them to low-paying, often unstable, work.[44]

Criticism. Although they were not saying the same thing, Moynihan, Lewis, and Banfield all came under heavy criticism during the 1960s and 1970s—the height of the civil rights movement—from commentators who felt they were blaming the victim. Critics argued that intergenerational poverty results from discrimination, structural conditions, or stratification rigidity. Fatalism, apathy, low aspiration, and other similar orientations found in lower-class culture are thus situational responses within each generation and not the result of cultural deficiencies transmitted from parents to children.

To William Ryan, blaming the victim results in misdirected social programs. If we rationalize away the socially acquired stigma of poverty as being the expression of a subcultural trait, we ignore the continuing effect of current victimizing social forces. As a result, we focus on helping the "disorganized" black family instead of on overcoming racism, or we strive to develop "better" attitudes and skills in low-income children rather than revamping the poor-quality schools they attend.[45]

Charles A. Valentine led an emotional attack on the culture-of-poverty thesis and on Lewis himself.[46] He argued that many of Lewis's "class distinctive traits" of the poor are either "externally imposed conditions" (unemployment, crowded and deteriorated housing, and lack of education) or "unavoidable matters of situational expediency" (hostility toward social institutions and low expectations and self-image).[47] Only by changing the total social structure and the resources available to the poor can we alter any subcultural traits of survival.

Yet Lewis was also saying this.[48] Michael Harrington, whose *The Other America* (1963) helped spark the federal government's War on Poverty program, defended Lewis.[49] Harrington—like Lewis—said that society was to blame for the culture of poverty: "The real explanation of why the poor are where they are is that they made the mistake of being born to the wrong parents, in the wrong section of the country, in the wrong industry, or in the wrong racial or ethnic group."[50]

Like Lewis, Valentine, and Harrington, others argued that all people would desire the same things and cherish the same values if they were in an economic position to do so. Because they are not, they adopt an alternative set of values to survive.[51] Eliot Liebow, in a participant-observer study of lower-class black males, concluded that they try to achieve many of the goals of the larger society but fail for many of the same reasons their fathers did: discrimination, unpreparedness, lack of job skills, and self-doubt.[52] The similarities between generations are due not to cultural transmission but to the sons' independent experience of the same failures. What appears to be a self-sustaining cultural process is actually a secondary adaptation to an adult inability to overcome structural constraints, such as racism, for example.

The debate continues over whether the culture of poverty results from **economic determinism** (structural barriers and discrimination) or from **cultural determinism** (transmission of cultural inadequacies). Some scholars continue to advance arguments about power relations and racial subjugation as the primary culprits, while others insist that cultural values and beliefs primarily explain a group's self-perpetuating world of dependence.[53]

Whatever the cause, most people's attitudes toward welfare and the urban poor (who are predominantly racial and ethnic minorities) reflect a belief in one position or the other. Interestingly, both viewpoints share a belief that determinism of some kind decides the fate of the poor, thereby reflecting the "free-will" thesis popular in Western thought—the notion that every individual "makes" his or her own luck. The two sociological viewpoints also support increased employment and educational opportunities to overcome the persistence of poverty.

However, functionalist explanations for inequality and the conditions of poverty differ significantly from conflict perspectives. Is poverty the result of personal deficiencies? Does long-term poverty result in the development of negative values passed from one generation to the next? Are personal characteristics of the poor the result of long-term poverty, or are they simply adjustments to conditions of poverty? Such questions of blaming the poor and/or existing socioeconomic systems for the existence of poverty, particularly among minority groups, evoke different analytical answers from the two perspectives. What if we used both perspectives instead of one over the other? How would we then answer this question: Is inequality an inevitable part of society?

INTERGROUP CONFLICT

Is conflict inevitable when culturally distinct groups interact? Do structural conditions encourage or reduce the probability of conflict? Robert E. Park argued that a universal, irreversible, perhaps slowly evolving cycle of events made conflict and subsequent resolution by assimilation inevitable. This "race-relations cycle" had four stages: (1) contact between the groups; (2) competition; (3) adjustment or accommodation; and (4) assimilation and amalgamation (or marital assimilation). (In Park's day, the term *race* referred to racial and ethnic groups, and his comments should be understood in this broader sense.) According to Park,

> The race relations cycle which takes the form, to state it abstractly, of contact, competition, accommodation, and eventual assimilation, is apparently progressive and irreversible. Customs regulations, immigration restrictions, and racial barriers may slacken the tempo of the movement; may perhaps halt it altogether for a time; but cannot change its direction, cannot, at any rate, reverse it. . . . It does not follow that because the tendencies to the assimilation and eventual amalgamation of races exist, they should not be resisted and, if possible, altogether inhibited. . . . Rising tides of color and oriental exclusion laws are merely incidental evidences of this diminishing distance. . . . In the Hawaiian Islands, where all the races of the Pacific meet and mingle . . . , the native races are disappearing and new peoples are coming into existence. Races and cultures die—it has always been so—but civilization lives on.[54]

Park's theory fit nicely into the prevailing assimilationist thinking of his time, but his race-relations cycle has several problems. By its very nature, the claim that all instances of interaction between subgroups in a society must end in assimilation is not testable because any instance of nonassimilation can be explained away as a case in which the cycle is not yet complete.[55] Indeed, Park never cited any example where his cycle had reached completion. Instead of seeing such negative data as refuting the theory, Park and other cyclical theorists attributed the lack of assimilation to temporary obstacles or interference. Such tautological reasoning, argues Stanford M. Lyman, leaves this theory deficient in an essential element of empirical science: It cannot be proved or disproved.[56] Perhaps, though, we might consider as one example the interaction between Anglo-Saxon residents and Norman-French invaders, both of whom gradually disappeared as the "English" emerged.

Meanwhile, the supposed universality of the stages identified in Park's cyclical theory is refuted by counterexamples in which conflict and competition did not occur when different groups came into contact. Brazil and Hawaii are only two places where relatively peaceful and harmonious interactions have existed among different, unassimilated peoples. In many other instances of intergroup relations, however, some form of stress, tension, or conflict does occur. In this chapter, we examine the major factors that may underlie such conflict: cultural differentiation and structural differentiation.

Cultural Differentiation

When similarities between the arriving minority group and the indigenous group exist, the relationship tends to be relatively harmonious and assimilation is likely to occur eventually.[57] Conversely, the greater and more visible the **cultural differentiation,** the greater the likelihood that conflict will occur. When large numbers of German and Irish Catholics came to the United States in the mid-19th century, Protestants grew uneasy. As priests and nuns arrived and Catholics built churches, convents, and schools, Protestants became alarmed at what they feared was a papal conspiracy to gain control of the country. Emotions ran high, resulting in civil unrest and violence.

Religion has often been a basis for cultural conflict in the United States as is demonstrated by the history of discriminatory treatment also suffered in this country by Mormons, Jews, and Quakers. Yet many other aspects of cultural visibility can serve as sources of contention as well. Cultural differences may range from clothing (e.g., Sikh turbans and Hindu saris) to leisure activities (e.g., Hispanic cockfights). Americans once condemned the Chinese as opium smokers, even though the British had introduced opium smoking into China, promoted it among the lower-class Chinese population, and even fought wars against the Chinese government to maintain the lucrative trade.

Cultural differentiation does not necessarily cause intergroup conflict. A partial explanation of variances in relations between culturally distinct groups comes from interactionist theory, which holds that the extent of shared symbols and definitions between intercommunicating groups determines the nature of their interaction patterns. Although actual differences may support conflict, interactionists say the key to harmonious or disharmonious relations lies in the definitions or interpretations of those differences. Tolerance or intolerance—acceptance or rejection of others—thus depends on whether others are perceived as threatening or nonthreatening, assimilable or nonassimilable, worthy or unworthy.

Structural Differentiation

Because they offer macrosocial analyses of a society, both functionalist theory and conflict theory provide bases for understanding how structural conditions (**structural differentiation**) affect intergroup relations. Functionalists seek explanations in the adjustments needed in the social system to compensate for other changes. Conflict theorists emphasize the conscious, purposeful actions of dominant groups to maintain systems of inequality.

Functionalists explain how sometimes economic and technological conditions facilitate minority integration. When the economy is healthy and jobs are plentiful, newcomers find it easier to become established and work their way up the socioeconomic ladder. In the United States today, however, technological progress has reduced the number of low-status, blue-collar jobs and increased the number of jobs requiring more highly skilled and educated workers. As a result, fewer jobs are available for unskilled, foreign, marginal, or unassimilated people.

Perhaps because of the importance of a job as a source of economic security and status, **occupational mobility**—the ability of individuals to improve their job position—seems to be an important factor in determining whether prejudice will increase or decrease. A number of studies have shown that a fear of economic insecurity increases ethnic hostility. One study of U.S. workers found that a perceived threat to either their cultural norms or economic well-being led to more negative attitudes toward immigrants.[58] Other researchers found that worsening economic circumstances intensify prejudicial stereotypes and attitudes about immigration.[59] In addition, upwardly mobile people are generally more tolerant than nonmobile individuals. It would appear that the loss of status and prestige

In this ESL class these Latino immigrants, like many other newcomers, seek to master English to ease their entry into the societal mainstream. Nationwide, there is a shortage of such classes in this important step in the acculturation process that helps reduce cultural differentiation and enhance opportunities for occupational mobility.

increases hostility toward outgroups, whereas upward gains enable people to feel more benevolent toward others.

ETHNIC STRATIFICATION

If one group becomes dominant and another becomes subservient, obviously one group has more power than the other. Social-class status partly reflects this unequal distribution of power, which also may fall along racial or ethnic lines. **Ethnic stratification** is the structured inequality of different groups with different access to social rewards as a result of their status in the social hierarchy. Because most Americans associate ethnicity with anything different from the mainstream, they don't realize that ethnicity also exists at the top. Ashley W. Doane Jr. reminds us that dominant-group ethnicity lies "hidden" because its status results in the taken-for-granted nature of dominant-group identity.[60]

Stratification is a normal component of all societies but typically falls along racial and ethnic lines in diverse societies. How does ethnic stratification continue in a democracy where supposedly all have an equal opportunity for upward mobility? Functionalists suggest that the ethnocentrism of those in the societal mainstream leads to discrimination against those in outgroups, as determined by their racial or cultural differences. Conflict analysts instead stress the subordination of minorities by the dominant group because that group benefits from such ethnic stratification. Two middle-range conflict theories offer helpful insights into this perspective. The power-differential theory helps explain the initial phases of domination and conflict, and the internal-colonialism theory examines the continuation of such subordination.

The Power-Differential Theory

Stanley Lieberson suggested a **power-differential theory**, in which intergroup relations depend on the relative power of the migrant group and the indigenous group.[61] Because the two groups usually do not share the same culture, each strives to maintain its own institutions. Which group becomes *superordinate* (superior in rank, class, or status) and which becomes *subordinate* (inferior in rank, class, or status) governs subsequent relations.

If the newcomers possess superior technology (particularly weapons) and social organization, conflict may occur at an early stage, with a consequent population decline due to warfare, disease, or disruption of sustenance activities. Finding their institutions undermined or co-opted, the local inhabitants may eventually participate in the institutions of the dominant group. In time, a group consciousness may arise, and sometimes the indigenous group even succeeds in ousting the superordinate migrant group. When this happened in many former African colonies and in Southeast Asia, interethnic fighting among the many indigenous groups led to new forms of superordination and subordination within countries (as with the Hutu and Tutsi peoples in Burundi and Rwanda).

Lieberson maintained that neither conflict nor assimilation is an inevitable outcome of racial and ethnic contact. Instead, the particular relationship between the two groups involved determines which alternative will occur. Conflict between a superordinate migrant group and a subordinate indigenous group can be immediate and violent. If the relationship is the reverse, and the indigenous group is superordinate, conflict will be limited and sporadic, and the host society will exert a great deal of pressure on the subordinate migrant group to assimilate, acquiesce, or leave.

In addition, a superordinate indigenous group can limit the numbers and groups entering to reduce the threat of demographic or institutional imbalance. Restrictive U.S. immigration laws against the Chinese in 1882 and against all but northern and western Europeans in 1921 and 1924 illustrate this process. Violent union attempts to remove Asian workers, labor union hostility to African Americans, and efforts to expel foreigners (e.g., Indians, Japanese, and Filipinos) or to revolutionize the social order (Native American boarding schools and the Americanization movement) illustrate the use of institutional power against minority groups.

Another sociologist, William J. Wilson, has suggested that power relations between superordinate and subordinate groups differ in paternalistic and competitive systems.[62] With **paternalism** (the system that once governed South Africa and the Old South of the United States), the dominant group exercises almost absolute control over the subordinate group and can direct virtually unlimited coercion to maintain societal order. In a competitive system (such as the United States has today), some degree of power reciprocity exists, so the dominant group in society is somewhat vulnerable to political pressures and economic boycotts.

Rapid social change—industrialization, unionization, urbanization, migration, and political change—usually loosens the social structure, leading to new tensions as both groups seek new power resources. If the minority group increases its power resources, through protective laws and improved economic opportunities, it may foresee even greater improvement in its condition. This heightened awareness is likely to lead to conflict unless additional gains are forthcoming. For example, the civil rights movement of the mid-1960s brought about legislation ensuring minority rights and opportunities in jobs, housing, education, and other aspects of life, but this led to new tensions. The 1960s were marked by urban riots and burnings, protest demonstrations and human barricades to stop construction of low-income housing sites, school-busing controversies, and challenges to labor discrimination.

The Internal-Colonialism Theory

In analyzing the black militancy of the late 1960s, Robert Blauner attempted to integrate the factors of caste and racism, ethnicity, culture, and economic exploitation.[63] His major point was that U.S. treatment of its black population resembled past European subjugation and exploitation of non-Western peoples in their own lands. Although he focused on black–white relations in the United States, he suggested that Mexican Americans might also fit his **internal-colonialism theory** and that Native Americans could be added as another suitable example:

> Of course many ethnic groups in America have lived in ghettoes. What makes the Black ghettoes an expression of colonized status are three special features. First, the ethnic ghettoes arose more from voluntary choice, both in the sense of the choice to immigrate to America and the decision to live among one's fellow ethnics. Second, the immigrant ghettoes tended to be a one- and two-generation phenomenon; they were actually way-stations in the process of acculturation and assimilation. When they continue to persist as in the case of San Francisco's Chinatown, it is because they are big business for the ethnics themselves and there is a new stream of immigrants.

The Black ghetto on the other hand has been a more permanent phenomenon, although some individuals do escape it. But most relevant is the third point. European ethnic groups like the Poles, Italians and Jews generally only experienced a brief period, often less than a generation, during which their residential buildings, commercial stores, and other enterprises were owned by outsiders. The Chinese and Japanese faced handicaps of color prejudice that were almost as strong as the Blacks faced, but very soon gained control of their internal communities, because their traditional ethnic culture and social organization had not been destroyed by slavery and internal colonization. But Afro-Americans are distinct in the extent to which their segregated communities have remained controlled economically, politically, and administratively from the outside.[64]

Several of these statements need to be modified. Chinatowns long persisted not because of any business advantage but because of racial discrimination. In proportion to the Chinatown population, only a few Chinese actually benefit from the tourist trade. Also, the Chinese and Japanese *always* had "control of their internal communities," although they differ greatly from each other in their structure and cohesiveness.

Blauner considers the exploitation phase that was temporary for other groups to be more nearly permanent for blacks and possibly Chicanos. He believes that conflict and confrontation, as well as real or apparent chaos and disorder, will continue, because this may be the only way an internally colonized group can deal with the dominant society. This conflict orientation suggests that the multigenerational exploitation of certain groups creates a unique situation and a basis for the often violent conflict that sporadically flares up in our cities (Table 2.2).

Origins of Ethnic Stratification

For ethnicity to become a basis for stratification, several factors seem necessary:

Ethnic stratification will emerge when distinct ethnic groups are brought into sustained contact only if the groups are characterized by a high degree of ethnocentrism, competition, *and* differential power. Competition provides the motivation for stratification; ethnocentrism channels the competition along ethnic lines; and the power differential determines whether either group will be able to subordinate the other.[65]

TABLE 2.2   Middle-Range Conflict Theories

The Power-Differential Theory	The Internal-Colonialism Theory
1. Neither conflict nor assimilation is inevitable.	1. American treatment of its black population resembles past European subjugation and exploitation of non-Western peoples.
2. The relative power of indigenous and migrant, groups determines events.	
3. If the migrant group is superordinate, early conflict and colonization will occur.	2. Black ghettos are more nearly permanent than immigrant ghettos.
4. If the indigenous group is superordinate, occasional labor and racial strife, legislative restrictions, and pressures to assimilate are common.	3. Black ghettos are controlled economically, politically, and administratively from the outside.
5. In a paternalistic society, the dominant group has almost absolute power.	4. Continual exploitation produces conflict and confrontation.
6. A competitive society is vulnerable to political pressures and economic boycotts.	5. Mexican Americans and Native Americans may also fit this model.

This power differential is of enormous importance in race and ethnic relations. If the stratification system is rigid, as in a slave or caste system, so that people have no hope or means of improving their status, intergroup relations may remain stable despite perhaps being far from mutually satisfactory. Dominant power, whether expressed in legalized ways or through structural discrimination, intimidation, or coercion, maintains the social system.

Challenges to the Status Quo. Even if the stratification system allows for upward mobility, some members of the dominant group may believe that the lower-class racial and ethnic groups are challenging the social order as they strive for their share of the "good life." If the dominant group does not feel threatened, the change will be peaceful. If the minority group meets resistance but retains hope and a sense of belonging to the larger society, the struggle for more power will occur within the system (e.g., by means of demonstrations, boycotts, voter-registration drives, or lobbying) rather than through violence.[66] The late-19th-century race-baiting riots on the West Coast against Chinese and Japanese workers and the 1919 Chicago race riots against blacks attempting to enter the meat-packing industry illustrate violent responses of a dominant group against a minority group over power resources. Similarly, the black–Korean violence in several urban neighborhoods during the late 20th century, including during the 1992 Los Angeles riots, and the violence between U.S. blacks and Cubans in Miami in 1988 typify minority-against-minority clashes over limited resources.

Social-Class Antagonisms. Conflict theorists, such as Ralf Dahrendorf, argue that social class is an important variable affecting conflict. Dahrendorf sees a correlation between a group's economic position and the intensity of its conflict with the dominant society. The greater the deprivation in economic resources, social status, and social power, the likelier the weaker group is to resort to violent conflict to achieve gains in any of these three areas. As the social-class position of a group increases, intergroup conflict becomes less intense and less violent.[67]

Years earlier, Max Weber argued that when economic resources become more evenly distributed among classes, relative status will become the issue of conflict—if conflict occurs at all.[68] Conflict occurs not only because a lower-class group seeks an end to deprivation but also because the group next higher on the socioeconomic ladder feels threatened. Often, the working-class group displays the greatest hostility and prejudice of all established groups in the society toward the upward-striving minority group. Other factors may be at work as well, but status competition is a significant source of conflict.

Social-class antagonisms influence people's perceptions of racial and ethnic groups, too.[69] Some social scientists maintain that the problem of black–white relations is more a problem of social class than of racism. James M. O'Kane illustrates this view:

> The gap exists between the classes, not the races; it is between the white and black middle classes on the one hand, and the white and black lower classes on the other. Skin color and the history of servitude do little to explain the present polarization of the classes. . . . Class differentials, not racial differentials, explain the presence and persistence of poverty in the ranks of the urban Negro.[70]

O'Kane suggests several parallels between Irish, Italian, and Polish immigrants and southern blacks who migrated to northern cities (the Chinese, some of the Japanese, and others also fit this model). All emigrated from agrarian poverty to urban industrial slums. Encountering prejudice and discrimination, some sought alternative routes to material success: crime, ethnic politics, or stable but unskilled employment.[71] Other social scientists, however, argue that the black experience does not equate with that of European immigrants. They hold, as did the Kerner Commission investigating the urban riots of the late 1960s, that the dominant society's practice of internal colonialism toward blacks deprived them of the strong social organizations that other groups had. Moreover, today's labor market offers fewer unskilled jobs for blacks than it offered other immigrant groups in earlier times, thereby depriving blacks of a means to begin moving upward.[72]

This debate over whether race or social class is the primary factor in assessing full integration of blacks in the United States continues to rage, particularly among black social scientists. We will devote more attention to this topic in Chapter 10.

IS THERE A WHITE CULTURE?

In the mid-1990s, interest in white studies rose significantly. White studies essentially focus on how whiteness has led to racial domination and hegemony, in which white American culture is simply called "American," thereby presuming that black, Native American, Asian, or Hispanic cultures are not "American" but instead racial and/or ethnic subcultures. The idea that a white culture also exists is difficult for many people to grasp, say the white studies advocates, much as a fish is unaware of water until out of it, because of its environmental universality.

The premise for a white culture existing independent of an "American" culture is that all racial groups have large social/cultural characteristics that change over time. These white values, attitudes, shared understandings, and behavior patterns—like many aspects of culture—are often unrealized by group members because they are part of a taken-for-granted world. Yet even though white culture may not be identifiable among its members, it is nonetheless real and easily recognizable by nonwhites. For example, says Jeff Hitchcock in *Lifting the White Veil*, in black culture feelings are given precedence over sensibilities. He explains that when a feeling comes on a person, black culture says it is appropriate to express it, but white culture

> . . . works hard to keep the volume down, lest we all go crazy from the demands we place on each other's capacity for self-control. Experience in the culture helps. We learn how not to step on toes, hurt other people's "feelings," to not make a scene, and all the other little social rules and practices of a lifetime. We rein it in, and trade spontaneity . . . for an orderly demeanor and generally predictable and controlled everyday existence.[73]

Lacking an understanding of the existence of white culture, say its proponents, results in the dominant group misinterpreting alternative cultural experiences as racial or else as the personal failings of someone of color. Recognizing its existence could be a first step toward building a truly multiracial society.

▲▲▲ RETROSPECT

Culture provides the normative definitions by which members of a society perceive and interpret the world about them. Language and other forms of symbolic interaction provide the means by which this accumulated knowledge is transmitted. Becoming acculturated requires learning both the language and the symbol system of the new society. Sometimes, though, situations become real in their consequences because people earlier defined them as real (the Thomas theorem). Unless it is isolated from the rest of the world, a society undergoes change through culture contact and the diffusion of ideas, inventions, and practices. Within large societies, subcultures usually exist. They may gradually be assimilated (convergent subcultures), or they may remain distinct (persistent subcultures).

Structural conditions, too, influence people's perceptions of the world—whether they live in an industrialized or agrarian society, a closed or open social system, a growing or contracting economy, a friendly or unfriendly environment, and whether their homeland, friends, and relatives are accessible or remote. Distribution of power resources and compatibility with the existing social structure greatly influence majority–minority relations as well. Interactionists concentrate on perceptions of cultural differences as they affect intergroup relations. Functionalists and conflict theorists emphasize structural conditions.

The interplay between the variables of race, ethnic group, and social class is important for understanding how some problems and conflicts arise. A feature interpreted as an attribute of a race or ethnic group may in fact be a broader aspect of social class. Because many attitudes and values are situational responses to socioeconomic status, a change in status or opportunities will bring about a change in those attitudes and values. Investigative studies have not supported the culture-of-poverty hypothesis of family disintegration and a self-perpetuating poverty value orientation.

Stratification along racial and ethnic lines is common in a diverse society. Functionalists think ethnocentrism leads to discrimination to cause this. One middle-range conflict perspective focuses on the power differential. Whether the indigenous group or migrant group possesses superior power determines the nature of subsequent intergroup relations. Another factor is whether the social system is paternalistic or competitive. Considering black and Hispanic ghettos or Native American reservations as examples of internal colonialism offers a second conflict perspective.

✦✦✦ KEY TERMS

Acculturation
Chain migration
Convergent subcultures
Cultural determinism
Cultural differentiation
Cultural diffusion
Cultural transmission
Culture
Culture of poverty
Culture shock

Economic determinism
Ethclasses
Ethnic stratification
Ethnic subcultures
Ethnogenesis
Internal-colonialism
    theory
Linguistic relativity
Marginality
Material culture

Nonmaterial culture
Norms
Occupational mobility
Paralinguistic signals
Parallel social
    institutions
Paternalism
Persistent subcultures
Power-differential theory
Reputational method

Social class	Structural assimilation	Vicious-circle
Social stratification	Structural differentiation	phenomenon
Social structure	Thomas theorem	

DISCUSSION QUESTIONS

1. What is the relationship among culture, reality, and intergroup relations?
2. What are subcultures? What forms do they take? What significance do these forms have for intergroup relations?
3. What is the relationship between ethnicity and social class?
4. What is meant by the *culture of poverty*? What criticisms exist about this thinking?
5. How do the functional and conflict perspectives approach the factors likely to contribute to intergroup conflict?

SUGGESTED READINGS

Anderson, Elijah, and Douglas S. Massey (eds.). *Problem of the Century: Racial Stratification in the United States.* New York: Russell Sage Foundation, 2001.
Offers sixteen essays on racial differentiation as measured by various demographic, economic, and educational indicators.

Griswold, Wendy. *Cultures and Societies in a Changing World,* 2nd ed. Thousand Oaks, CA: Pine Forge Press, 2003.
A thorough examination of the elements and dynamics of culture and the cultural diffusion spread by technology and the global economy.

Harrison, Lawrence E., and Samuel P. Huntington (eds.). *Culture Matters: How Values Shape Human Progress.* New York: Basic Books, 2001.
A collection of essays by leading social scientists that examines how culture affects prosperity, democracy, and social justice among both countries and immigrants.

Hitchcock, Jeff. *Lifting the White Veil: An Exploration of White Culture in a Multiracial Context.* Roselle, NJ: Crandall Dostie & Douglass Books, 2003.
An overview of the history of whiteness in U.S. society, with a personal, provocative argument on the need to recognize the existence of white culture and to "decenter" it.

Mangum, Garth L., Stephen L. Mangum, and Andrew M. Sum. *The Persistence of Poverty in the United States.* Baltimore: Johns Hopkins University Press, 2003.
A concise and coherent discussion of the causes and magnitude of poverty, with some strategic suggestions to alleviate the problem.

Ritzer, George. *The McDonaldization of Society,* 5th ed. Thousand Oaks, CA: Pine Forge Press, 2007.
Fine use of sociological imagination to show cultural diffusion in the organization of work throughout the world.

MYSOCKIT

Additional resources for this chapter can be found in MySocKit. If you have a subscription to MySocKit, go to www.mysockit.com to study, review, and go beyond the book to learn more about race and ethnic relations.

Prejudice and Discrimination

When strangers from different groups come into contact with one another, their interaction patterns may take many forms. So far, we have discussed the roles that ethnocentrism, social distance, culture, and social structure play in shaping perceptions of any outgroup. Prejudice and discrimination also emerge as major considerations in understanding intergroup relations. Why do they exist? Why do they persist? Why do certain groups become targets more frequently? How can we eliminate prejudicial attitudes and discriminatory actions?

◢◣◥ PREJUDICE

The word prejudice, derived from the Latin word *praejudicium*, originally meant "prejudgment." Thus, some scholars defined a prejudiced person as one who hastily reached a conclusion before examining the facts.[1] This definition proved inadequate, however, because social scientists discovered that prejudice often arose *after* groups came into contact and had at least some knowledge of one another. For that reason, Louis Wirth described **prejudice** as "an attitude with an emotional bias."[2]

Because feelings shape our attitudes, they reduce our receptivity to additional information that may alter those attitudes. Ralph Rosnow had this fact in mind when he broadened the definition of prejudice to encompass "any unreasonable attitude that is unusually resistant to rational influence."[3] In fact, a deeply prejudiced person is almost totally immune to absorbing such additional information. Gordon Allport offered a classic example of such an individual in the following dialogue:

Mr. X: The trouble with the Jews is that they only take care of their own group.

Mr. Y: But the record of the Community Chest campaign shows that they gave more generously, in proportion to their numbers, to the general charities of the community, than did non-Jews.

Mr. X: That shows they are always trying to buy favor and intrude into Christian affairs. They think of nothing but money; that is why there are so many Jewish bankers.

Mr. Y: But a recent study shows that the percentage of Jews in the banking business is negligible, far smaller than the percentage of non-Jews.

Mr. X: That's just it; they don't go in for respectable business; they are only in the movie business or run night clubs.*

It is almost as if Mr. X were saying, "My mind is made up; don't confuse me with the facts." He does not refute the argument; rather, he ignores each bit of new and contradictory information and moves on to a new area in which he distorts other facts to support his prejudice against Jews.

Prejudicial attitudes may be either positive or negative. Sociologists primarily study the latter, however, because only negative attitudes can lead to turbulent social relations between dominant and minority groups. Numerous writers, therefore, have defined *prejudice* as an attitudinal "system of negative beliefs, feelings, and action-orientations regarding a certain group or groups of people."[4] The status of the strangers is an important factor in the development of a negative attitude. Prejudicial attitudes exist among members of both dominant and minority groups. Thus, in the relations between dominant and minority groups, the antipathy felt by one group for another is quite often reciprocated.

Psychological perspectives on prejudice—whether behaviorist, cognitive, or psychoanalytic—focus on the subjective states of mind of individuals. In these perspectives, a person's prejudicial attitudes may result from imitation or conditioning (behaviorist), perceived similarity–dissimilarity of beliefs (cognitive), or specific personality characteristics (psychoanalytic). In contrast, sociological perspectives focus on the objective conditions of society as the social forces behind prejudicial attitudes and behind racial and ethnic relations. Individuals do not live in a vacuum; social reality affects their states of mind.

Both perspectives are necessary to understand prejudice. As psychologist Gordon Allport argued, besides needing a close study of habits, perceptions, motivation, and personality, we need an analysis of social settings, situational forces, demographic and ecological variables, and legal and economic trends.[5] Psychological and sociological perspectives complement each other in providing a fuller explanation of intergroup relations.

The Psychology of Prejudice

The psychological approach to prejudice is to examine individual behavior. We can understand more about prejudice among individuals by focusing on four areas of study: levels of prejudice, self-justification, personality, and frustration.

Levels of Prejudice.   Bernard Kramer suggested that prejudice exists on three levels: cognitive, emotional, and action orientation.[6] The **cognitive level of prejudice** encompasses a person's beliefs and perceptions of a group as threatening or non-threatening, inferior or equal (e.g., in terms of intellect, status, or biological composition), seclusive or intrusive, impulse gratifying, acquisitive, or possessing other positive or negative characteristics. Mr. X's cognitive beliefs are that Jews are

---

*Gordon W. Allport, *The Nature of Prejudice* (Reading, MA: Addison-Wesley, 1954), pp. 13–14.

intrusive and acquisitive. Other illustrations of cognitive beliefs are that the Irish are heavy drinkers and fighters, African Americans are rhythmic and lazy, and the Poles are thick-headed and unintelligent.

Generalizations shape both ethnocentric and prejudicial attitudes, but there is a difference. *Ethnocentrism* is a generalized rejection of all outgroups on the basis of an ingroup focus, whereas *prejudice* is a rejection of certain people solely on the basis of their membership in a particular outgroup.

In many societies, members of the majority group may believe that a particular low-status minority group is dirty, immoral, violent, or law breaking. In the United States, the Irish, Italians, African Americans, Mexicans, Chinese, Puerto Ricans, and others have at one time or another been labeled with most, if not all, of these adjectives. In most European countries and in the United States, the group lowest on the socioeconomic ladder has often been depicted in caricature as also lowest on the evolutionary ladder. The Irish and African Americans in the United States and the peasants and various ethnic groups in Europe have all been depicted in the past as apelike:

> The Victorian images of the Irish as "white Negro" and simian Celt, or a combination of the two, derived much of its force and inspiration from physiognomical beliefs . . . [but] every country in Europe had its equivalent of "white Negroes" and simianized men, whether or not they happened to be stereotypes of criminals, assassins, political radicals, revolutionaries, Slavs, gypsies, Jews or peasants.[7]

The **emotional level of prejudice** encompasses the feelings that a minority group arouses in an individual. Although these feelings may be based on stereotypes from the cognitive level, they represent a more intense stage of personal involvement. The emotional attitudes may be negative or positive, such as fear/envy, distrust/trust, disgust/admiration, or contempt/empathy. These feelings, based on beliefs about the group, may be triggered by social interaction or by the possibility of interaction. For example, whites might react with fear or anger to the integration of their schools or neighborhoods, or Protestants might be jealous of the lifestyle of a highly successful Catholic business executive.

An **action-orientation level of prejudice** is the positive or negative predisposition to engage in discriminatory behavior. A person who harbors strong feelings about members of a certain racial or ethnic group may have a tendency to act for or against them—being aggressive or nonaggressive, offering assistance or withholding it. Such an individual would also be likely to want to exclude or include members of that group both in close, personal social relations and in peripheral social relations. For example, some people would want to exclude members of the disliked group from doing business with them or living in their neighborhood. Another manifestation of the action-orientation level of prejudice is the desire to change or maintain the status differential or inequality between the two groups, whether the area is economic, political, educational, social, or a combination. Note that an action orientation is a predisposition to act, not the action itself.

Self-Justification. **Self-justification** involves denigrating a person or group to justify maltreatment of them. In this situation, self-justification leads to prejudice and discrimination against members of another group.

Some philosophers argue that we are not so much rational creatures as we are rationalizing creatures. We require reassurance that the things we do and the lives we live are proper, that good reasons for our actions exist. If we can convince ourselves that another group is inferior, immoral, or dangerous, we may feel justified in discriminating against its members, enslaving them, or even killing them.

History is filled with examples of people who thought their maltreatment of others was just and necessary: As defenders of the "true faith," the Crusaders killed "Christ-killers" (Jews) and "infidels" (Muslims). Participants in the Spanish Inquisition imprisoned, tortured, and executed "heretics," "the disciples of the Devil." Similarly, the Puritans burned witches, whose refusal to confess "proved they were evil"; pioneers exploited or killed Native Americans who were "heathen savages"; and whites mistreated, enslaved, or killed African Americans, who were "an inferior species." According to U.S. Army officers, the civilians in the Vietnamese village of My Lai were "probably" aiding the Viet Cong; so in 1968, U.S. soldiers fighting in the Vietnam War felt justified in slaughtering over 300 unarmed people there, including women, children, and the elderly. In recent years suicide bombers and terrorists have killed innocent civilians, also justifying their actions through their religious fanaticism.

Some sociologists believe that self-justification works the other way around. That is, instead of self-justification serving as a basis for subjugating others, the subjugation occurs first and the self-justification follows, resulting in prejudice and continued discrimination.[8] The evolution of racism as a concept after the establishment of the African slave trade would seem to support this idea. Philip Mason offers an insight into this view:

> A specialized society is likely to defeat a simpler society and provide a lower tier still of enslaved and conquered peoples. The rulers and organizers sought security for themselves and their children; to perpetuate the power, the esteem, and the comfort they had achieved, it was necessary not only that the artisans and labourers should work contentedly but that the rulers should sleep without bad dreams. No one can say with certainty how the myths originated, but it is surely relevant that when one of the founders of Western thought set himself to frame an ideal state that would embody social justice, he—like the earliest city dwellers—not only devised a society stratified in tiers but believed it would be necessary to persuade the traders and work-people that, by divine decree, they were made from brass and iron, while the warriors were made of silver and the rulers of gold.[9]

Another example of self-justification serving as a source of prejudice is the dominant group's assumption of an attitude of superiority over other groups. In this respect, establishing a prestige hierarchy—ranking the status of various ethnic groups—results in differential association. To enhance or maintain self-esteem, a person may avoid social contact with groups deemed inferior and associate only with those identified as being of high status. Through such behavior, self-justification may come to intensify the social distance between groups. As discussed in Chapter 1, *social distance* refers to the degree to which ingroup members do not engage in social or primary relationships with members of various outgroups.

Personality. In 1950, in *The Authoritarian Personality,* T. W. Adorno and his colleagues reported a correlation between individuals' early childhood experiences of harsh parental discipline and their development of an **authoritarian personality** as adults.[10] If parents assume an excessively domineering posture in their relations with a child, exercising stern measures and threatening to withdraw love if the child does not respond with weakness and submission, the child tends to be insecure and to nurture much latent hostility against the parents. When such children become adults, they may demonstrate **displaced aggression,** directing their hostility against a powerless group to compensate for their feelings of insecurity and fear. Highly prejudiced individuals tend to come from families that emphasize obedience.

The authors identified authoritarianism by the use of a measuring instrument called an F scale (the *F* stands for potential fascism). Other tests included the A-S (anti-Semitism) and E (ethnocentrism) scales, the latter measuring attitudes toward various minorities. One of their major findings was that people who scored high on authoritarianism also consistently showed a high degree of prejudice against all minority groups. These highly prejudiced people were characterized by rigidity of viewpoint, dislike for ambiguity, strict obedience to leaders, and intolerance of weakness in themselves and others.

No sooner did *The Authoritarian Personality* appear than controversy began. H. H. Hyman and P. B. Sheatsley challenged the methodology and analysis.[11] Solomon Asch questioned the assumptions that the F scale responses represented a belief system and that structural variables (e.g., ideologies, stratification, and mobility) do not play a role in shaping personality.[12] E. A. Shils argued that the authors were interested only in measuring authoritarianism of the political right while ignoring such tendencies in those at the other end of the political spectrum.[13] Other investigators sought alternative explanations for the authoritarian personality. D. Stewart and T. Hoult extended the framework beyond family childhood experiences to include other social factors.[14] H. C. Kelman and Janet Barclay pointed out that substantial evidence exists showing that lower intelligence and less education also correlate with high authoritarianism scores on the F scale.[15]

Despite the critical attacks, the underlying conceptions of *The Authoritarian Personality* were important, and research into personality as a factor in prejudice has continued. Subsequent investigators refined and modified the original study. Correcting scores for response bias, they conducted cross-cultural studies. Respondents in Germany and Near Eastern countries, where more authoritarian social structures exist, scored higher on authoritarianism and social distance between groups. In Japan, Germany, and the United States, authoritarianism and social distance were moderately related. Other studies suggested that an inverse relationship exists between social class and F scale scores: the higher the social class, the lower the authoritarianism.[16]

Although studies of authoritarian personality have helped us understand some aspects of prejudice, they have not provided a causal explanation. Most of the findings in this area show a correlation, but the findings do not prove, for example, that harsh discipline of children causes them to become prejudiced adults. Perhaps the strict parents were themselves prejudiced, and the child learned those attitudes from them—or, as George Simpson and J. Milton Yinger say,

> One must be careful not to assume too quickly that a certain tendency—rigidity of mind, for example—that is correlated with prejudice necessarily causes that prejudice. . . . The sequence may be the other way around. . . . It is more likely that both are related to more basic factors.[17]

For some people, prejudice may indeed be rooted in subconscious childhood tensions, but we simply do not know whether these tensions directly cause a high degree of prejudice in the adult or whether other powerful social forces are the determinants. Whatever the explanation, authoritarianism is a significant phenomenon worthy of continued investigation. Recent research, however, has stressed social and situational factors, rather than personality, as primary causes of prejudice and discrimination.[18]

Yet another dimension of the personality component is the role of self-esteem. Galinsky and Ku found that those with high self-esteem evaluated an outgroup more positively than those with low self-esteem.[19] Major, Kaiser, and McCoy reported that individuals' awareness of potential discrimination against themselves provided self-esteem protection, in contrast to the lower self-esteem experienced by those less aware of such external factors affecting themselves.[20] It would thus appear that the level of one's self-esteem affects attitudes both about oneself and others.

Frustration. Frustration is the result of relative deprivation in which expectations remain unsatisfied. **Relative deprivation** is a lack of resources, or rewards, in one's standard of living in comparison with those of others in the society. A number of investigators have suggested that frustrations tend to increase aggression toward others.[21] Frustrated people may easily strike out against the perceived cause of their frustration. However, this reaction may not be possible because the true source of the frustration is often too nebulous to be identified or too powerful to act against. In such instances, the result may be displaced aggression; in this situation, the frustrated individual or group usually redirects anger against a more visible, vulnerable, and socially sanctioned target that is unable to strike back. Minorities meet these criteria and are thus frequently the recipients of displaced aggression by the dominant group.

Blaming others for something that is not their fault is known as **scapegoating.** The term comes from the ancient Hebrew custom of using a goat during the Day of Atonement as a symbol of the sins of the people. In an annual ceremony, a priest placed his hands on the head of a goat and listed the people's sins in a symbolic transference of guilt; he then chased the goat out of the community, thereby freeing the people of sin.[22] Since those times, the powerful group has usually punished the scapegoat group rather than allowing it to escape.

There have been many instances throughout world history of minority groups serving as scapegoats, including the Christians in ancient Rome, the Huguenots in France, the Jews in Europe and Russia, and the Puritans and Quakers in England. Gordon Allport suggests that certain characteristics are necessary for a group to become a suitable scapegoat. The group must be (1) highly visible in physical appearance or observable customs and actions; (2) not strong enough to strike back; (3) situated within easy access of the dominant group and, ideally, concentrated in one area; (4) a past target of hostility for whom latent hostility still exists; and (5) the symbol of an unpopular concept.[23]

Some groups fit this typology better than others, but minority racial and ethnic groups have been a perennial choice. Irish, Italians, Catholics, Jews, Quakers, Mormons, Chinese, Japanese, blacks, Puerto Ricans, Mexicans, and Koreans have all been treated, at one time or another, as the scapegoat in the United States. Especially in times of economic hardship, societies tend to blame some group for the general conditions, which often leads to aggressive action against the group as an expression of frustration. For example, a study by

Carl Hovland and Robert Sears found that, between 1882 and 1930, a definite correlation existed in the South between a decline in the price of cotton and an increase in the number of lynchings of blacks.[24]

For over 20 years, Leonard Berkowitz and his associates studied and experimented with aggressive behavior. They concluded that, confronted with equally frustrating situations, highly prejudiced individuals are more likely to seek scapegoats than are nonprejudiced individuals. Another intervening variable is that personal frustrations (marital failure, injury, or mental illness) make people more likely to seek scapegoats than do shared frustrations (dangers of flood or hurricane).[25]

Some experiments have shown that aggression does not increase if the frustration is understandable.[26] Other experiments have found that people become aggressive only if the aggression directly relieves their frustration.[27] Still other studies have shown that anger is a more likely result if the person responsible for the frustrating situation could have acted otherwise.[28] Clearly the results are mixed, depending on the variables within a given social situation.

Frustration–aggression theory, although helpful, is not completely satisfactory. It ignores the role of culture and the reality of actual social conflict and fails to show any causal relationship. Most of the responses measured in these studies were of people already biased. Why did one group rather than another become the object of the aggression? Moreover, frustration does not necessarily precede aggression, and aggression does not necessarily flow from frustration.

The Sociology of Prejudice

The sociological approach to prejudice is not to examine individual behavior, as psychologists do, but rather to examine behavior within a group setting. Sociologist Talcott Parsons provided one bridge between psychology and sociology by introducing social forces as a variable in frustration–aggression theory. He suggested that both the family and the occupational structure may produce anxieties and insecurities that create frustration.[29] According to this view, the growing-up process (gaining parental affection and approval, identifying with and imitating sexual role models, and competing with others in adulthood) sometimes involves severe emotional strain. The result is an adult personality with a large reservoir of repressed aggression that becomes *free-floating*—susceptible to redirection against convenient scapegoats. Similarly, the occupational system is a source of frustration: Its emphasis on competitiveness and individual achievement, its function of conferring status, its requirement that people inhibit their natural impulses at work, and its ties to the state of the economy are among the factors that generate emotional anxieties. Parsons pessimistically concluded that minorities fulfill a functional "need" as targets for displaced aggression and therefore will remain targets.[30]

Perhaps most influential in staking out the sociological position on prejudice was Herbert Blumer, who suggested that prejudice always involves the "sense of group position" in society. Agreeing with Kramer's delineation of three levels of prejudice, Blumer argued that prejudice can include beliefs, feelings, and a predisposition to action, thus motivating behavior that derives from the social hierarchy.[31] By emphasizing historically established group positions and relationships, Blumer shifted the focus away from attitudes and personality compositions of individuals. As a social phenomenon, prejudice rises or falls according to issues that alter one group's position vis-à-vis that of another group.

Socialization. In the **socialization process,** individuals acquire the values, attitudes, beliefs, and perceptions of their culture or subculture, including religion, nationality, and social class. Generally, the child conforms to the parents' expectations in acquiring an understanding of the world and its people. Being impressionable and knowing of no alternative conceptions of the world, the child usually accepts these concepts without questioning. We thus learn the prejudices of our parents and others, which then become part of our values and beliefs. Even when based on false stereotypes, prejudices shape our perceptions of various peoples and influence our attitudes and actions toward particular groups. For example, if we develop negative attitudes about Jews because we are taught that they are shrewd, acquisitive, and clannish—all-too-familiar stereotypes—as adults we may refrain from business or social relationships with them. We may not even realize the reason for such avoidance, so subtle has been the prejudice instilled within us.

People may learn certain prejudices because of their pervasiveness. The cultural screen that we develop and through which we view the surrounding world is not always accurate, but it does permit transmission of shared values and attitudes, which are reinforced by others. Prejudice, like cultural values, is taught and learned through the socialization process. The prevailing prejudicial attitudes and actions may be deeply embedded in custom or law (e.g., the **Jim Crow laws** of the 1890s and early 20th century establishing segregated public facilities throughout the South, which subsequent generations accepted as proper and maintained in their own adult lives).

Although socialization explains how prejudicial attitudes may be transmitted from one generation to the next, it does not explain their origin or why they intensify or diminish over the years. These aspects of prejudice must be explained in another way.

Economic Competition. People tend to be more hostile toward others when they feel that their security is threatened; thus, many social scientists conclude that economic competition and conflict breed prejudice. Certainly, considerable evidence shows that negative stereotyping, prejudice, and discrimination increase markedly whenever competition for available jobs increases.

An excellent illustration relates to the Chinese sojourners in the 19th-century United States. Prior to the 1870s, the transcontinental railroad was being built, and the Chinese filled many of the jobs made available by this project in the sparsely populated West. Although they were expelled from the region's gold mines and schools and could obtain no redress of grievances in the courts, they managed to convey to some whites the image of being clean, hardworking, law-abiding people. The completion of the railroad, the flood of former Civil War soldiers into the job market, and the economic depression of 1873 worsened their situation. The Chinese became more frequent victims of open discrimination and hostility. Their positive stereotype among some whites was widely displaced by a negative one: They were now "conniving," "crafty," "criminal," "the yellow menace." Only after they retreated into Chinatowns and entered specialty occupations that minimized their competition with whites did the intense hostility abate.

One pioneer in the scientific study of prejudice, John Dollard, demonstrated how prejudice against the Germans, which had been virtually nonexistent in a small U.S. industrial town, arose when times got bad:

> Local Whites largely drawn from the surrounding farms manifested considerable direct aggression toward the newcomers. Scornful and derogatory opinions were expressed about the Germans, and the native Whites had a satisfying sense of superiority toward them. . . . The chief element in the permission to be aggressive against the Germans was rivalry for jobs and status in the local woodenware plants. The native Whites felt definitely crowded for their jobs by the entering German groups and in case of bad times had a chance to blame the Germans who by their presence provided more competitors for the scarcer jobs. There seemed to be no traditional pattern of prejudice against Germans unless the skeletal suspicion of all out-groupers (always present) be invoked in this place.[32]

Both experimental studies and historical analyses have added credence to the economic-competition theory. Muzafer Sherif directed several experiments showing how intergroup competition at a boys' camp led to conflict and escalating hostility.[33] Donald Young pointed out that, throughout U.S. history, in times of high unemployment and thus intense job competition, nativist movements against minorities have flourished.[34] This pattern has held true regionally—against Asians on the West Coast, Italians in Louisiana, and French Canadians in New England—and nationally, with the antiforeign movements always peaking during periods of depression. So it was with the Native American Party in the 1830s, the Know-Nothing Party in the 1850s, the American Protective Association in the 1890s, and the Ku Klux Klan after World War I. Since the passage of civil rights laws on employment in the 20th century, researchers have consistently detected the strongest antiblack prejudice among working-class and middle-class whites who feel threatened by blacks entering their socioeconomic group in noticeable numbers.[35] It seems that any group applying the pressure of job competition most directly on another group becomes a target of its prejudice.

Once again, a theory that offers some excellent insights into prejudice—in particular, that adverse economic conditions correlate with increased hostility toward minorities—also has some serious shortcomings. Not all groups that have been objects of hostility (e.g., Quakers and Mormons) have been economic competitors. Moreover, why is hostility against some groups greater than against others? Why do the negative feelings in some communities run against groups whose numbers are so small that they cannot possibly pose an economic threat? Evidently, values besides economic ones cause people to be antagonistic to a group perceived as an actual or potential threat.

Social Norms. Some sociologists have suggested that a relationship exists between prejudice and a person's tendency to conform to societal expectations.[36] **Social norms**—the norms of one's culture—form the generally shared rules defining what is and is not proper behavior in one's culture. By learning and automatically accepting the prevailing prejudices, an individual is simply conforming to those norms.

This theory holds that a direct relationship exists between degree of conformity and degree of prejudice. If so, people's prejudices should decrease or increase significantly when they move into areas where the prejudicial norm is different. Evidence supports this view. Thomas Pettigrew found that southerners in the 1950s became less prejudiced against blacks when they interacted with them in the army, where the social norms were less prejudicial.[37] In another study, Jeanne Watson found that people moving into an anti-Semitic neighborhood in New York City became more anti-Semitic.[38]

John Dollard's study, *Caste and Class in a Southern Town* (1937/1957), provides an in-depth look at the emotional adjustment of whites and blacks to rigid social norms.[39] In his study of the processes, functions, and maintenance of accommodation, Dollard detailed the "carrot-and-stick" method social groups employed. Intimidation—sometimes even severe reprisals for going against social norms—ensured compliance. However, reprisals usually were unnecessary. The advantages whites and blacks gained in psychological, economic, or behavioral terms served to perpetuate the caste order. These gains in personal security and stability set in motion a vicious circle. They encouraged a way of life that reinforced the rationale of the social system in this community.

Two 1994 studies provided further evidence of the powerful influence of social norms. Joachim Krueger and Russell W. Clement found that consensus bias persisted despite the availability of statistical data and knowledge about such bias.[40] Michael R. Leippe and Donna Eisenstadt showed that induced compliance can change socially significant attitudes and that the change generalizes to broader beliefs.[41]

Although the social-norms theory explains prevailing attitudes, it does not explain either their origins or the reasons new prejudices develop when other groups move into an area. In addition, the theory does not explain why prejudicial attitudes against a particular group rise and fall cyclically over the years.

Although many social scientists have attempted to identify the causes of prejudice, no single factor provides an adequate explanation. Prejudice is a complex phenomenon, and it is most likely the product of more than one causal agent. Sociologists today tend either to emphasize multiple-cause explanations or to stress social forces encountered in specific and similar situations—forces such as economic conditions, stratification, and hostility toward an outgroup.

Stereotyping

One common reaction to strangers is to categorize them broadly. Prejudice at the cognitive level often arises from false perceptions that are enhanced by cultural or racial stereotypes. A **stereotype** is an oversimplified generalization by which we attribute certain traits or characteristics to a group without regard to individual differences. Sometimes stereotypes are positive—for example, that African Americans are good athletes and that Asians are good mathematicians. Even here, however, they can create pressures and problems—for example, for African Americans who are not athletic or for Asians who are weak in math. Stereotypes distort sociocultural truths but nevertheless are socially approved images held by one group about another.[42]

Stereotypes, which easily become ingrained within everyday thinking, serve to enhance a group's self-esteem and social identity—in accord with Blumer's concept of prejudice as a sense of group position. Even if an outgroup is economically successful, stereotyping it as clannish, mercenary, or unscrupulous enables other groups to affirm their own moral superiority.

Not only do stereotypes deny individuals the right to be judged and treated on the basis of their own personal merit, but also, by attributing a particular image to the entire group, they become a justification for discriminatory behavior. Negative stereotypes also serve as important reference points in people's evaluations of what they observe in everyday life. Following is an excellent illustration of how prejudice leads a person to attribute stereotypical patterns to other people's behavioral motives and causes:

> Prejudiced people see the world in ways that are consistent with their prejudice. If Mr. Bigot sees a well-dressed, white, Anglo-Saxon Protestant sitting on a park bench sunning himself at three o'clock on a Wednesday afternoon, he thinks nothing of it. If he sees a well-dressed black man doing the same thing, he is liable to leap to the conclusion that the person is unemployed—and he becomes infuriated, because he assumes that his hard-earned taxes are paying that shiftless good-for-nothing enough in welfare subsidies to keep him in good clothes. If Mr. Bigot passes Mr. Anglo's house and notices that a trash can is overturned and some garbage is strewn about, he is apt to conclude that a stray dog has been searching for food. If he passes Mr. Garcia's house and notices the same thing, he is inclined to become annoyed, and to assert that "those people live like pigs." Not only does prejudice influence his conclusions, his erroneous conclusions justify and intensify his negative feelings.[43]

Once established, stereotypes are difficult to eradicate, even in succeeding generations. Evidence of the pervasiveness and persistence of stereotypes came from a study comparing responses of college students over three generations. Providing a list of 84 adjectives, the researchers asked the students to select 5 that they thought described the most characteristic traits of 10 racial and ethnic groups.[44] Although each group showed increasing reluctance to make such generalizations, a high level of uniformity nonetheless marked the responses.

Notably, students either tended to agree on the same adjectives others had chosen in earlier studies or to pick a similar new adjective. Positive stereotypes regarding work achievement continued for "Americans," Germans, Japanese, and Jews. Emotional stereotypes for the Irish and for Italians, a carefree image for "Negroes" (the accepted word then), a negative stereotype for Turks, a positive and conservative image for the English, and commitment to family and tradition for Chinese—all remained constant generalizations over the 35-year span of the study. Other recent studies have reported similar findings.[45]

Both majority-group and minority-group members may hold stereotypes about each other. Such generalized labeling often begins with some small basis in fact as applied to a few particular individuals that is then erroneously applied to everyone in that group. Social barriers between the two groups, mass-media portrayals reinforcing the stereotypes (see The Ethnic Experience box, page 72), and societal pressures to conform to the stereotype combine to give such thinking a false aura of validity, encouraging people to ignore contrary evidence.

Ethnophaulisms. An **ethnophaulism** is a derogatory word or expression used to describe a racial or ethnic group. This is the language of prejudice, the verbal picture of a negative stereotype that reflects the prejudice and bigotry of a society's past and present. Howard J. Ehrlich divides ethnophaulisms into three types: (1) disparaging nicknames (e.g., chink, dago, polack, jungle bunny, or honky); (2) explicit group devaluations (e.g., "jew him down" for trying to get something for a lower price, "luck of the Irish" suggesting undeserved good fortune, or "to be in Dutch" meaning to be in trouble); (3) irrelevant ethnic

The Ethnic Experience

The Impact of the Media

As a reflector of society's values, the media have a tremendous impact on the shaping of our personal and group identities. Radio, television, films, newspapers, magazines, and comics can convey the rich textures of a pluralistic society or they can, directly or indirectly (by omission and distortion), alter our perception of other ethnic groups and reinforce our defensiveness and ambivalence about our own cultural backgrounds. As an Italian American, I've realized this myself when comparing the ethnic invisibility of 1950s television with modern shows that concentrate on Mafia hit men and multiple biographies of Mussolini. Having squirmed as I watched some of these portrayals, I can empathize with Arabs who resent being characterized as villainous sheikhs, Jews seen as mendacious moguls, or even the current vogue for matching a Russian accent with a kind of oafish villainy. Although such stereotypes may or may not serve political ends, they share the cartoonlike isolation of a few traits that ignore the humanity and variety of a group's members.

What is the impact of ethnic stereotypes on TV and in film on how people feel about themselves and how they perceive other ethnic groups?

Although research in this area is limited, what is available suggests that TV and film's portrayal of ethnics does have a deleterious effect on perceptions of self and others. In my own clinical work, I have found that minority children and adults will often internalize negative stereotypes about their own group. Other studies have shown that ethnic stereotypes on television and in the movies can contribute to prejudice against a particular group—especially when the person is not acquainted with any members of that group. . . .

In studies of youngsters who commit hate acts—desecration of religious institutions, racial and anti-Semitic incidents—many apprehended youngsters reported they got the idea of performing vandalism from news coverage of similar acts (the copycat syndrome). They saw media coverage as conferring recognition and prestige, so was a means of temporarily raising their low self-esteem.

The combination of TV fiction and news with the rash of "truly tasteless" joke books, radio call-in shows that invite bigoted calls from listeners, and late-night TV hosts and comedians who denigrate ethnic groups has a considerable impact on people's perceptions. While the media cannot be blamed for creating the bigotry, their insensitive reporting and encouragement of inflammatory comments establishes a societal norm that gives license to such attitudes and behavior.

Source: Joseph Giordano, "Identity Crisis: Stereotypes Stifle Self-Development," accessed online at www.sicilianculture.com/news/2002-idcrisis.htm (January 19, 2008).

names used as a mild disparagement (e.g., "jewbird" for black cuckoos having prominent beaks, "welsh on a bet" for failure to honor a debt, or "Irish confetti" for bricks thrown in a fight).[46]

Both majority and minority groups coin and use ethnophaulisms to denigrate outgroups. Such usage helps justify discrimination, inequality, and social privilege for the majority, and it helps the minority cope with social injustices caused by others. Them-versus-us name-calling is divisive, but it also indicates the state of intergroup relations. Erdman Palmore, for example, concluded that all racial and ethnic groups use ethnophaulisms. He found a correlation between the number used and the degree of group prejudice, and he observed that they express and support negative stereotypes about the most visible racial or cultural differences.[47]

Sometimes members of a racial- or ethnic-minority group use an ethnophaulism directed against themselves in their conversations with one another. On occasion, they may use the term as a reprimand to one of their own kind for acting out the stereotype, but more often they mean it as a humorous expression of friendship and endearment. However, when an outsider uses that same term, they resent it because of its prejudicial connotations.

"Mutual: Both Are Glad There Are Bars between 'Em!"

This visual stereotype of an apelike Irishman reinforced prevailing beliefs that the Irish were emotionally unstable and morally primitive. This cartoon appeared in *Judge* on November 7, 1891, and is typical of a worldwide tendency to depict minorities as apelike. (Courtesy John and Selma Appel Collection)

The use of ethnophaulisms has behavioral consequences. For example, in an examination of archival research data spanning a 150-year period of U.S. history, Brian Mullen explored the effects of using ethnophaulisms in the representation of ethnic immigrant groups.[48] He found that the smaller, less familiar, and "more foreign" ethnic immigrant groups were typically portrayed in a simplistic and negative manner, with a corresponding tendency to exclude those groups from the host society. His study illustrates the "them" and "us" divisiveness, mentioned earlier, that results from the use of disparaging terms to refer to others.

The context of words is also important, as in the once derogatory expressions "Dutch treat" and "luck of the Irish," which now have a neutral or positive concept.

Ethnic Humor. Why do some people find ethnic jokes funny, whereas others find them distasteful? Studies show the response often reflects the listener's attitude toward the group being ridiculed. If you hold favorable or positive attitudes toward the group that is the butt of the joke, then you are less likely to find it funny than if you hold unfavorable or negative views. If you dislike a group about which a joke implies something negative, you will tend to appreciate the joke.[49]

A common minority practice is to use ethnic humor as a strategy for defining one's ethnicity positively. Lois Leveen suggests that, in telling ethnic jokes about one's own group, the speaker challenges stereotypes within the dominant culture.[50] If an ethnic tells the joke to the ethnic ingroup, the phenomenon of laughing together through joke sharing is "an ethnicizing phenomenon" that develops a sense of "we-ness" in laughing with others. If an ethnic tells that joke to outsiders, it can serve as a means to undermine the stereotype by ridiculing it. Ethnic humor can thus serve as a powerful force to facilitate a positive, empowered position for the ethnic individual within the dominant culture. Of course, we must realize that there is also the potential risk that the joke will confirm the stereotype, not undermine it.

The Influence of Television

Virtually every U.S. household owns at least one television set, and families in the United States watch more than seven hours of TV daily, on average. Does all this viewing make us think or act differently? Does it change our attitudes or shape our feelings and reactions about minority groups? Or is it only entertainment with no appreciable effect on perceptions and behavior? Abundant research evidence indicates television programming distorts reality, promotes stereotypical role models, and significantly shapes and reinforces our attitudes about men, women, and minority groups.

Perpetuation of Stereotypes. Twice in the late 1970s, the U.S. Commission on Civil Rights charged the television industry with perpetuating racial and sexual stereotypes in programming and news.[51] In 1982, media expert George Gerbner continued the criticism, arguing that little had changed since the commission's reports.[52] A tiny percentage of black characters, for example, were "unrealistically romanticized," but the overwhelming majority of them occupied subservient, supporting roles—such as the white hero's comic sidekick. Gerbner commented,

> When a black child looks at prime time, most of the people he sees doing interesting things are white. That imbalance tends to teach young blacks to accept minority status as naturally inevitable and even deserved.[53]

Despite some improvements since then, three studies published in 2003 revealed the continuance of stereotypes in commercials. One content analysis found that in the 21st century, prime-time commercials still perpetuate traditional stereotypes of women and men.[54] Another revealed that most major, active characters in commercials aired during children's cartoon programming were male, thus perpetuating stereotyped sex-typed behaviors, despite their decrease in the real world.[55] The third study found "distinct racial segregation" in prime-time ads, with whites appearing in ads for upscale, beauty, or home products, while people of color, in contrast, appeared in ads for low-cost, low-nutrition products (e.g., fast food and soft drinks) and in athletic and sports equipment ads. Such depictions raise questions about the continuance of racial stereotypes, notably a somewhat one-dimensional view of people of color as key consumers of low-cost products.[56]

Influencing of Attitudes. Television influences attitudes toward racial or ethnic groups by the status of the parts it assigns to their members, the kind of behavior they display within these parts, and even the type of products they promote. Television greatly influences children's attitudes in this area. Children watch television during prime time more than any other time of day. Yet according to a 2002 Children Now study, prime time remains overwhelmingly white, with people of color appearing largely in secondary and guest roles. Whites account for 73 percent of the prime-time population, followed by African Americans (16 percent), Hispanics (4 percent), Asian/Pacific Islanders (3 percent), and Native Americans (0.2 percent). However, prime-time diversity dramatically increases as the evening progresses, with the 8 p.m. hour the least racially diverse and the 10 p.m. hour the most racially diverse. Thus, children and youths are more likely to see a much more homogeneous prime-time world than are adults who watch television later in the evening.[57]

Critically acclaimed and honored, *The Sopranos* nevertheless drew complaints from many Italian American individuals and organizations for helping perpetuate the stereo-type linking Italians with organized crime. Yet in Italy the show drew no such criticism as Italians said, "Everyone knows it's just a show." What explains these different reactions?

Due to the near invisibility of characters of color (and the often negatively stereotyped portrayals when they do appear), children of color who watch television extensively may have low self-esteem, feel alienated, and be reluctant to participate in activities outside their own community.[58] This impact on identity development can be especially strong for Hispanic, Asian, and Native American children, who almost never see people who look like them on television. Children in these and other underrepresented groups can receive a strong, clear message that the majority culture does not value or respect them.[59]

All in the Family, a popular comedy series in the 1970s and still in syndicated reruns, received an NAACP award for its contribution to race relations but divided critics over the question of whether it reduced or reinforced racial bigotry.[60] Offering an explanation for both views, Neil Vidmar and Milton Rokeach reported findings that selective perception and prior attitudes governed viewers' affective responses.[61] Liberal viewers saw the program as satire, with son-in-law Mike effectively rebutting Archie's ignorance and bigotry or minority members besting Archie by the end of the program. In contrast, prejudiced viewers—particularly adolescents—were significantly more likely to admire Archie over Mike and to perceive Archie as winning in the end. Although most respondents indicated they thought Mike made better sense than Archie, highly prejudiced adolescents were significantly more likely to perceive Archie as making better sense. Thus, the program was probably doing more to reinforce prejudice and discrimination than to combat it.

The Influence of Advertising and Music

Social scientists are paying increasing attention to the impact of corporate advertising, rap music lyrics, and music videos on attitudes about men and women. Beyond the obviousness of marketing products and entertainment lie their powers of seduction, imagery, and conditioning of attitudes.

Advertising. The average American watches three years' worth of television ads over the course of a lifetime. What effect do they have on our attitudes? In a content analysis of popular 1990s TV commercials designed for specific target audiences, researchers found the characters in them enjoyed more prominence and exercised more authority if they were white or if they were male. Images of romantic and domestic fulfillment also differed by race and gender, with women and whites disproportionately shown in family settings and in cross-sex interactions. In general, the researchers found that these commercials tended to portray white men as powerful, white women as sex objects, African American men as aggressive, and African American women as inconsequential. They suggest that these commercial images help perpetuate subtle prejudice against African Americans by exaggerating cultural differences and denying positive emotions.[62]

Another study of prime-time television ads in 2001 found blacks generally portrayed in a more diverse, equitable manner compared to whites, but Asians, Hispanics, and Native Americans were underrepresented and sometimes negatively depicted. Hispanics were often suggestively clad and shown engaging in alluring behaviors and sexual gazing, thus stressing physical appearance and sexuality over intelligence. Asians were most commonly young, passive adults at work in technology ads, thus promoting the stereotype of submissiveness and superior achievements as measures of their self-worth.[63]

Exploitation of women in ads is worse today than ever before, writes Jean Kilbourne, best known for her documentary-film work (*Killing Us Softly; Pack of Lies*) and her college-lecture tours. Kilbourne's research points out that women—and girls in particular—need to be mindful of the influential power of advertising. Women's bodies, frequently portrayed as headless torsos, have long been used to sell everything from toothbrushes to chain saws. In addition, endless glossy spreads in women's magazines feature beauty products, fashion, and diets to keep women focused on exterior "problems." She doesn't blame ads alone for demonizing fat women or causing binge drinking, teenage pregnancy, and violence against women. The cumulative effect is what appalls her. Taken together, she says, advertising fosters an inescapable, poisonous environment in which sexist stereotypes, cynicism and self-hatred, and the search for quick fixes flourish. Consumers may think they are unaffected, but advertisers successfully create a false consciousness and teach young women that they are appetizing only when "plucked, polished and painted."[64]

Music. One of the major criticisms of rap music is that it may affect attitudes and behavior regarding the use of violence, especially violence against women. Although some rap artists, such as Arrested Development and Queen Latifah, reflect a concern for humanity and offer inspiration and hope, others—such as Eminem, 2 Live Crew, Apache, N.W.A., and Scarface—routinely endorse violence, homophobia, and portray women as punching bags, strippers, or simply sperm receptacles. Such portrayals prompted the National Black Women's

Political Caucus to seek legislation to control the access to rap music. In 2005, *Essence,* one of the leading magazines for black women, launched a one-year "Take Back the Music" campaign against antiwomen lyrics in rap music. In 2007, after the firing of radio personality Don Imus for his racist remarks about the Rutgers University women's basketball team, some black leaders next went after rap music producers to curtail offensive lyrics.

Pop culture has enormous influence on how young men and women see themselves and each other in terms of sexuality and gender. Sut Jhally, best known for his documentary film *Dreamworlds* (which MTV tried to stop), says the powerful sexual imagery in hundreds of music videos, produced mostly by men, objectifies and dehumanizes women, frequently portraying them as existing solely for males' sexual satisfaction. In fact, one study found a strong link between increased exposure to rap music videos and problems with the law, drugs, and sexually transmitted diseases.[65]

Can Prejudice Be Reduced?

Many organizations and movements dedicated to reducing prejudice have existed over the years. Although they have varied in their orientation and focal point of activity, they usually adopt two basic approaches: to promote greater interaction between dominant and minority groups in all aspects of living, by either voluntary or compulsory means, and to dispense information that destroys stereotypes and exposes rationalizations (self-justifications). Neither approach has been successful in all instances, probably because the inequalities that encourage prejudicial attitudes still exist.

Interaction. Contact between people of different racial and ethnic backgrounds does not necessarily lead to friendlier attitudes. In fact, the situation may worsen, as has happened frequently when schools and neighborhoods have experienced an influx of people from a different group. Often, however, interaction does reduce prejudice.[66] It would also appear that many other variables determine the effect of interaction, including the frequency and duration of contacts; the relative status of the two parties and their backgrounds; whether their meeting is voluntary or compulsory and competitive or cooperative; and whether they meet in a political, religious, occupational, residential, or recreational situation.[67]

A good example of the significance of the type of contact emerges from the experiments in the **jigsaw method** of Elliot Aronson and Neal Osherow.[68] This research team observed that classroom competition for teacher recognition and approval often wreaked special hardship on minority children less fluent in English or less self-assured about participating in class. The researchers created interdependent learning groups of five or six children, each member charged with learning one portion of the day's lesson in a particular subject. The children learned the complete lesson from one another and then took a test on all the material. Because it creates interdependent groups, this technique is *not* the same as the cooperative learning approach so common in U.S. schools. In fact, Australian researchers compared use of the two approaches among children in grades 4–6 and found that the jigsaw method produced significant improvements on measures of academic performance, liking of peers, and racial prejudice, in contrast to the effect of the cooperative approach that exacerbated preexisting intergroup tensions.[69] (See The Ethnic Experience box, page 78.)

The Ethnic Experience

Reducing Prejudice through the Jigsaw Method

The experience of a Mexican American child in one of our groups serves as a useful illustration. We will call him Carlos. Carlos was not very articulate in English, his second language. Because he was often ridiculed when he had spoken up in the past, over the years he learned to keep quiet in class. He was one of those students . . . who had entered into an implicit contract of silence with his teacher: he opted for anonymity and she called on him only rarely.

While Carlos hated school and was learning very little in the traditional classroom, at least he was left alone. Accordingly, he was quite uncomfortable with the jigsaw system, which required him to talk to his groupmates. He had a great deal of trouble communicating his paragraph, stammering and hesitating. The other children reacted out of old habits, resorting to insults and teasing. "Aw, you don't know it," Susan accused. "You're dumb, you're stupid. You don't know what you are doing."

One of the researchers, assigned to observe the group process, intervened with a bit of advice when she overheard such comments: "Okay, you can tease him if you want to. It might be fun for you, but it's not going to help you learn about Eleanor Roosevelt's young adulthood. And let me remind you, the exam will take place in less than an hour." Note how this statement brings home the fact that the reinforcement contingencies have shifted considerably. Now Susan does not gain much from putting Carlos down. And she stands to lose a great deal, not just from the teacher singling her out for criticism but because she needs to know Carlos's information.

Gradually, but inexorably, it began to dawn on the students that the only chance they had to learn about Carlos's segment was by paying attention to what he had to say. If they ignored Carlos or continued to ridicule him, his segment would be unavailable to them, and the most they could hope for would be an 80 percent score on the exam—an unattractive prospect to most of the children. And with that realization, the kids began to become pretty good interviewers, learning to pay attention to Carlos, to draw him out, and to ask probing questions. Carlos, in turn, began to relax more and found it easier to explain out loud what was in his head. What the children came to learn about Carlos is even more important than the information about the lesson that they got from him. After a couple of days, they began to appreciate that Carlos was not nearly as dumb as they had thought he was. After a few weeks they noticed talents in him they had not seen before. They began to like Carlos, and he began to enjoy school more and to think of his Anglo classmates as helpful friends and interested colleagues rather than as tormentors.

Source: Elliot Aronson and Neal Osherow, "Cooperation, Prosocial Behavior, and Academic Performance: Experiments in the Desegregated Classroom," *Applied Social Psychology Annual* 1 (1980): 174–175. Reprinted by permission.

Information. Most people have long cherished the hope that education would reduce prejudice. Some studies, such as that by Gertrude Selznick and Stephen Steinberg, have found a definite correlation between level of education and degree of tolerance.[70] Charles Stember's research, however, led him to conclude that more highly educated persons were not more tolerant—they were simply more sophisticated in recognizing measures of bias and more subtle in expressing their prejudices.[71] In sum, it appears that formal education is far from a perfect means of reducing prejudice.

One reason for this failure is that people tend to use **selective perception**; that is, they absorb information that accords with their own beliefs and rationalize away information that does not. Another reason is the almost quantum leap from the classroom to real-life situations. Dealing with prejudice from a detached perspective is one thing; dealing with it in actuality is quite another because emotions, social pressures, and many other factors are involved.

Despite these criticisms, courses in race and ethnic relations certainly have value because they raise the students' level of consciousness about intergroup dynamics. However, a significant reduction or elimination of prejudice is more

Cooperative learning is now a common teaching technique in U.S. elementary schools. Research shows that a variation of the approach, the jigsaw method, is also an effective means of reducing the walls of prejudice and social distance, while simultaneously building self-esteem and motivation in minority youngsters.

likely to occur by changing the structural conditions of inequality that promote and maintain prejudicial attitudes. As Herbert Blumer suggests, the sense of group position dissolves and racial prejudice declines when major shifts in the social order overtake the current definition of a group's characteristics.[72] As long as the dominant group does not react with fear and institute a countermovement, the improvement of a minority's social position changes power relations and reduces negative stereotypes. Therefore, continued efforts at public enlightenment and extension of constitutional rights and equal opportunities to all Americans, regardless of race, religion, or national origin, appear to be the most promising means of attaining an unprejudiced society.

One measure of shifting group positions is the expanding inclusiveness of the mainstream U.S. ingroup; previously excluded minority groups, once victims of prejudice, are gaining the social acceptance of structural assimilation. In its more than 225-year history, the United States has experienced a changing definition of *mainstream "American"*—from only those whose ancestry was English, to the British (English, Welsh, Scots, and Scots-Irish), to peoples from northern and western Europe, and now to all Europeans. People of color, however, have yet to gain entry into this national cultural-identity group, and that entry is the challenge before us.[73]

Diversity Training

A workplace environment that promotes positive intergroup interaction is more efficient, has higher morale, and retains experienced personnel. Conversely, a hostile work environment has lower productivity, disgruntled personnel, and a higher attrition rate. Moreover, if an organization develops a reputation for insensitivity to diversity, it will attract fewer qualified job applicants among women and people of color, and businesses will lose market share by attracting fewer clients from our increasingly diverse society for their goods and services.

With women and nonwhite males now constituting 75 percent of the people entering the U.S. labor force, and with 36 percent of the nation's enlisted military personnel identifying themselves as a minority, it has become critical for all organizations to take steps to prevent prejudice from creating dysfunctions within their daily operations.[74]

As someone who has conducted numerous diversity-training workshops for military leaders and corporate management (including healthcare), let me give you some insight into these programs. The best programs heighten awareness by providing informational insights into the diversity of cultural value orientations, as well as into the current and future demographics of employees and clients. Most valuable in broadening perceptions is the inclusion of interactive learning sessions such as role-playing demonstrations of the wrong and right handlings of situations and the creation of small groups to discuss and offer solutions to hypothetical but realistic problems. Although programs vary greatly in their length, structure, and content, the most effective ones are comprehensive, actively supported by management as part of the organization's general mission statement, and fully integrated into all aspects of the organization. The latter includes a diversity orientation session for new employees, occasional reinforcement sessions for continuing employees, and all levels of management working together to promote an inclusive, hospitable work climate. Such efforts can make a significant contribution in reducing prejudice in the workplace.

How effective are these programs? The majority of studies conclude that they are effective, but a key variable appears to be selection bias. That is, when participants attend by choice, the positive effects are stronger.[75] Critics, however, say most interventions are not grounded in theory and there is little evidence of program impact. They call for action research to study and improve diversity training to achieve greater prejudice reduction.[76]

◢◣◥◤ DISCRIMINATION

Discrimination is actual behavior, the practice of differential and unequal treatment of other groups of people, usually along racial, religious, or ethnic lines. The Latin word *discriminatus,* from which the English word is derived, means "to divide or distinguish," and its subsequent negative connotation has remained relatively unchanged through the centuries.

Levels of Discrimination

Actions, like attitudes, have different levels of intensity. As a result, discrimination may be analyzed at five levels.[77] The first level is *verbal expression,* a statement of dislike or the use of a derogatory term. The next level is *avoidance*, in which the prejudiced person takes steps to avoid social interaction with a group. Actions of this type may include choice of residence, organizational membership, activities located in urban centers, and primary relationships in any social setting.

At the third level, *exclusion* from certain jobs, housing, education, or social organizations occurs. In the United States, the practice of **de jure segregation** was once widespread throughout the South. Not only were children specifically assigned to certain schools to maintain racial separation, but segregationist laws kept all public places (theaters, restaurants, restrooms, transportation, etc.) racially separated as well. This exclusion can also take the form of **de facto segregation** as residential patterns become embedded in social customs and institutions. Thus, the standard practice of building and maintaining neighborhood schools in racially segregated communities creates and preserves segregated schools.

The fourth level of discrimination is *physical abuse*—violent attacks on members of the disliked group. Unfortunately, this behavior still occurs often in the United States. A new term, **ethnoviolence,** has entered our vocabulary. The Prejudice Institute defines *ethnoviolence* as encompassing a range of action—verbal harassment and threats, vandalism, graffiti, swastika painting, arson, cross burning, physical assault, and murder—committed against people targeted solely because of their race, religion, ethnic background, or sexual orientation.[78] Thousands of incidents of ethnoviolence against members of various minority groups occur each year throughout the nation on college campuses and in both suburban and urban areas.

The most extreme level of discrimination is *extermination:* massacres, genocide, or pogroms conducted against a people. Such barbarous actions continue to occur sporadically, as in Bosnia and Rwanda in the 1990s, in a Russian school in 2004, and in the Darfur region of the Sudan in 2006–2007.

Relationships between Prejudice and Discrimination

Prejudice can lead to discrimination, or discrimination can lead to prejudice, or neither can lead to the other. There is no simplistic cause-effect relationship. Our attitudes and our overt behavior are closely related, but they are not identical. We may harbor hostile feelings toward certain groups without ever making them known through word or deed. Conversely, our overt behavior may effectively conceal our real attitudes.

Prejudiced people are more likely than others to practice discrimination; thus, discrimination quite often represents the overt expression of prejudice. It is wrong, however, to assume that discrimination is always the simple acting out of prejudice. It may instead be the result of a policy decision protecting the interests of the majority group, as happens when legal immigration is curtailed for economic reasons. It may be due to social conformity, as when people submit to outside pressures despite their personal views.[79] Discriminators may explain their actions with reasons other than prejudice toward a particular group, and those reasons may be valid to the discriminators. Sometimes discriminatory behavior may precede prejudicial attitudes, as, for example, when organizations insist that all job applicants take aptitude or IQ tests based on middle-class experiences and then form negative judgments of lower-income people who do not score well.

Robert Merton has formulated a model showing the possible relationships between prejudice and discrimination (Figure 3.1). Merton demonstrates that quite conceivably a nonprejudiced person may discriminate and a prejudiced person may

FIGURE 3.1   Relationships between Prejudice and Discrimination

Prejudiced	Discriminates	
	No	Yes
No	All-weather liberal	Fair-weather liberal
Yes	Timid bigot	Active bigot

not. In his paradigm, Merton classifies four types of people according to how they accept or reject the American Creed: "the right of equitable access to justice, freedom and opportunity, irrespective of race or religion, or ethnic origin."[80]

The Nonprejudiced Nondiscriminator. Nonprejudiced nondiscriminators are neither prejudiced nor practicers of discrimination. Of course, as Merton observes, these are virtues of omission, not commission. He criticizes members of this class who show no inclination to illuminate others and to fight actively against all forms of discrimination. They talk chiefly to others who share their viewpoint, and so they deceive themselves into thinking that they represent the consensus of the community. Furthermore, because their "own spiritual house is in order," they feel no pangs of conscience pressing them to work collectively on the problem. In reality, some nonprejudiced nondiscriminators obviously are activists and do engage in dialogue with others who hold different viewpoints, thereby transforming belief into action.

The Nonprejudiced Discriminator. Expediency is the byword for those in the category of the nonprejudiced discriminator, for their actions often conflict with their personal beliefs. They may, for example, be free of racial prejudice, but they will join clubs that exclude people who belong to outgroups, they will vote for regressive measures if they would benefit materially from these, and they will support efforts to keep certain minorities out of their neighborhood for fear of its deterioration. These people frequently feel guilt and shame because they are acting against their beliefs.

The Prejudiced Nondiscriminator. Merton's term *timid bigots* best describes prejudiced nondiscriminators. They believe in many stereotypes about other groups and definitely feel hostility toward these groups. However, they keep silent in the presence of those who are more tolerant; they conform because they must. If there were no law or pressure to avoid bias in certain actions, they would discriminate.

The Prejudiced Discriminator. Prejudiced discriminators are active bigots. They demonstrate no conflict between attitudes and behavior. Not only do they openly express their beliefs, practice discrimination, and defy the law if necessary, but they consider such conduct virtuous.

The nonprejudiced discriminator and the prejudiced nondiscriminator are the most sociologically interesting classifications because they demonstrate that social-situation variables often determine whether discriminatory behavior occurs. The pressure of group norms may force individuals to act in a manner inconsistent with their beliefs.

Social and Institutional Discrimination

Discriminatory practices are encountered frequently in the areas of employment and residence, although such actions often are concealed and denied by those who take them. Another dimension of discrimination, often unrealized, is **social discrimination**—the creation of a "social distance" between groups that we discussed in Chapter 1. Simply stated, in their intimate primary relationships, people tend to associate with others of similar ethnic background and socioeconomic level; thus, dominant-group members usually exclude minority-group members from close relations with them. We can therefore make a distinction between *active* and *passive* discrimination. In the first, one takes action against someone, while in the second, one's silent acquiescence to others' discriminatory actions is still a form of discrimination, just as theologians speak of sins of omission as well as sins of commission.

Discrimination is more than the biased actions of individuals, however. In their influential book *Black Power* (1967), Stokely Carmichael and Charles Hamilton called attention to the fact that far greater harm occurs from **institutional discrimination,** the unequal treatment of subordinate groups inherent in the ongoing operations of society's institutions.[81] Entrenched in customs, laws, and practices, these discriminatory patterns can exist in banking, criminal justice, employment, education, healthcare, housing, and many other areas in the private and public sectors. Critical to understanding this concept is the fact that practices are so widespread that individuals helping to perpetuate them may be completely unaware of their existence. Examples are banks rejecting home mortgage applications of minorities at a higher rate, the sentencing inequities in our justice system, the concentration of minorities in low-paying jobs, the former "separate but equal" educational structure in the South, and segregated housing.

Another form of institutional discrimination can be found in religious bigotry. Numerous examples exist in U.S. history of religious minorities falling victim to systemic biased actions, as we will explore in Chapter 12. Hubert Blalock, offering conflict-perspective reasoning, suggests that, when the dominant group feels that its self-interests—such as primacy and the preservation of cherished values—are threatened, extreme discrimination usually results.[82] Blalock believes that the dominant group will not hesitate to act discriminatorily if it thinks that this approach will effectively undercut the minority group as a social competitor (see The International Scene, page 84).

The Affirmative-Action Controversy

At what point do efforts to secure justice and equal opportunities in life for one group infringe on the rights of other groups? Is justice a utilitarian concept—the greatest happiness for the greatest number? Or is it a moral concept—a sense of good that all people share? Is the proper role of government to foster a climate in which people have equal opportunity to participate in a competitive system of

The International Scene

Discrimination in Northern Ireland

Northern Ireland contains nearly 1.7 million people, close to 60 percent of them Protestants with loyalties to the overwhelmingly Protestant United Kingdom and 40 percent Catholics with a preference for unification with the Catholic-dominated Republic of Ireland. The Catholics outnumber Protestants in the western and southern areas, while the reverse is true in the eastern and northern areas. Despite progress toward reconciliation since the 1998 peace agreement, it remains today a polarized society, its sporadic violence fed by centuries of deep-seated hostility.

Sociologically, Catholics are the minority group, with limited political power. They are more likely than Protestants to be poor, to suffer prolonged unemployment, and to live in substandard housing in segregated communities. Catholics tend to be in low-status, low-skill jobs and Protestants in high-status, high-skill positions. It is difficult, however, to determine whether these employment patterns result from overt job discrimination, from structural factors of community segregation, education, and class, or from both.

Although the degree of actual discrimination employed to maintain their dominance is unclear, Protestants rationalize about the situation through a set of negative beliefs about Catholics. Many Protestants stereotype Catholics as lazy welfare cheats who are dirty, superstitious, and ignorant. They also view them as oversexed (as "proved" by the typically larger size of Catholic families) and brainwashed by priests, whose primary allegiance, they say, is to a foreign entity—the pope. Moreover, many Protestants suspect that Catholics are intent on undermining the Ulster government to force reunification with the Republic of Ireland. Most Protestants see no discrimination on the basis of religion in jobs, housing, and other social areas. Catholics "get what they deserve" because of their values, attitudes, and disloyalty.

For their part, most Catholics in Northern Ireland strongly believe that they suffer from discrimination as a direct consequence of their religion. They view Protestants as narrow-minded bigots who stubbornly hold onto political power and have no desire to relinquish any part of it. A vicious circle of prejudice and discrimination, despite the peace accord, intensifies Protestant resistance to sharing power and Catholic reluctance to support the government.

It is too soon to tell whether the hard-fought pragmatism and promise of the 1998 peace accord, still not fully implemented, will fall victim to political opportunism, fickle public opinion, or the evil intent of the radicals on both sides, who have never agreed to forswear the use of bombs and murder to pursue their political ends. In May 2007, though, a positive step occurred with restoration of power to the Northern Ireland Assembly, in which both factions participate, with the unionists in the majority.

In contrast, Protestants in the Republic of Ireland, who constitute only 3 percent of the population, live in harmony with their Catholic neighbors. They are fully integrated socioeconomically and do not, for the most part, experience prejudice.

Critical Thinking Question: What must be done to reduce the prejudice and discrimination that sow the seeds of violence in Northern Ireland?

---

occupations and rewards, or should government ensure equal results in any competition? These issues have engaged moral and political philosophers for centuries, and they go to the core of the affirmative-action controversy.

The Concepts of Justice, Liberty, and Equality. Over 2,300 years ago, Plato wrote in the *Republic* that justice must be relative to the needs of the people who are served, not to the desires of those who serve them. For example, physicians must make patients' health their primary concern if they are to be just. In *A Theory of Justice*, John Rawls interprets justice as fairness, which maximizes equal liberty for all.[83] To provide the greatest benefit to the least advantaged, society must eliminate social and economic inequalities by placing minority persons in offices and positions that are open to all under conditions of fair equality of opportunity.

Both philosophers see the ideal society as well ordered and strongly pluralistic: Each component performs a functionally differentiated role in working harmony; society must arrange its practices to make this so.

Anticipating the emergence of the equal-protection-under-the-law clause of the Fourteenth Amendment as a major force for social change, Joseph Tussman and Jacobus tenBroek examined the problems of the doctrine of equality five years before the 1954 Supreme Court school desegregation ruling. Americans, they argued, have always been more concerned with liberty than with equality, identifying liberty with the absence of government interference:

> What happens, then, when government becomes more ubiquitous? Whenever an area of activity is brought within the control or regulation of government, to that extent equality supplants liberty as the dominant ideal and constitutional demand.[84]

Tussman and tenBroek noted that those who insist on constitutional rights for all are not so much demanding the removal of government restraints as they are asking for positive government action to provide equal treatment for "minority groups, parties, or organizations whose rights are too easily sacrificed or ignored in periods of popular hysteria."[85] Responsibility for promoting individual rights has increasingly been placed on the federal government.

Affirmative Action Begins. We can trace the origin of government affirmative-action policy to July 1941, when President Franklin D. Roosevelt issued Executive Order 8802, obligating defense contractors "not to discriminate against any worker because of race, creed, color, or national origin." Subsequent executive orders by virtually all presidents continued or expanded the government's efforts to curb discrimination in employment. President John F. Kennedy's Executive Order 10925 in 1961 was the first to use the term **affirmative action;** it stipulated that government contractors would "take affirmative action that applicants are employed, and that employees are treated during employment, without regard to their race, creed, color, or national origin."

The legal basis for affirmative action appears to rest on two points. Stanford M. Lyman argued in 1987 that passage of the Thirteenth Amendment, which abolished slavery, set the precedent for action against any vestiges of slavery manifest through racial discrimination.[86] Both supporters and opponents, however, point to Title VII, Section 703(j), of the 1964 Civil Rights Act as the keystone of their positions on affirmative action.

Title VII seems to address the need for fairness, openness, and color-blind equal opportunity. It specifically bans preference by race, ethnicity, gender, and religion in business and government. Opponents claim that this clear language outlawing preferences makes affirmative action unnecessary and illegal.[87] Supporters contend that President Lyndon Johnson's Executive Order 11246 is linked to Title VII by mandating employer affirmative-action plans to correct existing deficiencies through specific goals and deadlines. This was, supporters say, a logical step from concern about equal rights to concern about actual equal opportunity.[88]

Addressing an expanded list of protected categories (Asians, blacks, Hispanics, Native Americans, women, the aged, people with disabilities, and homosexuals), an array of state and federal policy guidelines began to regulate many aspects of business, education, and government practices. Legislation in 1972 amended the 1964

Civil Rights Act, giving the courts the power to enforce affirmative-action standards. Preference programs became the rule through reserved minority quotas in college and graduate school admissions and in job hirings and promotions, as well as through government set-aside work contracts for minority firms.[89]

Court Challenges and Rulings. The resentment of whites over "reverse discrimination" crystallized in the 1978 *Regents of the University of California v. Bakke* case, when the U.S. Supreme Court ruled that quotas were not permitted but race could be a factor in university admissions. In a separate opinion, Justice Harry A. Blackmun stated,

> In order to get beyond racism, we must first take account of race. There is no other way. And in order to treat some persons equally, we must treat them differently. We cannot—we dare not—let the Equal Protection Clause perpetuate racial superiority.[90]

For the next 11 years, the Court upheld the principle of affirmative action in a series of rulings. Since 1989, however, a more conservative Court has shown a growing reluctance to use "race-conscious remedies"—the practice of trying to overcome the effects of past discrimination by helping minorities. This has been true not only in affirmative-action cases involving jobs and contracts but in school desegregation and voting rights as well. The 1995 *Adarand Constructors v. Peña* decision scaled back the federal government's own affirmative-action program, mandating "strict scrutiny and evidence" of alleged past discrimination, not just a "general history of racial discrimination in the nation." In another 1995 decision, the Supreme Court declared that race could no longer be the "predominant factor" in drawing congressional districts—or, by implication, any jurisdiction for any government body, from school boards to state legislatures.

In 1995, the California Board of Regents banned affirmative action for graduate and undergraduate admissions. The following year, California voters overwhelmingly passed the California Civil Rights Initiative, which prohibited the use of race, ethnicity, or gender "as a criterion for either discriminating against, or granting preferential treatment to, any individual or group," thereby dismantling state affirmative-action programs. Also in 1996, a sweeping ruling by the U.S. Circuit Court of Appeals in *Hopwood v. Texas* led the Texas attorney general to interpret the opinion as banning affirmative action in admissions, scholarships, and outreach programs.

Without affirmative action, California and Texas universities initially suffered minority enrollment drops in their undergraduate and graduate programs. However, both states then implemented percentage plans as a viable alternative to achieve a race/ethnic balance in higher education without the stigma of set-asides and lowered admission standards. California guaranteed university admission to the top 4 percent of high school graduates, while Texas guaranteed it to the top 10 percent. When Florida ended its affirmative-action program, it guaranteed college admission to the top 20 percent if students completed a minimum of two years of foreign language and other academic credits.

In 2003, a major Supreme Court decision preserved affirmative action in university admissions at the University of Michigan law school by a 5 to 4 vote, while at the same time striking down that university's undergraduate admissions program that used a point system based in part on race. In making a forceful endorsement of the role of racial diversity on campus in achieving a more equal

Prior to the 2003 Supreme Court ruling, thousands marched and demonstrated their feelings about the University of Michigan's affirmative action program. Although it endorsed programs promoting racing diversity to achieve a more equal society, the court also suggested such programs should have a time limit.

society, the court's ruling was a broad one that applies to all admissions programs. Moreover, this ruling strengthened the solitary view of Justice Lewis Powell at the time of the *Bakke* decision that there was a "compelling state interest" in racial diversity. At the same time, the court suggested a time limit on such programs, with Justice Sandra Day O'Connor writing in the majority opinion, "We expect that 25 years from now the use of racial preferences will no longer be necessary to further the interest approved today."[91]

Adding significance to this ruling is its strong signal to employers that they should continue their own affirmative-action plans to hire more women and minorities. Perhaps demonstrating the commitment of business to affirmative action were the series of friend-of-the-court briefs filed by 65 corporations (including General Motors and Microsoft) in support of the university.[92]

This ruling, however, is not the final word on affirmative action, as numerous groups still oppose it. With several Supreme Court justices about to end their careers on the bench, new challenges to a differently constituted court may result in different rulings.

Has Affirmative Action Worked? Evidence about the success of affirmative-action programs is as mixed as public debate on the subject. John Gpuhl and Susan Welch revealed in 1990 that the *Bakke* decision had had little impact on the enrollment of African Americans and Hispanics in medical and law schools; their enrollment had already leveled off two or three years before this 1978 ruling.[93] However, in a 1995 study, Alfred Blumrosen found that 5 million minority workers and 6 million women had better jobs than they would have had without preferences and antidiscrimination laws.[94]

Although some of the motivations behind the challenges to affirmative action may well be racist or sexist, the preservation of white privilege and conservative political ideology appear to be more significant underpinnings.[95] Addressing this point in defense of affirmative action, Tim J. Wise argues that reverse discrimination is a myth fueled by white hysteria, and he insists "affirmative action remains important and necessary because racism remains prevalent and damaging to the life prospects of people of color in the United States."[96]

Still, some minority group spokespersons, conservatives themselves, have spoken against affirmative action, arguing that it has had a destructive influence on their own communities. Thomas Sowell and Linda Chavez maintain that universities recruit talented minority students away from local colleges where they might do very well and into learning environments where the competition for grades is intense. Opponents also argue that affirmative action is "misplaced condescension" that has poisoned race relations—a view that seems to posit a golden age of race relations in the United States at some point prior to the advent of affirmative action. According to this line of reasoning, the achievements of minorities become tainted by the possibility that they resulted from special favorable treatment rather than being earned on merit.[97]

Public Opinion. Negative public opinion about affirmative action gathered strength in the 1990s as the United States experienced a slow-growth economy, stagnant middle-class incomes, and corporate downsizing, all of which made the question of who gets fired—or hired—unusually volatile. James Q. Wilson and Seymour Martin Lipset cynically suggested that the long-term resentment of affirmative action by whites influenced policy only when the remedy's effects finally touched the people who set the national agenda. The middle and upper classes, they argue, paid scant attention to mandated minority hirings among trade unionists or to busing orders in working-class neighborhoods. Now, however, women and minorities are competing for managerial positions that the elite once dominated and for admission to universities that the elites' sons and daughters also wish to attend.[98]

When asked in a 2006 CBS News poll what should happen to affirmative action, 12 percent thought it should be ended right away, while 37 percent thought it should be phased out. Another 36 percent thought it should be continued, while 19 percent were unsure.[99] However, while divided on preferences based on race and gender (blacks less in opposition than whites), most Americans seemed eager to support affirmative action based on economic class.[100] Under such a provision, for example, the white son of a poor coal miner in West Virginia could be eligible for special help, but the daughter of an affluent African American stockbroker would not.

Another poll, conducted by the Associated Press in 2003 just a few weeks before the Supreme Court ruling on the Michigan case, found that four of five Americans said it was important that colleges have racially diverse student bodies. However, only 51 percent thought affirmative-action programs were still needed to help blacks, Hispanics, and other minorities, while 43 percent did not and 35 percent wanted them abolished. Among blacks, 89 percent thought the programs were necessary. About six in ten young adults in the poll, from 18 to 34 years old, said affirmative action was still needed.[101] An obvious split along racial and generational lines exists on this subject.

Even as affirmative action withers in some states, it continues in others. Proposed federal legislation in Congress would end it everywhere. Supporters of affirmative action argue "mend it, don't end it," whereas opponents urge that it be dismantled completely. The next few years undoubtedly will see a continuing battle and significant changes in affirmative action as we know it.

Racial Profiling

Although racial profiling has a long history, only in recent years have the government and public given it much attention. **Racial profiling** refers to action taken by law enforcement officials on the erroneous presumption that individuals of one race or ethnicity are more likely to engage in illegal activity than individuals of other races or ethnicities. Such thinking led authorities routinely to stop vehicles driven by blacks and Hispanics in the expectation of finding drugs in their possession.

Some argued that overall discrepancies in crime rates among racial groups justified such profiling in traffic enforcement activities to produce a greater number of arrests for nontraffic offenses (e.g., narcotics trafficking). Critics contended that an emphasis on minority-group drug use would naturally result in more minority arrests, but the evidence shows that about 73 percent of all illicit drug users are white.[102]

In the 1990s, racial profiling received a great deal of attention through media exposés, special reports, commissions, and legislative initiatives. In 2001, the Bush administration became the first to take action to ban it in federal law enforcement. However, the terrorist attacks later that year changed the government view of racial profiling from an undesirable police activity to one of necessity for national security. As a result, airline security, customs officials, and police place Arab and Muslim Americans under special scrutiny, and immigration officials prosecute them for minor violations often ignored for resident aliens of other ethnic backgrounds.

In 2003, the U.S. Department of Justice issued guidelines rejecting racial profiling. It argued that such activity is immoral and perpetuates negative racial stereotypes that are "harmful to our diverse democracy, and materially impair our efforts to maintain a fair and just society." However, in that same statement, it included a broad and largely undefined exception when "national security" concerns come into play.[103] At the present time, then, a dichotomy exists in racial profiling attitudes and actions. For example, in 2007 the American Civil Liberties Union (ACLU) issued a detailed report on how racial minorities in Rhode Island were disproportionately stopped in virtually every municipality and were twice as likely as white drivers to be searched, even though they were *less* likely to be found with contraband.[104]

◢◣◥ RETROSPECT

The psychology of prejudice focuses on individuals' subjective states of mind, emphasizing the levels of prejudice held and the factors of self-justification, personality, frustration, and scapegoating. The sociology of prejudice examines objective conditions of society as social forces behind prejudicial attitudes; socialization, economic competition, and social norms constitute major considerations.

Stereotyping often reflects prejudice as a sense of group position. Once established, stereotypes are difficult to eradicate and often are manifest in ethnophaulisms and ethnic humor. Television has a profound impact in shaping and reinforcing attitudes; unfortunately, it tends to perpetuate racial and sexual stereotypes instead of combating them.

Increased contact between groups and improved information do not necessarily reduce prejudice. The nature of the contact, particularly whether it is competitive or cooperative, is a key determinant. Information can develop heightened awareness as a means of improving relations, but external factors (economic conditions and social pressures) may override rational considerations.

The imagery in advertising, rap music lyrics, and music videos can have a cumulative effect in shaping values about men and women. These images and words help perpetuate subtle prejudice and a false consciousness.

Diversity in the workplace, whether corporate or military, has prompted many organizations to create a more positive, inclusive environment through diversity training workshops. The most effective programs are comprehensive, actively supported by management, and fully integrated into all aspects of the organization.

Discriminatory behavior operates at five levels of intensity: verbal expression, avoidance, exclusion, physical abuse, and extermination. Discrimination is not necessarily an acting out of prejudice. Social pressures may oblige nonprejudiced individuals to discriminate or may prevent prejudiced people from discriminating.

The debate over affirmative action involves these questions: Is it a democratic government's responsibility to provide a climate for equal opportunity or to ensure equal results? If the latter, at what point do efforts to secure equality for one group infringe on the rights of other groups? After several decades of implementation, affirmative-action programs face dismantling through court decisions, public initiatives, and legislative action.

Racial profiling remains a serious concern, given its mixed interpretation since the 2001 terrorist attacks.

KEY TERMS

Action-orientation level of prejudice
Affirmative action
Authoritarian personality
Cognitive level of prejudice
De facto segregation
De jure segregation
Discrimination

Displaced aggression
Emotional level of prejudice
Ethnophaulism
Ethnoviolence
Institutional discrimination
Jigsaw method
Jim Crow laws
Prejudice

Racial profiling
Relative deprivation
Scapegoating
Selective perception
Self-justification
Social discrimination
Social norms
Socialization process
Stereotype

DISCUSSION QUESTIONS

1. What is prejudice? What are some of its manifestations?
2. What are some of the possible causes of prejudice?
3. What role do the media play in combating or reinforcing stereotypes?
4. What is discrimination? What are some of its manifestations?
5. What is the relationship between prejudice and discrimination?
6. Discuss the pros and cons of affirmative action.

SUGGESTED READINGS

Lester, Paul M. (ed.). *Images That Injure: Pictorial Stereotypes in the Media,* 2nd ed. New York: Praeger, 2003.
A collection of essays that discuss media stereotypes, their impact on individuals and society, and the motivations of those who made the images.

Pickering, Michael. *Stereotyping: The Politics of Representation.* New York: Palgrave Macmillan, 2001.
An interdisciplinary examination and critical assessment of stereotyping and the roots of prejudice and bigotry in modern societies.

Sowell, Thomas. *Migrations and Cultures: A World View.* New York: HarperCollins, 1997.
A provocative book that draws from case histories of the Germans, Italians, Japanese, Chinese, Jews, and Asian Indians that argues immigrants' habits and beliefs are more important to their fate than a country's economy, culture, or politics.

Van Ausdale, Debra and Joe R. Feagin. *The First R: How Children Learn Race and Racism.* New York: Rowman & Littlefield, 2002.
An important discussion of how preschool children grasp concepts of race and ethnic identity and can be active participants in prejudicial comments and actions.

Wang, Lu-In, *Discrimination by Default: How Racism Becomes Routine.* New York: New York University Press, 2006.
An intriguing explanation of how and why discrimination still plays a strong role in our society, with suggestions on how to overcome the default process.

Wise, Tim J. *Affirmative Action: Racial Preference in Black and White.* New York: Routledge, 2005.
A well-written, compelling, and provocative book about race, privilege, and education that offers an insightful defense of affirmative action.

MYSOCKIT

Additional resources for this chapter can be found in MySocKit. If you have a subscription to MySocKit, go to www.mysockit.com to study, review, and go beyond the book to learn more about race and ethnic relations.

Intergroup Relations

So far, we have looked at people's behavioral patterns in relating to strangers, the role of culture and social structure in shaping perceptions and interactions, and the complexity of prejudice and discrimination. In this chapter, we examine response patterns that dominant and minority groups follow in their dealings with each other.

The following pages suggest that these patterns occur in varying degrees for most groups regardless of race, ethnicity, or time period. They are not mutually exclusive categories, and groups do not necessarily follow all these patterns at one time. To some degree, though, each minority or dominant group in any society shares these pattern commonalities. Before we examine these patterns, we must consider two notes of caution. First, all groups are not alike, for each has its own unique beliefs, habits, and history. Second, variations *within* a group prevent any group from being a homogeneous entity.

MINORITY-GROUP RESPONSES

Although personality characteristics play a large role in determining how individuals respond to unfavorable situations, behavioral patterns for almost any group are similar to those of other groups in comparable circumstances. External factors play an important role, but social interpretation is also a critical determinant, as I will discuss in the formation of ethnic- and racial-group identity. Also, the minority group's perception of its power resource—its power to change established relationships with the dominant group in a significant way—to a large extent determines the response it makes.[1] The responses include avoidance, deviance, defiance, acceptance, and negative self-image.

Ethnic- and Racial-Group Identity

Any group unable to participate fully in the societal mainstream typically develops its own group identity. This is a normal pattern in ingroup–outgroup relationships. In the field of race and ethnic relations, group identity can serve as a basis for positive encounters, a source of comfort and strength, or entry into the mainstream. It can also be a foundation for prejudice and discrimination, negative self-image, a detriment to social acceptance, or a source of conflict.

Ethnic-group identity exists when individuals choose to emphasize cultural or national ties as the basis for their primary social interactions and sense of self. Leaving the taken-for-granted world of their homeland, immigrants—as strangers in a strange land—become more self-conscious of their group identity. Even as the acculturation process and ethnogenesis unfold, these group members retain some of the "cultural baggage" they brought with them and see themselves—as does the mainstream society—as possessing distinctiveness because of their ethnicity.

Many factors determine the duration of an ethnic-group identity. A cohesive ethnic community, continually revitalized by the steady influx of newcomers, will maintain a strong resilience. Ethnic-minority media can play a significant role in strengthening that sense of identity. Indeed, minority media can even affect the assimilation process, either by promoting it (as did the New York *Daily Forward* newspaper among Jewish immigrants in the late 19th and early 20th centuries) or by delaying that process by stressing the retention of language, customs, and values.

Socialization into one's own ethnic group also engenders this identity. Part of the growing-up process for minorities often involves the existence of a dual identity: one in the larger society and another within the person's own group. This multiple reality affects one's roles, behavior, and sense of self, depending on the social setting and other participants.

Ethnic-group identity can be especially protracted on the basis of religion. Some good examples are persistent subcultures, such as the Amish, Hutterites, and Hasidic Jews mentioned in Chapter 2. Although a group identity usually remains among the adherents of any faith, its existence along other ethnic lines depends on racial and assimilation considerations. For example, Catholic immigrants in the 19th century and other Catholic and Jewish immigrants in the early 20th century once stood apart not only for their religion but also for their other subcultural traits. Although traces of anti-Catholicism and anti-Semitism remain today in the United States, most members of these religious groups hold a mainstream-group identity alongside their religious-group identity, which was not the case a few generations ago. More recent arrivals—such as Buddhists, Hindus, Muslims, and Sikhs—are not only religiously distinct from the long-standing three main U.S. religions but are also culturally distinct in other ways along with their mostly racial differences. Currently, their ethnic-group identities embody all these aspects (religion, race, culture), and only time will tell what evolution in group identity will occur among them.

For most but not all European groups, everyday ethnicity eventually yields to assimilation over the generations, and ethnic-group identity fades. That change is possible because gradually the group identifies more and more with mainstream society and its own subcultural "marks" (clothing, language, customs, behavior, residential clustering) disappear, making the group less noticeable to the rest of society as its members become absorbed into the dominant white culture.

Because of the social definition of race, this metamorphosis is difficult for non-Europeans in a color-conscious society. Physical identification through skin color, facial features, and/or hair texture thus maintains differences between the mainstream racial group and others. With their race as an inescapable feature affecting their social acceptance and interaction patterns, non-Europeans typically develop a *racial-group identity*. This ingroup bonding satisfies the human need for a sense of belonging while simultaneously serving as a basis for racial and cultural pride. Such an arrangement can foster a healthier, more positive self-identity than would otherwise develop among racial minorities relegated to secondary social status.

People of color—whether black, brown, yellow, or red—typically affirm their identity and heritage in a variety of ways. These include combating their stereotypes, teaching the younger generation about their racial history and achievements, adopting slogans (e.g., "Black Is Beautiful") or special names (e.g., "La Raza" [the race]), and using a dual identity (e.g., African American, Mexican American, Korean American, Native American) as a positive designator of their dual reality. The more militant racial group members often use ethnophaulisms against their own whom they criticize for "thinking or acting white" and call them, depending on the racial group, "oreos," "coconuts," "bananas," or "apples"—that is, one color on the outside, but white on the inside.

Ethnic- or racial-group identity, then, can have positive and negative consequences. Examining it in both a social and historical context can lead to a more complete understanding of this social phenomenon, something we do in most of the following chapters.

Avoidance

One way of dealing with discriminatory practices is through **avoidance,** if this avenue is available. Throughout history, minority groups—from the ancient Hebrews to the Pilgrims to Kosovo Serbs in recent years—have attempted to solve their problems by leaving them behind. One motive for migrating, then, is to avoid discrimination. If leaving is not possible, minorities may turn inward to their own group for all or most of their social and economic activities. This approach insulates the minority group from antagonistic actions by the dominant group, but it also promotes charges of "clannishness" and "nonassimilation." Lacking adequate economic, legal, or political power, however, the minority group may find avoidance the only choice open to it.

By clustering together in small subcommunities, minority peoples not only create a miniature version of their familiar world in the strange land but also establish a safe place in which they can live, relax, and interact with others like themselves, who understand their needs and interests. For some minority groups, seeking shelter from prejudice is probably a secondary motivation, following a primary desire to live among their own kind.

Asian immigrants, for example, have followed this pattern. When the Chinese first came to this country, they worked in many occupations in which workers were needed, frequently clustering together in neighborhoods close to their jobs. In the United States, prejudicial attitudes had always existed against the Chinese, but in the post–Civil War period, they became even more the targets of bitter hatred and discrimination for economic and other reasons. Evicted from their jobs as a result of race-baiting union strikes and limited in their choice of residence by restrictive housing covenants, many had no choice but to live in insular Chinatowns within the larger cities. They entered businesses that did not compete with those of whites (curio shops, laundries, restaurants, etc.) and followed their old-country tradition of settling disputes among themselves rather than appealing to government authorities for adjudication.

Deviance

When a group continually experiences rejection and discrimination, some of its members can't identify with the dominant society or accept its norms. People at the bottom of the socioeconomic ladder, particularly members of victimized racial and ethnic groups, may respond to the pressures of everyday life in ways they consider reasonable but that others view as **deviance.** This situation occurs in particular when laws serve to impose the moral standards of the dominant group on the behavior of other groups.

Many minority groups in the United States—Irish, Germans, Chinese, Italians, African Americans, Native Americans, and Hispanics—have at one time or another been arrested and punished in disproportionate numbers for so-called crimes of personal disorganization. Among the offenses to the dominant group's morality have been public drunkenness, drug abuse, gambling, and sexual "misconduct." It is unclear whether this disproportion reflects the frequency of misconduct or a pattern of selective arrests. Moreover, some types of conduct are deviant only from the perspective of the majority group, such as cockfighting or female genital cutting, whereas other types, such as wife-beating, may also be deviant within the minority community.

Part of the problem with law enforcement is its subjective nature and the discretionary handling of violations. Many people criticize the U.S. criminal justice system for its failure to accord fair and equal treatment to the poor and to minority-group members as compared with people from the middle and upper classes.[2] Criticisms include (1) the tendency of police to arrest suspects from minority groups at substantially higher rates than those from the majority group in situations in which discretionary judgment is possible; (2) the overrepresentation of certain dominant social, ethnic, and racial groups on juries; (3) the difficulty the poor encounter in affording bail; (4) the poor quality of free legal defense; and (5) the disparities in sentencing for members of dominant and minority groups. Because social background constitutes one of the factors that the police and courts consider, individuals who belong to a racial or ethnic group with a negative stereotype find themselves at a severe disadvantage.

When a particular racial or ethnic group commits a noticeable number of deviant offenses, such as delinquency, crime, drunkenness, or some public nuisance problem, the public often extends a negative image to all members of that group even though it applies to only a few. Some common associations, for example, are Italians and gangsters, Irish and heavy drinking and fighting, Chinese and opium, African Americans and street crimes such as mugging and purse snatching, and Puerto Ricans and knife fighting. Even though a very small percentage of a group actually engages in such behavior, the entire group may become negatively stereotyped. A number of factors—including values, behavior patterns, and structural conditions in both the native and adopted lands—help explain the various kinds of so-called deviance among different minority groups. The appropriate means of stopping the deviance is itself subject to debate between proponents of corrective versus preventive measures.

Deviant behavior among minority groups occurs not because of race or ethnicity, as prejudiced people think, but usually because of poverty and lack of opportunity. Clifford Shaw and Henry McKay, in a classic study of juvenile delinquency in Chicago, suggested that structural conditions, not membership in a particular minority group, determine crime and delinquency rates.[3] They found that the highest rates of juvenile delinquency occurred in areas with poor housing, few job opportunities, and widespread prostitution, gambling, and drug use. The delinquency rate was consistently high over a 30-year period, even though five different ethnic groups moved in and out of those areas during that period. Nationality was unimportant; the unchanged conditions brought unchanged results. Other studies have demonstrated a correlation between higher rates of juvenile or adult crime and income level and place of residence.[4]

Because many minority groups are heavily represented among low-income populations, studies emphasizing social-class variables often provide insight into the minority experience. The most common finding is that a lack of opportunities encourages delinquency among lower-class males.[5] Social aspirations may be similar at all levels of society, but opportunities are not. Belonging to a gang may give a youth a sense of power and help overcome feelings of inadequacy; hoodlumism becomes a conduit for expressing resentment against a society whose approved norms seem impossible to follow.[6] Notwithstanding the economic and environmental difficulties they face, the large majority of racial-group and ethnic-group members do not join gangs or engage in criminally deviant behavior. However, because some minority groups are represented disproportionately in such activities, the public image of the group as a whole suffers.

Some social factors, particularly parental attitudes about education, appear related to delinquency rates. Generally, parental emphasis on academic achievement and extensive involvement in their children's schooling leads to more educationally committed adolescents. The greater their commitment, the lower the rates of delinquency, and vice versa.[7]

Defiance

If a minority group is sufficiently cohesive and conscious of its growing economic or political power, its members may act openly to challenge and eliminate discriminatory practices—**defiance**. In defying discrimination, the minority group takes a strong stance regarding its position in the society. Prior to this time, certain individuals of that group may have pioneered the movement (e.g., by challenging laws in court).

Sometimes the defiance is violent and seems spontaneous, although it usually grows out of long-standing conditions. One example is the Irish draft riot in New York in 1863 during the Civil War. When its volunteer armies proved insufficient, the Union used a military draft to secure needed troops. In those days, well-to-do males of draft age could legally avoid conscription by buying the military services of a substitute. Meanwhile, because the Irish were mostly poor and concentrated in urban areas, many of them had no recourse when drafted. Their defiance at what they considered an unfair practice blossomed into a riot in which blacks became the scapegoats, with lives lost and property destroyed or damaged. Similarly, the 1991 Washington, DC, Hispanic riot after a black female police officer shot a Salvadoran immigrant and the 1992 Los Angeles riot following the acquittal of police officers videotaped beating Rodney King may both have been spontaneous reactions, but only within the larger context of smoldering, deep-seated, long-standing resentments.

A militant action, such as the takeover of a symbolic site, is a moderately aggressive act of defiance. The late 1960s witnessed many building takeovers by African Americans and other disaffected, angry, alienated students on college campuses. In many instances, the purpose of the action was to call public attention to what the group considered society's indifference toward or discrimination against their people. Similar actions occurred in this period to protest the war in Vietnam. A small group of Native Americans took this approach in the 1970s to protest their living conditions; at different times, they seized Alcatraz Island in California, the Bureau of Indian Affairs in Washington, DC, and the village of Wounded Knee in South Dakota. Media attention helped validate and spread the idea of using militant actions to promote a group's agenda.

Any peaceful action that challenges the status quo, though less aggressive, is defiant nonetheless; parades, marches, picket lines, mass meetings, boycotts, and demonstrations are examples. Another form of peaceful protest consists of civil disobedience: deliberately breaking discriminatory laws and then challenging their constitutionality or breaking a discriminatory tradition. The Civil Rights actions of the 1960s—sit-ins, lie-ins, and freedom rides—challenged decades-old Jim Crow laws that restricted access by blacks to public establishments in the South. Shop-ins at stores that catered to an exclusively white clientele represented deliberate efforts to break traditional store practices by attempting to make purchases.

Acceptance

Many minority people, to the frequent consternation of their leaders and sympathizers, accept the situation in which they find themselves. Some do so stoically, justifying their decision by subtle rationalizations. Others are resentful but accept the situation for reasons of personal security or economic necessity. Still others accept it through false consciousness, a consequence of the dominant group's control over sources of information. Although **acceptance** maintains the superior position in society of the dominant group and the subordinate position of the minority group, it does diminish the open tensions and conflicts between the two groups.

In some instances, conforming to prevailing patterns of interaction between dominant and minority groups occurs subconsciously, the end result of social conditioning. Just as socialization can inculcate prejudice, so too can it cause minority-group members to disregard or be unaware of alternative status possibilities. How much acceptance of lower status takes this form and how much is characterized by resentful submission and mental rejection is never easy to determine.

African Americans, Mexican Americans, and Native Americans have experienced a subordinate position in the United States for multiple generations. Until the 1960s, a combination of structural discrimination, racial stratification, powerlessness, and a sense of the futility of trying to change things caused many to acquiesce in the situation imposed on them. Similarly, Japanese Americans had little choice when, following the bombing of Pearl Harbor and the subsequent rise in anti-Japanese sentiment, the U.S. government in 1942 dispossessed and imprisoned 110,000 of them in "temporary relocation centers."[8]

Acceptance as a minority response is less common in the United States than it once was. More aware of the alternative ways of living presented in the media, today's minorities are more hopeful about sharing in them. No longer do they passively accept the status quo, which denies them the comfortable life and leisure pursuits others enjoy. Simultaneously, through court decisions, legislation, new social services, and other efforts, society has created a more favorable climate for improving the status of minority groups. Televised news features and behavioral science courses may have heightened the public's social awareness as well.

CONSEQUENCES OF MINORITY–GROUP STATUS

Minority groups that experience sustained inequality face four possible outcomes: negative self-image, a vicious circle of continued discrimination, marginality, and status as middleman minorities.

Negative Self-Image

The apathy that militant leaders sometimes find among their own people may result from a **negative self-image**, a common consequence of prejudice and discrimination. **Labeling theory,** originally conceived by Howard Becker, helps us to understand this process. Based on racial or ethnic stereotypes, the mainstream group may single out a minority group through a process of "tagging, defining, identifying, segregating, describing, and emphasizing."[9] If the labeling process is pervasive and powerful enough, group members may come to accept the definition society forces on them and have lowered self-esteem.

Continual treatment as an inferior encourages a loss of self-confidence. If everything about a person's position and experiences—jobs with low pay, substandard housing, the hostility of others, and the need for assistance from government agencies—works to destroy pride and hope, the person may become apathetic. To remain optimistic and determined in the face of constant negative experiences from all directions is extremely difficult.

Kurt Lewin once observed that minority-group members had a fairly general tendency to develop a negative self-image.[10] The pervasiveness of dominant-group values and attitudes, which include negative stereotypes of the minority group, may cause the minority-group member to absorb them. A person's self-image includes race, religion, and nationality; thus, individuals may feel embarrassed, even inferior, if they see that one or more of the attributes they possess are despised within the society. In effect, minority-group members begin to perceive themselves as negatively as the dominant group originally did.

Negative self-image, or self-hatred, manifests itself in many ways. People may try to "pass" as members of the dominant group and deny membership in a disparaged group. They may adopt the dominant group's prejudices and accept their devalued status. They may engage in ego defense by blaming others within the group for the low esteem in which society holds them:

> Some Jews refer to other Jews as "kikes"—blaming them exclusively for the anti-Semitism from which all alike suffer. Class distinctions within groups are often a result of trying to free oneself from responsibility for the handicap from which the group as a whole suffers. "Lace curtain" Irish look down on "shanty" Irish. Wealthy Spanish and Portuguese Jews have long regarded themselves as the top of the pyramid of Hebraic peoples. But Jews of German origin, having a rich culture, view themselves as the aristocrats, often looking down on Austrian, Hungarian, and Balkan Jews, and regarding Polish and Russian Jews at the very bottom.[11]

Negative self-image, then, can cause people to accept their fate passively. It also can encourage personal shame for possessing undesired qualities or antipathy toward other members of the group for possessing them. Minority-group members may attempt to overcome their negative self-image by changing their name or religion, having cosmetic surgery, or moving to a locale where the stereotype is less prevalent.

But Lewin's view that negative self-image is a fairly general tendency among minority-group members may be too broad. For example, members of tightly cohesive religious groups may draw emotional support from their faith and from one another. The insulation of living in an ethnic community, having strong ingroup loyalty, and/or having a determination to maintain a cultural heritage may prevent minority-group members from developing a negative self-image.

Various social science studies show that people who are stigmatized can protect their self-esteem by attributing the negative feedback they receive to prejudice. In a study analyzing minority children's attitudes toward their own group, Frances E. Aboud suggested group visibility as a possible link to positive self-image. In another analysis, Margaret Beale Spencer argued that because parents are the first source of a child's "sense of self," their instilling racial pride contributes to resilience and may lead to coping strategies against prejudice that have positive consequences.[12]

The Vicious-Circle Phenomenon

Sometimes the relationship between prejudice and discrimination is circular. Gunnar Myrdal refers to this pattern as **cumulative causation**—a **vicious-circle phenomenon** in which prejudice and discrimination perpetuate each other.[13] The dynamics of the relations between dominant and minority groups set in motion a cyclical sequence of reciprocal stimuli and responses. For example, a discriminatory action in filling jobs leads to a minority reaction, poverty, which in turn reinforces the dominant-group attitude that the minority group is inferior, leading to more discrimination, and so on.

Myrdal points out that the pattern of expectation and reaction may produce desirable or undesirable results. Gordon Allport adds that the expectations held about the newcomers determine the pattern that develops.[14] If the dominant group makes the newcomers welcome, they in turn are likely to react in a positive manner, which reinforces their friendly reception. If the new group is ignored or made to feel unwelcome, the members may react negatively, which again reaffirms original attitudes and actions. As Allport says, "If we foresee evil in our fellow man, we tend to provoke it; if good, we elicit it."[15] In other words, negative expectations engender negative reactions, broadening the social distance between the groups, and causing the vicious circle to continue.

When Jews were denied access to many U.S. vacation resorts during the 19th century, their reactions served to reinforce their negative stereotype in the minds of some, reinforcing their discriminatory behavior. Some Jews demanded equal access, which the resort operators took as proof that Jews were "pushy." When Jews responded to this discriminatory policy by establishing and patronizing their own resorts in the Catskill Mountains, the majority group labeled them "clannish." Similarly, the Irish encountered severe job discrimination in the mid-19th century; the resulting poverty forced many of them to live in urban slums, where they often had trouble with the law. Given this evidence of their "inferiority" and "undesirability," majority-group employers curtailed their job opportunities further. In the same way, discrimination by whites against blacks, based partly on the low standard of living endured by many of the latter, exacerbates the problems of poverty, fueling even more the antipathy of some whites toward blacks.

Marginality

Minority-group members sometimes find themselves caught in a conflict between their own identity and values and the necessity to behave in a certain way to gain acceptance by the dominant group. This situation—**marginality**—usually arises when a member of a minority group is passing through a transitional period. In attempting to enter the mainstream of society, the *marginal* person internalizes the dominant group's cultural patterns without having gained full acceptance. Such individuals occupy an ill-defined position, no longer at ease within their own group but not yet fully a part of the *reference group,* the one by whose standards they evaluate themselves and their behavior.

Over the years, sociologists have differed in their interpretation of the effects of marginality. Robert E. Park, who gave this social phenomenon its name, believed that it caused the individual a great deal of strain and difficulty. A marginal person, he observed, is one "whom fate has condemned to live in two societies and in two not merely different but antagonistic cultures."[16]

According to Park, this situation can cause the marginal person, whether an adult or a child, to suffer anxiety over a conflict of values and loyalties. Adults leave the security of their cultural group and thereby risk being labeled renegades by their own people. They seek sustained social contacts with members of the dominant group, which may view them as outsiders. No longer comfortable with the old ways but nonetheless influenced by them and identified with them, marginal adults often experience feelings of frustration, hypersensitivity, and self-consciousness.

Children of immigrants likewise find themselves caught between two worlds. At home, their parents attempt to raise them in their social heritage, according to the established ways of the old country. Meanwhile, through school and other outside experiences, the children are exposed to the U.S. culture and want to be like other children in the society. Moreover, they may learn that the dominant group views their parents' ways as inferior and that they, too, are socially rejected because of their background. Consequently, many young people in transition develop emotional problems and are embarrassed to bring classmates home.

According to this view, marginality is an example of cultural conflict caused primarily by the clash of values within the individual. Many sociologists now believe, however, that the reaction to marginal status depends largely on whether the individual receives reassurances of self-worth from the surrounding community. Thus, successfully defining the situation and adjusting to it are contingent on the individual's sense of security within the community.[17] Supportive ethnic subcommunities and institutions and a sense of solidarity among members of the ethnic group contribute to that sense of well-being. These observations have led some sociologists to emphasize that the transitional phase involves stable individuals in a marginal culture rather than marginal persons in a dominant culture. Individuals in a marginal culture share their cultural duality with many others in primary-group relationships, in institutional activities, and in interacting with members of the dominant society without encountering any dichotomy between their desires and actuality.[18]

Whether this phase of the assimilation process represents an emotionally stressful experience or a comfortably protected one, minority-group members nonetheless pass through a transitional period during which they are not fully a part of either world. An immigrant group may move into the mainstream of U.S. society within the lifetimes of the first-generation members, it may choose not to do so, or it may not be permitted to do so. Usually, marginality is a one- or two-generation phenomenon. After that, members of the minority group either have assimilated or have formed a distinctive subculture. Whichever route they take, they are no longer caught between two cultural worlds.

Middleman Minorities

Building on theories of marginality, Hubert Blalock suggested the model of **middleman minorities**.[19] This model, based on a dominant–subordinate stratification system, places middleman minorities in an intermediate rather than a low-status position.[20] Feudal and colonial societies, with their ruling elite and large peasant masses, often rely on middleman minorities to forge mediating commerce links between the two. Consequently, such minorities commonly are trading peoples whose history of persecution (Jews, Greeks, and Armenians) or sojourner orientation (Chinese, Japanese, and Koreans) have obliged them to perform risky or marginal tasks that permitted easy liquidation of their assets when necessary.[21]

Middleman groups often serve as buffers and hence experience hostility and conflict from above and below. Jews in Nazi Germany and Asians in Uganda in the early 1970s, for instance, became scapegoats for the economic turmoil in those societies. Their susceptibility to such antagonism and their nonassimilation into the host society promoted high ingroup solidarity.

Systematic discrimination can prolong the duration of a group's middleman-

Once German, Irish, Italian, and Jewish merchants and small businesses served as middleman minorities to other ethnic groups. Today some Africans, Asians, and Hispanics repeat the pattern, such as in this black neighborhood pizzeria where a Hispanic cook sells slices and whole pies, along with other foods and drinks.

minority status, as in the case of European Jews throughout the medieval period. Sometimes the entrepreneurial skills developed in trade and commerce provide middleman minorities with adaptive capabilities and competitive advantages, enabling them to achieve upward mobility and to assimilate more easily; this occurred for Jewish immigrants to the United States and may similarly occur for Korean Americans. In other cases, a group may emerge as a middleman minority because of changing residential patterns. One example is Jewish store owners in city neighborhoods where they once served their own people; when their original neighbors moved away and they found themselves unable to follow them, these urban merchants served new urban minority groups that were situated lower on the socioeconomic ladder.

DOMINANT-GROUP RESPONSES

Members of a dominant group may react to minority peoples with hostility, indifference, welcoming tolerance, or condescension. The more favorable responses usually occur when the minority is numerically small, not perceived as a threat, or both. As the minority group's population increases, threatening the natives' monopoly on jobs and other claims to privileged cultural resources, the dominant group's attitude is likely to become suspicious or fearful. If the fear becomes great enough, the dominant group may take action against the minority group.

Dominant groups often use religion in varying aggressive ways against minority groups. Besides religious persecution (a push factor in many migrations throughout world history), they often use missionaries to convert minorities. Dominant groups do not necessarily conduct these sometimes forced conversions with the intent of assimilating a minority group. For example, teaching Christianity to slaves enabled southern whites to create a false consciousness among the Africans in accepting their fate by working hard to please their masters. In the case of Native Americans, the federal government gave reservation land to several Protestant religions in an effort to convert the "heathens" and remake them in the white man's image, while maintaining their isolated, segregated confinement.

Legislative Controls

If the influx of racial and ethnic groups appears to the dominant group to be too great for a country to absorb, or if prejudicial fears prevail, the nation may enact measures to regulate and restrict their entry. Australia, Canada, and the United States—the three greatest receiving countries in international migration—once had discriminatory immigration laws that either excluded or curtailed the number of immigrants from countries other than those of northern and western Europe. Through similar patterns of policy change, Canada (in 1962), the United States (in 1965), and Australia (in 1973) began to permit entry from all parts of the world.

To maintain a paternalistic social system, the dominant group frequently restricts the subordinate group's educational and voting opportunities. This denial assures the dominant group of maintaining its system of control, whether over internal minorities, such as blacks in the Old South and various ethnic minorities in the former Soviet Union, or over colonized peoples, such as those ruled by the Belgians, British, Dutch, French, Japanese, and Portuguese. Most colonial powers have committed themselves to stability, trade, and tapping the natural resources of a country rather than to developing its infrastructure and preparing it for self-governance. As a result, the usual experience of native populations under colonial rule has been largely ceremonial leadership from figureheads installed and approved by the colonial authority (who lack real power in important matters), limited educational opportunities, and restricted political participation. Other means of denying political power have included disenfranchising voters through high property qualifications (British West Indies), high income qualifications (Trinidad), and poll taxes (United States), although none of these practices exists today in these areas. The most conspicuous recent example of rigid social control was in South Africa, where a legislated apartheid society denied blacks not only equal education and the ballot but also almost every other privilege as well.

Segregation

Through a policy of containment—avoiding social interaction with members of a minority group as much as possible and keeping them "in their place"—the dominant group can effectively create both spatial and social segregation.

Spatial segregation is the physical separation of a minority people from the rest of society. This most commonly occurs in residential patterns, but it also takes place in education, in the use of public facilities, and in occupations. The majority group may institutionalize this form of segregation by law (*de jure* segregation) or establish it informally through pervasive practice (*de facto* segregation).

Spatial segregation of minorities has a long history. Since the days of the preindustrial city with its heterogeneous populations, the dominant group has relegated racial and ethnic minorities to special sections of the city, often the least desirable areas.[22] In Europe, this medieval ecological pattern resulted in minority groups being situated on the city outskirts nearest the encircling wall. Because this pattern remains in much of Europe today, Europeans, unlike people in the United States, consider it a sign of high prestige to live near the center of the city.[23]

The dominant group may use covert or overt means to achieve spatial segregation of a minority group. Examples of covert actions include restrictive covenants, "gentlemen's agreements," and collusion between the community and real estate agents to steer "undesirable" minorities into certain neighborhoods.[24] Overt actions include restrictive zoning, segregation laws, and intimidation. Ever since the 1954 *Brown v. Board of Education* desegregation ruling, U.S. courts have continually declared unlawful both covert and overt methods of segregation.

An important dimension of spatial segregation is that the dominant group can achieve it through avoidance or residential mobility. Usually referred to as the invasion-succession ecological pattern, this common process has involved different religions and nationalities as well as different races. The most widely recognized example in the United States is previously all-white neighborhoods becoming black, but any study of old urban neighborhoods would reveal the same pattern as successive waves of immigrants came here over the years. Residents of a neighborhood may resist the influx of a minority group but eventually abandon the area when their efforts are not successful. This pattern results in neighborhoods with a concentration of a new racial or ethnic group—a new segregated area.

Social segregation involves confining participation in social, service, political, and other types of activities to members of the ingroup. The dominant group excludes the outgroup from any involvement in meaningful primary-group activities and in secondary-group activities. Organizations use screening procedures to keep out unwanted types, and informal groups act to preserve their composition.

Segregation, whether spatial or social, may be voluntary or involuntary. Minority-group members may choose to live by themselves rather than among the dominant group; this is an avoidance response, discussed previously. In contrast, minority-group members may have no choice about where they live because of economic or residential discrimination.

Whether by choice or against their will, minority groups form ethnic subcommunities, the existence of which in turn promotes and maintains the social distance between them and the rest of society. Not only do minority-group members physically congregate in one area and thus find themselves spatially segregated, but they also do not engage in any social interaction with others outside their own group.

Under the right conditions, frequent interaction reduces prejudice, but when interaction is severely limited, the acculturation process slows considerably. Meanwhile, values regarding what is normal or different are reinforced, paving the way for stereotyping, social comparisons, and prestige ranking.

Expulsion

When other methods of dealing with a minority group fail—and sometimes not even as a last resort—an intolerant dominant group may persecute the minority group or eject it from the territory where it resides (**expulsion**). Henry VIII banished the Gypsies from England in the 16th century, Spanish rulers drove out the Moors in the early 17th century, and the British expelled the French Acadians from Nova Scotia in the mid-18th century. More recent examples include Idi Amin, who decreed in 1972 that all Asians must leave Uganda; Muammar al-Qaddafi, who expelled Libya's ethnic Italian community in 1970; and Serbs who forced ethnic Albanians out of Kosovo in 1999.

The United States also has its examples of mass expulsion. In colonial times, the Puritans forced Roger Williams and his followers out of Massachusetts for their nonconformity; the group settled in what became Rhode Island. The forcible removal of the Cherokee from rich Georgia land and the subsequent "Trail of Tears," during which 4,000 perished along the 1,000-mile forced march to Oklahoma Territory, is another illustration.

Mass expulsion is an effort to drive out a group that is seen as a social problem rather than attempting to resolve the problem cooperatively. This policy often arises after other methods, such as assimilation or extermination, have failed. Whether a dominant group chooses to remove a minority group by extermination or by expulsion depends in part on how sensitive the country is to world opinion, which in turn may be related to the country's economic dependence on other nations.

Xenophobia

If the dominant group's suspicions and fears of the minority group become serious enough, they may produce volatile, irrational feelings and actions. This overreaction is known as **xenophobia**—the undue fear of or contempt for strangers or foreigners. This almost hysterical response—reflected in print, speeches, sermons, legislation, and violent actions—begins with ethnocentric views. Ethnocentrism encourages the creation of negative stereotypes, which in turn invites prejudice and discrimination and can escalate through some catalyst into a highly emotional reaction (see The International Scene box).

Many examples of xenophobia exist in U.S. history. In 1798, the Federalists, fearful of "wild Irishmen" and "French radicals" and anxious to eliminate what they saw as a foreign threat to the country's stability, passed the Alien and Sedition Acts. When a bomb exploded at an anarchist gathering at Chicago's Haymarket Square in 1886, many Americans thereafter linked foreigners with radicals. The Bolshevik Revolution in 1917 led to the Palmer raids, in which foreign-born U.S. residents were illegally rounded up and incarcerated for their alleged Communist Party affiliation; some were even deported. In 1942, 110,000 Japanese Americans, many of them second- and third-generation U.S. citizens, were interned in concentration camps as a result of irrational suspicions that they would prove less loyal during the ongoing World War II than German Americans

The International Scene

Segregation and Defiance in France

In late 2005, three weeks of riots and violent clashes broke out in Paris and spread to other French cities, eventually engulfing all fifteen of the country's largest urban areas. By the time the riots ended, the counts were one dead, about 2,900 arrested, and thousands of vehicles and numerous public buildings burned, including a Roman Catholic Church.

The spiraling events began with the accidental electrocution of two teenagers—one the son of West African immigrants and the other the son of Tunisian immigrants—who ran from police (conducting one of their frequent identity checks of minorities) and hid in a power substation. A third teenager, the son of Turkish Kurdish immigrants, was injured and hospitalized. The three victims thus represented the primary minority groups in France—Arab, black, and Muslim—and became the catalyst to ignite the preexisting tensions.

For decades, French government policy had concentrated immigrants and their families in well-defined districts of poorly maintained public housing projects on the edges of cities. Isolated from the city center, these *de facto* ethnic ghettos have little activity at night or on Sundays, and there is limited public transportation to the center. In addition, much higher unemployment for the foreign-born compared to the native-born—even worse among college graduates—contributed extensively to the mounting frustration and desperation.

Amid charges of job discrimination and police harassment, the common use by the media and general population of the expression "second generation of immigrants" (even for those born in France) suggested a cultural mindset that differentiated who was "really" French. (At age 18, immigrant children born in France may go through a bureaucratic application process to be citizens; their birth there does not automatically bestow citizenship on them as it does in the United States.)

Experts cite the racial and social discrimination against persons with dark skin or Arabic- and/or African-sounding names as a major cause of unhappiness in the riot-torn areas. Although such discrimination is illegal, children of immigrants claim that they frequently encounter economic segregation, problems getting a job or renting an apartment, or even getting into a nightclub, just because of their name or the color of their skin. Since the riots, little has changed, and thus the potential for another violent outbreak remains.

Critical Thinking Questions: How similar or dissimilar are the experiences of U.S. minorities today? Does the difference in French and U.S. citizenship laws have any impact on the acceptance and integration of minorities into society? If so, how?

and Italian Americans. The U.S. English movement's current efforts to pass English-only laws reflect a xenophobic fear that foreigners won't learn English.

Annihilation

The Nazi extermination of more than 6 million Jews brought the term *genocide* into the English language, but the practice of **annihilation**—killing all the men, women, and children of a particular group—goes back to ancient times. In warfare among the ancient Assyrians, Babylonians, Egyptians, Hebrews, and others, the usual practice was for the victor to slay every member of an enemy civilization, partly to prevent their children from seeking revenge. For example, preserved in Deuteronomy are these words of Moses:

> Then Sihon came out against us, he and all his people, to fight at Jahaz. And the LORD our God delivered him before us; and we smote him, and his sons, and all his people. And we took all his cities at that time, and utterly destroyed the men, and the women, and the little ones, of every city, we left none to remain: Only the cattle we took for a prey unto ourselves, and the spoil of the cities which we took.
>
> Then we turned, and went up the way to Bashan: and Og the king of Bashan came out against us, he and all his people, to battle at Edrei. . . . So the LORD our God delivered into our hands Og also, the king of Bashan, and all his people: and we smote him until none was left to him remaining. And we took all his cities at that time, there was not a city which we took not from them, threescore cities, all the region of Argob, the kingdom of Og in Bashan. . . . And we utterly destroyed them, as we did unto Sihon king of Heshbon, utterly destroying the men, women, and children, of every city. But all the cattle, and the spoil of the cities, we took for a prey to ourselves.[25]

In modern times, various countries have used extermination as a means of solving a so-called race problem. Arnold Toynbee once said that the "English method of settlement" followed this pattern.[26] The British, through extermination and close confinement of survivors, annihilated the entire aboriginal population of Tasmania between 1803 and 1876.[27] The Dutch considered South African San (Bushmen) less than human and attempted to obliterate them.[28] When native peoples of Brazil resisted Portuguese settlement of their lands, the whites solved the problem by systematically killing them. One favored means of doing so was to place the clothing of recent smallpox victims in their villages and allow the contagion to destroy the native population.[29] In the 1890s and again in 1915, the Turkish government systematically massacred hundreds of thousands of Armenians, events still solemnly remembered each year by Armenian Americans. One of the largest genocides in U.S. history occurred at Wounded Knee in 1890, when the U.S. Seventh Cavalry killed about 200 Native American men, women, and children. In the past 50 years, campaigns of genocide have occurred around the globe in such countries as Sudan, Burundi, Rwanda, Nigeria, Indonesia, Iraq, Bangladesh, Bosnia, and Kosovo.

Lynchings are not a form of annihilation because the intent is not to exterminate an entire group but to set an example through selective, drastic punishment (most frequently, hanging). Nonetheless, the victims usually are minority-group members. Although lynchings occurred throughout U.S. history, only since 1882 do we have reasonably reliable statistics on their frequency (Figure 4.1). Archived data at the *Chicago Tribune* and the Tuskegee Institute reveal that at least 5,000

FIGURE 4.1   Lynchings in the United States Since 1882

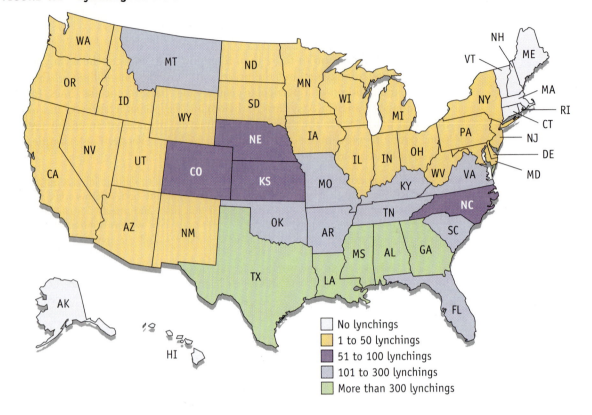

lynchings have occurred since 1882. They happened in every state except the New England states, with the Deep South (including Texas) claiming the most victims. In fact, 90 percent of all lynchings during this period occurred in the southern states, with blacks accounting for 80 percent of the victims. The statistics do not, however, cover lynchings during the nation's first 100 years, including those in the western frontier, when many Native Americans and Hispanics also met this fate.[30]

Annihilation sometimes occurs unintentionally, as when whites inadvertently spread Old World sicknesses to Native Americans in the United States and Canada, to Inuit (Eskimos), and to Polynesians. With no prior exposure to ailments such as measles, mumps, chicken pox, and smallpox, the native populations had little physiological resistance to them and thus succumbed to these contagious diseases in unusually high numbers. Other forms of annihilation, usually intentional, occur during times of mob violence, overzealous police actions, and the calculated actions of small private groups.[31]

Hate Groups

Like most nations, the United States has had its share of hate groups and hate crimes. Most prominent among hate groups of the past were the Know-Nothings of the mid-19th century and the Ku Klux Klan in the late 19th and early 20th centuries. As you will read in subsequent chapters, bias crimes against Europeans,

Native Americans, Asians, and numerous religious groups occurred frequently in the 19th and 20th centuries. Deplorably, in the 21st century, this ugly pattern remains a brutal force in U.S. society.

The Intelligence Project of the Southern Poverty Law Center—the nation's preeminent monitor and analyst of American extremism—reported that the number of hate groups in the United States increased by 40 percent since 2000, driven in large measure by the immigration issue. (Figure 4.2).[32] Of the 844 organized hate groups in 2006, neo-Nazi organizations comprised 191 of the total, followed by the Ku Klux Klan (165), white nationalists (110), neo-Confederates (102), and black separatist groups (88), including the Nation of Islam. Although the Nation of Islam is not involved in political violence, its tenets are based on racial hatred according to the Intelligence Project. Other hate groups are racist skinheads (78) and Christian Identity groups (37), which identify whites as the Bible's chosen people and Jews as satanic. The remaining 73 groups followed a hodgepodge of hate-based doctrines.

California contains the largest number of hate groups (63), followed by Texas (55), Florida (49), South Carolina (45), Georgia (44), Tennessee (35) New Jersey (34), North Carolina (33), Ohio and Virginia (31 each), Mississippi (28), Pennsylvania (27), Louisiana and New York (24). Every state except North Dakota, South Dakota, and Rhode Island had at least one hate group in 2006.

FIGURE 4.2   Hate Groups in the United States

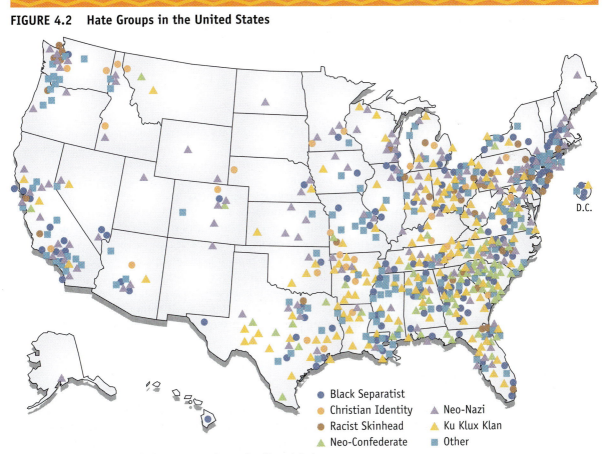

● Black Separatist
● Christian Identity   ▲ Neo-Nazi
● Racist Skinhead   ▲ Ku Klux Klan
▲ Neo-Confederate   ■ Other

Source: Adapted from the Southern Poverty Law Center, Intelligence Project.

Sadly, about 20 hate crimes occur daily in the United States. Almost one-third are acts of intimidation, while another third are assaults against individuals. Nearly one-third involve vandalism or property damage, such as the arsonist who gutted this Middle Eastern store in Everett, Washington, in July 2004.

Hate Crimes

Hate crime offenses—only some of which are committed by members of organized hate groups—numbered 9,080 in 2006 and claimed 9,652 victims. Racial bias motivated 52 percent of the incidents, religious bias another 18 percent, sexual-orientation bias 16 percent, and ethnicity/national origin bias 14 percent (Table 4.1). Crimes against persons accounted for 60 percent of hate crime offenses, while damage/destruction/vandalism of property constituted 40 percent.[33]

To combat hate crimes—commonly defined as any criminal offense against a person or property that is motivated in whole or part by the offender's bias against a race, religion, ethnic/national origin, group, or sexual orientation—many states have passed laws mandating severe punishments for persons convicted of these crimes. Federal law (18 U.S.C. 245) also permits federal prosecution of a hate crime as a civil rights violation if the assailant intended to prevent the victim from exercising a "federally protected right" such as voting or attending school. Despite such sanctions, however, the numbers of hate groups and hate crimes continue to rise.

EXPLOITATION

Countless writings have documented instances of the **exploitation** of minority groups in various countries. Sometimes the perpetrators of this abuse are members of the same group—the operators of Asian sweatshops in U.S. cities, for instance, and the *padroni* of old Italian immigrant communities, both of whom

TABLE 4.1   Bias Motivation of Hate–Crime Incidents in 2006, by Percentage

	Percentage of Category	Percentage of Total
Race		**52.2**
Antiblack	66.2	
Antiwhite	21.3	
Anti-Asian	4.9	
Antimultiracial group	6.1	
Anti–Native American	1.5	
Religion		**17.6**
Anti-Jewish	64.3	
Anti-Islamic	12.0	
Anti-Protestant	3.9	
Anti-Catholic	5.1	
Antimultireligious group	5.5	
Other	9.2	
Ethnicity/National Origin		**13.6**
Anti-Hispanic	62.4	
Other	37.6	
Sexual Orientation		**15.6**
Antimale homosexual	62.3	
Antifemale homosexual	13.6	
Antihomosexual	20.7	
Antiheterosexual	2.0	
Antibisexual	1.5	

Source: Adapted from Federal Bureau of Investigation, *"Hate Crimes" Crime in the United States: 2006,* accessed online at http://www.fbi.gov/ucr/hc2006/table1.pdf [January 20, 2008].

often benefited at the expense of their own people. Most often, however, members of dominant groups exploit minority groups.

Middle-range conflict theories are often helpful in understanding specific forms of exploitation, such as the internal-colonialism theory discussed in Chapter 2. Another analytical explanation comes to us from Edna Bonacich, who suggests a **split-labor-market theory** as a means of understanding the ethnic antagonism arising from economic exploitation.

To understand how a split labor market works, we must first understand its structural context. Racial or ethnic differences do not in themselves create labor price differentials, because they arise out of the resource conditions of both groups. As Bonacich says:

> With the possible exception of sojourners, cheaper labor does not intentionally undermine more expensive labor. It is paradoxically its weakness that makes it so threatening, for business can more thoroughly control it.[34]

Bonacich theorizes that ethnic antagonism results from a combination of economic exploitation by employers and economic competition between two or more groups of laborers that produces a wage differential for labor. She contends that much ethnic antagonism is based not on ethnicity and race but on the conflict between higher-paid and lower-paid labor—the split-labor-market theory:

> Ethnic antagonism is specifically produced by the competition that arises from a price differential. An oversupply of equal-priced labor does not produce such antagonism, though it too threatens people with the loss of their job. However, hiring practices will not necessarily fall along ethnic lines. . . . All workingmen are on the same footing, competing for scarce jobs. When one ethnic group is decidedly cheaper than another (i.e., when the labor market is split), the higher paid worker faces more than the loss of his job; he faces the possibility that the wage standard in all jobs will be undermined by cheaper labor.[35]

The lower-paid group—its wages nonetheless higher than its members can find elsewhere—threatens the higher-paid labor group with possible displacement with such wage undercutting. In turn, higher-paid labor may respond, says Bonacich, in one of three ways.

First, if the higher-paid labor group is strong enough, it may be able to block the cheaper competition through exclusion. To some degree, the U.S. restriction of Chinese and Japanese immigrant labor and Australia's restriction of Asian and Polynesian immigrants represented victories for organized labor against lower-paid competition.

Second, it may create a caste system of occupational segregation. In a caste system, higher-paid labor exclusively controls certain high-paying jobs and limits the minority group to other lower-paying jobs (often lacking health benefits and

Today, sweatshops remain a form of economic exploitation just as they did three generations ago. The labor union movement of the early 20th century ended this practice for European immigrants, but now Asian and Hispanic newcomers—many undocumented aliens—work long hours for low pay without any advocates for them.

pension plans). This creates an aristocracy of labor and submerges the labor-market split by stratifying the differentially priced workers. This phenomenon can be seen in the job differentials between blacks and whites and between men and women in certain trade unions.

A third response is radicalism, in which the workers form a multi-ethnic coalition against the employers. Here the action may include mass demonstrations and protests, sometimes provoked into violent outbreaks by counterdemonstrations, employer race-baiting, or police activity.

Among the factors that lower the price of one group's labor are exploitation by management, unfamiliarity with wage standards, limiting language skills and customs, and lack of economic resources. All these factors force them into low-paying jobs, into making contractual commitments before emigrating, or into seeking political support from a labor organization or government:

> Governments vary in the degree to which they protect their emigrants. Japan kept close watch over the fate of her nationals who migrated to Hawaii and the Pacific coast. . . . In contrast Mexican migrant workers to the United States have received little protection from their government, and African states were unable to intervene on behalf of slaves brought to America.[36]

When a labor market splits along ethnic lines, racial and ethnic stereotyping becomes a key factor in the labor conflict, and prejudice, ethnic antagonism, and racism become overt. The conflict is not due to religious differences—and does not depend on which group was first to move into the area—because examples of ethnic antagonism can be found in which these variables were controlled. Bonacich argues that the one characteristic shared by all societies in which ethnic antagonism is acute is an indigenous working class that earns higher wages than do immigrant workers.

This common characteristic fuels anti-immigration sentiments, intensified even more these days by the concern over the millions of undocumented immigrants in the country. The generations-old complaint that "they're taking jobs away from Americans" has at its core the fear of higher-priced American labor being displaced by cheaper immigrant labor.

Employers are seldom passive observers of this clash between higher-priced and cheaper labor along racial and ethnic lines. They are the ones, after all, who control the lower wages offered to the minority workers. Moreover, employers will often actively manipulate the situation to keep the groups divided. For example, they could practice *majority paternalism* (promoting a racial hierarchy to cultivate majority-group loyalty) or *minority paternalism* (cultivating minority-group loyalty through jobs, home loans, or funds for community projects to encourage company unionism). A more militant approach would be a divide-and-rule strategy either by hiring minorities as strikebreakers or by encouraging state intervention to demobilize a possible coalition of workers.[37]

Employers can more easily persuade a group to work for a lower price if that group's initial standard of living—either in the United States or in the homeland left behind—is low, than it could tempt another group coming from a more favorable economic resource position. In addition, employers' political resources may affect the price of labor, by using the law to criminalize labor protest and thus prevent a threat to their control over wages.[38]

▰▰▰ MINORITY-MINORITY RELATIONS

Most of the research studies and literature in the field of race and ethnic relations focuses on the interactions between the dominant group and minority groups, as did the preceding pages in this chapter. However, another important aspect of intergroup relations is the interactions that occur *between* minority groups. Sometimes these can be positive, as in coalitions formed to fight for a cause at the local or national levels. Jesse Jackson's Rainbow PUSH Coalition is an example of the latter; with a diverse racial and ethnic membership, this organization seeks to "educate, demonstrate, boycott, and litigate" by "focusing on cures for social, economic, and political ills."[39]

Most times, however, tensions and conflicts arise between minority groups either jockeying for power, competing for jobs, seeing the other as gaining an "unfair" advantage, or becoming resentful of the other's presence in their neighborhood. In the chapters that follow, for example, you will read about how split labor market created conflicts between the Irish and Germans, Hungarians, Chinese, and Syrians. You will also read about tensions between Korean storeowners and the black communities they serve, about a black–Cuban riot in Miami in 1980, and about a multiracial Los Angeles riot in 1992. These are but a few of many such instances of violent outbursts.

In the 21st century, relations among peoples of color will no doubt be a central concern. With Hispanics now the largest U.S. minority group and still growing rapidly, the African American community worries about the potential erosion of its political strength. Both groups live in close proximity to one another in urban areas; and, in many of these school districts, Hispanics are the majority. Also, often African Americans and Hispanics compete against one another for elected and appointed offices previously occupied by whites. Adding to the tension is the growing number of Hispanic immigrants, whom African Americans, particularly in the lower class, see as an economic threat.

While it is true that accommodation and cooperation versus conflict between black and Hispanic Americans will depend on the local context, several factors will clearly affect black–brown relations in the years to come. Increasing numbers of Hispanic newcomers, legal and illegal, will not only generate further competition for resources and status, but also put into close proximity two groups with little direct knowledge or interaction with one another. Such limited awareness, plus the prevalence of cultural and language differences, will affect perceptions, attitudes, and behaviors on both sides. The resultant social distance sets the stage for friction, misunderstandings, and negative stereotyping. Intergroup relations will thus rest on whether consensus on or conflict over issues will prevail.[40]

▰▰▰ THEORIES OF MINORITY INTEGRATION

More than 71 million immigrants have come to the United States since its founding as a nation. Over the course of this extensive migration, three different theories have emerged regarding how these ethnically different peoples either should or did fit into U.S. society. These theories are (1) assimilation, or majority-conformity, theory; (2) amalgamation, or melting-pot, theory; and (3) accommodation, or pluralistic, theory.

The type of interaction between minority peoples and those of the dominant culture has depended partly on which ideology was then accepted by those already established in the community and partly on the ideology of the minority groups. People formulate attitudes and expectations based on the values they hold. If those values include a clear image of how an "American" should look, talk, and act, people who differ from that model will find their adjustment and acceptance by others more difficult. Conversely, if those values allow for diversity, a greater possibility exists that harmonious relationships will evolve.

Assimilation (Anglo-Conformity) Theory

Generally speaking, **assimilation (Anglo-conformity) theory** refers to the functioning within a society of racial or ethnic minority-group members who lack any marked cultural, social, or personal differences from the people of the majority group. Physical or racial differences may persist, but they do not serve as the basis for group prejudice or discrimination. In effect, members of the minority groups no longer appear to be strangers because they have abandoned their own cultural traditions and successfully imitated the dominant group. Assimilation may thus be described as $A + B + C = A$.[41]

Anglo-Conformity. Because most of the people in power in the United States during the 18th century were of English descent, English influence on the new nation's culture was enormous—in language, institutional forms, values, and attitudes. By the first quarter of the 19th century, a distinct national consciousness had emerged, and many U.S. citizens wanted to deemphasize their English origins and influences. However, when migration patterns changed the composition of the U.S. population in the 1880s, the "Yankees" reestablished the Anglo-Saxon as the superior archetype.[42] Anglo-Saxonism remained dominant well into the 20th century as the mold into which newcomers must fit.

To preserve their Anglo-Saxon heritage, people in the United States have often attempted, sometimes with success, to curtail the large numbers of non–Anglo-Saxon immigrants. Social pressures demanded that new arrivals shed their native culture and attachments as quickly as possible and be remade into "Americans" along cherished Anglo-Saxon lines. The schools served as an important socializing agent in promoting the shedding of cultural differences.

Sometimes insistence on assimilation reached feverish heights, as evidenced by the **Americanization movement** during World War I. The arrival of a large number of "inferior" people in the preceding 30 years and the participation of the United States in a European conflict raised questions about nationals who were not "100 percent American." Government agencies at all levels, together with many private organizations, acted to encourage more immediate adoption by foreigners of U.S. practices: citizenship, reverence for U.S. institutions, and use of the English language.[43] Because this policy required that all minority groups divest themselves of their distinctive ethnic characteristics and adopt those of the dominant group, George R. Stewart suggested (some decades later) that it be called the "transmuting pot" theory.[44]

Other assimilation efforts have not been very successful—for example, with people whose ancestral history in an area predates the nation's expansion into that territory. Most Native American tribes throughout the United States as well as the *Hispanos* of the Southwest have resisted this cultural hegemony.

Types of Assimilation. Milton Gordon suggested assimilation has several phases.[45] One important phase is **cultural assimilation (acculturation)**— the change of cultural patterns to match those of the host society. **Marital assimilation**—large-scale intermarriage with members of the majority society— and **structural assimilation**—large-scale entrance into the cliques, clubs, and institutions of the host society on a primary-group level—best reveal the extent of acceptance of minority groups in the larger society.

Other types of assimilation are *identificational assimilation,* the development of a sense of peoplehood or ethnicity based exclusively on the host society and not on one's homeland; *attitude-receptional assimilation,* reaching the point of encountering no prejudiced attitudes; *behavior-receptional assimilation,* reaching the point of encountering no discriminatory behavior; and *civic assimilation,* the absence of value and power conflicts with the native-born population.

Gordon states, "Once structural assimilation has occurred, either simultaneously with or subsequent to acculturation, all other types of assimilation will naturally follow."[46] Other sociologists disagree, claiming that cultural assimilation does not necessarily result from structural assimilation. Some studies have shown that in the United States no significant structural assimilation has yet occurred for racial and ethnic groups other than those of northern and western European origin.[47]

Sociologists prefer to divide structural assimilation into two subprocesses: primary and secondary. **Secondary structural assimilation** typically involves the more impersonal public sphere of social interaction. Examples are a nondiscriminatory sharing by dominant- and minority-group members of settings such as those in civic, recreational, school, or work environments. **Primary structural assimilation** typically involves close, personal interactions between dominant- and minority-group members in settings such as those in churches, families, social clubs and organizations, or small social gatherings.

Louis Wirth maintained that situational variables are important in the assimilation of minority groups.[48] Wirth distinguished among pluralism, assimilation, secession, and militancy as successive orientations by minorities in response to majority-group prejudice and discrimination. As groups begin to gain some power, they generally attempt to gain social tolerance of the group's differences (*pluralism*) and then become absorbed by the dominant society (*assimilation*). Those groups that are prevented from assimilating eventually withdraw from the societal mainstream (*secession*); however, if conflict then ensues, they seek more extreme remedies (*militancy*).

Assimilation may be both a majority-group and a minority-group goal, but one or both may view assimilation as undesirable in some cases. Accordingly, the preceding typologies are not always helpful when examining dominant–minority relationships. Gordon shows the complexity of the assimilation process; Wirth suggests that the dynamics of the situation shape the evolution of dominant–minority relations throughout the assimilation process. The larger question of whether the assimilation process is linear remains in all cases. Not all groups seek assimilation, and not all groups that seek assimilation attain it.

Assimilation as a belief, goal, or pattern helps explain many aspects of dominant–minority relations, particularly acceptance and adjustment. For many members of the dominant society, assimilation of minorities has meant their absorption into the mold, reflecting what Barbara Solomon calls "the Anglo-Saxon complex."[49] For physically or culturally distinct groups (e.g., blacks, Native Americans, Asians, or Muslims), this concept has raised a seemingly insurmountable barrier. Even without the Anglo-Saxon role model, assimilation is preceded by a transitional period in which the newcomer gradually blends in with majority-group members. In doing so, the individual acquires a new behavioral identity, perhaps at some personal cost.

Amalgamation (Melting-Pot) Theory

The democratic experiment in the United States fired many imaginations. A new society was being shaped, peopled by immigrants from different European nations and not slavishly dependent on the customs and traditions of the past. This set of circumstances generated a romantic notion of the United States as a melting pot. The **amalgamation (melting-pot) theory** states that all the diverse peoples blend their biological and cultural differences into an altogether new breed—the American. This concept may be expressed as $A + B + C = D$.[50]

Advocates. J. Hector St. John de Crèvecoeur, a French settler in New York, first popularized the idea of a melting pot. Envisioning the United States as more than

This cartoon pictures Uncle Sam annoyed by groups that were seen as unassimilable. Both racial differences (blacks, Chinese, and Native Americans) and religious differences (Catholics and Mormons) were cause for being kicked out of the symbolic bed. This cartoon appeared in a San Francisco illustrated weekly, *The Wasp*, on February 8, 1879. (Courtesy John and Selma Appel Collection)

just a land of opportunity, Crèvecoeur in 1782 spoke of a new breed of humanity emerging from the new society. That he included only white Europeans partly explains the weakness of this approach to minority integration:

> What is an American? He is either a European, or the descendant of a European; hence that strange mixture of blood which you will find in no other country. I could point out to you a man whose grandfather was an Englishman, whose wife was Dutch, whose son married a French woman, and whose present four sons have now four wives of different nations. He is an American, who, leaving behind him all his ancient prejudices and manners, receives new ones from the new mode of life he has embraced, the new government he obeys and the new rank he holds. . . . Here individuals of all nations are melted into a new race of men, whose labors and posterity will one day cause great changes in the world.[51]

This idealistic concept found many advocates over the years. In 1893, Frederick Jackson Turner updated it with his frontier thesis, a notion that greatly influenced historical scholarship for half a century. Turner believed that the challenge of frontier life was the catalyst that fused immigrants into a composite new national stock within an evolving social order:

> Thus the Middle West was teaching the lesson of national cross-fertilization instead of national enmities, the possibility of a newer and richer civilization, not by preserving unmodified or isolated the old component elements, but by breaking down the line-fences, by merging the individual life in the common product—a new product, which held the promise of world brotherhood.[52]

In 1908, the play *The Melting-Pot* by English author Israel Zangwill enthusiastically etched a permanent symbol on the assimilationist ideal:

> There she lies, the great melting pot. Listen! Can't you hear the roaring and the bubbling? There gapes her mouth—the harbor where a thousand mammoth feeders come from the ends of the world to pour in their human freight. Ah, what a stirring and a seething—Celt and Latin, Slav and Teuton, Greek and Syrian. America is God's Crucible, the great Melting Pot where all the races of Europe are melting and reforming!—Here you stand good folk, think I, when I see you at Ellis Island, here you stand, in your fifty groups, with your fifty languages and histories, and your fifty hatreds and rivalries. But you won't be long like that, brothers, for these are the fires of God you come to—these are the fires of God! . . . Germans and Frenchmen, Irishmen and English, Jews and Russians, into the Crucible with you all! God is making the American! . . . the real American has not yet arrived. . . . He will be the fusion of all races, perhaps the coming superman. . . . Ah, Vera, what is the glory of Rome and Jerusalem, where all races and nations come to worship and look back, compared with the glory of America, where all races and nations come to labor and look forward.[53]

Both the frontier thesis and the melting-pot concept have since come under heavy criticism. Although many commentators still pay homage to the melting-pot concept, few social scientists accept this explanation of minority integration into society. Nevertheless, many people in the United States hold this view. The "English-only" movement, arguments against bilingual education, and exclusive emphasis on Western heritage are examples of some U.S. citizens rejecting multiple cultures and wanting others to "blend in," although they really mean that they want people of ethnic subgroups to assimilate.

Did We Melt?   Over several generations, intermarriages frequently occur between people of different nationalities, less frequently between people of different religions, and still less frequently between people of different races. One could thus argue that a biological merging of previously distinct ethnic stocks, and to a smaller extent of different races, has taken place.[54] However, the melting pot theory spoke not only of intermarriages among the different groups but also of a distinct new national culture evolving from elements of all other cultures. Here the theory has proved to be unrealistic. At its founding, the United States was dominated by an Anglo-Saxon population and thus by the English language and Anglo-Saxon institutional forms. Rather than various cultural patterns melting into a new U.S. culture, elements of minority cultures metamorphosed into the Anglo-Saxon mold.

Milton Gordon suggests that only in the institution of religion did minority groups alter the national culture.[55] From a mostly Protestant nation in its early history, the United States has become a land of four major faiths: Protestantism, Catholicism, Judaism, and Islam. In the mid-20th century, some social observers viewed the United States as a **triple melting pot**. From her studies in New Haven, Connecticut, Ruby Jo Reeves Kennedy reported on extensive intermarriage between various nationalities but only within the three major religious groupings.[56] Will Herberg echoed this analysis, arguing that ethnic differences were disappearing as religious groupings became the primary foci of identity and interaction.[57] Today, the high religious intermarriage rate (discussed in Chapter 12) and the increasing numbers of U.S. believers in Islam, Hinduism, and other non-Western religions render the concept of a triple melting pot obsolete.

In other areas, the entry of diverse minority groups into U.S. society has not produced new social structures or institutional forms in the larger society. Instead, subcultural social structures and institutions have evolved to meet group needs, and the dominant culture has benefited from the labors and certain cultural aspects of minority groups within the already existing dominant culture. For example, minority influences are found in word usage, place names, cuisine, architecture, art, recreational activities, and music.

Sociologist Henry Pratt Fairchild offered a physiological analogy to describe how the absorption of various cultural components or peoples produces assimilation and not amalgamation. An organism consumes food and is somewhat affected (nourished) by it; the food, though, is assimilated in the sense that it becomes an integral part of the organism, retaining none of its original characteristics. This is a one-way process. In a similar manner, U.S. culture has remained basically unchanged, though strengthened, despite the influx of many minority groups.[58]

Most social scientists now believe that the melting-pot theory is a myth. Its idealistic rhetoric continues to attract many followers, however. In reality, the melting meant **Anglo-conformity**—being remade according to the idealized Anglo-Saxon mold, as Herberg so eloquently observed:

> But it would be a mistake to infer from this that the American's image of himself—and that means the ethnic group member's image of himself as he becomes American—is a composite or synthesis of the ethnic elements that have gone into the making of the American. It is nothing of the kind; the American's image of himself is still the Anglo-American ideal it was at the beginning of our independent existence. The "national type" as ideal has always been, and

remains, pretty well fixed. It is the *Mayflower,* John Smith, Davy Crockett, George Washington, and Abraham Lincoln that define the American's self-image, and this is true whether the American in question is a descendant of the Pilgrims or the grandson of an immigrant from southeastern Europe.[59]

The rejection of the melting-pot theory by many people, coupled with an ethnic consciousness, spawned a third ideology: the accommodation (pluralistic) theory.

Accommodation (Pluralistic) Theory

The **accommodation (pluralistic) theory** recognizes the persistence of racial and ethnic diversity, as in Canada, where the government has adopted multicultural-ism as official policy. Pluralist theorists argue that minorities can maintain their distinctive subcultures and simultaneously interact with relative equality in the larger society. In countries such as Switzerland and the United States, this com-bination of diversity and togetherness is possible to varying degrees because the people agree on certain basic values (see Table 2.1). At the same time, minorities may interact mostly among themselves, live within well-defined communities, have their own forms of organizations, work in similar occupations, and marry within their own group. Applying our descriptive equation, pluralism would be $A + B + C = A + B + C$.[60]

Early Analysis. Horace Kallen is generally recognized as the first exponent of cultural pluralism. In 1915, he published "Democracy versus the Melting Pot," in which he rejected the assimilation and amalgamation theories.[61] Not only did each group tend to preserve its own language, institutions, and cultural heritage, he maintained, but democracy gave each group the right to do so. To be sure, minority groups learned the English language and participated in U.S. institu-tions, but what the United States really had become was a "cooperation of cultural diversities." Seeing Americanization movements as a threat to minority groups and the melting-pot notion as unrealistic, Kallen believed that cultural pluralism could be the basis for a great democratic commonwealth. A philoso-pher, not a sociologist, Kallen nonetheless directed sociological attention to a long-standing U.S. pattern.

Pluralistic Reality. From its colonial beginnings, the United States has been a pluralistic country. Early settlements were small ethnic enclaves, each peopled by different nationalities or religious groups. New Amsterdam and Philadelphia were exceptions; both were heavily pluralistic within their boundaries. Chain-migration patterns resulted in immigrants settling in clusters. Germans and Scandinavians in the Midwest, Poles in Chicago, Irish in New York and Boston, French in Louisiana, Asians in California, Cubans in Miami, and many others illustrate how groups ease their adjustment to a new country by re-creating in miniature the world they left behind. Current immigrant groups and remnants of past immigrant groups are testimony to the pluralism in U.S. society.

Cultural pluralism—two or more culturally distinct groups living in the same society in relative harmony—has been the more noticeable form of pluralism. **Structural pluralism**—the coexistence of racial and ethnic groups in subsocieties within social-class and regional boundaries—is less noticeable.

As Gordon observes, "Cultural pluralism was a fact in American society before it became a theory—at least a theory with explicit relevance for the nation as a whole and articulated and discussed in the general English-speaking circles of American intellectual life."[62] Many minority groups lose their visibility when they acculturate. They may, however, identify with and take pride in their heritage and maintain primary relationships mostly with members of their ethclass. Despite this pluralistic reality, criticism of such self-segregating diversity remains a problem within U.S. society.

Dual Realities. Although Americans give lip service to the concept of a melting pot, they typically expect foreigners to assimilate as quickly as possible. Mainstream Americans often tolerate pluralism only as a short-term phenomenon, believing that sustained pluralism is the enemy of assimilation, a threat to the cohesiveness of U.S. society.

Assimilation and pluralism are not mutually exclusive, however, nor are they necessarily enemies. In fact, they have always existed simultaneously among different groups, at different levels. Whether as persistent subcultures or as convergent ones gradually merging into the dominant culture over several generations, culturally distinct groups have always existed. And even when their numbers have been great, they never threatened the core cultures, as we will see. Assimilation remains a powerful force affecting most minority groups, despite the assertions of anti-immigration fearmongers and radical multiculturalists. Although proponents of one position may decry the other, both pluralism and assimilation have always been dual realities within U.S. society.

As Richard D. Alba reminds us, assimilation occurs in different ways and to different degrees, and it does not necessarily mean the obliteration of all traces of ethnic origins. It can occur even as ethnic communities continue to exist in numerous cities and as many individuals continue to identify with their ethnic ancestry.

> [*Assimilation*] refers, above all, to long-term processes that have whittled away at the social foundations for ethnic distinctions. These processes have brought about a rough parity of opportunities to attain such socioeconomic goods as educational credentials and prestigious jobs, loosened the ties between ethnicity and specific economic niches, diminished cultural differences that serve to signal ethnic membership to others and to sustain ethnic solidarity, shifted residence away from central-city ethnic neighborhoods to ethnically intermixed suburbs, and finally, fostered relatively easy social intermixing across ethnic lines, resulting ultimately in high rates of ethnic intermarriage and ethnically mixed ancestry.[63]

In a 1997 special issue of the *International Migration Review* on "Immigrant Adaptation and Native-Born Responses in the Making of Americans," several leading sociologists addressed the unnecessary intellectual conflict over the dual realities. Herbert Gans suggested that reconciliation between assimilation and pluralism may be found by recalling the distinction between acculturation and assimilation. Acculturation has always proceeded more quickly than assimilation, providing evidence in support of both traditional assimilationist theory and recent pluralist—or ethnic retention—theory. Moreover, researchers of past and present immigrations have studied different generations of newcomers and have approached their research with "outsider" and "insider" values, respectively.[64] Richard D. Alba and Victor Nee add that the evidence shows that assimilation is occurring among recent arrivals, albeit unevenly, and suggest that some fine-tuning of assimilationist theory to address these variances in settlement, language acquisition, and mobility patterns may improve our understanding of the contemporary ethnic and racial scene.[65]

◢◣◥ RETROSPECT

Ethnic- and racial-group identity is a normal pattern in ingroup–outgroup relationships. It can have positive and negative results depending on the social context in which it exists. A group identity based on immigrant status is normally of shorter duration than one based on religion or race. Minorities typically experience a dual identity, one in the larger society and another within their own group.

Minority-group responses to prejudice and discrimination include avoidance, deviance, defiance, and acceptance, depending in large measure on the group's perception of its power to change the status quo. After prolonged treatment as an inferior, a person may develop a negative self-image. Continued inequality intensifies through a vicious circle or cumulative causation.

Marginality is a social phenomenon that occurs during the transitional period of assimilation; it may be either a stressful or a sheltered experience, depending on the support system of the ethnic community. Some groups become middleman minorities because of their historical background or sojourner orientation; they may remain indefinitely in that intermediate place in the social hierarchy, a potential scapegoat for those above and below them, or they may achieve upward mobility and assimilation.

Dominant-group actions toward the minority group may take various forms, including favorable, indifferent, or hostile responses. When the reaction is negative, the group in power may place restraints on the minority group (e.g., legislative controls and segregation). If the reaction becomes more emotional or even xenophobic, expulsion or annihilation may occur. Sensitivity to world opinion and economic dependence on other nations may restrain such actions. Another dominant response is exploitation, as illustrated by the internal-colonialism theory discussed in Chapter 2, or by the split-labor-market theory, in which differential wage levels can spark ethnic antagonism. An ethnic bourgeoisie may arise that is both exploitive and benevolent.

Three theories of minority integration have emerged since the nation's beginning. Assimilation, or majority-conformity, became a goal of many, both native-born and foreign-born; yet not all sought this goal or were able to achieve it. The romantic notion of amalgamation, or a melting pot, in which a new breed of people with a distinct culture would emerge, proved unrealistic. Finally, accommodation, or pluralism, arose as a school of thought recognizing the persistence of ethnic diversity in a society with a commonly shared core culture. Assimilation and pluralism are not mutually exclusive; both have always existed simultaneously, with assimilation exerting a constant, powerful force.

KEY TERMS

Acceptance
Accommodation
 (pluralistic) theory
Amalgamation
 (melting pot)
 theory
Americanization
 movement
Anglo-conformity
Annihilation
Assimilation (majority-
 conformity) theory
Avoidance

Cultural assimilation
 (acculturation)
Cultural pluralism
Cumulative causation
Defiance
Deviance
Exploitation
Expulsion
Labeling theory
Marginality
Marital assimilation
Middleman minorities
Negative self-image

Primary structural
 assimilation
Secondary structural
 assimilation
Social segregation
Spatial segregation
Split-labor-market theory
Structural assimilation
Structural pluralism
Triple melting pot
Vicious-circle
 phenomenon
Xenophobia

DISCUSSION QUESTIONS

1. What are some common minority-group responses to prejudice and discrimination?

2. What are some common majority-group responses to minorities?

3. What is marginality? Why may it be a stressful experience in some cases but not in others?

4. What are middleman minorities? How do they affect acceptance?

5. Discuss the split-labor-market theory.

6. Discuss the major theories of minority integration.

SUGGESTED READINGS

Bender, Daniel E., and Richard A. Greenwald (eds.). *Sweatshop USA: The American Sweatshop in Historical and Global Perspective.* New York: Routledge, 2003.
An examination of the exploitation of minorities in U.S. sweatshops, their role in global migration and economics, and efforts to control and eradicate them.

Cheadle, Don, and John Prendergast. *Not on Our Watch: The Mission to End Genocide in Darfur and Beyond.* New York: Hyperion, 2007.
The star of *Hotel Rwanda* and his activist friend offer an inspiring firsthand account of the Darfur genocide and concrete tips on how

all of us can make a real contribution to stop such crimes against humanity.

Connolly, William E. *Pluralism.* Durham, NC: Duke University Press, 2005.
A leading political theorist on pluralism weaves a compact analysis about the future possibilities of democratic pluralism.

Dennis, Rutledge (ed.). *Marginality, Power and Social Structure,* Vol. 12: Issues in Race, Class, and Gender Analysis. Greenwich, CT: JAI Press, 2005.
A collection of articles about the evolution of the concept of marginality and the issues surrounding its social structural foundation.

Levin, Jack, and Jack McDevitt. *Hate Crimes: The Rising Tide of Bigotry and Bloodshed.* Boulder, CO: Westview Press, 2002. Analysis of how seemingly random hate crimes share certain characteristics and are encouraged by stereotypes, a "culture of hate," and economic hard times.

Massey, Douglas S., and Nancy A. Denton. *American Apartheid: Segregation and the Making of the Underclass,* reprint ed. Cambridge, MA: Harvard University Press, 1998. A richly documented account of how segregation and dissociation from other cultures and ways of life lie at the root of many problems facing African Americans today.

Wachtel, Paul L. *Race in the Mind of America: Breaking the Vicious Circle between Blacks and Whites.* New York: Routledge, 1999. Examines how blacks and whites unknowingly perpetuate and maintain racial problems that inhibit progress toward resolution and offers guidance on how to break the cycle.

MySocKit

Additional resources for this chapter can be found in MySocKit. If you have a subscription to MySocKit, go to www.mysockit.com to study, review, and go beyond the book to learn more about race and ethnic relations.

European Americans

"America is God's Crucible, the great melting-pot where all the races of Europe are melting and reforming."
Israel Zangwell, 1908

Northern and Western Europeans

Although Native Americans lived on this continent in rich cultures for centuries before the Europeans arrived, this part of the book deliberately begins with the northern and western Europeans (Figure 5.1). This group established the foundation for the dominant culture to which others have had to adjust. To understand fully the dynamics of intergroup relations involving Native Americans and all immigrants, past and present, we must first examine how the creation of a white Anglo-Saxon Protestant (WASP) society set the stage for conflict. As we will see, religion, nationality, and social class were causal factors for conflict even within this northern and western European grouping. Even though a trickle of immigrants from almost all parts of the world arrived during the early history of the United States, the story of its colonial period and first 100 years as an independent nation is primarily the experience of immigrants from the British Isles, France, Holland, Germany, and Scandinavia and of their descendants.

▲▲ SOCIOHISTORICAL PERSPECTIVE

Like all immigrants, the first European colonists to reach the Americas were strangers to these shores, and they responded with wonder and excitement in their journals and reports about the vastness, resources, and promise of the New World. In those early years, all shared in the adventure of creating a new society. First the necessity to survive, then religious preference, and finally pro- or anti-British sentiments dominated relations among diverse peoples in the North American colonies. As life stabilized and a common culture evolved, other newcomers found themselves not only in strange surroundings but also perceived as strangers in a society in which WASP homogeneity was the norm. Thus, many Irish and Germans—with their cultural, religious, and social-class differences—experienced open hostility on their arrival.

Before we examine the connection between theory and the experiences of any group, we need to recognize the pitfall in considering ethnic groups within a limited historical framework: Immigration patterns vary among countries and peak at different times. The word

FIGURE 5.1   Northern and Western Europe

peak provides a clue as to how we should view the experiences of each racial or ethnic group. Although most minority groups experience one especially intensive period of migration, which provides a logical time frame to emphasize, most countries have sent a continual flow of immigrants over the years. Consequently, the immigrants' experiences have varied with changing conditions, and each nationality usually has a first-generation American grouping at any given time.

The Colonial Period

Members of each ethnic group came to the New World for economic, political, or religious reasons, or sometimes for the adventure of beginning a new life in a new land. As strangers, most encountered yet another ethnic group—the Native

Americans. Although limited social interaction between the European settlers and the natives occurred, their cultural differences frequently resulted in **xenophobic** reactions from both sides, as will be discussed in Chapter 7.

Cultural Diversity. From the moment the first Europeans settled in what became the United States, cultural differences existed among them. The settlements were culturally distinct from one another in nationality or religion, such as the Puritans in Massachusetts and Congregationalists in Connecticut. Some settlements, even in their early stages, were a mixture of ethnic groups. To strengthen his Pennsylvania colony, the English Quaker William Penn recruited several hundred Dutch and many more German settlers. In fact, the "Pennsylvania Dutch" are actually of German descent, the word *Dutch* being a corruption of *Deutsch,* which means "German." The settlement of New Amsterdam in the colony of New Netherland was also a pluralistic community, reflecting the home country's positive attitude toward minorities and refugees within its borders:

> In 1660, William Kieft, the Dutch governor of New Netherland, remarked to the French Jesuit Isaac Jogues [later canonized as a saint] that there were eighteen languages spoken at or near Fort Amsterdam at the tip of Manhattan Island. . . . The first shipload of settlers sent out by the Dutch was made up largely of French-speaking Protestants. British, Germans, Finns, Jews, Swedes, Africans, Italians, Irish [quickly] followed, beginning a stream that has never yet stopped.[1]

Religious Intolerance. Religious differences caused social problems more frequently than did nationality differences during this period. Many people who first crossed the Atlantic as immigrants had been religious dissenters in their native land and were seeking a utopia in the new land—a place of religious harmony. Unfortunately, they brought with them their own religious prejudices. Although they themselves came seeking religious freedom, many were intolerant of others with different religious beliefs.

The expulsion of religious dissident Roger Williams from the Massachusetts colony led to the founding in 1639 of the Baptist Church in Rhode Island. For the rest of the 17th century, Baptists were the most persecuted sect in New England. Fines, beatings, and whippings of adherents were not uncommon, and not until 1708 could Baptists legally maintain a house of worship in Connecticut. In contrast, Baptists thrived in the more tolerant Middle Colonies, establishing in Philadelphia, by 1700, the strongest Baptist center in the colonies.

When the 1691 Massachusetts Charter extended "liberty of conscience" to all Christians, including Baptists, it specifically excluded "Papists" (Catholics). Dislike of Catholics was the one common ground on which all Protestants could agree.

The Presbyterians, Baptists, Quakers, German Reformed, and Lutherans along the "frontier" were intolerant of one another, but they shared a strong dislike of Anglicans. The Anglicans, strongest in Virginia but prevalent throughout the South, looked disdainfully on the New England Puritans, and the New Englanders reciprocated and jealously guarded their communities against any inroads by Anglicans in their region.

Religious clashes in the 18th century were not uncommon. Prior to the American Revolution, clashes in the Chesapeake colonies between Anglicans and Baptists were frequent, the result of class antagonism between the planter elite on one side and poor whites on the other. Armed bands of planters and law officials forcibly broke up Baptist meetings, where preachers were condemning the planters' lifestyle of horse racing, gambling, whoring, and cock fighting.

Animosity between England-loyalist Anglicans and England-hating Scots-Irish Presbyterians was common. The latter group, living along the western frontier from Maine to Georgia, where they frequently fought the Native Americans, also often came into dispute with the pacifist Quakers and with German sectarian groups that advocated peaceful coexistence with the Native Americans.

Even though many colonists shared a common nationality, religious intolerance created wide cultural gulfs and social distance among the various denominations. As Gary B. Nash stated, "Any attempt to portray the colonies as unified and homogeneous would be misguided."[2]

The Early National Period

As a new nation, the United States was forged under the cultural, economic, and political dominance of Anglo-Americans. Their culture, however, was at first a diverse one of Puritans, Anglican Cavaliers, Quakers, and Scots-Irish Presbyterians. With a common language and history, though, they soon coalesced into what Lawrence H. Fuchs calls a "civic culture."[3] This common culture became reasonably solidified by 1820, when the first great wave of non-Protestant immigrants began. The civic culture included strong beliefs in Protestantism, individual enterprise, and political democracy.

Because no single religion dominated the colonies, religious tolerance slowly evolved. When the Constitution was drafted in 1789, the nation's leading statesmen put aside their prejudices to institutionalize such tolerance, creating a bedrock principle of U.S. culture: the separation of church and state. Congregationalists in New England retained a privileged tax position for a few more decades though, until their diminishing political power could no longer sustain that contradiction. In addition, some states barred Catholics and Jews from running for elected office in the early years of the republic. But this institutionalized bias eventually yielded, though not without a struggle, to the democratic principle of freedom of religion that had emerged from the primeval diversity of the nation's beginnings.

The 1790 Census. Although WASPs were the dominant group in 1790, the nation's first census revealed a society that was both culturally and racially diverse. As Table 5.1 shows, one in every five people in the 13 states was a member of a racial minority (African American or Native American); this compares to the one in four found in the 2000 census. The English constituted less than half the total population, and one in nine was not English (Dutch, French, German, Swedish). If we include the Irish Catholics who were clearly not part of the WASP mainstream, we find that at least one in seven was an ethnic minority.

Scots-Irish Presbyterians lived mainly on the western frontier, away from the more established English American towns and cities. The Dutch lived in mostly self-contained communities, primarily in New York and New Jersey. The Germans also clustered within their own urban or rural communities in a

TABLE 5.1   Total U.S. Population in 1790

Nationality	Percentage
English	48.3
African	18.9
German	6.9
Scots	6.6
Unassigned	5.2
Scots-Irish	4.8
Irish	2.9
Dutch	2.7
Native American	1.8
French and Swedish	1.8

Source: U.S. Census Bureau.

"German belt" that began in the Middle Atlantic states and soon stretched westward into the Midwest.

Early Signs of Nativist Reactions. Many new immigrants arrived during the immediate post-Revolution period, and a broad-based antiforeign attitude—sporadic and localized until then—asserted itself. Both the Jeffersonian and the Federalist political factions feared that their opponents would benefit from the newcomers. The populist Jeffersonians were alarmed at the arrival of so many refugees, particularly French, from collapsing European aristocracies. Meanwhile, the Federalists, the conservatives of their day, feared that the ranks of anti-Federalists would grow because poor immigrants, particularly the Irish, had no commitment to preserving a strong central government.

Whatever their motives, the dominant English Americans' beliefs about and actions toward the newly arriving northern and western European immigrants followed what was to become a familiar pattern in dominant–minority relations. Suspicious of those who differed from themselves, the members of the dominant culture felt threatened.

In a letter to John Adams in 1798, George Washington indicated his reservations about newcomers, especially when they settled in their own separate communities. His words anticipate what many others have uttered ever since:

> My opinion, with respect to immigration, is that except of useful mechanics and some particular descriptions of men or professions, there is no need of encouragement, while the policy or advantage of its taking place in a body (I mean the settling of them in a body) may be much questioned; for, by so doing, they retain the language, habits and principles (good or bad) which they bring with them.[4]

Xenophobia. Many Federalists, in fact, believed that the large foreign-born population was the root of all evil in the United States. In letters, speeches, and newspapers, they expressed fear that

> coming from "a quarter of the world so full of disorder and corruption" as Europe, it was to be feared that immigrants would "contaminate the purity and simplicity of the American character"; warned "their principles spread like the

leaven of unrighteousness; the weak, the ignorant and the needy are thrown into a ferment, and corruption threatens the whole mass." True some immigrants were industrious, peaceable, and voted the Federalist ticket—but for one such "good" European, lamented Noah Webster, "we receive three or four discontented, factious men—the convicts, fugitives of justice, hirelings of France, and disaffected offscourings of other nations." "Generally speaking," said a Federalist, "none but the most vile and worthless, none but the idle and discontented, the disorderly and the wicked, have inundated upon us from Europe." Clearly, the property and the virtue of the United States would not be secure until foreign immigration had been reduced to a mere trickle of hand-picked newcomers of approved political sympathies.[5]

William Smith Shaw, the young nephew of President John Adams, wrote to the First Lady in 1798: "The grand cause of our present difficulties may be traced . . . to so many hordes of Foreigners immigrating [sic] to America. . . . Let us no longer pray that America may become an asylum to all nations."[6]

These xenophobic remarks, and thousands of similar ones throughout this period, illustrate some of the dynamics of Anglo-conformity and assimilation. It really was not the presence of *all* foreigners that disturbed the Federalists but rather the increasing numbers of non-English foreigners. Wrapped in the dominant group's negative perceptions were concerns that those newcomers' cultures, religions, political ideologies—indeed, their very essence as people—were so unlike themselves as to make their blending into the mainstream a virtual impossibility. Such ethnocentrism blinded these early nativists from any other consideration except that of an undermining of their culture and society, a reaction similar to nativist reactions still heard in the 21st century.

Legislative Action. The Federalists attempted to limit all office holding to the native-born and to extend the period for naturalization from 5 to 14 years. Although they succeeded in having the longer period enacted, the states—faced with the problems of establishing a new nation—successfully fought office-holding restrictions.

In 1798, with a volatile situation in Europe and a distinct possibility of war with France, the Federalists passed a series of laws known collectively as the Alien and Sedition Acts, designed to discourage political activity by pro-French immigrants. One factor contributing to the successful passage of this notorious legislation was the widespread belief that a large foreign-born population threatened the stability of the United States. Significantly, the legislation passed because of sectional block voting, with New England almost unanimously in favor of the bills. Few foreigners resided in New England, and hence, little contact had occurred there; nonetheless, negative **stereotyping** flourished in that region. Jefferson's election to the presidency in 1800 ended this xenophobia, and the acts were abrogated.

The Pre–Civil War Period

Not until 1820 did the national census include a person's country of origin as part of its data, and new regulations required shipmasters to submit passenger lists to customs officials. The 1820 census (which excluded Native Americans) listed approximately 9.6 million Americans, of whom 20 percent were blacks and most of the remainder white Protestants from northern and western Europe.

Between 1820 and 1860, over 5 million immigrants—more than half the U.S. population of 1820 and more than the entire population of 1790—crossed the Atlantic and Pacific Oceans to disembark on U.S. shores.

In these 40 years preceding the Civil War, the first great wave of immigrants produced additional arrivals from England and Scandinavia. Ireland and Germany, however, supplied the greatest numbers. In fact, so large was Irish immigration that the Irish accounted for 44 percent of all immigration in the 1830s and 49 percent of all immigration in the 1840s. Consequently, they accounted for 7 percent of the total population by the end of the Civil War. The fact that so many of the newcomers were Catholic—a religion toward which many Protestant groups were openly hostile—made the rising tide of foreigners even harder for the dominant group of U.S. nativists to accept.

Structural Conditions

Along the East Coast and in the newer cities west of the Appalachian Mountains, life was stable and established. Although regional variations existed as did differences in religion and social status, the prevailing cultural norms were relatively homogeneous.

Urban living conditions, particularly among the poor Irish immigrants, were substandard, even for those days. The poverty-stricken newcomers, forced to live in squalid slums, suffered high disease and mortality rates, and endured the condemnation of the dominant society for living as they did. Like so many others in succeeding generations, these critics did not realize that their own attitudes and actions may have helped to create the situation in the first place:

> Typical of overcrowded cellars was a house in Pike Street which contained a cellar ten feet square and seven feet high, with one small window and an old-fashioned inclined cellar door; here lived two families consisting of ten persons of all ages. The occupants of these basements led miserable lives as troglodytes amid darkness, dampness, and poor ventilation. Rain water leaked through cracks in the walls and floors and frequently flooded the cellars; refuse filtered down from the upper stories and mingled with the seepage from outdoor privies. From such an abode emerged the "whitened and cadaverous countenance" of the cellar dweller.[7]

Xenophobia. U.S. citizens saw the large influx of immigrants between 1820 and 1860 as a threat to their institutions and their social order. Not only were many of the newcomers Catholic, but they came from countries embroiled in political turmoil. Anxiety mounted over the imagined radical threat as well as the Catholic threat.

In the 1830s, antiforeign organizations, calling themselves "native" American organizations, arose in many cities. They frequently became "mobs to burn Catholic convents, churches and homes, assault nuns, and murder Irishmen, Germans, and Negroes."[8] These sporadic outbursts gradually coalesced into the powerful Know-Nothing movement of the 1850s. The Know-Nothings unleashed a vicious hate campaign, frequently accompanied by brutal violence, particularly in large cities, where many immigrants lived. Surprisingly successful, the Know-Nothings "became the magnet for all dazed elements in the political whirlpool; they fed on pathological fears and fanned to white heat all the petty animosities that had bored into the public mind."[9]

Irish Catholic and Protestant tensions spurred the New York Orange Riots on July 12, 1870 and 1871, when the Orangemen marched to celebrate a 1690 battle in Ireland when Protestants defeated Catholics. In the 1871 riot shown here, more than 60 Irish Catholics, but no Protestants, were killed.

A Whig presidential candidate, General Winfield Scott, waged an anti-Catholic, antiforeign campaign with Know-Nothing support but lost badly to Democrat Franklin Pierce in 1852. By 1854, the Know-Nothing Party was strong enough to elect 75 congressmen and many city, county, and state officials.[10] In 1855, the party elected six governors, and many contemporaries believed that this reactionary movement would capture the White House in the 1856 election.[11] A candidate familiar to the electorate, former President Millard Fillmore, sought to return to office on the Know-Nothing ticket. The conservative Whig party endorsed Fillmore, but a serious split within its ranks, with defections to Republican candidate John C. Frémont, enabled Democrat James Buchanan to win the three-way race. The bitter sectional rivalry of the Civil War period then effectively ended this ethnocentric-turned-xenophobic movement.

Not all voices were raised against the European expatriates. In defense of the newcomers, Harriet Martineau (often called the "mother of sociology") answered some of the criticisms:

> It would certainly be better that the immigrants should be well-clothed, educated, respectable people (except that, in that case, they would probably never arrive). But the blame of their bad condition rests elsewhere, while their arrival is, generally speaking, a pure benefit. . . . Every American can acknowledge that few or no canals or railroads would be in existence now in the United States, but for the Irish labor by which they have been completed; and the best cultivation that is to be seen in the land is owing to the Dutch and Germans it contains.[12]

Ralph Waldo Emerson, an articulate literary figure of the times, was also a popular speaker on the lyceum lecture circuit. (In those days, many communities had a lyceum, or association, for lectures, discussions, and entertainment.) One of his journal entries in 1845 shows how he tried to combat the **nativism** movement in those lectures by stressing the "smelting-pot" concept:

> I hate the narrowness of the Native American Party. It is the dog in the manger. It is precisely opposite of true wisdom. . . . Well, as in the old burning of the Temple at Corinth, by the melting and intermixture of silver and gold and other metals, a new compound more precious than any, called Corinthian brass, was formed; so in this continent—asylum of all nations—the energy of Irish, Swedes, Poles, and Cossacks, and all the European tribes—of the Africans, and of the Polynesians, will construct a new race, a new religion, a new state, a new literature, which will be as vigorous as the new Europe which came out of the smelting-pot of the Dark Ages, or that which earlier emerged from Pelasgic and Etruscan barbarism.[13]

Currents and countercurrents occurred then, as now. Not all members of the same ethnic group encountered problems, nor did all native-born Americans react negatively to the newcomers. Yet patterns of harmony or conflict did exist, and they often depended on the degree of cultural and structural differentiation that existed in each region, as well as on economic prosperity or whatever competition the newcomers appeared to present.

THE ENGLISH

Despite earlier explorations by other countries, the English were the first white ethnic group to establish permanent settlements in the New World. The first two successful ones were Jamestown and Plimmoth (Plymouth) Plantation (the word *plantation* was first used in the North).

These two settlements were culturally quite different from one another; they offer an excellent example of cultural diversity within the same nationality, as opposed to a stereotyped concept of a single entity. Jamestown was the seed from which the southern aristocracy and the slave-based agrarian economy of the South grew, and Plymouth was the precursor of town meetings (participatory democracy), the abolition movement, and "Yankee ingenuity" (capitalistic enterprise). Many factors, such as the different purposes of the settlements and different religions, climates, and terrains, played a role in the unfolding of events and lifestyles.

The writings of William Bradford, the first governor of the Plymouth colony, provide evidence that the English were an ethnically conscious people. Nearly 400 years have passed since the time of the Pilgrims, but Bradford's words in the following sections regarding their experiences could apply to many other immigrant groups—past, present, and future.

The Departure

Leaving one's native land for another country known only by reputation is usually an emotional experience. For many, it is a time of joy and sorrow, anticipation and trepidation. People know what they are leaving behind, but they are uncertain what they will find. The Pilgrims first fled England for Holland, which opened its doors to all refugees, and later they journeyed to the New World. In the following passage, Bradford speaks about the Pilgrims' journey to Holland, but the locale is only incidental to the expression of the immigrant's typical sensations:

> Being thus constrained to leave their native soil and country, their lands and livings, and all their friends and familiar acquaintances, it was much, and thought marvelous by many. But to go into a country they knew not but by hearsay, where they must learn a new language and get their livings they knew not how, it being a dear place and subject to the miseries of war, it was by many thought an adventure almost desperate; a case intolerable and a misery worse than death.[14]

Culture Shock

Arrival at one's destination brings with it unfamiliar cultural contact, which jolts one's world of reality—that subconsciously accepted way of life—as the group encounters a different civilization. Bradford continues,

> Being now come into the Low Countries, they saw many goodly and fortified cities, strongly walled and guarded with troops of armed men. Also, they heard a strange and uncouth language, and beheld the different manners and customs of the people, with their strange fashions and attires, all so far differing from that of their plain country villages (where they were bred and had so long lived) as it seemed they were come into a new world.[15]

Resisting Assimilation. Not all immigrants desire to become full, participating citizens in the country to which they move. Many, in fact, never become naturalized citizens. Although they are starting a new life, they do not necessarily intend to forsake their cultural heritage. More often, they seek to preserve that heritage as a familiar world in a strange land and to pass it on to their children. Often, the children become *assimilated* into the new ways despite their parents' efforts. The Pilgrims feared that their children would be assimilated into the Dutch culture and viewed such an outcome as an evil to be avoided:

> But that which was more lamentable, and of all sorrows most heavy to be borne, was that many of their children, by these occasions and the great licentiousness of youth in that country, and the manifold temptations of the place, were drawn away by evil examples into extravagant and dangerous courses, getting the reins off their necks and departing from their parents. . . . So that they saw their posterity would be in danger to degenerate and be corrupted.[16]

English Influence. English immigrants' greatest impact on U.S. culture occurred during the colonial period. Settling in the 13 original colonies, they so established themselves that succeeding generations were culturally and politically dominant by the time of the American Revolution. In 1790, about 63 percent of the U.S. population could claim nationality or descent from the British Isles (see Table 5.1). This large majority of English-speaking citizens made an indelible imprint on U.S. culture in language, law, customs, and values. The wars of 1776 and 1812 notwithstanding, the descendants of English immigrants prided themselves on their heritage, as indicated in their contemporary writings. For example, in his *Sketchbook* (1819–20), Washington Irving encouraged Americans to pattern themselves after the English nation rather than any other.

After 1825, when the British Parliament repealed its ban on the emigration of artisans, many English, Scottish, and Irish mill hands found work in U.S. textile factories, often at more than twice the salary they had been earning at home. Many British coal miners also came, but by the latter part of the 19th century, Slavic and Italian workers had largely replaced them—at least in the North. Those who remained in the coal industry tended to be supervisors and foremen. Some British farmers also immigrated to the United States, scattering throughout the Midwest. British immigrants of any occupation seldom concentrated in any one area, though, going instead wherever the job market led them.[17]

As foreigners with the same language and original cultural heritage as the dominant society, British immigrants seldom experienced **prejudice** or **discrimination** in the United States. Rowland Berthoff cites numerous studies and reports indicating that the English were rarely ridiculed on the vaudeville stage except as titled fops (not relevant to English Americans). Relatively few ethnophaulisms for the English existed, except such terms as "John Bull" or "limey," and even these were not widely used.[18]

Yet the British were not always comfortable in the new land. Ilja M. Dijour found similar results among immigrants to other countries and reported, "The return of British from Australia, South Africa, and Canada or of Portuguese from Brazil, or Spaniards and Italians from the rest of Latin America is incomparably higher than the re-emigration of say Japanese from Brazil, Slavic people from Australia or Canada, or others." Dijour concluded that the first group had exaggerated expectations of similarity between the new country and the old, whereas the second group was psychologically prepared to find everything different in the new country.[19] Those not expecting to be strangers were unprepared when they realized that they actually were strangers.

During the first 100 years after U.S. independence, many British immigrants found the new country less attractive than England. Comparing the criticisms of 75 returnees prior to 1865, Wilbur Shepperson found some common themes reflecting a failure of the new land to live up to their expectations:

> Rather than vigorous, they found America boring; rather than questioning and vital, republican communities were suspicious and moribund. Although they were often unemployed, Americans boasted of their economic opportunities; although they condemned politicians, they defended the political system; although they advocated freedom, they enforced conformity. . . .
>
> Knowledge of the language allowed for rapid assimilation of English immigrants, but at the same time it permitted them to compare critically American authors, newspapers, and theaters with those at home. Acquaintance with English government and legal traditions provided easy understanding of American law, but it sometimes provoked censure of political methods and frontier justice. Nearness to markets, cheap labor, and advanced technological methods in Britain often led immigrants of the entrepreneur class to despair of the New World's inefficient agricultural methods and unorthodox business practices. British workers once associated with the trade union or Chartist movements found American labor groups lacking in organization, leadership, and purpose.[20]

In the post–Civil War period, an undercurrent of Anglophobia prevailed, and British immigrants discovered that they had to exercise self-restraint to be accepted among U.S. natives. An ethnic consciousness led many British to resent this necessity and to dislike the ways of the new country. Between 1881 and

1889, more than 370,000 British and Irish aliens left the United States to return to their native lands.[21]

> In fact, in all things but money and quick promotion, British-Americans thought the United States a debased copy of their homeland. Many seemingly familiar customs and institutions had lost their British essence. "The Land of Slipshod," one immigrant in 1885 called the country, its language not English but a "silly idiotic jargon—a mere jumble of German idioms and popular solecisms, savored by a few Irish blunders," the enforcement of its basically English legal code "totally farcical," and its children half-educated, spoiled, and unruly. . . . Many returned home discontented with "the manners and habits of the people."
>
> . . . Although as the years passed the immigrants' personal ties came to be in America rather than in Britain, their fondness for and pride in the old country waxed. British travelers found them everywhere, "British in heart and memory, . . . always with a touch of the exile, eager to see an English face and to hear an English voice!"[22]

Despite certain similarities, enough differences and ethnic consciousness remained to restrain British immigrants from merging in a totally smooth fashion. Second-generation British Americans, however, had no such problem and identified the United States as their country.

The United Kingdom has been the source of a great many immigrants over the years; between 1820 and 2006, over 5.3 million of its people came to the United States. It ranks third in the list of nations that have supplied immigrants to the United States since 1820, and an average of 17,000 new British immigrants still arrive yearly.[23] Southern California, particularly Santa Monica, has become the permanent home of several hundred thousand first-generation British Americans, who maintain their pubs and traditions amidst the surfers and rollerbladers.[24] (See The International Scene box for a discussion on how Britain handles its own immigrant minorities.)

THE DUTCH

The two greatest periods of Dutch immigration were 1881 to 1930, with 1.6 million, and 1941 to 1970, with nearly 98,000 new arrivals. Since 1971, the level of immigration has been relatively low, averaging about 1,500 annually.[25] In any case, the most significant impact of Dutch influence on U.S. society occurred at a much earlier period.

Pearl Street in present-day New York City marks the limit of dry land in the days of New Amsterdam, where palisades had been erected against Native American raiders. In Dutch, these were called *de wal,* and thus the northern boundary gave its name to the Wall Street of today. Breukelen (later Brooklyn) became a town in 1646. Peter Stuyvesant's farm, or *bouwerij,* in Manhattan, where Stuyvesant lived after the English takeover in 1664 until his death in 1672, gave its name to the Bowery, a well-known street in New York.

Other Dutch settlements sprang up in the Bronx, on Staten Island, in New Jersey at Bergen (named after a town in Holland, and later known as Jersey City), at Ridgewood, at Hackensack, in the Raritan and Ramapo valleys, and in South Carolina at St. James Island. So widespread were the Dutch settlements and so strong was the Dutch imprint that Dutch remained a major language in this region for generations.

The International Scene

Britain's Approach toward Ethnic Minorities

The British government's terminology and policies regarding immigrants—most of whom are people of color—have some interesting effects on dominant-minority relations.

About 8 percent of Britain's population—some 4.8 million people—are nonwhite ethnic minorities, almost all of them present as a consequence of immigration. Called "new commonwealth peoples"—the euphemism for ex-colonials of color—they have managed to become naturalized citizens fairly easily. Nevertheless, nationality often carries biological connotations among native-born Britons—"British stock," as Margaret Thatcher once phrased it. Thus, many supposedly indigenous Britons view the new minorities as not belonging—even the growing numbers of the second- and third-generation minority citizens who have lived only in the United Kingdom (U.K.).

To combat this mindset, the government—in its statistical and legal classifications and the publications of official bodies such as the Commission for Racial Equality—use the term *ethnic minority* instead of *immigrant* to refer to immigrants and to their U.K.-born descendants. This nomenclature deliberately ignores the reality that most ethnic-minority-group members are immigrants. It serves in job monitoring and in the census to identify and rectify problems of inequality, not to settle arguments about the number or growth rate of immigrant subgroups per se.

Many experts view Britain's Race Relations Act of 1976 (RRA), amended in 2000, as a model for Europe in addressing discrimination. The law expanded the concept of discrimination to include indirect discrimination (i.e., seemingly neutral rules that have an indefensibly discriminatory effect), and it created a new body, the Commission for Racial Equality (CRE), to undertake formal investigations under the law and to encourage equality of opportunity more broadly. The core of the law is its definition of racial discrimination, which is race neutral: "A person discriminates against another . . . if on racial grounds he treats that other less favourably than he treats or would treat other persons" (RRA, Part I, Section 1).

The law permits but does not require employers to offer racial minorities "access to facilities or services to meet the special needs of persons of that group in regard to their education, training or welfare, or any ancillary benefits" (RRA, Part VI, Section 35). This enables minorities to overcome seniority or test competence limitations through employer initiatives. The law emphasizes encouraging employers to seek minority inclusiveness rather than mandating preferential policies that would affect outcomes. The law does not set positive-action requirements in employment, mandate recordkeeping of minority employment statistics, or establish quota set-asides for government to do business with set percentages of minority-owned businesses—all of which exist in the United States.

The prevailing belief is that government cannot build good race relations by implementing laws or policies that create resentment. As a result, preferential treatment, quotas, and set-aside policies are not part of British antidiscrimination practice. Rather than imitating U.S. practice, Britain pursues its own model of equal opportunity policy.

Critical Thinking Question: Why does the shorter history of nonwhite settlement in Britain free that country to attempt a less-prescriptive solution to racial inequality?

Structural Conditions

During the colonial period, few Dutch were willing to exchange the security at home for the hardships of the New World. With their stable economy and harmonious society, they had few inducements or "push" factors to migrate in such great numbers as had other ethnic groups. Urban areas in Holland had heterogeneous populations because the Dutch had offered shelter to many refugees from other countries. When seeking to establish trading settlements in the New World, the Dutch therefore sought other minority-group members willing to journey to the New World. As a result, immigrant Dutch settlements became as heterogeneous as their counterparts in Holland.

The spirit of 17th-century Holland resulted in a cosmopolitan and tolerant atmosphere in New Amsterdam that outlasted Holland's rule. The somewhat more relaxed atmosphere of New Amsterdam contrasted with that of the English colonies, whose rigid "blue laws" limited behavior, particularly on Sundays. Sports were popular, too. The colonists loved boat and carriage races, and from Holland they imported the game of *kolf,* or golf.

The English takeover of New Amsterdam in 1664 caused no hardship for the Dutch settlers. They enjoyed a basically favorable social environment during the colonial and post–Revolutionary War periods and thereafter. A relatively tolerant people in an intolerant age, similar in physical appearance and religious beliefs to other Americans, the Dutch were generally accepted, though sometimes they were the butt of gentle humor, as illustrated in the writings of Washington Irving about the Dutch in New York.

In 1846, a group of Dutch religious separatists settled in what became Holland, Michigan. Spurred by religious and economic motives, a new wave of immigrants from the Netherlands followed suit, settling mostly in Michigan, Iowa, Wisconsin, and Illinois because of favorable soil and climate conditions. The social bond proved to be religion rather than nationality, and sectarian schisms ensued, resulting in the Dutch Reformed Church, the Christian Reformed Church, and the Netherland Reformed Church. The first group's efforts to propagate the faith and achieve higher social standing rested partly on Hope College in Holland, Michigan. Its success encouraged the Christian Reformed Church, a more conservative group, to establish Calvin College in Grand Rapids to achieve similar objectives for its people.

Pluralism

For several reasons, Dutch culture and influence persisted for many generations despite the Anglo-Saxon cultural dominance. The Dutch were self-sufficient and enjoyed high social standing in the new society. Their church, rather than mainstream secular ways, formed the basis of their social life; the more orthodox they were, the more they resisted assimilation. A steady migration into concentrated residential communities reinforced the old ways. Finally, a friendly atmosphere enabled the Dutch to coexist with other groups in a pluralistic society.

Not until 1774—more than 100 years after New York became an English colony—were Dutch American children taught English. The following passage gives some insight into the extensive use of the Dutch language and the resistance to using the English language:

> In 1764 Dr. Archibald Laidlie preached the first English sermon to the Dutch Reformed congregation in New York City. Ten years later English was introduced in the schools. In Kingston, Dutch was used in church as late as 1808. A few years before, a traveler had reported that "on Long Island, in New York, along the North River, at Albany, how Dutch was in general still the common language of most of the old people." Francis Adrian van der Kemp, who had come to this country as a refugee in 1788, wrote that his wife was able to converse in Dutch, with the wives of Alexander Hamilton and General George Clinton. Much later, in 1847, immigrants from Holland were upon their arrival welcomed in Dutch by the Reverend Isaac Wyckoff of New York, a descendant of one of the first settlers in Rensselaerwyck, who only in school had learned to speak English; and until very recently many communities in New Jersey adhered

to the tradition of a monthly church service in Dutch. As late as 1905, Dutch was still heard among the old people in the Ramapo Valley of that state.[26]

President Martin Van Buren illustrated Dutch endogamy and social isolation during the colonial and federal periods when he wrote in his autobiography that his family was

> without a single intermarriage with one of different extraction from the time of the arrival of the first emigrant to that of the marriage of my eldest, embracing a period of over two centuries and including six generations.[27]

Van Buren's comment could have applied to most of the Dutch families and other ethnics of his time. Fluent in Dutch, Van Buren was chided, rather unfairly, by critics such as John Randolph for his inability to "speak, or write, the English language correctly," a complaint often made today about newcomers.[28]

Although most of the Dutch immigrants came to the United States during the same period as did the southern, central, and eastern Europeans (1880–1920), they did not encounter ethnic antagonism and eventually assimilated. Their physical features, their religion, and their relatively urbanized background enabled them both to adapt to and gain approval from the dominant society more easily than other groups.

Today, more than 5 million Americans claim Dutch ancestry. Although they are found in many fields of work and heavily represented in business, a substantial number of dairy farmers settled in Texas and brought that state—where the vast majority of cattle are raised for beef—from no ranking in milk production to sixth in the nation.[29] While maintaining certain aspects of their culture through their churches and private schools maintained by multiple-generation Dutch Americans, the newcomers typically acclimate easily to U.S. culture.

THE FRENCH

French Americans fall into three population segments: migrants from France, migrants from French Canada (who settled primarily in New England), and French Louisianans. Many of the latter, also known as Cajuns, were expelled from Acadia (now the predominantly Canadian province of Nova Scotia) by the British in 1755; and, by 1790, about 4,000 of them had resettled in Louisiana. Each group's experience has been somewhat different, illustrating varying patterns in dominant–minority relations.

Marginality and Assimilation

In the 17th century, the Huguenots fled either to Holland or to colonial America to escape religious persecution. Their Protestantism, willingness to work hard, conversion to the Anglican Church, and rapid adoption of the English language eased the Huguenots' **assimilation** into colonial society. However, the transition was not altogether smooth, and members of the second generation apparently agonized over their marginal status much as those in other groups did:

> By 1706, sufficient time had elapsed since the Revocation [in 1685 Louis XIV formally eliminated religious liberty, causing the renewal of persecution and

extermination of the Huguenots] to give rise to a younger generation unsatisfied with the adherence to old French forms, a generation adverse to a language not in general use in the province, clamoring for the new and the popular. . . . The children of many of the refugees were even ashamed to bear French names. The idea of remaining foreigners in a land in which they were born and reared was alien to their thought.[30]

Encountering distrust and occasional violence from the dominant society, partly explained by the frequent hostilities between England and France, the Huguenots tried to Anglicize themselves as quickly as possible to avoid further unpleasantness. They changed their names and their customs, learned to speak English, and soon succeeded in assimilating completely into the host society. For them, assimilation and loss of ethnic identity were the desired goals. By 1750, the Huguenots were no longer a distinct ethnoreligious group.

Francophobia

While the French Revolution was still in its moderately liberal stage, the Jeffersonians were French sympathizers and the Federalists were vehemently anti-French. Then the infamous XYZ Affair arose, when French officials demanded bribes before permitting U.S. diplomats to secure desired conferences or agreements. This inflamed public opinion against the French and their sympathizers. The lives of French immigrants during those passionate times were at best uncomfortable and at worst filled with trouble and turmoil:

> The fear and detestation in which American "Jacobins" were held were no less powerful than the abhorrence felt for the French revolutionists themselves. "Medusa's Snakes are not more venomous," declared a Federalist, "than the wretches who are seeking to bend us to the views of France." "The open enemies of our country," declared the *Albany Centinel,* "have never taken half the pains to render our Government and our rulers infamous and contemptible in the eyes of the world, than those wretches who call themselves Americans, Patriots and Republicans." This "Gallic faction" was believed to be in close communication with Paris, "the immense reservoir, and native spring of all immorality, corruption, wickedness and methodized duplicity."
> . . . In the eyes of the Federalists, however, every Frenchman was a potential enemy; whether royalists or revolutionists, they were eager to extend French influence over the United States, and actuated by national pride, they might join a French army of invasion. Moreover, their notoriously loose morals and irreligion threatened to infect Americans.[31]

By 1801, the Republicans had effectively ended the Federalists' political dominance in the United States. President Thomas Jefferson purchased the Louisiana Territory from France in 1803 and, with it, the French city of New Orleans, which retains much of its ethnic flavor to this day, including the famed Mardi Gras celebration.

Pluralism

Two vibrant, persistent French subcultures give testimony to the cultural pluralism that is a constant feature of U.S. society, the Louisiana French and the French Canadians.

Louisiana French. The French subculture in southern Louisiana suggests ethnic homogeneity to the outsider, but its communities include two subgroups: the Creoles and the Acadians (or Cajuns). Creoles are people of color—a blend of French and African American, Native American, Jamaican American or other ethnic groups of color. Cajuns are a blend of French and German, Italian, Polish, or other white ethnic groups. Both groups practice endogamy, usually based around skin color, hair texture, and shared cultures.

The Cajun subculture was at one time so strong that it absorbed other ethnic groups in the area, as T. Lynn Smith and Vernon Parenton observed in 1938:

> The French assimilated the Germans while both were under Spanish rule and both subject to strenuous programs designed to stamp them with a Spanish cultural heritage. But the virile French culture was not content with this, even made a beginning at swallowing the politically dominant Spaniards themselves, a beginning which has been practically consummated during the American period while both were enveloped in the so-called melting pot which was heralded as bringing about Americanization. Under American rule the Louisiana French have, to the present time, perpetuated their language and culture and, at the same time, have absorbed most of the diverse Anglo-Saxon elements which have settled among them.[32]

Two years later, these same observers noted some changes in the previously insulated subculture, although they believed that the movement toward the U.S. mainstream was limited:

> Today, urbanizing influences are permeating the entire section. These include improved communication, mechanization of agriculture (with its concomitant social implications) and, particularly, mass media of education (radio, movies, and newspapers) as well as increased contacts outside French-speaking Louisiana. Nevertheless, the system of common values which was generated by language, national origin, settlement pattern, as well as familial, kinship, and religious ties, has thus far retained its societal integrative forces in this period of rapid and far-reaching technological changes now operative among these people.[33]

The emergence of television in the 1950s accelerated the process of ethnogenesis. Cajun parents typically gave their children Anglicized names and encouraged them to go to college, thereby doubling their numbers in the 1960s at southern Louisiana universities. However, these upwardly mobile, college-educated Cajuns did not completely abandon their parents' subculture, and by the late 1960s they again embraced their heritage.[34] One outcome was a reaffirmation not only of Cajun identity but also of the French language, whose use had been declining. By the early 1970s, French window signs and bilingual programs in the schools were commonplace.

Lafayette, a city of about 110,000 located 135 miles west of New Orleans, is essentially the Cajun capital. It is the principal city of an area known as Acadiana, comprising about one-third of the state and home to about 522,000 people. Here is where you'll find the heart of Cajun culture in food, music, dancing, a fondness for large, extended families, and where street signs say *rue*, not *street*.[35]

The 2000 census revealed a dramatic decline among Cajuns, from more than 407,000 in 1990 to about 44,000. However, refined analyses showed the change resulted more from changes in the wording and interpretation of the survey form, including dropping "Cajun" as an example of ancestry or national origin while

Three generations of Cajun women, displaying one form of extended family bonding, sit quilting under an old oak tree in Catahoula, Louisiana. This shared craft activity helps maintain a cohesive subculture through the cultural transmission of traditional designs, skills, and time-honored practices.

adding "French Canadian" to the form. The distinctiveness of Cajun culture may be fraying a bit, but this ethnic group remains a strong presence in Louisiana.[36] Today, Cajun music and cuisine remain resilient entities, as do nuclear-family cohesiveness and extended-family bonds.

French Canadians. Another persistent subculture exists among the Americans of French/French Canadian ancestry living in New England. In 2000, the 2.3 million people of French Canadian ancestry comprised 10.3 percent of New Hampshire's population, 8.8 percent of Vermont's, 8.6 percent of Maine's, and 5 percent of Massachusetts's.[37]

Although some French Canadians immigrated to the United States prior to the Civil War, the largest movement came after the Civil War. The Industrial Revolution brought rapid expansion to the New England factories, and the owners actively recruited labor in Quebec. In response, many Quebecois flocked to the mill towns, competing with the Irish and others for jobs. The heaviest migration occurred in the 40-year period between 1841 and 1880. By 1873, approximately 400,000 French Canadians were living in the United States, half of them in New England and most of the remainder in the Midwest, primarily in Illinois and Michigan.[38]

As in Louisiana, in French New England the family and the church serve as strong cohesive units for retaining language and culture. French parochial schools also have a unifying effect on the community. Ethnic French Canadians remain a distinct subgroup, and their loyalties to their institutions and to their original home, Quebec, suggest that they will retain their identity as a strong subculture in the foreseeable future. Moreover, their proximity to Quebec—with its French-language press, radio, and television stations, as well as its cultural influences—fosters a vibrant ethnicity.

THE GERMANS

Germany has supplied the greatest number of immigrants to the United States—over 7.2 million since 1820. Today, 42.8 million people, nearly one of six Americans, trace at least some of their forebears to Germany (Table 5.2). In several earlier periods, the large concentrations of German Americans raised nativist fears, but today's average citizen no longer thinks of them as a distinct ethnic group, even though an average of 10,000 new German immigrants arrive annually.

Early Reactions

William Penn was so successful in recruiting German immigrants to his Pennsylvania colony that by the outbreak of the Revolutionary War, they numbered over 100,000—a third of the colony's total population. England's deployment of Hessian (German) mercenary troops in this territory during the Revolutionary War may have been done in part to secure sympathetic German colonial assistance in such areas as provision of supplies and intelligence reports.

TABLE 5.2   U.S. Population of European Ancestry in 1990 and 2000

	1990		2000	
	Number (in millions)	Percentage	Number (in millions)	Percentage
German	57.9	23.3	46.5	17.0
Irish	38.7	15.6	33.0	12.1
English	32.7	13.1	28.3	9.6
Italian	14.7	5.9	15.9	5.8
Scottish and Scots-Irish	11.0	4.5	10.6	3.9
French	10.3	4.1	9.8	3.6
Polish	9.4	3.8	9.1	3.3
Scandinavian	9.2	3.8	10.4	5.1
Dutch	6.2	2.5	5.2	1.9
Russian	2.9	1.2	3.0	1.1

Note: The most dramatic changes since the 1990 census were large declines in Americans of European ancestry except among Italians, Russians, and Scandinavians. Still more than half of all Americans trace their bloodlines to northern and western Europe.

Americans claiming German, Polish, Scandinavian, or Dutch ancestry are most concentrated in the northern Midwest. Those of Irish, English, Italian, French, or Russian descent are most concentrated in the Northeast. Scottish and Scots-Irish concentrations are scattered around the nation.

Source: U.S. Census Bureau, 1990 Special Tabulations, 1990 CPH-L-89, p, 1; *Profile of Selected Social Characteristics: 2000*, Table 2.

The German immigrants' experience provides a good example of how a distinct minority group sometimes incurs the hostility of the dominant culture. The Germans were different in language, customs, and religion (mostly Lutherans), as were other groups. But their high visibility because of their numbers and settlement patterns set them apart and brought them to public attention as a perceived threat to the majority group.

By 1750, the influx of German immigrants had become so great that a concerned Benjamin Franklin asked,

> Why [should] the Pennsylvanians . . . allow the Palatine Germans to swarm into our settlements, and by herding together to establish their Language and Manners to the exclusion of ours? Why should Pennsylvania, founded by the English, become a colony of Aliens, who will shortly be so numerous as to Germanize us instead of our Anglifying them?[39]

These fears were expressed repeatedly in later years by other representatives of the dominant group about other immigrant groups. Indeed, Franklin's worries about the duality of language markedly resemble some contemporary concerns about the Spanish-speaking populace and bilingual education. Franklin particularly opposed the Mennonites on the grounds that members of this religious sect were pacifists. Maurice Davie reports that Franklin also had misgivings about the Germans because of their clannishness, their meager knowledge of English, their separate German press, and their increasing need for interpreters. Speaking of the latter, Franklin said, "I suppose in a few years they will also be necessary in the Assembly, to tell one-half of our legislators what the other half say."[40] Franklin was not arguing for restrictions on immigration but rather for rapid assimilation (**Anglo-conformity**).

The Second Wave: Segregation and Pluralism

The German immigrants of the 18th century settled first in Pennsylvania and then in other mid-Atlantic states, but the 19th-century immigrants predominantly went to the Midwest, settling in the Ohio, Mississippi, and Missouri river valleys. There they became homesteaders, preserving their heritage through their schools, churches, newspapers, language, mutual-aid societies, and recreational activities. Various colonization societies in Germany also sent thousands of German settlers to the St. Louis region in the 1830s, to Texas in the 1840s, and to Wisconsin in the 1850s.

The failure in 1848 of an attempted liberal revolution in Germany brought many political refugees to the United States. Known as "Forty-Eighters," these Germans settled in the large cities of the East and Midwest—in particular, Baltimore, New York, St. Louis, Milwaukee, and Minneapolis. Political activists in their homeland, the Forty-Eighters quickly became active in U.S. politics. Many Germans even gave serious thought to forming an all-German state within the Union, with German as the official language; later, some considered creating a separate German nation in North America in the event that the slavery issue caused the dissolution of the Union.

Although more dispersed throughout the country than the Irish, in the cities they concentrated in "Germantown" communities. Here Germans owned and operated most of the businesses, and German functioned as the principal spoken language. An array of parallel social institutions—fraternal and mutual aid societies, newspapers, schools, churches, restaurants, and saloons—like those of other immigrant groups, aided newly arrived Germans in adjusting to their new country.

Gymnastic societies and cultural centers known as *Turnvereine* provided libraries, reading rooms, discussion groups, and singing and dramatic groups for German Americans. They became controversial, however, as a result of their radical reform proposals and political activism on behalf of social-welfare legislation, direct popular election of all public officials, tax and tariff reform, abolition of slavery, and their militant opposition to prohibition.

In the Midwest, from Wisconsin to Texas, the Germans achieved success either in farming or in urban enterprises, becoming a significant part of the region's identity. By 1850, Milwaukee contained 6,000 German-born Americans and 4,000 native-born Americans. In the "German triangle"—the area defined by Cincinnati, Milwaukee, and St. Louis—the presence of hundreds of thousands of German Americans resulted in state statutes authorizing the use of the German language in public schools for all classroom instruction.[41] The use of German in the schools served an additional purpose: It was intended to preserve the whole range of German culture, much as some Hispanic leaders hope Spanish-language instruction today will bolster Hispanic culture.

Societal Responses

A diverse group in their religions, occupations, and residence patterns, German Americans came under increasing criticism for being clannish and for attempting to preserve their culture. Their large numbers added to rising tensions, which culminated in violent confrontations. One of the more notorious incidents occurred in Louisville, Kentucky, on August 5, 1855. On that day, which became known as Bloody Monday, a mob of Know-Nothings, incited by fiery articles in the Louisville *Journal,* stormed into the Germantown section intent on mayhem. When the riot was over, 22 men had been killed, several hundred wounded, and 16 houses burned.

Following the Civil War, German Americans were well positioned economically and suffered little interethnic conflict until the outbreak of World War I. As a wave of anti-German hostility and patriotic zeal swept the land, German Americans became targets of harassment, business boycotts, physical attacks, and vandalism of their property. Several states even banned the German language, and towns changed German-named street signs. Attempting to prove their loyalty to the United States, many German Americans abandoned their cultural manifestations. After the war, the number of German-language newspapers was one-fourth the number published in 1910, and various ethnic institutions either had been shut down or had suffered major losses in membership.[42]

Since 1920, more than 1.7 million German immigrants have arrived in the United States, one-fourth of this total in the 1920s and another one-fourth in the 1950s (see The Ethnic Experience box, page 148). Such numbers have given resilience to a German ethnic subculture, but nothing like the one that flourished prior to 1914. Newcomers tend to assimilate fairly rapidly, although pockets of ethnicity exist in many parts of the country.

Cultural Impact

American speech, eating, and drinking reflect German influence. Frankfurters, sauerkraut, sauerbraten, hamburgers, Wiener schnitzel, pumpernickel bread, liverwurst, pretzels, zwieback, and lager beer were introduced by German immigrants.

The Ethnic Experience

Health Inspection at Ellis Island

"When I got to Ellis Island, we all had to line up and they would examine us. Some people could pass and they marked their coat. Some they marked on the left and some they marked on the right lapels. Those that were marked on one side could go through right away. Maybe they had been here before, I don't know. But I got a mark—'This is back.' So they led us through a big hall and we had to strip naked: And we met two fellas, they were doctors with stethoscopes. I didn't know what a stethoscope was—I learned that after. They tapped us on the chest and on the back and then I had to run around. I was the only one they examined.

"All of a sudden one raised his fist. He was gonna knock the other fella down, the other doctor. I didn't know what it meant. I was told afterward. One said I had consumption and the other doctor said there was nothing wrong with me—all I needed was a bellyful of food for a couple of months, I was undernourished. Well, finally, I got passed. And when I got out, I had to go before an examiner. My brother had arranged for relatives that lived in Brooklyn. The examiner said to my cousin, 'You will have to put up $50,000 bail so this young man will not become a burden of the United States.'

"... Then the examiner said, 'You are free to go.' And [voice breaking] when I—I tell the news 'you are free,' I choke up. The judge says, 'The boy [pause, tears streaming] may be undernourished [Pause, then very emotionally] but he has a wonderful mind.' And he said again, 'You are free to go,' and we went out."

Source: German immigrant who came to the United States in 1910 at age 16. Taped interview from the collection of Vincent N. Parrillo.

The words *stein* and *rathskeller* are of German origin, as are the concepts of the kindergarten and the university. Germans dominated the U.S. brewing industry, founding Anheuser-Busch, Coors, Schaefer, Schlitz, Schmidt's, Pabst, Ruppert, and many other breweries.

German immigrant industrialists who made a major mark on U.S. society included Meyer Guggenheim (mining), Frederick Weyerhaeuser (lumber), John Jacob Astor (fur trade), Bausch and Lomb (optical instruments), Henry Steinway and Rudolph Wurlitzer (pianos), and H. John Heinz (food canning). Thomas Nast, a German immigrant and the first great U.S. caricaturist and political cartoonist, created the Democratic donkey, the Republican elephant, and Uncle Sam.

THE IRISH

Most prerevolutionary immigrants from Ireland were Ulster Irish, Presbyterian descendants of Scottish immigrants who had migrated to Northern Ireland a generation earlier. Settling chiefly in New England at first (around 1717), they clustered together, preserving their ethnicity and seldom mingling with the English Americans. The latter regarded these newcomers contemptuously, labeling them ill-tempered ruffians who drank and fought too much. Soon the friction escalated into Boston newspaper denunciations, the destruction of an Irish Presbyterian meetinghouse, and a mob blocking the disembarkation of Irish ship passengers.[43]

William Penn's recruitment in Europe for his colony led the next wave of Scots-Irish immigrants to choose Pennsylvania as their preferred destination. However, the tendency of the newcomers to be land squatters without paying for the land and their frequent conflicts with the Germans living there spurred Pennsylvania authorities to discourage further immigration. Scots-Irish immigration then flowed to the frontier regions, from Pennsylvania to Georgia, in the area known today as Appalachia.[44] By the end of the 18th century, cultural assimilation had occurred, but structural and marital assimilation lagged behind.

Unlike the Scots-Irish Protestants, the Irish Catholics fared poorly. The Irish Catholics' religion, peasant culture, and rebelliousness against England marked them as strangers to the dominant culture and set the stage for the most overt discrimination and hostility any ethnic group had thus far encountered. Originally made unwelcome in the New England settlements, most of the early Irish Catholic immigrants settled in Pennsylvania or in Maryland; the latter, founded as an English Catholic colony in 1634, fell under Protestant control by the mid-18th century.

By 1790, Irish Catholics accounted for nearly 4 percent of the almost 3.2 million total population. Their growing numbers became a source of increasing concern to the Federalists, especially during the presidency of John Adams. Fearing that "wild Irish" rebels would attempt to turn the United States against England and that they would join the Republican Party, the Federalists strongly opposed the incoming "hordes of wild Irishmen." Rufus King, U.S. ambassador to England, was among the foremost opponents of Irish emigration to the United States. He expressed to Secretary of State Timothy Pickering his fear that the disaffected Irish would "disfigure our true national character," which was purest in untainted New England. Massachusetts-born John Quincy Adams agreed that the United States had "too many of these people already."[45]

After 1820, emigration to the United States became increasingly essential to the Irish Catholics, who suffered under oppressive British rule in their native land. Failure of the potato crop in successive years and the resulting famine during the late 1840s accelerated the exodus. About 1.2 million Irish emigrated between 1847 and 1854; in the peak year of 1851, almost a quarter of a million Irish Catholics arrived.

The immigrants settled mostly in coastal cities; their living conditions in these overcrowded "Dublin Districts" were deplorable. With many families living in poorly lighted, poorly heated, and badly ventilated tenements, contagious, deadly diseases—such as cholera—were widespread. Moreover, when the immigrants were drawn elsewhere to work in mines or to build canals and railroads, shantytowns sprang up in many locales; their presence became a symbol to native-born U.S. residents that an "inferior" people had appeared in their midst.

Cultural Differentiation

The Irish attracted attention because of their sheer numbers, their Catholicism, and their strong anti-British feelings. These factors weighed heavily against them in Anglo-Saxon Protestant America. In addition, they were a poverty-stricken rural people who settled in groups mainly in the slum areas of cities on the East Coast. Because they could find only unskilled jobs, they began life in the United States with a lower-class status, bearing that stigma at a time when the country was becoming increasingly class conscious.

The Irish were the first ethnic group to come to the United States in large numbers as a minority whose culture differed from the dominant culture of the country. They were to be the harbingers of the "new" immigrants yet to come. As Charles Marden and Gladys Meyer point out,

This was America's first confrontation with a peasant culture. The English, Scandinavians, or Germans who came to America in the nineteenth century came from towns or from freehold farming patterns. The Irish had been long exploited by the English landholding system. The unchallenged position of the Catholic church cemented bonds of identity. A history of famine, a family and inheritance system that led to late marriage and many unmarried men and women, the ambivalent situation of being English-speaking but not part of English-derived institutions, and migration in large numbers put the Irish in a peculiar relationship to dominants. Some welcomed them as a necessary working-class contingent; others engaged in flagrant discrimination.[46]

Even those who welcomed the Irish as people who had come to fill working-class jobs did so with an **ethnocentric** attitude of superiority over a lowly breed of people, typified by these comments of a Massachusetts senator in 1852:

> That inefficiency of the pure Celtic race furnishes the answer to the question: How much use are the Irish to us in America? The Native American answer is, "none at all." And the Native American policy is to keep them away.
>
> A profound mistake, I believe. . . . We are here, well organized and well trained, masters of the soil, the very race before which they have yielded everywhere besides. It must be, that when they come in among us, they come to lift us up. As sure as water and oil each finds its level they will find theirs. So far as they

THE AMERICAN RIVER GANGES.
THE PRIESTS AND THE CHILDREN.—[See Page 915.]

Many consider this the most vicious anti-Catholic, anti-Irish cartoon ever printed in a mass-circulation magazine. It illustrates the belief that Irish Catholics were endangering public education (symbolized by the upside-down American flag). Notice the Irish harp and papal tiara flying above Tammany Hall, the teachers being led to the gallows, and the children being thrown to the riverbank by Democratic politicians. One Protestant teacher (the Bible tucked into his jacket) is protecting children from the crocodiles, which represent Catholic bishops. Their jaws are mitres, their scales are vestments, and their faces are Irish stereotypes. This cartoon by German immigrant Thomas Nast appeared in *Harper's Weekly* on September 30, 1871. (Courtesy John and Selma Appel Collection) are mere hand-workers, they must sustain the head-workers, or those who have any element of intellectual ability. Their inferiority as a race compels them to go to the bottom; and the consequence is that we are, all of us, the higher lifted because they are here.[47]

Societal Reaction

Native U.S. citizens blamed the Irish for their widespread poverty and resented the heavy burden they placed on charitable institutions. They also stereotyped the Irish as inherently prone to alcoholism, brawling, corruption, and crime—and derisively dubbed police vans "paddy wagons." Viewed as an unwelcome social problem, the Irish served as the rallying point for opponents of immigration.

Nativism, briefly evident in the immediate post–Revolutionary War period, now swept across the land in a shameful display of bigotry and intolerance. Aiding the growth of anti-Irish feeling was anti-Catholicism. Fears of "Popery" arose, partly in response to the influx of priests to minister to the needs of the Irish Catholics. Know-Nothing violence targeted the Irish far more than it did the Germans, as destruction of property, brutal beatings, and loss of life occurred in the Irish sections of many cities. Besides starting frequent street brawls, anti-Catholic mobs sometimes burned churches and convents.

Nonviolent antagonism toward the Irish was manifest most strongly in social and job discrimination. For a long time, job advertisements in Boston and elsewhere included the words "No Irish Need Apply" or the acronym "NINA."

> Indeed, they suffered severe discrimination in the new land and most often found employment only in the lowest-paying and hardest-working jobs: as ditchdiggers, or dockers, or "terriers" working on the railroads and in the canal beds. In some respects (clearly not in all), the urban experience for Blacks in the twentieth century—in terms of the attitudes of others and in terms of occupations—has its parallel in the Irish experience in the middle of the previous century.[48]

Large-scale Irish immigration continued between 1871 and 1910, with the arrival of about 1.9 million newcomers. Women outnumbered men among these immigrants, the reverse of other arriving groups' gender imbalance. Many unmarried women migrated, primarily to seek domestic service as maids; others sought work in textile mills or clothing factories.[49] Male occupational fields were more diverse, ranging from labor in factories, mines, railroads, and canals to business entrepreneurship, store clerking, and teaching (see The Ethnic Experience box, page 152).[50]

Irish labor played a key role in the industrial expansion of the United States, particularly in building the great systems of canals, waterways, and railroads. As Roman Catholicism—through increased membership and the power of the church hierarchy—evolved into a major faith in a Protestant country, Irish Americans exerted great moral force on the nation. As the Irish began to assimilate, they often served as a middleman minority, aiding new European immigrant groups in work, church, school, and city life.[51] The Irish were less hospitable to the Chinese, however, often clashing with them in the cities and in railway labor disputes.

Minority Response

The experience of the Irish was the prototype for the experiences of later immigrants, not only in their hostile reception by the host society but also in their

The Ethnic Experience

Immigrant Expectations

"Like many more immigrants like myself, I came to this country to seek a living because living over there was very, very poor. Work was scarce and hard. I decided that I ought to try the United States to make a living.

"I left home in Ireland on a Friday morning. I went to a place then called Queenstown in County Cork. I was there for the greater part of Friday and Saturday because you had to go through quite a number of tests and screening to be allowed to board ship. On Sunday morning around eight o'clock I boarded the ship.

"We arrived in the United States a week from that Monday, around two o'clock in the afternoon in the harbor of New York. The nicest thing I saw after being so seasick—and I might say I was very, very seasick—the nicest thing I ever experienced was seeing the Statue of Liberty.

It meant we were here and we were all right. We had landed and we were safe. Then, of course, I had to go through customs and things like that.

"I had heard a great deal about the United States, that it was a good country, and I might very well say that it was a good country, although all that time I was disappointed because I wasn't the one to find the gold in the streets. I really had to go out and look for a job. I worked for awhile in a doctor's office and from there I went to work for a chemical company. There was disappointment. There were loans from my family and my friends. It's something you wonder if you can make it. Thank God I did."

Source: Irish immigrant who came to the United States in 1920 at age 18. Taped interview from the collection of Vincent N. Parrillo.

---

reaction to the prejudice and discrimination they frequently encountered. We should not underestimate the hardship involved in leaving one's native land—alone or with family—journeying to a distant country, feeling both anxieties and hopes, and then finding oneself an unwanted stranger in a strange land.

Actions and Reactions. The response of the Irish was alternately retreatist and aggressive, as their social behavior and their involvement in the labor movement and in the urban political machine demonstrate. Because these activities frequently offended U.S. norms of behavior, they confirmed the suspicions of native-born Americans, thereby reinforcing the stereotypes of the Irish and prolonging the vicious circle:

> Unable to participate in the normal associational affairs of the community, the Irish felt obliged to erect a society within a society, to act together in their own way. In every contact therefore the group, acting apart from other sections of the community, became intensely aware of its peculiar and exclusive identity.[52]

The small degree of intermarriage both reflected and buttressed the distinction between the Irish American and other U.S. residents. Among the Irish, religious and social considerations encouraged a tendency to marry their own kind. As Catholics, they were repeatedly warned that union with Protestants was tantamount to loss of faith, and the great majority of non-Irish in the city considered marriage with them degrading. As a result, the percentage of Irish marrying outside their ethnic group was extremely low.

The number of Irish households headed by women, mostly widows, was fairly high in the mid-19th century, about 18 percent in 1855 and dropping only to 16 percent in 1875.[53] Such high percentages normally reflect a tendency of the men in a community either to marry younger women or to meet early death in dangerous occupations. A household expanding to include other relatives was quite common, as was taking in boarders to help meet living expenses.

In building their parallel social institutions, the Irish succeeded in helping one another. Besides offering informal aid for kin and neighbors, the Irish created their own mutual-welfare system through trade associations (the predecessor of labor unions), fraternal organizations, and homes for the aged that were staffed by nuns. These efforts assisted and protected the Irish from societal indifference and hostility, but they also isolated them and slowed their acculturation.[54] The Irish community was further united through family, church, and school, as well as through social and recreational activities. Such "clannishness" added fuel to the fires of resentment among assimilationists.

Labor Conflict. Irish labor was diversified, but it was concentrated in low-status unskilled or semiskilled occupations. The Irish worked at the hard, physical jobs in the cities, in the mines of Appalachia, or in railroad construction from the Alleghenies to the Rockies. With their knowledge of the English language, the Irish provided strong, articulate membership and leadership in such early labor movements as the Knights of Labor. Their greatest notoriety came from the violence and murders committed by the Molly Maguires, a secret terrorist group that aided Irish miners in their struggles with mine owners. Following infiltration of the group by a secret agent for the Pinkerton Detective Agency and a highly questionable court proceeding, the Molly Maguire movement ended in the hanging of 20 men, one of the largest mass executions in U.S. history.

Bonacich's split-labor-market theory helps explain much of the conflict involving the Irish. Irish-German conflict, particularly in Pennsylvania, was intense in the late 18th and early 19th centuries because of economic competition and the use of Germans as strikebreakers.[55] On the West Coast, Irish workers held meetings and demonstrations to demand the curtailment of further Chinese immigration, viewing the lower-paid Chinese as a serious economic threat.[56] The Irish also fiercely resisted abolition, fearing labor competition from released slaves. Anti-black riots in Chicago, Cincinnati, and Detroit followed.[57] Most notorious was the so-called Draft Riot of 1863 in New York City, in which about 400 rioters were killed, as well as dozens of blacks, police, and soldiers. This riot, the worst in U.S. history, was led by Irish longshoremen angry over the recent use of black strikebreakers to undermine their efforts to secure better wages.[58]

Upward Mobility

Unlike other immigrant groups in the 19th century, the Irish experienced little occupational or social **upward mobility.** Grassroots politics gave them a power base, however, triggering a nativist concern over Catholic priests controlling U.S. politics. Through political machine organization, the Irish controlled Tammany Hall in New York by the 1860s and the Brooklyn Democratic Party by the 1870s.[59] By the 1890s, they also controlled city governments in Boston, Buffalo, Chicago, Philadelphia, St. Louis, and San Francisco. Through a tightly organized patronage system, the boss-controlled urban political machine offered economic and political opportunities, as well as social-welfare provisions for the Irish community.[60]

Irish Catholics made slow but steady progress in entering the societal mainstream. Antipathy against them gradually declined as their command of English, improved economic position, and physical appearance made them less objectionable to English American Protestants than were the new immigrants arriving from other parts of Europe.

The New Irish

In the 1980s, half the population of Ireland was under the age of 28, and the nation wrestled with a fairly constant 18 percent unemployment rate. As a result, a new wave of emigrants left their native land. Almost 32,000 Irish entered the United States legally in the decade from 1981 to 1990; but, faced with a two-year waiting list, perhaps 50,000 more came illegally. Only 1,300 of these Irish undocumented aliens applied for amnesty under provisions of the 1986 Immigration Reform and Control Act because most had not been here long enough to meet residency requirements.[61] Since the 1990s, greatly improved economic conditions in Ireland and a low birth rate reduced emigration to the United States to a current average of 1,500 annually, compared to 23,000 in 1990.[62] Those realities, plus the crackdown by Homeland Security on undocumented aliens motivating their return to Ireland, has resulted in a shrinking of the Irish presence in Boston and other cities.[63]

Like their predecessors, the new Irish cluster in the big cities, working in construction or in the care of children and the elderly. Reflecting the chain-migration pattern, Boston receives immigrants from the west of Ireland, whereas those from

Celebrating their ethnic heritage, these participants march along New York's Fifth Avenue during the 2007 St. Patrick's Day parade. Several generations ago, such parades were also militant demonstrations of Irish power and ethnic resiliency, serving to inspire ethnic pride despite harsh judgments and responses by an often-hostile society.

Donegal, Fermanagh, and other northern counties go to Philadelphia. Cleveland attracts newcomers from Achill Island, off the coast of Mayo. Other Irish settle along Bainbridge Avenue in New York City's borough of the Bronx, known as the "Irish Mile."

Well represented in the professions, in financial services, and in the executive suites of corporate America, the old Irish—the descendants of earlier immigrants—now live mostly in suburbia, enjoying higher incomes and status. Once a despised minority group and victims of blatant discrimination, the Irish now are part of the American mainstream. Even many non-Irish share in the St. Patrick's Day celebrations.

THE SCANDINAVIANS AND FINNS

Some Swedes and Finns came to what is now the United States as early as 1638, making their landfall at the mouth of the Delaware River. They established a colony, New Sweden—a land encompassing parts of modern-day Delaware, Pennsylvania, and New Jersey—and there constructed the first log cabin in the New World.

Although small numbers of Norwegians, Swedes, and Danes continued to immigrate to the United States over the next 200 years, they did not come in substantial numbers until after 1865. Thereafter, motivated by religious dissension, voting disenfranchisement, crop failures, and other economic factors, the Scandinavians emigrated in large numbers.

Many of these immigrants settled in fertile soil regions of the northern Midwest and established rural communities where they could enjoy social and political equality. These farmland settlements became strongholds of church-centered Norwegian and Swedish traditions. Isolation from the dominant drift of U.S. social patterns permitted widespread, long-lived retention of indigenous lifeways, which continue in some measure to this day.[64] Ole Rölvaag presented an eloquent and poignant saga of late-19th-century Norwegian pioneers in the Dakota Territory in *Giants in the Earth,* a vivid sociopsychological portrait of pioneer life. Capturing the exuberant hopes, fears, despair, struggles, and interactions of the immigrants in the heartland of the United States, this monumental work offers vivid testimony to the human quest of a dream:

> And it was as if nothing affected people in those days. They threw themselves blindly into the Impossible, and accomplished the Unbelievable. If anyone succumbed in the struggle—and that happened often—another would come and take his place. Youth was in the race; the unknown, the untried, the unheard-of, was in the air; people caught it, were intoxicated by it, threw themselves away, and laughed at the cost. Of course it was possible—everything was possible out here. There was no such thing as the Impossible any more. The human race had not known such faith and such self-confidence since history began. . . . And so had been the Spirit since the day the first settlers landed on the eastern shores; it would rise and fall at intervals, would swell and surge on again with every new wave of settlers that rolled westward into the unbroken solitude.[65]

Copper and iron mining in northern Michigan and eastern Minnesota attracted the majority of emigrating Finns. By 1920, 52 percent of all Finnish

Americans lived in these two states. Another 25 percent lived in the West, working in the mining, lumber, and fishing industries. The great concentration of Finns in Astoria, Oregon, earned it the nickname "the Helsinki of the West." In the East, Finns settled mostly in small Massachusetts towns or in the Red Hook section of Brooklyn in New York, near a Norwegian community.[66]

Peter Kivisto suggests that Finns were perhaps the most radical ethnic group to come to the United States. Between 25 and 40 percent of the Finnish immigrants participated in national leftist organizations, including the Finnish Socialist Federation of the Socialist Party and the International Workers of the World (IWW).[67] Gus Hall, longtime chairman of the U.S. Communist Party, was a Finnish American from this radical tradition. By 1920, marital assimilation was increasingly the norm among Finnish Americans, except in the western Great Lakes region and Astoria, where endogamy remained high. Upward mobility and the decline of ethnic institutions further acculturated Finnish Americans and simultaneously brought about the decline of the Finnish American left.[68]

Ingroup Solidarity

Like other immigrant groups, the Scandinavians attempted to resist Americanization and to cling to their Old World traditions. Intermarriage was frowned on, often far into the 20th century. An ethnic newspaper's 1897 lament about exogamy illustrated the concern "that the national spirit is not particularly strong among the Danes of this region" and that intermarriage would "strike out our mother tongue and all we received as a heritage from our fathers."[69]

Ethnic festivals and parades provide opportunities for Americans to learn and appreciate other cultures, and for that culture's descendants to touch base with their roots and celebrate their heritage, such as this Norwegian-American Day parade in Bay Ridge, Brooklyn, New York.

As greater numbers of Norwegians settled in Minnesota and Wisconsin, they eventually outnumbered the native-born population, creating social tensions and political competition. A typical example occurred in 1878 in Trempealeau County, Wisconsin, a beautiful region of wooded hills and valleys. When the Norwegians practiced their custom of picnicking and drinking on Sunday afternoons, their neighbors increasingly censured them. When a Norwegian running as an independent was elected sheriff on a vote split along party lines, the Sunday custom continued without further interference; political party leaders then realized they could no longer ignore or dictate to this ethnic majority.[70]

Ethnicity, however, is an ever-changing dialogue between immigrants and the host society. When Presidents Theodore Roosevelt and Woodrow Wilson launched attacks, prior to U.S. entry into World War I, on hyphenated Americans for their language retention, ethnic press, and ethnic organizations, local attacks on Scandinavian ethnicity followed. (In the past use of hyphens was common, such as, for example, "Scandinavian-American".) In 1915, the *Minneapolis Journal* published an editorial titled "The Hyphen Must Go!" It argued that in the upper Midwest the melting pot was not functioning properly because immigrant communities were retaining too much of their Old World cultures, and too many "hyphenated" newspapers, schools, and societies were still using the immigrant languages.[71]

Ethnic Identity

Norwegians, Swedes, and Danes came to the United States from lands with different governments, different traditions, and different languages. Nonetheless, because of physical similarities among the three groups and because they frequently settled together in the new land, use of the term *Scandinavian* to designate all three groups became common throughout U.S. society:

> The common use of the term *Scandinavian* to describe Swedes, Norwegians, and Danes in a broad and general way is one of the products of the commingling of these three peoples on the American side of the Atlantic. The word really fits even more loosely than does the word *British* to indicate the English, Welsh, and Scotch. It was applied early in the history of the settlements in Wisconsin and Illinois, to groups which comprised both Norwegians and Danes on the one hand, or Norwegians and Swedes on the other hand, when no one of the three nationalities were strong enough to maintain itself separately, and when the members of one were inclined . . . to resent being called by one of the other names; for example, when a Norwegian objected to being taken for a Swede. The Scandinavian Synod of the Evangelical Lutheran Church, organized in 1860, included both Norwegians and Danes.
>
> . . . The use and acceptability of the word steadily grew; the great daily paper in Chicago took the name *Skandinaven*; in 1889, the editor of *The North* declared: "the term has become a household word . . . universally understood in the sense in which we here use it to designate the three nationalities."[72]

In addition to farming, the Scandinavians primarily worked as lumberjacks, sailors, dock workers, and craftsmen in the building and machine trades. Because they came from countries with compulsory education, their literacy rate was high, and a significant percentage acquired U.S. citizenship. Danes tended to spread out more and to downplay the role of the church and fraternal organizations in comparison to Norwegians and Swedes. For that reason, the Danes assimilated more quickly, although all groups succeeded in blending into the social fabric fairly easily. The Swedes hit their peak year of immigration in 1913, and the Norwegians hit their peak in 1924. The total number of Scandinavians who have immigrated to the United States since 1820 exceeds 2.1 million.

THE SCOTS

The first wave of Scottish migration occurred during the colonial period; by 1790, the Scots were third in number behind only the English and the Germans, as the Scots constituted 6.6 percent of the population, compared with the English (48 percent) and the Germans (6.9 percent). Scottish Americans therefore played a prominent role during the formative years of the new nation. For example, 11 of the 56 signers of the Declaration of Independence were Scottish Americans. Almost 80 percent of all Scottish emigrants came to the United States later, however; between 1871 and 1930, more than 640,000 Scots arrived. This group was primarily drawn from the working class of Scotland, and its members entered various semiskilled occupations.

Although the Scots-Irish supported the rebel cause during the Revolutionary War, the Scots from the Highlands of Scotland tended to be loyalists. They settled in established areas rather than along the frontier, and their ethnic identity—particularly the rigid discipline of Scottish church life (either Presbyterian or Episcopalian)—was reflected in their lifestyle. Deeply religious, they adhered to a strict moral code; the Protestant ethic of hard work, frugality, and honesty was as evident among them as among Calvinist New Englanders. Like many other communities, they also sought to preserve their culture and to duplicate the way of life from the old country. Nonetheless, they were easily assimilated almost from the outset.

Scottish emigration dropped sharply after 1936, as did their proportional representation in the total population, and the assimilation process substantially decreased their visibility. Efforts to maintain Scottish ethnic identity proved largely unsuccessful. The Scots did continue, however, to wear disguises on Halloween (a practice subsequently adopted by most children in the United States on this holiday) and to celebrate regularly the January 25 birthday of Robert Burns, the Scottish poet. Today, western North Carolina hosts annual Highland Games, with pipe bands, caber tossing, and a formal ball afterward, at which the men appear in formal evening kilts and the women in white ball gowns with their clan tartan sashes over their shoulders.

THE WELSH

Although frequently lumped together with the English, the Welsh were a distinct ethnic minority in the United States. Sufficient numbers lived here during the pre–Civil War period to warrant the printing of newspapers and some books in Welsh.

Welsh immigrants came to North America with the other early northern European colonists, settling together to a much greater degree than did the English. They were active during the Revolution, and five Welsh Americans—William

Floyd, Button Gwinnett, Thomas Jefferson, Francis Lewis, and Lewis Morris—signed the Declaration of Independence.

Like other immigrants, the Welsh had economic and religious motives for immigrating to the United States. Many Baptists and Quakers left Wales, followed later by Anglicans and Presbyterians. Primarily farmers and miners, many Welsh immigrants settled in Cambria County, Pennsylvania, where they exerted a strong social and political influence; others settled in Oneida County, New York, a region where "Welsh butter" became famous. By the late 19th century, many Welsh miners—like their English counterparts—had become superintendents and foremen of coal mines in many states, including Ohio, Illinois, and Washington.

◆◆◆ SOCIAL REALITIES FOR WOMEN

Social class and ethnic background were important variables in determining women's places in the social order in the 19th century. Women in affluent families had servants to do menial tasks, while they themselves could devote their free time to such activities as playing a musical instrument, creating fine embroidery, or perhaps reading good books, particularly Scripture. Working-class women would likely either produce goods for sale (cheese, cloth, shoes, yarn) or render services (working as cooks or domestics or possibly as servers at inns, restaurants, or taverns).

Among those ethnic groups living even just a short distance from cities—especially the Germans, Scots-Irish, and French Canadians—women would normally perform a variety of agricultural tasks, working in barns, fields, meadows, stables, or wherever they were needed.[73]

Many Irish were single women taking jobs as domestics or nannies for the native-born urban elite. In 1800, there was 1 domestic servant for every 20 families, but by 1840, the ratio had dropped to 1 servant for every 10 families. Young unmarried Irish (and Scandinavian) women often came first and worked in U.S. homes. Their daily typical workload was 16 hours of cooking, cleaning, tending to the children, and nursing the sick, six days a week. With little time to themselves, these women saved their earnings for passage money for other family members. Records from the Boston Society for the Prevention of Pauperism offer one illustration of the difficulties women had seeking jobs in a household compared to men finding work in labor gangs. Between 1845 and 1850, it received employment applications from 14,000 female foreigners in contrast to 5,034 male applications.

The loss of husbands through accident, desertion, or sickness left many women without means to support large families except perhaps by taking in boarders or hiring out to do others' laundry or sewing at home. Among the Irish, as mentioned earlier, female-headed households reached 18 percent by 1855. Although it dropped to 16 percent by 1875, this proportion remained significantly higher than the national average for native-born Americans.

Among working-class, rural, and frontier families, women continued working at many tasks that genteel ladies of the mercantile and upper classes did not do. However, one commonality almost all women shared, regardless of social class or residence, was that they married at a young age, had many children, and were usually grandmothers by the time they were 40.

By 1820, the number of children under age 5, per 1,000 women between the ages of 20 and 44, was 1,295, about three times what it is today. Child rearing, keeping of home and hearth, and working in the fields if a farmer's wife, were the areas of responsibility for most women. Only 6.2 percent of the women were in paid employment outside the home. For most women, the house or perhaps the farm was their world, their reality, and their fate.[74]

NORTHERN AND WESTERN EUROPEAN ASSIMILATION

The differing experiences of these ethnic groups illustrate the roles that ethnocentrism and social distance play in the assimilation process. At first, cultural and religious differences kept the groups socially segregated for the most part, but eventually those with greater similarities (the English, Scots, Welsh, and Ulster Irish) coalesced into what became the mainstream group. Such was not the case with many other groups with pronounced ethnic differences, and this difference was often sharpened even more by their numbers and geographic isolation:

> In 1890, the "melting pot" had not yet absorbed the 80,000 Dutch, 200,000 Swiss, or 1.2 million Scandinavians in the Midwest, most of whom had arrived after 1870. Likewise, the 150,000 French immigrants, 200,000 Cajuns in Louisiana, and 500,000 French Canadians in New England and the Great Plains remained culturally, linguistically, and religiously separated from the larger society. So too did many of the 8 million Germans in the rural Midwest or concentrated in many large cities. Their poverty and Catholic faith kept 6 million Irish in the Northeast . . . in social isolation. . . .
>
> Race, culture, and/or social class shaped group relations in the United States in 1890, keeping the nation a patchwork quilt of cultural diversity. All three variables influenced perceptions, receptivity and interactional patterns.[75]

Their ingroup solidarity strengthened by social isolation, endogamy, and vibrant ethnic communities, these groups remained pluralistic entities throughout much of the 19th century, even if some of their number had assimilated.

By the 19th century's end, however, an industrializing America lured millions of new immigrants, vastly different from the ethnic groups already here. Mainstream Americans would view these new white ethnics as so culturally and physically different as to be even farther removed on the social distance scale than the "old" immigrants. Consequently, they judged these previously excluded older groups as more like themselves and thus more socially acceptable. A redefined mainstream American identity emerged, bringing people of northern and western European origins into this classification in contrast to the newer, "less desirable" newcomers, even though it took decades for this redefinition to fully manifest.[76]

SOCIOLOGICAL ANALYSIS

Thus far, we have examined the experiences of northern and western European immigrants within a sociohistorical context, as well as studied the specific patterns of dominant–minority interaction. To understand better the meaning of those patterns, we now appraise them within the conceptual frameworks of the three major sociological perspectives: functionalist, conflict, and interactionist.

The Functionalist View

With their emphasis on a societal network of interrelated parts working cooperatively for survival or stability, functionalists see as highly desirable the arrival of large groups of people to forge a civilization out of a vast, undeveloped country rich in natural resources. The New World offered the new arrivals economic opportunity and freedom from religious and political oppression, while benefiting from their presence. Unskilled newcomers helped build cities, canals, and railroads; cleared land for farming; and created demand for goods and services. Others used their entrepreneurial skills or craftsmanship to supply the growing nation with needed commerce. The evolution of an independent U.S. society and of the poor immigrants Crèvecoeur had called "useless and withered plants" that "have taken root and flourished" proceeded from a smoothly functioning social system.[77]

Sometimes the large numbers of Irish and Germans entering the country led to dysfunctions because the society could not absorb them quickly enough. They clustered together, culturally distinct from the dominant English American model, creating a situation that generated prejudice and discrimination against them. The ensuing conflict, like that involving French Americans in earlier years, disrupted the social system, obstructed cooperative efforts toward common goals, and prevented many newcomers from attaining personal goals. In time, the necessary adjustments occurred; education and upward mobility through economic growth and the civil service (in the case of the Irish) allowed both acceptance and assimilation.

The Conflict View

The beginning point of the conflict perspective is the dominance of English Americans in the new nation. Not only did they influence the adoption of language, customs, and social institutions derived from Great Britain, but they also held economic and political power. In this context, Federalist hostility toward the French and the Irish becomes more than ethnic antagonism. The propertied elite saw the influx of so many "common" people and the possible spread of Jacobin (French radical) revolutionary ideas as threats to their power, and they took various actions to safeguard their interests (e.g., passing the Alien and Sedition Acts and forming the Native American Party). Political considerations also weighed heavily in dealings with the Irish and the Germans. The rise in power of Irish city politicians and the political activism of the Forty-Eighters caused nativist reactions through mob violence, political movements, and state legislative countermeasures.

Economic exploitation, particularly in the case of the Irish, brought prosperity to the owners of mines, factories, and railroads. Working under brutal conditions in physically demanding jobs, many Irish struggled to survive in the slums where their subsistence wages obliged them to reside. The captains of industry, when confronted with strikes or labor organization efforts, used their power to thwart such efforts through the courts, through law enforcement personnel or vigilante groups to break up demonstrations, or by hiring other workers. Much of the industrial expansion in the 19th century, conflict theorists maintain, came at the expense of the immigrant workers who made it possible. The resulting conflict did eventually bring about change, as Irish and Germans organized and gained a greater share of the nation's wealth.

Lieberson's power-differential theory (Chapter 2) seems quite appropriate for the Irish in particular. As unskilled, peasant migrants, the Irish were subordinated to the English Americans. The conflict was sporadic and limited, with the Irish locked into their subservient role until they, too, gained a share of power.

The Interactionist View

Understanding how people perceive and define the strangers in their midst is the basis of interactionist analysis. The Dutch in New Amsterdam and the Quakers in Philadelphia, for example, were receptive to cultural pluralism; as a result, harmonious relations ensued between them and the diverse peoples in their respective colonies. In contrast, the Puritans were intolerant of anyone different, which resulted in the expulsion of such religious dissidents as Roger Williams and his followers. Longstanding violent conflict in Europe between the English and the Irish and between the English and the French partially explains the negative perceptions English Americans had of French Americans and Irish Americans; cultural prejudices, transmitted from generation to generation, helped foster ethnic antagonism in the United States, often on a reciprocal basis.

In a country predominantly Protestant throughout its colonial and early national periods, the arrival of large numbers of German and Irish Catholic immigrants disturbed the native population. The Protestants interpreted the presence of these groups as a threat to the "American" way of life, labeling them as inferiors and worse. Note the use of *hordes* (William Shaw) and *swarm* and *herding* (Benjamin Franklin)—words used frequently by other dominant-group commentators as well. Words are symbols, and here they connote both animalistic qualities and massive numbers, the latter often perceived as a contaminating menace to society. With this social interpretation of reality, confrontations and conflict were inevitable.

◢◣◥ RETROSPECT

Structural and cultural differentiation played important roles in determining the nature of intergroup relations among northern and western European immigrants in the United States. Generally, while the social structure remained in its formative (and thus very fluid) period, the ethnic groups did not experience discrimination or low status for long. Living in relative isolation from European influences and sharing the commonality of forging a new life in the wilderness helped reduce nationalistic biases. Although sporadic flare-ups occurred because of Old World rivalries, the different ethnic groups were usually hospitable to one another, welcoming strangers coming to settle because they themselves would benefit from the community's growth.

As life became more settled, residential patterns more densely clustered, and the social structure more solidified, new arrivals became more conspicuous. Their cultural differences were often accentuated by their relative poverty. German and

Irish immigrants of the 19th century, for example, encountered hostility not only because of their religion and culture but also because of their lack of power. Many settled in established areas and so started a new life in a region already dominated by others, who looked on them with scorn. Immigrant subgroups who kept to themselves by settling in rural areas—the Scandinavian, the French, and some German immigrants—fared better than those who tried to settle in already urbanized areas.

Prevailing attitudes were crucial to a minority group's experience. The Dutch and Quakers, tolerant of people who differed from themselves, encouraged religious and cultural diversity within their settlements. Cultural diffusion and assimilation were least likely among the religiously orthodox. This was true not only for the dominant groups in most New England colonies—who expelled or denied welcome to dissenters, Quakers, Catholics, and Jews—but also for minority groups who resisted intermarriage and assimilation, such as the 19th-century Dutch, Scandinavians, and Irish.

Cultural diversity was a reality from the outset. Each settlement was an ethnic enclave in which people of similar beliefs and values clustered together and helped one another to adjust in a new land. As the settlements became more populous, growing into towns and cities, the ethnic enclaves formed by newer immigrants became subcommunities within a larger society. Although not as physically isolated as earlier ethnic groups, they were, nonetheless, socially and spatially segregated—often voluntarily—from those unlike themselves.

All immigrants faced varying degrees of hardship in adjusting to the strangeness of a new land and people. To ease that adjustment, they tried to re-create the familiar old country here in the new, through their churches, schools, newspapers, and fraternal and mutual-aid societies. These efforts to preserve their language and culture helped them gain a measure of security, but the attempts also often led to suspicion, dissension, and hostility between the dominant and minority cultures.

Discrimination and xenophobia occur especially when the superordinate group views the size and influence of the subordinate group as posing a threat to the stability of the job market, the community, or the nation itself. The nativist movements against the French and the Irish during John Adams's presidency and against the Germans and the Irish during the mid-19th century testify to that pattern. Through legislative efforts and violent actions, the dominant group's members sought to justify their discriminatory behavior as necessary to preserve the nation's character.

For the "old" immigrants, the Civil War brought an end to the difficulties they had encountered because of their background; they now became comrades-in-arms for a common cause. Then, too, a new threat loomed on the horizon, as "new" immigrants—shorter and swarthier, with unfamiliar dress, foods, and customs—began the second great wave of migration to the United States. These new immigrants seemed totally unlike all that U.S. citizens were or should be. People found a new target for their fears, mistrust, prejudices, and discrimination in these "undesirable" aliens.

The functionalist perspective stresses the young nation's need for newcomers and sees the problems arising from the arrival of large numbers of Irish and German immigrants as being caused by sheer size of the influx, which hampered more rapid absorption. Conflict theorists emphasize English American dominance and the economic exploitation of other nationalities. Interactionists discuss how differing social interpretations of strangers—Dutch toward Puritans, Federalists toward foreigners, Protestants toward Catholics—set the stage for ethnic conflict.

KEY TERMS

Anglo-conformity	Nativism	Upward mobility
Assimilation	Pluralism	Xenophobia
Discrimination	Prejudice	
Ethnocentrism	Stereotyping	

DISCUSSION QUESTIONS

1. How is it significant that British Americans comprised 63 percent of the U.S. population at the nation's beginning?

2. What are some examples of cultural pluralism among the Dutch, French, German, and Irish peoples in the United States?

3. What similarities in dominant–minority patterns were shared by most northern and western European immigrants?

4. Apply the various sociological concepts about strangers to immigrant groups against whom dominant groups had xenophobic reactions.

5. Apply the three major theoretical perspectives to the experiences of the immigrant groups discussed in this chapter.

SUGGESTED READINGS

Fabend, Firth H. *Zion on the Hudson: Dutch New York and New Jersey in the Age of Revivals*. New Brunswick, NJ: Rutgers University Press, 2000.
A fine social history of the evolution of ethnic identity, changing roles of women, reform movements, persistence and eventual fading of Dutch culture.

Higham, John. *Strangers in the Land: Patterns of American Nativism, 1860–1925*, 2nd ed. New Brunswick, NJ: Rutgers University Press, 2002.
Excellent and detailed historical narrative of the patterns of native-born xenophobic responses to culturally different immigrant groups.

Hirsch, Arthur H., and Bertrand Van Ruymbeke. *The Huguenots of Colonial South Carolina*, reprint ed. Charleston, SC: University of South Carolina Press, 1999.
Historical portrait of the rapid social and religious disintegration, by choice, of this ethnic group in the United States.

McCaffrey, Lawrence J. *Textures of Irish America*. Syracuse, NY: Syracuse University Press, 1998.
Engaging book on Irish adaptation to urban life, Irish upward mobility, Irish public figures and personalities, and the role of Irish nationalism in developing the personality of Irish America.

O'Hanlon, Ray. *The New Irish Americans*. Niwot, CO: Roberts Rinehart, 1998.
An insider's portrait of the new generation of Irish in America who are in the United States under much different circumstances from those their ancestors experienced.

Tolzmann, Don H. *The German-American Experience*. Amherst, NY: Humanity Books, 2000.
A comprehensive account of this ethnic group from colonial times to the present, with an analysis of German American influences on all aspects of U.S. society.

Webb, James. *Born Fighting: How the Scots-Irish Shaped America*. New York: Broadway, 2004.
A passionate social history that depicts Scots-Irish culture as a bedrock of working-class America, fundamentalist Christianity, and fierce individualism.

MYSOCKIT

Additional resources for this chapter can be found in MySocKit. If you have a subscription to MySocKit, go to www.mysockit.com to study, review, and go beyond the book to learn more about race and ethnic relations.

Southern, Central, and Eastern Europeans

CHAPTER **6**

During the colonial period, immigrants came to the United States from southern, central, and eastern Europe, as well as from northern and western regions of the continent. Many, in fact, played important roles in the Revolutionary War and during the early years of the new nation. Not until the late 19th century, however, did immigrants from this part of the world come in significant numbers. The same economic changes that earlier caused emigration from northern and western Europe (particularly industrialization) spread south and east, creating agrarian difficulties, famine, and unemployment and triggering a major shift in the source of European emigration.

SOCIOHISTORICAL PERSPECTIVE

The 1870s saw a dramatic increase in the number of Russians, Italians, and Austro-Hungarians arriving in the United States (see the Appendix). By 1896, a turning point occurred, as immigrants from the rest of Europe outnumbered those from northern and western Europe. Their physical appearance and **cultural differentiation** easily identified the newcomers as strangers, and they often were broadly categorized as alike despite their many intrinsic differences as individuals and as separate ethnic groups. They arrived in large enough numbers to be able to preserve their various old-country cultures and social boundaries within the new urban subcultural setting, but this circumstance also increased the probability of prejudice and discrimination against them.

The Push–Pull Factors

Helpful to our understanding of why people migrate are **push–pull factors**, those forces that encourage migration from one place to another. "Push" factors are those negative elements (e.g., persecution, repression, hard economic times) that discourage one from remaining in the country of origin, and "pull" factors are positive inducements (e.g., family or friends already there, freedom, opportunity, living standards) that lure people to seek a better life elsewhere.

167

FIGURE 6.1   Total Immigration to the United States from 1820 to 2000, by Decade

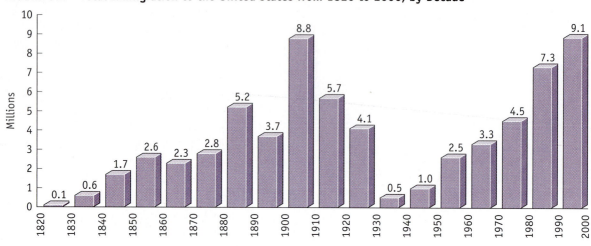

Source: U.S. Office of Immigration Statistics.

A number of elements contributed to the great wave of immigration from 1880 to 1920 (Figure 6.1). During that time, U.S. industry was growing rapidly, requiring ever larger numbers of workers. Improved transportation—quicker, sturdier steamships with highly competitive rates for steerage ($10 or less per person)—encouraged transoceanic migration.

Peasant life was especially harsh in Europe. The ruling classes and local estate farm owners ruthlessly exploited the common people. They crushed most peasant revolts and protests instead of reforming the basic agricultural economy. Peasants saw their sons drafted into the army for periods of 12 to 31 years. Trying to eke out an existence amid poverty, unemployment, sickness, and tyranny, many of Europe's poor looked elsewhere for a better life.

Letters from friends or relatives already in the United States were eagerly read and circulated among villagers. Newspapers, books, pamphlets, transportation advertisements, and labor-recruiting agents all stimulated "America fever." Following a familiar minority pattern of avoidance, Europe's poor and persecuted peoples fled their homelands for the promise of "Golden America."

Political and economic unrest in Europe also encouraged the exodus. Old World governments faced pressures of overpopulation, chronic poverty, the decline of feudalism, dissident factions, and a changing agrarian economy. For them, large-scale emigration to the United States provided an expedient means of easing societal pressures without actually addressing the root causes of many institutional problems, so they sponsored emigration drives, further increasing the European migration.

Hundreds of thousands of immigrants thus came to the United States: Italians, Portuguese, Greeks, and Armenians from the southern part of Europe; Hungarians, Poles, Czechs, Slovaks, and others from the central plains; Austrians and Swiss from the high mountain country; Byelorussians, Ukrainians, Ruthenians, and others from the western regions of Czarist Russia; and Jews from all parts of eastern and central Europe (Figure 6.2). All these different peoples came, leaving behind their familiar world and seeking a new destiny.

FIGURE 6.2   Pre–World War I Southern, Central, and Eastern Europe

Structural Conditions

The United States that the immigrants came to differed considerably from the land earlier immigrants had found. The frontier was rapidly disappearing; industrialization and urbanization were changing the nation's lifestyle. The immigrants, mostly illiterate, unskilled, rural peasants, were plunged into a new cultural and social environment.

With virtually no resources, many immigrants settled in their ports of entry or in inland cities along railroad lines, such as Chicago. At the turn of the century, living conditions in cities were far worse than they are today. Overcrowding, disease, high mortality rates, crime, filth, and congestion were endemic. Crowded into poorly ventilated tenements and cellars, the immigrants often lived in squalor.

Settling in the oldest city sections, immigrants formed ethnic subcommunities, re-creating the nationality quilt of Europe. Although they were neighbors out of necessity, intermarriage and joint organizational activities were rare. To find security in a strange land, they repeated the adjustment patterns of the "old" immigrants. They sought and interacted with their own people, establishing their own churches, schools, and organizations to preserve their traditions and culture.

As unskilled workers, most found employment in the low-status, manual labor jobs in the factories, mines, needle trades, and construction. At that time, workers had no voice in working conditions, for labor unions had not yet become effective. The 84-hour workweek (14 hours per day, 6 days per week) for low wages was common. Jobs offered no paid vacations, sick pay, or pension plans. Child labor was commonplace, and entire families often worked to provide a subsistence-level family income. Lighting, ventilation, and heating were poor (see

The Ethnic Experience

Immigrant Working Conditions

"Working conditions were terrible, terrible. If you have to sit two–three hours overtime for ten cents, what can I explain you? It don't get worse. But these ten cents I need. Whenever it was overtime, I was the first one to raise my hand.

"The boss watches you. You shouldn't talk to one another. He watches you between lunch and supper, you know. So you want something, you have something in your drawer like candy. He watches. No, no, no, nothing. You can't eat while you're working. So, you watch, you put the candy in your mouth.

"It was so hot in the shop, the sweat was running from the body and from the hand and the material got stained. The boss didn't care, the foreman didn't care. Once two policemen came in. They stopped the power. They said we couldn't work in such a heat. You haven't even got a fan here to have a little coolness. Nothing! People used to faint. Big people used to faint.

"In winter—it was such a hard winter. When I opened the door in the morning to go to work, I couldn't take away my hand from the knob—the frost. Terrible, terrible. At work in the big shop in the middle was a stove. It kept us a little warm. But, you know, young people, young blood—we put on a sweater. Yeah, the conditions was terrible. Can't be worse. Can't be worse. It was terrible. And the boss had a fresh mouth always for the workers."

Source: Austrian Jewish immigrant who came to the United States in 1914 at age 17. Taped interview from the collection of Vincent N. Parrillo.

The Ethnic Experience box above); in the factories, moving parts of machinery were dangerously exposed, leading to numerous horrific accidents. There was no workers' compensation, although many laborers were injured on the job. A worker who objected was likely to be fired and blacklisted. Exploited by the captains of industry, the immigrants became deeply involved in the labor union movement, so much so that to tell the story of one without the other is virtually impossible:

> It is true that many immigrants embraced the industrial ethos and found fulfillment in it. But many could not adjust to the new work discipline required of them and drifted from job to job; a good percentage returned to the Old Country, defeated and disillusioned. Some tried and failed to find work for which their skills and previous experience equipped them. Others turned to collective action—temperance societies, workers' educational associations, fraternal benefit societies, cooperatives, and unions—either to protect themselves from a system that was often pitiless, or to try in a small way to change the social and economic environment in which they found themselves. Still others resorted to radical and "direct" action to forcibly change a system which did not yield what they had crossed the Atlantic to find.[1]

Faced with these adverse circumstances, many immigrants worked hard and made sacrifices. Conditions, though bad, were better than what they had left behind. More important, the United States gave them hope and a promise of better things—if not for themselves, then surely for their children.

Societal Reaction

Although the immigrant groups segregated themselves socially from one another, outsiders saw them mainly as unacculturated strangers and tended to lump them together. Italians and Jews stood out from others because of their large numbers, residential clustering, religions, languages, appearance, and cultural practices. Although many viewed all "new" immigrants as undesirable and unassimilable,

U.S. society directed the greatest antagonism against the more visible Italians and Jews (see The International Scene box, page 173).

Racism. Negative reactions to incoming minority groups had occurred many times before. This time, however, it developed a new dimension—actions based on physical features:

> The arrival on American shores of these darker swarms of migrants—the so-called "new immigration"—was countered by the development of a new note in American **nativism:** the racist claim of ineluctable biological superiority for those with lighter skins, fairer hair, and earlier debarkation dates. Together with the older nativist themes of anti-Catholicism, fear of "foreign radicalism," and general **xenophobia,** this newer development in collective hatred, along with an awakening anti-Semitism, combined to produce the onslaught on the immigrant's culture, social organization, and self-regard known as the Americanization movement—a development which . . . was brought to its highest pitch by the events of World War I and the immediate post-war period.[2]

Probably the most influential blending of nativist and racist strains of thought during this period occurred in Madison Grant's 1916 book, *The Passing of the Great Race.* Relying on what he considered scientific truth, Grant identified race as the key factor in determining culture and behavior. He argued that racial hybridism can lead only to a reversion to the "lower type." As his pessimistic title suggests, Grant saw the vastly superior native U.S. stock as disap-

"An Interesting Question"

"How long will it be," asked the caption, "before the rats own the garden and the man gets out?" This cartoon shows Uncle Sam asleep in his garden, unaware of the invasion of foreign rats. Their faces are stereotyped depictions of Jews, Russians, Italians, Greeks, and other immigrants from southern and eastern Europe. This cartoon by E. M. Ashe appeared in *Life* on June 22, 1893. (Courtesy of Library of Congress [LC-USZ62–7386])

FIGURE 6.3   Staging Areas for Illegal Immigration into Italy

pearing (through "racial suicide") as a result of lower birth rates, which reflected their desire not to sully their racial purity:

> [Native U.S. citizens of colonial stock] will not bring children into the world to compete in the labor market with the Slovak, the Italian, the Syrian and the Jew. The native American is too proud to mix socially with them and is gradually withdrawing from the scene, abandoning to these aliens the land which he conquered and developed. The man of the old stock is being crowded out of many country districts by these foreigners just as he is today being literally driven off the streets of New York City by the swarms of Polish Jews. These immigrants adopt the language of the native American, they wear his clothes, they steal his name and they are beginning to take his women, but they seldom adopt his religion or understand his ideals; and while he is being elbowed out of his own home, the American looks calmly abroad and urges on others the suicidal ethics which are exterminating his own race.[3]

Grant's book struck a responsive chord with other writers and with congressional leaders. Popular magazines, such as the *Saturday Evening Post,* quoted and praised Grant. Other "scholars" followed with eugenic explanations purporting to establish a correlation between racial physique and culture:

> Previously vague and romantic notions of Anglo-Saxon peoplehood were combined with general ethnocentrism, rudimentary wisps of genetics, selected tidbits of evolutionary theory, and naive assumptions from an early and a crude imported anthropology (later, other social sciences, at a similar stage of scientific development added their contributions) to produce the doctrine that the English, Germans, and others of the "old immigration" constituted a superior race of tall, blonde, blue-eyed "Nordics" or "Aryans." Whereas the peoples of Eastern and Southern Europe made up the darker Alpines or Mediterraneans—both inferior breeds whose presence in America threatened, either by intermixture or supplementation, the traditional American stock and culture.[4]

Ronald M. Pavalko maintains that **racism** was at the core of the negative response to the "new" immigrants and that any economic argument for immigration restrictions was a smokescreen.[5] He cites economist Isaac A. Hourwich, who

The International Scene

Anti-Immigrant Backlash in Italy

Italy attracts more illegal immigration than other European countries because its long coastline and close proximity to other countries make it especially vulnerable. The most popular clandestine sea routes for Africans are from Libya or Tunisia to the Italian island of Lampedusa (which is closer to Africa than to Italy) or to Sicily (see Figure 6.3). A second underground gateway is a 60-mile speedboat ride by smugglers from Albania across the Adriatic Sea. Albanians, Afghans, Kurds, Turks, and Chinese are the most frequent arrivals this way. A third route is by truck over the Slovenian border, across northern Italy, and into Milan [see map in Figure 6.3 on p. 172].

With a limit of 20,000 to 30,000 legal immigrants per year, and an estimated 2 million others waiting for transit to enter, the "backdoor" of illegal entry became the only viable choice for many. About 2.5 million (4.3 percent) of Italy's 58 million people are foreign-born, about half of them beneficiaries of four amnesties between 1986 and 1998. These amnesties, however, did not solve the problem and instead tended more to attract tens of thousands of new illegal migrants rather than to lower their numbers. Each year, hundreds drown in unsafe, overcrowded boats in attempts to reach Italy.

Africans and Asians are visible everywhere, selling cheap merchandise on the streets, trying to clean windshields at intersections, or pumping gas. Native Italians disparagingly refer to the newcomers by the **ethnophaulism** *vu compra,* which is a slang version of the phrase, *Vuoi comprare* (Do you want to buy?).

The arrival of so many physically and culturally distinct newcomers in so short a period created an anti-immigrant backlash, transforming Italy from a relatively open country into a closed one. The nation expelled thousands of illegal aliens and turned back ten of thousands of others at its borders and on the seas. Racial incidents, including firebombings, became commonplace. In March 2002, after nearly 1,000 Kurdish refugees landed in Sicily in a rusting boat, Italy declared a state of emergency and launched an aggressive deportation of illegals. Even so, the growing backlash has resulted in the formation in 1991 of the *Lega Nord* (Northern League), an anti-immigration party that received about 5 percent of the vote in the 2006 general election, forcing the ruling political party to maintain its actions against illegal immigrants.

Critical Thinking Question: How and why does the Italian government action against illegal immigrants differ from that of the U.S. government?

Source: Drawn in part from the author's several visits to Italy and in part adapted from various news reports.

reported that in reality unemployment rates tended to be lowest in years of *high* immigration and highest during years of *low* immigration.[6] However, "specific economic and political events—industrial conflict, World War I, and the Russian Revolution—contributed to [a] redefinition" of these groups in nonracial terms.[7] As the emphasis shifted to national loyalty and stability, the Americanization movement reached a "crucial turning point":

> The transformation of the new immigrants from a stigmatized racial entity to a threat to economic and political order represents a shift in the definition of them as unassimilable to one emphasizing the point that they must be assimilated. We can only speculate on whether the new immigrants would have continued to be the focus of a racist ideology if this redefinition had not occurred. It does seem clear that the conscious and explicit emphasis on "Americanization" did not represent a rejection of racist assumptions about them as much as the substitution of economic and political concerns as more pressing.[8]

Americanization. Without government assistance and with little knowledge of the language or customs, the immigrants were expected to fit into U.S. society quickly. Native U.S. residents expected them to speak only English, strip away their old culture, and avoid ethnic institutions or organizations. These demands often led to ethnic self-hatred or a negative self-image because of the newcomers' ambivalence about assimilation or their inability or slowness to achieve it.[9]

To preserve the stability of the country, many people attempted to hasten the **assimilation** of the new immigrants already here. They looked on the schools as agents of socialization, a key force in effecting Anglo-conformity. The following quotation by an educator of the early 20th century reflects the prevailing dominant-group attitudes of that period:

> These southern and eastern Europeans are of a very different type from the north Europeans who preceded them. Illiterate, docile, lacking in self-reliance and initiative, and not possessing the Anglo-Teutonic conceptions of law, order, and government, their coming has served to dilute tremendously our national stock, and to corrupt our civic life. The great bulk of these people have settled in the cities of the North Atlantic and North Central states and living, moral and sanitary conditions, honest and decent government, and proper education have everywhere been made more difficult by their presence. Everywhere these people tend to settle in groups or settlements, and to set up here their national manners, customs, and observances. Our task is to break up these groups or settlements, to assimilate and amalgamate these people as a part of our American race, and to implant in their children, so far as can be done, the Anglo-Saxon conception of righteousness, law and order, and popular government, and to awaken in them a reverence for our democratic institutions and for those things in our national life which we as a people hold to be of abiding worth.[10]

Children of immigrants felt the **marginality** conflicts between majority-group expectations and their minority perspective more keenly than their parents. They were truly caught between two worlds. Schools vigorously promoted the shedding of cultural differences as the children grew up in a society contemptuous of foreigners. Wanting to be accepted, the children began to feel self-conscious. Many were even embarrassed to bring friends to their homes, where a foreign language, foreign cooking, and different atmosphere prevailed.

Xenophobia. Historians point to the Haymarket Affair as perhaps the single most important factor inciting a xenophobic reaction against all immigrants. In Chicago in May 1886, at the height of a general strike for an eight-hour workday, the strike's anarchist organizers—almost all immigrants—held a rally in Haymarket Square. As nervous police approached the peaceful gathering, someone threw a bomb at them, killing an officer and wounding 70 people. The bomb thrower's identity was never discovered, but the courts sentenced six immigrants and one native-born U.S. citizen to death; another immigrant received a long prison term. Newspapers promoted a negative stereotype of immigrants as troublemakers and national hysteria and fear of anarchy mushroomed, particularly in the large cities of the Northeast and Midwest. Reflecting this public hostility, one editorial writer said,

> These people are not Americans, but the very scum and offal of Europe . . . long-haired, wild-eyed, bad-smelling, atheistic—reckless foreign wretches, who never did an honest hour's work in their lives . . . crush such snakes . . . before they have time to bite.[11]

A magazine writer warned Americans that anarchy was a "blood disease" unknown to the Anglo-Saxons but common to the "darker swarms" from Europe: "I am no race worshipper but . . . if the master race of this continent is subordinated to or overrun with the communistic and revolutionary races, it will be in grave danger of social disaster."[12]

For a long time after the Haymarket Affair, the words *foreign* and *radical* were linked. Negative **stereotyping** and nativist movements increased. Calls for restrictions on immigration continued until the Immigration Law of 1921 was passed.

"Spoiling the broth!" ran the caption to this February 1921 cartoon, which, if "Europe" were changed to "Latin America" could easily fit today's public sentiment. The fear of inundation by and nonassimilation of immigrants led to the passage of a restrictive immigration law later that year. (*Source:* John and Selma Appel Collection)

Legislative Action.   In 1907, in response to public pressure, Congress established a joint Senate–House commission to investigate the entire immigration situation. The Dillingham Commission (previously discussed in Chapter 1) issued a voluminous report in 1911, concluding that the "new" immigrants tended to congregate, slowing the assimilation process, whereas the "old" immigrants had dispersed immediately on arrival. Moreover, "new" immigrants were less skilled and less educated, had greater criminal tendencies, and were more willing to accept low wages and a low standard of living. As a solution, the commission suggested instituting either a mandatory literacy test for immigrants or tighter immigration restrictions.

Congress's first response, in 1913, was to pass a literacy bill requiring all immigrants over 16 to be able to read some language. Outgoing President Taft vetoed the bill, however, just as President Cleveland had vetoed a similar proposal in 1896. Finally, in 1917, Congress overrode President Wilson's veto of yet another literacy bill of the same type. This law did little to stem the tide of immigrants, however, for it exempted the many refugees fleeing religious persecution. Meanwhile, the literacy rate in Europe had risen since 1900, so the literacy test was not a serious obstacle for most. Because of the continual flow of immigrants from war-ravaged Europe, the fear that such political upheavals as the Bolshevik Revolution would spread to the United States, and the general U.S. mood of isolationism at the close of World War I, pressures for immigration restrictions mounted.

Although outgoing President Wilson vetoed a new congressional bill dealing with immigration, it was reintroduced in a special session of Congress and signed by President Harding soon afterward. The National Origins Quota Act of 1921, adopting a proposal that the Dillingham Commission had made a decade earlier, limited the numbers of immigrants. It imposed a quota system, allowing only 3 percent of the number of people of each nationality already in the United States in 1910. The effect of this legislation was to reduce the number of southern, central, and eastern European immigrants from the 780,000 annual average in the years 1910–1914 to about 155,000 annually.

When the act expired, it was replaced by the even tougher Johnson–Reed Act of 1924, which reduced each country's annual quota to 2 percent of its emigrants already in the United States as of 1890; this discriminated even more severely against the "newer" immigrant countries, and the worldwide quota dropped to near 165,000. In 1929, however, the quota of 3 percent was restored, with a total ceiling of 150,000 (Table 6.1).

Henry Pratt Fairchild, a sociologist, summed up the **ethnocentric** attitudes of his time when he said,

> The highest service of America to mankind is to point the way, to demonstrate the possibilities, to lead onward to the goal of human happiness. Any force that tends to impair our capacity for leadership is a menace to mankind and a flagrant violation to the spirit of liberalism.
>
> Unrestricted immigration was such a force. It was slowly, insidiously, irresistibly eating away at the very heart of the United States. What was being melted in the great Melting Pot, losing all form and symmetry, all beauty and character, all nobility and usefulness, was the American nationality itself.[13]

Although an exception was made to receive approximately 400,000 displaced persons following World War II, the 1929 legislation remained in effect until the McCarran–Walter Act of 1952 was passed. This new law, passed over President Truman's veto, still reflected nativist biases. It simplified the quota

TABLE 6.1   Major Immigration Acts

1875	First direct federal regulation of immigration, barring criminals, prostitutes, and "coolie" labor.
1882	Established a system of central control of immigration through state boards under the Secretary of the Treasury.
1882	Chinese Exclusion Act suspended immigration of Chinese laborers for ten years, extended in 1892 for another ten years, and in 1902 for an indefinite period.
1891	Established the Bureau of Immigration.
1917	Further restricted immigration of Asian persons creating the "barred zone" (known as the Asia—Pacific triangle), natives of which were declared inadmissible.
1921	Limited immigration to 3 percent of foreign-born persons of each nationality living in the United States in 1910.
1924	Banned Japanese immigration and temporarily set other immigration limits to 2 percent of foreign-born persons of each nationality living in the United States in 1890; in 1929 returned to 3 percent in equal ratio to a total ceiling of 150,000.
1952	Set an annual quota of one-sixth of 1 percent of ancestry or national origin recorded in 1920, with a minimum quota of 100 and a ceiling of 2,000 for countries in Asia–Pacific triangle.
1965	Abolished the national-origins quota system; numerical limitations of 120,000 from Western hemisphere and 170,000 from Eastern hemisphere, with a 20,000-per-country limit for the latter only; excluded spouses, children, and parents from numerical restrictions.
1976	Added a 20,000-per-country limit to the Western hemisphere.
1978	Combined the separate hemisphere ceilings into one worldwide limit of 290,000.
1986	Granted amnesty and eligibility for permanent-resident status to undocumented aliens residing in the United States before 1982.
1990	Set an immigrant ceiling of 700,000 for 1992 through 1994, dropping to 675,000 thereafter.

Source: U.S. Citizenship and Immigration Services, *Immigration Legislation* (Washington, DC: U.S. Government Printing Office, 2007).

formula to one-sixth of 1 percent of the foreign-born population from each country in the 1920 census.

The Immigration and Nationality Act of 1965 ended the proportional-representation quota system. Numeric limits of 120,000 from the Western Hemisphere and 170,000 from the Eastern Hemisphere were set; the numbers were based on a complicated preference system stressing job skills and close family kinship. In 1976, a 20,000-per-country annual limit was established, followed in 1978 by replacement of hemisphere quotas with a single worldwide ceiling of 290,000; this number then changed in 1980 to 270,000, excluding refugees. Immediate relatives of immigrants were admitted above the 270,000 limit, however, bringing annual legal immigration totals to over 500,000 annually in the

1980s. Then, 1990 legislation set a new ceiling of 700,000 through 1994, after which it dropped to 675,000.

The collapse of communism in Europe in 1989 had a major impact on immigration. In the 1990s, hundreds of thousands migrated to the United States from central and eastern Europe, most particularly from Poland and the former Soviet Union. Their coming revitalized old ethnic neighborhoods and created new ones, as a once-declining white ethnic presence reasserted itself in many parts of the country.

THE SLAVIC PEOPLES

Often included under the general classification "Slavic peoples" are Poles, Russians, Ukrainians, Ruthenians, Bulgarians, Romanians, Czechs, Serbs, Croats, Slovaks, and Slovenians. The first three groups came to the United States in much greater numbers than the others during the 1880–1920 mass migration period, and more information is available about their experiences. However, U.S. public opinion during this period usually made no distinctions among these groups; and, as a result, their experiences in this country tended to be similar.

Earlier Immigrants

Slavic people had been in the New World since colonial times. New Amsterdam and New Sweden, for example, received Protestant refugees from this region in the 17th century, and Moravians fled to the Quaker colony of Pennsylvania in the 18th century. In the mid-19th century, many Slavic political refugees came to the United States, and almost all of them remained. In the post–Civil War period, however, Slavic people began to come in steadily increasing numbers, and this influx continued until the Immigration Act of 1921 sharply curtailed it.

These "new" immigrants scattered throughout the country, although many concentrated in mining and industrial areas of Pennsylvania and the Midwest. Beginning as unskilled workers, they formed the large majority of the workers in the Chicago slaughterhouses, the coal fields, and the iron and steel factories. By 1917, they outnumbered all other ethnic groups in those places of occupation. The normal pattern was for the males to come first and their families later, if at all. Like many Greek and Italian males, numerous Slavic males came merely as sojourners to earn money for land, dowries, or just a better life, returning to their native land after a year or two. Members of these three ethnic groups accounted for the majority of the more than 2 million aliens who returned from the United States to Europe between 1908 and 1914.

In his book *The Slavic Community on Strike,* Victor R. Greene vividly depicted the immigrant experience in the mining industry. In the following excerpt, he described the anxiety and arrival of a newcomer to the Pennsylvania coal region:

> The typical greenhorn would have alighted from the immigrant train in the Pennsylvania hard-coal region undoubtedly apprehensive if he had not yet met his correspondent. With luck, one or both had a photograph to aid in recognizing the other. Otherwise, the weary traveler at the depot asked or shouted the

name of his sponsor. One can imagine the tears of joy on both sides when to the immigrant's call his countryman responded, and their relief was expressed in a demonstrative embrace. . . .

The sponsor then led his charge to a group of shacks usually at the edge of town. This ghetto was separated from the rest of the populace, just as in other places in America where the East Europeans lived. Here in the coal country inhabitants term the foreign nest the Slavic mining "patch." If he arrived at night, the bundle-laden traveler would have to grope through the darkness, as no street illumination, paved roads or signs (even if he could have read them) facilitated this last, short trip.[14]

Here we can visualize the **social segregation** and the resulting ethnic enclave so common in immigrant groups. Although their languages and customs varied, the Slavic peoples all experienced economic hardship. Children were often put to work to help the family survive, instead of being sent to school. This not only deprived these immigrant children of a "normal" childhood but also delayed upward mobility by at least a generation:

The sight of so many children employed in mining along with their fathers appalled many Americans. The Slav would give a ready answer when accused of practising child labor—economic necessity. Popular American abhorrence of the evil forced through minimum age laws, but to little avail, as parents and employers violated them with rare penalty. Some child labor reformers announced that they had found boys as young as six working at the mines; nine or ten was probably the actual minimum. A leading reformer sympathized with the East European youngster as the "helpless victim of the frugality, ignorance, and industrial instincts of his parents." The value placed by Americans on educating the young little interested the Slav, for the valuable child was the working one. Above a minimum education was useless, and the pressing need for income forced sons into the pits at or before their teens. . . . All of the workers here, men and boys, labored the normal ten-hour, six-day week, when at full time.[15]

In the case of Slavic immigrants, a combination of factors—their peasant background, economic deprivation, child labor, and little education—slowed their rise up the socioeconomic ladder. A high proportion of second- and third-generation Slavic Americans, for example, had lower income and educational levels than did Greek and Jewish Americans through the 1960s.[16] Many Slavic Americans today are middle class and less recognizable as a distinct ethnic subgroup because of high rates of intermarriage.

Recent Immigrants

About 20,000 refugees fled to the United States from Hitler-occupied Czechoslovakia, most of them professionals, scholars, and artists. When the communists seized control in the late 1940s, thousands more sought refuge in the United States. Still other Czech refugees were admitted into the United States in 1968 after the Soviet invasion ended their country's brief flirtation with liberalization. Since 1971, over 23,000 Czechs (and Slovakians) have migrated to the United States.

After the breakup of Yugoslavia, the tragic violence that raged in the 1990s among Serbians, Croats, and Bosnians sparked a large refugee exodus, with more than 137,000 refugees from this strife-torn land fleeing to the United States, although far more of the displaced sought refuge in nearby European countries.

Between 1993 and 2003, the United States resettled over 143,000 Bosnian Muslim refugees; by 2006, the program came to a close as fewer than 100 additional Bosnian refugees arrived. In addition, immigrants from Yugoslavia to the United States exceeded 156,000 in the 1990s and more than 100,000 from Bosnia and Herzegovina between 2000 and 2006.[17]

THE POLES

Included among other Slavic groups until 1899, when they began to be counted separately, the Poles constituted the third-largest ethnic group of the "new" immigration. With their homeland partitioned among Germany, Russia, and Austria-Hungary, 1 million Poles came to the United States between 1899 and 1914, fleeing poverty and seeking economic opportunity. In fact, the desire for economic improvement was so common to almost all the new immigrants that the English expression "after bread" is found in the vocabularies of most central and eastern Europeans who migrated to the United States.

Nobel Prize–winning Polish writer Henryk Sienkiewicz, who visited the United States from 1876 to 1878, illustrated this point in his classic observation of the difficulties his people first encountered here. Notice also the traces of ethnocentrism in his observation of Americans:

> Their lot is a severe and terrifying one and whoever would depict it accurately would create an epic of human misery. . . . Is there anyone whose hand is not against them? Their early history is a tale of misery, loneliness, painful despair and humiliation. . . . They are primarily peasants and workers who have come in quest of bread. Thus you will easily understand that in a country inhabited by a people who are not at all sentimental, but rather energetic, industrious, and whose competition it is difficult to survive, the fate of these newcomers, poorly educated, unfamiliar with American conditions, ignorant of the language, uncertain how to proceed, must be truly lamentable.[18]

Elsewhere, Sienkiewicz found vibrant Polish communities in Radom, Illinois; Krakow, Missouri; Polonia, Wisconsin; and Panna Maris, Texas.[19] Buffalo, Detroit, and Milwaukee all had sizable Polish populations, too; Chicago had the largest Polish community.

Culture Shock

The effects of **culture shock**—bewilderment and disorganization, particularly in family life—can be seen in many immigrants' writings and in the records of courts and social-service agencies. One of the early sociological classics, *The Polish Peasant in Europe and America,* by William I. Thomas and Florian Znaniecki, explored this theme, and influenced subsequent studies of Polish American life.[20]

Leaving behind a *gemeinschaft* society with behavior regulated by custom and habit, the Polish immigrants found themselves surrounded by unsympathetic, even hostile, people whose language and customs they did not comprehend. Thomas and Znaniecki maintained that, even if active demoralization and antisocial behavior did not result, those who made the transition suffered a "partial or general weakening of social interests, a growing narrowness or shallowness of the individual's social life." In fact, many immigrant families found the adjustment too difficult, and crime, delinquency, divorce, desertion, prostitution, and economic dependence were the by-products of family disorganization. Such tendencies also occurred in other immigrant communities caught in a web of economic and social instability.

Community Organization

The values and forms of village life in rural Poland were reintegrated, although not completely, in the parish structure of the urban American Roman Catholic Church.[21] For example, St. Stanislaus Kostka Church in Chicago in 1899 held the world's largest parish. The church blended staunch Roman Catholicism, Polish culture, and a full range of social services to help the immigrants become acculturated.

Not all Poles desired assimilation, however, and many wanted the church to reflect Polish culture. Frustrated also by futile attempts to have Polish priests elevated in a church hierarchy dominated by Irish and German prelates, representatives from various "independent" parishes formed the Polish National Catholic Church; Lithuanians formed a similar church. Both church groups used their native languages in the Mass rather than Latin. They added other elements of their culture (patriotic songs, patron saint feast days) to their church activities, too.

Culture also affected Polish attitudes toward U.S. education. Summarizing the numerous scholarly references to this point, Helena Znaniecki Lopata reported,

> The attitudes of the Polish peasants toward education—which defined it as a waste of time at best, and as a dangerous thing undermining the traditional way of life at worst—were transplanted to the American soil. Ideally, the children of Polonia began working at an early age to help the family in its endless struggle for money. The United States Immigration Commission, which undertook an intensive study of immigrants in 17 American cities in 1911, found the children of Poles following this typical educational career: parochial school from the ages of 8 to 12, first communion, public school for two years, and then work.[22]

At that time, the Polish immigrant merely wanted the educational system to provide children with a strict moral upbringing in a well-disciplined atmosphere.

The Polish community did not fall into complete family disorganization and demoralization, as predicted by Thomas and Znaniecki. Its immigrant peasant culture was not a rigid set of norms subject to collapse from constant attack; indeed, that culture was as receptive to **ethnogenesis** as any other ethnic community. Poles formed some of the earliest and strongest ethnic associations, such as the Polish National Alliance.

> The history of Polonia over the years, locally or as a superterritorial community, indicates that its cultural fabric was much more flexible and viable, based on the social structure and gradually changing, bending, and modifying as new norms were introduced purposely or through unconscious diffusion by its members.[23]

Several studies conducted in the 1960s showed the rate of Polish **upward mobility** as trailing that of other ethnic groups.[24] While this was true of the first two generations, changes occurred in the mid-1970s; the older Polish Americans were at the top of the blue-collar world, and most of their offspring were entering the professions and the white-collar world.[25] By 1980, Polish American high school graduation was higher than all other European American groups.[26]

Examining the Polish American community in Los Angeles, Neil C. Sandberg found an inverse correlation between social class and ethnicity, with a decline in cultural ethnicity among the third- and fourth-generation members as they experienced upward mobility.[27] In other words, greater individualism and less group cohesiveness accompanied a climb up the socioeconomic ladder.[28]

Polonia Today

Of the 9 million Americans claiming Polish ancestry in 2000, about 80 percent are clustered in nine northeastern and midwestern states. Chicago still claims the world's largest concentration of ethnic Poles outside Poland: about 1 million. There and elsewhere, however, traditional inner-city Polish neighborhoods have yielded to other minority groups, as the better educated and more successful Polish Americans have moved to the suburbs. St. Stanislaus Kostka Church, for example, still stands, but the second language of the mass is no longer Polish but Spanish.[29]

New Polish immigrants still arrive—more than 172,000 in the 1990s and over 75,000 between 2000 and 2006. Each year, over a third of the new arrivals choose the Chicago metropolitan area as their intended settlement area.[30] Their numbers keep Polish ethnic neighborhoods somewhat resilient, but their assimilation occurs with relative ease.

THE RUSSIANS

The first Russian immigrants were Mennonites, who actually were of German origin and had maintained their German language and German customs within Russian borders for a century. As they became targets of forced assimilation, military conscription, and persecution during the 1870s, they began to leave Russia and emigrate to the Great Plains of North America. Although the Mennonites were never very numerous in the United States—only 30,000 to 40,000 in total by 1900—they made a significant contribution to U.S. agriculture by introducing Turkish wheat, a hard winter wheat that by the turn of the century had become the leading first-class wheat product.

Of the more than 3 million Russian immigrants who arrived in the United States between 1881 and 1920, approximately 43 percent were Jewish.[31] In Chapter 12, on religious minorities, we examine the Jewish experience in the United States. This section focuses primarily on the non-Jewish Russian immigrants, the great majority of them members of the Russian Orthodox Church.

The peak Russian migration occurred between 1881 and 1914, with poor, illiterate peasants emigrating for economic reasons and others seeking political or religious freedom. Forced to adjust to an industrial environment from a rural one, they joined other immigrants in the grueling labor in mines and factories. Severely exploited, they often complained about the harshness of their work situation, became active in the labor movement, and sought to improve their working conditions.

Following the 1917 Bolshevik Revolution, a new type of Russian immigrant sought asylum in the United States. Czarist army officers, landowners, professional people, and political activists all fled from the new regime (see The Ethnic

The Ethnic Experience

Immigrant First Impressions

"The closer we came to the United States the better we felt after being so dizzy and nauseous. The trip took us ten days and we landed in Ellis Island in 1924. We saw a big, big building. It was like an armory and, yes, we went through inspection. Before we went on the boat we went through inspection and the physical, and when we came to Ellis Island it was the same thing. They inspected all the clothing of ours and the physical too. Everything was all right with us. Some people didn't pass the inspection and they had to go back, with their health and all.

"All the immigrants were holding their bundles, the baggage, by them. Also we ate by huge tables and most of the food they served was herring. There were some young immigrant boys and they played the mandolin and I was dancing and I didn't think about anything. We were laughing and dancing. I didn't understand what they were saying but we had a lot of fun. We stayed in Ellis Island three days because we came in on a Friday and on the weekend they didn't let anyone out. So we stayed there three days.

"When my father came in—they told me it's my father, of course, but I didn't know him because I hadn't seen him in ten years—I was thrilled to see him. And, of course, as a young girl, I was very happy and I was giggling a lot and that worried my father because he heard a lot of girls came here in this country and they got in trouble. He asked me, "My dear daughter, why are you giggling so much?" I didn't have an answer for him then. I never saw my father and yet I saw him worry for me and giving me orders what to do, what not to do. It was very strange to me, but we were all very happy to see him and finally he took us on a subway. The subway was very new to me. This I didn't see in Europe.

"Now I see it wasn't such a big palace my father took us in. It was four rooms but everything looked so nice. It was a piece of carpet on the floor with a victrola with the letters, chairs, and a little sofa, and I thought we came into a palace and I used to correspond with my girlfriends overseas and I told them what beautiful things we have. But now when I look back it wasn't really so beautiful."

Source: Russian immigrant who came to the United States in 1923 at age 15. Taped interview from the collection of Vincent N. Parrillo.

Experience box above). Thereafter, Soviet restrictions sharply curtailed Russian emigration, except for those Russians who succeeded in coming to the United States as displaced persons (DPs) after World War II.

Life in the United States

During the boom immigration period, the transplanted Russian peasants stood at the bottom of the socioeconomic ladder in their newly adopted country. Two excerpts, although referring to Russian immigrants, are excellent illustrations of the recurring pattern of any minority experience. They could just as easily be applied to other groups who live or have lived in urban slums. In the first, the editor of a religious newspaper tells in 1916 of the toll exacted by long working hours under wretched conditions:

> Each working day shortens the worker's life for a few months, saps the living juice out of him, dries out the heart, dampens the noblest aspirations of the soul; transforms a living man into a sort of machine, embitters the whole life. The ragged soul and body of the worker bring forth to the world half-sick children, paralytic, idiotic—therefore the factory's poison kills not merely the unfortunate workers, but also whole generations.[32]

Closely related to inhumane working conditions were poor living conditions necessitated by low wages. This timeless commentary by a social worker of the same early period analyzes the effects of the urban ghettos' squalor and apathy on the Russian immigrants:

> Parental neglect, congestion of population, dirty milk, indigestible food, uncleaned streets, with the resulting contaminated atmosphere, the prevalence of infectious diseases, multiplied temptations to break the law. . . . Add a twelve-hour day, and a seven-day week, irregular, casual employment, sub-standard wages, speeding processes which have no regard to human capacities or nervous strains for which the system is unprepared, indecent housing, unsanitary conditions both in home and factory, and we have an explanation amply adequate to account for sub-normal wage earners.[33]

Xenophobia

Many Russian Americans who had worked hard to achieve some economic security in the United States found themselves jobless and unable to find work after the Bolshevik Revolution in 1917. Employers, fearful of any threat to capitalism in the United States, fired their Russian workers lest they be Bolsheviks. Most Russian peasant immigrants were probably ignorant of the ideology of Bolshevism or, in the case of second-generation Americans, more attuned to U.S. **values** and attitudes, but they were identified as "Bolsheviks" simply because of their nationality. Some may have been sympathetic to the Bolshevik regime but only because the Bolsheviks had participated in the overthrow of the hated Czarist government. The thought of spreading the Bolshevik Revolution to the United States, where the political, labor, and social conditions were so different, appears to have been in the minds of only a very small percentage.[34]

Nevertheless, labor unrest and radical agitation during that period caused a strong xenophobic reaction against many foreigners. A. Mitchell Palmer, U.S. Attorney General, stepped into the federal power vacuum caused by the incapacitation of President Wilson. His first target was the Union of Russian Workers, and his men raided 11 of their meeting places in various cities. About a month later, 249 immigrants were deported, many of them forced to leave their wives and children behind in most dire circumstances. The Palmer raids continued with a vast dragnet of eastern Europeans, primarily Russians:

> Officers burst into homes, meeting places, and pool rooms, as often as not seizing everyone in sight. The victims were loaded into trucks, or sometimes marched through the streets handcuffed and chained to one another, and massed by the hundreds at concentration points, usually police stations. . . . Many remained in federal custody for a few hours only; some lay in crowded cells for several weeks without a preliminary hearing. For several days in Detroit eight hundred men were held incommunicado in a windowless corridor, sleeping on the bare stone floor, subsisting on food which their families brought in, and limited to the use of a single drinking fountain and single toilet. Altogether, about three thousand aliens were held for deportation, almost all of them eastern Europeans.[35]

Homegrown opposition to these illegal actions arose, and many of the immigrants were freed, although more than 500 were deported. Expulsion remained an effective weapon of the U.S. government. Eventually, the growing strength of the Congress of Industrial Organizations (CIO) within the labor movement brought immigrant workers a measure of economic security and domestic tranquility.

The Brighton Beach section of Brooklyn, New York, is home to over 50,000 Russian immigrants, many of them Jewish. A walk along the streets of this 25-block neighborhood will reveal numerous examples of its ethnicity in signs, cooking aromas, and spoken language. The signs offering customers a variety of ethnic and U.S. foods illustrate one form of ethnogenesis that immigrants typically experience.

Recent Immigrants

Russian immigration dropped sharply while the communists were in power. Altogether, about 163,000 new immigrants came to the United States between 1921 and 1990. That number was easily surpassed between 1996 and 2006, with the arrival of more than 173,000 Russian immigrants.[36]

Among the many settlement locations of first-generation Russian Americans, large concentrations can be found in Boston, Minneapolis, and Rockville, Maryland. In a 25-block section of Brooklyn called Brighton Beach, nicknamed "Little Odessa" after the Black Sea port, lives the nation's largest Russian population, about 50,000 of the New York City area's 120,000 Russian Jews. Here the emigrés have settled just outside the central shopping district in regional ethnic neighborhoods. The community itself is distinctly Jewish and so thoroughly Russian in its sights, sounds, smells, window signs, and spoken language that the outsider can quickly be either charmed or disoriented.

Thousands of descendants of Russian immigrants belong to the Russian Orthodox Church, which has 157 parishes in the United States.[37] Found in virtually every profession and occupation, Russian Americans preserve their heritage with history centers, newspapers, publishing houses, and organizations.

THE UKRAINIANS

Sometimes called Carpatho-Russians or Little Russians, and until 1992 simply included as part of Soviet Union immigration and refugee statistics, the Ukrainians are among the nationalities who regained independence following the dissolution of the Soviet Union. They have a language and culture distinct from the Russians' and have always maintained their own group identity. The parallel social institutions of Ukrainian Americans not only reflected this fact but became even stronger after World War II to preserve the unity and heritage of U.S.-born generations.

About 700,000 Ukrainians immigrated to the United States by 1914, some of them settling as farmers in the western United States and Canada, but most settling in the urban industrial centers of the Northeast and Midwest, working in factories or coal mines. Wasyl Halich offers a representative example of one Ukrainian group's early contacts with Americans and its fights with Irish American miners, who saw the group as a serious economic threat:

> The experience of the first Ukrainian group in America contains some of the basic elements of that of other pioneers on this continent. When they landed in New York, they did not understand a word of English; their colorful attire attracted much attention, and they were regarded as a curiosity. Being unable to get lodgings, they had to leave the city. They walked to Philadelphia, being forced to sleep outdoors because people were afraid to give shelter to such curious strangers. . . .
>
> This group of immigrants arrived in the mining communities during a labor strike. Not understanding the conditions, or probably because of necessity, they went to work as strike-breakers; consequently they brought upon themselves the hatred of old miners, mostly Irishmen. There were frequent assaults on the strike-breakers which ended in riots. The influx of fresh immigrants tended to keep the wages low, and this prolonged the racial and labor antagonism between the Ukrainian and Irish groups. In connection with this racial animosity not infrequently the newcomer became a victim of "accidental" injury in the mine, or even death.[38]

After World War II, in 1948, Congress passed the Displaced Persons Act, allowing homeless people from war-ravaged Europe to enter, in addition to the annual quota under existing immigration laws. Under this special legislation and with the assistance of many Ukrainian Americans, about 85,000 Ukrainian refugees came to the United States (see The Ethnic Experience box). The new arrivals were better educated, more politically oriented, and better able to adapt to U.S. life than the older immigrants had been.

Since the creation of the independent Ukraine nation in 1992, its citizens have led all other former Soviet "republics," except Russia, in immigrating to the United States. Between 1997 and 2006, over 141,000 Ukrainian immigrants arrived, making the Ukraine one of the largest European suppliers of present-day immigrants.[39]

THE HUNGARIANS

In the 19th century, the Hungarians, or Magyars, were a minority in control of the Kingdom of Hungary. They began a campaign of "Magyarization"—imposing the Magyar language and culture—on all peoples living within their boundaries. As emigration to the United States increased, the Hungarian government financed both Catholic and Protestant churches and various immigrant societies in an unsuccessful effort to maintain its influence over Hungarians living in the United States.

The Ethnic Experience

Education In and Out of the Classroom

"My sister and I were sent to a public school in the local town. This experience was devastating to me since I did not know one word of English. The teacher, who seemed like a friendly person, must have tried with much frustration to communicate with me, but I was frustrated too, and so did what most children do under those circumstances—I turned her off and did what my imagination led me to do. I colored, cut, played imaginary games and had an all-around good time till I finally started to put some of the sounds together and began to realize the meaning of a few English words.

". . . Because we lived in Maryland, race **prejudice** was the first unpleasant and embarrassing situation which my family had to encounter. My father was the only white man to work in the fields. During the lunch break he was allowed to come into the farmhouse to eat while the others ate their lunch outside. Soon my father learned that dark-skinned men were not allowed to eat with fair-skinned men. I heard my parents discussing this problem. Since they did not know American history and did not speak English, they had to figure that for some reason the dark people were not liked in this country. We did not even know what they were called except that the farmer sometimes called them 'niggas,' which later I learned was niggers.

"One day the farmer became very angry because he learned that we were entertaining the other farm hands in our home. My mother, being a good neighbor, invited the other workers to our house for supper. We had pirogis and the men drank corn liquor. The Negro families reciprocated and we were invited to their homes. It seemed a very natural thing to do and we could not understand why the farmer became so excited. During our first six months stay in Maryland, our home must have been the first case of integration in the South and we were not even aware of it.

"Although I was only seven years old at the time, my observations of the treatment which the whites inflicted on the blacks had a lasting effect on me. While riding in the all-white school bus, I was shown the shabby school for the 'niggas.' I could not understand why two schools were needed in the first place. While stopping for food in the town, I saw only whites were served in most stores. No matter where I went, the Blacks were excluded. . . . Looking back, I guess that my education in Maryland did not take place in the segregated public school but on the farm, where I learned more about human behavior than any college course could ever offer."

Source: Ukrainian refugee who came to the United States in 1949 at age 7. Taped interview from the collection of Vincent N. Parrillo.

Like others before and after them, the Hungarians congregated in their own ethnic clusters. Most settled in New Jersey, New York, Ohio, Pennsylvania, Illinois, Indiana, and West Virginia. Cleveland and New York City attracted the greatest concentration of immigrants. In 1920, with more than 76,000 ethnic Hungarian residents, New York City was the "third largest Hungarian city in the world."[40]

In each such ethnic community, the Hungarians established their own institutions and organizations, embodying the same religious division among Catholics, Protestants, and Jews as in their homeland. They established their own social and fraternal organizations to provide benefits to the sick and to pay for funerals. They also founded their own newspapers and nationalistic cultural groups.

Labor Conditions

The United States was seeking industrial workers, so the Hungarians forsook farming and worked instead in the mines, steel factories, and other heavy industries. The labor agitation of the late 19th century—which often turned violent and bloody—usually included Hungarian as well as Lithuanian and Slavic workers.

The most violent episode occurred outside of Hazelton, Pennsylvania in 1897. A posse, headed by a sheriff who was a former mine foreman, fired several vollies [sic] into an unarmed group of 150 strikers, mostly Hungarian, who were marching to a nearby town to urge other miners to join the strike. Twenty-one immigrants were killed and another forty wounded. There was general agreement among other mine foremen that there would have been no bloodshed if the strikers had not been foreign-born.[41]

The prominence of Hungarian immigrants in such brawny occupations as mining and steel, as well as in the labor unrest, led to whites using the **ethnophaulism** *hunky,* an alteration of their proper name, to refer generally to all central European laborers. By the turn of the century, *hunky* had evolved into a universal term for a white roughneck laborer—a redneck—and blacks simply extended it to all whites, using the dialectal pronunciation *honky.* The term *hunky* has now fallen into disuse, but *honky* lingers on as a racial epithet.[42]

A sizable number of these turn-of-the-century immigrants originally came as sojourners, but most eventually stayed. Consequently, their becoming U.S. citizens was a slower process. Members of the Hungarian American community who were naturalized citizens totaled only 15 percent before World War I, 21.1 percent by 1920, and 55.7 percent by 1930.[43]

The number of Hungarians who came to the United States is somewhat difficult to determine exactly because the U.S. government did not distinguish Hungarians from Austrians until 1905, and even ethnic Poles who emigrated from Hungary were recorded as Hungarians until 1919. On the basis of immigration records and the research of Emil Lengyel, however, it appears that more than 2 million Hungarians came to the United States between 1871 and 1920, many from the middle Danube region. As many as half may have returned to their homeland once they had saved enough money.

Recent Immigrants

In the mid-1950s, an entirely different group of Hungarians came to the United States for political rather than economic reasons. When the Soviet Union crushed the Hungarian rebellion in 1956, Congress passed special legislation to circumvent the restrictive national quotas of the McCarran–Walter Bill of 1952. The United States airlifted refugees—families, minors unaccompanied by parents, and students—and gave them temporary shelter at Camp Kilmer, New Jersey. Many volunteer agencies and Hungarian Americans assisted the 30,000 newcomers in their readjustment.

Over 32,000 Hungarians have come to the United States since 1961, averaging now about 1,200 each year. These low numbers suggest the continuing decline of ethnicity in Hungarian American communities, except to observe occasions of situational or symbolic ethnicity as now occur for many European American groups.

THE GYPSIES

Gypsies are perhaps the most elusive U.S. minority. The numbers range from less than 100,000, according to the Census Bureau, to more than 1 million, according to some of their leaders.[44] Several factors account for this: census and immigration authorities have never kept official statistics on them; Gypsies actively discourage any form of "snooping"; and often they do not reveal themselves to be Gypsies.

Who are the Gypsies? Their major distinguishing characteristics are language and culture. They speak Romany, a form of Sanskrit, which has enabled researchers to trace their origins to northern India.[45] Gypsy culture distinguishes between the Rom (Gypsies) and the *gadje* (others). Words that distinguish between the ingroup and the outgroup in this way are quite common in tribal societies. When individual Gypsies assimilate into the dominant culture, they are no longer considered Gypsies by the Rom. Thus, we must view the Gypsies as a persistent subculture maintaining a unique cultural system.

Throughout the second half of the 17th century, Gypsies from Scotland came to work on Virginia plantations. Records indicate that Gypsies also settled among the French in Louisiana, the Germans in Pennsylvania, and the Dutch in New Amsterdam.[46] Repressive actions against them in England in the 1840s prompted Gypsy migration to the United States in substantial numbers.[47] The Nazis exterminated somewhere between 300,000 and 500,000 Gypsies, and they remained generally unwelcome throughout Europe after World War II, so many legal and illegal Gypsy immigrants undoubtedly came to the United States during the postwar period. Our only evidence for this, however, is their increased visibility at that time.

Cultural Differentiation

At the core of Gypsy culture is the family (the *familia*), which is actually a functional **extended family**. Parents, siblings, aunts, uncles, cousins, assorted other relatives, and adopted children all live and work together, caring for one another in times of joy and sorrow.[48] The *familia* is an effective support institution for all problems, offering also a safe refuge from the *gadje*. The second unit of identity for the Rom is the *vitsa*, a clan or band of a few to more than a hundred *familiyi*, forming a cognitive kinship group of affiliation through which Gypsies classify one another.[49]

The *familia* is strongly patriarchal, with males working for short spans of time in various trades: roofing, driveway blacktopping, auto-body repair, scrap metal, and carnival work.[50] Women provide a valuable source of income, usually from fortune-telling, which the Rom practice only with the *gadje*, not among themselves.[51] Parents do not force matches, but are the principals in the mate-selection process, encouraging marriages within the *vitsa* beyond first-cousin relationships. A bride price, or *daro* goes toward the bride's trousseau, wedding festivities, and household articles for the new couple.[52]

Most Gypsies marry between the ages of 12 and 16, seldom over 18 for a first marriage—their youthfulness no doubt contributing to the high rate of failed Gypsy marriages. The wife traditionally lives with her husband's family and is known as a *bori*, subject to the supervision of her in-laws.[53] Elopements have increased and romantic love is more accepted preceding still-arranged marriages, but Rom–*gadje* intermarriages account for fewer than 6 percent of all Gypsy marriages.[54]

Rom culture has as its linchpin the concept of *marimé*, which extends to all areas of life. The term, which means "defilement" or "pollution," refers to rigid lines between good and bad, clean and unclean, health and disease, Rom and *gadje*.[55] Most notable is its application to the upper and lower halves of the human body. The pure and clean upper portion cannot come into contact in any way with the lower portion, which is *marimé*, or with objects that have been in contact with it. For example, each person uses soaps and towels of different colors for the two body portions.[56] A woman brings shame on herself for exposing too much leg, but breasts are unashamedly squeezed by both men and women.[57] A *marimé* woman—one who has recently given birth or is having her monthly period—cannot cook or serve food to men, step over anything belonging to a man, or allow her skirts to touch his things.[58]

> The *gadje* are conceived as a different race whose main value is economic, and whose raison d'être is to trouble the Rom. The major offense of the *gadje*, the one offense the Rom can never forgive, is their propensity to defilement. *Gadje* confuse the critical distinction between the pure and the impure. They are observed in situations which the Rom regard as compromising; forgetting to wash in public bathrooms; eating with the fork that they rescued from the floor of the restaurant; washing face towels and tablecloths with underwear at the laundromat; relaxing with their feet on the top of the table.
>
> Because they do not protect the upper half of the body, the *gadje* are construed as *marimé* all over, head to foot.[59]

Gypsy sexual mores concerning intimacy are very strict, an outgrowth of their normally confined living arrangements and their social structure. Premarital chastity remains highly regarded, and Gypsy women rarely resort to prostitution. Birth control and abortions are rare, so their birth rate is very high. Because Gypsies do not officially record births, our only information on the birth rate comes from case studies. Peter Maas, for example, reported in 1975 on one couple who had 14 children and 76 grandchildren, most under 30 years of age; these grandchildren had already produced 183 children, with more likely to come.[60] Although most Roma families today may not be as large, their high birth rate continues to increase their U.S. population size.

The safety valve within the social organization is the *kris*, or Gypsy court. Through an effective grapevine, Gypsies send word to the different tribes of the time and place of the *kris*. Much like Native American chieftains at a powwow, the tribal leaders confer, settle disputes, and place restraints on more powerful members. The most potent social sanction is shunning—no longer acknowledging someone as a Rom. Because Gypsies spend virtually all their waking moments in group activities with other Rom, shunning is a feared social death that keeps the Rom effectively in line.[61] The *kris* operates with ceremonial dignity; it forms the social cement that binds Gypsy society together. Once the court matters are concluded, the *kris* becomes an occasion for general feasting, renewal of friendships, bartering, and bridal matchings because such large gatherings are infrequent.

Evasive Pluralism

Although most Gypsies have a home base, they maintain a fondness for travel. This mobility orientation rests partly on their association of travel with freedom, health, and good luck and of settling down with illness and bad luck. Job opportunities, social visits, and evasion of *gadje* authorities are other motives. Part of their avoidance pattern includes posing as Arabs, Armenians, Greeks, Mexicans, Puerto Ricans, and other local ethnics to obtain jobs, housing, and welfare. They are so successful in doing so that many Americans are unaware that there are any Gypsies in America.[62]

The Gypsies have kept their tribal codes and morals virtually unchanged in an urbanized and industrialized society by remaining outside the educational institutions and being passively antagonistic to the larger society. Although they are highly conscious of ritual, Gypsies survive through adaptation to their environment. Despite enormous pressure from every society in which Gypsies have lived, they have retained their identity and resisted assimilation. Gypsies live mostly in cities, about 10,000 in Chicago and 15,000 in Los Angeles. They reside in all states, but their largest concentrations are in New York, Virginia, Illinois, Texas, Massachusetts, and along the Pacific Coast.[63]

THE ITALIANS

Despite their small numbers, the first Italians to come to the New World included some important early explorers. Cristoforo Colombo (Columbus), Giovanni Cabotto (John Cabot), Amerigo Vespucci, and Giovanni de Verrazano all explored and charted the new land. Father Marcos da Nizza explored Arizona in 1539, and other Italians were among the settlers throughout the colonies. Filippo Mazzei influenced the writings and the farming of his neighbor Thomas Jefferson. Many Italians fought in the American Revolution, the Civil War, and the other wars that followed. Antonio Meucci invented the first primitive version of the telephone 26 years before Alexander Graham Bell, and Constantino Brumidi painted the frescoes in the rotunda of the U.S. Capitol building.

Throughout the 19th century, parallels and relationships existed between Italians and blacks. In some pre–Civil War southern localities, futile efforts were made to replace black slaves with Italian workers. In other areas, Southerners barred Italian children from white schools because of their dark complexions. Union General Edward Ferraro commanded an all-black combat division during the Civil War. In 1899, five Sicilian storekeepers were hanged in Tallulah, Louisiana, for the crime of treating black customers the same as whites.

The Great Migration

Of the more than 5.4 million Italians who have come to the United States throughout its history, 80 percent came between 1880 and 1920 (see The Ethnic Experience box, page 192). Many Italian males engaged in "shuttle migration," going back and forth between the United States and Italy. Fleeing abject poverty and economic disaster in the harsh *Mezzogiorno* east and south of Rome, they quickly became so visible to U.S. society that they were subject to vicious anti-Italian bigotry.

Most Italian immigrants were peasants from rural areas and thus ill prepared for employment in an industrial nation. As a result, they labored in low-status, low-paying manual jobs as railroad laborers, miners, and longshoremen; in construction, they dug ditches, laid sewer pipes, and built roads, subways, and other basic structures in urban areas.

Societal Hostility

Strong hostility against Italian immigrants sometimes resulted in violence and even killings. Several Italians were lynched in West Virginia in 1891. That same year, when 10 Sicilians were acquitted by a jury of having killed the New Orleans police

The Ethnic Experience

Bewilderment and Adjustment

"We came here on a large ship in 1910. We had a rough time coming here with storms and all, and my big sister was deadly sick. She never lifted her head up from her berth. It was a very long trip, about thirteen days, and the waters were rough. And when we got to Ellis Island, we were so happy to get out of that ship.

"When we got there my daddy was waiting for us and we got some nice gifts from the attendants in Ellis Island—who got a doll, who got a jumping jack. But the funniest part was when they were selling bananas in the room, and my brother thought they were peppers and he wanted a pepper and discovered they were bananas.

"When my father took us down to the street, we heard a different language. We looked at each other. We went to my mother. We didn't know what they were saying, maybe they were talking about us. My father said, 'Don't worry. That's the language they speak here and you'll learn it yourself very fast.'

"Then my dad took us on a train to Old Forge, Pennsylvania, where he had rented rooms for us and we lived there six months. They were mostly all Polish people and German, and my mother didn't feel at home with no Italians around. My mother wanted to move to Paterson, New Jersey, because there were more Italian people there, but here she didn't understand anybody. And that's what we did. There were all Italians on the street where we lived. My dad was a musician but the other Italian immigrants worked on the trolley tracks, digging trolley tracks or to make streets.

"I got in right away with all the kids. They were all very friendly with me. As soon as recess used to come, they used to be in a playground. They would all come around me and they would talk to me in English, which helped me pick it up right away."

Source: Italian immigrant who came to the United States in 1910 at age 8. Taped interview from the collection of Vincent N. Parrillo.

chief, an angry mob that included many of the city's leading citizens stormed the prison and executed them, adding an 11th victim who had been serving a minor sentence for a petty crime. Four years later, coal miners and other residents of a southern Colorado town murdered six Italians. In 1896, three Italians were torn from a jail in Hahnsville, Louisiana, and hanged. In a southern Illinois mining town, after a street brawl in 1914 that left one Italian and two native-born U.S. citizens dead, a lynch mob hanged the only survivor, an Italian, seemingly with the approval of the town's mayor. A few months later, another Italian was lynched in a nearby town after being arrested on suspicion of conspiracy to murder a mining supervisor. No evidence to substantiate the charge existed other than his nationality.

In Massachusetts, Nicola Sacco and Bartolomeo Vanzetti—an immigrant shoe-factory worker and a poor fish peddler—were charged with and convicted of robbery and murder in 1920. The prosecutor insulted immigrant Italian defense witnesses and appealed to the prejudices of a bigoted judge and jury. Despite someone else's later confession and other potentially exonerating evidence, their seven-year appeals fight failed to win them retrial or acquital; they were executed in 1927. At his sentencing in 1927, Vanzetti addressed presiding Judge Webster Thayer, saying,

I would not wish to a dog or a snake, to the most low and misfortunate creature of the earth—I would not wish to any of them what I have had to suffer for the things that I am not guilty of. . . . I have suffered because I was an Italian, and indeed I am an Italian.[64]

These incidents are extreme examples of U.S. reaction to the Italian immigrants. Because they arrived in large numbers, the public became increasingly aware of their presence, and Italian Americans quickly became stereotyped as possessing all the objectionable traits the dominant group perceived in the "swarm" of immigrants coming to the United States. When an Italian got into trouble, newspaper headlines often magnified the event and stressed the offender's nationality.[65] Italians, like Jews, found certain occupations, fraternities, clubs, and organizations closed to them, and restrictive covenants excluded them from certain areas of the city and suburbs.

Social Patterns

The Italians settled mainly in urban "Little Italys"—such as the North End of Boston, Mulberry Street in New York City's Lower East Side, the area to the northwest of Chicago's Loop, and San Francisco's North Beach district. Often, families from the same village lived together in the same tenement. Earning poor wages as part of the unskilled labor force, the new Italian immigrants moved into rundown residential areas vacated by earlier arrivals whose children and grandchildren had moved up the socioeconomic ladder. Their numbers enabled them to create an Italian community replete with Italian stores, newspapers, theaters, social clubs, parishes, and schools. Because of their parochial and family orientations, however, they failed to establish groupwide institutions.[66]

New York's Little Italy section no longer teems with hundreds of thousands of first-generation Italian American residents as it did in the past. Each year, however, it easily attracts millions of visitors, Italian and non-Italian alike, to its restaurants and sidewalk cafés throughout the year and to its Feast of San Gennaro street fair each September.

A variant of the extended-family system of southern Italian society was adapted to Italian life in the United States. Relatives were the principal focus of social life, and non-Italians were usually regarded as outsiders. True interethnic friendships rarely developed. Moreover, individual achievement (a U.S. tradition) was not strongly encouraged. More important were family honor, group stability, and social cohesion and cooperation. Each member of the family was expected to contribute to the economic well-being of the family unit.

In the old country, absentee landowners had commonly exploited Italian tenant farmers, and priests and educators had silently supported this inequitable system, rarely welcoming peasant children in the schools. Landowner resistance to the political unification of Italy, which finally occurred in 1870, further increased the hardships of tenant farmers and small landholders. Consequently, Italian immigrants generally mistrusted priests and educated people.[67] In the United States, as in Italy, the common people—especially males—had little involvement with the church, and schooling was regarded as having limited practical value. Children attended school, for the most part, only as long as the law demanded; then they were sent to work to increase the family income. A few families did not follow this pattern, but most second-generation Italian Americans who attended college did so against the wishes of their families.

> The outside world continued to be a source of deprivation and exploitation. . . . Situated on the lowest rung of the occupational hierarchy, they were exploited by their employers and by the "padrone," the agent who acted as middleman between the immigrants and the labor market. Moreover, the churches in the immigrant neighborhoods were staffed largely by Irish priests, who practiced a strange and harsh form of Catholicism, and had little sympathy for the Madonna and the local saints that the Italians respected. The caretaking agencies and the political machines were run by Yankees and other ethnic groups. As a result of the surrounding strangeness, the immigrants tried to retain the self-sufficiency of the family circle as much as they could. They founded a number of community organizations that supported this circle, and kept away from the outside world whenever possible.[68]

Marginality

First-generation Italian Americans, reinforced by the great majority of their compatriots, retained much of their language and customs. The second generation became more Americanized, producing a strain between the two generations. Italians who did not settle or remain long in the Little Italys assimilated much more quickly. Some changed their names and religion to accelerate the process.

In his study *Street Corner Society,* William Foote Whyte commented on the problems of marginality experienced by Italian American boys:

> Some ask, "Why can't those people stop being Italians and become Americans like the rest of us?" The answer is that they are blocked in two ways: by their own organized society and by the outside world. Cornerville people want to be good American citizens. I have never heard such moving expressions of love for this country as I have heard in Cornerville. Nevertheless, an organized way of life cannot be changed overnight. As the study of the corner gang shows, people became dependent upon certain routines of action. If they broke away abruptly from these routines, they would feel themselves disloyal and would be left helpless, without support. And, if a man wants to forget that he is an Italian, the

society around him does not let him forget it. He is marked as an inferior person—like all other Italians. To bolster his own self-respect he must tell himself and tell others that the Italians are a great people, that their culture is second to none, and that their great men are unsurpassed.[69]

Social Mobility

Upward mobility occurred more slowly for the Italians than for other groups arriving in the United States at about the same time, such as the Greeks, Armenians, and Jews. Many factors we have already discussed contributed to this situation—a retreatist lifestyle, disdain for education, negative stereotyping, and overt dominant-group hostility protracted by the continuing flow of new Italian immigrants. Sheltered within their ethnic communities in various large U.S. cities, the Italians gradually adapted to industrial society. They joined the working class and encouraged their children to do likewise as soon as they were able.

Second-generation adults, although drawn to *la via nuova*—"the new way"—through schools, movies, and other cultural influences, still adhered to a **social structure** centered on the extended family. Expected to contribute to the family's support early in life, they followed their parents into working-class occupations without benefit of the extended education necessary to secure higher-status jobs. Today, the picture has changed. Third- and fourth-generation Italian Americans are attaining educational levels comparable to those of other white ethnic groups; they are mostly middle class and well represented in the professional fields.

Intermarriage, or marital assimilation, is a primary indicator of structural assimilation, the last phase of minority-group mainstreaming. Exogamy among Italian Americans, especially among those three and four generations removed from the old country, exceeds 40 percent, which is similar to that of most European American groups.[70] As structural assimilation proceeds, Richard D. Alba suggests, all Americans of European ancestry are entering "the twilight of ethnicity." Twilight, says Alba, is an appropriate metaphor because ethnic community remnants and differences do remain, with occasional flare-ups of ethnic feelings and conflicts; still, this ethnicity is "little more than flickers in the fading light" as social assimilation increases.[71]

Today, Italian Americans still find themselves the target of prejudicial accusations concerning their allegedly prominent role in criminal activities, a stereotype perpetuated in films and television. Despite their progressive assimilation, the perception of members of this group as potential criminals or as part of the Mafia-connection stereotype still persists. Its persistence haunts politicians of Italian descent, undermines voters' trust in them, and thus limits their political success.[72]

▰▰▰ THE GREEKS

Most of the Greeks who came to the United States in the early 20th century did not expect to stay long. They came as sojourners, planning to make money and then return to Greece. For many, the dowry system was an important "push" factor. Fathers and brothers found they could earn more money in the United States than in their homeland, so these Greek men journeyed here to earn the money necessary to provide substantial dowries for the prospective brides in their families. The fact that 95 percent of all Greek immigrants were male encouraged them to return home to their women.

Occupational Distribution

Many Greeks worked as laborers on railroad construction gangs or in factories. Those who did often were under the control of a *padrone,* who, like the Italian *padroni,* acted as a labor agent and paternal figure. Abuses were common in this system. Other Greek immigrants operated small businesses of many types, although Greeks came to be identified particularly with candy stores and restaurants:

> The association of Greeks with candy and food was proverbial. Chicago became the center of their sweets trade, and in 1904 a Greek newspaperman observed that "Practically every busy corner in Chicago is occupied by a Greek candy store." After World War II the Greeks still maintained 350 to 450 confectionary shops and eight to ten candy manufacturers in the Windy City. Most Americans still connect the Greeks with restaurants and for good reason. Almost every major American city boasts of its fine Greek eating establishments, a tradition that goes back more than half a century. After World War I, for example, estimates were that the Greeks owned 564 restaurants in San Francisco alone.[73]

For many Greeks, the restaurant provided a relatively stable economic base and higher social status. Restaurant owners enjoyed more esteem than peddlers or manual laborers. Because so many immigrants sought a career in the restaurant business (and still do), they continuously interacted with the general public. A 1901 government survey showed Greeks faring better than Poles; at present, most Greeks, except the newest arrivals, are economically secure, and many are in the upper middle class.[74] Greek Americans hold jobs in most middle-class occupations, although the restaurant business appeals mostly to the first generation.

Social Patterns

Although they came from a predominantly agricultural country, Greeks settled primarily in the cities. Like so many other ethnic groups, they gathered in ethnic residential enclaves, or "Greek colonies," within the major cities. A *kinotis,* or community council, served as the governing body; it was responsible for establishing and staffing schools and churches and for promoting the general welfare of the community. The *kaffeneion,* or coffeehouse, played a very important role, as Theodore Saloutos reports:

> It was to the coffeehouse that the immigrant hurried after his arrival from Greece or from a neighboring community. It was in the coffeehouse that he sought out acquaintances, addresses, leads to jobs, and solace during the lonely hours. . . .
>
> The coffeehouse was a community social center to which the men returned after working hours and on Saturdays and Sundays. Here they sipped cups of thick, black Turkish coffee, lazily drew on narghiles, played cards, or engaged in animated political discussion. Here congregated gesticulating Greeks of all kinds: railroad workers, factory hands, shopkeepers, professional men, the unemployed, labor agitators, amateur philosophers, community gossips, card-sharks, and amused spectators.[75]

Favorable working conditions induced many Greek males to remain in the United States. But because they preferred **endogamous** marriage, they often returned home to marry a Greek woman, or they sent money home to pay for the passage of a wife or wife-to-be. Like other immigrant peoples of this period, the Greeks maintained close family ties. The father was the unchallenged head of the household. Children were raised to be strictly obedient and had specific chores assigned to them. They studied Greek in addition to their regular classes at public schools and were frequently admonished to work hard and take advantage of the opportunities their parents had not had. Greeks placed a high value on education and encouraged their children to enter the professions.

The Greek church—the Eastern Orthodox Church—and the Greek press bolstered Greek American solidarity. In addition, many organizations encouraged cohesiveness. The most notable of these was the American Hellenic Educational Progressive Association (AHEPA), founded in 1922. Its purpose was to preserve the Greek heritage and to help immigrants understand the new country's way of life.

In their process of ethnogenesis, Greek Americans have blended aspects of **pluralism** (fierce love of homeland, pride in their heritage, slowness to become citizens, endogamy, and institutional agencies) with aspects of assimilation (geographic and occupational dispersion, low visibility, and relatively high socioeconomic status). Cultural pluralism has been an important element in their adaptation to U.S. society.

Societal Reaction

Not all early Greek immigrants adjusted smoothly to U.S. society. Many young males, unencumbered by family discipline and village controls, got into trouble with the law. Sociologist Henry Pratt Fairchild held a prejudiced, stereotyped view of the Greeks and other foreigners in the United States. He was especially concerned about the overrepresentation of Greek immigrants among law violators. His comments about the effects of concentration in Greek communities reflect his pessimism about their assimilating or even being a benefit to U.S. society, and his underlying ideas contain elements of the culture-of-poverty thesis developed in the 1960s with respect to Puerto Ricans, Mexicans, and blacks. Fairchild stated that the negative values in the Greek community would remain until effective interaction commenced with members of the better (i.e., middle) class. He also favored diffusion and dispersal of Greeks:

> It seems likely that the presence of this race [Greeks] in the country will add to, rather than diminish, the growing indifference to law as such, which is one of the most threatening signs of the times. This lack of reverence for law, and every form of authority, seems to be characteristic of every race. But the Greeks appear to have it when they come. What the character of their children will be in this respect we can only conjecture. . . . It has been frequently remarked in the course of the preceding discussion, that the evil tendencies of Greek life in this country manifest themselves most fully when the immigrants are collected into compact, isolated, distinctively Greek colonies, and that when the Greek is separated from the group and thrown into relations with Americans of the better class, he develops and displays many admirable qualities.[76]

Today, Greek Americans are a model of a nationality group that has been accepted by the dominant group, has achieved economic security, and has become

Americanized, yet has also retained a strong pride in its ethnicity. New Greek arrivals are low, about 1,200 annually, but the Greek American community retains its ethnic vitality, and its church and festivals provide continuing sources of ethnic pride and identity. Greek coffee shops, benefiting from the recent popularity of espresso bars, prosper, as do Greek restaurants, such as in Manhattan, near 86th Street and Second Avenue, where a dozen Greek merchants vie with one another in providing authentic and varied cuisine.[77]

THE PORTUGUESE

Although it is a relatively small country, Portugal has provided the United States with more than half a million immigrants of varying economic and cultural backgrounds. Whether their manner of adaptation was assimilationist or nonassimilationist has depended on the part of the United States to which they migrated.

Early Immigrants

In the 18th and 19th centuries, Portuguese immigrants—whites from the Azores Islands and blacks from the Cape Verde Islands—primarily settled in New England and occupied an important place in the fishing industry. These Portuguese had been whalers and fishermen for many generations. Recruited by business agents for their expertise, they came and settled in such coastal port cities as New Bedford and Newport. Although the Portuguese were predominantly Catholic, the Jews among them erected one of the first synagogues in the United States, in Newport in 1763.

Other Portuguese, some from the mainland and of Moorish lineage, worked on farms and in dairies. They started as farm laborers and then rented and eventually bought old New England farms as these became available. As new Portuguese immigrants continued to arrive and U.S. industry grew, the newcomers turned to factory work; the majority of New England's Portuguese Americans were working in factories shortly after the turn of the 20th century.

A few thousand Portuguese went to California, lured by the gold rush. Many others followed in typical chain-migration fashion. Some Portuguese went to the Hawaiian Islands in the late 19th century. By 1920, about 84,000 Portuguese lived in New England; most of the rest lived in California and Hawaii. Because transportation for laborers and their families was guaranteed, and they had labor contracts from the Hawaiian plantation owners, they willingly made the long journey.

Those in Hawaii assimilated, whereas those in California, encountering little conflict, retained their ethnic identity and sense of community to a much greater extent. The reason for this difference seems to be that the Portuguese quickly became a sizable portion of the workforce on Hawaiian pineapple and sugar plantations—about 12 percent of the population. The dominant group, from northern Europe, identified itself separately through a special census classification and stereotyped the Portuguese as inferior. The Portuguese reacted by continuing to work hard, moving into crafts and skilled trades that paid better, and intermarrying and surrendering the usual accouterments of ethnic visibility—

language, customs, residential clustering, and sometimes even their names—to achieve greater respect from the dominant group.

> There is a wide cultural differentiation between the Portuguese in the Island setting and those in California today [1941]. Four decades of separation have shown the influence that environment can have in remolding a people. Although there have been changes in the cultural patterns of the Portuguese in California, it is in Hawaii, where the Portuguese people have gone through the processes of competition, conflict, accommodation, and assimilation and have broken down social distance, that the distinction from old-world family patterns [is most evident].[78]

As demonstrated by the experiences of other groups, once again the adaptation of strangers in a new land moved along a continuum that could or could not end in total assimilation. The Portuguese in Hawaii and in California present two distinct yet successful patterns that reflect different structural conditions.

Later Immigrants

As it inspired other immigrant groups, the Industrial Revolution spurred the Portuguese to migrate to the United States. Beginning in the late 19th century and peaking in 1921 (after which immigration quotas restricted their numbers), 200,000 came, many to work in the mills of Massachusetts and Rhode Island. Their adaptation from Old World life as rural peasants to low-level laborers in an urban setting also parallels that of other ethnic groups. Initially, they clung to their old ways and restricted their social relations to their own kind.

In an analysis of two Portuguese American communities in New England in the late 1920s, Donald Taft noted a high rate of infant mortality and a low level of educational achievement. This lack of interest in education may have been due to an occupational preference for farming and fishing, as well as to a high rate of adult illiteracy.[79] Like Judge Thayer with the Italians and Fairchild with the Greeks, Taft allowed his ethnocentric biases about social class disparities to color his assessment of the Portuguese:

> There seems no doubt that for the majority of Portuguese, immigration to New England has meant an improved status. Granting that they are poverty-stricken here, that they live far below our standards of comfort and decency, that women often work outside the home and that children leave school as soon as the law allows, that homes are unattractive and wages low; nevertheless their lot is far better than in the homeland, except perhaps in its picturesqueness. America gives the Portuguese a small wage but a higher one, a poor house but a better one, a meager sixth grade education but more than they know enough to want, and it is universal and compulsory.
>
> . . . The presence of these people undoubtedly handicaps the public health organizations, increases the births where they should be fewest, and the death rates of all ages but especially of little children. It also makes possible economic and political exploitation whether by unscrupulous natives or by their own leaders. Indeed the presence of the Portuguese goes far to account for the poor record of our two communities [Fall River and Portsmouth] in official statistics and for the not altogether enviable reputation which they may have among sociologists.[80]

Portuguese Americans partied in the Ironbound section of Newark, New Jersey, when Portugal defeated four opponents to reach the 2006 World Cup semi-finals, before bowing to France. This four-generations-old Portuguese neighborhood is popular for its many ethnic restaurants, cafes, bakeries, and grocery stores.

Although they are now scattered throughout the nation, Portuguese Americans are concentrated in Massachusetts, Rhode Island, California, Hawaii, and Newark, New Jersey, where *Luso-American,* the only Portuguese-language national weekly newspaper in the United States, is still published. A steady flow of new immigrants from Portugal has replenished the Portuguese communities. In the 1960s, the numbers of arrivals increased sharply because of political unrest and worsening economic conditions in Portugal, ultimately reaching a total of about 76,000. Chain migration and continuing push–pull factors caused the number of Portuguese immigrants to rise to about 102,000 in the 1970s. In recent decades those numbers dropped dramatically, and presently just slightly more than 1,000 arrive annually (see Appendix).

THE ARMENIANS

Armenian immigrants settled in Jamestown in 1619. In that year, Armenian workers, together with some Germans and Poles, went on strike to secure political rights that were denied to them as "inferiors." The Virginia House of Burgesses granted them full colonist's rights in response to this early civil rights protest.[81]

Confusion over Refugee Identity

After coming under the rule of the Ottoman Empire after 1375, as Christians in a Muslim country, the Armenians became a special target of authoritarian, religiously intolerant rulers. Better educated and more prosperous than the Turks, the latter suspected them of wanting political power. Over the years, Armenians migrated to the United States for religious, political, and economic reasons, but the Turkish government's campaign of **annihilation** against them between 1894 and 1916 was the primary reason for their movement to the United States. In 1915–1916 alone, the Turks and their surrogates killed 1 million Armenians.[82]

Because they traveled with Turkish passports and the U.S. government identified immigrants by country of origin, Armenians and Syrian Christians were classified upon entry into the United States as Turks. It is therefore difficult to determine exactly how many Armenians came to the United States in the late 19th century. However, government estimates place the number of Armenian immigrants for the period between 1895 and 1899 at 70,982. The Turkish government then cut off further emigration until 1915. Because of World War I, only a few thousand reached the United States until the 1920s, when 26,000 Armenians arrived.[83] After that, although Armenians continued to emigrate, their actual numbers were further obscured because the U.S. government identified them by their point of departure (usually Egypt, France, Lebanon, Iraq, Iran, Turkey, or Syria). However, in the 2000 Census, more than 385,000 Americans declared Armenian ancestry.

Societal Reaction

As indicated in the early social distance scales of Emory Bogardus, U.S. public opinion and stereotypes of the Turks were extremely negative, in part because of the atrocities committed against the Armenians.[84] Nonetheless, when Armenians attempted to become U.S. citizens, the federal government tried to stop them. The issue was resolved in 1925 in a U.S. district court case brought by Tatos O. Cartozian, an Armenian rug merchant in Portland, Oregon. The government argued that Armenians were of Asiatic descent and thus not eligible for citizenship under the 1790 Naturalization Act, which allowed only whites to become citizens. By this time, Asians were the only group of people ineligible for citizenship; persons of African descent were accorded the right to citizenship by the Fourteenth Amendment. After hearing expert testimony to the effect that Armenians were Indo-European in language and origin, the court ruled in favor of Cartozian.

Cultural Differentiation

Armenians have a long cultural history because of their resilience in maintaining their cultural identity. Their language and religion are two contributing factors. Not only do Armenians speak their own language, but they have their own alphabet, increasing ingroup solidarity. The Armenian Apostolic Church—the oldest national Christian church in the world, dating from the third century—never sought converts among other nationalities and functions as more than a religious institution. Armenian art, architecture, literature, philosophy, and music are heavily interwoven in the fabric of the church. As Gary Kulhanjian reports,

The Armenian Church was and still is a fortress for preserving the cultural identity of Armenians in the world. Religion, social organizations, ethnocentrism, family life, and endogamy had all been potent social forces by which Armenians or Americans of Armenian descent have been culturally identifiable.[85]

Another important factor in Armenian cohesiveness has been family life, but the assimilation process appears to be weakening some traditional practices, particularly that of endogamy. Although some second- and third-generation Armenian Americans still marry within their group, a greater number do not, and most still retain their subcultural identity with the Church.[86]

Armenians Today

Approximately half of the Armenian American population resides in California, largely in the cities of Glendale, Fresno, Los Angeles, and San Francisco. They have their own state-approved American-Armenian International College at LaVerne, in Los Angeles, as well as two endowed chairs in Armenian Studies at UCLA.[87]

Other large concentrations are in Michigan, New Jersey, New York, and New England. About 50,000 Armenians currently live in and around Boston. A walk around Watertown's Coolidge Square (the "Main Street" of the Boston area's Armenian community) today finds a concentration of Armenian-run businesses. It is common to hear the Armenian language spoken and see it written on store signs. The region is home to many Armenian organizations, including more than a dozen churches, three newspapers, and the Armenian Library and Museum of America.[88]

IMMIGRANT WOMEN AND WORK

Within the immigrant communities, gender played an important role in the organization of economic activities. Although men sought employment in a variety of occupations, cultural norms dictated that married women should not work outside the home. Indeed, less than 5 percent did so in 1890, often only because their husbands were disabled, missing, or unemployed. Typically, the wife's role was to maintain the house. If family needs required her income because the children were too young to work, then she would take on work at home (e.g., laundry, sewing, or crafts) or else care for boarders (a common practice given the high number of male immigrants).[89]

The world of work for women thus fell mostly to the young and single. More than half of all gainfully employed women at the turn of the century were between 16 and 24 years old. These young women were often employed in factories or mills in "suitable" positions such as machine tenders or seamstresses, perhaps, or else as assemblers, inspectors, packers, and the like in various types of garment, textile, tobacco, or other manufacturing plants.[90]

About a third of all employed female workers at this time were blue-collar workers. Another third were domestic workers: maids, cooks, nannies, and so on. The final third of female workers were usually not first-generation Americans. Employed women in this category were in such white-collar positions as nurse, teacher, or salesclerk.[91]

An expanding economy and population and the institution of child labor laws (not applicable to agriculture) brought about an increase in jobs for women. Included in the significant rise of female participation in the nonfarm labor force were married women as well. By 1920, 1 in 5 paid workers was a woman, and 1 in 10 married women (twice that of 1890) had become a wage earner.[92]

SOUTHERN, CENTRAL, AND EASTERN EUROPEAN ASSIMILATION

With so massive and complex a migration and settlement pattern, no general assessment of acculturation and assessment is possible for these many ethnic groups. Strikingly different in appearance, culture, customs, language, and often religion, societal reaction (often negative, sometimes exploitive) was more uniform to their presence than was their adjustment to the new society. At first, most experienced the social isolation and social distance that new-comers typically do, but these were also accentuated this time by racism, as illustrated in Madison Grant's book discussed earlier in this chapter.[93] Whether in rural or urban locales, most remained socially segregated in flourishing ethnic communities with a strong social network and where endogamy was the norm.

For many immigrants, the transition from an agrarian to an industrial society was difficult. Those who came from an urban background or had to adapt as a subordinate minority group in Europe, such as the Jews and Armenians, adjusted to city life more easily. They took advantage of educational opportunities, climbed the socioeconomic ladder when possible, and adapted to U.S. society. Others, consisting predominantly of illiterate peasants, took longer to get established. Not all the immigrants became citizens, and not all were successful; some did not even learn English.

Although educational values and opportunities aided the assimilation of Armenians, Greeks, and Jews, other groups from this part of Europe took one or two generations longer to enter the mainstream. The labor movement, filled with sacrifice and turmoil, was a significant factor in their achieving economic security, which in turn led to better education for the children and eventual entry into the mainstream. Still, by 1971, their assimilation was far from complete, leading social critic Michael Novak to call this group of Europeans the "unmeltable ethnics."[94]

Yet over the generations, even as they shed their ethnolinguistic marks that distinguished these white ethnics from other white Americans, those who were Catholics and Jews still encountered prejudice because of their faiths. Their continuance as the target for ethnophaulisms, ethnic "humor," and stereotyping is an unfortunate legacy from those intolerant times. Interestingly, just as their cultural and physical differences aided the social acceptance of northern and western Europeans in earlier times, so too are the cultural and physical differences of the majority of today's immigrants enhancing the social acceptance of those whose heritage is from southern, central, or eastern Europe.

▰▰▰ SOCIOLOGICAL ANALYSIS

In this chapter, our examination of immigrants from diverse backgrounds has necessarily covered a wide range of material. By applying the three major sociological perspectives, however, we can identify unifying themes of common experiences in dominant–minority relations.

The Functionalist View

From the functionalist viewpoint, the arrival of significant numbers of immigrants served the rapidly industrializing nation well. Immigrants provided a valuable labor pool to meet the needs of an expanding economy, enabling the United States to emerge as an industrial giant. Unemployment during this era was not a problem, and the poor of Europe were able to build a better life for themselves in their adopted land. Despite nativist fears, the freedom and economic opportunities created fervently patriotic citizens among the newcomers. Later, political and war refugees, many of them talented and highly skilled people, augmented this hardworking, freedom-loving population. The U.S. social system evolved into a complex, interdependent, and prosperous society, in large measure through the efforts of its first- and second-generation European Americans.

Accompanying problems of overcrowded tenements, social disorganization, crime, harsh working conditions, labor strife, and ethnic antagonism can all be understood within the context of rapid social change. For poor immigrants unable to afford better housing, the tenements at least offered a place to begin life anew, while also providing a dense concentration of compatriots for a social support system.

For many, the abrupt change of life—language, customs, and urban living—introduced problems of adjustment resulting in various pathologies of behavior. The abuses of the industrial age—child labor, poor wages, wretched working conditions, and lack of security—caused severe hardship for many workers, but these factors were overcome in time through legislative safeguards and labor union organization. Massive immigration, especially during the first two decades of the 20th century, further strained society's capacity to absorb the newcomers, prolonging the assimilation process and fostering negative reactions from the U.S. native-born population. Gradually, the necessary adjustments occurred through labor regulations, housing codes, acculturation, and upward mobility. With the corrective actions taken, harmonious interrelations ensued, restoring the social system to a stage of equilibrium.

The Conflict View

A focus on the use and abuse of power, rather than on societal inability to cope with rapid change, marks the conflict approach. U.S. industrialists exploited immigrant workers, maximizing profits by minimizing wages and maintaining poor working conditions. When workers protested or went on strike, employers blacklisted them, hired other ethnics as strikebreakers, secured court injunctions, or used vigilantes, police, or state militia to break up the efforts. Employers possessed absolute economic power to curtail worker agitation because their position was reinforced by other social institutions aligned with the powerful against the powerless. The power-differential theory (Chapter 2) suggested by Lieberson places such actions in a conceptual framework consistent with the earlier experiences of the Irish. Bonacich's split-labor-market theory (Chapter 4) becomes applicable, for example, in the use of Hungarians and Italians as strikebreakers, generating interethnic conflict as a means of thwarting "troublemakers" in the labor force.

Upward mobility for these "white ethnics" occurred not from gradual societal adjustments but from an organized worker movement in opposition to the power structure. First- and second-generation workers fought hard through the labor union movement—often at great risk and with great sacrifice against strong pressures—to secure their share of the American Dream. Change thus resulted from conflict, from class consciousness, and from an unrelenting social movement against entrenched economic interests. With economic gains came stability and respectability, enabling these ethnic groups to gain acceptance and overcome the prejudice and discrimination directed against them.

The Interactionist View

Imagine yourself a native-born American living in a northeastern or midwestern city at the turn of the 20th century. From two-thirds to three-fourths of your city is populated by foreign-born people, most of whom are dark-skinned and dark-haired or physically distinctive because of their clothing. Everything about them—their religion, lifestyle, and behavior—seems so different, so alien. The people you associate with do not live clustered together in such crowded slums. And there are so many of them! You constantly read about them getting arrested for breaking some law or other. The city has changed—and not for the better. You worry that the country itself will lose its "true" identity as it is overrun by these European "misfits" who exhibit little appreciation for the national values and democratic principles of the United States.

Such a mental picture is not difficult to construct. Industrialization, urbanization, social disorganization, economic exploitation, and a host of other factors may have created the social problems regarding immigrants then, but the native-born tended to see only the symptoms manifest in the immigrant communities. Believing such conditions had not existed until "these people" came, members of the dominant group defined the problems as inherent in the "new" immigrants. Indeed, everything the typical U.S.-born citizen saw or heard reinforced the perception that the current flood of immigrants threatened the entire social fabric. The demands for immigration restrictions, eventually enacted, and the acts of avoidance, discrimination, and occasional violence all reflected the negative stereotyping of those who looked "different."

RETROSPECT

The period from 1880 to 1920 was one of the greatest immigration epochs in U.S. history; 23 million people left everything behind for the promise of "Golden America." Social and economic forces at work on both continents combined to encourage this mass migration. Europe's inability to offer a decent standard of living and this country's massive need for laborers were the major push–pull factors. Recruited or attracted to the United States because of its rapid industrialization, European immigrants met an important need in the nation's growth and development.

Yet the "new" immigrants were hardly welcomed with open arms. Ethnocentric preconceptions of how an "American" should look and behave prejudiced large segments of the society against them. Their physical and cultural differences marked them as strangers and heightened nativist fears about an undesirable element populating the country. By 1900, one-third of the total population consisted of first- or second-generation Americans, a fact that spurred demands to close the "floodgates" to stem the "immigrant tide." Finally, in 1921, the first restrictive legislation against Europeans was enacted. Not until the mid-1960s would the discriminatory quota system based on national origin end.

Many theoretical considerations in majority–minority relations apply to these European immigrants. Their cultural and structural differences set the stage for stereotyping, all three levels of prejudice, and discrimination. Progressive stages of culture shock, community organization, development of subcultural areas, and marginality were common. Dominant patterns of nativism, antagonism, social and spatial segregation, and legislative controls appeared frequently, as did the minority responses of avoidance, deviance, defiance, and acceptance.

The immigrants settled in ethnic clusters and established their own institutions, and they generally followed the broad patterns of earlier groups of immigrants. The various new peoples differed from one another in language, customs, and value orientations, although many U.S. natives found those who were not Italians or Jews indistinguishable and lumped them together. Not all of them wanted to stay, and not all who did assimilated. The new immigrants in their ethnic clusters exhibited the same sort of cultural pluralism as, in more isolated settings, the "old" immigrants had shown. But the times were different. Urbanization had introduced a greater degree of functional interdependence, a reliance of all residents on one another for the exchange of goods and services. Thus, the newcomers were less isolated than many earlier immigrants had been. Their numbers were great, and the dominant society wanted them to assimilate, although it also feared that they could not.

U.S. industry employed the immigrants because it needed them. The work was hard, the hours long, and the pay low, but most believed that the opportunities were better in the United States than in their homelands. Exploitation of workers led to labor unrest and the growth of the union movement. Some immigrants were attracted to radical movements, and others returned home, but most toiled, indoors or outdoors, to succeed in their adopted land for themselves and their children.

KEY TERMS

Annihilation	Ethnophaulism	Racism
Assimilation	Extended family	Social segregation
Cultural differentiation	Marginality	Social structure
Culture shock	Nativism	Stereotyping
Endogamy	Pluralism	Upward mobility
Ethnocentrism	Prejudice	Values
Ethnogenesis	Push–pull factors	Xenophobia

DISCUSSION QUESTIONS

1. How had structural conditions in the United States changed for the "new" immigrants?

2. What factors aroused dominant-group antagonism against the newcomers? In what ways was this hostility expressed?

3. In what ways were the various ethnic groups' adaptations to U.S. society similar?

4. Apply the concepts of stereotyping and the vicious-circle phenomenon to immigrant experiences.

5. How does the power differential relate to these immigrants' experiences and to the labor union movement?

6. How do the three major sociological perspectives explain the experiences of southern, central, and eastern Europeans?

SUGGESTED READINGS

Erdmans, Mary P. *Opposite Poles: Immigrants and Ethnics in Polish Chicago, 1976–1990*. University Park: Pennsylvania State University Press, 1998.
Thorough overview of immigrants and refugees, cultural differences, national loyalty versus communism, power, competition, and multigenerational acculturation.

Fonseca, Isabel. *Bury Me Standing: The Gypsies and Their Journey*, reprint ed. New York: Vintage Books, 1996.
Revealing portrait of the Rom, discussing their traditions, folklore, social institutions, and repression throughout history.

Greene, Meg. *Immigrants in America: The Russian-Americans*. Farmington Hills, MI: Lucent Books, 2002.
Traces the first arrivals in 1740 to the present, examining their push–pull factors, their diverse culture and history, and insights into their presence in North America.

Kourvetaris, George A. *Studies of Greek Americans*. New York: Columbia University Press, East European Monographs, 1997.
Combines theory and research in the study of ethnicity and identity among first- and second-generation Greek American entrepreneurs and professionals.

Mangione, Jerre, and Ben Morreale. *La Storia: Five Centuries of the Italian American Experience*. New York: HarperPerennial, 1993.
An excellent, detailed account as well as an in-depth discussion of the social

consequences faced by immigrant Italians and their children.

Petrini, Catherine M. *Immigrants in America: The Italian-Americans*. San Diego, CA: Greenhaven Press, 2001.

Examines push–pull factors, immigrant acculturation, problems of acceptance, efforts to preserve their heritage, and persecution of Italian Americans during World War II.

MySocKit

Additional resources for this chapter can be found in MySocKit. If you have a subscription to MySocKit, go to www.mysockit.com to study, review, and go beyond the book to learn more about race and ethnic relations.

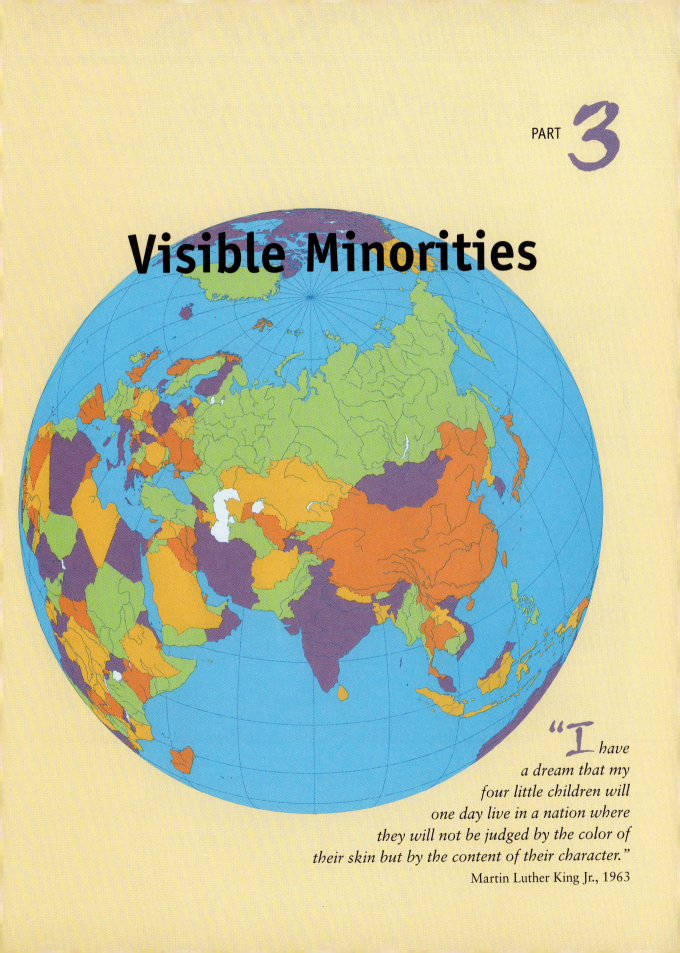

PART 3

Visible Minorities

"*I have a dream that my four little children will one day live in a nation where they will not be judged by the color of their skin but by the content of their character.*"

Martin Luther King Jr., 1963

The Native Americans

*D*ifferent in race, material culture, beliefs, and behavior, the Europeans and the Native Americans initially were strangers to each other. The Europeans who first traded with and then conquered the natives showed little interest in or understanding of them. Brutalized and exploited, the Native Americans experienced all the dominant-group response patterns: legislative action, segregation, expulsion, xenophobia, and—for some tribes and groups—annihilation. In turn, they reacted with varying patterns of avoidance, defiance, and acceptance, steadfastly remaining numerous and persistent subcultures with a marginal existence.

SOCIOHISTORICAL PERSPECTIVE

Most ethnohistorians place the pre-European colonization number of Native Americans who lived in what later became the United States at between 6 and 10 million. Divided into several hundred tribes with discrete languages and lifestyles, these original inhabitants had cultures rich in art, music, dance, life-cycle rituals, belief systems, social organization, coping strategies, and instruction of their young. Although tribes varied in their values, customs, beliefs, and practices, their cultures rested primarily on living in harmony with the land.

Early European explorers and settlers, reflecting ethnocentric views, condemned the aspects of Native American culture that they did not understand and related to other aspects only in terms of their own culture. Some considered the indigenous people to be savages, even though Native American societies had a high degree of social organization. Others idealized them as uncorrupted children of nature who spent most of their time engaging in pleasurable activities. In Europe, intellectual debate raged over how the presence of people so isolated from other human beings could be explained. Were they descended from the inhabitants of Atlantis, Carthage, ancient Greece, East Asia? Were they the Lost Tribes of Israel?[1] Were they no better than beasts, or were they intelligent, capable beings? In colonial and frontier days, the **stereotype** of the Native Americans often was negative, especially when they obstructed Europeans from occupying the Native Americans' land. As a result of *self-justification*—the denigration of others to justify maltreating them—some whites viewed Native Americans as cruel, treacherous, lying, dirty heathens. Supposedly, all they desired during the frontier period were scalps, firearms, and "fire-water." Even today many stereotype contemporary Native Americans as backward, unmotivated, or continually drunk, or else regard them as romantic anachronisms.

Outsiders frequently generalize about Native Americans, thinking of the many tribes as one people even though the tribes have always differed from one another in language, social structure, values, and practices. Of the approximately 300 different Native American languages spoken in 1492 within what became the United States, only about half still exist. At present, there are 275 Native American reservations, and the Bureau of Indian Affairs recognizes 561 different tribal entities in the United States.[2] Figure 7.1 shows the principal Native American tribes living in the United States today.

The Native Americans' experiences in the colonial period were unique in one respect: The whites, not the Native Americans, were the newcomers, and the whites were the minority for many years. The relationship between Native Americans and whites often was characterized by distrust, uneasy truces, or violent hostilities. Even in colonial Massachusetts and New Netherland, where peaceful coexistence initially prevailed, the situation deteriorated.

As the two peoples interacted more fully, each group grew more antagonistic toward the other. The Native Americans could not understand the European settlers' use of beatings, hangings, and imprisonment as means of social control. The settlers could not understand the Native Americans' resistance to Christianity and to the whites' more "civilized" way of life. These were but peripheral considerations, however; the major issue was whose way of life would prevail and whether the land would be further developed or allowed to remain in its natural state, abounding with fish and wildlife.

In the mid-19th century, the U.S. government adopted a policy of forced relocation of Native American tribes to encourage westward expansion by nonnatives. The government used military force to displace the many tribes and resettle them on wilderness reservations, where they remained unless new settlement plans or the discovery of oil and valuable minerals (such as gold in the Black Hills of South Dakota) caused further displacement. This program of compulsory segregation and dependence—compounded by attempts at "Americanization"—reduced the Native Americans' status to that of a subordinate colonized people—wards of the government—living at a subsistence level. Reflecting changing attitudes and interests in the late 19th and early 20th centuries, Congress enacted various legislative acts ostensibly designed to help the Native Americans but that actually worked to the Native Americans' further disadvantage, worsening their already low and dependent status (see The Ethnic Experience box, page 214, for a similar governmental interaction with Hawaiians).

One short-lived Pan-Indian association of the 20th century, the Society of American Indians (1910–1920), failed to unify the tribes into an effective pressure group or to generate much outside support. In 1944, a group of World War II veterans formed the National Congress of American Indians (NCAI). In the early 1960s, another organization, the National Indian Youth Council (NIYC) came into existence. New moves toward unity began in the 1960s, and new legislation and greater government sympathy helped the Native Americans' cause.

The most significant factor in the Native Americans' success, however, was the Civil Rights movement, which heightened the nation's social consciousness and inspired the Native Americans to renew their campaign for self-determination.

FIGURE 7.1   Principal Native American Tribes in the Continental United States (Where They Live Today)

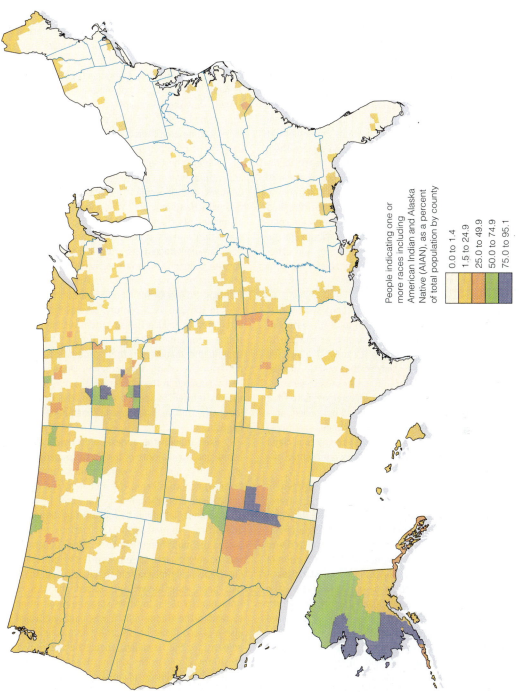

People indicating one or
more races including
American Indian and Alaska
Native (AIAN), as a percent
of total population by county

0.0 to 1.4
1.5 to 24.9
25.0 to 49.9
50.0 to 74.9
75.0 to 95.1

Source: Based on data from U.S. Department of the Interior, Bureau of Indian Affairs, "Indian Land Areas, General" (map), (Washington, DC: U.S. Government Printing Office, 2001).

The Ethnic Experience

Hawaiians Lose Their Independence

Hawaii's history—preserved in the oral tradition through chants and legends—dates back to about 700 BCE with migration of Polynesians from the Marquesas. As with Native Americans, life changed dramatically for the indigenous people in Hawaii after European contact in 1778.

In the centuries before European contact, Hawaiian society was a highly stratified system. Under the king were the *ali'i,* or chiefs, who ruled over portions of the land at the whim of the king, who could remove and replace them according to a system of rewards and punishments. Below the chiefs in temporal power, but often far above them in spiritual power, were the *kahuna,* or priest craftsmen—specialists in such areas as canoe building, medicine, and casting and lifting spells. Most people, however, were commoners (*makaainana*) or laborers, who paid tributes to the king and chief in the form of food, clothing, and other goods, and also provided warriors for the chief's army. At the bottom were a small number of slaves known as *kauwa* and outcastes.

Social control rested on a *kapu* (taboo) system that dominated all aspects of life from birth to death, with violators swiftly punished by being strangled or clubbed to death. Commoners could not even let their shadows fall across the person of a high chief, so they quickly kneeled or lay down in the presence of such sacred persons. Commoners performed simple religious ceremonies to their personal gods (*aumakua*), and the *kahuna* performed more elaborate rituals (sometimes including human sacrifices) for the *ali'i* in the large temples (*heiau*) to the four major gods (*Ku, Kanaloa, Lono,* and *Kane*), who represented the universal forces of nature.

In the late 18th century, foreign ships arrived in increasing numbers, bringing domestic animals, trees, fruits, and plants never before seen in Hawaii. They also brought diseases, alcohol, and firearms. With little immunity to new diseases, the Hawaiians soon began to die in alarming numbers as survivors witnessed the destruction of their traditional way of life. By the time missionaries—mostly from Puritan New England—arrived in 1820, the Hawaiian people had already dismantled their *heiaus,* rejecting earlier religious beliefs, and soon many converted to Christianity. Early missionaries disliked the *hula,* originally a religious rite to honor the gods and the chiefs. The sight of scantily clad women moving in rhythm to poetry offended their puritan ethics, and they nearly succeeded in abolishing this aspect of ancient Hawaiian culture.

The first newcomers were of European ancestry, beginning with the English under Captain James Cook and then Americans who came as explorers, adventurers, businessmen, and missionaries. At first, all foreigners were known as *haole* (outsiders), or non-Hawaiians. Since the first foreigners that the Hawaiians saw were Europeans, the word soon came to refer strictly to persons of European ancestry. This meaning continues to this day, although sometimes it can also be used derogatorily.

Among the Caucasians who came in small groups as agricultural workers were Russians, Portuguese, Spaniards, Germans, and Norwegians. Many of these groups intermarried with Hawaiians and other racial groups. Larger waves of immigrants then came, beginning with the Chinese as plantation workers in the 1850s. Quite a few Chinese married Hawaiian women. As a result, Hawaiian Chinese families are common in Hawaii today. Over the next 70 years, other groups arrived, first the Japanese, then the Koreans, Filipinos, Puerto Ricans, and Samoans.

In the late 19th century, several Hawaiian monarchs attempted to reduce the agitation fomented by the sugar planters for annexation to the United States to secure a dependable market for their product. The divisiveness between the ruling and economic power structures was best illustrated in the legislature, though, where white legislators refused to speak Hawaiian, the kingdom's official language, and native Hawaiian members refused to use English.

Even though the annexationists were badly outnumbered, and the majority of the Hawaiian people—as well as many white residents—were against annexation, these businessmen considered the monarchy too inept to safeguard their property interests and profits. In 1893, their armed companies of militia took over government buildings and offices, supported by U.S. marines and sailors who landed the night before "to keep order." Queen Lili'uokalani was powerless and surrendered under protest. President Cleveland's administration concluded that the monarchy had been overthrown and raised the U.S. flag over Honolulu. In 1895, loyalists staged a revolt in an attempt to restore the throne, but it was quickly crushed and the queen placed under house arrest. As a condition to obtain amnesty for the Hawaiian rebels, she was forced to relinquish any claim to the throne. President McKinley then signed the resolution of annexation on July 7, 1898, to seal the fate of the forever-lost kingdom.

Although they had never been silent, they now became more vocal, organized, and militant, while finding outsiders more receptive. A new generation of "Red Power" advocates took up the fight for Native American rights. Some attempted to achieve their goals through a national, or Pan-Indian, movement, whereas others preferred to emphasize individual tribal culture and practices.

Throughout their 500-year history with whites, Native Americans consistently rejected the notion that the whites' religions and lifestyles were superior to theirs. To understand the nature of the relations between these two groups, we must comprehend the roles of **ethnocentrism**, stereotyping, cultural differences, and power differentials in intergroup relations.

EARLY ENCOUNTERS

In the first encounters between Native American and Europeans, two races with vast differences in culture, knowledge, and lifestyle saw each other's physical distinctions for the first time. Each group was a source of wonder to the other. Columbus's first impressions of the Arawak tribe in the Caribbean reflected his ethnocentrism:

> I knew they were a people who would better be freed and converted to our Holy Faith by love than by force. . . . they are all generally of good height, of pleasing appearance and well built. . . . They must be good servants and intelligent . . . and I believe that they would easily become Christians, as it appeared to me that they had no sect.[3]

The landing of Columbus on the island of San Salvador in the Bahamas on October 12, 1492, marked the beginning of dramatic social upheaval in the lives of the indigenous peoples throughout the Americas. Conquest, subjugation, exploitation, annihilation, and the loss of a centuries-old way of life soon followed.

Although he admired the Native Americans, Columbus essentially saw them as potential servants, and he assumed that they had no religious convictions because he found no trappings of religion or written codes such as he was accustomed to seeing in Europe.

Although some Europeans romanticized Native Americans and a positive mystique about the Native Americans swept Elizabethan England and other parts of Europe, others viewed them as bloodthirsty barbarians and cruelly exploited them. The early phases of Spanish military activity in the New World involved enslavement, plunder, rape, and slaughter. For example, the Spanish put the peaceful Arawak tribe of the Caribbean islands into forced labor for land clearing, building, mining, and plantation work. Because they had no weapons to match those of their conquerors, the subjugated peoples often responded by committing mass suicide and mass infanticide. Within a few decades of the European discovery of the New World, the Native American population began to decline rapidly as a result of disease, warfare, and self-destruction.

Native American populations in Latin America and North America were decimated by various sicknesses that resulted from earlier contact with white explorers or traders. When the early settlers in New England found deserted Native American villages, they rejoiced; they considered this to be mute testimony of the judgment of Divine Providence on these "heathens" as well as on their own undertaking. The Lord had smitten the pagan to make way for the righteous! This accidental annihilation often resulted from a serious contagion such as smallpox, tuberculosis, or cholera. Native Americans were also fatally susceptible to such diseases as measles, mumps, and chicken pox because they had not developed immunities to these Old World illnesses.

Epitomizing the **dichotomy** of views of the Native American either as a Noble Savage or as a bloodthirsty barbarian was the great debate between Bartolomé de las Casas, a bishop serving in the New World, and Juan Ginés de Sepulveda, a Renaissance scholar. The latter considered the Native Americans no better than "beasts" who should be enslaved. Las Casas presented a picture of the Native Americans as naifs, both artistically and mechanically inclined, with intellectual capabilities for learning and a willingness to coexist with the Spanish intruders.[4] In 1550, King Charles V appointed the Council of the Indies, a panel of distinguished theologians and counselors, which met at Valladolid. The council heard the arguments of the two antagonists, agreed in large measure with Las Casas, and thereupon fundamentally altered Spanish policy toward the Native Americans.

As part of his long struggle to protect the Native Americans, Las Casas had returned to Spain in 1517 to plead their case directly to the king. In doing so, he revealed the extent of their decimation: "At my first arrival in Hispaniola [1497], it contained a million inhabitants and now there remain scarce the hundredth part of them." He believed the Native Americans could survive only if another labor force replaced them. By convincing the Spanish authorities that Africans were sturdier and better adapted to agricultural operations, he opened the doors for the subsequent massive slave trade of blacks to the Spanish possessions in the New World. It is cruelly ironic that the humane efforts of Las Casas on the Native Americans' behalf encouraged the brutalization and exploitation of black people and racial discrimination against them that has lasted for more than 400 years.

The Native American populations in the United States and Latin America differ in their social, economic, and political status. Nevertheless, Native Americans are indigenous to the land, regardless of present-day national boundaries (e.g., the Mohawk in New York State and Canada). Several factors, including habitability of terrain, migration patterns, degree of industrialization, and especially different governmental and social attitudes in the various countries, have accounted for the differences. In the United States, the 19th-century policy of removal, relocation, and Native American dependence on the federal government prevented most tribes from becoming full participants in U.S. society.

In Latin America in 1550, however, Spain adopted a more benevolent policy toward the Native Americans, following the recommendations of the Council of the Indies, and greater interaction, intermarriage, absorption, and gradual acculturation occurred among the Native Americans and the Spanish. Except for those living in the central Andes and other remote areas, the indigenous peoples became fuller participants in their society than did their counterparts in the United States and lived in relative cultural and racial harmony with the white, black, *mulatto* (of mixed black and white ancestry), and *mestizo* (of mixed Native American and white ancestry) populations. Along with the other nonwhite groups, they were part of the large low-ranking social class, in sharp contrast to the small high-ranking class. Despite this comparative racial harmony, however, they have had little opportunity for upward mobility, and most Latin American nonwhites live in economic stagnation. In contrast, most North American tribes have experienced both economic stagnation and a lack of racial harmony.

Cultural Strains

In many areas, when the white settlers were few in number and depended on Native American assistance, the Native Americans were hospitable and the whites were receptive to them. The Native Americans along the East Coast helped the colonists get settled by teaching them what to plant and how to cultivate their crops, as well as imparting to them the knowledge and skills they needed to survive in the wilderness. With stabilization of the settlements, relations between the two races became more strained, as the following excerpt from Douglas Edward Leach's study of 17th-century New England reveals:

> Ever since the coming of the white men there had been economic intercourse between Indians and English traders. At first it had seemed that the flourishing trade in furs, tools, cloth, and foodstuffs was as beneficial to the Indians as to the colonists, but as time went on and the English extended their activities the Indians grew more and more dissatisfied with the situation. It became apparent that they were gradually sinking into a position of complete economic subservience. Indian villages which had once enjoyed almost total self-sufficiency were now increasingly dependent upon products of English manufacture. . . .
>
> In the meantime, some of the Indians were exchanging their forest ways for the security and comfort of English habitations by engaging themselves as servants or laborers to the settlers, whose ambitious expansionism was fostering a continual shortage of labor. This meant that members of the two races were now being brought into frequent contact with each other on the streets of colonial villages, producing still more interracial friction. Furthermore, the migration of individual Indians to the English plantations was disturbing to the other Indians who chose to cling to their old independence, and who saw with dismay the weakening of tribal and family bonds. . . .

At the same time, the English colonists were being hardened in the conviction that the Indians were a graceless and savage people, dirty and slothful in their personal habits, treacherous in their relations with the superior race. To put it bluntly, they were fit only to be pushed aside and subordinated, so that the land could be occupied and made productive by those for whom it had been destined by God. If the Indians could be made to fit into a humble niche in the edifice of colonial religion, economy, and government, very well, but if not, sooner or later they would have to be driven away or crushed.[5]

Throughout the westward movement, if contact led to cooperation between the two cultures, the resulting interaction and cultural diffusion usually worked to the disadvantage of the Native Americans. They lost their self-sufficiency and became economically dependent on whites. The whites, in turn, insisted on full compliance with their demands as the price of continued peaceful relations. Even if the Native Americans complied with the whites' demands, however, many whites continued to regard them as inferior people destined for a subservient role in white society.

Differing Values

Benjamin Franklin offered a classic example of different values in his account of a treaty signed between the whites and the Iroquois in 1744:

> After the principal Business was settled, the Commissioners from Virginia acquainted the Indians by a Speech, that there was at Williamsburg a College, with a Fund for Educating Indian youth; and that, if the Six Nations would send down half a dozen of their young Lads to that College, the Government would take care that they should be well provided for, and instructed in all the Learning of the White People. . . . [The Indians'] Speaker began . . . "We are convinc'd . . . that you mean to do us Good by your Proposal; and we thank you heartily. But you, who are wise, must know that different Nations have different Conceptions of things; and you will therefore not take it amiss, if our Ideas of this kind of Education happen not to be the same with yours. We have had some Experience of it; Several of our young People were formerly brought up at the Colleges of the Northern Provinces; they were instructed in all your Sciences; but, when they came back to us, they were bad Runners, ignorant of every means of living in the Woods, unable to bear either Cold or Hunger, knew neither how to build a Cabin, take a Deer, or kill an Enemy, knew our Language imperfectly, were therefore neither fit for Hunters, Warriors, nor Counsellors; they were totally good for nothing. We are however not the less oblig'd by your kind Offer, tho' we decline accepting it; and, to show our grateful Sense of it, if the Gentlemen of Virginia will send us a Dozen of their Sons, we will take great Care of their Education, instruct them in all we know, and make *Men* of them."[6]

Almost 100 years later, George Catlin offered insight into another manifestation of differing value orientations. Catlin, a 19th-century artist famous for his paintings of Native Americans and his sensitivity to their ways, described how each of the two cultures viewed the other:

> The civilized world look upon a group of Indians, in their classic dress, with their few and simple oddities, all of which have their moral or meaning, and laugh at them excessively, because they are not like ourselves—we ask, "why do the silly creatures wear such great bunches of quills on their heads?—Such loads and streaks of paint upon their bodies—and bear's grease? abominable"! and a thousand other

equally silly questions, without ever stopping to think that Nature taught them to do so—and that they all have some definite importance or meaning which an Indian could explain to us at once, if he were asked and felt disposed to do so—that each quill in his head stood, in the eyes of his whole tribe, as the symbols of any enemy who had fallen by his hand—that every streak of red paint covered a wound which he had got in honourable combat—and that the bear's grease with which he carefully anoints his body every morning, from head to foot, cleanses and purifies the body, and protects his skin from the bite of mosquitoes, and at the same time preserves him from colds and coughs which are usually taken through the pores of the skin.

At the same time, an Indian looks at the civilized world, no doubt, with equal, if not much greater, astonishment, at our apparently, as well as really, ridiculous customs and fashions; but he laughs not, nor ridicules, nor questions—for his natural good sense and good manners forbid him,—until he is reclining about the fireside of his wigwam companions, when he vents forth his just criticisms upon the learned world, who are a rich and just theme for Indian criticism and Indian gossip.

An Indian will not ask a white man the reason why he does not oil his skin with bear's grease, or why he does not paint his body—or why he wears a hat on his head, or why he has buttons on the back of his coat, where they can never be used—why he wears whiskers, and a shirt collar up to his eyes—or why he sleeps with his head towards the fire instead of his feet—why he walks with his toes out instead of turning them in—or why it is that hundreds of white folks will flock and crowd round a table to see an Indian eat—but he will go home to his wigwam fireside, and "make the welkin ring" with jokes and fun upon the ignorance and folly of the knowing world.[7]

These two selections sharply illustrate how culture shapes an individual's view of reality. When people use their own group as a frame of reference in judging another group, the resulting ethnocentric judgments declare the outgroup to be strange and inferior.

One Native American nation, the Iroquois, had a pronounced influence on some of the provisions of the U.S. Constitution. Iroquois is a name given to five Native American tribes located in New York State and the Ohio River Valley—the Cayuga, Mohawk, Oneida, Onondaga, and Seneca—that united in a league in 1570. They added a sixth tribe—the Tuscarora—in 1722 and took other groups, including the Delaware, under their protection. The League was still expanding and maturing when it was curtailed by white settlers; by 1851, it had virtually disappeared.

In its time, the League's democratic processes were so effective that romanticists called the Iroquois the "Greeks in America," and many aspects of their system served as models for the colonists. Called the Great Law of Peace, the Iroquois constitution gave each of the five tribes an equal voice, guaranteed freedom of political and religious expression, and had amendment and impeachment processes.[8]

VALUES AND SOCIAL STRUCTURE

Although the cultures of the many tribes differed (and still do) from one another, some marked similarities have existed among them. Native Americans have lived in close and intimate relationship with nature, respecting and not abusing the land. They have traditionally maximized the use of any animal prey—using its skin for clothing and shelter, its bones for various tools and implements, its sinews for thread, its meat for food, its bladder for a container, and so on.

Native American approaches toward possessing the land itself ranged from individual to joint to tribal ownership depending on the tribe. Most frequently, the land belonged to the tribe; as tribal members, individuals or families could live on and possibly farm certain portions. Land no longer cultivated by one Native American could be cultivated by another. However, the nominal owner could not dispose of the property without considering the land-use rights of the current user. More emphasis was thus placed on the rights of the user than on the rights and power of the nominal owner.[9] In terms of shared access, this practice resembles a law in present-day Sweden that roughly translates as "every person's right." In that country, a landowner cannot deny others access to the land, since all are entitled to enjoy its beauty. Thus, campers and hikers do not encounter no-trespassing signs; because all respect the land, littering and other forms of abuse are quite rare.

With regard to personal interaction, Native Americans established primary relationships either through a clan system (descent from a common ancestor) or through a friendship system, much like the systems of other tribal societies:

> Kin relationships were the basic building blocks of Indian society. These blocks were formed into social and political structures ranging from nuclear families to vast empires. The Indians, in their initial attempts to establish a basis of cooperation with the immigrant whites, attempted to incorporate the newcomers into the familiar kinship system. When proffered marriage alliances were turned down by the whites, the Indians sought to establish relationships based on the reciprocal responsibilities of brother to brother, nephew to uncle, and, finally, children to father. The white man refused the proferred relationships, misinterpreted Indian speech as weakness, and increasingly imposed his will on the disheartened remnants of once proud Indian nations.[10]

Native American children grow up under the encouragement and discipline of the extended family, not just the nuclear family. A generalized love of all children in the tribe, rather than just their own progeny, is common among Native Americans.[11] This factor may help explain the permissive and indulgent child-rearing practices many early Europeans reported.[12] Whether the Native American tribe was a hunting, fishing, or farming society, the children were raised in a cooperative, noncompetitive, affectionate atmosphere. Considered from the outset as an individual, the child developed a sense of responsibility and interdependence at an early age. Unrestrained displays of affection or temper and the use of corporal punishment have rarely been part of traditional Native American childcare practices. Instead, the means of social control are shame and ridicule, and the Native American matures into an individual keenly aware of any form of conduct that would lead other members of the tribe to react negatively. Sometimes the price of emphasizing these forms of social control is heavy, for shame and ridicule can cause a great deal of psychological harm.

Closely related to sensitivity to shame and ridicule is the Native American concept of personal honor, including the honor of one's word. Once pledged, whether to a white person or to another Native American, that word was considered inviolate. Exceptions did exist, for chiefs might lie, but only as a war measure, and later, in an attempt to please a white person. Some tribes had no word for *thief*, although an enemy's goods were always fair game. Sometimes, as among the Lakota (Sioux), Crow, and Blackfeet, young men of one tribe would steal from another tribe as a form of sport or a joke, but normally, they would not steal from one another.[13]

The Native American woman's role differed from the man's. Women's functions were to work and to raise children. However, the notion that women held a subservient position and labored long and hard while the men idled away their time is inaccurate. Actually, a cooperative but not egalitarian arrangement existed between the sexes, with the men doing the heavy work and the women doing tasks that would not conflict with their child-rearing responsibilities. In hunting and fishing societies, the men would be away from the village for extended periods searching for food. In farming societies, the men cleared and cultivated the land, and the women tended the crops, collected edible foods, and gathered firewood while the men sought a fresh meat supply. Each member of the tribe, according to sexually defined roles, had kinship and tribal responsibilities to fulfill. Moreover, in some tribes—such as the Cherokee, Cheyenne, and Iroquois—women held high esteem and influence.

STEREOTYPING

One popular misconception was that the Native American was a bloodthirsty savage. Some tribes, such as the Apache and Ute, were warlike, but most sought to avoid conflict if they could. Rivalries did exist among various tribes, however, and the French, English, and (later) U.S. settlers often exploited these rivalries for their own advantage. Native Americans believed strongly in retributive justice: a wrong had to be repaid, even if it took years, but not to a greater degree. Scalping, often depicted in films as a standard Native American practice, was not common. Even tribes that did scalp frequently did so because of their belief in retributive justice. Some historians argue that the Native American first learned about scalping from white settlers:

> Whatever its exact origins, there is no doubt that scalp-taking quickly spread over all of North America, except in the Eskimo areas; nor is there any doubt that its spread was due to the barbarity of White men rather than to the barbarity of Red men. White settlers early offered to pay bounties on dead Indians, and scalps were actual proof of the dead. Governor Kieft of New Netherland is usually credited with originating the idea of paying for Indian scalps, as they were more convenient to handle than whole heads, and they offered the same proof that an Indian had been killed. By liberal payment for scalps, the Dutch virtually cleared southern New York and New Jersey of Indians before the English supplanted them. By 1703 the colony of Massachusetts was paying the equivalent of about $60 for every Indian scalp. In the mid-eighteenth century, Pennsylvania fixed the bounty for a male Indian scalp at $134; a female's was worth only $50. Some White entrepreneurs simply hatcheted any old Indians that still survived in their towns.[14]

Another side of the Native American stereotype is the portrayal of them as silent or aloof. This image probably grew out of normal behavior in ambiguous situations, such as those faced by Native Americans transported to Europe for exhibition, transported to Washington, DC, for treaty negotiations, or interacting with strangers. Because they had developed from childhood a strong inclination to avoid acting in any way that might bring about shame or ridicule, Native Americans often remained silent for fear of speaking or acting improperly. This

Throughout the American Southwest, Native Americans selling handcrafted jewelry are a common sight at numerous roadside stands or at sidewalk bazaars, such as this scene in Albuquerque Old Town. With limited occupational choices available, utilizing artistic skills of one's heritage preserves the past and helps meet present-day economic needs.

practice is still common in courtship, in the greeting that parents offer to children returning from boarding school, and in the face of harsh, angry words from a white. In each instance, the practice among most tribes is to allow some time, perhaps days or months, to elapse before the uncertainty is sufficiently reduced to permit conversation. Native American silence is a precautionary device to preserve respect and dignity on both sides.[15] It does not represent aloofness, and it is temporary, continuing only until the situation lends itself to speaking.

In a larger context, William Lang identified the fundamental difference in values that separates European Americans from Native Americans. European Americans have a tendency to separate and categorize elements of experience in the belief that this process leads to ultimate knowledge. Statistical truth thus becomes the key to knowledge and to understanding human behavior. This approach has led to spectacular advances in science and technology but also to an "attitude of arrogant superiority" that dismisses other approaches as unsophisticated and inadequate. In contrast, says Lang, Native Americans have a holistic, or symbiotic, view of existence, seeing it as a great circle, or sacred hoop, representing unity and equality, linking all aspects of culture—art, religion, ritual, social organization, language, law, and lifestyle. Life is thus a complex matrix of entities, emotions, revelations, and cooperative enterprises, and the hallmark of the Native American approach is to experience rather than to interpret human existence. Because everything is interconnected, Native Americans believe a unified approach to life is more satisfying than a fragmentary one.[16]

CHANGES IN GOVERNMENT POLICY

Official European and U.S. government policy toward Native Americans has changed frequently over the years (see The International Scene box below and Table 7.1). In 1763, King George III of England issued a proclamation declaring that thenceforth the Native American tribes would be treated as independent nations and denying the colonies any jurisdiction over them. Thereafter, if the colonists wanted to obtain additional Native American lands or negotiate trade pacts, they had to do so through the English government and not directly with the Native Americans.

Historians cite enforcement of this policy as an indirect cause of the American Revolution. In addition to the delay involved in drawing up petitions, crossing the ocean back and forth, and waiting for bureaucratic processing, the colonists fumed over the fact that heathens were being accorded higher official status than they themselves enjoyed. Yet when the colonies declared their independence from England, they adopted the same policy in 1778, and the tribes retained quasi-national status. Congress reaffirmed this policy when it passed the Northwest Territory Ordinance in 1787, declaring the federal government—and not the states—responsible for Native American property, rights, and liberty.

The International Scene

A New Treaty Ends Exploitation

Throughout the 20th century, fishing, lumber, and mining companies removed millions of dollars' worth of natural resources from the rugged Nass Valley in northwestern British Columbia. The Native American Nisga'a who live in this spectacular mountain valley laid claim to the fish, timber, and minerals taken from their territory all along but never received any compensation whatsoever. With no control over their own land and few other economic options, the Nisga'a lived in poverty in substandard housing and typically had a 60 percent unemployment rate.

The Nisga'a had sought a treaty since 1887 to protect their rights and land claims. After two decades of negotiations, the Canadian government and the tribe reached agreement in 1998. The 5,500-member tribe would receive $126 million in cash over a 15-year period, title to 745 square miles in the Nass Valley, and return of about 250 Nisga'a artifacts from museums in Hull, Quebec, and Victoria, British Columbia. In return, the tribe would relinquish claim to the other nine-tenths of their original land claim as well as their tax-exempt status, although they would retain the right to self-government, with their own justice system (judges, police, and jails).

Some dissenters in the tribe thought too much was given up, and the opposition British Columbian Liberal Party objected to creating "a whole new order of government" and "entrenching inequality based on race." For its part, the right-wing Reform Party opposed the treaty as "an unwelcome step toward creation of mini-states for each of British Columbia's native communities." Nevertheless, the Nisga'a approved the treaty in 1998, and a year later, both the British Columbian and Canadian legislatures did the same. In May 2000, the treaty—the first between a North American tribe and a national government since the 19th century—went into effect. The government transferred the land to the Nisga'a Nation and created Bear Glacier Provincial Park and a water reservation. Two months later, the British Columbia Supreme Court upheld the legislation and treaty as "constitutionally valid."

Critical Thinking Question: Why doesn't the United States negotiate treaties with its Native American tribes?

Source: Adapted from David Crary, "Indian Treaty Splits British Columbia," Associated Press, August 4, 1998.

TABLE 7.1 Government Actions toward Native Americans

1763	English Royal Proclamation: Tribes accorded independent nation status; all lands west of the Appalachian Mountains are Native American country; the royal government must approve all land purchases.
1778	Continental Congress: Reaffirms the old British policy as U.S. policy.
1787	Northwest Territory Ordinance: Opens the Midwest for settlement; declares the U.S. government responsible for Native American property, rights, and liberty.
1824	Bureau of Indian Affairs (BIA) is created under the jurisdiction of the secretary of war.
1830	Indian Removal Act: Mandates all Native Americans must move west of the Mississippi River.
1830–1843	Except for Iroquois and Seminole, more than 100,000 eastern Native Americans are forcibly relocated westward. About 12,000 die on the "Trail of Tears."
1850–1880	Most reservations are established, as forced segregation becomes the new Native American reality.
1871	Appropriations bill rider: Declares tribes no longer are independent nations; legislation, not negotiation, is to determine any new arrangements.
1887	Dawes Act: Reservations surveyed, divided into tracts, and allotted to individual tribal members; surplus land sold.
1898	Curtis Act: Terminates tribal governments that refuse allotment; the president is to appoint tribal chiefs henceforth.
1906	Burke Act: Eliminates Native Americans' right to lease their Land, with the intent to force Native Americans to work the land themselves.
1924	Indian Citizenship Act: Grants U.S. citizenship to Native Americans.
1934	Indian Reorganization Act: Ends allotment; encourages tribal self-government; restores freedom of religion; extends financial credit; promotes the revival of Native American culture and crafts.
1952	Relocation Program: Moves Native Americans at government expense to urban areas for better job opportunities.
1953	Termination Act: Authorizes elimination of reservation systems, with an immediate end to federal services and tax immunity.
1973	Menominee Restoration Act: Revokes termination and restores the Menominee's reservation and tribal status.
1974	Indian Finance Act: Facilitates financing of Native American enterprises and development projects through grants and loans.
1975	Indian Self-Determination and Education Assistance Act: Expands tribal control over reservation programs; provides funding for new public schools on or near reservations.
1976	Indian Health Care Improvement Act: Provides funds to build or renovate hospitals, add more personnel, and give scholarships to Native Americans to enter Indian Health Service.
1978	Education Amendments Act: Gives substantial control over education programs to local Native American community.
1978	Tribally Controlled Community College Assistance Act: Provides grants to tribal community colleges.
1978	Indian Child Welfare Act: Restricts placement of Native American children by non-Native American social agencies in non-Native American homes.
1978	American Indian Religious Freedom Act: Protects religious rights of Native Americans, including their use of peyote.
1993	Religious Freedom Restoration Act: Restores standards of review for American Indian Religious Freedom Act that were overturned by a Supreme Court ruling in 1990.
1993	Omnibus Indian Advancement Act: Establishes foundation for gifts to BIA schools; increases economic development opportunities for tribes; improves tribal governance.
2002	Improper Payments Information Act: Reassesses each federal agency to review annually its programs to identify erroneous payments.
2004	American Indian Probate Reform Act: Facilitates consolidation of Indian land ownership to restore economic viability to Native American assets.

Indian Removal Act

In 1830, by a close vote, Congress passed the Indian Removal Act recommended by President Andrew Jackson. This act called for **expulsion** of all Native Americans from the southeastern states and their relocation to the territory west of the Mississippi River. The legislation was prompted in part by the state of Georgia, which for several years had been annexing the fertile land of the

Cherokee for its expanding cotton industry. The Cherokee had rejected Georgia's assertion of legal authority to settle disputes over all lands within its borders and petitioned the U.S. Supreme Court for protection, citing their "foreign nation" status and treaties with the federal government.

Combining two cases, *Cherokee Nation v. Georgia* and *Worcester v. Georgia,* Chief Justice John Marshall delivered the majority opinion on February 28, 1832, establishing the foundation that has shaped U.S. Native American policy ever since. The Cherokee were not a foreign nation, the Court ruled, and therefore could not sue Georgia. They were instead a "domestic dependent nation," a "distinct community, occupying its own territory." Because of this definition, the Court said, the laws of Georgia had no jurisdiction, and the Court thus ruled in favor of the Cherokee keeping the land.

President Jackson reportedly responded, "John Marshall has rendered his decision, now let him enforce it." Indeed, two of the three branches of government favored removal of the Cherokee, and Jackson interpreted his overwhelming reelection in November as a mandate from the electorate to pursue that policy. Jackson thus moved to enforce the Indian Removal Act, launching one of the ugliest episodes in the nation's history.

Expulsion. After signing the Treaty of Dancing Rabbit Creek (1830) under compulsion, the Choctaw of Mississippi were the first to face removal. The government forcibly relocated 20,000, of whom 5,000 died from famine and disease along the march to Indian Territory in Oklahoma. In 1836, the army moved against the Creek in Alabama, forcing 17,000 westward; 2,000 died from exposure, famine, and disease en route, and another 3,500 died within three months of arrival. About 1,000 Chickasaw in Mississippi died during their forced march.[17] The Seminole in Florida successfully resisted expulsion by adapting guerrilla warfare tactics in the Everglades, killing almost 2,000 soldiers and costing the U.S. Army more than $20 million before it gave up the fight.[18]

The Cherokee. In about 1790, the Cherokee, after some 14 years of warfare with the whites, decided to adopt U.S. customs and culture. In other words, they actively sought assimilation in an effort to live harmoniously with a different civilization. Over the next 40 years, their success in achieving this goal was remarkable. They converted their economy to one based on agriculture and commerce, strengthened their self-governing political system, and prospered. They cultivated farmlands in the fertile soil of the tristate region of Georgia, Tennessee, and North Carolina and reaped bountiful harvests. The Cherokee patterned themselves after the whites, setting up churches, schools, sawmills, grist mills, and blacksmith shops. They acquired spinning wheels, looms, plows, and all the other implements of white society.

Most extraordinary of all was the achievement of a Cherokee named Sequoyah. In 1821, after a determined 12-year effort, he succeeded in inventing a phonetic syllabary notation system for the Cherokee language. This immense accomplishment was unprecedented in world history. A man, untrained in linguistics, had been able to write a language by himself and do so in a way that could be learned easily. Remarkably, within three years, almost all the Cherokee could read and write their own language. By 1828, the tribe had its own newspaper and had adopted a written constitution, a code of laws, a bicameral legislature, and an appellate judiciary.

By U.S. standards, the Cherokee were the most "civilized" tribe in the country. Driven by a desire for self-improvement, they educated themselves, converted to Christianity, and learned the whites' ways of agriculture, business, and government. They successfully acculturated. Only one problem remained: the whites wanted their rich land for growing cotton, and, consequently, the Cherokee now faced eviction, too.

With U.S. public opinion against the Cherokee, the voices of John Marshall, Daniel Webster, Henry Clay, Sam Houston, Davy Crockett, and others could not help the Cherokee cause. Georgia confiscated Cherokee lands and redistributed them to whites through land lotteries, with the state militia stationed in the region to preserve the peace should the Native Americans resist:

> The premeditated brutality of the militia's daily conducts suggested their commanders' hope of provoking a Cherokee reaction which might provide an excuse for their immediate physical expulsion. The carefully disciplined Cherokee instead patiently submitted even when the provocations extended to the burning of their homes, the confiscation of their property, the mistreatment of their women, the closing of their schools, and the sale of liquor in their churches.[19]

The Cherokee retreated into the forests and continued their desperate legal maneuvering to avoid expulsion. Although federal troops removed the Choctaw and Chickasaw in Mississippi and the Creek in Alabama, they did not move against the Cherokee, who had won worldwide sympathy and whose efforts to obtain recognition of their rights in the courts continued to be successful. Instead, the federal government intensified its efforts to promote disunity among the Cherokee through bribery, jailings, persecution, and denial of the services and support guaranteed under treaties. Most of the Cherokee remained loyal to their president, John Ross, and rejected the proposed treaty of removal and its $5 million compensation payment.

Government officials finally succeeded in getting the treaty signed on December 29, 1835, by convening an ad hoc council of President Ross's Cherokee opponents. Fewer than 500 of the 17,000 Cherokee appeared, but they signed the treaty, and the Senate ratified the pact on May 18, 1836. Ross and the Cherokee people fought this fraudulent treaty; and, in January 1838, Ross presented the Senate with a petition signed by 15,665 Cherokee repudiating the document. The Senate rejected the petition by a vote of 37 to 10. A new wave of public protest against the government's conduct toward the Cherokee swelled in the North, including an impassioned open letter to President Van Buren by Ralph Waldo Emerson, but these results did not alter the outcome. On April 10, 1838, Van Buren ordered General Winfield Scott to remove the Cherokee immediately, using whatever military force was necessary. The U.S. government, through its military forces, acted against an entire people who had willingly adapted to the changing world around them. Soldiers forced them at gunpoint from their homes, first to stockades and then westward, far from all that had been theirs:

> Families at dinner were startled by the sudden gleam of bayonets in the doorway and rose up to be driven with blows and oaths along the weary miles to the stockade. Men were seized in their fields or going along the road, women were taken from their wheels and children from their play. In many cases, on turning for one last look as they crossed the ridge, they saw their homes in flames, fired

by the lawless rabble that followed on the heels of the soldiers to loot and pillage. So keen were these outlaws on the scent that in some instances they were driving off the cattle and other stock of the Indians almost before the soldiers had fairly started their owners in the other direction. Systematic hunts were made by the same men for Indian graves, to rob them of the silver pendants and other valuables deposited with the dead. A Georgia volunteer, afterward a colonel in the Confederate service, said: "I fought through the Civil War and have seen men shot to pieces and slaughtered by thousands, but the Cherokee removal was the cruelest work I ever knew."[20]

The Cherokee suffered extensively during this mass expulsion. Beginning in October 1838, army troops marched the Cherokee westward along what the Cherokee later called the Trail of Tears: 10 to 20 Native Americans died each day from exposure and other miseries. By March 1839, fewer than 9,000 of the 13,000 who had set out survived to reach the Indian Territory, which is now Oklahoma. At the midpoint of this sad episode—December 3, 1838—President Van Buren's message to Congress announced,

> It affords me sincere pleasure to apprise the Congress of the entire removal of the Cherokee Nation of Indians to their new homes west of the Mississippi. The measures authorized by Congress at its last session have had the happiest effects. . . . They have emigrated without any apparent reluctance.[21]

Reservations and Dependence

A shift in U.S. government policy in the mid-19th century changed Native American lifestyles to such an extent that its aftereffects remain visible today on any reservation. Instead of using annihilation and expulsion to deal with the Native Americans, the government embarked on a policy of segregation and isolation. Between 1850 and 1880, it established most of the nation's Indian reservations, which now number 275.

In 1871, Congress ended federal recognition of the Native American tribes as independent, **sovereign** nations—or "domestic dependent nations," for that matter—and made them wards of the government instead. Bureaucrats became responsible for the welfare of the Native American peoples, issuing them food rations and supervising every aspect of their lives. The results were devastating. Proud and independent people who had been taught self-reliance at an early age now depended on non–Native American government agents. Many of the tribes, once nomads, found it difficult to adjust to reservation life. Such problems as inadequate administration by government agents and irregular delivery of food, supplies, and equipment made matters worse.

The government was not done restructuring Native American lifestyles. Americanization became the goal. This meant destroying tribal organizations, suppressing "pagan" religions and ceremonies, allowing only English as the language of instruction in the schools, requiring "white" clothing and hair styles, and teaching only the dominant (white) group's culture and history:

> Most of the attention of the Americanizers was concentrated on the Indian children, who were snatched from their families and shipped off to boarding schools far from their homes. The children usually were kept at boarding school for eight years, during which time they were not permitted to see their parents, relatives or friends. Anything Indian—dress, language, religious

practices, even outlook on life (and how that was defined was up to the judgment of each administration of the government's directives)—was uncompromisingly prohibited. Ostensibly educated, articulate in the English language, wearing store-bought clothes, and with their hair short and their emotionalism toned down, the boarding-school graduates were sent out either to make their way in a white world that did not want them, or to return to a reservation to which they were now foreign.[22]

One value promulgated was the rugged individualism of white society rather than the cooperative, noncompetitive approach of the Native American. This was the purpose of the General Allotment Act of 1887. Its sponsor, Senator Dawes, genuinely believed that the law would engender in the Native American that spirit of self-interest that he considered the major force in white civilization.

In reality, this legislation deprived Native Americans of even more land. Its goal was to break the backbone of Native American culture by ending communal ownership of reservation lands and instead giving each Native American a share. Many Native Americans had no technical knowledge of farming and neither the cash nor credit to obtain farm implements. Some Native American peoples believed it was sacrilegious to plow the earth. Loopholes in the Dawes Act enabled unscrupulous whites to plunder the Native Americans' lands, either through low-cost, long-term leases or by convincing Native American owners to write wills leaving their property to white "friends." This practice was widespread, and a mysterious increase in the number of Native American deaths followed; some of these deaths were later proved to have been murders.[23]

In 1898, faced with tribes that refused to accept the allotment policy, the government passed the Curtis Act. This law terminated the tribal governments of all tribes that resisted allotment, and it made their tribal chiefs presidential appointments thereafter. By 1914, the 138 million acres of Native American holdings had been reduced to 56 million acres of eroded, poor-quality land.[24]

Indian Reorganization Act

After 1933, Franklin Roosevelt's administration shifted from a policy of forced assimilation to one of pluralism. One outcome was the Indian Reorganization Act of 1934, which ended the land-allotment program, encouraged tribal self-government, extended financial credit to the tribes, gave preference in Bureau of Indian Affairs (BIA) employment to Native Americans, and permitted consolidation of Native American lands split up through inheritance. Furthermore, Native Americans were encouraged to revive their ancient arts and crafts, their languages, their religions and ceremonies, and their customs and traditions. In keeping with an administrative philosophy of treating Native Americans with dignity, the act was permissive, not mandatory; each tribe could vote to accept or reject the new law. Most chose to accept it.

In the 1950s, new top administrative personnel in President Eisenhower's Interior Department and the BIA espoused a different philosophy and tried to shift the BIA back to assimilationist policy. Some critics of the 1934 legislation considered it regressive. Believing that the only way to end the chronic poverty, disease, overpopulation, and hopelessness among the Native Americans was to end the isolation of reservation life, the new administration tried other approaches.

The Relocation Program

Beginning in the 1950s, the Bureau of Indian Affairs offered assistance to individuals or families who wanted to relocate in urban areas to obtain jobs and living accommodations. For many Native Americans, the word *relocation* had terrible connotations. That was the euphemism used for the internment camps in which 110,000 Japanese Americans had been placed during World War II. Furthermore, Dillon S. Myer, the government administrator who had been in charge of those camps, was now in charge of the Native American relocation program.

Most of the 40,000 Native Americans who enrolled in this program went to work in low-status unskilled or semiskilled jobs and found housing in the poorer sections of the cities. Some adjusted and became acculturated; others felt uprooted, became alcoholics, and fared poorly. More than one-fourth of the total number returned to the reservations. The program tapered off after 1960, due mostly to other efforts to improve Native American life.

The Termination Act

A series of bills passed in 1953–1954 sought to end federal responsibility for welfare and administration of Native Americans by ending all federal services and federal liaison with tribal organizations and by dispensing receipts from the sale of reservation land among all tribal entities. Medical care, schools, road maintenance, and other federal services guaranteed under treaty obligations were immediately halted, instead of gradually withdrawn to allow a period of transitional adjustments. The termination acts affected 109 tribes and bands, a total of 13,263 Native Americans, and over 1.3 million acres of trust land.[25]

Two of the more prosperous tribes—the Klamath of southern Oregon and the Menominee of Wisconsin (both of whom owned considerable tracts of valuable timberland)—as well as some Paiute and Ute in Utah, and several other tribes, were among the first to suffer from this legislation. For the Klamath, a tribe of 668 families totaling some 2,000 individuals, termination threatened to obliterate their tribal identity. In the spring of 1968, when 77 percent of the tribe's members voted to withdraw from the tribe and receive a cash payment for their share of the landholdings, many government and business officials feared that liquidating tribal assets when the lumber market was already depressed would threaten the Pacific Northwest economy. Instead of selling the lumber, Congress voted to purchase the land, which it used to create the Winema National Forest. A federal trusteeship for adults declared incompetent to handle their own affairs and for minors kept the government involved in the affairs of 48.9 percent of the tribe members.[26]

In the case of the Menominee, the new policy brought economic disaster:

> Almost overnight, many millions of dollars of tribal assets disappeared in the rush to transform the Menominee reservation into a self-supporting county. The need to finance the usual hospital, police, and other services of a county and pay taxes imperiled the tribe's sawmill and forest holdings, alienated tribal lands, threatened many Indians with the loss of their homes and life savings, and saddled Wisconsin with a huge welfare problem which it could not underwrite and which had to be met by desperate appeals for help from the same federal government that had thought it had washed its hands of the Menominees.[27]

The standard of living dropped sharply as the tribe lost its ability to furnish water, electricity, and healthcare. Shortly after termination, a tuberculosis

TABLE 7.2 Formerly Terminated Native American Tribes Now Restored

Tribe or Band	State	Population	Acres
Alabama-Coushatta	Texas	450	3,200
California Rancherias (37–38 rancherias)	California	1,107	4,315
Catawba	South Carolina	631	3,388
Coyote Valley Ranch	California	NA	NA
Klamath	Oregon	2,133	862,662
Lower Lake Rancheria	California	NA	NA
Menominee	Wisconsin	3,270	233,881
Ottawa	Oklahoma	630	NA
Peoria	Oklahoma	640	NA
Ponca	Nebraska	442	834
Southern Paiute	Utah	232	42,839
Western Oregon (61 tribes and bands)	Oregon	2,081	3,158
Wyandotte	Oklahoma	1,157	94

Note: NA = not available.

Source: Bureau of Indian Affairs.

epidemic swept through the Menominee. Washington's reckless policy shift cost the Menominee their hospital, their saw mill, and some of their best land, lakefront property which they had to sell because they could not afford the taxes on it. President Nixon officially repudiated the termination policy in 1970, and Congress reversed the termination of the Menominee in December 1973. The Restoration Act re-created their reservation, but the Menominee never got back their old hospital or their sawmill.

The following year, the Menominee took over the abandoned 64-room Alexian Brothers monastery to serve as their new hospital. It had been built on Menominee land at a time when any church group could take as much Native American reservation land as it needed to build religious structures. Local whites, who had bought tribal land cheaply when the tribe had to sell, objected, although the Alexian Brothers did not. When bloodshed seemed imminent, the governor of Wisconsin called out the National Guard to maintain order. A peaceful accommodation was reached, and the Menominee won permanent possession of the building. Between 1977 and 1990, most of the other tribes that had been terminated also had their federal recognition restored (Table 7.2) but, in many cases, not their land.

PRESENT-DAY NATIVE AMERICAN LIFE

Of all the minorities in the United States, according to government statistics on income, employment, and housing, Native Americans are "the poorest of the poor." It is cruelly ironic that most of the Native Americans' problems are due not only to their subordinate position as a result of conquest but also to their insistence on their right to be different, to continue living as Native Americans. In a society that has long demanded assimilation, this insistence has not been popular.

Population

The Census Bureau reported in 2007 that the Native American and Alaska Native population was 2.2 million for those claiming only that race, and about 4.3 million if combined with two or more races. They have a higher fertility rate than the non-Hispanic white population, 66 births per 1,000 women aged 15 to 50, than non-Hispanic white women (50 per 1,000).[28]

As Figure 7.2 indicates, the age distribution of the Native American population (including Alaska Natives) is weighted toward the younger years to a much greater extent than that of the total U.S. population. The greater ratio of the population in childbearing age groups suggests continued faster rates of population increase among Native Americans. They are far from being the "vanishing Americans" some observers once claimed.

Education

Significant changes have occurred since 1969, when a Special Senate Subcommittee on Indian Education issued a scathing report on the BIA school system, particularly its boarding schools. Nothing changed, though, until the American Indian Policy Review Commission criticized the BIA in 1976 for still failing to resolve any of the problems. Singled out for especially sharp condemnation were the 19 boarding schools described as "dumping grounds for students with serious social and emotional problems," which "do not rehabilitate" but "do more harm than good." Moreover, the BIA violated official policy by not sending students to the school

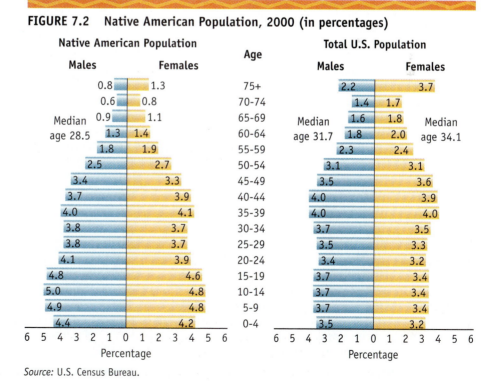

FIGURE 7.2   Native American Population, 2000 (in percentages)

	Native American Population			Total U.S. Population	
	Males	**Females**	**Age**	**Males**	**Females**
	0.8	1.3	75+	2.2	3.7
	0.6	0.8	70-74	1.4	1.7
Median age 28.5	0.9	1.1	65-69	1.6	1.8	Median age 34.1
	1.3	1.4	60-64	1.8	2.0
	1.8	1.9	55-59	2.3	2.4
	2.5	2.7	50-54	3.1	3.1
	3.4	3.3	45-49	3.5	3.6
	3.7	3.9	40-44	4.0	3.9
	4.0	4.1	35-39	4.0	4.0
	3.8	3.7	30-34	3.7	3.5
	3.8	3.7	25-29	3.5	3.3
	4.1	3.9	20-24	3.4	3.2
	4.8	4.6	15-19	3.7	3.4
	5.0	4.8	10-14	3.7	3.4
	4.9	4.8	5-9	3.7	3.4
	4.4	4.2	0-4	3.5	3.2

Median age 31.7

Percentage

Source: U.S. Census Bureau.

closest to their homes, but often hundreds of miles away.[29] Not financial considerations, but the conscious intention of forcing a separation between children and their parents and between "children and the idea of the reservation" determined the location of schools.[30] (See The Ethnic Experience box below.)

The Educational Amendments Act of 1978 gave substantial control over school policy and programs to the Native American communities. Local school boards and school authorities now ensure that the curriculum addresses the unique aspects of Native American culture and heritage. Further, bilingual Native American language

The Ethnic Experience

Boarding School Experiences

"We lived for a few years on Devil's Lake Reservation in North Dakota. . . . I spoke no English until I was four years old. Everything we spoke in the house was Sioux. The religion that my mother and my father both professed was that of their respective tribes. My father had taken on the Sioux religion and my mother was Mohawk. . . .

"I can tell you more about the actual life of a reservation-born Indian, drawing from my mother's experience, than on my own. When my mother was eight years old, economic pressures and also family pressures from the point of view of social justice forced all of the five children of her family to be sent to the Haskell Indian Institute for their education. There was so little future for them if they remained on the reservation, so little possibility of an education. . . .

"My mother was still on crutches. She had had a very serious operation and she was six years between crutches and wheelchair and had to have the operation repeated. Yet she was never excused from any one of the regimental disciplines that were rampant at Haskell. For example, the first statement off the bus was, 'You will be up at five o'clock in the morning. From this moment on there is to be no Indian spoken and the punishments are very severe for anyone who violates this law. You must speak English.'

"My mother had learned first Indian and then some French. She knew not a word of English and yet no one was allowed to ask any companion [for] even the slightest translation. My mother saw severe punishments inflicted on my aunts and uncles, but she herself, because she was so sick, was never punished. However, she was very careful not to violate the rules. Despite the fact she was still in a wheelchair, she had to be out at reveille in the morning. They were up at five o'clock. By five-fifteen they had reveille: You had to be dressed, your face washed, and you had to be standing in military formation. Then the roll call

was called. It was all with the viewpoint of checking who had escaped during the night, because escape was rampant. There was actually some kind of barbed wire around the enclosure at that time.

"My mother, however, did say she had never found a better school. Afterward she went to different schools and she had to admit the education she received at Haskell was superior. She went all the way to business college, and she got six good years of violin training, which prepared her well enough so that she was accepted by the Juilliard School of Music. So she always had admiration for the education that was afforded the Indians. However, the absolute cutoff and isolation from the tribal customs and from the language brought about a lot of culture shock. And the big thing at Haskell was to try to fool the white folks. The Indians always felt that they were on the other side of the line and that nothing would ever overcome that barrier. . . .

"The Indians were forced to take on a Christian religion. Either you adhered to a Christian religion or you were assigned to heavy duty on Sunday mornings, and nobody wanted that. So my mother simply joined the Methodist Church not out of any conviction whatsoever, but because she had had a delicate operation on the hip; and when she saw that the Catholics were bundled off in a pickup truck whereas those who went to the Methodist church had a comfortable, plush school bus, that was the cause for her choice of religion. She never, however, really joined the church, was never baptized. She simply conformed because she said that was the way to keep the white people off her back.

"Now they say that the whole setup has changed a lot and there is none of that rigid discipline."

Source: Sioux–Mohawk woman whose mother went to boarding school in the 1940s. Taped interview from the collection of Vincent N. Parrillo.

programs in 17 states help preserve ancestral languages and teach English to children who were raised in households where only their tribal language was spoken.

Improvement. Significant improvements in educational achievement have occurred in recent years, but Native Americans still lag behind the rest of the U.S. population. Fewer Native Americans graduate from high school (72 percent versus 84 percent), and fewer still will complete college (12 percent versus 27 percent).[31] On average, if 100 Native American students enter the ninth grade, only 77 will graduate from high school. Of these graduates, about half will enter college, and only about 12 will earn a degree (see Table 7.3 and Figure 7.3).

Tribally Controlled Colleges. The tribal college movement began in 1968 when the Navajo Nation established the first such institution, Navajo Community College in Arizona (now called Diné College). Accelerating this movement was federal legislation in 1978 that provided funding for the establishment and continued operation of such colleges. Then, in 1996, President Clinton issued the Tribal Colleges Executive Order—renewed by President Bush in 2002—that directed federal agencies to provide more resources to tribal colleges.

Yet the tribal colleges have an uneven growth. While 17 new ones have opened in the past 25 years, seven others have closed.[32] Today, over 25,000 students are enrolled in over three dozen institutions. With student enrollments increasing by 62 percent in the 1990s and their growth still continuing, tribal colleges offer a family-like support system and serve as cultural intermediaries for Native American college students, reaffirming their group identity while preparing them to succeed in the contemporary world.[33]

Employment

Although the situation is improving, chronic unemployment remains a serious problem, exceeding 50 percent on many reservations and reaching as high as 82 percent at the Rosebud reservation in South Dakota.[34] However, as educational attainment improves, so do employment opportunities. About 25 percent of

TABLE 7.3   Socioeconomic Characteristics of Native Americans, 2000

	Number of Persons	% High School Graduates	% College Graduates or Higher	% Families Below Poverty	% Persons Below Poverty
Cherokee	302,569	76.1	15.7	14.9	18.1
Navajo	276,775	62.7	6.9	33.8	37.0
Sioux	113,713	76.2	10.8	34.3	38.9
Chippewa (Ojibwe)	110,857	77.9	10.3	20.1	23.7
Choctaw	88,692	79.6	16.4	15.8	18.5
Pueblo	59,621	76.3	9.6	26.7	29.1
Apache	57,199	69.0	8.5	26.7	33.9
Iroquois	47,746	79.6	16.3	15.6	19.0
Lumbee	52,614	64.7	12.5	16.4	18.2
All Native Americans	2,447,989	72.5	12.1	21.9	25.8

Source: U.S. Census Bureau, *Characteristics of American Indians and Alaska Natives by Tribe and Language, 2000* (PHC-5).

FIGURE 7.3   Social Indicators About Native American Progress (in percentages)

Age by percent

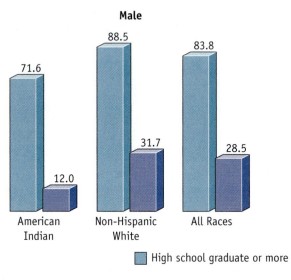

Education (of persons age 25 and over)

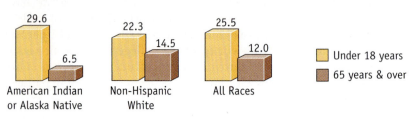

Economic Status

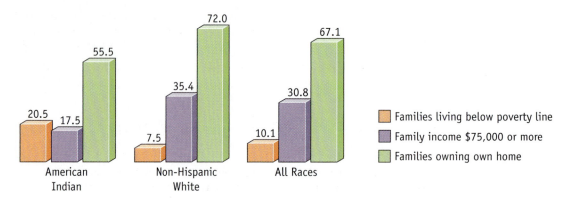

Source: U.S. Census Bureau, *Census 2000,* Summary File 3.

Native Americans aged 16 and older work in management, professional, and related occupations, compared with about 38 percent of employed non-Hispanic whites. About 23 percent work in sales and office occupations, compared with about 27 percent of non-Hispanic white workers. Native Americans are also employed in a variety of other occupations, including about 22 percent in service occupations; about 15 percent in construction, extraction, and maintenance occupations; and about another 15 percent in production, transportation, and material moving occupations, compared to 14 percent, 10 percent, and 12 percent, respectively, for non-Hispanic white workers.[35]

Tribal Enterprise. Some tribes have succeeded through their own efforts. The Mississippi Choctaw are one of the 10 largest employers in that state, with enterprises that include five auto parts factories and one greeting card operation; overall, they employ more than 8,000 permanent full-time workers.[36] Similar successful operations can be found among the Salt River Pima Maricopa of Arizona, New Mexico's Jicarilla Apache, and the Devil's Lake Sioux of North Dakota. The Oklahoma Cherokee now receive half of their funds from commercial ventures, including Cherokee Nation Industries, which constructs military components. The Maine Passamaquoddy had limited success after receiving a multimillion dollar land settlement in 1980. Although they took losses in some investments, their $53 million dollar profit from sale of their cement factory in 1988 enabled them to build a community center, fund some social welfare programs, and distribute $2,000 a year to each tribal member over a five-year period. Today, they maintain an 1,800-acre blueberry farm, making them one of the nation's largest blueberry producers. Harvesting about 3.2 million pounds each years pumps about $500,000 into each of the Passamaquoddy's two reservations, where poverty is common and unemployment can reach 50 percent.[37]

The Pequot tribe in Mashantucket, Connecticut, owns Foxwoods, a spectacularly successful gambling casino bringing great wealth to its members. However, it is the exception; most tribal casinos are small-time bingo or poker gambling halls, whose revenues do little to combat the poverty plaguing so many reservations.

The "New Buffalo." Because federal law permits them to offer any form of gambling not prohibited in other parts of the state, about half of all tribes have casinos. About 300 casinos operate in 28 states and make a staggering $5 billion in profit each year. Nicknamed the "new buffalo" because of their role in providing for the tribes' well-being, most of these casinos barely break even because they are too small and too remote. To illustrate, five states—Montana, Nevada, North Dakota, Oklahoma, and South Dakota—contain nearly half the total Native American population but generate less than 3 percent of all casino proceeds. In contrast, casinos in California, Connecticut, and Florida—totaling only 3 percent of the total Native American population—take in 44 percent of all revenue, about $100,000 per tribal member. Thus only a few wealthy tribes benefit from lucrative casinos; for hundreds of thousands of Native Americans living in poverty, the casinos do nothing. Meanwhile, the white backers of the casinos are earning billions of dollars on their investments.[38]

Health Concerns

Demographic statistics (Table 7.4) testify to the harshness and deprivation of reservation life and the despair accompanying it. The Indian Health Service reports that Native Americans born today have a life expectancy that is 2.4 years less than that of the U.S. population as a whole, and their infants die at a rate of nearly 10 per every 1,000 live births, as compared to 7 per 1,000 for the U.S. population of all races. Moreover, they die at higher rates than other Americans from tuberculosis (500% higher), alcoholism (550% higher), diabetes (200% higher), unintentional injuries (150% higher), homicide (100% higher), and suicide (60% higher).[39] Why have Native Americans long experienced lower health status in comparison to other Americans? In the words of the Indian Health Service:

> Lower life expectancy and the disproportionate disease burden exist perhaps because of inadequate education, disproportionate poverty, discrimination in the delivery of health services, and cultural differences. These are broad quality of life issues rooted in economic adversity and poor social conditions.[40]

TABLE 7.4   Age-Adjusted Death Rates in the United States per 100,000 Population, 2004

Cause of Death	Native Americans	All Races	Ratio
Heart disease	148.0	217.0	0.7
Malignant neoplasms (cancer)	124.9	185.8	0.7
Cerebravascular disease	35.3	50.0	0.7
Motor vehicle accidents	26.0	15.2	1.7
Diabetes mellitus	39.2	24.5	1.6
Chronic liver disease and cirrhosis	22.7	9.0	2.5
Pneumonia, influenza	17.6	19.8	0.9
Suicide	12.2	10.9	1.1
Homicide	7.0	5.9	1.2
HIV (AIDS)	2.9	4.5	0.6

Source: National Center for Health Statistics, *Health, United States* 2006 (Hyattsville, MD: NCHS, 2006), Table 29, pp. 179–180.

In a thorough review of the Native American healthcare system and the role of the federal government, the U.S. Commission on Civil Rights concluded "that persistent discrimination and neglect continue to deprive Native Americans of a health system sufficient to provide health care equivalent to that provided to the vast majority of Americans."[41]

Suicide and Violence. The number of deaths by suicide among Native Americans is generally higher than for all other groups. Suicide among Native American males aged 15 to 24 (30.7 per 100,000) is nearly twice that of the general population's youths (16.8 per 100,000).[42] Recent studies reveal that risk factors for suicide among Native American youth include: strained interpersonal relationships, family instability, depression, low self-esteem, alcohol use or substance abuse, negative school attitudes, and perceived discrimination.[43]

Suicide isn't the only violence in the world of Native Americans. In 1999, the U.S. Justice Department, in its first-ever comprehensive analysis of Native Americans and violent crime, reported that their victimization rate was twice that of the national average. Although their murder rate is no higher than for whites and only a fifth as high as among blacks, they are three times as likely as whites and twice as likely as blacks to be victims of rape or aggravated assault. Alcohol abuse, tensions with non–Native Americans, poor law enforcement services, and other factors may all play a part in generating such high rates of violent crime.[44]

Alcohol Abuse. A serious social problem facing Native Americans today is alcohol abuse, which is also a major factor in their high **mortality rate.** Native Americans have a rate of terminal liver cirrhosis 2.5 times the national rate,[45] and the majority of Native American suicides and motor vehicle deaths involve the use of alcohol. Crimes related to consumption of alcohol and other drugs occur up to 20 times more often among Native Americans than among whites in the same geographic areas.[46]

Scientific evidence suggests, but does not yet clearly prove, that Native Americans are more susceptible to alcohol problems. Philip A. May reports that they metabolize alcohol as rapidly as, or more rapidly than, matched controls of non–Native Americans. Nevertheless, alcohol metabolism and alcohol genetics are traits of individuals, and there is more variation within any ethnic group than there is between ethnic groups.[47] However, according to one national study, Native Americans may actually drink less than the total U.S. population. Surveyed tribes reported a 40 percent drinking rate compared to the national rate of 70 percent. This suggests that those Native Americans who do drink may experience more adverse consequences than others, and that perhaps alcoholism among Native Americans is not innate.[48]

Problem drinking sets in early among Native American youths. Age at first involvement with alcohol is younger than all other groups, the frequency and the amount of drinking are greater, and the negative consequences are more common. Although white youths' alcohol consumption begins to diminish after age 22, no comparable decline occurs among Native American youths.[49]

Cultural marginality is an important factor in understanding alcohol and drug abuse, as studies have shown that Native Americans with a stronger sense of ethnic pride are more likely to adhere to antidrug norms than those with little pride.[50] On the one hand, Native Americans seek to maintain their tribal identity and traditional cultural heritage, even though they are not always certain what their heritage means in the context of modern life; on the other hand, they desire respect, success in the world of work and careers, and the standard of living enjoyed by the dominant society. Inner conflict occurs because the two sets of standards that Native Americans attempt to reconcile are not always consistent. What mainstream society deems appropriate may be undesirable according to tribal values, and vice versa.[51]

Housing

One of the most visible signs of Native Americans' economic deprivation is reservation housing, called "open-air slums" by some critics. Mostly located down back roads and therefore rarely seen by reservation visitors, the various tribes live in small, overcrowded western-style houses, in mobile homes, or in hogans—traditional one-room, eight-sided log houses with sod roofs. The 2000 Census revealed that 18 percent of Native households live in crowded units (more than one person per room) compared to 6 percent of households nationwide. One out of ten households lacked adequate plumbing, ten times the national average, and 17 percent lack telephone service, compared to 2 percent of the U.S. population.[52]

Because many Native Americans live in crowded dwellings, have limited sanitation facilities, and are exposed to smoke from wood-burning stoves, they are more likely to suffer from respiratory and other infectious diseases than other population groups.[53]

NATURAL RESOURCES

Encroachment on Native American land to obtain natural resources or fertile land continues. The need for water and energy has led government and industry to look covetously at reservation land once considered worthless. Moreover, many Native Americans have serious concerns about their lands being used as dumping grounds. Another issue that divides the Indian community is balancing their environmental concerns against the need for economic development.

Exploitation and Emerging Control

Under 53 million acres held by 22 western tribes lie some of the nation's richest reserves of natural gas, oil, coal, and uranium, worth billions of dollars. In fact, one-third of the nation's low-sulfur coal and at least half its uranium deposits are on tribal land. Some tribes, such as the oil-rich Osage in Oklahoma, benefit from the sale of these resources. Only 14 percent of Native Americans, however, live on reservations that receive natural-resource revenues, and even then, the Department of the Interior routinely allows energy companies to shortchange the Indians on royalties.[54]

Even when a tribe thinks its timber, mining, or fishing royalties have secured it a measure of financial stability, such may not be the case. Because the BIA was unable to account for billions of dollars in Native American trust fund accounts, a 1996 class-action suit on behalf of all tribes brought results. In December 1999, a federal judge held officials in the Department of the Interior (who oversee the BIA) in contempt of court for failing to provide relevant materials. A court-appointed special investigator determined government officials had shredded 162 cartons of ledgers listing transactions and disbursements plus records of uncashed checks—some 100 years old—that never reached their intended Native American recipients. Finally, Department of the Treasury officials admitted it received many millions of dollars from the Department of the Interior with no instructions, so they just put it in a general fund where it was used, among other things, to bail out New York City during its 1975 fiscal crisis, to save Chrysler Corporation from going under, and even to reduce the national debt. The BIA had also leased large tracts of Indian land to gas and oil companies and failed to collect any money.[55]

Calling the situation "fiscal and governmental irresponsibility in its purest form," the court fined the government $625,000, officially assumed oversight on efforts to reform the trust program, and required quarterly updates. An appeals court panel upheld the ruling, and the administration opted not to appeal. Based on four reports from the court monitor and with still no resolution, in October 2004, the federal judge held Interior Secretary Gale Norton in contempt of court for lying, going after whistleblowers, and mishandling the Native American trust fund. In July 2006, an appeals court removed the judge from the case, ruling that he "appeared to have lost his objectivity."[56]

Blackfeet. The Sweet Grass Hills are 1,000-foot-high volcanic pyramids standing on the plains of Montana. The hills receive twice the rainfall the plains do, and some observers say the grass grows sweeter in the meadows of these hills than anywhere else. Native Americans from across the continent travel here to collect it for their ceremonies, braiding and drying it, then burning it to "smudge" (purify) people and objects with its sweet, sacred smoke.

As both a burial ground and a place where the Blackfeet of Montana have practiced their religion, the hills are sacred to this tribe, once the fiercest of the northern Plains peoples. In 1995, the land faced the threat of strip mining for gold under the Mining Act of 1872. About 150 miles east-southeast of the Sweet Grass Hills are the Little Rocky Mountains, where previous gold mining has scarred the land, silted in the creeks, and leached cyanide (used by miners to bond and remove finely disseminated gold) into the water. Because the hills are a critical source of water for surrounding ranches and farms, an unusual coalition of environmentalists, farmers, ranchers, and the Blackfeet fought to stop two mining companies from changing the Sweet Grass Hills forever. In 1997, the Bureau of Land Management placed a ban on new oil and gas drilling in this region for 20 years, but this moratorium does not impact valid existing mineral rights, and so the hills are not protected until the claims of the two mining companies are purchased or exchanged.[57]

Navajo. More than 210,000 Navajo live on the nation's largest Native American reservation, larger than the state of West Virginia; its 16 million acres surround the four-corner junction of Arizona, New Mexico, Colorado, and Utah. Beneath this harsh, barren land, 2.5 billion tons of coal and 55 million pounds of uranium deposits lie untouched in the ground.[58] Ironically, high-voltage wires run across vast tracts of the Navajo Nation, carrying electricity to California but not to two-thirds of the Navajo living under them.[59]

The 12,000 Navajo who lived on Big Mountain in northern Arizona fell victim to another form of exploitation. An attorney, working secretly as a hired agent of Peabody Coal Company—the world's largest privately owned coal company—helped persuade Congress to pass the Navajo–Hopi Land Settlement Act in 1978, dividing 1.8 million acres between the two tribes. Any member of either tribe on the wrong side of the line was forced to move. At the time, 100 Hopi were living on territory assigned to the Navajo, and 10,000 Navajo were on lands now officially Hopi. Coincidentally, the Hopi side contains most of the region's known coal reserves, which Peabody wanted for strip mining. The attorney then concocted a "Hopi tribal council" of pro-mining leaders from 3 of the 12 Hopi villages, which signed leases to his company covering 100 square miles of coal reserves. Peabody was already strip-mining coal at nearby Black Mesa, an operation that had destroyed over 4,000 burial and other sacred sites and caused wells to run dry across both Navajo and Hopi reservations.[60]

By 1993, all but 200 Navajo families had moved, motivated partly by a $5,000 stipend they received in return for abandoning their small adobe shelters and moving to government-built housing, and partly by a federal law requiring an immediate 90 percent reduction in livestock grazing on lands now assigned to the Hopi and giving Hopi tribal police the right to impound Navajo livestock.

Strip mining is one of the most irreversible abuses of land, as it removes all soil and vegetation, pollutes groundwater with heavy metals, and permanently alters the condition of the ecosystem. These peaks, north of Flagstaff, Arizona, are sacred to the Navajo, who succeeded in getting the mine closed in 2000, when the U.S. government paid the mine owners $1 million to shut down. However, the scarring of the land is permanent.

Ill-equipped to succeed in an urban economy, many of the relocated Navajo soon lost their homes after the $5,000 was gone. These Navajo suffered far higher rates of unemployment, alcoholism, and suicide than other Navajo.[61]

As the 1993–1994 winter approached and the 200 remaining families attempted to cling to their ancestral homes, BIA agents began confiscating their firewood, along with their axes and saws, and denied the Navajo access to the area water supply. They demolished all new construction projects, began daily raids to confiscate all the free-range Navajo livestock (mostly sheep) they could find, and increased the fee for recovering impounded livestock 10-fold. Still the families held out, unwilling to renounce their claim to sacred sites in the area or to accept the prohibition against burying their dead on the land—a stipulation that strikes at the very core of Navajo custom.

Finally, in 1997, unsuccessful in addressing their grievances in U.S. courts, the Navajo filed a complaint with the United Nations, accusing the U.S. government of violating the Universal Declaration of Human Rights through forced relocation, religious persecution, and environmental degradation of native lands. In the summer of 1998, for the first time in history, the UN Commission on Human Rights conducted a formal investigation of alleged human-rights violations inside the United States. An organized, international protest march in 2000 did nothing to stop the remaining two dozen families from receiving eviction notices. By 2001, however, the U.S. government, facing mounting public pressure at home and abroad, relented and allowed these families to remain.[62]

Meanwhile, the tribal government banned uranium mining, as mercury contaminants from this operation have sickened and killed some Navajos. New Mexico has warned children and pregnant women not to eat the carp and catfish in the San Juan River that passes through the reservation. Nevertheless, in 2007 the Navajo-owned Diné (pronounced dee-NAY) Power Authority moved forward with plans to build the Desert Rock coal plant, one of the largest new plants to be built in recent years, to sell electric power to Phoenix and Las Vegas. Once it opens in 2012, each year it will emit 12 million tons of carbon dioxide, the equivalent of adding 1.5 million average cars to the road. Furthermore, since coal is the most polluting of all fossil fuels, it will add to the air pollution (already exceeding federal standards) in an area where two other coal plants already exist and where 15 percent of the population now suffers from lung disease. The indigenous Diné people, already unable to see the sunrise their ancestors revered because of coal smog, are divided about building this plant, while environmentalists and state officials have been fighting it. However, the Navajo have sovereignty over the land.[63]

Southern Ute. In pleasant contrast, the Southern Ute tribe, located on a 700,000-acre reservation in southwest Colorado, have become an energy powerhouse and a model for other resource-based tribes. Sitting atop one of the world's richest deposits of methane, they control the distribution of about one percent of the nation's natural gas supply, after buying back the drilling rights in the 1990s. With a net worth of about $4 billion and wisely diversifying, mostly through real estate investments, they have donated land for a new county hospital, built a new elementary school and a plush $9.4 million recreation and community center, and offer full scholarships and living stipends for the tribe's college students.[64]

Council of Energy Resource Tribes. Twenty-five Native American tribes formed the Council of Energy Resource Tribes (CERT) in 1975. Modeling the council after the OPEC (Organization of Petroleum Exporting Countries) oil cartel, Native American leaders believed this new organization could prevent further exploitation and secure far greater revenues in return for tribal mineral resources. By 2007, the number of CERT member tribes increased to 54 in the United States and 4 in Canada.[65] The organization offers technical assistance, focuses on internal energy needs of the tribes, and seeks to increase the employment of Native American youths by increasing their engineering and technical skills and by developing proposals to industrialize reservations with royalties from resource development. Critics, including other Native Americans, worry about environmental destruction and disruption of traditional values and culture caused by tapping into the natural resources.

"Dances with Garbage and Nuclear Waste"

With landfills filling up or shutting down because pollutants are leaching into groundwater, disposal companies are looking for cheap new sites for the 320 billion tons of solid-waste materials and 6 billion tons of toxic-waste materials produced annually in the United States.[66] Native American lands are not subject to the same set of environmental regulations as the rest of the country. Poor, but possessing large tracts of isolated land, Native Americans in recent years have seen their reservations recommended as toxic-waste dumping grounds. Although more than 100 tribes have been approached, most of them have rejected the disposal companies' cash offers and employment promises.[67]

In contrast, the Rosebud Sioux tribal council in South Dakota voted to allow O&G Industries of Connecticut to build a 6,000-acre megaregional trash site on the reservation. Previously rejected by the Sioux community at the neighboring Pine Ridge reservation, the huge dump will hold millions of tons of garbage, incinerator ash, coal ash, sewage-sludge ash, and shredded tires. Despite company promises of financial riches for the tribe's 13,600 members, they receive only $1 per ton of trash even though similar dumps charge up to $80 a ton.[68]

The Mescalero Apache—a 5,300-member tribe living in southern New Mexico—made a controversial $2 billion deal with the nation's nuclear utilities to house radioactive waste (spent uranium fuel rods) in a remote corner of their scenic 720-square-mile reservation. Similarly, the 412-member Skull Valley Goshute band, part of the Shoshone nation, agreed to a nuclear waste storage facility, but a lawsuit by the state of Utah has delayed the project for several years. Called everything from hapless victims of environmental racism to unscrupulous opportunists selling out their heritage by despoiling Mother Earth for profit, tribal leaders reject all such criticism, seeing these projects as a means to fight high unemployment rates and gain millions of dollars annually.[69]

Another tribe had little choice about its contact with waste. The St. Regis Mohawk reservation on the St. Lawrence River near Massena, New York, was inundated with chemical garbage for decades. Located downstream, downwind, and downgradient in an industrial corridor extending 100 miles west to Lake Ontario, the reservation suffered from both aquatic poisoning and airborne toxins and experienced a high number of birth defects, thyroid disease, and diabetes.[70] Its water and land food chains are permeated with PCBs (polychlorinated biphenyls) discharged by General Motors (GM), Reynolds Metal, and other corporate polluters. The Environmental Protection Agency fined GM $507,000 for illegal use and disposal of PCBs—the largest fine ever levied for violating of the Toxic Substance Control Act—and it dredged 30 tons of contaminated soil from the St. Lawrence and hauled toxic sludge from lagoons on company property. Yet problems with the two resulting waste sites, their 35-foot high mounds covered by impermeable sheaths, still remain. An impasse presently exists between GM, which wants to seal the dumps permanently, and the Mohawk, who want the toxic sludge dug out and removed forever. Meanwhile, the Mohawk lifestyle has changed: no one fishes or lives off the land now.[71]

Water Rights

Nevada's Pyramid Lake, a spectacular 30-mile expanse of water, belongs to the Paiute, whose water rights the federal government was and is supposed to protect. Instead, in 1906, the government developed an irrigation project to divert 9.8 billion gallons of water each year before it reached the lake. By the 1940s, the water level had dropped 80 feet, killing the trout on which the Paiute depended. In 1944, the U.S. Supreme Court decided the water-rights case, awarding the tribe $8 million in damages. However, in settling the case on their behalf, the Department of Justice did nothing about the fish crisis, the water level in the lake, or imposing restrictions on future irrigation. Finally, the Department of Justice, formally confessing its "breach of faith with the Indians," petitioned the Supreme Court in 1983 to reopen the case to allow the Paiute to refill their lake.[72] A 1996 agreement settled the lawsuit, as three localities and the Department of the Interior agreed to fund a $24 million program to improve river flows, water levels, and wildlife conditions over a five-year period. Today the Paiute economy centers on permits it issues for fishing, camping, and recreational activities at the lake.

Water disputes are sharpest in the Southwest, where the water table is the lowest. Urban sprawl and agribusiness have prompted whites to sink deep wells around reservations in Arizona, siphoning off the water reserves of several tribes. In New Mexico, for example, farmers similarly undermined a viable water system the Pueblo Tribe had built 200 years before the Spanish arrived, leaving that tribe without an adequate water supply. In 2006, a water rights settlement agreement was reached between the Taos Pueblo, the state of New Mexico, and affected non-Native American parties that mutually resolved Pueblo water rights claims and provided basic rules for groundwater production without injuring surface water supplies or underground aquifers.

Water rights are the western tribes' most valuable rights, providing a basis for achieving economic independence. Loss of water dooms them to an even worse existence. On the bright side, since the 1980s most water rights cases were settled in favor of the affected tribes, resulting in tens of millions of dollars awarded in each case. In 2001, the U.S. Supreme Court supported claims by five tribal reservations to water rights for the Colorado River, reflecting the continuing struggle for water in the Southwest.[73]

Suburban sprawl is not only impacting water usage. As it encroaches on the nation's green spaces, a growing number of sacred Native American sites are under threat from housing developments and industrial plants. From North Dakota and Minnesota to Arkansas, from Florida to Nevada, Native American groups are fighting battles with state and federal governments to protect places, including burial sites, to prevent construction from destroying the cultural integrity of these locations.[74]

RED POWER

As Alvin M. Josephy Jr. noted, Native Americans have never been silent about their needs and wishes.[75] Beginning with Seneca Chief Red Jacket's visit to Washington, DC, in 1792, Native Americans have repeatedly told the federal authorities what their people wanted and what was acceptable to them. Because they were seen as "savages," Native Americans found that government representatives usually ignored their views. After the forced-removal programs and the bloodshed came to an end in the late 19th century, the government tried to change the reservation Native Americans' way of life, to eliminate their poverty, and to encourage further integration.

In the 20th century, Native American militancy was quite rare until the 1960s. In the mid-1960s, Native Americans changed their approach, partly because the social climate was different. Many social forces were at work—the Civil Rights movement, the Vietnam protests, the idealism of the Great Society, and a growing social awareness within mainstream society itself. Perhaps taking their cue from other movements, a new generation of Native American leaders asserted themselves.

Pan-Indianism

Pan-Indianism—a social movement attempting to establish a Native American ethnic identity instead of just a tribal identity—has its roots in the past. The growing Iroquois Confederation of the 17th century, the mobility and social interaction among the Plains Tribes in the 19th century, and the spread of the Ghost Dance religion in the 19th century are earlier examples of Pan-Indianism. As Native American youths found comfort in one another's presence, first in boarding schools and later in urban areas, they discovered a commonality in their identity as Native Americans.

Several organizations dedicated to preserving Native American identity and gaining greater political clout evolved from this emerging group consciousness. First organized in Denver in 1944, the National Congress of American Indians (NCAI) effectively lobbied for creation of the Indian Claims Commission (1946), a judicial body allowing the tribes to sue the U.S. government. Like the NAACP (National Association for the Advancement of Colored People), it remains a major civil rights organization acting on behalf of its people. Subsequently, the National Indian Youth Council (NIYC), founded in Gallup, New Mexico, in 1961, and the American Indian Movement (AIM), founded in Minneapolis in 1968, attracted many young people who objected to discrimination and white domination. Both began with militant activism, but the NIYC—with funding support from the Department of Labor—works within the system to improve Native American quality of life, while AIM remains confrontational, with an ideological rift among some of its leaders and other leaders—most prominently Leonard Peltier and Arlo Looking Cloud—in prison on murder convictions.

The Pan-Indian movement lacks complete acceptance, even among young people. Many Native Americans prefer to preserve their tribal identities and to work for the cultural enrichment and social betterment of their own tribe rather than to engage in a national movement. As part of this tribal emphasis, these individuals also learn and teach their people silversmithing, pottery and blanket making, and other crafts that are part of their heritage. In an effort to increase tribal pride and economic welfare, they also establish cultural centers to exhibit ceremonial dances and to sell their artistic works and wares.

Alcatraz

On November 20, 1969, a group of 78 Native Americans under the name Indians of All Tribes occupied Alcatraz Island, a former federal prison. This move, the first militant Native American action in the 20th century, was both symbolic and an effort to establish a cultural center. The sarcasm in this excerpt from their proclamation attacks the paternalism, neglect, and deprivation fostered on Native American tribes past and present:

> We will give to the inhabitants of this island a portion of that land for their own, to hold in perpetuity—for as long as the sun shall rise and the rivers go down to the sea. We will further guide the inhabitants in the proper way of living. We will offer them our religion, our education, our life-ways, in order to help them achieve our level of civilization and thus raise them and all their white brothers up from their savage and unhappy state. We offer this treaty in good faith and wish to be fair and honorable in our dealings with all white men. We feel that this so-called Alcatraz Island is more than suitable for an Indian Reservation, as determined by the white man's own standards. By this we mean that this place resembles most Indian reservations in that
>
> 1. It is isolated from modern facilities, and without adequate means of transportation.
> 2. It has no fresh running water.
> 3. It has inadequate sanitation facilities.
> 4. There are no oil or mineral rights.
> 5. There is no industry and so unemployment is very great.
> 6. There are no health care facilities.
> 7. The soil is rocky and nonproductive; and the land does not support game.
> 8. There are no education facilities.
> 9. The population has always exceeded the land base.
> 10. The population has always been held as prisoners and kept dependent upon others.
>
> Further, it would be fitting and symbolic that ships from all over the world, entering the Golden Gate, would first see Indian land, and thus be reminded of the true history of this nation. This tiny island would be a symbol of the great lands once ruled by free and noble Indians.[76]

This militant action did not succeed. The group's cohesiveness collapsed when the 12-year-old daughter of its leader, Michael Oakes, a Mohawk, fell down an elevator shaft on the island and died. Oakes, the unifying and motivating force, left Alcatraz with his daughter's body. Federal authorities then stepped in and removed the remaining protesters. Oakes himself was later shot to death in California, supposedly mistaken for a trespasser. Today, Alcatraz Island is a tourist attraction as a former prison.

Wounded Knee

On February 27, 1973, about 200 AIM members seized control of the village of Wounded Knee, South Dakota, taking 11 hostages. The location was symbolic as the site of the last Native American resistance in 1890, when 150 Miniconjou Sioux from the Cheyenne River reservation, including men, women, and children, were massacred by the U.S. Cavalry. Many were killed from behind, and the wounded were left to die in a blizzard the following night.[77]

AIM's 71-day siege was a staged media event aimed at directing national attention to the plight of the Native Americans. Some Native American leaders criticized the action as rash, but most Native Americans appeared to sympathize with it. The holdout ended May 8, 1973, with two Native Americans killed, injuries on both sides (including a U.S. marshal paralyzed), and $240,000 in damage to property.[78]

The militants had demanded, among other things, that the government deal with the Sioux on the basis of an 1868 treaty that guaranteed them dominion over the vast northern Plains between the Missouri River and the Rocky Mountains, land that the U.S. government confiscated in 1876. Sioux representatives describe their land claim as the "largest, most historically and socially significant and, in terms of time taken in the courts, the oldest Native American land claim on record."

◢◣◤ THE COURTS

In 1980, the U.S. Supreme Court reaffirmed a lower court's award of $105 million to compensate 60,000 Sioux living on eight reservations in South Dakota, Montana, and Nebraska for the government's illegal seizure of their sacred Black Hills (Paha Sapa), part of the aforementioned Sioux land claim. AIM leader Russell Means urged Sioux chiefs to reject the U.S. offer and demand the land instead, claiming that the Black Hills land was "our graveyard, our church, the center of our universe and the birthplace of our people . . . everything we hold sacred and dear, and this is the reason it is not for sale."[79] With interest, that amount today exceeds $500 million, but the Lakoto Sioux, despite their poverty status, continue to reject an offer that would allow each of them to live comfortably without ever working again. They simply want their land back instead.

The cash settlement offer for the Black Hills rested in part on a 1950 precedent, when the U.S. Court of Claims awarded $31.2 million to the Colorado Ute for lands illegally taken from them. This amounted to about $10,000 for each tribal adult and child. A precedent also existed for the return of land. The Taos Pueblo of New Mexico had regarded the lands at and near Blue Lake as sacred since the 14th century. Demanding the land back from the

Forest Service instead of a proffered cash settlement, the Taos ultimately regained 48,000 acres in 1970 through congressional action at President Nixon's urging.

In 1977, the Passamaquoddy and Penobscot laid claim to about 5 million acres, or nearly one-third of Maine. The Carter administration threw its support behind the Native Americans and in 1978 reached an out-of-court settlement: a lump-sum payment of $25 million cash, plus an additional $1.7 million a year for 15 years, and the sale to the two tribes of 300,000 acres at $5 an acre. The basis for the claim was that the Native American land had been bargained away in violation of the Nonintercourse Act of 1790, which reserved to Congress the power to negotiate with Native American tribes. As mentioned in an earlier section on tribal enterprise, these tribes still have problems due to poor investment decisions.

Elsewhere, after losing 76 of 80 court battles with various Native American tribes, the state of Washington broke new ground, dealing with the tribes as if they were governments. Reaching agreement on salmon management, they also cooperated on health policy, child welfare agreements, and water rights. Wyoming, Colorado, and New Mexico have also negotiated directly with tribes to avoid costly and possibly losing court battles.[80] In New York, the Mohawk, Oneida, Cayuga, Onondaga, Seneca, and Tuscarora nations of the Iroquois Confederacy all have filed sizable land claims, given impetus by a 1985 Supreme Court ruling that New York's treaty with the Oneida violated the Nonintercourse Act, setting a precedent for its treaties with the other Iroquois tribes. In 2007, a federal judge ruled that the Oneida cannot take back land they sold more than a century ago, but that they may be entitled to profits the state made in reselling the land. With interest that amount could be as high as $500 million.[81]

BUREAU OF INDIAN AFFAIRS

The Bureau of Indian Affairs was created in 1824. It has many critics among federal officials, sociologists, anthropologists, and Native Americans (see The Ethnic Experience box, page 248). Some observers view it as a bureaucracy staffed by able, dedicated people (90 percent of them Native Americans) whose ability to act is frustrated by an inefficient organization; others see it as an inept agency that "loses" trust funds, administers ineffective programs that are supposed to reduce unemployment and poverty, and maintains a paternalistic trustee relationship with the tribes, with non–Native Americans holding many of the top positions.

Native American hostility toward the BIA goes beyond complaints about unsympathetic, incompetent, or patronizing personnel; it is directed against the bureau's very structure. Although different government agencies touch all Americans in some ways, few non–Native Americans realize how thoroughly the BIA dominates the lives of Native Americans residing on reservations. The agency is in charge of everything, from tribal courts and schools to social services and law enforcement. It must approve virtually every tribal decision regarding the use of tribal resources—even the disposition of cash settlements that the Navajo and other tribes have won in lawsuits against the BIA itself.

The Ethnic Experience

A Formal Apology to the Indian People

"The works of this agency have at various times profoundly harmed the communities it was meant to serve. From the very beginning, the Office of Indian Affairs was an instrument by which the United States enforced its ambition against the Indian nations and Indian people who stood in its path. . . .

"As the nation looked to the West for more land, this agency participated in the ethnic cleansing that befell the western tribes . . . In these more enlightened times, it must be acknowledged that the deliberate spread of disease, the decimation of the mighty bison herds, the use of the poison alcohol to destroy mind and body, and the cowardly killing of women and children made for tragedy on a scale so ghastly that it cannot be dismissed as merely the inevitable consequence of the clash of competing ways of life. This agency and the good people in it failed in the mission to prevent the devastation. . . .

"Nor did the consequences of war have to include the futile and destructive efforts to annihilate Indian cultures. After the devastation of tribal economies and the deliberate creation of tribal dependence on the services provided by this agency, this agency set out to destroy all things Indian.

"This agency forbade the speaking of Indian languages, prohibited the conduct of traditional religious activities, outlawed traditional government, and made Indian people ashamed of who they were. Worst of all, the Bureau of Indian Affairs committed these acts against the children entrusted to its boarding schools, brutalizing them emotionally, psychologically, physically, and spiritually. Even in this era of self-determination, when the Bureau of Indian Affairs is at long last serving as an advocate for Indian people in an atmosphere of mutual respect, the legacy of these misdeeds haunts us. The trauma of shame, fear and anger has passed from one generation to the next, and manifests itself in the rampant alcoholism, drug abuse, and domestic violence that plague Indian country. Many of our people live lives of unrelenting tragedy as Indian families suffer the ruin of lives by alcoholism, suicides made of shame and despair, and violent death at the hands of one another. So many of the maladies suffered today in Indian country result from the failures of this agency. Poverty, ignorance, and disease have been the product of this agency's work.

"And so today I stand before you as the leader of an institution that in the past has committed acts so terrible that they infect, diminish, and destroy the lives of Indian people decades later, generations later. These things occurred despite the efforts of many good people with good hearts who sought to prevent them. These wrongs must be acknowledged if the healing is to begin.

"Let us begin by expressing our profound sorrow for what this agency has done in the past. Just like you, when we think of these misdeeds and their tragic consequences, our hearts break and our grief is as pure and complete as yours. We desperately wish that we could change this history, but of course we cannot. On behalf of the Bureau of Indian Affairs, I extend this formal apology to Indian people for the historical conduct of this agency. . . .

"Never again will this agency stand silent when hate and violence are committed against Indians. Never again will we allow policy to proceed from the assumption that Indians possess less human genius than the other races. Never again will we be complicit in the theft of Indian property. Never again will we appoint false leaders who serve purposes other than those of the tribes. Never again will we allow unflattering and stereotypical images of Indian people to deface the halls of government or lead the American people to shallow and ignorant beliefs about Indians. Never again will we attack your religions, your languages, your rituals, or any of your tribal ways. Never again will we seize your children, nor teach them to be ashamed of who they are. Never again.

"We cannot yet ask your forgiveness, not while the burdens of this agency's history weigh so heavily on tribal communities. What we do ask is that, together, we allow the healing to begin: As you return to your homes, and as you talk with your people, please tell them that the time of dying is at its end. Tell your children that the time of shame and fear is over. Tell your young men and women to replace their anger with hope and love for their people. Together, we must wipe the tears of seven generations. Together, we must allow our broken hearts to mend. Together, we will face a challenging world with confidence and trust. Together, let us resolve that when our future leaders gather to discuss the history of this institution, it will be time to celebrate the rebirth of joy, freedom, and progress for the Indian Nations. The Bureau of Indian Affairs was born in 1824 in a time of war on Indian people. May it live in the year 2000 and beyond as an instrument of their prosperity."

Source: Excerpts from a speech by Assistant Secretary of the Interior for Indian Affairs Kevin Gover at a ceremony on September 8, 2000, commemorating the BIA's 175th anniversary, at the BIA in Washington, DC.

Yet the BIA continues with its sorry record of waste, corruption, and fiscal mismanagement. A 1999 study by the National Academy of Public Administration (NAPA) detailed acute shortcomings in the agency's ability to manage finance, information technology, records, and procurement operations. Its overall ranking by the Federal Performance Project in 2000 was a "D." Years of fiscal mismanagement continued, as a 2007 audit by the inspector general's office of the U.S. Department of Education revealed that the BIA could not adequately account for more than $100 million in funding for students at special education schools on the reservations and expressed concern about an additional $217 million in other education funding.[82] In 2001, the executive director of the Harvard Project on American Indian Economic Development said, "We can't find a single case of sustained economic success where the BIA is in control."[83] In fact, when tribes took over the managing and management of tribal forests, they surpassed the BIA in harvest productivity and selling price.[84]

URBAN NATIVE AMERICANS

About 70 percent of all Native Americans live in urban areas or away from reservations (Figure 7.4).[85] New York claims the largest concentration (more than 41,000), but that constitutes only 0.5 percent of the city's total population. The Native American population in Los Angeles is over 29,000, or 0.8 percent of the total. Other cities with sizable numbers are Anchorage, Albuquerque, Chicago, Dallas, Detroit, Houston, Oklahoma City, Phoenix, San Antonio, Tucson.[86]

FIGURE 7.4   Major Cities with Largest Native American Populations

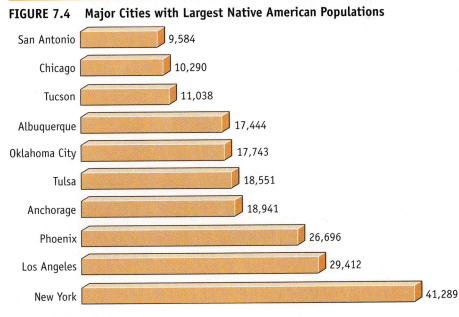

San Antonio	9,584
Chicago	10,290
Tucson	11,038
Albuquerque	17,444
Oklahoma City	17,743
Tulsa	18,551
Anchorage	18,941
Phoenix	26,696
Los Angeles	29,412
New York	41,289

Source: U.S. Census Bureau.

Although urban Native Americans are more widely dispersed in residence than are blacks and Hispanics, twice as many live in poverty compared to all other racial and ethnic groups combined.[87] Often lacking job skills and adequate education, these Native Americans generally experience the same poverty they left behind but without the familiar environment and tribal support system. Researchers have found that urban migration does not immediately improve Native American well-being. Findings consistent with those of other studies show that, although urban Native Americans are more likely to be employed than those who remain behind on the reservations, they do not achieve any improved income earnings, on average, until after five years of residence in the city.[88]

Even though urban Native Americans are not gathered in ethnic enclaves, their other behavior patterns are similar to those of European immigrants. Situated in a social arena where they constitute a minority, new arrivals experience the culture shock of urban living away from the solidarity of the tribe. This shock sometimes leads to personal disorientation, and Native Americans seldom get relief or assistance from the dominant society. These appear also to be reasons that Native American college enrollment is so low outside the tribal colleges.

Members of urban Native American populations generally drink more and have a higher rate of problem drinking than do most members of reservation populations. Such heavy drinking is most common among the lower social strata of urban Native Americans and relates highly to such occupational considerations as prestige and satisfaction.[89] A 2006 public health study of urban Native Americans and Alaska Natives in 19 states revealed that the percentages of disabled, of infant mortality, of teenage mothers, and deaths

In December 2006, the Seminole of Florida, buoyed by income from government compensation for seized lands and casino revenues, diversified their new wealth and became the first Native American tribe to acquire a major international corporation, paying $965 million for 124 Hard Rock Cafés in 45 countries.

from unintentional injuries or liver disease were all higher than for the general population.[90]

Native Americans who succeed in adapting to urban living, usually over a two- to five-year period, settle into semiskilled or skilled jobs. Once they have gained some economic security, they frequently move out of the city to racially mixed suburban areas. Although this shows some degree of acculturation and convergent social adaptation, the trend appears to be limited. Many middle-class urban-adapted Native Americans form their own ethnic institutions, including churches, powwow clubs, social centers, and athletic leagues.[91]

CULTURAL IMPACT

Perhaps no other ethnic group has had as great an impact on U.S. culture as the Native Americans, primarily because they were already here when the first Europeans arrived. The whites, who had to adapt to a new land, found it advantageous to learn from those **indigenous** people. Cities, towns, counties, states, rivers, lakes, mountains, and other geographic entities by the thousands bear Native American names today. More than 500 words in our language are Native American, including *wigwam, succotash, tobacco, papoose, chipmunk, squash, skunk, toboggan, opossum, tomahawk, moose, mackinaw, hickory, pecan, raccoon, cougar, woodchuck,* and *hominy.*[92]

The Native Americans' knowledge of wild herbs and the more than 80 plants they domesticated brought whites a wide variety of new tastes. Native Americans introduced the Europeans to corn, white and sweet potatoes, kidney beans, tomatoes, peanuts, peppers, pumpkins, avocados, pineapples, maple sugar, chicle (as chewing gum), and cacao, as well as tobacco and long-fiber cotton. The Native Americans' knowledge of medicinal plants is also part of their legacy:

> At least fifty-nine drugs, including coca (for cocaine and novocaine), curare (a muscle relaxant), cinchona bark (the source of quinine), cascara sagrada (a laxative), datura (a pain-reliever), and ephedra (a nasal remedy), were bequeathed to modern medicine by the Indians.[93]

Native Americans also made various articles that many people still use today—canoes, kayaks, snowshoes, toboggans, moccasins, hammocks, pipes, parkas, ponchos, dogsleds, and rubber syringes, among other items. Native American influence on jewelry, clothing, art, architecture, literature, and scouting is substantial. Traditional Native American reverence for the land parallels beliefs that conservationists support. In addition, appreciation and adaptations of Native American child-rearing practices, group-directed activities, cooperatives, and ministrations to a patient's mental state are common today.[94]

NATIVE AMERICAN ASSIMILATION

That hundreds of thousands of Native Americans are not assimilated into mainstream society has certainly not been through lack of effort by the dominant group. After following a policy of frontier genocide, expulsion, and forced segregation on reservations, the federal government adopted other methods to "kill the Indian, but save the man," according to a popular saying between 1860 and 1930.[95]

As mentioned earlier in the "Reservations and Dependence" section, a concerted effort at forced assimilation through authoritarian boarding schools attempted to "civilize" Native American youth into mainstream society. On the reservations, meanwhile, the Dawes Act of 1887 disrupted their traditional approach to communal landholding in an attempt to force them to conform to the social and economic structure of the dominant society.[96] Another dimension to this cultural onslaught occurred in the 1890s with the outlawing of indigenous religions. In the 1950s, the termination and relocation programs represented another federal effort to get Native Americans to assimilate.

These efforts had a major impact on the Native American way of life, much of it negative. Earlier sections of this chapter, for example, offered statistics about rates of suicide, alcoholism, violence, disease, poverty, educational attainment, and unemployment. Today, many live in two worlds—their own ethnic community and the mainstream community—forcing them to maintain a bicultural ethnic identity.

Native Americans are not a homogeneous group and differ greatly in their level of acceptance of and commitment to tribal values, beliefs, and practices through a variance of customs, language, and family structure. Moreover, their socioeconomic status and geographic setting (urban, rural, or reservation) affect other individual differences.[97] Michael Garrett and Eugene Pichette suggest that a five-level continuum of acculturation would best describe Native Americans:

- **Traditional:** May or may not speak English, but generally speak and think in their native language; hold only traditional values and beliefs and practice only traditional tribal customs and methods of worship.
- **Marginal:** May speak both the native language and English; may not, however, fully accept the cultural heritage and practices of their tribal group; not fully identify with mainstream cultural values and behaviors.
- **Bicultural:** Generally accepted by dominant society and tribal society/nation; simultaneously able to know, accept, and practice both mainstream values/ behaviors and the traditional values and beliefs of their cultural heritage.
- **Assimilated:** Accepted by dominant society; embrace only mainstream cultural values, behaviors, and expectations.
- **Pan-traditional:** Assimilated Native Americans who have made a conscious choice to return to the "old ways." They are generally accepted by dominant society but seek to embrace previously lost traditional cultural values, beliefs, and practices of their tribal herbal heritage. Therefore, they may speak both English and their native tribal language.[98]

Caught between two cultures, many Native Americans experience pressure to compromise their basic cultural values and behaviors to meet societal expectations and standards. Thus, acculturation influences serve as a mediating factor in maintaining one's cultural values in the process of identity development.[99] When American Indian and Alaskan Native students feel alienated within a school environment because of a clash of cultures, the failure to reconcile cultural differences leads to a high percentage of school dropouts.[100] The challenge remains to find ways for Native Americans to establish a healthy and meaningful cultural identity through bicultural competence.

SOCIOLOGICAL ANALYSIS

Both Hollywood and the BIA rely on stereotypes in their characterization and treatment of Native Americans, even though extensive differences among tribes have always existed. In this chapter, we looked at their similarities and differences, noting changes in attitude and public policy over the years. Our three theoretical frameworks not only provide a coherent approach to understanding the experiences of Native Americans but also provide insights into their problems.

The Functionalist View

Whites may never have fully understood the traditional Native American social system, but anthropologists have found that these tribal societies functioned with a high degree of social organization. Kin relationships, from the nuclear family to a vast clan system, formed the basis of interaction. Clearly defined interdependent work roles for young and old, male and female, in cooperative tasks of living fostered a rather stable society. Living off the land and espousing a pantheistic belief system, they were conservationists, maintaining a harmonious relationship with their natural environment. They were self-sufficient people with institutionalized practices of gift giving and property control—such as the willful destruction of personal property in a competitive display of wealth among some Pacific Coast tribes—which helped sustain a fairly equitable society without great extremes of poverty or riches.

Early contacts with white explorers, trappers, and settlers were mostly harmonious, with both sides benefiting from what each had to offer the other. Dysfunctions occurred as Native Americans slipped into economic subservience, their way of life further threatened by encroachment on their land by steadily increasing numbers of white settlers. Whites saw Native Americans as a hindrance to their making the land productive, so they forcibly removed them. Forced segregation on nonproductive reservations completely destroyed Native American society as a self-sufficient entity while reinforcing other cultural aspects. The systemic disorganization of the society—entrenched for over 100 years—restricted life opportunities. Continued poor education, low income, bad housing, poor health, alcoholism, and other pathologies are costly to society and the people who endure them.

Functionalists stress that the most effective method of resolving these problems is to reorganize our social institutions to put the Native American social system back into balance. However, the plight of the Native Americans is functional to the few reservation Native Americans employed by government agencies to provide services and to BIA employees whose jobs rest on continued paternalistic control, as well as to whites living near reservations who dominate these regions' economy. These individuals, Native American and white alike, would find adjustments in the system dysfunctional to themselves and therefore oppose such changes.

The Conflict View

Lieberson's power theory provides an obvious model for studying Native American–white relations. As discussed in Chapter 2, the white newcomers, superior in technology compared to the indigenous population, engaged in early conflict. The native population suffered numeric decline from warfare, disease, and disruption of sustenance activities, and its social institutions were undermined. Westward expansion, the nation's "Manifest Destiny," occurred by pushing aside the people who already possessed the land without regard for their rights or wishes. Formal government agreements and treaties became meaningless to those in power if further land confiscation or exploitation for natural resources offered profits.

What about today? Who benefits from Native American deprivation now? The battle over the precious commodity of water in the Southwest offers one answer. Water might enable these tribes to gain some income, but it has been stolen out from under them by mining companies, farmers, and land developers. Prolonged court battles enable powerful business interests to maintain their dams, wells, and aqueducts at the expense of the Native Americans. You have read of abuses of other natural resources as well.

Why doesn't Congress do something? Legislators respond to public pressure. Those not living near Native Americans are not motivated or sufficiently concerned to insist on corrective action. Those living near Native Americans have a vested interest in maintaining the status quo, and they are the constituency with the power to influence their legislators.

Yet Native Americans have achieved some positive results. They did so through an emerging group consciousness, whether tribal or Pan-Indian (involving all Native Americans). Protest marches and demonstrations, militant acts of defiance—the Alcatraz, Wounded Knee, and BIA occupations—and class-action lawsuits have all brought public attention and some efforts to remedy their situation. Conflict theory suggests that organized social movements by the exploited can bring about social change. Native Americans are increasingly discovering that redress of their grievances will not occur without concerted public pressure.

The Interactionist View

Consider again the words of Columbus, Franklin, and Catlin earlier in this chapter. Ethnocentric views of Native American culture prompted a definition of the native population as inferiors, savages, and even nonhumans! Once you create such social distance between groups by dehumanizing them, it is easy to justify any action taken against them. Compounding the negative labeling process was racial differentiation. European Americans viewed even the acculturated Native Americans working as servants or laborers in colonial villages, or the entire Cherokee people, as members of an inferior race fit to be subordinated and relegated to a noninterfering, humble role in society.

For their part, the Native Americans at first found whites' customs, fashions, and behavior outlandish and astonishing. Later, they perceived the whites as threats to their existence and as liars and treacherous people. The ensuing hostilities reaffirmed each group's negative view of the other, and the conflict ended with total subjugation of the Native Americans.

Government policy today mistakenly interprets the needs of all tribes in broad terms and treats all tribes alike: the biggest and smallest, the agrarian and fishing, the ones with economic land bases and the ones without. Many dominant-group people in the United States view Native Americans as perpetuating their own problems by remaining on reservations, depending on government support, and refusing to blend in with white society. Growing up on reservations, Native Americans find security in tribal life, viewing the outside world as alien and without promise. Now the strangers in their own land, they believe they have the right to preserve their culture and to receive government assistance because of past abuses, including broken treaties. With so many different interpretations of the current situation, the problems of the reservation appear difficult to resolve.

High levels of prejudice against Native Americans still exist in the West, especially on the edges of the reservations where there is a climate that tolerates violence, say the experts. A 1999 study released by the Department of Justice revealed that Native Americans are the victims of violent crime at a rate of more than twice the national average for blacks. Unlike blacks and whites, they are most likely to be the victims of violent crimes committed by members of a race other than their own. Clearly, the negative labeling and dehumanizing processes that led to past acts of violence against Native Americans remain problems today.[101]

ᐱᐱᐱ RETROSPECT

The white strangers who appeared among the Native Americans eventually outnumbered them, overpowered them, and changed their way of life. Once a proud and independent people, the Native Americans were reduced to a state of poverty, despair, and dependence. The land they had known so well and roamed so freely was no longer theirs. Forced to live within an alien society that dominated all aspects of their lives, they became strangers in their native land. Misunderstood and categorized as savages, they observed the taken-for-granted world of the whites more keenly than most whites did theirs.

Physical and cultural differences quickly became the basis for outgroup hostility as the groups competed for land and resources. Like other groups, the Native Americans faced the familiar patterns of stereotyping, prejudice, discrimination, and conflict because of their alleged inferiority and actual lack of power. Isolation on the reservations not only prevented assimilation (which most Native Americans did not desire anyway) but also created for them a world of dependence and deprivation. Subsequent efforts at forced assimilation—boarding schools, relocation, and termination of the reservations—failed because of Native American resilience and the Bureau of Indian Affairs' lack of thoroughness in personal preparation, assistance, and follow-through.

The Native Americans are still misunderstood and exploited. One, two, or three hundred years ago, people who lived far from the Native Americans idealized them, and those who lived nearest often abused and exploited them. It is no different today. Many people are oblivious to their problems and consider them quaint relics of the past; others find them either undesirable or in the way. Some want their land and will use almost any means to secure it. Native Americans still encounter discrimination in stores, bars, and housing, particularly in cities and near the reservations. They are frequently beaten or killed, and their property rights infringed on.

Since the 1960s, some Native Americans have become more assertive. Many young, better-educated Native Americans are forgetting tribal differences and finding a common bond—Pan-Indianism—uniting in the struggle to protect what they have and to restore what they have lost. Others prefer a more individualistic approach within the tribe. Some gains have been made, and more non–Native Americans are becoming aware of the situations; however, at present, the Native Americans still are one of the poorest minorities in the United States.

KEY TERMS

Dichotomy	Indigenous	Sovereign
Ethnocentrism	Mortality rate	Stereotype
Expulsion	Pan-Indianism	

DISCUSSION QUESTIONS

1. Why do some social scientists call the Native Americans the first victims of racism? Why is racism an integral part of their experiences?

2. Cite some examples of ethnocentrism and stereotyping regarding Native Americans.

3. Why is the power differential so crucial in understanding the Native Americans' past and present problems?

4. Why have most government efforts to "help" the Native Americans failed?

5. In what ways has little changed in the exploitation of the Native Americans?

6. How many Native American names of cities, towns, counties, states, rivers, lakes, mountains, and other geographic entities are there in your area?

SUGGESTED READINGS

Brown, Dee. *Bury My Heart at Wounded Knee*, reprint ed. New York: Holt Paperbacks, 2007.
A Native American viewpoint of past Native American–white interrelations, offering a valuable corrective to traditional historical coverage.

Deloria, Vine, Jr. *God Is Red*, rev. ed. Golden, CO: Fulcrum Books, 2003.
A thought-provoking book that contrasts Christianity with the Native American perspective that, despite a few flaws, is a fascinating read.

Fixico, Donald L. *The Urban Indian Experience in America*. Tucson, AZ: University of Arizona Press, 2000.
An ethnohistorical narrative that deals with such issues as relocation, stereotypes,

alcoholism, the Indian middle class, and the urban–Native American identity crisis.

Fixico, Donald L. *The Invasion of Indian Country in the Twentieth Century: American Capitalism and Tribal Natural Resources*. Niwot, CO: University Press of Colorado, 1998.
A bicultural perspective on the cultural conflict over land and natural resources, with case studies of the Muskogee Creek, Osage, Pueblo, Klamath, Chippewa, and Sioux.

Prucha, Francis P. *American Indian Treaties: The History of a Political Anomaly*. Berkeley, CA: University of California Press, 1997.
Analyzes ratified and unratified treaties, the treaty system during various periods and its collapse, and 20th-century issues related to treaties.

Taylor Colin F., and William C. Sturtevant. *The Native Americans: The Indigenous People of North America*. San Diego, CA: Advanced Protecting Services, 1999.
A comprehensive portrait (with many photographs) of Native American culture, divided into nine geographic areas.

Weatherford, J. McIver. *Native Roots: How the Indians Enriched America*. New York: Ballantine Books, 1992.
A rich, detailed account of the cultural legacy of Native Americans found in many aspects of present-day U.S. society.

MySocKit

Additional resources for this chapter can be found in MySocKit. If you have a subscription to MySocKit, go to www.mysockit.com to study, review, and go beyond the book to learn more about race and ethnic relations.

FIGURE 8.1   Southeast Asia

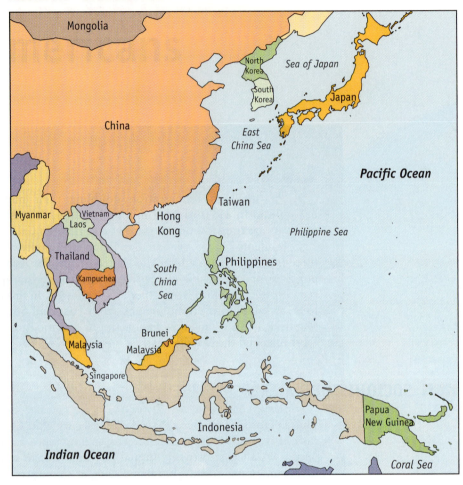

A major social problem affecting most Asian immigrants through the 1940s was the shortage in this country of Asian women. Not only was this imbalance in the sex ratio significant in their personal, social, and community life, but it also provided the basis for racist complaints about prostitution and miscegenation. For the Chinese, the sojourner orientation, the custom that wives should remain in the household of the husband's parents, and subsequent immigration restrictions all help explain this disproportionate sex ratio. By the turn of the century, the shortage of Chinese women in the United States had led to the rise of brothels in Chinatowns and public condemnation. The Filipinos also were mostly male and similarly affected by the shortage of same-ethnicity women. Whether the Asians patronized prostitutes or sought the company of white women who were not prostitutes, racist whites expressed moral indignation, and negative racial stereotypes resulted. Legislators in 14 states passed laws against **miscegenation** (interracial marriage) to prevent Asians from marrying whites.

By 1920, the Japanese sex ratio was largely balanced. Following World War II, a greater number of Asian women migrated to the United States, and the sex ratio for other Asian immigrant groups improved as well. Refugees and war brides from the Japanese, Korean, and Vietnam wars account for part of the change, as do the brides of servicemen stationed overseas during the intervening years. The Immigration Act of 1965, which included provisions giving preference to relatives of U.S. residents, finally ensured both sexes equal opportunity to enter the United States.

After World War II, immigrants from these countries and from other parts of East and Southeast Asia entered a much more industrialized society. Many also came from lands affected by Western contact. Some were political refugees, better educated and more skilled than earlier Asian immigrants. Many preferred living in California, and others moved to the East Coast or elsewhere. Entering various occupations, these postwar immigrants were spared the violent hostility of previous times, although many encountered resentment and discrimination nonetheless.

CULTURAL ATTRIBUTES

The great social distance between themselves and Asians often causes white and black Americans to view Asians as a homogeneous group. They are not. Not only do they differ in their nationality, language, religion, and culture, but they are also diverse within each of their own cultures. Consequently, no single model can reflect the wide disparities in occupational choices or acculturation and acceptance experiences.

Although we need to look beyond racial stereotypes to understand the different Asian immigrant groups more fully, we can identify certain cultural hallmarks that Asians tend to share. The degree to which individuals internalize these norms and values depends significantly on social class, length of residence in the United States, and acculturation.

Generally, traditional Asian values emphasize appropriate behavior, strict control of aggressive or assertive impulses, and a self-conscious concern for conduct in the presence of others. Sibling rivalry is discouraged, and older children are socialized to set an example for younger siblings in politeness, gentleness, and unselfish sacrifices for another's pleasure. Unlike U.S. children, who are encouraged to develop an inner sense of guilt as a social-control mechanism, Asian children experience the external sanctions of shame, or losing face—of bringing disgrace or dishonor to the family name.

Within the family, open displays of emotion or affection are rare, except with infants and small children. Uniting the family is the important value of filial piety. Elders in the family (even those only slightly older) command respect and obedience; younger family members never talk back to them. Traditional sex-role definitions require the men to provide for and protect the women and the women to submit to the decisions of the men. Fathers and eldest sons are thus the most powerful family members.

As in most immigrant groups, the extended family is predominant among Asian Americans. A cohesive structure exists, encouraged in part by the sense of duty and responsibility arising out of filial piety but also by values stressing ancestor worship and the importance of the family name. Loneliness and isolation for the unmarried or aged seldom occur because the extended family embraces and absorbs them. No typical Asian American family model exists, however, and the blending of U.S. and Asian cultures affects the family structure, especially in promoting a more egalitarian role for women.

THE CHINESE

U.S. residents on both coasts of North America knew something about the Chinese long before they first came to the United States. The United States had established trade relations with China as early as 1785, and many Protestant missionaries went there after 1807. Newspaper reports and magazine articles, inspired by the Anglo-Chinese War (1839–1842)—the so-called Opium War— and subsequent rebellions and incidents, featured lurid descriptions of filth, disease, cruel tortures, and executions. Americans gradually developed an unfavorable image of the Chinese based on these ethnocentric distortions and exaggerations. In 1842, seven years before the gold rush, the *Encyclopaedia Britannica* offered this unflattering portrait of the Chinese people:

> A Chinaman is cold, cunning and distrustful; always ready to take advantage of those he has to deal with; extremely covetous and deceitful; quarrelsome, vindictive, but timid and dastardly. A Chinaman in office is a strange compound of insolence and meanness. All ranks and conditions have a total disregard for truth.[3]

Structural Conditions

Most Chinese who came to the United States in the 19th century were farmers, artisans, craftsmen, political exiles, and refugees. The discovery of gold in California proved to be an opportunity not only for easterners and Europeans but for the Chinese from Kwangtung Province, who could reach the gold rush country easily and who sought to recoup their losses from flood, famine, and the Taiping Rebellion (1850–1864). A combination of push–pull factors thus brought the Chinese to the United States. The first wave of migrants came as sojourners, intending to earn some money and then return home.

Visible because of their race, appearance, and behavior, the Chinese aroused both curiosity and suspicion. The sounds and characters of their language seemed most peculiar to the non-Chinese, as did their religion. Their "strange" clothes and hair worn in *queues* (a braid of hair in the back of the head) also seemed out of place in the crude pioneer surroundings. With little or no command of English, they kept mostly to themselves and viewed California as a temporary workplace. As a result, the Chinese remained an enigma to most Americans.

By 1860, California's population included a large and varied ethnic segment. About 38 percent were foreign born, and many others were Spanish-speaking natives or children of European immigrants.[4] The Chinese constituted about 9 percent of the state's population in 1860, but because they were mostly adult males, they accounted for close to 25 percent of the labor force.[5] As the general population increased, however, the percentages of the total and working populations that they represented decreased.

Hired as laborers who worked in gangs, the Chinese built much of the western portion of the transcontinental railroad for the Central Pacific. As many as 9,000 Chinese a year toiled through the High Sierra country, digging tunnels and laying tracks, and the task was completed sooner than expected. Leland Stanford, then president of the Central Pacific Railroad, described the Chinese as "quiet, peaceable, industrious, economical." Although Chinese laborers received the same wages as non-Chinese, they fed and housed themselves, unlike the white workers, and thus cost the railroad company two-thirds as much as whites to maintain.[6] The Chinese did not, however, pose an economic threat to the non-Chinese workers:

> Hiring Chinese resulted not in displacement of non-Chinese but in their upgrading. To the unskilled white railroad laborer of 1865, the coming of the Chinese meant his own advancement into that elite one-fifth of the labor force composed of straw-bosses, foremen, teamsters, skilled craftsmen. And one final reason was perhaps more cogent than all the others. No man with any choice would have chosen to be a common laborer on the Central Pacific during the crossing of the High Sierra.[7]

The end of the Civil War, however, brought veterans seeking jobs and eastern manufacturing concerns seeking West Coast markets, helped by efficient, low-cost shipment of goods over the transcontinental railroad. Fired when their work was completed, Chinese railroad laborers sought other jobs, but economic conditions worsened across the nation, culminating in the Panic of 1873. Labor supply exceeded demand, and laborers, union organizers, and demagogues mounted racist denunciations of Chinese "competition."

Among the most popular ethnophaulisms directed against the Chinese during this period of labor agitation were accusations of their being "dirty" and "disease-ridden." These epithets had originated decades earlier. In the 1840s, Americans first became aware of the relationship between germs and dirt and disease. Negative stereotypes about the supposed Chinese preference for eating vermin and the crowded, unsanitary Chinatowns caused whites to associate the Chinese with leprosy, cholera, and bubonic plague. By the 1870s, the labor issue had become predominant, but as the labor unions closed ranks against the Chinese, they labeled them a menace to both the economy and the health of U.S. society. The *real* issue by 1877, however, was race, disguised as labor conflict.

Societal Reaction

Racist attacks against the Chinese continued throughout the remainder of the 19th century. Some antagonists compared them with blacks in terms of "racial inferiority"; others attacked the "vices" of the "Oriental" race. In the 1850s, one antislavery southerner attempted to draw parallels among several groups that were supposedly inferior:

> No inferior race of men can exist in these United States without becoming subordinate to the will of the Anglo-Americans. . . . It is so with the Negroes in the South; it is so with the Irish in the North; it is so with the Indians in New England; and it will be so with the Chinese in California. . . . I should not wonder, at all, if the copper of the Pacific yet becomes as great a subject of discord and dissension as the ebony of the Atlantic.[8]

Cries for restrictions on Chinese immigration increased as racial antagonism rather than economic competition came to the forefront. In particular, the myth of an Asian inclination for despotic government was propagated by hostile Western media. "Oriental despotism" soon became as much a catch-phrase as "heathen Chinese." In 1865, the *New York Times* expressed alarm at the supposed effect of increased Asian immigration on U.S. civilization, religion, morals, and political institutions:

> Now we are utterly opposed to the permission of any extensive emigration of Chinamen or other Asiatics to any part of the United States. There are other points of national well-being to be considered beside the sudden development of material wealth. The security of its free institutions is more important than the enlargement of its population. The maintenance of an elevated national character is of higher value than mere growth in physical power.
>
> . . . We have four millions of degraded negroes in the South . . . and if there were to be a flood-tide of Chinese population—a population befouled with all the social vices, with no knowledge or appreciation of free institutions or constitutional liberty, with heathenish souls and heathenish propensities, whose character, and habits, and modes of thought are firmly fixed by the consolidating influence of ages upon ages—we should be prepared to bid farewell to republicanism and democracy.[9]

In 1867, California Democrats used an anti-Chinese platform to such advantage that they swept the state elections, including the gubernatorial chair. Democrats elsewhere saw a bonanza in this issue because many Republicans were identified with the railroads and with companies that recruited and employed the Chinese and because the Democrats—identified with the defeated Confederacy and slavocracy—could not use Negro-baiting effectively outside the South after 1865. Republicans secured the Burlingame Treaty of 1868 between China and the United States, providing for unrestricted travel between both countries "for the purpose of curiosity, or trade, or as permanent residents." Still, public hostility in the United States against the Chinese continued to grow.

To some, the Chinese posed a serious immigrant threat to the idealized concept of the melting pot. Individuals who held this belief argued that German and Irish Catholics, at least, were physically similar to the Protestant northern and western Europeans. An 1868 *New York Times* editorial offered this display of racial bigotry:

> Although they are patient and reliable laborers, they have characteristics deeply imbedded which make them undesirable as part of our permanent population. Their religion is wholly unlike ours, and they poison and stab. The circumstance would need be very favorable which would allow of their introduction into our families as servants, and as to mixing with them on terms of equality, that would be out of the question. No improvement of race could possibly result from such a mixture.[10]

As the prejudices of the 1850s distilled into the almost hysterical sinophobia of the 1870s and 1880s, the negative stereotype of the "yellow peril" emerged. In 1879, Senator James G. Blaine of Maine, a Republican Party leader and presidential hopeful, even attacked Chinese family values because of the sojourner orientation:

> The Asiatic cannot go on with our population and make a homogeneous element. This idea . . . comparing European immigration with an immigration that had no regard to family, that does not recognize the relation of husband and wife, that does not observe the tie of parent and child, that does not have in the slightest degree the enabling and civilizing influence of the hearthstone and the fireside.[11]

His erroneous comments ignored not only the intense cohesiveness of Chinese family structure but also the common practice of European males coming to the United States ahead of their families.

Legislative Action

More than 225,000 Chinese came to the United States between 1850 and 1882. As Chinese sojourners came to the United States and returned to China in steady numbers, steamship companies found passenger trips a highly profitable operation and so encouraged Chinese immigration. In 1881, about 12,000 Chinese disembarked; in 1882, the number jumped to almost 40,000.[12]

Another cycle of economic woes and labor agitation against the Chinese led to increasing pressures for restrictions. President Arthur vetoed the first restriction bill, which would have barred all Chinese immigration for 20 years. A few months later, however, he signed a revised bill that barred Chinese laborers for a 10-year period but permitted Chinese businessmen, clergy, students, and travelers to enter. The Chinese Exclusion Act of 1882 marked a significant change in national policy toward immigrants. For the first time in the nation's history, the federal government enacted a human embargo on a particular race of laborers. Sufficient exceptions remained to allow 8,000 legal Chinese immigrants in 1883, but legislative action in 1884 tightened the restrictions further, and in 1885, the number of Chinese immigrants dropped to 22.[13]

This 1882 political cartoon—the year of passage of the Chinese Exclusion Act—depicts an Irishman, African American, Civil War veteran, Italian, Frenchman, and a Jew—most victims of prejudice themselves—building a wall against the Chinese, using blocks of prejudice. Across the sea, an American ship enters China, as the Chinese tear down their own wall to permit trade of such goods as rice, tea, and silk. (*Source:* The Library of Congress [LC-USZC4-4138]).

Violence directed against Chinese immigrants, which had sporadically flared up prior to the legislation, continued. In 1871, 21 Chinese had been massacred in Los Angeles, and anti-Chinese riots had occurred in Denver in 1880. Such hostile actions became much more widespread after 1882. For example, at Rock Springs, Wyoming, in September 1885, a mob attacked and murdered 28 Chinese, wounded many others, and drove hundreds from their homes. Labor unions and politicians took action against the Chinese in various localities across the western United States. In Tacoma, Seattle, Oregon City, and many smaller towns, angry mobs expelled hundreds of Chinese residents, with considerable loss and destruction of property.

Congress extended the Chinese Exclusion Act for 10 years in 1892, then extended it indefinitely in 1902. Other Anglo-Saxon–dominated countries on the Pacific Rim also restricted Chinese immigration. Australia passed legislation in 1901, but Canada did not take such action until 1923. Before then, Americans frequently criticized Canada, especially the province of British Columbia, because Chinese entered the United States from there. Reverse migration also occurred after 1858, when the United States served as a point of entry into Canada for many Chinese.

Organized labor's creation and instigation of the anti-Chinese issue is illustrated in an 1893 American Federation of Labor (AFL) convention resolution, which held that the Chinese brought to the United States "nothing but filth, vice, and disease." It also maintained they had corrupted "a part of our people on the Pacific Coast to such a degree that could it be published in detail the American people would in their just and righteous anger sweep them from the face of the earth."[14] These wild, racist charges had little basis in fact except that filth and disease did exist in some Chinatown districts—as indeed they did in Irish, Italian, and other ethnic urban slums.

Avoidance and Segregation

How did the Chinese immigrants react to all the abuse, vilification, and discriminatory legislation? Some reluctantly returned to China. Some sought redress in the courts, winning all cases involving state immigration restrictions but few based on assault or property damage complaints. The latter were difficult to maintain in California, at least, because from 1854 to 1870 the California courts did not allow Chinese to testify against whites.

Expelled from various trades and occupations as well as from many residential areas, Chinese immigrants had little choice but to congregate in Chinatowns and rely on their own benevolent and protective associations for assistance. A large number congregated in San Francisco, but others moved to the larger eastern and midwestern cities and formed ethnic enclaves there. These Chinatowns were in low-rent ghetto areas, usually situated close to major means of transportation, which at least gave the Chinese ready access to friends and relatives. For example, in New York City and San Francisco, they are near the docks, and those in Boston, Pittsburgh, and St. Louis are near the railroad stations (Figure 8.2).

In seeking redress of grievances through the courts, the Chinese petitioned for equal rights. They won the right to have their children attend public schools, and then they fought to desegregate the schools. Housing codes kept them in the ghetto, where they found themselves segregated both socially and spatially.

FIGURE 8.2   Percent Asian Alone or in Combination: 2000

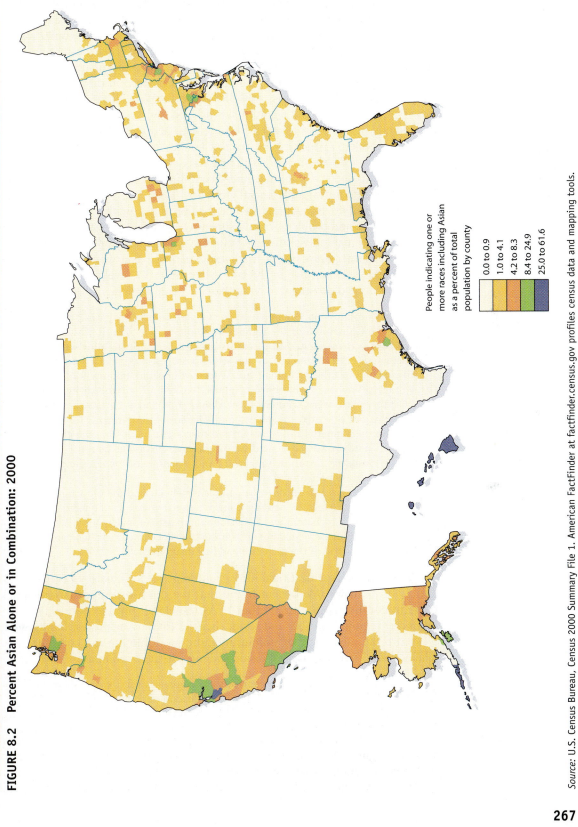

People indicating one or
more races including Asian
as a percent of total
population by county

0.0 to 0.9
1.0 to 4.1
4.2 to 8.3
8.4 to 24.9
25.0 to 61.6

Source: U.S. Census Bureau, Census 2000 Summary File 1. American FactFinder at factfinder.census.gov profiles census data and mapping tools.

Securing jobs through the associations or from Chinese merchants, most entered occupations that either did not compete with whites (e.g., in art and curio shops or Chinese restaurants) or that involved serving only their own people. They settled disputes among themselves, partly because this was their custom and partly because they distrusted the white people's court. The traditional associations and the family clan offered them the familiarity and protection they needed. Chinese temples, newspapers, schools, and Old World festivals all represented efforts to preserve their cultural and traditional practices.

Examining the early growth of Chinatowns across the United States and analyzing the modern status of New York's Chinatown, D. Y. Yuan identified a four-stage process of development.[15] The first stage was marked by involuntary choice in response to societal prejudice and discrimination. Defensive insulation came next, as protection against racial hostility. Then, as a group consciousness emerged, voluntary segregation became the third stage, with Chinatown residents sharing culture and problems of adjustment. The final stage was gradual assimilation, a process markedly slowed by voluntary segregation and social isolation.

Albert Palmer drew on his firsthand experience as a white growing up near San Francisco's Chinatown in the late 19th century to develop his social analysis of the stereotyped dominant view of these "foreign settlements":

> Those who know only the picturesque Chinatown of today can hardly realize what the Chinatown of the eighties and nineties was like. It was dirty, overcrowded, rat-infested, and often diseased. It was poorly built with narrow alleys and underground cellars and secret passages, more like a warren of burrowing animals than a human city. It seemed uncanny because inhabited by a strange yellow race who wore "pigtails," talked an outlandish lingo in high falsetto voices, were reputed to eat sharks' fins and even rats, and to make medicine out of toads and spiders, and who sprinkled garments for ironing by sucking their mouths full of water and then squirting it out over the clothes. And Chinatown was accounted vicious because it was the haunt of gambling, opium smoking, lotteries, tong wars and prostitution, where helpless little slave-girls were bought and sold. . . .
>
> Now, fear is a great disturber, and it largely created the old Chinatown. It did this partly, in fact, by herding Chinese into narrow, squalid quarters and surrounding them by hatred and suspicion; and partly in imagination, by creating the weird and distorted picture of their outlandish character. . . . Chinatown was never quite so bad as the prejudice and fear imagined it.[16]

In analyzing organizational life in San Francisco's Chinatown between 1850 and 1910, Stanford M. Lyman found that the traditional associations quickly came in conflict with one another.[17] As the clans (lineage bonds), *hui kuan* (ethnic or regional bonds), and secret societies (outlaw or protest bonds) fought to secure the allegiance of immigrants and to dominate the community, the Chinese faced strife from both inside and outside their community:

> Principles of clan solidarity, barriers of language and dialect, allegiance to rebellious secret societies, and their own competitive interest in making enough money to permit retirement in China divided the loyalties of the Chinese immigrants. Yet during the same period the depredations of anti-Chinese mobs, the difficulties and indignities imposed by restrictive immigration legislation, the occupational discrimination created by state and local laws prohibiting or limiting the employment of Chinese, and the active opposition of the American labor movement to the Chinese workingman all seemed

to call for a community united in the face of its enemies. What emerged out of this condition of pressures from without the ghetto and divisions within was a pattern alternating between order and violence. By 1910 this pattern had assumed a complex but recognizable sociological form: that of the community whose members are bound to one another not only because of external hostility but also because of deadly internal factionalism.[18]

One constant of Chinese immigrant life was discrimination and hostility in the white world:

> During most of this period, the lives of average Chinese in the United States were difficult and irregular. No matter how well educated they were, in their living quarters they were confined to a crowded Chinatown. . . . College training in engineering or other technical subjects did not guarantee decent positions to Chinese. If one should go out, dressed casually for a walk, or go to a club, or even to a church, he was liable to be picked up by the immigration officers on suspicion of illegal residence. For many years officials made a practice of picking up persons in the street or in public places on the suspicion that they were aliens illegally in this country. Such arrests were reported to be very common, especially in the late 1920s.[19]

Not all Chinese migrated to the crowded Chinatowns of the cities. A few hundred, many of whom became merchants, settled in the Mississippi Delta. Chinese grocers catered mostly to blacks, extending them credit and providing other essential services (e.g., assisting illiterate rural blacks with government forms and making telephone calls). Some Chinese married black women; others brought their families over from China.

In this transition from sojourner to immigrant, Chinese men with families tried to evade their "black" status and avoid discrimination against their children, who were attending white public schools. In the 1920s, however, as a result of segregationist actions, Chinese children were expelled from the white schools, and the action was upheld by the courts "to preserve the purity and integrity of the white race, and prevent amalgamation." Separate schools for the Chinese were established, as the Mississippi Chinese developed parallel institutions when they were excluded from the white prototypes. By 1950, their status improved, as white churches and schools opened to them.

Social Factors

In the 19th century, single Chinese women rarely ventured alone to the United States in search of economic opportunity, and Chinese tradition demanded that the wife remain with her husband's parents, even if he worked far from home. About half the Chinese sojourners were married. The imbalance in the male–female ratio in the United States was very significant: 1,858:1 in 1860; 2,106:1 in 1880; 2,678:1 in 1890; and 1,887:1 in 1900. By 1920, the gender ratio, although still very much out of balance, had lessened to 695:1.[20] The ratio continued to decline steadily thereafter. By 1990, Chinese immigration had reached parity in sex distribution: 49 percent male and 51 percent female from mainland China, and 47 percent male and 53 percent female from Taiwan.[21]

In earlier years, however, the overabundance of Chinese males and the scarcity of Chinese females led to organized prostitution in Chinatowns. Numerous brothels dotted the Chinatowns, some of them run or protected by the secret societies and staffed with young women kidnapped from their villages, sold by impoverished parents, or lured abroad by the deceit of a proxy marriage.[22]

With the vast Pacific Ocean separating him from domestic joys and companionship, the Chinese sojourner relied on the tong-controlled brothels for sex, attending the gambling and opium dens for recreation and respite from the day's toil, and paid homage and allegiance to his clansmen, *Landsmänner,* and fraternal brothers to secure mutual aid, protection, and a job.[23]

Intermarriage was extremely difficult for the Chinese; indeed, 14 states had passed laws expressly forbidding miscegenation. Furthermore, in 1884, a federal court ruled that only wives of those males exempt from the Chinese Exclusion Act of 1882—namely, merchants and businessmen—could emigrate to the United States. For nearly all the Chinese laborers in the United States, establishing a family was impossible. By 1890, 40 years after the Chinese had first arrived, only 2.7 percent of the total Chinese population was U.S.-born. The figure climbed to 30 percent by 1920. Legislation in 1943 allowed Chinese women to enter the country, enabling the U.S.-born Chinese population to pass the halfway point in 1950. By 1960, U.S.-born Chinese accounted for approximately two-thirds of the total Chinese American population.[24]

Recent Immigrants

Congress ended the ban on immigration from China in 1943 and in its place instituted a quota system despite lingering anti-Chinese feeling. Speaking against the repeal, however, Congressman Compton White of Idaho in 1943 condemned the Chinese as a race unable to accept U.S. standards, citing the actions of a few to create a false stereotype of an entire group:

> The Chinese are inveterate opium-smokers most of the day. They brought that hideous opium habit to this country. . . . There is no melting pot in America that can change their habits or change their mentality. . . . If there are any people who have refused to accept our standard and our education, it is the Chinese.[25]

In any case, the 1943 legislation permitted only 105 Chinese immigrants to enter the United States each year, and that quota included anyone in the world of Chinese descent, not just citizens of China. Special and separate legislative acts covering refugees, displaced persons, and brides allowed more Chinese to enter. Not until passage of the Immigration Act of 1965, however, could the Chinese enter under regular immigration regulations.

Since 1965, the Chinese American population has increased rapidly, growing more than fivefold since 1970 to about 2.4 million in 2000 (Table 8.1). More than 342,000 arrived in the 1990s, a total already surpassed between 2000 and 2006 with 385,000. As a result, the Chinatowns in San Francisco, Los Angeles, and New York doubled in population in a decade, spilling over their traditional boundaries and into adjacent neighborhoods. The arrival of so many "FOB" (fresh off the boat) immigrants and refugees has raised commercial rents, squeezing out old-line shops. With the Chinatowns unable to absorb all the newcomers, Chinese are flourishing in outlying areas as well—such as the Corona, Flushing, and Jackson Heights sections of Queens in New York City and the Richmond and Sunset neighborhoods of western San Francisco. Upward mobility and outward migration have converted Monterey Park, east of Los Angeles, from an almost entirely white residential suburb into "Little Taipei," where the majority of people are now Chinese Americans (Figure 8.3).[26]

TABLE 8.1   East and Southeast Asian American Populations

Nationality	1970	1980	1990	2000
Chinese	435,000	806,000	1,645,000	2,423,000
Filipino	343,000	775,000	1,407,000	1,864,000
Vietnamese*	NA	262,000	615,000	1,110,000
Korean	70,000	355,000	799,000	1,073,000
Japanese	591,000	701,000	848,000	795,000
Cambodian*	NA	16,000	147,000	178,000
Laotian*	NA	48,000	149,000	168,000
Hmong*	NA	5,000	90,000	170,000
Thai*	NA	45,000	91,000	111,000

Note: NA = not available.

*Virtually all have entered the United States since 1970.

Source: U.S. Census Bureau.

The San Francisco, Los Angeles, and New York Chinatowns, paradoxically, are both tourist attractions and slum communities. They are filled with overcrowded, dilapidated buildings and troubled by the problems of youth gangs and high tuberculosis rates; nonetheless, they retain historical, picturesque, and commercial importance. Less evident to tourists are the Chinese garment shops, or sweatshops, notorious for their long hours and meager compensation.[27] Also hidden above and behind the street-level storefront façades is a population density that is 10 to 12 times the city average and a tuberculosis risk rate that is far greater than the general population's.[28]

FIGURE 8.3   Cities with Largest Asian Populations, 2000

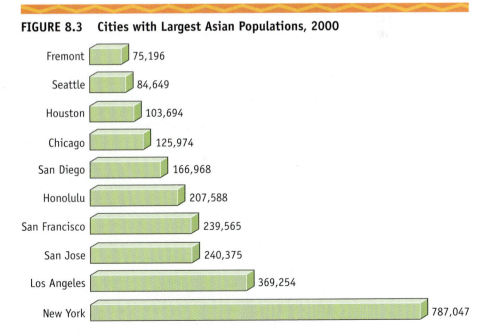

Fremont	75,196
Seattle	84,649
Houston	103,694
Chicago	125,974
San Diego	166,968
Honolulu	207,588
San Francisco	239,565
San Jose	240,375
Los Angeles	369,254
New York	787,047

Source: U.S. Census Bureau.

Compounding the problem are crime syndicates in China, known as *triads,* that smuggle perhaps as many as 80,000 Chinese into the United States each year (only about 10 percent are caught). Estimates place the number of illegal aliens in big-city Chinatowns as one in five residents.[29]

Within the Chinatowns, streets mark off the sections containing residents of different regional origins and dialects, much as in an early 20th-century Little Italy. In New York City, for example, which is the largest Chinese enclave in the Western Hemisphere, Burmese Chinese concentrate on Henry Street, Taiwanese on Centre Street, Fujianese on Division Street, and Vietnamese Chinese on East Broadway.[30]

A Chinatown concern in recent years has been the increasing rebelliousness, criminality, and radicalism of many Chinese American youths. The formation of delinquent gangs, particularly in New York City and San Francisco, has resulted in a growing number of gang wars and killings. The rise of youthful militancy and delinquency appears to reflect the marginal status of those in the younger generation, who experience frustration and adjustment problems in the United States. Many recent arrivals from Hong Kong are unfamiliar with the language and culture; they are either unemployed or in the lowliest of jobs, and they live in overcrowded, slumlike quarters with no

In a scene photographed around 1912, U.S. flags fly in New York City's Chinatown. This blend of the distinctive features of an ethnic community and the U.S. influence illustrates the ongoing processes of acculturation and ethnogenesis—the absorption of some cultural elements of the host society while elements from one's own cultural heritage are retained or adapted.

recreational facilities. For some youths, gang behavior helps fulfill status and identity needs.[31]

Socioeconomic Characteristics

Chinese Americans present a bipolar occupational distribution: 30 percent occupy professional and technical positions as against 15 percent of the white labor force, but the Chinese are also heavily overrepresented among low-skilled service workers, with 24 percent as compared to 7 percent of the white labor force. Such employment characteristics reflect in part educational and immigration patterns. Also notable is a higher median family income for Chinese Americans than for other U.S. ethnic groups. However, more than 62 percent of Chinese families have more than one wage earner, compared to the 57 percent of the total population of families, which may account for the difference.[32]

THE JAPANESE

When Commodore Matthew Perry sailed into Tokyo Bay in 1853, his arrival marked the beginning of a new era for Japan. For more than 200 years, the Japanese had lived in government-enforced isolation. The emperors had prohibited travel and foreign visitors, although castaways were treated hospitably and allowed to leave unharmed. No one was permitted to build large boats, and any attempt to emigrate was punishable by death.

The situation began to change in 1860, when the Japanese government sent its first official emissaries to Washington, DC. U.S. observers thought the Japanese lacked emotional expression:

> [A San Francisco reporter wrote:] "This stoicism, however, is a distinguishing feature with the Japanese. It is part of their creed never to appear astonished at anything, and it must be a rare sight indeed which betrays in them any expression of wonder."
>
> In the 85 years which passed between the arrival of Japan's first embassy and the end of World War II, this "distinguishing feature" of the Japanese became the cardinal element of the anti-Japanese stereotype. Characterized by journalists, politicians, novelists, and film-makers as a dangerous enemy, the Japanese were also pictured as mysterious and inscrutable.[33]

Beginning in 1868, the Japanese began emigrating, first as laborers and eventually as permanent settlers. Their numbers on the U.S. mainland were small at first. U.S. Census Bureau records show only 55 in 1870 and 2,039 in 1890. After that, they came in much greater numbers, reaching 24,000 in 1900, 72,000 in 1910, and 111,000 in 1920.

Economic Competition

Because many families in Japan still followed the practice of **primogeniture** (in which the eldest son inherits the entire estate), many second and third sons came to the United States to seek their fortunes. They settled in the western states, where anti-Chinese sentiment was still strong, most of them becoming farmers or farm laborers. Their growing numbers, their concentration in small areas, and their racial visibility led to conflict with organized labor, vegetable growers, and shippers in California.

Early Japanese immigrants entered various manufacturing and service occupations. Hostility from union members, who resented Asians' willingness to work for lower wages and under poor conditions, produced the inevitable clashes. Members of the shoemakers' union attacked Japanese cobblers in 1890, and members of the union for cooks and waiters attacked Japanese restaurateurs in 1892. Finding that employment was difficult to obtain, most Japanese gravitated to the outlying areas and entered agricultural work, first as laborers and eventually as tenant farmers or small landholders; other Japanese became contract gardeners on the estates of whites.

Their industriousness and knowledge of cultivation placed the Japanese in serious competition with white and Hispanic farmers, and they encountered further acts of discrimination. In 1913, the California legislature passed the first alien landholding law, prohibiting any person who was ineligible for citizenship from owning land in the state and permitting such persons to lease land for no more than three years in succession. Under the U.S. Naturalization Act of 1790, then still in effect, citizenship was available to "any alien, being a free *white* person" (italics mine). In 1868, the government had modified this law to extend citizenship to persons of African descent (the recently freed slaves), but the Japanese continued to be excluded.

Because their children born in this country were automatically U.S. citizens, the Japanese held land in their children's names, either directly or through landholding companies whose stock they owned collectively. After World War I, new agitation arose against the Japanese. In 1920, the California legislature passed a law prohibiting aliens from being guardians of a minor's property or from leasing any land at all. The U.S. Supreme Court upheld the constitutionality of this law in 1923, and New Mexico, Arizona, Louisiana, Montana, Idaho, and Oregon passed similar statutes. Because their opportunities were still best in agriculture, many Japanese continued to work as tenant or truck farmers. Morton Grodzins suggests that their immense success (the Japanese raised 42 percent of California's truck crops by 1941) helps to explain why white vegetable growers and shippers pressed for their evacuation during World War II.[34]

National Policy

Most non-Californians had no strong feelings about Japanese immigrants, but they were aware of Japan's growing military power after the Japanese defeated Russia in 1905 after two years of warfare. The catalyst that triggered a change in national policy toward the Japanese was a local incident. In 1906, the San Francisco Board of Education passed a resolution transferring 93 Japanese children scattered throughout the city's 23 schools into a segregated "Oriental" school in Chinatown. This action made national headlines and had international ramifications. Under pressure from the Japanese government, President Theodore Roosevelt instructed the attorney general to initiate lawsuits challenging the constitutionality of this action.

As a compromise, the school board rescinded its resolution, the government dropped its legal action, and Roosevelt issued an executive order (which remained in effect until 1948) barring the entry of Japanese from a bordering country or U.S. territory. Thus, Japanese who stayed even briefly in Hawaii, Canada, or Mexico could no longer enter the mainland United States. In addition, President Roosevelt secured the so-called Gentlemen's Agreement of 1908, whereby Japan agreed to restrict, but not eliminate altogether, the issuance of passports. The big loophole in the Gentlemen's Agreement was permission for wives to enter. Many Japanese married by proxy and then sent for their "picture brides." Several thousand Japanese entered the United States every year until World War I, and almost 6,000 a year came after the war.

As men brought their wives here and children were born, fearful nativists made exaggerated claims that the Japanese birth rate could lead to the Japanese "overrunning" the country. Questions about Japanese immigration began to shift from economic competition to the "assimilability" of the Japanese because of their race, lifestyle, and alleged birth rate. The anti-Japanese stereotype, long a part of dominant-group attitudes, played a key role:

> The anti-Japanese stereotype was so widespread that it affected the judgments of sociologists about the possibilities of Japanese assimilation. Thus, in 1913 Robert E. Park was sufficiently depressed by anti-Japanese legislation and popular prejudice to predict: "The Japanese . . . is condemned to remain among us an abstraction, a symbol, and a symbol not merely of his own race, but of the Orient and of that vague, ill-defined menace we sometimes refer to as the 'yellow-peril.'" Although Park later reversed his doleful prediction, his observations on Japanese emphasized their uncommunicative features, stolid faces, and apparently blank character.[35]

The Immigration Law of 1924—which severely restricted the number of southern, central, and eastern Europeans who could enter the United States—specifically barred the Japanese because it denied entry to all aliens ineligible for citizenship. The bill passed by large majorities (323 to 71 in the House and 62 to 6 in the Senate), indicating widespread support for limiting immigration to the supposedly "assimilable" peoples. The Japanese government vehemently denounced this legislation, taking it as a national affront, a violation of the terms of the Gentlemen's Agreement, and an insult to a world power only recently courted by the United States. Nevertheless, the legislation remained in effect until 1952 (see The International Scene box about a latent function of Japanese national policy on immigrants).

Expulsion and Imprisonment

By 1940, about 127,000 ethnic Japanese lived in the United States, 94,000 of them in California. About 63 percent were U.S.-born, and only 15 percent were of voting age. Japan's attack on Pearl Harbor in 1941 and the subsequent war led to what was subsequently referred to as "our worst wartime mistake."[36] More than 110,000 Japanese, many of them second- and third-generation Americans with as little as one-eighth Japanese ancestry, were removed from their homes and placed in "relocation centers" in Arkansas, Arizona, eastern California, Colorado, Idaho, Utah, and Wyoming.[37]

> The evacuees loaded their possessions onto trucks. . . . Neighbors and teachers were on hand to see their friends off. Members of other minority groups wept. One old Mexican woman wept, saying, "Me next. Me next."
>
> . . . People were starting off to 7 o'clock jobs, watering their gardens, sweeping their pavements. Passers-by invariably stopped to stare in amazement,

The International Scene

The Difference between Race and Culture

After decades of Japanese refusal to let in unskilled foreigners, tens of thousands of Bangladeshis, Pakistanis, Thais, and other Asians entered Japan in the 1980s on tourist visas and stayed illegally. Worried that it might be flooded by foreigners, as France and Germany had been, Japan enacted tougher immigration curbs on unskilled workers in 1989 and began expelling the estimated 100,000 illegal immigrant Asians. Still needing a labor pool and not wanting to open its doors to outsiders, Japan next changed its immigration laws in 1990 to encourage immigration of foreigners whose parents or grandparents already lived in Japan, expecting a homogeneous blending.

About 150,000 unskilled ethnic Japanese fleeing the troubled economy of Brazil quickly entered Japan to take dirty, difficult, and dangerous jobs at construction sites, factories, and foundries or low-status jobs in restaurants and shops unwanted by native-born Japanese. But what objectively appeared to be a mutually beneficial arrangement created numerous adjustment problems for both sides, neither of which was prepared for the resulting culture shock.

The Japanese expected the Brazilians to be Japanese, but culturally they were not. They spoke Portuguese—and little or no Japanese—when they arrived and for a long time afterward. They dressed differently, talked more noisily, and laughed and embraced one another in public, all unlike the native-born Japanese.

Their ethnicity became more visible with the advent of numerous Portuguese-language radio programs and newspapers, restaurants, stores, and social clubs. Brazilian street festivals in Tokyo flavored with samba and salsa attracted large crowds.

The immigrants complain that they are looked down on and treated with suspicion. They say they suffer discrimination in stores and restaurants, where they are either made to feel unwelcome or treated as probable shoplifters. Another problem they face is the lack of health benefits and worker's compensation if they are injured at work. The government, meanwhile, has opened a dozen centers to assist the foreign-born laborers.

Today, about 280,000 Brazilians live in Japan, about 3,500 of them in a public-housing complex in Toyota City. Numerous slights by Japanese against Brazilians, and the natives' generalization that all Brazilians are criminals, served as preludes to confrontations and in May 1999 to a brawl between Japanese and immigrant youth gangs. The Toyota City government then formed a committee to work on improving relations between the two nationalities, but the committee did not include any Brazilians.

Critical Thinking Question: What similarities to the above situation do you find between native-born African Americans and immigrants from Africa?

perhaps in horror, that this could happen in the United States. People soon became accustomed to the idea, however, and many profited from the evacuation. Japanese mortgages were foreclosed and their properties attached. They were forced to sell property such as cars and refrigerators at bargain prices.[38]

The mass expulsion of the Japanese from the West Coast was unnecessary for national security, despite claims to the contrary. The traditional anti-Asian sentiment on the West Coast, fear of the "perfidious" character of the Japanese, and opposition to Japanese American success in agriculture may all have been factors. No mass evacuation of the 150,000 ethnic Japanese occurred in Hawaii, which was much more strategically important and vulnerable to attack because of its location. The differences in the Japanese experience in Hawaii and on the mainland are perhaps best understood by looking at the differences in structural discrimination. In Hawaii, the Japanese were more fully involved in economic and political endeavors, partly because they lived in an environment of greater racial harmony. On the West Coast, the

Japanese American evacuees, most of them born in the United States, return to their barracks after leaving church on a wintry morning at Manzanar Relocation Center, California. Only in 1988 did the government begin making token reparations payments for losses they sustained by this wartime imprisonment.

Japanese were more isolated from mainstream U.S. society, and certain labor and agricultural groups saw them as an economic threat. Also, anti-Asian attitudes and actions had prevailed in that area for almost 100 years.

Besides the trauma that resulted from being uprooted and interned, the Japanese had to adjust culturally to their new surroundings. Instead of their preferred deep hot baths, they had only showers and common washrooms. Central dining halls prevented families from eating together intimately as a family unit. Outside and sometimes distant toilet facilities, not partitioned in the early months, were a hardship for the old and for the parents of small children. Almost 6,000 babies were born while these centers were in existence, and proper hospital facilities were not always available. Only partial partitions divided rooms occupied by different families in the same barracks, permitting minimal privacy. Ted Nakashima, a second-generation Japanese American, offered a frightening portrait of what the early months of life in the Tule Lake, California, camp were like:

> The resettlement center is actually a penitentiary—armed guards in towers with spotlights and deadly tommy guns, fifteen feet of barbed wire fences, everyone confined to quarters at nine, lights out at ten o'clock. The guards are ordered to shoot anyone who approaches within twenty feet of the fences. No one is allowed to take the two-block-long hike to the latrines after nine, under any circumstances. The apartments, as the army calls them, are two-block-long stables, with windows on one side. Floors are . . . two-by-fours laid directly on the mud, which is everywhere. The stalls are about eighteen by twenty-one feet; some contain families of six or seven persons. Partitions are seven feet high, leaving a four-foot opening above. . . .

> The food and sanitation problems are the worst. We have had absolutely no fresh meat, vegetables or butter since we came here. Mealtime queues extend for blocks; standing in a rainswept line, feet in the mud, waiting for the scant portions of canned wieners and boiled potatoes, hash for breakfast or canned wieners and beans for dinner. Coffee or tea dosed with saltpeter and stale bread are the adults' staples. Dirty, unwiped dishes, greasy silver, a starchy diet, no butter, no milk, bawling kids, mud, wet mud that stinks when it dries, no vegetables—a sad thing for the people who raised them in such abundance. . . .
>
> Today one of the surface sewage-disposal pipes broke and sewage flowed down the streets. Kids played in the water. Shower baths without hot water. Stinking mud and slops everywhere.
>
> Can this be the same America we left a few weeks ago? . . . What really hurts most is the constant reference to us evacuees as "Japs." "Japs" are the guys we are fighting. We're on this side and we want to help.
>
> Why won't America let us?[39]

Although the harsh physical conditions and sanitation problems improved, the Japanese Americans remained prisoners. They tried to make life inside the barbed wire fences a little brighter by fixing up their quarters and planting small gardens. However, these "residents" of the "relocation centers" still lived in what were actually concentration camps. About 35,000 young Japanese Americans left these centers by the end of 1943, going voluntarily to the East and Midwest for further schooling or a job. For those obliged to remain in the camps, life was monotonous and unproductive. The evacuation brought financial ruin to many Japanese American families; they lost property, savings, income, and jobs for which they were never adequately compensated.

By weakening Japanese subcommunities and institutions, the evacuation program encouraged acculturation. The traditional authority of the first-generation Japanese Americans (*Issei*) declined; family structure and husband–wife roles underwent changes and became more equal because of camp life; and the second-generation Japanese (*Nisei*) who resettled found new opportunities. Of the Japanese who relocated to the Midwest and to the East Coast, a large number later returned to the West. Many became more a part of U.S. society in the postwar period because they had been forced to do so.

In 1944, the Supreme Court upheld the Japanese evacuation by a 6 to 3 vote (*Korematsu v. United States of America*), although the dissenting justices gave strong minority opinions. Justice Francis Murphy called approving the evacuation "the legalization of racism." Justice Robert H. Jackson, who later prosecuted the Nazi war criminals at Nuremberg, wrote,

> But once a judicial opinion rationalizes such an order to show that it conforms to the Constitution, or rather rationalizes the Constitution to show that the Constitution sanctions such an order, the Court for all time has validated the principle of racial discrimination in criminal procedure, and of transplanting American citizens. The principle then lies about like a loaded weapon ready for the hand of any authority that can bring forward a plausible claim of an urgent need. Every repetition imbeds that principle more deeply in our law and thinking and expands it to new purposes.[40]

Soon after, another case, *Endo v. United States*, brought an end to this forcible detention—as of January 2, 1945—when the U.S. Supreme Court unanimously ruled that all loyal Japanese Americans be set free unconditionally.

Justice Jackson's 1944 dissenting opinion seemed prophetic 35 years later, when the seizure of U.S. hostages at the U.S. Embassy in Iran prompted calls by some politicians for Iranian students then attending U.S. colleges to be rounded up and detained in the very same concentration camps.

After their release Japanese Americans sought redress through the Japanese American Citizens League (JACL). This organization fought to restore and reopen frozen bank deposits to their owners, obtain compensation for owners of confiscated land, and regain lost retirement benefits owed to civil service workers. The Evacuation Claims Act of 1948 brought token repayment of about 10 percent of actual Japanese American losses.[41] In 1988, new legislation brought a formal apology to the former internees for violating their "basic civil liberties" because of "racial prejudice." The bill also awarded a tax-free payment of $20,000 to each of the 60,000 surviving detainees.[42]

Recent Immigrants

Because homeland influences are important in understanding immigrant orientations, changes in Japan since World War II are worth mentioning. U.S. occupation of the country and foreign aid–based reconstruction led to significant and rapid social change in Japan. Westernization and industrialization affected Japanese values and lifestyles; it also altered U.S. attitudes. The 25,000 Japanese war brides who accompanied returning GIs to the United States at first encountered suspicion and hostility, but such attitudes eventually disappeared. Some were not accepted by the Japanese American ethnic community, but Japanese wives of whites were usually looked on as unthreateningly exotic by the dominant group.[43]

Traditionally, Japanese parents have encouraged their children to get a good education; and, since the 1940s, Japanese American males and females have performed well above the national norms of those completing high school and college. The culture's emphasis on conformity, aspiration, competitiveness, discipline, and self-control helps to explain the high educational attainments of Japanese Americans.[44] Encouraged by their *Nisei* (second-generation) elders and the upwardly mobile *Sansei* (third generation), the *Yonsei* (fourth generation) and *Gosei* (fifth generation) have increasingly entered professional fields, especially engineering, pharmacy, electronics, and other technical fields. Most Japanese Americans are U.S.-born, and their higher education levels translate into their having incomes above those of any other ethnic group, including all white Americans.[45]

With half their number now native-born Americans, Japanese Americans have become arguably the best-assimilated of all Asian Americans. Both of Hawaii's U.S. senators, Daniel Akaka and Daniel Inouye, are of Japanese ancestry. On the mainland, structural assimilation, for example, is evident among the *Sansei* and *Yonsei,* whose outgroup dating and exogamy have significantly increased, surpassing 50 percent.[46] This trend suggests that Japanese Americans are becoming the first nonwhite group to merge biologically into the dominant U.S. society.

Japanese immigration to the United States amounted to about 67,000 in the 1990s—far less than the totals of most other East Asian countries.[47] Consequently, the Japanese American population represents a steadily declining proportion of the Asian American community (8 percent in 2000). Two of every three Japanese Americans live either in California (36 percent) or Hawaii (29 percent). About half of all new arrivals are skilled and professional workers who find many similarities between U.S. society and their homeland. Most are adherents of Buddhism, a religion whose U.S. membership is growing because of the continuing entry of Japanese and other Asian believers in this faith.

One special group in the United States is comprised of businesspeople and employees of the *kai-sha* (large corporations) on two- or three-year assignments with their companies' U.S. branch offices. Their presence is extremely noticeable in the New York metropolitan region. Many suburban towns near New York City, particularly those along the Metro train line north into Westchester County and northeast along the New Haven line have experienced a large influx of *kai-sha* employees and their families, particularly such suburban communities as Scarsdale, Hartsdale, Larchmont, and Mamaroneck.[48]

THE FILIPINOS

The Filipinos came to the United States with a unique status. In 1898, the Philippines became a U.S. possession, so for the next several decades, the inhabitants were considered U.S. nationals, although not U.S. citizens. Not therefore designated as aliens, they faced no quota restriction on their entry until 1935. The geographic locale of their homeland and their Spanish heritage complicated their status, however, because the federal government argued that they were not whites. The U.S. Supreme Court upheld this official position in a 1934 ruling on a case challenging the 1790 naturalization law limiting citizenship to foreign-born whites:

> "White persons" within the meaning of the statute are members of the Caucasian race, as Caucasian is defined in the understanding of the mass of men. The term excludes the Chinese, the Japanese, the Hindus, the American Indians and the Filipinos.[49]

Early Immigrants

Like so many other immigrant groups, the early Filipino immigrants did not think of themselves in nationalist terms. Instead, they placed themselves in one of several native language subgroupings: the Tagalogs, Visayans, or Ilocanos. Their social hangouts—the clubhouse, bar, or poolroom—often reflected that separation. U.S. society lumped them together, however, and soon societal hostility forged a common ethnic identity among them.

After the Gentlemen's Agreement of 1908 curtailed Japanese emigration, the Hawaiian Sugar Planters' Association recruited laborers from the Philippines to work the plantations. Fifteen years later, the modest number of Filipinos in the continental United States (5,603 in 1920) began to increase. Why? California growers, faced with the loss of Mexican labor because of quota restrictions in the pending Immigration Act of 1924, turned to the Filipinos as an alternative labor source. By 1930, the number of Filipinos in the continental United States had increased to over 45,000, with more than two-thirds living in California.

Many Filipinos worked in agriculture at first, particularly in California and Washington. However, the lure of the city attracted many young Filipino males to urban areas, where they sought jobs. Discrimination, along with lack of education and job skills, resulted in their getting only low-paying domestic and personal-service work in hotels, restaurants, other businesses, and residences. They were employed as bellboys, waiters, cooks, busboys, janitors, drivers, house boys, elevator operators, and hospital attendants. By 1940, their employment in these areas peaked, with 9 of 10 Filipinos so employed.[50] Feeling exploited by their employers, they often joined unions (or formed their own unions when denied membership in existing unions) and went on strike, intensifying management resentment. Ironically, the union hierarchy also disliked them and later joined in efforts to bar them from the United States.

Race riots erupted in Exeter, California, on October 24, 1929, and in Watsonville, California, on January 19, 1930, when one Filipino was killed. In both instances, several hundred white men beat Filipinos, shattered windows in cars and buildings, and wrecked property. As the Depression of the 1930s worsened and jobs became scarcer, dominant-group critics increased their objections to the presence of the Filipinos Other clashes occurred in San Jose and San Francisco, followed on January 28, 1930, by the bombing of the Filipino Federation of America Center in Stockton, called "the Manila of California" because of its large Filipino population.

The Scarcity of Filipino Women

Of every 100 Filipinos coming to California between 1920 and 1929, 93 were male; almost 80 percent were single and between 16 and 30 years of age. With few Filipino women available, these males sought the company of women of other races, thereby enraging many white men, as the following racist statement illustrates:

> The Filipinos have . . . demanded the right to run dance halls under the alias of clubs, with white girls as entertainers. And the excuse they have openly and brazenly given for their demand is that the Filipinos "prefer" white women to those of their own race and that besides there are not enough Filipino women in the country to satisfy their lust. . . . If that statement is not enough to make the blood of any white man, of any other decent man boil, then there is no such thing as justified indignation at any advocacy of immorality.[51]

This bigoted, demagogic statement reflects the sort of sexually oriented charges often directed against minority racial groups. Filipino men's association with white women through intermarriage, dance hall encounters, and affairs led to increased tensions in Filipino–white relations. The Filipinos' reputation as great lovers emerged as a stereotype and probably was enhanced when a San Francisco judge commented:

> Some of these boys, with perfect candor, have told me bluntly and boastfully that they practice the art of love with more perfection than white boys, and occasionally one of the girls has supplied me with information to the same effect. In fact, some of the disclosures in this regard are perfectly startling in nature.[52]

Filipino responses followed quickly. Sylvester Saturday, editor of the Filipino Poets League in Washington, DC, stated,

> We Filipinos are tickled at being called "great lovers." Surely, we are proud of this heritage. We love our women so much that we work ourselves to death to gain and keep their affections.[53]

A Filipino from Chicago chided,

> And as for the Filipinos being "great lovers," there is nothing surprising about that. We Filipinos, however poor, are taught from the cradle up to respect and love our women. That's why our divorce rate is nil compared with the state of which Judge Lazarus is a proud son. If to love and respect our womenfolks is savagery, then make the most of it, Judge. We plead guilty.[54]

Whites were not amused. Several western states passed laws prohibiting marriages between Filipinos and whites. The Tyding–McDuffie Act of 1935 granted deferred independence to the Philippines and imposed an immediate rigid quota of 50 immigrants a year. Repatriation efforts from 1935 to 1937 succeeded in returning only 2,190 U.S. residents to the Philippines.[55]

Because of the lack of Filipino women and legal restrictions on intermarriage, many Filipino males remained single. These early immigrants became lonely old men with no family ties, living in poverty after years of hard work, although a small number did intermarry with Mexicans, Native Americans, mulattos, Asians, and whites.[56]

Unlike the Chinese, who had a tradition of being sojourners and who formed benevolent and protective associations, the Filipinos did not establish the support institutions usually found in immigrant communities. Their lack of families and the seasonal, transitory nature of their employment were primary reasons for this. As a result of housing discrimination, they lived in hotels and rooming houses in less desirable sections of town. The pool hall and taxi-dance hall became their recreational outlets.[57]

Recent Immigrants

With the Philippines a strategically important ally during World War II, the social climate in the mainland United States became more liberal toward Filipinos. In January 1942, legislation enabled Filipino residents to become naturalized U.S. citizens. They could buy land in California, and many did—often from Japanese Americans who were being removed from certain areas, such as Los Angeles. Many Filipinos bought farms in the San Fernando Valley, the San Joaquin Valley, and the Torrance–Gardena area.[58]

Since the Immigration Act of 1965, Filipino immigration has been quite high. An unstable political situation at home toward the end of the Marcos regime (which was peacefully overthrown in 1986) and continuing economic deprivation in the Philippines have served as the major push factors. Like the Japanese, new Filipino arrivals tend to have better educational and occupational skills than most of their ethnic cohorts born in the United States. Over two-thirds are professional and technical workers in medicine, law, engineering, and education. Because of licensing and hiring problems, however, many are unable to secure jobs commensurate with their education, skills, and experience (Figure 8.4).[59]

Filipinos are fragmented socially, linguistically, and politically. Unlike the Koreans, few are entrepreneurs, and seldom do Filipinos form cooperative credit

FIGURE 8.4   Occupation Distribution of the Employed Civilian Labor Force by Sex: 2002

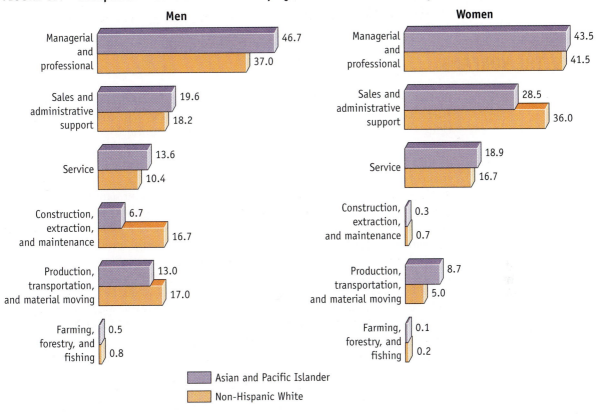

	Men		Women	
	Asian and Pacific Islander	Non-Hispanic White	Asian and Pacific Islander	Non-Hispanic White
Managerial and professional	46.7	37.0	43.5	41.5
Sales and administrative support	19.6	18.2	28.5	36.0
Service	13.6	10.4	18.9	16.7
Construction, extraction, and maintenance	6.7	16.7	0.3	0.7
Production, transportation, and material moving	13.0	17.0	8.7	5.0
Farming, forestry, and fishing	0.5	0.8	0.1	0.2

Asian and Pacific Islander
Non-Hispanic White

Source: U.S. Census Bureau.

associations to raise business capital. Filipino youths, unlike other East Asian American youths but like the Indochinese, often reject traditional family discipline and become assimilated. About half of all Filipino Americans speak only English.[60]

The largest concentration of Filipinos living outside the Philippines is in Hawaii, where they comprise 60 percent of all hotel maids and porters. On the mainland, Filipinos tend to settle on either the West Coast or the East Coast. Mostly Roman Catholics, with a strong loyalty to family and church, today's Filipino Americans otherwise present diverse socioeconomic characteristics of education, occupation, income, and residence. Time of immigration and age appear to be the key variables. The old-timers—retired laborers—usually are single males with meager incomes. Second and third generations born in the United States typically share such problems as lack of social acceptance, low income, low educational achievement, and negative self-image. In contrast, new arrivals often are college graduates seeking white-collar jobs in the economic mainstream.[61]

Filipino Americans more than doubled in number between 1970 and 1980, going from 343,000 to 775,000, and doubled again—to nearly 1.9 million—by 2000. Today, they are the second-largest Asian and Pacific Islander ethnic group in the United States, comprising 18 percent of the total U.S. Asian population. More than 534,000 newcomers arrived in the 1990s, a number that will probably be matched in this decade.[62]

THE KOREANS

By the middle of the 19th century, English, French, and Russian whaling ships sailed Korean waters, and many Catholic missionaries had come to Korea. The United States, however, became the first Western nation to sign a treaty with Korea, when it formalized a relationship of friendship and trade in 1882. Other nations quickly followed suit, and all attempted to displace China as the then preeminent foreign power in Korea.

Despite various treaties and declarations by the different nations purporting to guarantee Korea's independence, emerging Japanese hegemony (both political and economic) became the reality. Japan's victory over Russia in 1905 solidified Japanese domination of Korea, and Japan exercised colonial control until the end of World War II. Even then, Korea did not gain national independence, however, for an Allied military agreement in 1945 mandated that Soviet troops accept the Japanese surrender in the region north of the 38th parallel and U.S. troops do the same in the region south of it. This temporary line, created out of military expediency, became a permanent demarcation that still defines the split between North and South Korea.

Early Immigrants

The Hawaii Sugar Planters' Association, needing laborers to replace the Chinese, who were excluded by the 1882 legislation, recruited 7,226 Koreans, 637 of them women, between 1903 and 1905. This was the first large group of Koreans to migrate to the United States. The Koreans, mostly peasants, sought economic relief from the famines plaguing their country at the turn of the century. In Hawaii, they worked long hours for meager wages under harsh conditions. Of the original group, about 1,000 returned to Korea, but 2,000 males and 12 women went on to the mainland United States, and the rest remained in Hawaii. The males were almost all between the ages of 20 and 40.[63] (See The Ethnic Experience box.)

Between 1907 and 1924, several thousand more Korean immigrants—mostly "picture brides," political activists fighting Japanese oppression, and students— migrated to the United States. As a result of the age disparity between the picture brides and the older males, many second-generation Korean Americans spent a good portion of their formative years with non–English-speaking widowed mothers who had limited formal schooling.[64]

Recent Immigrants

Not until the end of the Korean War and passage of the Refugee Relief Act in 1953 did Koreans emigrate in substantial numbers. As refugees or war brides, Koreans came to the United States in growing numbers beginning in 1958. The continued presence of U.S. troops in South Korea and the cultural influence on South Korea that resulted were constant inducements to intermarry or contemplate living in the

The Ethnic Experience

The First Korean Women in the United States

The following comments, through the courtesy of Harold and Sonia Sunoo, are a composite of taped interviews with three of the first 12 Korean women to come to the U.S. mainland:

"We left Korea because we were too poor. We had nothing to eat. . . . There was absolutely no way we could survive.

"At first we were unaware that we had been 'sold' as laborers. . . . We thought Hawaii was America in those days. . . . We cut sugar canes, the thing you put in coffee. . . .

"I'll never forget the foreman. No, he wasn't Korean—he was French. The reason I'll never forget him is that he was the most ignorant of all ignoramuses, but he knew all the cuss words in the world. . . . [I] could tell by the sound of his words. He said we worked like 'lazy.' He wanted us to work faster. . . . He would gallop around on horseback and crack and snap his whip. . . . He was so mean and so ignorant!

". . . If all of us worked hard and pooled together our total earnings, it came to about fifty dollars a month, barely enough to feed and clothe the five of us. We cooked on the porch, using coal oil and when we cooked in the fields, I gathered the wood. We had to carry water in vessels from water faucets scattered here and there in the camp area. . . .

"My mother and sister-in-law took in laundry. They scrubbed, ironed, and mended shirts for a nickel apiece. It was pitiful! Their knuckles became swollen and raw from using the harsh yellow laundry soap . . . but it was still better than in Korea. There was no way to earn money there."

On the mainland, the Koreans encountered even worse problems than in Hawaii because of the more highly charged racial tension and the severe weather conditions, as the following account indicates:

"We had five children at that time—our youngest was three and a half. I was paid fifteen cents an hour for weeding. Our baby was too young to go to school, so I had to take him along with me to the fields—it was so early when we started that he'd be fast asleep when we left so I couldn't feed him breakfast. Returning home, he'd be asleep again because he was so tired. Poor child, he was practically starved. He too suffered so much. . . . [In February] the ground . . . was frozen crisp and it was so cold that the baby's tender ears got frozen and blood oozed from him. . . . For all this suffering, I was paid fifteen cents an hour."

Source: Three Korean immigrants who came to Hawaii between 1903 and 1905 at ages ranging from 19 to 25. Taped interview from the collection of Vincent N. Parrillo.

United States. The liberalized immigration law of 1965 opened the doors to Asian immigrants and allowed relatives to join family members already in the United States. This chain-migration pattern resulted in an impressive fivefold population increase in 10 years, from 70,000 in 1970 to 355,000 in 1980, and in a doubling of that number to 799,000 in 1990. The 2000 Census revealed an increase of the Korean American population by a third to 1.1 million.

The Role of the Church

Almost 70 percent of the Korean American population identifies itself as Christian, a significantly higher proportion than the 30 percent Christian population living in Korea. Mostly Presbyterian and Methodist, Korean American congregations now exceed 2,000, compared to fewer than 75 in 1970. Ethnic churches, including Korean ones, make important contributions to immigrant communities, serving more than religious purposes. The church becomes a social organization, providing religious and ethnic fellowship, a personal community, and a family atmosphere within an alien and urban environment.[65]

As in many North American churches, Korean American churches often use praise music to include and appeal to the younger generation who have spent all or most of their lives in the United States. To further attract the second generation, some worship services are now in English, unlike past years when they were typically all in Korean for the immigrant community.

One study of the role of Korean churches in the ethnic community of Chicago, where more than 100,000 Koreans live, found patterns reminiscent of those of earlier European immigrants.[66] Their church involvement—much higher than in Korea—was strongly motivated by their sense of marginalization from the larger society. Providing institutional transmission of Korean culture, the ethnic church thus legitimizes traditional ethnic values and moral standards. For many second-generation Korean Americans who believe that complete assimilation is not possible because of their race, the Korean ethnic church—particularly the evangelical Protestant church—provides a significant sense of belonging and group identity. Because the greater the participation, the greater the identification with homeland and culture, Korean American churches, like similar institutions in other ethnic communities, serve as a focal point for enhancing ethnic identity.

Occupational Adaptation

Korean Americans have one of the highest self-employment rates of all ethnic or racial groups, including whites, although they want their children to find "good jobs" elsewhere in the open labor market.[67] Whereas about 1 in 8 Korean

Americans is a business owner, for blacks it is 1 in 67 and for non-Hispanic whites 1 in 15. In many cities and **exurbs,** Korean small businesses and firms are especially conspicuous. At first, these business owners followed the usual immigrant practice of hiring their fellow co-ethnics, since such a practice was mutually beneficial to employers and employees. Lately, however, a new pattern has emerged. For example, in Los Angeles and New York City—cities with large Hispanic populations—Mexicans and Central Americans are increasingly visible as employees in Korean-owned businesses, partly as an available labor pool and partly to render customer service to the nearby Hispanic clientele with limited command of English. In another example of **minority-minority relations,** in Los Angeles the two groups are learning each other's language to communicate before learning English.[68]

Widespread use of rotating credit associations has greatly aided the Koreans in establishing their own businesses. Like the *hui* among the Mandarin Chinese, the *tanomoshi* among the Japanese, and the *susu* of Caribbean Islanders, the *kye* of the Koreans provides startup funds for their ethnic entrepreneurs. In the arrangement's simplest form, each member contributes a fixed amount monthly to a fund and has rotating access to the pot. The first borrowers pay extra loan interest. Dating back to Korean farming villages of the 16th century, the *kye* helps newcomers get started in business while simultaneously functioning as a social club to bind immigrants together.

Overall, Koreans are more highly educated than most other nonwhite groups. Their income, however, in proportion to their number of college graduates, lags behind that of native-born Americans, although their earnings are similar to those of most other Asian American groups. Koreans have fared rather poorly in social acceptance, as indicated by social distance measures, an important indicator of structural assimilation. In his 1956 and 1966 studies, Emory S. Bogardus found Koreans at or near the bottom in preference rankings, below all other East Asian peoples. In my 2001 study, I found that Koreans had improved in preference rankings, although they remained in the bottom tier (see Chapter 1).[69]

THE VIETNAMESE

In April 1975, as the Vietnam War ended, 127,000 Vietnamese and 4,000 Cambodian refugees entered the United States. As they waited in relocation centers at military bases for sponsors to materialize, public opinion polls showed that most U.S. citizens, especially members of the working class, believed the refugees would take jobs away from people already living in the United States. Labor and state officials raised serious objections to "flooding" the labor market and welfare rolls with so many aliens at a time when the economy was mired in a recession. Yet all the refugees were resettled within seven months across all 50 states with little disruption.

Like the Cuban exiles of the 1960s, many of these Vietnamese were middle class, migrating for political rather than economic reasons. Many were well educated, with marketable skills, and nearly half spoke English.[70] They were relatively cosmopolitan people, mostly from the Saigon region, and many had previously lived elsewhere, particularly in North Vietnam.

The Ethnic Experience

A Desperate Bid for Freedom

"Our boat was kind of lucky, 'cause 70 percent of boats get captured by Vietnamese Coast Guard. That day there was no moon. It was totally dark. . . . Luckily we make it. . . . After one day and one night we get out of the control of the Vietnamese. Now we know we're free! . . . Our boat was 30 feet long and about 7 feet wide and, totally, we had about 103 people. It was so crowded, almost like a fish can, you know? Can you imagine?

". . . There was only enough water for one cup for each person in one day. So we rarely drank the water for, if we don't have water, we're going to die in the sea. The first day everyone got seasick. Nobody got used to it, the kind of high waves and ocean. So everyone got seasick and vomited. . . . But by the second day and the third day, we felt much better.

"We kept going straight into the international sea zone and we met a lot of ships. We tried to get signal for help, we tried to burn our clothes to get their attention. We wrote the big S. O. S. letter in our clothes and tried to hang it above the boat. No matter how we tried, they just passed us by. I think they might feel pity for us, have the good compassion, but I think they're afraid their government going to blame them because the law is, if you pick up any refugee in the ocean, your country got to have responsibility for those people. So finally we so disappointed because we got no help from anybody and our boat is now the only boat and we have only 3 h.p. motor.

"We have too many people and the wave is extremely high, about 5 feet. It is so dangerous. You can see the boat only maybe like 1 feet distant from the sea level. But we got no choice. We decide to keep going straight to Malaysia. The fifth day, the sixth day, we saw nothing. The only thing we saw is water, sun, and at night the stars. It's just like upside-down moon. And the sea. If you look down into the ocean, you get scared, because the water—color—is so dark. It's like dark blue. If you look down into the water, you had the feeling like it invite you, say 'Go down with me.' Especially at night, the water—it's black, like evil waiting for you. Say, 'Oh, 103 people, I was waiting for you. Come down with us.' We kept going, but we don't know where we're going to be, if we have enough food and water to make it. . . . We don't even know if we're going the right way . . . we just estimate by looking at the sun and the stars.

". . . The sixth day we saw the bird and a couple of floating things, so we are hoping we are almost come to the shore. We had some hope and we kept traveling one more day, the seventh day. That day is the day—our water—we have only one more day left. And the gasoline is almost gone. And we saw some fire, very little fire, very far away. And we went to that fire. One hour, two hours. And finally we saw that fire offshore drilling platform of Esso Company. Everybody's screaming and so happy because we know at least we have something we can turn to. . . . We know we cannot go any further. Most of the women and children in my boat are exhausted, and some of the children unconscious. Some of the children had been so thirsty, they just drank the water from the sea. And the water from the sea is terrible. The more you drank, the more you got thirsty. And the children, starving, got a bad reaction from the seawater. We all got skin disease and exhausted. . . . They took us in their boat to the refugee camp in Malaysia."

Source: Vietnamese refugee who came to the United States in 1980 at age 17. Taped interview from the collection of Vincent N. Parrillo.

In 1979, tens of thousands of Vietnamese "boat people"—many of them actually ethnic Chinese residents of Vietnam—sought refuge in other countries, setting sail in flimsy, overcrowded boats. Many drowned or were killed by pirates, but several hundred thousand reached refugee camps in Thailand and other countries (see The Ethnic Experience box). President Carter authorized admitting an additional 200,000 Indochinese refugees into the United States.

Immigration from Vietnam remains significant. About 275,000 Vietnamese immigrated to the United States in the 1990s, a total likely to be surpassed in this decade. From a virtual nonpresence in the United States in 1970, the Vietnamese numbered 1.1 million in 2000, making them the third largest East Asian group, and constituting 11 percent of the total Asian American population. Most of these more recent arrivals speak little English and have few occupational skills, making their adjustment and attainment of economic self-sufficiency more difficult.

Cultural Differentiation

Unlike most people in the United States, who believe in free will and self-determination, many Vietnamese believe in predestination, with very limited individual control over events.[71] Two of the more important factors that the Vietnamese believe determine a person's destiny are *phuc duc* and astrology. These are core elements within the family infrastructure of filial piety and ancestor worship, and they provide important insights into the Vietnamese ability to adapt to a new society with minimal emotional anxiety.

The concept of *phuc duc* refers to the amount of good fortune that comes from meritorious or self-sacrificing actions. This accumulation of rewards, secured primarily by women for their family, also affects the lives of succeeding generations into the fifth generation. *Phuc duc* is quantifiable, in that improper conduct diminishes the amount one has, whereas the nature of one's actions and one's degree of personal sacrifice determine the amount one acquires:

> To a great extent phuc duc acts as the social conscience of the nation, a collective superego. The children are conscientiously instructed in the ways of living that result in phuc duc. It is, in great part, related to the Confucian concept of Li [propriety and etiquette], although it is actually Buddhist-Confucian in origin and unique to Vietnam. It has its place in future reincarnations but primarily it relates to the family and to future generations of the family. Thus the responsibility that it represents is impressively exacting: the future destiny of one's loved ones and those yet unborn depends upon one's conduct.[72]

So strong is the Vietnamese belief in horoscopes that parents accept no responsibility for a child's personality, believing that the configuration of the celestial bodies at the moment of conception fixes the character of that individual. At the time of birth, a Vietnamese astrologer specifically predicts the personality and events to come for the newborn infant. This often becomes a self-fulfilling prophecy because the predictions influence actual behavior (the parents' child-rearing practices as well as the child's own actions, including mate selection as an adult). The Vietnamese way of life thus includes belief in a deterministic life force over which the individual has minimal control. This concept has greatly influenced the accommodation of the Vietnamese to the United States:

> For many this is the second or third time that they have been refugees. It is not something that one ever gets used to, but there is a philosophic acceptance of fate. And this the Vietnamese can accept. It is assigned to bad *phuc duc*, to the heavens, to the land on which one's ancestors are buried, or whatever. The cause, however, is externalized and inasmuch as this is universally concurred in by one's peers, these adverse events are integrated into one's psychic apparatus with a minimum of emotional dislocation.[73]

Vietnamese are strongly tradition bound, revering their ancestors, homeland, and family traditions. Their culture is oriented toward achievement of group goals, primarily within the extended family. In addition, the cultural values of courage, stoicism, and adaptation through conformity helped make the refugees' adjustment somewhat easier.

Acculturation

Vietnamese refugees who possessed relatively traditional views faced the greatest culture shock and difficulty in adapting. Women were more likely than men to suffer from depression, anxiety, and tension. A greater frequency of feelings of inadequacy, anger, tension, and sensitivity occurred among these Vietnamese refugees than in the general population. Principal causes of mental stress were loneliness, lack of community life, breakup of the family, uncertainty about the future, homesickness, grief over losses in fleeing the homeland, and frustration in coping with life in the United States. As found in earlier studies of Cuban and Hungarian refugees, assuming hostile and aggressive attitudes toward the host society or fellow refugees often proved an effective adaptive style. This emotional arousal helped Vietnamese to overcome the passivity of their traditional cultural values and find better ways to survive and surmount their problems.[74]

Contributing to Vietnamese immigrants' adjustment problems was the federal government's policy of scattering the refugees throughout the United States. Intended as an integration program to accelerate acculturation, it denied the Vietnamese a social and emotional support network of ethnic communities comparable to those developed and used by other immigrant groups. Initially, no mutual assistance organizations were formed, and early studies showed varying degrees of success in the refugees' adaptation to life in the United States.

Gradually, Vietnamese Americans began to relocate near one another, particularly in California, Texas, Virginia, and New York. Here their concentrations,

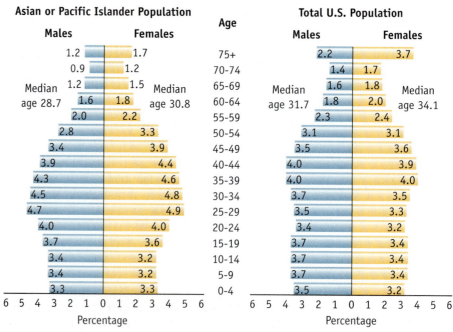

FIGURE 8.5   Asian and Pacific Islander Population, 2000 (in percentages)

| Asian or Pacific Islander Population | | Age | Total U.S. Population | |
Males	Females		Males	Females
1.2	1.7	75+	2.2	3.7
0.9	1.2	70-74	1.4	1.7
1.2 (Median age 28.7)	1.5 (Median age 30.8)	65-69	1.6 (Median age 31.7)	1.8 (Median age 34.1)
1.6	1.8	60-64	1.8	2.0
2.0	2.2	55-59	2.3	2.4
2.8	3.3	50-54	3.1	3.1
3.4	3.9	45-49	3.5	3.6
3.9	4.4	40-44	4.0	3.9
4.3	4.6	35-39	4.0	4.0
4.5	4.8	30-34	3.7	3.5
4.7	4.9	25-29	3.5	3.3
4.0	4.0	20-24	3.4	3.2
3.7	3.6	15-19	3.7	3.4
3.4	3.2	10-14	3.7	3.4
3.4	3.2	5-9	3.7	3.4
3.3	3.3	0-4	3.5	3.2

Percentage — Percentage

Source: U.S. Census Bureau.

aided by subsequent "normal" immigration, led to the development of ethnic neighborhoods and social networks characteristic of first-generation Americans. "Little Saigons" have blossomed in numerous cities where the language, signs, shops, offices, and music all convey a distinctly Vietnamese atmosphere. The largest of these are in Orange County and San Jose, California, and in Houston. In many Chinatowns, a distinct Vietnamese presence is also visible.

As with most immigrants, age determines the degree of acculturation (Figure 8.5). The elderly come to be with their families but show little interest in giving up their cultural values or assimilating. Youths find their traditional family values inconsistent with those of the dominant group in U.S. society. Traditionally, Vietnamese parents play a major role in determining their adolescents' social interactions. Vietnamese culture emphasizes achieving one's identity and sense of worth through close relationships with family adults and as a member of an extended family. U.S. adolescents are more autonomous and concerned about peer approval. These ways attract Vietnamese youths, encouraging them to reject parental guidance and enter into situations without parental consent. Intergenerational conflict is thus exacerbated by the gap between the cultural values of the adults and those learned by their children.[75]

Vietnamese—like other Southeast Asians—have lower labor force participation and median family incomes, higher poverty and unemployment rates, and disproportionate representation in low-skill, low-paying jobs than most East Asian American groups (Figure 8.6). These economic disadvantages particularly manifest themselves among the refugee population and seem likely to continue, although second- and third-generation Southeast Asians should fare better thanks to their higher education levels and English proficiency.[76]

OTHER SOUTHEAST ASIANS

Cambodians and Laotians, like the Vietnamese, came from the area of Southeast Asia formerly colonized and administered as French Indochina. For centuries prior to the arrival of the French, however, these three groups were linguistically, culturally, and ethnically distinct from one another, and differences exist within each nationality group as well. Of the approximately 1 million Indochinese Americans identified by the 2000 Census, about 24 percent were from Laos, 15 percent were from Cambodia (Kampuchea), and 61 percent were from Vietnam.

Thailand, formerly Siam, is another Southeast Asian nation that has sent significant numbers of immigrants to the United States. Although about 111,000 Thai now live in the United States, relatively little has been written about this group, except in groupings with other Southeast Asians (see The Ethnic Experience box, page 293).

THE LAOTIANS

About 168,000 Laotians now call the United States home. These refugees include several subgroups, including the Tai Dam, over 3,000 of whom live prosperously in Iowa. Most refugees from Laos, however, are the lowland

FIGURE 8.6   Social Indicators About Asian-Americans (in percentages)

Age by percent

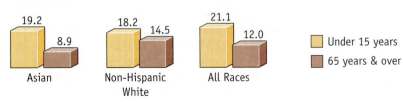

Education (of persons age 25 and over)

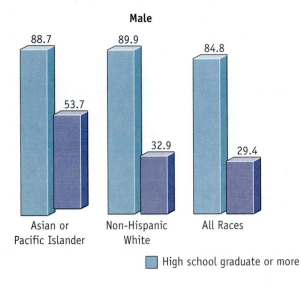
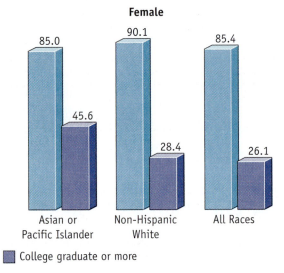

Economic Status

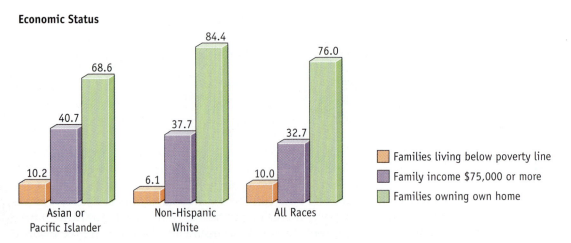

Source: U.S. Census Bureau, *The Asian and Pacific Islander Population in the United States,* March 2004.

The Ethnic Experience

The Struggle to Adapt

"I came to the U.S. for the adventure. I had heard much about this country and seen many American films. My parents are Chinese and migrated to Thailand about twenty years before I was born. My father is a very successful businessman, having his own lumber business and a few hotels. So I really came here only to satisfy my own curiosity, but I stayed here for my undergraduate and graduate course work and I haven't returned yet.

"It's almost as if I sensed this before I left. I was going to America because I wanted to see that country, but before my parents took me to the airport, I cried. At the airport a lot of people came to say farewell to me and I just waved to them. I had the feeling I would never come back here. Especially when I got into the airplane, I felt that I was losing the things that I really love, and I wanted to get off. It's a very lonely and scary feeling. . . .

"Things seemed strange to me at first. Oriental people all have dark hair. Here I saw many people with different features, with blond hair, brown hair, and so on. At that time they looked funny to me. I had seen some American soldiers in Thailand, but they were a small minority. Now everyone around me was so very different. Another thing was being driven [so fast] on the highways. . . . We have few good highways in Thailand and this was a new experience.

"I can't describe to you how lonely and depressed I was in this country. I at first wished I had never come. The family I stayed with in New Hampshire was friendly and tried to teach me about America, but the language and cultural barriers were overwhelming in those first six or eight months. I was withdrawn because I was afraid of the people and didn't know how to do. Most people were impatient with me and so avoided me. I was sad and didn't like this country, but I felt obliged to my parents to stay for the year even though I was very homesick.

"At the end of the school year I went back home. I discovered I had changed. I was more independent and stubborn, and I enjoyed doing some things that Thai people thought were silly, like getting a suntan. Also, I really wanted to be somebody and make my parents proud, and I thought the best way was to get an education in the U.S. So I came back here and earned my bachelor's degree. This summer I'll finish my master's degree and then I'll go back home to my parents and give them my diplomas. They really belong to my parents because they gave me material and emotional support. I'll come back here . . . and maybe someday be a college professor."

Source: Thai immigrant who came to the United States in 1971 at age 19. Taped interview from the collection of Vincent N. Parrillo.

Lao, although more has been written about the Hmong (pronounced *mung* and meaning "free people").

A traditional mountain people living north of the Plain of Jars in Laos, the Hmong had been little exposed to the modern world—Western or Eastern—practicing slash-and-burn farming on hilltops, attributing disease to evil spirits, and relying on the stories of their parents and grandparents for their education. Their belief in spirits includes the idea that a frightening or shameful experience leads to illness caused by the individual spirit fleeing the body. To lock the soul inside so it cannot leave, the Hmong wear copper or silver bracelets, anklets, and necklaces as special protective jewelry.[77]

Recruited as U.S. allies during the secret war in Laos in the early 1970s, thousands of Hmong men and boys went to work for the CIA (U.S. Central Intelligence Agency), rescuing downed U.S. pilots, sabotaging communist war supplies, and gathering intelligence on North Vietnamese troop movements. About 15,000 Hmong were killed in combat with the Viet Cong. When communist Pathet Lao forces took control of Laos, the new government systematically attempted to wipe out the Hmong, forcing them to flee.

Many Americans felt a special concern and commitment to the Hmong, and tens of thousands were admitted into the United States as refugees. Coming from a society that had no written language until four decades ago and no cash economy, the Hmong have faced enormous difficulties in making the quantum leap to living in U.S. society.

Hmong society is patrilineal: the traditional role of the wife is devotion to her husband. An extremely strong extended family and clan system binds the individuals together. This is why, after initially being scattered across the country by the U.S. government, many Hmong have resettled near kin and clan members. Today, 89 percent of the Hmong population in the United States reside in three states: California, Minnesota, and Wisconsin.[78] Although problems of language, economic naiveté, and lack of job skills initially plagued the Hmong, placing a large percentage on welfare, some recent studies suggest that a gradual, successful acculturation has begun.[79]

As the children become "Americanized" adolescents, cultural dissonance typically affects the Hmong family. Parents lack personal experience and role models for dealing with the adolescent experience in the United States because adolescence as such did not exist in Laos. There, succeeding generations married young and assumed parental responsibilities early. Dating without an adult chaperone, and any overt public display of affection, such as kissing or holding hands in public, violates Hmong tradition. Attracted to the U.S. way of life, Hmong teenagers often challenge their parents' authority on these matters.[80]

Although the Hmong have suffered from poverty since their arrival in the United States, their experience of severe destitution earlier in refugee camps in Thailand appears to have helped them cope. Moreover, they do not expect to stay poor because they encourage many family members to work, and they show a strong commitment to educating their children.

ETHNOVIOLENCE

A report of the Asian American Justice Center identified 275 bias-motivated hate crimes against Asian Pacific Americans in 2002, far lower than the 507 reported in 2001 and the 392 reported in 2000. However, the percentage of assault and battery crimes increased from 12 to 15 percent.[81] Nevertheless, the number of incidents has dropped dramatically since the wave of anti-Asian violence in the 1980s.

When the May 1992 Los Angeles riots erupted, damaging or destroying about 2,300 Korean-owned stores and causing losses estimated in excess of $400,000, a nationwide pattern of black–Korean conflict had been well established.[82] Like Jewish and Italian immigrants before them, thousands of Koreans owned inner-city retail stores, serving as a middleman minority to blacks and Hispanics in virtually every major U.S. city. Working long hours and relying on low-paid family labor to eke out a profit, they succeeded in neighborhoods where many area residents lived a marginal existence.

Black resentment stems partly from the Koreans' ease in borrowing through the *kye* and their mercantile success in black neighborhoods. Blacks accurately complain that Koreans take money out of the community but rarely hire non-Koreans. They also interpret Koreans' limited English and brusque cultural interactions with customers as rudeness. Social distance, economic frustration, envy, alienation, and a sense of being exploited all help explain the racial tensions that sometimes erupt into **ethnoviolence.** An increase in the number of inner-city

On April 29, 1992, a Korean shopping mall in Los Angeles burns on the second day of one of the worst modern-day riots in U.S. history. Other Korean store owners brandished rifles and shotguns to deter arsonists and looters. This multi-ethnic riot left 55 people dead and more than 2,300 injured.

black entrepreneurs and concerted outreach by Korean merchants to the communities they serve would do much to lessen the problem.[83]

Occasional incidents of harassment, intimidation, graffiti, vandalism, and assault continue to serve as painful reminders of the continuing presence of widespread racism, bigotry, and discrimination. These violent episodes may match the familiar pattern of actions taken against earlier immigrant groups, but that offers no comfort for the victims or for a U.S.-born generation that considers itself more sophisticated and tolerant than past generations.

THE MODEL-MINORITY STEREOTYPE

Since 1966, when William Petersen first praised Asian Americans as a "model minority," the term has become entrenched in the public mind.[84] Images of Chinese engineers, Japanese financiers, Filipino nurses, Korean entrepreneurs, and Vietnamese restaurateurs abound, helping to reinforce this positive stereotype. Asian American educational and economic successes apparently demonstrate that people of color can realize the American Dream through hard work and self-reliance. These achievements are seeming testimony to the possibility of color-free, problem-free, government-intervention–free integration into U.S. society. Moreover, advertising in mainstream news magazines helps perpetuate the stereotype by frequently depicting Asian Americans as highly educated, affluent, and proficient with technology.[85] Like all stereotypes, however, that of the model minority is misleading and ignores the diversity of the Asian American population. Many Asian Americans, in fact, are poor and poorly educated, people who need help in attaining economic and educational success.[86]

Other examples also contradict the stereotype. Many Southeast Asian refugees still require welfare aid. Not all Asian American students are strong academically.[87] The criminal activities of major Asian American drug rings, smaller-scale Asian American extortion gangs, and Asian American youth gangs are seen as an often brutal menace. Some Asian Americans live in crowded dwellings and suffer from tuberculosis or depression, and some live without hope.

The idea of a model minority also creates a harmful and unrealistic example for the dominant group to use as a cudgel to blame others for their difficulties in achieving success. Commentators often unfairly criticize other minority groups for failing to attain comparable levels of achievement, ignoring that much of the success of Asian American youths is attributable to their being (in many cases) children of professionals, as well as to their coming from cultures that have prized educational achievement for many generations.

EAST AND SOUTHEAST ASIAN ASSIMILATION

As with all groups, rates of acculturation and assimilation vary widely both among and within them, depending on various socioeconomic factors and length of residence. We can, however, make a few general observations. Because minority groups have less economic, political, and social power than the societal mainstream, such indicators as income, education, political participation, residential patterns, and intermarriage provide insights into the comparative status of Asian Americans.

As a group, Asian Americans have the highest median family income ($61,094 in 2005 compared to $50,784 for non-Hispanic whites). They have the lowest poverty rate of all minority groups, by half—one that is only slightly higher than that of whites.[88] About 44 percent have at least a college degree, compared to 25 percent of non-Hispanic whites, and 24 percent of all races (see Figure 8.6).[89] These positive indicators suggest substantial progress in the area of civic assimilation.

Citizenship is the first step toward political participation and influence. A greater proportion of Asian immigrants become U.S. citizens than any other immigrant group, a pattern partly influenced by the greater distance between their homelands and the United States.[90] Although their numbers will not give them the same political muscle as the larger black and Hispanic groups, their influence is growing.

Residential segregation is an important dimension of social relations between minority- and majority-group members. Although Asian Americans are predominantly concentrated in just a few states and are a mostly urban population, they tend to live in less segregated areas than other minority groups. Moreover, the 2000 census revealed that they are dispersing more and more throughout the United States.[91]

Racial intermarriages do not necessarily indicate complete acceptance between members of two groups, as racial boundaries may still exist despite their meaninglessness to those who do intermarry.[92] Nevertheless, comparative intermarriage statistics can give us some indication of a group's social acceptance, at least with respect to other groups. By 2000, about half of all U.S.-born Asian Americans had a non-Asian spouse, reflecting a growing trend. As more Asian Americans outmarry, future generations of Asian Americans may increasingly blend with other U.S. racial and social groups, mirroring the experience of European ethnic groups in the last century.[93]

Finally, Kyeyoung Park discussed an acculturation pattern found among Korean American families that we could easily apply to most other Asian groups as well.[94] Frequently the balance of power between generations shifts as older parents become dependent on their children, who must translate for them. Often, more successful younger brothers usurp the position of the esteemed oldest son because they frequently immigrate before him. Women's labor force participation in the United States is an important factor in changing relations between husbands and wives and in the capital-accumulation process.

SOCIOLOGICAL ANALYSIS

Some of this chapter's discussion of Asian immigrants covered events that occurred in previous generations; other parts focused on the contemporary scene. If we apply the sociological perspective to these individual group chronologies, we find that the time span involved is irrelevant to understanding the continuing patterns of intergroup relations.

The Functionalist View

The Chinese who came to the United States in the 19th century fulfilled important social needs—working on railroads, farms, and ranches and in stores and factories. Their work contributed significantly to the building of a transcontinental transportation system, the manufacture of needed goods, and the provision of valuable services. Although racial antagonism existed earlier, nationwide economic hard times in the 1870s made the situation much worse. Economic dysfunctions set off intensified labor antagonism, culminating in a system adjustment of immigration restrictions. Despite occasional internal strife, the withdrawal of the Chinese into their Chinatowns helped to promote ethnic solidarity and to offer an interactive social network in a hostile white society. Later, these Chinatowns functioned as absorption centers for tens of thousands of new arrivals, once the immigration restrictions were lifted.

Japanese, Korean, and Filipino farm laborers, both in Hawaii and on the mainland, helped agriculture expand and prosper. An urbanizing West Coast offered many domestic and personal service jobs—jobs filled mostly by Filipinos who liked city life and its educational opportunities. Major societal dysfunctions—a severe, long-lasting economic depression and the trauma of a desperate war begun with a surprise attack—triggered negative actions against the Filipinos and Japanese, respectively. Eventually, a restoration of system balance enabled these minority groups to overcome past discrimination and become more fully assimilated. Problems remaining with Filipino immigrants stem from their unemployment or underemployment and their rapid increase in population, compounded by the recent recession and the changing occupational structure of society.

Cultural traditions and family cohesiveness have been positive functions easing the adjustment of most East and Southeast Asian immigrants into U.S. society. Family dysfunctions also occurred, however, particularly with Americanized Asian adolescents. These difficulties range from disputes over dating to problems with self-identity and esteem, leading some Asian youths—unsupervised because of their parents' working long hours—into gangs.

Korean, Vietnamese, and other Asian refugees gave Americans the opportunity to act on one of their commonly held values—humanitarianism—by opening their doors to people from war-ravaged lands. Just as the U.S. host society provided freedom and opportunity for these Asian peoples, so, too, did society gain from their labors and contributions to U.S. culture.

The Conflict View

When employers—railroads, farmers, urban businesses, and Hawaiian plantation owners—needed inexpensive alien labor, they recruited it and reaped the profits. When times turned bad, those with power used intergroup ethnic antagonisms to divide the working class and thereby protect their interests. So it was that the series of electoral victories by the anti-Chinese Workingmen's Party in California caused the Republican and Democratic political parties to commandeer the anti-Chinese cause to defuse this new political movement. Similarly, white California growers advocated Japanese removal in 1942 to eliminate their competition in the marketplace. Labor organizations campaigned against the Chinese in the 1870s and against the Filipinos and other groups in the 1930s to prevent their taking increasingly scarce jobs.

Originally applied to the historical example of labor antagonism against the Chinese, the split-labor-market theory (see Chapter 4) explains the experiences of several other Asian groups equally well. Coming from low-income countries, Asian workers accepted wages that, although reasonable by their standards, undermined the wage scale of the native workers. For instance, when the Chinese entered the shoemaking trade extensively in the 1870s, weekly wages in the trade dropped from $25 to $9. Complaints about unfair competition by Japanese farm laborers included their "willingness" to work for less than whites or to accept payment in crops or land instead of wages. In the late 20th century, white shrimpers burned Vietnamese-owned boats in Galveston Bay, Texas; blacks in Harlem and Brooklyn urged boycotts of Korean stores; Hispanics in Denver housing projects attacked Indochinese refugees; and black–Filipino animosity on the East Coast occasionally manifested itself among medical service workers competing for certain hospital jobs.

Economic exploitation or competition generates other forms of ethnic antagonism. The Chinatown sweatshops exploit immigrant labor and undermine the position of unionized garment workers, who are further affected adversely by imports from developing countries. Auto workers and steel workers experience layoffs and job insecurity because of Japanese products. As black, white, and Hispanic workers treat Asian Americans as the enemy, the real culprits are those who benefit most—the sweatshop employers, the corporations that avoid capital modernization expenditures to maximize profits, and the U.S.-based multinational corporations that establish factories in low-income countries, marketing their products in the United States and elsewhere for higher profits.

The Interactionist View

Westerners have used the word *inscrutable* almost exclusively to describe Asians, especially the Chinese and Japanese. The concept that Asians defy understanding rests on their markedly non-Western physical appearance, language, belief systems, customs, stoicism, and observable behavior. Consistent with the connection between perceived similarity factor and acceptance of strangers, the wide social distance between native-born U.S. citizens and Asian immigrants becomes understandable. As groups farther from the dominant group's interaction patterns, Asians offer easy targets for negative stereotyping, prejudice, scapegoating, and discrimination. Cultural differences become intertwined with physical differences in the minds of many Americans, allowing racism to predominate in value judgments and avoidance–dominance responses.

Asian immigrants in the late 19th and early 20th centuries gave the West Coast an immigrant experience similar to the European migration in the eastern United States. Hispanic Americans and Native Americans were already indigenous to the West, so Asians created the new subcommunities, worked for low wages, and received the scorn and resentment of earlier arrivals. The Asian newcomers were replicating patterns already exhibited by European immigrants in the eastern United States, but people in the West interpreted these as threats to their own economic security and mainstream culture. This social interpretation of reality set in motion the interaction problems that followed. Attitudes translated into actions, setting off reactions and reinforcing attitudes on both sides; thus, the vicious circle intensified and perpetuated the ingroup's perception of the outgroup.

Recent Asian immigrants offer a bipolar model. Those who come from preliterate societies wedded to a tradition of subsistence living face a bewildering leap into an urban society. Schutz's observation, discussed in Chapter 1, that every taken-for-granted situation for the native presents a crisis for the stranger, is overwhelmingly true for many Southeast Asians. Their adjustment and integration into U.S. society may be long and difficult. Other Asians bring education and skills that enable them to enter the economic mainstream more easily. Nonetheless, their racial and cultural differences presently limit their social integration or structural assimilation.

RETROSPECT

A combination of racial and non-Western cultural differences caused a great many Asian immigrants from 1850 to 1940 to remain outside the U.S. mainstream all their lives. Lack of acceptance and social interaction in the dominant society and frequent hostile actions directed against them reinforced the Asians' awareness of the differences in the people and culture around them. Each succeeding wave of Asian immigrants, from whatever country, encountered some degree of hostility because of their racial and cultural visibility. To some Americans, the Asians posed a serious challenge to the cherished notion of a melting pot because of their race, their non-Christian faith (though some were Christians), their language and alphabet, and their customs and practices. That many chose to settle on the West Coast near their port of entry, much as European immigrants had in the East, only underscored their presence and led whites to exaggerate their actual numbers. Many also believed that these immigrants posed an economic threat to U.S. workers, which further encouraged racist reactions.

Many white Americans came to accept negative stereotypes, first about the Chinese and later about the Japanese and Filipinos. Normal ethnocentric judgments about a culturally distinct people, coupled with racial visibility that offered a distinct link to the stereotype, caused generalized societal antagonism toward the Asians. The vast differences in culture and physical appearance, augmented by racist fears and fantasies of threats to economic security or to white womanhood from "lascivious Orientals," led to sporadic outbreaks of violence and a continuing current of hostility.

Until 1940, Japanese Americans settled mostly in rural areas on the West Coast. On the mainland, racist antagonisms and fears culminated in 1942 with the militarily supervised removal of Japanese Americans from their homes and jobs. Although a few Japanese Americans were rounded up in Hawaii, no mass evacuation occurred there because Hawaii presented a less racist environment and offered fuller political and economic participation.

Filipinos, too, encountered overt racial discrimination prior to 1940. Following changes in U.S. immigration law in 1965, over 1.6 million Filipinos have migrated to the United States. Although many are underemployed, they and new arrivals among the Chinese and Japanese encounter less hostility today than did their predecessors.

Koreans, Vietnamese, Cambodians, Laotians, and Thais are more recent East and Southeast Asian immigrants. Some are war refugees, and all come from non-Western cultures and are racially distinct from white and black Americans. They enter a country that is far less racially hostile toward Asians than in the past. Many are either dependents of U.S. servicemen or individuals with marketable job skills. Most come from a region of the world where patience, stoicism, quiet industriousness, and the cohesiveness of an extended family are longstanding traditions. These values aid the newcomers' transition to a new life.

Asia is currently the major source outside the Western Hemisphere of immigrants to the United States. Approximately one-third of all immigrants now come from Asia. Obviously, that part of the world is profoundly altering the ethnic composition of the U.S. population. In the years ahead, the United States will become even more a land of racial and cultural diversity.

KEY TERMS

Ethnoviolence	Minority-minority	Primogeniture
Exurbs	relations	Sojourners
Kye	Miscegenation	

DISCUSSION QUESTIONS

1. Discuss the interrelationship between labor conflict and racism with regard to the Chinese, Japanese, and Filipinos.

2. How did the Chinese immigrants of the late 19th century respond to hostility and discrimination?

3. What explains the different treatment of Japanese Americans in Hawaii and on the mainland during World War II?

4. How do the concepts of "ethnic church" and "middleman minority" apply to Korean Americans?

5. What are some cultural characteristics of Vietnamese Americans?

6. Discuss the legislation and court rulings historically directed against Asian Americans.

7. How do today's Asian immigrants differ from their predecessors? How and why does society respond to them differently?

8. How do the three major sociological perspectives approach the Asian experience in the United States?

SUGGESTED READINGS

Bloom, Barbara Lee. *Immigrants in America: The Chinese-Americans*. Farmington Hills, MI: Lucent Books, 2002.
Despite discrimination and legal exclusion in their early years of labor in the United States, the book recounts how Chinese Americans found success and acceptance.

Bonus, Rick. *Locating Filipino Americans: Ethnicity and the Cultural Politics of Space*. Philadelphia: Temple University Press, 2000.
An engaging ethnographic study that presents a multidisciplinary cultural analysis of the relationship between ethnic identity and social space.

Kim, Kwang Chung (ed.). *Koreans in the Hood: Conflicts with African Americans*. Baltimore: Johns Hopkins University Press, 1999.
A series of essays offering informative insights into recent conflicts between these two racial groups in Chicago, Los Angeles, and New York City.

Kitano, Harry H. L., and Roger Daniels. *Asian Americans: Emerging Minorities*, 3rd ed. Upper Saddle River, NJ: Prentice Hall, 2000.
A thorough sociohistorical profile of each of the different Asian peoples who have migrated to the United States.

Min, Pyong Gap. *Asian Americans: Contemporary Trends and Issues*. Thousand Oaks, CA: Pine Forge Press, 2005.
Examines such issues as socioeconomic status, educational achievement, intermarriage, intergroup relations, and settlement pattern of each group.

Springstubb, Tricia. *Immigrants in America: The Vietnamese-Americans*. Farmington Hills, MI: Lucent Books, 2001.
Portrays how the traditional values of these refugees from war and repression serve them well in retaining their old culture and in playing an increasingly large role in their new culture.

MYSOCKIT

Additional resources for this chapter can be found in MySocKit. If you have a subscription to MySocKit, go to www.mysockit.com to study, review, and go beyond the book to learn more about race and ethnic relations.

Other Asian and Middle Eastern Americans

West Asian and Middle Eastern immigrants come from a part of the world situated between the area of Western thought and history on one side and the area of Eastern thought and philosophy on the other (Figure 9.1). From Turkey through the Middle East to Bangladesh, the Muslim religion predominates, but the cultures are as diverse as elsewhere in the world.

Although some of these peoples immigrated to the United States before 1965 and had encounters similar to those of earlier racial and ethnic groups, most have come since the 1965 Immigration Act. Their acceptance as strangers and their adjustment to U.S. life have differed from the experiences of pre-1920 immigrants because structural conditions in both the sending and the host countries have changed. As before, some immigrants have limited job skills and educational levels. Many other newcomers, however, are professional, managerial, or technical workers. Some are underemployed, but others find employment in their occupational roles. Either way, most tend to be isolated from informal social contact with other people outside their nationality group. As with many East and Southeast Asians, the social distance between most first-generation West Asian or Middle Eastern Americans and native-born U.S. citizens is considerable.

SOCIOHISTORICAL PERSPECTIVE

Aside from special legislation of temporary duration allowing political or war refugees to enter the United States, immigration regulations before 1965 effectively limited the number of immigrants from the non-Western world. Because few had migrated to the United States prior to 1890, the year on which the 1924 immigration legislation based its quotas, few non-Western immigrants were able to gain approval to migrate to the United States. Eliminating this restrictive national-origins quota system thus opened the door to many different peoples who previously were denied entry.

Since the 1965 change in the immigration laws, a third major wave of immigration has occurred, again creating dramatic changes in the composition of the nation's population.

FIGURE 9.1   The Middle East and West Asia

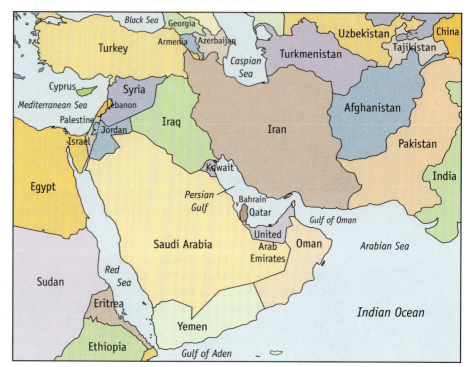

For example, immigration from India since 2000 has more than tripled that from Germany, Ireland, and Italy combined, previously three of the top suppliers of immigrants.[1] The 2000 census count identified over 400,000 foreign-born Arab Americans, a number that exceeds the combined foreign-born population from Greece and Spain.[2]

The Push–Pull Factors

For many non-Western immigrants, overpopulation and poverty so seriously limit the quality of life in their homelands that they seek a better life elsewhere. Sometimes restrictive government actions or limited socioeconomic opportunities push people to look elsewhere. The United States, with its cultural diversity, economic opportunities, and higher living standards, is influential throughout the world and a magnet to those dissatisfied with their situation. For others, the United States offers educational, professional, or career opportunities. Rapid air travel and instant communications, which reduce the psychological distance from a person's native country, are further inducements.

Structural Conditions

The non-Western immigrants discussed in this chapter follow the same patterns as have other ethnic groups that immigrated to the United States. They usually settle in urbanized areas near their compatriots, with whom they develop close primary social contacts.

Because many are trained professionals or skilled technicians, however, their job situation differs markedly from that of the mostly unskilled poor in the 1880–1920 immigrant groups. They usually do not settle in decaying sections of cities because their income enables them to find better places to live. The economic profile of these non-Western Americans ranges from the older and more affluent to the newer and struggling. Some are suburbanites, some live in working-class urban neighborhoods, and others cope with poverty. Wherever they congregate to live and work, various support facilities have arisen: churches or temples, grocery stores and restaurants specializing in native foods, social clubs or organizations, and perhaps their own schools and newspapers. They soon send for other members of their family or write home telling of their good fortune, prompting others to come to the United States. The chain-migration pattern of earlier immigrants recurs.

Many of the new immigrants do not fit the acculturation patterns that worked for other immigrant groups. For instance, prosperity in oil-rich Middle Eastern countries and the Western world's generalization of Arabs as a single group not only have strengthened that group's ethnic solidarity in the United States but also have encouraged some to plan to return to their native country eventually. A Saudi Arabian, for example, might return from the United States after acquiring an advanced education or experience that will permit a better life back home. Saudi Arabia collects no taxes whatsoever and offers free education and medical care, and its standard of living is improving rapidly. Although the number of immigrants from Saudi Arabia may be extremely low, a greater number of newcomers from other Arab countries are seeking permanent residence in the United States, as Table 9.1 indicates.

Because many members of this group of non-Western immigrants have marketable skills, they can obtain professional and salaried jobs without first having to adopt a subservient role in the economy. They need not yield to pressures to assimilate fully to gain middle-class respectability. Their income is high enough to enable them to enjoy the lifestyle they want; and, as a result, they are free to continue their own cultural behavior patterns. Some Americanization undoubtedly occurs, but these first-generation

TABLE 9.1   Arabic Immigrants Admitted to the United States

Country	1971–1980	1981–1990	1991–2000	2001–2006
Algeria	1,123	1,511	6,326	5,889
Egypt	25,495	34,259	46,714	37,339
Iran	46,152	165,267	112,597	69,045
Iraq	23,404	22,211	40,749	34,730
Jordan	29,578	36,032	38,749	22,725
Lebanon	33,846	45,770	43,469	23,714
Morocco	4,431	7,158	20,442	24,993
Saudi Arabia	700	4,180	7,716	6,148
Syria	13,339	22,230	26,109	15,884
Yemen	5,170	5,634	16,319	13,663

Source: Adapted from Office of Immigration Statistics Annual Report. *Statistical Yearbook 2006* (Washington, DC: U.S. Government Printing Office, 2007), Table 3.

immigrants do not have to make substantial cultural sacrifices to "make it" in U.S. society.

Another sizable segment of non-Westerners in the United States consists of nonimmigrant (sojourner) students, workers, and businesspeople. Although they usually remain for only two to five years, their growing numbers make their presence a matter of significant concern in the field of race and ethnic relations. In 2005, for example, over 457,000 Asian students and exchange visitors arrived in the United States, and about 4.3 million Asians came to this country as temporary business visitors.[3]

In many respects, these temporary visitors—visible to others in work, residential, shopping, and entertainment settings—resemble U.S. citizens who work for multinational corporations overseas. Even if assigned to another country for a considerable number of years, they seldom lose their sense of ethnic or national identity. They live within the culture and enjoy the available opportunities without contemplating abandoning their own cultural ties and becoming assimilated in the host country. Many aliens working in the United States have no interest in U.S. citizenship or assimilation, whether they work for one of their own country's multinational corporations or for some U.S. employer. Today's sojourners may be more sophisticated than their predecessors, but their resistance to assimilation is just as strong. At the same time, however, other non-Western immigrants are highly motivated to become part of U.S. society, as demonstrated by the fact that, among immigrants admitted since 1982, those from Cambodia, China, India, Korea, Laos, the Philippines, Taiwan, and Vietnam were proportionately higher than most other countries in becoming U.S. citizens. Since 2001, Asia has been the leading region of naturalizations.[4]

Societal Reaction

About 5,000 Asian Indians and 325,000 Middle Easterners migrated to the United States between 1880 and 1920. These early arrivals encountered far more prejudice and discrimination in the United States than their compatriots do today. Americans are now more tolerant of the differences in appearance and customs of non-Western immigrants. Terrorist attacks on September 11, 2001, in New York City and Washington, DC, however, increased suspicions about Arab Muslims, although their social acceptance remains fairly strong (see Table 1.1). People do categorize others and make judgments based on visible impressions, and this often leads to stereotyping. Distinguishing racial features and distinctive apparel, such as a dashiki, turban, or sari, set the newcomers apart. Although little overt discrimination occurs, limited social interaction takes place in most cases.

In recent surveys of social distance among various minority groups, racially distinct non-Western immigrants scored at the bottom, most notably Arab and Muslim Americans since September 11, 2001.[5] Many newcomers find themselves accepted in their professional, managerial, and technical occupational roles by members of the dominant society but excluded from outside social activities. Once the workday or workweek ends, they seldom receive social invitations from dominant-group members; thus, they interact mostly with family and compatriots. Economic mainstreaming may have occurred for many non-Western immigrants, but they have yet to achieve social integration.

✦✦✦ THE ASIAN INDIANS

Emigration from India to the United States happened in two distinct phases. In the early 20th century, several thousand poorly educated Indian agricultural laborers migrated to the West Coast and settled in rural regions in Washington (lumbering) and California (agriculture). Almost all the early immigrants were Sikh males who came from the Punjab region of northern India. Distinctive in their traditionally worn beards and turbans, they soon experienced hostile racism and violent attacks. In the 1970s and 1980s, a second group of immigrants—many of them provisioned with substantial monetary capital and "cultural capital" in terms of college education or professional training—arrived. More recently, less educated relatives of earlier immigrants have come, typically entering such family-owned businesses as groceries, motels, and newspaper stores or driving taxis or limosines.[6]

Early Immigrants

Between 1820 and 1900, fewer than 800 immigrants came to the United States from India. In the next two decades, a small wave of almost 7,000 agricultural laborers from northern India journeyed to the West Coast of the United States, and still others entered Canada. Almost entirely male, this group—like so many other immigrant groups—intended to accumulate some savings and then return home. Between 1908 and 1920, a total of 1,656 did leave, and another 249 were deported as undesirable aliens.[7]

Societal Reaction

Even though the Japanese, Chinese, and Filipinos far outnumbered the Asian Indians, the latter, too, experienced discrimination and dominant-group aggression because of their visibility and identification as Asians. Near a lumber camp in Bellingham, Washington, on September 5, 1907, several hundred whites raided the living quarters of Indian workers, forcing about 700 of them to flee across the Canadian border. Two months later, in Everett, Washington, several hundred whites drove the Indian workers out of town. Racial prejudice manifested itself also in Port Angeles, Washington, where real estate brokers published in the local newspaper the terms of their covenant not to sell to "Hindoos or Negroes." They justified their action on grounds that wherever these groups settle, they "have depreciated [the] value of adjacent property and injured the reputation of the neighborhood, and are generally considered as undesirable."[8]

The San Francisco–based Asiatic Exclusion League quickly included Asian Indians among its targets and warned the public that these people were a "menace." League officials declared that the East Indians were untrustworthy, immodest, unsanitary, insolent, and lustful.[9] National hostility toward Asian Indians from 1908 to 1910 led immigration officials to reject 1,130 would-be immigrants from India at their ports of entry. Pro-immigration pressure from the Western Pacific Railroad in 1910 enabled 1,462 of them to enter between 1911 and 1920, but another 1,762 were denied entry, mostly on grounds that they would become public charges.[10] The popular magazine *Collier's*, influenced by the Asiatic Exclusion League's exaggerated claim that 10,000 Asian Indians already lived in California, printed an article warning its readers about the "Hindu invasion."[11]

Hindu was a popular ethnic epithet for Indians in those days, undoubtedly used because so much of the Indian subcontinent (including 80 percent of India's population today) was Hindu. However, these immigrant victims were mostly Sikhs, a religious minority composing just 2 percent of present-day India's population.

> In this atmosphere of marked hostility toward Asians, the few thousand East Indians gradually established themselves primarily in California and relied chiefly on agriculture as a means of livelihood. Typically the Indians sought work in groups with a leader serving as their agent in negotiating with employers. Owing in part to the desire of many farmers to break the Japanese monopoly on the labor supply in those areas, they had little difficulty finding employment in the Sacramento and San Joaquin valleys. Also, Indians moved into the Imperial Valley, another rapidly growing agricultural area.[12]

In 1923, the U.S. Supreme Court reversed previous lower-court decisions and ruled that Asian Indians were nonwhites and thus ineligible for citizenship under the terms of the 1790 Naturalization Act. The government then revoked naturalization certificates that had previously been granted to 60 or 70 Asian Indians. The decision also prevented Asian Indians in California from owning or leasing land in their own names because state legislation prohibited alien landholding. The Asian Indians thus became itinerant farm laborers. Few of them had any family life because of the migrant nature of their work and the lack of women they could marry.

Minority Response

Juan Gonzales Jr. pointed out that the social and economic restrictions imposed by discriminatory immigration and **miscegenation** laws created and magnified the social isolation of the early immigrants. Unable to travel, send for wives or future brides, or marry women outside their own group, East Indian immigrants could neither participate fully in U.S. society nor produce a second generation of U.S. citizens to aid their movement into the mainstream of American life.[13]

About 3,000 Asian Indians returned home between 1920 and 1940. A few hundred more were deported. The population dwindled from 5,441 in 1920 to 3,138 in 1930 and to 2,405 in 1940.[14] A few of those who remained married Mexican American women. Most, however, lived in communal groups apart from the rest of society. Some Sikhs congregated in Stockton, California—the site of a large Filipino community—and built a temple there for worship.

In July 1946, the Luce–Celler Bill removed Asian Indians from the "barred zone" established in 1917 to prevent most Asians and Pacific Islanders from immigrating to the United States. Thenceforth, 100 Asian Indians could enter annually. In addition, males already living here could bring over their wives and children or make marital arrangements with women living in their homeland. Finally, Asian Indians were permitted to become naturalized citizens, an opportunity taken by 1,772 of them between 1948 and 1965.[15]

By the mid-1950s, Gary R. Hess reports, the Asian Indian community in Sutter County in north-central California numbered about 900 and had grown stronger and more unified.[16] This came about because the men preferred to marry Asian Indian women and because the caste system in India had a negligible influence in the United States, except perhaps in terms of status. Because they rarely intermarried and they retained important aspects of their culture, the rural Asian Indians, Hess concluded, remained only slightly acculturated even though they had adopted certain material comforts, dress, and other features of life in the United States.

Physical appearance was an important factor setting these immigrants apart. In the early 20th century, the full beards prescribed by the Sikh religion were not fashionable. Moreover, all the men wore turbans and were sometimes belittled as "ragheads." The Indian women who arrived before the Depression—like those who have arrived since the more liberal Immigration Act of 1965—were quite distinct in wearing the *sari,* a lightweight outer garment with one end wrapped about the waist and the other draped over the shoulder or covering the head. Most cultural differences—appearance, food taboos, and social interaction—were an integral part either of the Hindu caste system or of the Sikh religion in India. Therefore, Asian Indians not only seemed strange to non-Indian U.S. natives but had difficulty assimilating because they were reluctant to abandon their customs and practices.

Recent Immigrants

Statistics reveal a dramatic change in the number of immigrants from India. Only 15,513 entered the United States over the 65-year period from 1901 to 1965. In the next five years, that total was easily surpassed: 24,587 immigrated between 1966 and 1970. Then the immigrant totals sky-rocketed: About 148,000 newcomers from India arrived in the 1970s; 232,000 in the 1980s; and 352,000 in the 1990s. Between 2001 and 2006, that last total was surpassed, with 362,000 new legal permanent residents.[17] The Asian Indian presence is now substantial, exceeding 2.2 million (more than twice the number in 1990). A higher percentage of individuals aged 15 and older are married (69 percent), and Asian Indians also have a higher birth rate than any other Asian group. Currently the third largest Asian American population, 35 percent of all Asian Indians live in the Northeast, 24 percent in the South, 23 percent in the West, and 18 percent in the Midwest.[18]

Of the post-1965 immigrants from India, the largest numbers have been Hindu-speaking, followed by Gujarati, Punjabi, and Bengali speakers. Ethnic Asian Indians also emigrate from East Africa and Latin America, particularly from the Caribbean islands and Guyana, where earlier generations had immigrated as indentured plantation laborers.[19]

The Immigration Act of 1965 alone does not explain the increase in Asian Indian migration. Conditions in India are an important "push" factor. India is the world's second most populous country after mainland China, with 16 percent of the world's population occupying 2.5 percent of the world's land mass. The population density is nearly 11 times greater in India than in the United States.

The problem of overpopulation is quite serious. India's population grew from 439 million in 1960 to over 1.1 billion in 2006. The rapid rise is not due to any increase in the birth rate but to a decline in the mortality rate. Even with a slowing population growth rate due to a gradually declining birth rate, about 18 million babies are born in India each year. Vast differences in access to health services, sanitary conditions, and education level result in variances in life expectancy for one area to another, ranging from 57 years in Madhya Pradesh to 74 in Kerala, for a national average of 63 years.[20]

With nearly three-fifths of the population engaged in agriculture, a literacy rate of 75 percent among males and 54 percent among females, and problems of severe poverty, hunger, and inadequate resources, India offers many of its citizens little economic security.[21] However, many recent immigrants to the

Dressed in their traditional clothing in their temple in Philadelphia, these women celebrate the Hindu New Year, which is on the day following the new moon on or after the spring equinox in March. Year 2009 begins the year 2062 on Friday, March 27th in the Hindu calendar and this celebration is a means of preserving cultural traditions among U.S. immigrants.

United States have been professionals such as physicians, dentists, teachers, and skilled workers—the very people India needs most to retain if the quality of life there is to improve. Most developing nations face this **brain drain** problem.

With their education and occupational skills, many of these newcomers achieve economic security but also experience cultural strains. For example, they are uneasy with the sexual mores in the United States. Parents have considerable difficulty convincing their children that the Indian custom of not dating before an arranged marriage has merit. Although some second-generation Indian young people still yield to their parents' traditional prerogative to arrange marriages, this is one area in which **ethnogenesis** is apparent. Most young people tolerate their parents' introduction to eligible mates but insist that the final choice is entirely their own.[22]

More than two-thirds of all newly admitted Asian Indians pursue professional or managerial occupations.[23] The others typically operate convenience stores, gas stations, or family-managed hotels and motels. In fact, with Asian Indian ownership of the latter now constituting half of all economy lodging in the United States, they have found a family-labor economic niche as ubiquitous as the Korean greengrocery.[24] (See The International Scene box for insights into the Asian Indian experience in South Africa.)

Jonathan Brooks reported that Gujarati-speaking Asian Indians gravitated toward the lodging industry partly because of widespread opportunities presented by an aging hotel-owning population leaving the business, and partly because this endeavor:

> . . . required little English, skills, or education to run the business. Moreover, the family could live and work at the hotel which saved on expenses; and the

The International Scene

Asian Indians in South Africa

Of the 47.4 million people living in South Africa, more than 1.1 million are Asian Indians. They are mostly descendants of laborers recruited since the 1860s to work on the sugar estates or of traders who migrated before enactment of restrictive immigration laws in the early 20th century.

Their heritage of struggling against white oppression began a century ago with the arrival of a young lawyer named Mohandas (Mahatma) Gandhi. His efforts to improve the circumstances of his compatriots living in South Africa led to the development of his strategy of *satyagraha,* or nonviolent mass defiance of discriminatory laws, later used in India's independence struggle. In 1894, Gandhi became the first secretary of the Natal Indian Congress (NIC), and before returning to India in 1914, he won concessions from Afrikaner leaders on taxes, marriage law, and rights of movement. In many respects, the NIC served as a model for the African National Congress (ANC), whose leader, Nelson Mandela, became president of South Africa when majority rule was finally achieved.

The infamous Group Areas Act in 1950 forced 75,000 Indians and 8,500 "Coloured" (mixed-race people) to vacate what had become valuable inner suburban land for more distant settlements with rudimentary services. When the ANC was banned in 1960 and its leaders arrested or exiled, Indian leaders and the NIC played a key role in keeping the ANC together. By the 1980s, their political alliance was indicated by the presence of eight Indians on the 50-member ANC executive council.

As a middleman minority, the Indians fared better than the indigenous Africans, moving into middle-echelon jobs in accounting, sales, banking, and factory management, as well as becoming owners of many business and service enterprises. Their success has generated some African resentment and hostility. Violent attacks in 1992 against Indian businesses in black areas forced their owners to sell out and move back to major cities.

In postapartheid South Africa, the economic success of Indians initially caused tension. Polls in 1994 showed that the majority of Indian voters, a group that had previously supported the ruling ANC Party, leaned toward the National Party. This conservative shift was attributed to an Indian fear of losing economic power to the growing black business class.

Finding themselves both courted and pressured by various black and white political factions, South Africa's Indians apparently felt reassured, for in the 2004 general election, the most historically Asian Indian areas voted for the ANC candidates.

Critical Thinking Question: How similar or dissimilar is the Asian Indian experience in the United States compared to that in South Africa?

---

business was a piece of real estate that appreciated over time. The factors that facilitated the entrance into and success in the business were the class, ethnic, and family resources that were mobilized by Gujarati hoteliers. Class resources included financial and human capital. Ethnic resources included access to training, information, labor, networks, and most importantly, capital from within the Gujarati community. It is precisely because Gujaratis were able to mobilize these resources that they were able to establish a foothold and later dominate the industry.[25]

Racial ambiguity marks the Asian Indian acceptance pattern. The skin colors of Asian Indians range from light brown to almost black, although most of the U.S. immigrants are of a light hue. Americans perceive them as racially different but have difficulty categorizing them. Defined as "white" sometimes, "Asian" at other times, and "brown" or "black" at still other times, Asian Indians tend to classify themselves as "white" and identify with the majority group (see The Ethnic Experience box, page 312).

The Ethnic Experience

Values, Identity, and Acceptance

"You ask me if I came here to settle down. Yes, I came here to settle down. I changed myself a lot. I cut my hair. I took my sari off and I wore skirts and dresses. I dressed all-American. So it hurt to go outside and have people ask, 'Are you Indian?' We don't ask a white person, 'Are you French, British, Polish?' We are all Americans.

"I made a choice when I came to this country. My choice was to become an American citizen, and I have become one. I think we are wrong going into all these labels of cultural heritage. Our main goal is to keep America strong—America No. 1. And we can do that by communicating with each other; and in order to communicate and understand each other, we need to have one channel of culture and language.

"And it is difficult for us to forget about India because it is part of our culture. I spent 29 years there. I consider India as my mother—my womb. It gave me birth and my values. America is my father: It gave me my dream. They are both equally important. Maybe my children won't have to fight bigotry if we stop putting these labels on government forms, job applications, and on television. We must stop that. We should want to help people be part of us. We are Americans of Asian heritage. As long as they don't classify us, it will be easier for our children to be all Americans.

"My children are completely Americanized. I believe when in Rome, do as the Romans. I never forced on them the Indian language. In fact, they don't speak one word of the Indian language. They are very strong with Indian values, but I don't think they are Indian values alone. Those are universal values. Every American, Indian, Chinese, Japanese, Black, Puerto Rican—no matter what nationality you are, what racial group, all parents want that their children are well behaved, go to school, have good careers, don't hang out in the street and get into drugs or other trouble. I don't think the values are, you know, set for any one ethnic group. I don't find any American mother different from any Indian mother.

"The news media plays a very big role in spreading diversity. I'll give you an example. Every news media on television labels a person Black, White, Indian, and so on. Why? We are all Americans!

"What happened with my older daughter, who graduated college, was people kept asking her all the time, 'Are you Indian?' 'Are you Indian?' 'Are you Indian?' And then, at the age of 22, she turned around and said, 'Hey, gee, if they're always asking me if I'm Indian, why don't I think about India, find something out about India.' And if you're going to see after 50 years, different pockets of different ethnic groups, we too have to blame our own television media and our news media. If we keep giving people labels then, I don't know what is going to happen in America in the future."

Source: Asian Indian woman who came to the United States in 1970 at age 29. Taped interview from the collection of Vincent N. Parrillo.

⬗ ARAB AMERICANS

Arab is a broad term covering people of diverse nationalities, religions, and socioeconomic backgrounds. Although Arab Americans may share a sense of peoplehood, they come from 22 nations of North Africa and the Middle East (Figure 9.2). Not surprisingly, many cultural differences separate them from one another, and their ethnic identities remain rooted in their nationalities and specific homelands.

Over 1.2 million people identified themselves as Arab Americans in the 2000 Census. About half trace their ancestry to immigrants who arrived between 1880 and 1940, and the rest are immigrants or descendants of immigrants who arrived after World War II. More than 250,000 Arab Americans live in southeastern Michigan, giving that area one of the largest concentrations of Arabs outside the Middle East (Figure 9.3).

FIGURE 9.2   Arab Americans by Origin, 2000

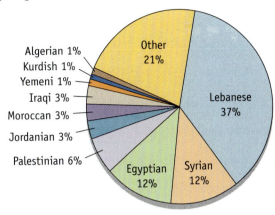

Algerian 1%
Kurdish 1%
Yemeni 1%
Iraqi 3%
Moroccan 3%
Jordanian 3%
Palestinian 6%
Other 21%
Lebanese 37%
Egyptian 12%
Syrian 12%

Source: Council on American-Islamic Relations.

FIGURE 9.3   Cities with Largest Arab American Populations, 2000

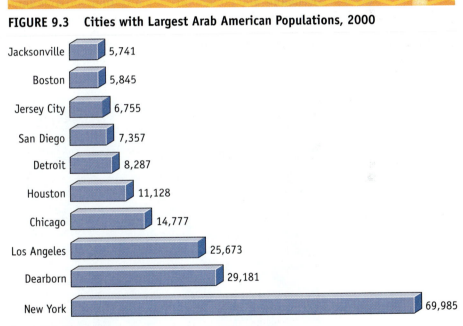

Jacksonville	5,741
Boston	5,845
Jersey City	6,755
San Diego	7,357
Detroit	8,287
Houston	11,128
Chicago	14,777
Los Angeles	25,673
Dearborn	29,181
New York	69,985

Source: U.S. Census Bureau.

Dearborn, Michigan, a suburb of Detroit, became a favorite destination of many working-class Arab immigrants after the 1967 Arab–Israeli war. Several thousand Muslim Palestinians, Yemenis, and southern Lebanese arrived there, making it today the largest Muslim community in the United States. Because of the concentration of so many first-generation Arab Americans, Dearborn today resembles more completely a "Little Arabia" than any other Arab American community. Nearby Detroit suburbs, such as Livonia, house large numbers of middle-class Arab Americans.

Despite the large concentration of Arab Americans in some urban areas, they are fairly evenly divided among the four regions of the United States (Figure 9.4). About 27 percent of all Arab Americans live in the Northeast, compared to about 24 percent in the Midwest, 26 percent in the South, and 22 percent in the West.[26] Arab Americans in the Northeast are more likely to be U.S.-born, whereas those in the West are more likely to be immigrants. Different Arab subgroups are fairly evenly dispersed, although Saudi Arabians are concentrated in the West, Assyrians in the Midwest, and Syrians in the Northeast.[27]

Social Organization

Many of today's Arab Americans are sophisticated, cosmopolitan people whose lifestyle matches that of other middle- or working-class U.S. citizens. Like many other past and present immigrant groups, Arab Americans have established institutions to help preserve their cultural heritage, strengthen their ethnic identity, and unite the community. More than four dozen Arabic newspapers are published and some 50 Arabic radio programs broadcast in such cities as Chicago, Detroit, New York, and San Francisco to aid in this effort. Religious and community organizations provide important emotional, social, and financial services to help sustain the Arab community. Among professional organizations, two of the better known are the National Association of Arab Americans and the Association of Arab American University Graduates.

Enjoying a slice of pizza, these children of Arab immigrants, like most immigrant children, will likely acculturate more rapidly than their parents. Through the impact of the media, schools, and everyday life, and with their ability to learn a new language more easily than adults can, they will identify more closely with the land where they grow up than with the land of their parents' youth.

FIGURE 9.4   Arab Ancestry: 2000

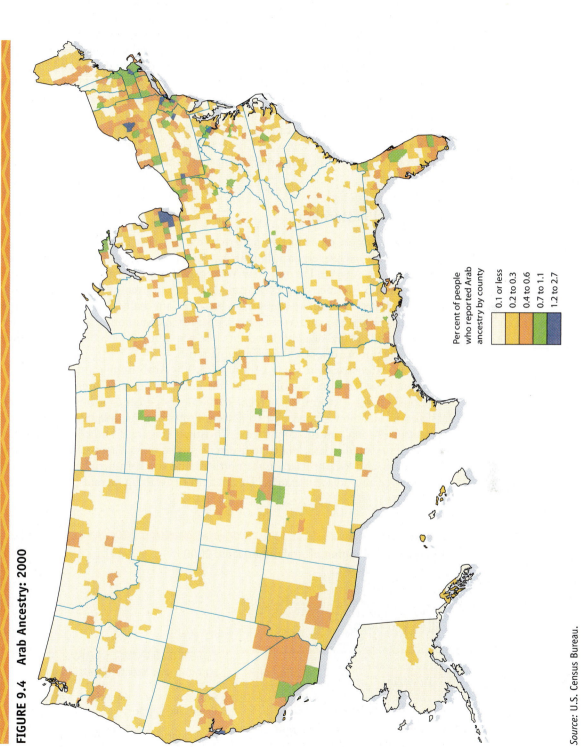

Per cent of people
who reported Arab
ancestry by county

- 0.1 or less
- 0.2 to 0.3
- 0.4 to 0.6
- 0.7 to 1.1
- 1.2 to 2.7

Source: U.S. Census Bureau.

As with most immigrant groups, kinship links play an important role in stabilizing community life.[28] Exchanges of letters, gifts, and family visits help maintain bonds between the immigrants and their relatives back home. Another important element is belief in an integrated economic family unit. Family members pool their income and resources in a common fund for all to share, even if the family is dispersed. Each month, many Arab Americans send vast amounts of money overseas to their relatives, helping them buy land, build homes, or purchase modern agricultural equipment such as tractors, plows, and irrigation pumps. Ironically, greater acculturation appears to be associated positively with satisfaction with life in the United States but negatively with family satisfaction.[29] Perhaps marginality and the clash of values contribute to this outcome.

Residential Patterning

Arab Americans are repeating the pattern of many earlier European immigrants by settling almost exclusively in urban areas. About 94 percent live in metropolitan areas, with Los Angeles, Detroit, New York/New Jersey, Chicago, and Washington, DC, as the top five metro areas of Arab American concentration. They live in all 50 states, but two-thirds reside in just 10 states and half of that number live in California, New York, and Michigan.[30] Some first-generation Arab Americans live in recognizable ethnic neighborhoods in close proximity to one another, but others adopt slightly more dispersed residential patterns.

In an extensive field study of almost 3,000 Arab immigrants living in the Paterson, New Jersey, metropolitan area, my investigators and I found them to be a religiously diverse group: 34 percent Muslim, 30 percent Orthodox Christian, 25 percent Melkite Catholic, and 10 percent Protestant. As in Paterson, most Arab Americans throughout the country are Christians (Figure 9.5). Lebanese refugees, mostly of the middle class, tended to live in nearby suburbs; Circassians, Jordanians, Palestinians, and Syrians lived on the northern and southern peripheries of the city, spilling over into adjacent exurbs. This pattern of Arab immigrants settling on the

FIGURE 9.5   Religion of Arab Americans, 2000

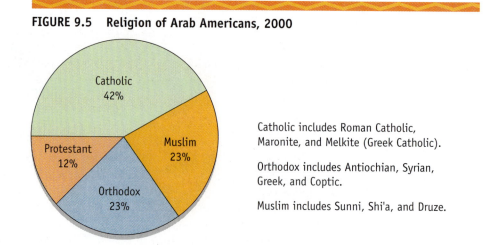

Catholic includes Roman Catholic, Maronite, and Melkite (Greek Catholic).

Orthodox includes Antiochian, Syrian, Greek, and Coptic.

Muslim includes Sunni, Shi'a, and Druze.

Source: Based on data from Zogby International, February 2000.

edges of cities instead of in historically inner areas or transition zones has been found in other U.S. cities, too.[31]

In the Paterson area, we found that a few families would live fairly close to one another but that the next grouping would be situated several blocks away. Nevertheless, a shared sense of community and frequent interactional patterns existed. Ethnic solidarity was maintained through a cosmopolitan network of communication and life-cycle rituals, homeland concerns, political activism, or limited social situations (work, school, and nearby families). Instead of maintaining a territorial ethnic community as other immigrant groups have done, Arab immigrants often maintained an interactional community. In recent years, however, the steady influx of new arrivals has resulted in the creation of more visible Arab neighborhoods in numerous states.

In the Paterson study, racial composition of the neighborhood did not appear to be a factor in choice of residence or desire to relocate. No interracial tensions or conflicts were reported; Arab Americans shared a common assumption that those who lived where they did—white or black—were respectable people. Coming from a part of the world steeped in religious rather than racial prejudices, Arab Americans appear to be unconcerned about racial differences in the more secular society of the United States.

Fighting Stereotypes and Group Blame

Any discussion of Arab American problems with stereotyping or violence must distinguish conditions before and after September 11, 2001, the day of major terrorist attacks on the United States. Although Islamic radicals committed these atrocities, some Americans saw little distinction between those radicals and anyone identified as Arab, Muslim, or both.

Before those attacks, films and television shows rarely portrayed Arabs as ordinary people. More often, they were oil-rich billionaires or cold-blooded terrorists. They ranged from such broadly stereotypical TV wrestling villains as Abdullah the Butcher to cartoon villains such as Ali Boo-Boo, the desert rat in a Heckle and Jeckle animated feature. In the 1987 film *Wanted Dead or Alive,* starring Gene Simmons of the rock group Kiss, an Arab terrorist conspired with Arab Americans to poison the people of Los Angeles. The 1992 Disney film *Aladdin* gave the villainous Jaffar a distinctly Arabic accent, whereas Aladdin and Jasmine sounded like typical U.S. teenagers. In *Martial Law* (1999), Middle Eastern terrorists detonate bombs in New York City, and the federal government forces all Arab and Muslim Americans into detention camps.

Such widespread media portrayals have a cumulative, conditioning effect, and it is not a positive one. Adding to their difficulty in overcoming these stereotypical perceptions, Arab Americans have had to dissociate themselves from real-life terrorism. Bombings of the World Trade Center in 1993 and of U.S. embassies in Africa in 1998 caused the Arab American community some anxiety about the potential stigmatizing of all Arabs for the violent acts of just a few radicals.

The mass destruction and killing of nearly 3,000 people in attacks on the World Trade Center and Pentagon shocked everyone, including Arab Americans, many of whom had migrated here to get away from violence in their homelands. Although most Americans did not assign group blame, anti-Arab invective and sporadic acts of violence did occur. Such actions were remindful of the backlash that many Irish Americans felt in the 1870s over the terrorist activities of the Molly Maguires or that many immigrants experienced when a bomb exploded in the midst of police officers at an immigrant labor rally at Haymarket Square in Chicago in 1886. Perhaps, though, it is a tribute to the increased tolerance of U.S. society of 2001 that there were no calls for an action similar to that taken against Japanese Americans in 1942 after the bombing of Pearl Harbor.

However, it became more difficult to be an Arab American. Taking a flight anywhere made one an immediate subject of intense scrutiny. Verbal abuse, vandalism, and physical attacks occurred.[32] Because some of the hijackers had lived in communities a year or more, many first-generation Arab Americans found their loyalties questioned. Ingroup–outgroup boundaries solidified more between Arab and other Americans, as reported in the 2001 social distance survey discussed in Chapter 1. Federal arrests of numerous Arab Americans also increased fear and resentment in the Arab American community.

Presented with so much negative stereotyping and suspicions, one might falsely conclude that predominantly Arab nations are our enemy. In fact, the United States maintains friendly relations with 19 of 21 such countries, and most were allies during Operation Desert Storm in 1991. The million-plus Arab Americans living in the United States are normal human beings pursuing the American Dream, but the media seldom report that. Failure to grasp the humanity of the Arab people increases the social distance between non-Arabs and Arabs.

THE SYRIAN/LEBANESE

A number of factors contributed to a confusion of ethnic identities and a lack of accurate official U.S. statistics regarding immigrants from Syria and Lebanon. In the late 19th and early 20th centuries, the entire Arabian Peninsula and the lands directly north of it were part of the Ottoman Empire, and its inhabitants were Turkish citizens until the end of World War I. Although much cultural diversity existed in this geographic region, all the inhabitants spoke Arabic and, except for the Sinai Egyptians, used the term *Syrian* to identify themselves. Still, the immigrants had Turkish passports, so U.S. officials identified them as Turks until 1899, when a separate category for Syrians began. Although approximately 85 percent of the immigrants came from the area now known as Lebanon, only in the 1930s did the term *Lebanese* gain acceptance. Some Lebanese resisted the change in designation, preferring to continue calling themselves Syrians, whereas some people from what is now Syria began calling themselves Lebanese.

Ethnic Identity

In the past, Arab Americans tended to identify themselves by family name, religious sect, and village of origin. Rarely did they cross religious or village lines to set up common organizations. Instead, social clubs and fraternal organizations had a clannish focus, often leading to factionalism within the community. Neither political authority nor specific regional residence determined group affinity; rather, religion defined the goals and boundaries of the "Syrian" community in the United States. The theological differences of Jews, Christians, and Muslims translated into social and structural realities keeping each community socially separate from the others.[33]

Migration and Settlement

Although religious differences kept the three groups separate, the push–pull factors that led them to emigrate to the United States affected them similarly. Essentially, a combination of harsh living conditions—hunger, poverty, and disease—and Turkish oppression, particularly of Christians, led many Syrians to leave. The pull of the United States was the result of reports by missionaries and steamship agents of economic opportunities and religious and political freedom. Emigration to the United States began in the 1870s, reaching an estimated 100,000 between 1890 and 1914 as the harshness of Turkish rule increased. The peak years were 1913 and 1914, when more than 9,000 migrated to avoid conscription into the Turkish army on the eve of World War I combat.

A seven-block area along Washington and Rector Streets in lower Manhattan became a thriving Syrian community during the late 19th century. Other Syrians settled in downtown Brooklyn and elsewhere throughout the entire country. Another center for immigration was Worcester, Massachusetts. Most Syrian immigrants came either from cities or from densely populated villages; they usually chose to reside in U.S. cities of 100,000 or more and had little difficulty adjusting to urban life.[34]

Between 1890 and 1895, the New York community established three Arab Christian churches: Melkite, Maronite, and Eastern Orthodox. Before then, Syrians had simply joined U.S. churches. Maronites and Melkites usually

Although many Americans think otherwise, the majority of Arab Americans are Christians, and only one-fourth are Muslims. About one-fifth are Orthodox Christians, which includes Antiochian, Coptic, and Syrian sects. This photo shows a priest leading a Sunday morning service at an Antiochian church in Syracuse, New York.

became Roman Catholics; members of the Eastern Orthodox Church generally became Episcopalians.[35]

Culture Conflicts

Newly arrived Syrians often replaced departing Irish American residents in old city neighborhoods. This is an example of the sociological concept of **invasion–succession,** in which one group experiencing upward mobility gradually moves out of its old neighborhood. Another group then replaces it, living at the previous residents' original socioeconomic level. Sometimes hostility develops between the old and new groups. In the case of the Syrians, religious tension resulted in a clash with the Irish, as this 1920 account about the Dublin District of Paterson, New Jersey, reveals:

> When the Syrians came to live there, the rentals became higher. This caused hard feelings between the Irish and the Syrians, which developed into a feud between the two nationalities. The fight started in the saloon on Grand and Mill Streets, first with bitter arguments and harsh words, and then threatening fist fights. From the saloon, the fight came out to the streets. It was like two armies in opposition facing each other. . . . The police force was called in to put an end to this fight. All they could do was to throw water on them to disperse them. These fights continued for three days in the evening. Finally, a committee of Syrians went to talk to Dean McNulty of St. John's, explaining to him that they were Christians coming from the Holy Land, not Mohammedans or Turks, as the Irish used to call them. They were good Catholics and they wanted to live in peace with everybody. Then the good Dean, at Sunday masses, urged the Irish to stop fighting with the Syrians, who were like them, Catholics. He succeeded in stopping this fighting better than the police.[36]

Another problem the Syrian immigrants encountered before World War I was racial classification. In 1909, the U.S. District Court in St. Louis ruled them ineligible for naturalization on the basis of the 1790 legislation, declaring them to be nonwhite. Many Syrian Christians were blond and blue-eyed, but the racial barrier was determined by their country of origin. The Circuit Court of Appeals reversed this decision. Shortly thereafter, the matter came up again, this time in the U.S. District Court in New York, which ruled that they could be naturalized.

Early Patterns

Syrian males usually came alone and then sent for their wives and children. Although poor, most were literate and insisted that their children complete primary school. Married Syrian women were more emancipated and less dependent on their husbands than were their counterparts in other ethnic groups at that time. Both mother and children—after they completed grade school—worked together for the family's economic welfare. The family structure proved to be an important factor in the Syrians' economic success.

Generally, Syrians preferred to work as traders and shopkeepers because trading was a time-honored occupation in their native land. Many Syrians became peddlers and traveled throughout the United States, bringing essential and exotic goods to far-flung communities. In the late 19th and early 20th centuries, these peddlers filled an economic need and were welcome visitors to remote homes and communities. About one in three Syrian men became peddlers; others tried various commercial ventures, started restaurants, or in a few cases, worked in factories.

The choice of peddling by so many Syrians expedited their acculturation. It took them into U.S. homes, quickly teaching them the hosts' language and customs. It prevented their cultural isolation by way of ghetto settlement patterns, instead dispersing them throughout the country. By 1914, most Syrian peddlers had switched to being shopkeepers, with the majority operating grocery or dry goods stores.

Upward Mobility

Syrian Americans achieved economic security quickly, often in the first generation. This is especially significant because fewer than one-fourth of those who came were professional or skilled workers. Aiding them in their adjustment, acceptance, and upward mobility were (1) wide dispersal, negating any significant opposition to their presence; (2) business expertise and self-employment, which allowed them greater rewards; and (3) cultural values of thrift, industriousness, and investment that were comparable to the middle-class values of the host society:

> Even while they were still in the lower income brackets and in working class occupations, the "Syrians" displayed the social characteristics of the middle classes in American urban centers. Studies of these Arab immigrants in Chicago, Pittsburgh and the South reveal a common pattern: low crime rates, better than average health, higher I.Q.'s, and more regular school attendance among the children, few intermarriages and divorces.[37]

Coming from a country in which nearly every man owned the house he lived in, determined to be independent, and highly motivated to succeed, the Syrians accumulated money rapidly and invested it either in property or in business ventures. By 1911, Syrians worked in almost every branch of commerce, including banking and import–export houses, and the government reported that their median income was only slightly lower than the $665 annual income of the adult native-born male.

> Unlike other immigrant groups who had to wait two or three generations to exert their independence from ghetto life and to satisfy their desire for mobility, it was the Syrian immigrants (first generation) who amassed the wealth that their sons used as a lever for bringing themselves into wider contacts with society.[38]

Rapid economic success and lack of either unfavorable stereotypes or discrimination barriers once they were known as Syrians rather than Turks allowed Syrian/Lebanese immigrants to assimilate into U.S. society quite easily, so they did not need to duplicate the host society's institutions. True, they had social organizations and their own newspapers, but their mobility, wide dispersal, differing religions, and emphasis on the extended family rather than on ethnic organizations resulted in their being assimilated rather easily (see The Ethnic Experience box, page 322).

By the mid-1950s, Syrian Americans had completely abandoned their "nomadic" occupations. They had entered the mainstream of U.S. economic and social life and were represented in virtually every industry and profession.[39] Because they were prosperous, their children were able to enter the sciences, the professions, politics, and the arts, and many have distinguished themselves in these fields.

The Ethnic Experience

First Encounters with U.S. Ethnicity and Language

"I am of Circassian origin, having been born in Syria. My father worked in government with the interior ministry. When the government changed from a moderate socialist to a radical socialist government following the Arab–Israeli War in 1968, my father was arrested as a pro-Western sympathizer. He escaped from jail, and we all fled to Jordan, where we received asylum. We migrated to West Germany, but very few Circassians live there, and so we came to the U.S. where other Circassians who had fled from Russia now lived.

"Before we came here, the idea I had about America was that the people were the same, that everybody was an American except the blacks because they were different in color. I thought everybody would be an American, but when we came here—especially as soon as I went to high school—I found everyone identified with their parents' origin. In other words, they would call themselves Italian-American, Dutch-American, and so on. It was a little confusing to me because I expected them to say they were Americans. Instead they said their nationality first and then said American.

"Most Circassians live in northern New Jersey or in California, and so we settled in New Jersey where my father already knew some people. I did have a lot of trouble with the language here. I spoke two languages—Circassian and Arabic—but starting as a sophomore in high school, I had trouble relating to the people. You know how high school kids are. They're immature. Sometimes in class I might say something with a super-heavy accent, and perhaps even say it completely wrong, and they would laugh at me. I didn't have many friends in high school because I worked after school, and besides, we didn't interact very much with the Americans because the Circassian community had its own activities and clubs. Our language and culture were different and the Americans weren't so friendly. Besides, once you know you have an accent, that does stop you from even trying to make friends. It's a barrier. You're still trying to learn a language and it's hard. With my brothers I spoke Arabic, with my parents who were so nationalistic we had to speak Circassian, and in school I had to learn English, and it was all very confusing."

Source: Syrian immigrant who came to the United States in 1968 at age 15. Taped interview from the collection of Vincent N. Parrillo.

Over 27,000 Lebanese and 20,000 Syrians have left their homeland for the United States since 2000. Either joining friends and relatives who are already assimilated and dispersed or coming as middle-class refugees, they usually blend in easily with the rest of U.S. society in their work and residence. Syrian and Lebanese Americans maintain a strong social network of communication and interaction in social events. Their extended families have tended to do things together, including vacationing and relocating to different geographic areas.[40] In recent years, large-scale intermarriage has occurred, which Milton Gordon asserts is the last stage of the assimilation process.[41]

THE PALESTINIANS

More than 72,000 Arabs claimed Palestinian ancestry in the 2000 Census, with most of them living in Palestinian communities clustered in California, Illinois, Michigan, New Jersey, New York, and Texas.[42] Most Palestinian Americans are Muslims, although a significant proportion are Christian, mostly members of the Antiochian Orthodox Church. Many Palestinians first work as sojourners in other Arab countries and then come to the United States directly from these countries.

Homeland Influence

Until recently, most Palestinian Americans tried to keep a low profile. Faced with stereotypes that labeled them as terrorists, they became disheartened by the actions of Palestinian extremists in their homeland. Yet they also felt bitterness over violent acts against their people, such as when, prior to the creation of Israel by international fiat later that year, Irgun (the Zionist underground army led by Menachem Begin) massacred as many as 254 Arab men, women, and children at Deir Yassin in 1948 as they fled from their houses. In 1998, Palestinian Americans created and passed from city to city a gigantic quilt composed of 418 patches to commemorate the 50th anniversary of the many Palestinian communities eliminated when the Jewish state came into existence.

When the Palestinian *intifada* uprisings against Israel began in 1988, Palestinian Americans took a strong interest in the cause, watching network news telecasts and listening to shortwave radio reports. Inspired by the demonstrations and by the Arab League's recognition of an independent Palestinian state, second- and third-generation Palestinian Americans have gained a new sense of ethnic identity and belonging. Changes in Israeli leadership and government policy culminated in the agreement signed by Palestinian leader Yasir Arafat and Israeli Prime Minister Yitzhak Rabin in 1995 that transferred control over much of the West Bank of occupied Jordanian territory to its Palestinian residents. Despite Rabin's assassination in 1996 and the subsequent impasse in Israeli–Palestinian talks, Palestinian self-rule continues to evolve, and that homeland influence has renewed the pride of Palestinian Americans in their ethnic identity. Continued Israeli–Palestinian conflict, especially the suicide bombers, the radicalism of Hamas, and links to terrorist motivation against U.S. targets contribute to strained relations between Palestinian Americans and other U.S. citizens.

The American Federation of Ramallah

Many recent Palestinian arrivals from the Middle East lack advanced education or occupational skills for various white-collar positions, so they find employment in various working-class trades. One source of assistance is the American Federation of Ramallah, named after a Palestinian city 10 miles north of Jerusalem. It is a nationwide ethnic organization, with local and regional social clubs designed to help people of Palestinian heritage adjust to life in the United States. The organization provides financial assistance, guaranteed bank loans, and expertise to enable the newcomers to start mom-and-pop grocery, liquor, and variety stores. The newcomers gradually repay the loans, adding a small percentage to help others who follow them.

The federation also conducts many social activities, such as parties and picnics, through its local chapters. These events help maintain ethnic bonding and provide opportunities for young people to meet potential marriage partners. A youth department offers summer camp programs and cultural heritage classes.

Community Life

For middle-class Palestinian Americans, the community's mosques and churches serve many purposes. They meet religious needs, of course, but they also function as ethnic centers for social occasions, temporary hostels for new

On September 14, 2001, three days after the terrorist attacks, more than a thousand Arab-American worshipers at the Passaic County Mosque in Paterson, New Jersey, prayed for America and victims of the World Trade Center and Pentagon terrorist attacks before lining up to donate blood for the wounded.

arrivals not yet situated, cultural learning centers for youths, meeting places for Arab organizations, and reception centers for visiting dignitaries.

Working-class Palestinian American males, many of whom live in urban neighborhoods, often congregate in coffeehouses in their free hours, much as earlier Greek immigrants did. These neighborhood social centers provide places to relax, exchange news about the community or homeland, and perhaps learn of work opportunities.

Endogamy remains the norm among Palestinian Americans. Each summer, marriage-age Palestinian American singles throng East Jerusalem, the West Bank, and the Gaza Strip in search of a spouse. Some engagements last one to two years, but it is not uncommon for a couple—with their families' assistance—to meet, become engaged, and marry within a few weeks. Most such couples are college educated and happy with the nuptial arrangement because they share the same culture, religion, and expectations as they start new families in the United States.[43]

THE IRANIANS

Iran, formerly called Persia, is not an Arab country. The great majority of its people speak their own language, Farsi, not Arabic, and their culture has unique qualities that set it apart from the culture of neighboring Arab states. Immigration patterns and societal reaction to Iranian immigrants have fluctuated greatly in the past 30 years depending on the political climate. Immigration to the United States from Iran is a relatively new phenomenon. During the reign of the westernizing Shah Mohammed Reza Pahlevi, about 50,000 Iranian students studied in the United States annually. They maintained a sense of community among themselves, forming associations and interacting with one another. Fear of political repression under the shah kept many from returning to their homeland until after his fall from power in 1979.

Other Iranians living in the United States in the late 1970s were skilled professionals working as sojourners, who had no intention of remaining, or political refugees hoping to return home someday. At that time, only the Iranian college students maintained an ethnic community or network. Other Iranians kept to themselves, partly for fear that members of the shah's secret police force (SAVAK) would report something about them, bringing harm to relatives still in Iran. Minority emigrants from Iran—Armenians, Baha'is, and Jews—showed great cohesiveness, intending to become U.S. citizens, but they constituted a very small percentage of all Iranian immigrants.

In a study of his fellow Iranian immigrants, Maboud Ansari found that the Iranian migration in the late 1970s consisted mostly of male middle-class professionals. Although physically separated from their families, typical Iranian immigrants still viewed their extended family at home as their only source of primary relations, which they maintained through regular telephone calls. These men did not form a territorially compact community or develop close ties with their compatriots.[44] Most remained physically and socially distant from other Iranians in the United States and did not come together except at Now-Ruz, the Iranian New Year, celebrated on the first day of spring:

> The Now-Ruz party (which takes place in many major American cities) is the only major national event for Iranians in America. As the only publicly visible ceremony, it creates an atmosphere of national identity and a sense of belonging. However, it seems that somehow the ceremony has lost the meaning originally attached to it. For example, one of the most important aspects of Now-Ruz is to review or to extend friendships. The Iranians who attend the festivities in America are apt to come together as strangers and leave without exchanging any addresses or gaining any new friendships. Most of the festivities are characterized by a lack of intimacy and excessive self-consciousness in maintaining of social distance.[45]

In the 20 years since this study, Iranians have become more organized and socially interactive with one another, no longer fearful of Iranian secret police or repercussions against family members still in Iran. Both older and more recent arrivals openly participate in a variety of ethnic activities, and few yearn to return to Iran.

In the 1970s, though, Ansari found that Iranians fell into four self-designated categories. Only about 20 percent called themselves *mandegar* (settlers), or Persian Yankees. Many of these were older, former exchange students who opted to stay permanently. The majority were in the second category, the *belataklif,* or ambivalent Iranians. Torn by a nostalgic love and guilt feeling for what had been left behind, yet growing attached to what lay ahead in the United States, the *belataklif* remained undecided about staying or returning. Yet the longer one remained, the less likely one was to return, thus becoming a *mandegar.* The other two categories were the *siyasi,* political exiles who viewed their host society only as a necessary refuge, and the *cosmopolitans,* who were committed to their profession and not to their nationality—citizens of the world at home anywhere.[46] Today, the first and fourth categories primarily describe Iranian Americans.

Anti-Iranian feelings ran high in the United States in 1980 when the hostage crisis at the U.S. Embassy in Iran remained unresolved. Verbal abuse, boycotts, arson against Iranian American businesses, and physical attacks against Iranian students on several college campuses occurred. Iranian Americans who harbored no anti-U.S. feelings themselves became the scapegoats of U.S. frustration, suffering indignities and discrimination. In the 1990s and still in this decade, political rhetoric from leaders in both countries has continued to make for a difficult situation for Iranian Americans who desire, as most immigrants have always done, to maintain ethnic pride.

Iranian immigration, which peaked in the 1980s at 98,000, dropped to 77,000 in the 1990s, and reached 50,000 between 2000 and 2006.[47] About half of all Iranian immigrants choose California as their state of intended residence. With more than 338,000 Americans now claiming Iranian ancestry, the presence of Iranian Americans is more readily noticed by outsiders. Although found in most major cities, distinct Iranian neighborhoods exist in Queens, New York, and Beverly Hills, California. As in the Washington, DC–Arlington, Virginia, area, classes in Farsi, the primary Iranian language, take place in these enclaves. Also located in these four areas are Islamic centers and mosques, further evidence of the sizeable Iranian community.

Born to mostly middle-class professional parents, today's second-generation Iranian Americans grow up in a child-centered family with egalitarian norms, quite unlike the patriarchal and authoritarian character of families in Iran.[48] Nonetheless, many parents are concerned about preserving their Iranian heritage and make efforts to preserve the positive aspects of the culture, despite the inevitable Americanization process.[49]

Living as a despised and persecuted religious minority in Iran, many Baha'is have immigrated to the United States, establishing centers in several major U.S. cities. The population of Baha'is in the United States is greater than anywhere else in the world, including the religion's cradle, Iran.

THE IRAQIS

We must distinguish between the immigrants from Iraq who arrived before and those who came after World War II, as well as the most recent immigrants, because political, social, and economic changes in the Middle East over the generations resulted in distinctive differences among these groups of immigrants. Studying one Iraqi subcultural group of Chaldeans living in the Detroit metropolitan area, Mary Sengstock observed significant pre- and postwar changes caused by the evolution of Iraq into a modern nation-state and the heightened Arab consciousness caused by Arab–Israeli tensions.[50]

The early immigrants formed a community of village-oriented entrepreneurs whose religious traditions served as their self identification. They maintained a *gemeinschaft* subsociety within U.S. society. Family orientations were strong, and many Iraqis were self-employed, operating grocery stores and other small businesses. They were, for the most part, a self-enclosed ethnic community.

Not only did the post–World War II immigrants to Detroit have different value orientations from their predecessors, reflecting their increased education and more urbanized backgrounds, but these newer orientations had an effect on the self-perceptions and behavior of the earlier immigrants. Although the Chaldeans are Christian, they felt the pull of Arab nationalist loyalties, and this national consciousness was infectious.[51] Most came to think of themselves as Arabs or Iraqis, not as Chaldeans or Telkeffes (another Iraqi subcultural group). These immigrants were less likely to be self-employed and more likely to interact with people of different backgrounds, including close friendship ties and intermarriage.

The most recent Iraqi immigrants come from a country suffering from civil war, continual violence, and the deaths of innocents. At the present time, few are refugees; they are immigrants, often departing for the U.S. from another country. About 30,000 Iraqi immigrants have arrived since 2000. In typical chain migration patterning, they settle where other Iraqis live, most particularly in Michigan (36 percent), California (13 percent), and Illinois (9 percent).[52]

Interestingly, neither the 1990 Gulf War against Saddam Hussein's troops nor the Iraqi war begun in 2003 generated subgroup-specific hostility against Iraqi Americans living in the United States. Several factors probably contributed to this lack of societal animosity. Given their relatively small numbers and tendency to live within the larger Arab American community, Iraqi Americans are not that visible. Furthermore, they were mostly supportive of the brief military action against their homeland's dictator and fled the violence ravaging Iraq. When the turmoil finally ends, we will see how that change affects future Iraqi immigration.

THE TURKS

The U.S. Office of Immigration Statistics reports that about 480,000 Turkish immigrants have come to the United States since 1820. Ordinarily, that number would place Turkey in the top 20 suppliers of emigrants. However, various subjugated peoples of different languages and cultures left the Ottoman Empire with only Turkish passports prior to World War I. Over 300,000 people, three-fourths of the total "Turkish" immigrants, entered the United States during this period (see the Appendix). Although immigration officials identified them as Turkish by their passports, many actually were Armenians, Syrians, Lebanese, or other nationalities. Over 88,000 ethnic Turks immigrated between 1980 and 2006, making this the period of their largest immigration.

Factors against Immigration

Several factors explain the earlier low level of emigration from Turkey in comparison with other poor, undeveloped nations during the great migration period. Perhaps foremost, Muslim Turks had waged a relentless campaign against the Christians within their empire and would hardly be inclined to settle in an almost exclusively Christian country. Second, the Turks had traditionally migrated in large groups. Consequently, there was little beyond the country's borders to attract families or individuals. In 1923, Turkey barred any emigrant from ever returning, even as a visitor. This law remained in force until 1950. With laws against emigration, few Turks chose to seek a better life elsewhere. Since 1965, however, an increasing number of Turkish immigrants have migrated to the United States because Turkey has been a military ally of the United States for several generations.

Societal Attitudes

Although relatively few Turks immigrated to the United States before World War I, feelings toward the Turks in the United States were mostly negative, primarily because of the Ottoman Empire's political and religious repression. Perhaps both that hostility and the desire to adopt a Turkish identity may explain the high level of return to Turkey after the end of the Ottoman Empire:

> Between 1890 and 1924, an estimated 25,000 to 50,000 Muslim Turks arrived in the United States. . . . Anecdotal evidence indicates that the creation of a Turkish national identity among the "Turkish" immigrants who remained in the United States paralleled the process being carried out in the new Republic of Turkey after 1923. Given the opportunity to ascribe to a "Turkish" identity, many apparently did so in the Republican, post-Ottoman era. This question of identity becomes more complex and therefore more intriguing when one considers that perhaps eighty percent of the Turks who arrived in the U.S. before 1924 returned. . . . If this is true, it is one of the highest return rates recorded for any immigrant group. Certainly the high rate can, in large part, be linked to the concept of sojourning—staying to earn enough money for a better life upon return—as well as the inability to deal with the extensive cultural disconnect in the host country.[53]

The Ottoman Empire's efforts to suppress Armenian and Syrian/Lebanese Christians were often brutal. Annihilation of enemies occurred frequently, and Turkish massacres of thousands of Armenians in the 1890s and again in 1915 stirred the wrath of many Americans. To this day, many Americans of Armenian descent mark the anniversary of these Turkish pogroms. American hostility toward the Turks was common during those times, which helps explain the initial hostility Syrian/Lebanese immigrants encountered in the United States when they were misidentified as Turks. In his survey of **social distance** in 1926, Emory S. Bogardus found that Turks ranked 27th of 30, above only Chinese, Koreans, and Asian Indians. In the 1946, 1956, and 1966 studies, Turks remained near the bottom, while Armenians ranked from 5 to 11 positions above them.[54]

Immigrant Patterns

When the Balkan War of 1912 began, many young unmarried Turkish males came to the United States to avoid military service. When war-ravaged Europe achieved peace again in 1919, more than 30,000 of them returned to Turkey. The few thousand who remained settled primarily in New York, Massachusetts, Michigan, Illinois, and Indiana.

Most Turkish immigrants who came before World War II were illiterate and secured jobs as unskilled laborers. They settled mostly in New York City and Detroit, and they kept to themselves. Some gradually became acculturated, while others remained socially segregated within U.S. society. Turkish Americans live in all 50 states, but the largest concentrations are in Brighton Beach in Brooklyn, Sunnyside in Queens, and in the cities of Paterson and Clifton, New Jersey.[55]

More recent Turkish immigrants are better educated than their predecessors. Almost half of all Turks in the United States have a bachelor's degree (nearly twice that of the total population), and about one-fourth of Turkish American adults have a graduate degree. Many are professionals or experienced businesspeople who settle in a relatively dispersed pattern. Others are working-class tradesmen and laborers who usually cluster together in urban areas in sufficient numbers to induce the establishment of bilingual programs in neighborhood schools.

> Turkish immigrants with limited skills are often dependent on community-survival strategies for finding work and housing. . . . [They] are mainly lower-class workers in the lowest-paid wage jobs in mostly Turkish-owned businesses, such as restaurants, gas stations, and grocery stores. . . . Such occupational concentrations play an important role in shaping their identities, as the impact of common occupational activity and interpersonal interactions in work spaces can provide a sense of difference. Many . . . have little or no contact with anyone outside their own ethnic community, for they work and socialize with others from Turkey.[56]

The negative image of Muslims among the U.S. public shapes the Turkish American sense of identity. As is the government in their homeland, they consider themselves secular and declare their differences from other Muslims. In particular, they emphasize their similarities with Europeans as one means to distance themselves from the unpopular Arab image.

THE PAKISTANIS

In the 2000 Census more than 253,000 Americans claimed Pakistani ancestry, and between 2000 and 2006 about 99,000 additional immigrants from Pakistan arrived, giving this group a significant presence in the United States—larger than, for example, the Nicaraguans or Turks.[57] Three in five are white-collar workers or professionals, and the rest are craftsmen, service workers, or laborers. Another common occupation of Pakistani immigrants in many cities is taxicab driver. In New York City, for example, immigrants from Pakistan, Bangladesh, and India made up less than 0.5 percent of the population but constitute 30 percent of its taxicab drivers.[58] Another common endeavor is family ownership of discount stores.[59]

Pakistani Americans have a widely dispersed settlement pattern, although 25 percent settle in the New York City metropolitan region. The Chicago, Washington, DC, Houston, and Los Angeles metropolitan areas are other locuses of residential clustering. The Pakistanis' acculturation and assimilation patterns are similar to those of other groups considered in this chapter.

OTHER ASIAN AND MIDDLE EASTERN ASSIMILATION

Structural assimilation among immigrant groups is rarely a first-generation occurrence. Because most people claiming ethnicity from this part of the world are newcomers, sufficient time has not yet elapsed to give us a perspective

Just as first-generation European Americans were distinctive in the old world clothing and/or kerchiefs they wore, so too do many Asian immigrants stand out today by their apparel. At this Pakistani street festival in Brooklyn, New York, the newcomers can buy additional articles of clothing to maintain this aspect of their cultural traditions.

on their assimilation. However, studies are emerging to give us some insights into their acculturation as immigrants. First, though, let us consider the assimilation of those who are not foreign born. This would include the descendants of Asian Indians, Lebanese, Syrians, and Turks who arrived in the early or mid-20th century. For the most part, their multigenerational life in the United States means only vestiges of ethnicity remain, and they are as much a part of the U.S. mainstream as the descendants of European immigrants.

Those recent arrivals of middle-class backgrounds whose education and occupational skills enabled them to settle in upscale urban neighborhoods or suburban communities are part of the economic mainstream, but they often have not yet overcome social barriers to full acceptance. Like the similarly situated Asian Americans discussed in the previous chapter, everyday ethnicity is still a real part of their lives, even though they may be living and working in a larger society. They are living in two worlds—private and public—old and new.

In a study of Asian Indian immigrants in Dallas–Fort Worth, Caroline Brettell found that their spatial, social, and political incorporation involved a process of inclusion through which their cultural identity is reinforced even as a new identity is adopted.[60] Other researchers examining ethnic identity formation among adolescents of Asian Indian, Chinese, Filipino, Vietnamese, and Salvadoran descent concluded, as have other studies, that the family plays a critical role in this process.[61] Together, these studies help us understand that family and an ethnic support system do not simply reinforce ethnicity but they also provide the foundation that eases the acculturation process.

On a related point, researchers studying Arab American adults found that acculturation and satisfaction with life in the United States and with family life were stronger with longer U.S. residence, younger age at immigration, not having recently visited their country of origin, and being Christian. Discrimination experiences influenced reduced satisfaction with life in the United States but not with acculturation in general.[62] Such findings would seem to reinforce assimilationist theory that length of residence and cultural affinity are key determinants of adjustment and acceptance.

SOCIOLOGICAL ANALYSIS

Most non-Western immigrants discussed in this chapter arrived since 1965. Since most are therefore first-generation Americans, their experiences lack sufficient historical perspective to permit full analysis. Furthermore (as noted at the beginning of the chapter), because many are educated with marketable occupational skills, not all entirely fit the theoretical framework of past immigrants. How well do the three theoretical perspectives explain their situation? As we will see, each provides a focus that promotes further understanding.

The Functionalist View

How has the social system been able to adapt relatively smoothly in absorbing the newcomers, many of whom are racially and religiously different? Functionalists would point to the immigration laws ensuring either sufficient earning power in occupational preference (higher admission priorities for skilled workers) or a support system in relative preference (higher admission priorities for close relatives). These better educated, better skilled, and/or better connected individuals quickly adjust, contribute to the economy, and seem to integrate into society with a minimum of problems. Most currently rank low on the social distance scale, but they become functionally integrated fairly easily. Their economic power allows them to live in middle-class neighborhoods, accessible through fair-housing laws. Some may even integrate areas, their comparable values and lifestyle making their native-born neighbors more receptive to them as a racially or culturally distinct people.

Less skilled non-Westerners help fill a population void in urban and exurban neighborhoods. Although they may encounter some minor problems, these newcomers bring stability to neighborhoods, preventing their decline and helping maintain a racial balance. Urban density gives the immigrants close proximity to one another, enabling ethnic solidarity to develop and be sustained. Living near their work, these newcomers find jobs other U.S. residents are unwilling to take. They also fulfill societal needs. As they struggle to succeed in the United States, they find better opportunities than they had known in their home countries, while society benefits from their work, purchasing power, and cultural contributions.

The Conflict View

Early non-Western immigrants provide grist for the analytical mill of conflict theorists. Industrialists often used Syrian/Lebanese men as strikebreakers in the Northeast, particularly during the intense labor unrest in the early 20th century. Just as the Syrian/Lebanese offered factory owners a cheaper labor alternative, Asian Indians on the West Coast enabled farmers, lumber companies, and railroads to benefit from their low-cost labor. Other workers resented their presence, fearing that the newcomers' growing numbers would jeopardize their own positions. Once again, the split-labor-market theory seems applicable. Economic competition between two wage level groups generated ethnic antagonism and violence.

More recent arrivals suggest a different analysis. In this case, tensions arise in the United States among African Americans and Hispanics at the bottom of the socioeconomic ladder, who see foreign-born non-Westerners leapfrogging over them. Resentment builds against the new arrivals whose hiring appears to deny upward mobility to native-born minority groups. Foreigners benefit at the expense of U.S. natives, they think. In addition, the movement of non-Western immigrants into white, middle-class apartment complexes and suburban neighborhoods changes the prior racial or cultural homogeneity, which sometimes stirs hostilities among the old-timers against the newcomers.

Although conflict may be less intense regarding these groups than toward previous waves of immigrants, an undercurrent of tension and resentment may exist, as evidenced by occasional eruptions of public protest over the building of a Sikh temple in a suburban community or over the effort to provide bilingual education to a group of Turkish American children in an urban school (two actual incidents). Fear of further terrorist attacks and racial profiling add to underlying tensions between the Arab American community and host society.

The Interactionist View

Because visual clues are a major means of categorizing strangers, people with different clothing or physical characteristics get classified as dissimilar types. Is it surprising to learn that the racially different (Africans and Asians) and the religiously different (Buddhists and Muslims) score lower on the social distance scale? If this perception of others as different couples with a sense of overwhelming numbers of newcomers, fears of a "Hindoo invasion" or something similar can easily lead to acts of exclusion, expulsion, and violence. Consider the case of the Irish in Paterson who attacked the Syrians moving into their neighborhood, supposing them to be Turks or "Mohammedans." Only when a respected religious leader from their own community redefined the situation for the Irish did the fighting stop. In recent years, Palestinian Americans struggled against U.S. natives who presumed they were all terrorists because of a few extremists. Misinterpretations about an ethnic group often cause problems for the group's members, and the peoples in this chapter are no exception.

Because many recent immigrants join the economic mainstream, their co-workers or neighbors assume that they have integrated socially as well. Interaction may occur in work-related relationships, but socially, the middle-class newcomers tend to become "unknown ethnics," at least in primary relationships. Socially isolated for the most part, the non-Westerners thus interact with compatriots and so remain a generalized entity in the minds of members of the dominant group. This social segregation appears to result more from an attraction toward similarly perceived others than from overt avoidance. Whatever the reason, non-Westerners are mostly social outcasts in the leisure activities of other U.S. residents. Variety may be the spice of life, but we do not apply that principle to racial and ethnic personal relationships.

RETROSPECT

Relatively few members of the racial and ethnic groups discussed in this chapter came to the United States before 1965. The experiences of those who did were generally similar to the experiences of other non-Western peoples in the United States and depended on the then-prevailing policies and regional attitudes.

For the most part, the immigrant experience of people from central and southwestern Asia is current. Although identifiable because of physical and cultural differences, they usually experience little difficulty because of their occupational status, their urban locale, and the relaxation of U.S. norms about newcomers. Nevertheless, as strangers they are keenly aware of the society in which they find themselves, and U.S. natives generally tend to avoid interacting with them in meaningful primary relationships. These non-Westerners are somewhat unusual in that many are able to secure a respectable social status via education, occupation, income, and residence, but because of their cultural differences, they have minimal social participation with native-born U.S. residents. This often is a two-way arrangement.

As larger numbers of immigrants from central and southwestern Asian countries come to the United States, they make their presence felt more and more. One aspect of this impact is in religion. Waves of earlier European immigrants changed the United States from an almost exclusively Protestant country to one of three major faiths. Now this Judeo-Christian population composition is expanding again, as increasing numbers of Muslims, Hindus, Buddhists, and adherents of other Eastern religions arrive.

As the United States becomes more diverse in religion, physical appearance, and value orientations, more U.S. residents are becoming aware of the differences in the people around them. Some argue that Americans today are more tolerant because of a resurgence of ethnicity and a more liberal government attitude toward cultural pluralism. Others contend that the past nativistic reaction to Asians in the West and to southern and eastern Europeans in the East is finding new form today against the non-Western immigrants. Riots and violent confrontations may have disappeared, but more subtle and sophisticated acts of discrimination occur, including calls for increased immigration restrictions against non-Western immigrants. Others dispute this claim.

Recent central and southwestern Asian immigrants are better educated and better trained, often speak English before they arrive, and thus enter U.S. society at a higher socioeconomic level than earlier immigrants did. Their ethnic community is more interactional than territorial for the most part, although some groups are more clustered and visible than others. They seem to adjust fairly easily to life in the United States, although ingroup socializing is quite common, as was the case with past immigrant groups. Perhaps we are still a generation away from being able to measure the full impact of their role within U.S. society.

KEY TERMS

Brain drain	Invasion–succession	Structural assimilation
Ethnogenesis	Miscegenation	
Gemeinschaft	Social distance	

DISCUSSION QUESTIONS

1. Why do differences in economic power between non-Western immigrants and earlier immigrants make assimilation less necessary now than before?

2. What parallels exist between Asian Indian and East and Southeast Asian immigrant experiences, both past and present?

3. How have structural conditions in the home countries reshaped ethnic identity and attitudes among Arab immigrants to the United States?

4. Discuss problems of stereotyping and prejudice encountered by non-Westerners because of outgroup perceptions and the media.

5. What insights do the three sociological perspectives offer about non-Western immigrants?

SUGGESTED READINGS

Angelo, Michael. *The Sikh Diaspora: Tradition and Change in an Immigrant Community.* New York: Garland Publishing, 1997. Explores the dynamics of acculturation and the maintenance of cultural traditions in a compact, middle-class Sikh immigrant community in upstate New York.

Marschner, Janice. *California's Arab Americans.* Sacramento, CA: Coleman Ranch Press, 2003. A detailed portrait of a cross-section of Arab American families, with detailed information about various aspects of Arabic culture.

Naff, Alixa. *The Arab Americans.* New York: Chelsea House, 1998. A clear, well-written introduction to Arab Americans, examining their culture and acculturation experiences in the United States.

Sheth, Pravin. *Indians in America: One Stream, Two Waves, Three Generations.* Jaipur, India: Rawat Publishing, 2001. An ambitious portrayal of a multigenerational saga within a multilingual ethnic group, covering its historical, cultural, and economic elements.

Suleiman, Michael (ed.). *Arabs in America: Building a New Future*. Philadelphia: Temple University Press, 2000.
An interdisciplinary anthology that examines the status of Arabs in various communities in North America and their prospects for the future.

Sullivan, Zohreh. *Exiled Memories: Stories of the Iranian Diaspora*. Philadelphia: Temple University Press, 2000.
A moving portrait of the Iranian émigré community grappling with life and identity transformation in the United States.

MySocKit

Additional resources for this chapter can be found in MySocKit. If you have a subscription to MySocKit, go to www.mysockit.com to study, review, and go beyond the book to learn more about race and ethnic relations.

Black Americans

ost Africans who arrived in America from 1619 until the end of the slave trade, in 1808, immigrated unwillingly, but 20th-century voluntary emigration to the United States from Africa has been substantial (Figure 10.1). Between 1899 and 1922, 115,000 African blacks and over 25,000 West Indian blacks arrived. The restrictive immigration law of 1924 reduced the number of new immigrants from these groups; Africans, for example, were limited to only 122 newcomers annually.[1] Africa sent more than 300,000 immigrants between 2001 and 2006, and nearly 600,000 West Indians arrived in the same time period.

Differences in culture have prevented any unifying racial bond from forming between black immigrants and native-born blacks. The newcomers are strangers in a new land; many native-born blacks—like Native Americans—are strangers in their own land, and both groups are strangers to each other. The new arrivals come from areas where (1) their race is the majority, (2) a tripartite color system prevails, or (3) color is not a primary factor in group life, but they enter a society where color is an important determinant of social and cultural identity. They find that white Americans identify Africans with a partially assimilated and socially restricted native black population that itself does not accept or relate well to them.

This chapter attempts to place black–white relations in perspective by showing their similarities with and differences from the patterns of dominant–minority interaction of other racial and ethnic groups. Other major themes are the long-lasting impact of cultural conditioning and the changes wrought by the Civil Rights movement.

SOCIOHISTORICAL PERSPECTIVE

During the age of exploration, black crew members served under Columbus and under such 16th-century Spanish explorers as Balboa, Cortéz, Pizarro, and de Soto. The first-known group of African immigrants consisted of 20 voluntary immigrants who landed in Jamestown in August 1619, a year before the Pilgrims

FIGURE 10.1 Africa

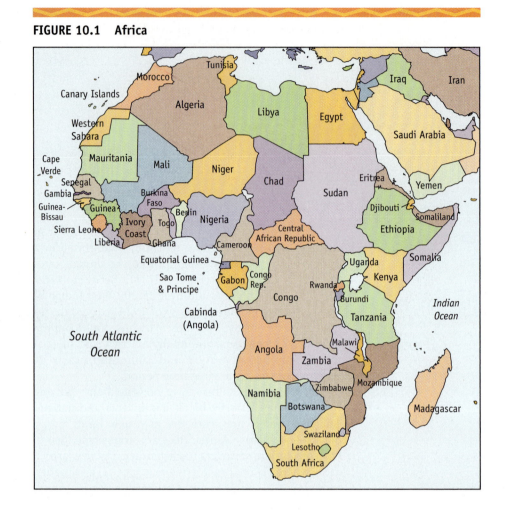

landed at Plymouth Rock. They came as indentured servants (as did many whites), worked off their debt, and became masters of their own destiny. They were the fortunate few, for the labor demands of the southern colonies soon resulted in the enslavement of millions of other Africans and their forced migration to the United States.

The Years of Slavery

To ease their transition to a new land, other ethnic groups re-created in miniature the society they left behind, but the Africans who came to the United States were not allowed to do so. Other groups could use education to give themselves and their children a better future, but state laws in the South made educating black slaves a criminal offense. Other groups may have encountered some degree of hostility and discrimination, but through hard work and perseverance, many were able to overcome nativist fears and prejudices. For blacks, however, 200 years of master–slave relations did much more than prevent their assimilation; they shaped values and attitudes about the two races that still linger today.

Indeed, some black leaders have lobbied for **slavery reparations,** similar to those given to Japanese Americans in 1988 for their incarceration in the 1940s. Arguing that if President Andrew Johnson had not stripped the freed slaves of the land given them by General William Tecumseh Sherman under Special Field Orders No. 15, their descendants might now control a much larger share of U.S. wealth, proponents seek cash payments now to right an old wrong. Opponents insist that, unlike other reparation payments, no victims are alive today, the statute of limitations has long expired, and descendants of slaves are impossible to identify since such descent is not identical with racial self-identification.

As the industrial North and the slaveholding, agrarian South evolved into different societies, they developed different norms. To be sure, the institution of slavery created an inferior status for blacks and led to much prejudice and discrimination. Yet there were free blacks in the South, too (nearly half a million by 1860)—people who had been emancipated by their owners, had purchased their freedom, or were descendants of free mothers. They lived in such urban areas as New Orleans, Mobile, and Charleston; in the tidewater regions of Virginia and Maryland; and in the Piedmont region of western North Carolina and Virginia. Those who lived in southern cities worked in a wide variety of skilled and unskilled occupations; some were architects, teachers, store and hotel managers, clerks, and milliners. In the North, although there was some variance, blacks faced considerable discrimination in education, housing, employment, and voting rights. Because in the North no operative caste system delineated norms and interaction patterns, many whites reacted more strongly to blacks in their midst. As a result, northern blacks had considerable difficulty achieving economic security.

Racism and Its Legacy

Although some ancient civilizations considered themselves superior to others, they typically did so on the basis of culture or special religious status, not race. Most historians agree that racism did not emerge as an ideological phenomenon until the 16th and 17th centuries.[2] This was the period of European exploration and imperialism, during which Europeans were brought into contact with many physically different, less technologically advanced peoples. The physical characteristics, values, and ways of life of these people differed from their own, so the Europeans naively concluded that there must be some relationship between how the people looked and how they behaved. This was another instance in which prejudices and stereotyping resulted from ethnocentric rationalization.

Myths about the racial inferiority of blacks emerged as a rationalization of slavery. Although slavery was by no means uncommon in earlier societies, ancient civilizations did not link skin color and social status. Statues and paintings from ancient Egypt, for example, depict slaves and rulers alike as both white and black.[3] Speculation about how racism arose includes such factors as (1) the rise of seagoing power among European nations and increased contact with red, brown, black, and yellow peoples; (2) the influence of Christianity, linking slavery and skin color with the Curse of Ham (Noah's second son, cursed by his father in Genesis 9:20–29); and (3) European technological and military superiority over native peoples throughout the world. In the 19th century, with racism firmly implanted in U.S. culture, a mangled and scientifically unsound form of evolutionary theory emerged to support racist thinking, for some argued that the white race was more highly evolved than the others.

W. E. B. DuBois interpreted the rise of racism as follows:

Labor was degraded, humanity was despised, the theory of "race" arose. There came a new doctrine of universal labor: mankind were of two sorts—the superior and the inferior; the inferior toiled for the superior; and the superior were the real men, the inferior half men or less. . . . Luxury and plenty for the few and poverty for the many was looked upon as inevitable in the course of nature. In addition to this, it went without saying that the white people of Europe had a right to live upon the labor and property of the colored peoples of the world.

In order to establish the righteousness of this point of view, science and religion, government and industry, were wheeling into line. The word "Negro" was used for the first time in the world's history to tie color to race and blackness to slavery and degradation. The white race was pictured as "pure" and superior: the black race as dirty, stupid, and inevitably inferior; the yellow race as sharing, in deception and cowardice, much of this color inferiority; while mixture of the races was considered the prime cause of degradation and failure in civilization. Everything great, everything fine, everything really successful in human culture, was white.[4]

Once established, the master–slave social system and the theory of racial inferiority supporting it conditioned values, attitudes, and the development of capacities that lasted far beyond the Civil War. Treated as if they were biologically inferior, blacks became socially inferior, first as a result of slavery and then as a result of discrimination in jobs, housing, and education. Blacks thus remained more thoroughly excluded from participation in the free community than did the former slaves of Latin America, trapped in a vicious circle of stereotyping, prejudice, and discrimination.[5] (See the discussion of the vicious-circle phenomenon in Chapter 4.)

Although many laws now protect people against discrimination, racist beliefs continue to exist. They can be seen in the reasons people give for moving out of racially changing neighborhoods or in their attitudes toward cities, crime, and welfare. Fear of crime, violence, and other problems of the inner city may be justified, but some individuals incorrectly attribute such troubles to race. Deviance, it must be remembered, occurs among all groups that are poor, powerless, and victims of discrimination.[6] (See the discussion of deviance in Chapter 4.)

The problem with racism is twofold: its legacy and its subtlety. *Legacy* here refers not only to its institutionalization within society but also to its transmission from one generation to the next. Slavery and segregation may end, but some people continue to believe blacks are inferior. This is part of the subtlety of racism because people usually draw such conclusions from their observable world. They are not aware that this "objective" reality is a multi-generational social construct. The alleged inferiority is a myth, except as a social product. People see primarily the effects of prolonged racist attitudes and actions. Even a person's own attitudes, actions, and reactions may unwittingly contribute to the propagation of racism.[7] (See the discussion of the Reality Construct and the Thomas Theorem in Chapter 2.)

◆◆◆ INSTITUTIONALIZED RACISM

Institutionalized racism, which occurs when laws attempt to legitimize differential racial treatment, took a new form after slavery in the United States was abolished. At first, though, racial equality seemed to have some chance of developing.

During the Reconstruction period and almost to the end of the 19th century, southern blacks generally had greater access to stores, restaurants, public transportation, bars, and theaters than in the first half of the 20th century. A typical pattern was for whites to live on one street in large homes, while behind them on the parallel street were the lesser dwellings of blacks, many of whom worked as domestics. Although a clear status distinction existed, in most places no severe social distance divided the two races. Blacks lived in close proximity to whites and frequently interacted with them in secondary relationships through their occupational roles as domestic or service workers. In education, marriage, political participation, and major economic enterprises, however, blacks did not share any commonality with whites (see The Ethnic Experience box below).

Immigration and Jim Crow

The change in black–white relations during the late 19th and early 20th centuries is an example of **cultural drift,** a gradual and pervasive change in a people's values. Economic problems, scandals, and frustrations endured by southern whites appear to be some of the factors that reshaped their attitudes. In a region where they had long been considered inferior, many blacks were achieving socioeconomic respectability and becoming economic competitors. Resentment at black

The Ethnic Experience

How Northerners Differ from Southerners

"I had heard so much talk about New York. People would say things were so good in New York until I felt that if I would get to New York, I would find money on the streets and wouldn't have no more worries. All my problems would be solved. When I got to New York, things were much different than that. Jobs were very hard to find, and the people were very different than in West Virginia.

"Finally I did get a job through the State Employment Office, working as a cook in the Brooklyn Navy Yard in a private canteen. I stayed there a year and then the war closed up—was over. Then I got another job in a seafood house on 34th Street and 3rd Avenue and I stayed there a year. Then a friend of mine and I went into our own business selling raw fish. Opened a store in Brooklyn selling raw fish. And, of course, it didn't pan out that way. The problem with that business was that we didn't have enough capital to carry us over the rough spots. And then my wife started having babies, and so I had to give up that job and seek another, which I did, and finally I got a job right away at another seafood house.

"In the South we had whites live here, Colored live there and everybody would speak to you whether they knowed you or not. But when I got to the North, I'd be out on the street, maybe walking around, before I got the jobs, looking around, trying to find my way around, and I would be saying, 'Good morning,' and 'Good evening,' whichever way the situation was, and people would look at me as if I was some dope or something. People would say, 'What's wrong with him?' People are not as friendly up here.

"And I also found out when we bought a house here, that the whites started right away moving out. They started selling their houses, putting up signs for sale. That didn't bother me any. Only thing was that I was just saying to myself that I thought New York was so great. Why should this be happening? And in the South, where I was living, it didn't happen that way. Blacks and whites lived side-by-side there, and we didn't have no problems with that. That kind of upset me that in New York, after hearing so much about it, this did go on."

Source: Black migrant from West Virginia who came North in 1944 at age 26. Taped interview from the collection of Vincent N. Parrillo.

upward mobility, amplified by a historical undercurrent of racist attitudes, was further increased by economic troubles (declining cotton prices and unemployment). Blacks became a convenient scapegoat for the frustrations and hostility of southern whites.

When Reconstruction ended in 1876, blacks once again found themselves in a formalized inferior status through segregation laws, voting disfranchisement, **black codes** (state laws designed to keep blacks in subservient positions), job discrimination, and occupational eviction. Not until the 1960s did many of these segregationist practices end in the South.

Less liberal attitudes in the North were another factor that led to an increased incidence of racist acts of discrimination in housing, labor, associations, unions, schools, and churches throughout the United States.[8] What caused this change in the North? The change in racial attitudes occurred just when great numbers of southern and eastern European immigrants were settling in northern urban areas. The arrival of so many dark-eyed, dark-haired, dark-complexioned newcomers set in motion a nativist reaction culminating in restrictive immigration laws. Northerners became more sensitive to the influx of foreigners and "anarchists" as well as to southern blacks coming north to seek work. The overtones of racism in the North's ethnocentric reaction to the "new" immigrants prompted greater empathy among Northern nativists for the South's reaction to blacks. As a result, the North ceased to pressure the South regarding its treatment of blacks and allowed the Jim Crow laws to emerge without a challenge.

In the 1870s and 1880s, Californians succeeded in making the Chinese question a national issue and cleverly related it to that of blacks whenever necessary. Political deals were made; and, later, southern representatives voted overwhelmingly in favor of the Chinese Exclusion Act of 1882 and the 1921 immigration bill restricting southern and eastern Europeans, most of whom were settling in the North.

In 1896, the U.S. Supreme Court ruling on *Plessy v. Ferguson* upheld the principle of "separate but equal" railroad accommodations for blacks and whites. Only a few southern states had had mandatory segregation laws covering train passengers before the turn of the century. Between 1901 and 1910, though, most southern states passed multiple, activity-specific **Jim Crow laws** as part of a rolling snowball effect of such legislation. Segregation became the norm in all areas of life—bars, barbershops, drinking fountains, toilet facilities, ticket windows, waiting rooms, hotels, restaurants, parks, playgrounds, theaters, and auditoriums. Through literacy tests, poll taxes, and other measures, the southern states also succeeded in disfranchising black voters.

Effects of Jim Crow

The segregation laws, mostly of 20th-century vintage, reflected racist attitudes that remained strong throughout the South decades after slavery had ended. When the 1954 Supreme Court ruling overturned school segregation laws, 17 states had mandatory segregation: Alabama, Arkansas, Delaware, Florida, Georgia, Kentucky, Louisiana, Maryland, Mississippi, Missouri, North Carolina, Oklahoma, South Carolina, Tennessee, Texas, Virginia, and West Virginia. Four other states—Arizona, Kansas, New Mexico, and Wyoming—permitted segregation as a local option.

The South. It is impossible to exaggerate the impact on society of legalizing such discriminatory norms. These laws existed for two or three generations. During that time, both white and black children grew up in a racially stratified society. Because the white world of reality was one in which differential treatment was the norm, the inferior status of blacks was taken for granted. For most whites growing up in such an environment and in turn transmitting values and attitudes to their children, this reflected objective reality.

Structural discrimination in the South was pervasive. Despite legal challenges by the National Association for the Advancement of Colored People (NAACP) and by other groups and individuals, most blacks and whites appeared to accept the situation. To whites, the inferior status of blacks in southern society appeared to justify continued differential treatment. It was, as Gunnar Myrdal concluded in his study of U.S. race relations, a perfect example of the vicious-circle phenomenon, in which "discrimination breeds discrimination."[9] Because blacks' education and job opportunities were restricted, the consequences of deprivation and limited opportunity only aggravated the situation. Blacks did not hold lucrative jobs or become educated; they lived in squalor amidst poverty, disease, crime, and violence; and so they were not "good enough" to use the same facilities as whites. This gave whites more ammunition to bolster their aversion to blacks and

For the first six decades of the 20th century, Jim Crow laws maintained a racially segregated society in the South. All aspects of public interaction, including the entrance and seating accommodations of this movie theater, determined use and accessibility by race. Such pervasive norms socialized many people into accepting a world of institutionalized discrimination as "normal."

increased their prejudicial attitudes and discriminatory actions. Myrdal calls this intensification a **cumulative causation,** in which an almost perpetual sequence of reciprocal stimuli and responses produces complex interactive results.[10]

The North. But what about the North, where few segregationist laws existed? Although there had been some migration to the North earlier, prior to 1914 almost all blacks resided in the South; then, however, large numbers of blacks began to migrate to the northern urban areas. Clearly, the Jim Crow laws and poor economic conditions were the major push factors for moving north, and promises of better wages, education, and political freedom were the primary pull factors (see The Ethnic Experience box below).

> By 1915, the North needed labor. The war was under way in Europe and Northern industry was reaping the benefits from it. The large supply of foreign immigrant labor was rapidly dwindling. In the fourteen years after 1900, over twelve million immigrants found their way to the United States. More than one million immigrants reached the United States in 1914 alone. The next year this figure was cut to about one third, in 1916 to about one fourth, and, by 1918, only 110,618 new arrivals landed on the shores of the United States, while 94,585 left. Other sources of labor were needed and Southern Negroes appeared as an available and willing substitute. . . .
>
> The larger pay and increased economic opportunities in the North were heady inducements to migrants. But it was not only for economic reasons that the desire to come North existed in so many. . . . The desire of adults to see their children able to obtain an education caused many to move North. . . . According

The Ethnic Experience

Adjusting to Northern Urban Life

"I came to the North not because of a lack, not being able to cope with economic situations in the South, because I was doing all right economically. I came, more or less, for a change of environment and for a higher income for the work I was doing.

"I was educated in the South and by the time I left I was not sharecropping any longer. I was teaching and so my standard of living was different from back when I was a child growing up. I had heard many rumors about the North when I was a child. I had heard there was no segregation in the North. You were at liberty to ride buses, use all facilities, no discrimination in jobs. And I found all of this was, more or less, a fairy tale in a lot of respects. As an adult, I had a more accurate picture of what the North was all about since I had relatives living in Detroit, Washington, and New Jersey.

"I worked at different jobs—office worker, in a nursery school, a dietician—before going to grad school and becoming a public school teacher as I was in the South.

"The biggest adjustment to me going from a rural to an urban setting was getting accustomed to rushing, rushing, rushing city life. To me the people were always running instead of walking. There was always the hustle-bustle to catch the buses and catch subways and this kind of thing. And this was the hardest thing for me to get accustomed to, and the rate at which people worked. The people in the North move much, much faster than people in the South.

"I lived in an apartment with my sister four months, got married and moved to another apartment with my husband. We lived there a year and then moved to the suburbs where we bought our house. Now things here have deteriorated to the extent we have higher unemployment in the North than we do in the South. The overcrowding situation and your housing situation is badly in need of improvement, too."

Source: Black migrant from South Carolina who came north in 1954 at age 22. Taped interview from the collection of Vincent N. Parrillo.

to a *New York Times* editorial (January 21, 1918), higher wages would have been far less attractive if the colored man had not felt, and felt for a long time and bitterly, that in the North and West he would not, as in his southern home, be reminded of his black skin every time he met a policeman, entered a street car, railway station or train, and in a hundred other less conspicuous ways in the course of a day.[11]

By 1925, more than 1.5 million blacks lived in the North. As their counterparts on the West Coast had done in response to Asian immigrants, labor unions in the North organized against the blacks. Seeing them either as an undesirable social element or as economic competition, many workers quickly became antagonistic toward them. Although African Americans found greater freedom in the North, the dominant group's animosity toward them led to majority patterns of avoidance and discrimination.

Race riots, basically an urban phenomenon reflecting the growing hostility in the North, swept through a number of cities during World War I. In 1917, in East St. Louis, Illinois, 39 blacks and 8 whites were killed and hundreds seriously injured in one of the worst of these riots. In 1919, the crisis became even more acute, with returning war veterans seeking jobs and more blacks moving north:

> That year there were race riots large and small in twenty-six American cities including thirty-eight killed in a Chicago riot of August, from twenty-five to fifty killed in Phillips County, Arkansas; and six killed in Washington. For a day, the city of Washington, in July, 1919, was actually in the hands of a black mob fighting against the aggression of the whites with hand grenades.[12]

The riots intensified the hostile racial feelings even more. The South had *de jure* **segregation,** but Jim Crow—as a cause of black migration and a model for northern attitudes and actions—played an important role in the development of *de facto* **segregation** in the North. With race the determinant for various life opportunities in both the North and the South, succeeding generations of blacks encountered the same obstacles to upward mobility. So the effects of Jim Crow on black assimilation into the mainstream of U.S. society went beyond the South and lasted longer than just the first half of the 20th century.

The Ku Klux Klan

Originally organized in the South during Reconstruction, primarily to intimidate blacks so that they would not exercise their new political rights, the Ku Klux Klan (KKK) reorganized in the 20th century with a broader range of target groups. In 1915, William J. Simmons resurrected the movement, formalized its rituals and organization, and dedicated it to white supremacy, Protestant Christianity, and "Americanism." A combination of factors—the agricultural depression, Prohibition, immigration, and isolationism—enhanced the Klan's rapid expansion. By 1923, it claimed 3 million enrolled members and operated in virtually every state in the union, with public ceremonies and parades.

At first, the Klan concentrated on maintaining white supremacy by intimidating white employers as well as black workers and potential voters. Although this remained an important theme, as the Klan spread northward, its racist orientation broadened into a more general nationalism and nativism. Fears and condemnation of Jews and foreigners, especially Catholics, led the Klan into a campaign of promoting an Anglo-Saxon version of Americanism with evangelical zeal. The hooded Klansmen used mass raids, tarring and featherings, floggings, and other strong-arm tactics to enforce their notions of moral propriety or to stabilize the old order. In reality, their actions only fomented additional strife and cruelty.

The Ku Klux Klan thus evolved into a multixenophobic organization in which southern and eastern European Catholics and Jews, as well as blacks, were seen as a threat to the nation's character. The Klan's enormous popularity in the early 1920s reflected the times because these minority peoples were considered an economic threat to more established residents. As prosperity increased and immigration decreased, thereby reducing the tensions, support for the Klan ebbed. Its success, though, like the success of the Native American Party and the Know-Nothing Party of the 19th century, indicates that many people were receptive to its philosophy and goals.

The Ku Klux Klan is not just a relic from the past. Wherever racial strife occurs, its members come to sermonize, recruit, and stir up trouble. They have harassed and intimidated blacks in southern California and Vietnamese along the Texas Gulf Coast. When unemployment rises, they seek out the vulnerable white victims, offering a convenient black scapegoat for their troubles. In the backwoods of several states, they run paramilitary camps, practicing riflery and battle tactics for what they see as an inevitable racial war. Klan members indoctrinate their children at these camps, too, passing on a legacy of hate. Meanwhile, on equal-access local cable channels, they telecast programs promoting their bigotry.

THE WINDS OF CHANGE

In the past, blacks made many concerted efforts to improve their lot. The Colored National Farmers' Alliance claimed 1,250,000 members in 1891, but it faded from the scene by 1910. In the 20th century, several black leaders arose to rally their people: Booker T. Washington, W. E. B. DuBois, Marcus Garvey, and A. Philip Randolph. In the next three decades, the NAACP and other groups filed court cases that achieved limited success but laid the basis for the 1954 school desegregation ruling, which produced a massive restructuring of black–white relations.

Desegregation: The First Phase

Having experienced life outside their cultural milieu, many blacks who fought in World War II returned home with new perspectives and aspirations. The GI Bill of Rights, the Veterans Authority, and the Federal Housing Authority offered increased opportunity for education, jobs, and housing. Expectations increased, and the growing popularity of television sets brought into more and more homes insights into lifestyles that previously could only be vaguely imagined.

Several court cases challenging school segregation laws of Delaware, Kansas, South Carolina, and Virginia reached the U.S. Supreme Court in 1954. After consolidating the several suits, the justices ruled unanimously that the "separate but equal" doctrine was unconstitutional. Social science data, through *amicus curiae* briefs, played an important role in the decision.[13] The following year, the Court established a means of implementing its decree by giving the federal district courts jurisdiction over any problems relating to enforcement of the ruling. The

Court insisted that the states move toward compliance with "all deliberate speed," but this guideline was vague enough to allow the states to circumvent the ruling at first.

Although the NAACP quickly began a multipronged challenge to school districts in the 17 states where statutorily mandated school segregation existed, its efforts met with mixed success. Many whites, perceiving their values, beliefs, and practices threatened by outsiders, resisted desegregation. State legislatures passed bills to stave off integration, whites used economic and social pressures to intimidate any blacks who attempted to integrate local schools, and the school districts themselves procrastinated in dealing with the problem. For three years, the battle of wills resulted in a stalemate, continuing the status quo despite the Supreme Court ruling.

On another front, an event occurred in Montgomery, Alabama, in 1955 that foreshadowed other minority actions in the 1960s. Rosa Parks, a tired black seamstress on her way home from work, found the seats in the black section of the bus all occupied and so sat down in an open seat in the section reserved for whites; when she refused the bus driver's demand that she relinquish the seat, she was arrested. Through the organizing efforts of Martin Luther King Jr., the black community staged a successful bus boycott in protest. Four months later, the NAACP argued the case in the federal district court, which ruled against segregated seating on municipal buses and the U.S. Supreme Court upheld the decision.

The confrontation in the fall of 1957 at Little Rock Central High School in Arkansas was a watershed event in desegregation. Here the state's defiance of the Supreme Court could not be ignored because the governor called out the National Guard to forcibly block implementation of a federal court order to integrate the high school. President Eisenhower, who had personally opposed the 1954 ruling, acted decisively by federalizing the National Guard and sending regular army troops to Little Rock to ensure compliance.

With all legal avenues of appeal exhausted and the federal government insisting that all citizens, including black children, be accorded equal rights, southern resistance ebbed. Desegregation in the public schools, although sometimes slight in effect because of neighborhood-based districting plans, became the norm throughout the southern states. That is not to say that everything was harmonious. Some whites established private academies to avoid sending their children to integrated schools, and some southern leaders publicly committed themselves to upholding southern tradition at all costs. Still, Jim Crow had been dealt a severe blow, and opponents readied themselves for the next assault.

Desegregation: The Second Phase

In the 1960s, the Civil Rights movement gained momentum, attracted many followers, and moved against the remaining Jim Crow legislation. Sit-in demonstrations began in Greensboro, North Carolina, on February 1, 1960, when four freshmen from the all-black Agricultural and Technical College sat at the all-white lunch counter at the local Woolworth's store and refused to leave. During the spring of 1960, similar sit-ins occurred throughout the South. From the sit-ins evolved a fourth social organization—the Student Nonviolent Coordinating Committee (SNCC)—to compete with the NAACP, the Congress on Racial Equality (CORE), and the Southern Christian Leadership Conference (SCLC), which Dr. King had formed after the bus boycott.

The success of the sit-ins convinced many people that direct action was a quicker and more effective means of achieving total desegregation than protracted court battles. James Farmer of CORE organized Freedom Rides from Washington, DC, to selected southern locations in 1961 to challenge the segregated facilities in bus terminals. These were followed by freedom marches, voter registration drives, and continued litigation challenging the constitutionality of Jim Crow legislation.

All of these movements were symptomatic of the times. John Kennedy's election as president in 1960 and his speaking of "a new generation of leadership" had inaugurated a period of high hopes and ideals. It was a time of political commitment and societal change, of VISTA and the Peace Corps, of promise and reachable goals. As the Civil Rights movement grew, "We Shall Overcome" became the rallying theme song, and Bob Dylan's "Blowin' in the Wind" captured the spirit of the times.

Civil rights activity met with fierce resistance. Dr. King urged nonviolence, but younger black activists grew impatient with such an approach:

> The aim was "to awaken a sense of moral shame in the opponent." Such a philosophy presumed that the opponent had moral shame to awaken, and that moral shame, if awakened, would suffice. During the 1960s many civil rights activists came to doubt the first and deny the second. The reasons for this did not lie primarily in white Southern terrorism as manifested in the killing of NAACP leader Medgar Evers, of three civil rights workers in Neshoba, Mississippi, of four little girls in a dynamited church in Birmingham, and many others. To a large extent, white Southern violence was anticipated and expected. What was not expected was the absence of strong protective action by the federal government.
>
> Activists in SNCC and CORE met with greater and more violent Southern resistance as direct action continued during the sixties. Freedom Riders were beaten by mobs in Montgomery; demonstrators were hosed, clubbed, and cattle-prodded in Birmingham and Selma. Throughout the South, civil rights workers, Black and White, were victimized by local officials as well as by nightriders and angry crowds. It was not surprising, then, that student activists in the South became increasingly disillusioned with nonviolent tactics of resistance.[14]

Two events in 1963—the March on Washington and the integration of the University of Alabama—gave King and Kennedy the opportunity to express the mood of the times. On August 28, 1963, tens of thousands of marchers of all races from all over the country and from many walks of life gathered before the Lincoln Memorial. Dr. King addressed them (in part) as follows:

> There are those who are asking the devotees of civil rights, "When will you be satisfied?" We can never be satisfied as long as the Negro is the victim of the unspeakable horrors of police brutality. We can never be satisfied as long as our bodies, heavy with the fatigue of travel, cannot gain lodging in the motels of the highways and the hotels of the cities. We cannot be satisfied as long as the Negro's basic mobility is from a smaller ghetto to a larger one. We can never be satisfied as long as a Negro in Mississippi cannot vote and a Negro in New York believes he has nothing for which to vote. No, no, we are not satisfied, and we will not be satisfied until justice rolls down like waters and righteousness like a mighty stream. . . .

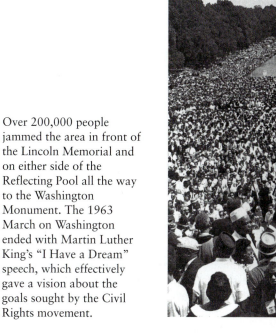

Over 200,000 people jammed the area in front of the Lincoln Memorial and on either side of the Reflecting Pool all the way to the Washington Monument. The 1963 March on Washington ended with Martin Luther King's "I Have a Dream" speech, which effectively gave a vision about the goals sought by the Civil Rights movement.

> I say to you today, my friends, that in spite of the difficulties and frustrations of the moment I still have a dream. It is a dream deeply rooted in the American dream.
>
> I have a dream that one day this nation will rise up and live out the true meaning of its creed: "We hold these truths to be self-evident; that all men are created equal." . . . I have a dream that my four little children will one day live in a nation where they will not be judged by the color of their skin but by the content of their character.

On April 4, 1968, an assassin's bullet prevented Martin Luther King from seeing his dream move closer to reality. President Kennedy had been assassinated 4½ years earlier, on November 22, 1963, before Congress could pass the civil rights legislation he had proposed after sending troops to enforce the integration of the University of Alabama that same year. In explaining that action, Kennedy had told the public in a television address:

> This nation was founded by men of many nations and backgrounds. It was founded on the principle that all men are created equal, and that the rights of every man are diminished when the rights of one man are threatened. . . .
>
> It ought to be possible, therefore, for American students of any color to attend any public institution they select without having to be backed up by troops. It ought to be possible for American consumers of any color to receive equal service in places of public accommodation, such as hotels and restaurants, and theaters and retail stores without being forced to resort to demonstrations in the street.

And it ought to be possible for American citizens of any color to register and to vote in a free election without interference or fear of reprisal.

It ought to be possible, in short, for every American to enjoy the privileges of being American without regard to his race or his color.

In short, every American ought to have the right to be treated as he would wish to be treated, as one would wish his children to be treated. But this is not the case. . . .

One hundred years of delay have passed since President Lincoln freed the slaves, yet their heirs, their grandsons, are not fully free. They are not yet freed from the bonds of injustice; they are not yet freed from social and economic oppression.

And this nation, for all its hopes and all its boasts, will not be fully free until all its citizens are free.

The Civil Rights Act of 1964 was the most far-reaching legislation against racial discrimination ever passed. It mandated that equal standards be enforced for voter eligibility in federal elections. It prohibited racial discrimination and refusal of service on racial grounds in all places of public accommodation, including eating and lodging establishments and places of entertainment, recreation, and service. It gave the attorney general broad powers to intervene in private suits regarding violation of civil rights. It banned racial discrimination by employers and unions and by any recipient of federal funds, and it directed federal agencies to monitor businesses and organizations for compliance and to withhold funds from any recalcitrant state or local agency.

Congress passed additional legislation in 1965 to simplify judicial enforcement of the voting laws and to extend them to state and local elections. In 1968, further civil rights legislation barred discrimination in housing and gave

Lt. Vernon Baker, the only living African American World War II hero, received the Medal of Honor from President Clinton at a 1997 White House ceremony, 52 years after his courageous actions. The action overturned a policy of systematic racial discrimination in the criteria for awarding medals during the war.

Native Americans greater rights in their dealings with courts and government agencies at all levels. Congress also set stiff federal penalties for persons convicted of attempting or conspiring to intimidate or injure anyone who was exercising any of the civil rights provided by congressional action.

In 1966, Stokely Carmichael, the head of SNCC, advanced the slogan "Black Power"—a declaration that civil rights goals could be achieved only through concerted black efforts. It symbolized the attainment of what Kurt Lewin called a "sense of peoplehood" and what Franklin Giddings identified as a "consciousness of kind." The word *black* rather than *Negro* became the accepted way of referring to this racial group in the 1970s. Unfortunately, Carmichael was also a major force in the purge of whites from the SNCC leadership—an isolationist act that alienated many white sympathizers to SNCC's cause.

Four decades later, we can readily see the gains in black power in the political arena. The number of black elected officials increased dramatically, from about 170 in 1964 to over 9,000 today, about two-thirds of these in the southern states.[15] Blacks also improved their rate of participation in other areas, including voter registration. Perhaps "stateways" will change "folkways," as legislation opens doors to blacks, thereby providing long-term opportunities for the social conditioning of people's attitudes toward racial harmony.

URBAN UNREST

As the Civil Rights movement gained momentum, it spread northward as well. Protests against discrimination in employment and housing and against *de facto* segregation in northern schools began in the early 1960s, in New York City and Philadelphia, and quickly spread:

> None of the problems of the blacks in the North—slum schools, unemployment or residential segregation—were new, but an intensified awareness of them had grown. Part of this new awareness reflected the economic cramp that developed during the latter part of the fifties, particularly in the burgeoning ghettoes of northern and western cities. Ideological cramp was being felt outside the South, too. The promise of a new equality for all blacks, the struggle of southern blacks to realize this promise, and the complacency of white America as the white South turned the new equality into token equality spread disillusionment into black neighborhoods all over the nation. Ironically, the plaintive and oft-repeated plea of white southerners that the problem of race relations was not just a Southern problem finally began to be heard—but only because it was now sounded by black voices.[16]

In the North, ideological support for the black cause waned as the percentages of blacks in northern cities increased. Changes—in particular, open housing and busing—were demanded nearer home. By 1964, Charles Silberman observed,

> And so the North is finally beginning to face the reality of race. In the process, it is discovering animosities and prejudices that had been hidden in the recesses of the soul. For a brief period following the demonstrations in Birmingham in the spring of 1963—a very brief period—it appeared that the American conscience had been touched; a wave of sympathy for the Negro and of revulsion over white brutality seemed to course through the nation. But then the counteraction set in, revealing a degree of anti-Negro prejudice and hatred that surprised even the most sophisticated observers.[17]

As blacks experienced some gains and some frustrations, a pattern of increased alienation, cynicism, hostility, and violence ensued. When a social movement achieves some goals, its expectations are increased and so are its frustrations, which leads to greater militancy.[18] Militant leaders such as Malcolm X, Eldridge Cleaver, Huey Newton, and Bobby Seale emerged to speak of the grievances of northern blacks. New organizations, such as the Black Panthers, and older ones, such as the Black Muslims, attracted many followers as they set out to meet the needs of northern blacks in the ghettos.

The 1960s Riots

In the summer of 1964, blacks rioted in the tenement sections of Harlem, Rochester, and Philadelphia, attacking both police and property. The following summer, the violence and destruction were more massive; outbursts occurred first in the Watts section of Los Angeles and then in Chicago; Springfield, Massachusetts; and Philadelphia. Ghetto violence continued. In the summer of 1966, 18 different riots occurred, and in the summer of 1967, 31 cities experienced riots, of which those in Newark (26 killed) and Detroit (42 killed) were the worst.

The increase in the number and intensity of riots in 1967 prompted an in-depth study of 75 of the disorders, including those in Newark and Detroit, by the National Advisory Commission on Civil Disorders. It concluded that, although specific grievances varied somewhat from city to city, there were consistent patterns in who the rioters were, how the riots originated, and what the rioters wanted. The most intense causal factors were police practices, unemployment and underemployment, and inadequate housing. In its 1968 report, the so-called Kerner Commission warned that the United States was "moving toward two societies, one black, one white—separate and unequal."[19]

The assassination of Martin Luther King Jr. in April 1968 prompted violence to erupt anew in 125 cities. The Department of Justice reported 46 people killed in one week of unrest. Several years of civil rights legislation now set changes in motion. Government action at all levels sought to correct the conditions that encouraged the violence, and U.S. cities experienced no further major disturbances for several years.

Several factors contributed to the cooling of black urban violence. First, a new social movement protesting the war in Vietnam, to which many black youths were sent, became a focus of public concern. Second, many black leaders were assassinated (King, Evers, and Malcolm X) or imprisoned (Carmichael, Newton, and Seale) or went into exile (Cleaver). Third, many blacks redirected their energies toward community self-help programs, some leaders were co-opted into leadership roles within the system, and other blacks began to strive for the black power goal Carmichael had enunciated. Perhaps, also, the realization that the destruction of their neighborhoods had left a trail of economic devastation without producing any tangible benefits helped stop the rioting.

The 1980s Miami Riots

In Miami in May 1980, black economic frustrations and resentment against the growing Cuban community—sparked by an all-white jury's acquittal of four white police officers accused of bludgeoning a black man to death—set off three days of the worst outbreak of racial violence in 13 years. When it ended, 18 were dead, more than 400 were injured, and property damages exceeded $200 million.[20] In January 1989, violence erupted in Miami again, in the Overtown section, after a policeman shot and killed a black motorcycle rider.

The 1992 Los Angeles Riot

Five days of rioting erupted in Los Angeles in 1992, after a jury acquitted four white city police officers of criminal wrongdoing in the videotaped beating of black motorist Rodney King. In the aftermath of the prolonged riot, officials reported 58 deaths, 4,000 injuries, 11,900 arrests, and damage ranging as high as $1 billion.[21] The events seemed like a flashback to the 1960s, and some observers predicted a new wave of rioting across the United States in response to a decade of retreat by the federal government from its earlier role as a champion of the disadvantaged. But U.S. society had changed. Most of the nation's 30 million African Americans did not take to the streets. Those who did were part of a relatively small urban underclass clearly distinct from the 40 percent of all African American families now middle class or upwardly mobile working class. Moreover, whereas the 1965 Watts riot was black versus white, the 1992 riot was *multiracial* warfare: blacks preying on other blacks, Latinos on whites, blacks and Latinos on Koreans and other Asian Americans.[22] The Rodney King verdict was the spark that detonated a powder keg built of the pathologies resulting from poverty—squalid living conditions, frustration, alienation, anger, and family disintegration.

In Chapter 8, I discussed some aspects of the black–Korean conflict. Part of that animosity stems from the growing presence and economic success of Korean merchants in black neighborhoods where poverty and unemployment are widespread. Limited education is not a barrier to self-employment for Korean Americans because of their informal networks of assistance and advice. Poorly educated African Americans, however, lack similar support networks and are less likely to become entrepreneurs in the central city.[23] As these blacks witness the economic gains of strangers in their midst while they themselves are mired in deprivation, their resentment sometimes reaches the flashpoint of violence when triggered by an incident.

How can the United States prevent such violence? The primary answer lies in taking steps to meet black expectations and to eliminate the economic despair that fuels riots. We must focus on overcoming depressed urban economies, chronic unemployment, a poorly skilled and poorly educated labor force, substandard housing, and unsafe streets.

Reducing the social distance among urban residents through community interaction offers another promising approach. When "we" replaces "us versus them," violence becomes less likely. Still another approach is to increase the number of African American entrepreneurs in the central city. African American proprietors would act as positive role models and could provide initial employment opportunities to urban African American youths. Local mom-and-pop stores could become bonding anchors in the neighborhood, reinforcing community life around work and thereby helping generate and sustain informal associations.[24]

Postviolence Exodus

For several complex reasons, a significant white middle-class migration from cities to suburbs began in the 1950s, and urban violence has clearly been a major factor in this movement. The 1960s riots gave added impetus to white flight, with many stores and businesses following close behind. Because many major cities—especially in the Northeast and Midwest—also experienced population declines, this resulted in a larger concentration of people of color in these cities.

Riots also induced many middle-class minorities to leave the embattled neighborhoods in south-central Los Angeles and elsewhere.[25] Violence, burning, and looting thus destroy the neighborhood economy, stability, and potential as its middle class flees.

THE BELL-CURVE DEBATE

In 1994, *The Bell Curve,* by Richard Herrnstein and Charles Murray, set off a fire-storm of controversy.[26] Rejecting conventional theories about the role of environment and culture in creating dependence and crime, the authors argued that intelligence is the best single explanation of wealth, poverty, and social status. They asserted that the United States was becoming increasingly stratified by intellectual ability—with a "cognitive elite" of brilliant, highly educated business leaders, politicians, and professionals; a large cognitive middle class of about 125 million with IQs measuring between 91 and 110; and a growing underclass of dullards with IQs of 90 or below.

The authors also contended that social pathologies such as poverty, welfare dependence, illegitimacy, and crime were all strongly related to low IQ. Most explosive was their argument that blacks as a group were intellectually inferior to whites as a group because the mean, or average, IQ score for blacks was 15 points lower than that for whites. Herrnstein and Murray then attacked affirmative action in college admissions and in the workplace, characterizing it as a futile policy designed to help the cognitively disadvantaged; not-so-smart people, they implied, can never become middle class.

Another volatile theme of the book was the proposition that the cognitive elite pass on their genetic advantages to their children while members of the low-IQ underclass pass on genetic disadvantages. Herrnstein and Murray, noting the higher birth rate among the underclass, argued that government subsidies to welfare mothers were responsible for a gradual decline in the national IQ. Therefore, they argued, such programs as Aid to Families with Dependent Children should be terminated.

Critics attacked the book for its selective use of data to fit its political arguments, such as ignoring the difference between actual intelligence and IQ as measured by tests. Others found factual contradictions, such as the claim that the national IQ had declined when actually group scores have been rising slowly but steadily since the 1930s.[27] Still others attacked the book's scholarship, methodology, and analytical techniques.[28]

Early IQ Tests

Although Herrnstein and Murray offered some new wrinkles, their argument is an old, discredited one. The intelligence test, first developed by Alfred Binet in 1905, became a popular means of comparing the intelligence of different racial and ethnic groups, although that was not Binet's intention. This supposedly objective, scientific instrument was intended to measure an individual's innate intelligence, uninfluenced by any beneficial or detrimental effects of environment. As misappropriated and applied to groups of people, however, the test invited researchers to compare groups' intellectual ability. Early studies showed that northern and western Europeans—and often the Chinese and Japanese—scored consistently and decidedly higher than southern and eastern Europeans, blacks, Mexicans, and Native Americans.[29] Conveniently ignoring the results for Asians, nativists and segregationists seized on these studies as arguments for immigration restrictions against "inferiors," for the forced assimilation of Native Americans, and for Jim Crow laws in the South.

Gradually, as nativist antipathy against the "new" immigrants abated, the argument shifted primarily to intelligence differences between blacks and whites. The disparity in the test results, which most authorities believe actually reflects a cultural bias within the tests, became a basis for claiming white intellectual superiority.

In 1958, Audrey Shuey's book *The Testing of Negro Intelligence* appeared and caused a furor. Shuey surveyed some 240 studies of 60 different intelligence tests that had been given over a 44-year span to hundreds of thousands of servicemen from World Wars I and II and thousands of schoolchildren of all ages through college, from all regions of the country. She concluded that the "remarkable consistenc[ies] in test results . . . all point to the presence of some native differences" between blacks and whites "as determined by intelligence tests."[30]

For any scientist, the interpretation of findings is as crucial as the findings themselves and the methods employed to obtain them. Shuey was accurate in observing the consistent lower scoring of blacks on intelligence tests. However, many scientists disagreed with her conclusion that this was due to racial intellectual inferiority. The conclusion of innate or genetic differences was a quantum leap from her findings, which did not prove any such thing.

In the late 1960s, the IQ controversy centered on claims made by two California professors: Arthur R. Jensen, an educational psychologist at the University of California (Berkeley), and William B. Shockley, a Nobel Prize–winning physicist at Stanford University. Jensen argued that the 10- to 20-point IQ differential between blacks and whites involved only certain mental functions. He pointed out that blacks and whites tested equally well in such brain functions as rote learning and memory but that blacks did more poorly in problem solving, in seeing relationships, and in abstract reasoning. Because this material does not depend on specific cultural information, he maintained, the blacks' lower scores must be due to their genetic heritage.[31] Shockley declared that the conceptual intelligence of blacks, as measured by many different IQ tests, was significantly lower than that of whites and that some of this variance was genetically caused and therefore not correctable.

IQ Test Performance by Other Groups

Refuting this position, Thomas Sowell argued that, on average, white ethnic groups, such as the Poles, Jews, and Italians, scored in the 80s on IQ tests administered during the 1920s but as a group had gained 20 to 25 points by the 1970s after experiencing upward mobility.[32] Groups of European ancestry who have not experienced upward mobility, as well as Mexican Americans and Puerto Ricans, continued to score in the 80s on IQ tests. Most significantly, at various times and places, other low-IQ groups have also done poorly on the abstract portions of mental tests. Studies of immigrant groups in 1917, of white children in isolated mountain communities, of working-class children in England, and of early Chinese immigrants all show marked deficiencies on the abstract sections. Concerning the Chinese Americans, recent studies show them to be strongest on the abstract portions of the mental tests, suggesting that upward mobility helps to improve powers of abstract reasoning. Other patterns—children's IQ scores declining as they become adults and females consistently scoring higher than males—also are frequent among low-IQ groups, not just blacks. Again, these results change once the group achieves a higher socioeconomic status.

Another problem with IQ tests is that they purport to measure only some forms of intelligence—analytical, conceptual, and verbal (Table 10.1). We are only beginning to understand how and why the brain functions as it does. Until we know more, any assumption of intellectual superiority or inferiority based on IQ scores is conjectural. Moreover, the only demonstrated value IQ scores have is in predicting how well students will do in a traditional school setting. They do not predict performance in nontraditional approaches to education or in any job situation. Does a professor with a 135 IQ teach better than one with 120? Not necessarily, and that is another reason IQ scores should not be a factor in questions of social interaction.

TABLE 10.1 Black Intelligence Test of Cultural Homogeneity

The purpose of this tongue-in-cheek "test" was to demonstrate both the subcultural language or understandings of a group and the unfairness of culture-loaded IQ tests on low-income people. Many of you will probably do badly on these questions, regardless of your ability, if the questions are alien to your cultural background, and that is the point of demonstrating cultural bias in tests.

1. Alley Apple is a (a) brick, (b) piece of fruit, (c) dog, (d) horse.
2. CPT means a standard of (a) time, (b) tune, (c) tale, (d) twist.
3. Deuce-and-a-quarter is (a) money, (b) a car, (c) a house, (d) dice.
4. The eagle flies means (a) the blahs, (b) a movie, (c) payday, (d) deficit.
5. Gospel Bird is a (a) pheasant, (b) chicken, (c) goose, (d) duck.
6. "I know you, shame" means (a) You don't hear very well. (b) You are a racist. (c) You don't mean what you're saying. (d) You are guilty.
7. Main Squeeze means (a) to prepare for battle, (b) a favorite toy, (c) a best girlfriend, (d) to hold up someone.
8. Nose Opened means (a) flirting, (b) teed off, (c) deeply in love, (d) very angry.
9. Playing the dozens means (a) playing the numbers, (b) playing baseball, (c) insulting a person's parents, (d) playing with women.
10. Shucking means (a) talking, (b) thinking, (c) train of thought, (d) wasting time.
11. Stone fox means (a) bitchy, (b) pretty, (c) sly, (d) uncanny.
12. T. C. B. means (a) that's cool baby, (b) taking care of business, (c) they couldn't breathe, (d) took careful behavior.

Answers 1-a, 2-a, 3-b, 4-c, 5-b, 6-d, 7-c, 8-c, 9-c, 10-d, 11-b, 12-b.

Source: Robert L. Williams, Ph.D.

LANGUAGE AS PREJUDICE

Words are symbols connoting meanings about various phenomena in the world around us. That the very words used to describe the two races—*white* and *black*—usually convey positive and negative meanings, respectively, is unfortunate. For example, *white* often symbolizes cleanliness, purity, or heroes (clothes, armor, hats, and horses), and *black* often stands for dirt, evil, or villains. A snow-covered landscape is beautiful, but a sky laden with black smoke is not. Black clouds are seen as threatening, but white clouds are not.

The power of words is such that the pervasiveness of positive and negative meanings for these two words can easily influence minds and attitudes. Ossie Davis had such concerns in mind when he said,

> A superficial examination of Roget's *Thesaurus of the English Language* reveals the following facts: the word "whiteness" has 134 synonyms, 44 of which are favorable and pleasing to contemplate. For example: "purity," "cleanness," "immaculateness," "bright," "shiny," "ivory," "fair," "blonde," "stainless," "clean," "clear," "chaste," "unblemished," "unsullied," "innocent," "honorable," "upright," "just," "straight-forward," "genuine," "trustworthy," and only 10 synonyms of which I feel to have been negative and then only in the mildest sense, such as "gloss-over," "whitewash," "gray," "wan," "pale," "ashen," etc.
>
> The word "blackness" has 120 synonyms, 60 of which are distinctly unfavorable, and none of them even mildly positive. Among the offending 60 were such words as "blot," "blotch," "smut," "smudge," "sullied," "begrime," "soot," "becloud," "obscure," "dingy," "murky," "low-toned," "threatening," "frowning," "foreboding," "forbidding," "deadly," "unclean," "dirty," "unwashed," "foul," etc. In addition, and this is what really hurts, 20 of these words—and I exclude the villainous 60 above—are related directly to race, such as "Negro," "Negress," "nigger," "darkey," "blackamoor," etc.
>
> If you consider the fact that thinking itself is subvocal speech (in other words, one must use words in order to think at all), you will appreciate the enormous trap of racial prejudgment that works on any child who is born into the English language.[33]

When *black* has so many negative connotations—blackening the reputation, being black-hearted, blacklisting or blackballing someone, being a blackguard, using black magic, running a black market, and so on—it is easy to see how language by itself can precondition a white person's mind against black people and can lead a black person's mind into possible self-hatred.

Ebonics, sometimes called *Black English* or *African American Vernacular English,* survives as a cultural vestige of the West African origins of many black American slaves. It is not slang, as some say, but a systematic language dialect in terms of its grammar, pronunciation, and vocabulary. A center of controversy in 1996 when the Oakland, California school board officially recognized it as a language some children used while mastering standard English, Ebonics today continues in the speech patterns of low-income or rural blacks, and in rap music.[34]

SOCIAL INDICATORS OF BLACK PROGRESS

As Figure 10.2 shows, a larger percentage of blacks than the total population are young. This demographic fact suggests both a more rapid future population growth for blacks and the importance of the socioeconomic environment in

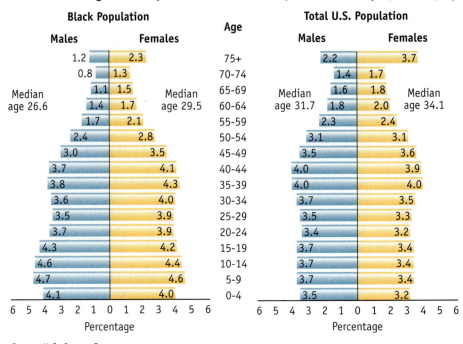

FIGURE 10.2   Age-Sex Composition of the Black Population, 2000 (in percentages)

Source: U.S. Census Bureau.

which young people grow up. The more enriched their childhood socialization, the greater their adult life opportunities. The more deprived their environment, the more limited their adult life opportunities.

Where are we today? How far has the United States gone toward true equality for blacks and whites? Sociologists use quantifiable measurements of social indicators to identify specifically a group's achievements in comparison with others', as well as its mobility within the stratification system. Three of the most common variables—education, income, and occupation—offer an objective portrait of what gains have been made and of how much the gap between the two races has narrowed.

Education

Since 1960, as a greater proportion of the population stays in school longer, the percentage gap between blacks and whites completing four years of high school or beyond has steadily lessened for both males and females. At the college level, more blacks than ever before are completing four years of college or more, but proportionately, the gap between black attainment compared to white attainment has widened a bit (Figure 10.3.) Improvement in high school completion also manifests itself in the changed dropout rates. From a dropout rate twice that of white students in 1970, the black student dropout rate fell considerably, then increased in 2005, widening the gap between black and white males (see Table 10.2). These statistics offer a hopeful sign for the next generation's socioeconomic progress but also suggest the need for further improvement.

FIGURE 10.3   Social Indicators about Black Americans (in percentages)

Age

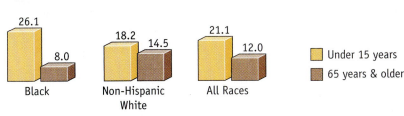

Education (of persons age 25 and over)

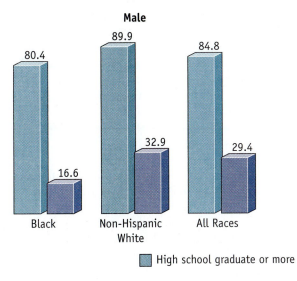

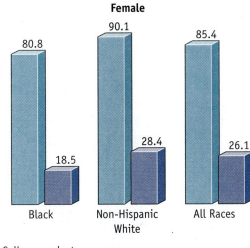

Economic Status

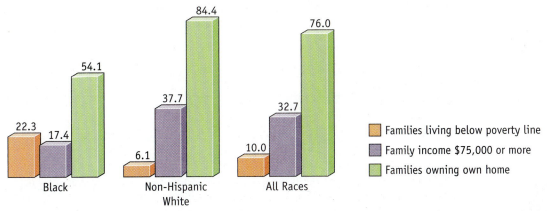

Source: U.S. Census Bureau, *The Black Population in the United States,* March 2004.

TABLE 10.2 High School Dropouts, Grades 10–12, by Race and Gender (in percentages)

	1970	1980	1990	2000	2005
Blacks	11.2	8.3	5.1	5.6	6.9
Black females	9.9	8.0	6.0	3.8	7.5
Black males	12.6	8.5	4.1	7.6	6.2
Whites	5.0	5.6	3.8	4.3	3.1
White females	5.3	4.9	3.5	4.0	3.4
White males	4.7	6.4	4.1	4.7	2.7

Source: U.S. Census Bureau.

Another barometer is comparative test scores. The College Entrance Examination Board, which administers the Scholastic Assessment Test (SAT), reports that between 1996 and 2007 the mean SAT scores of black students increased by 1 point in critical reading and by 7 points on the math section, whereas the mean scores of whites rose by 1 point in critical reading and by 13 points on the math section. A significant difference in scores thus remains: 527 to 433 in critical reading scores, 518 to 425 in writing scores, and 534 to 429 in math scores for whites and blacks, respectively.[35]

Income

Historically, black family income has always been significantly lower than white family income. Civil rights legislation and the War on Poverty began to create a slow, steady improvement until the 1980s, when economic problems and a reduction in federal support for remedial programs eroded some of the gains. As Table 10.3 indicates, the 2006 median family income was $52,423 for non-Hispanic whites and $31,868 for blacks. Put differently, the average black family earned 61 cents for every $1 the average white family earned, the slippage from 2000 partly caused by an economic downturn and lower earnings by new black immigrants. The actual income gap between the two groups has also increased.[36]

TABLE 10.3 Median Family Income, 1950–2006, Selected Years

Year	White Income	Black Income	Black Income as a Percentage of White Income	Actual Income Gap
1950	$ 3,445	$ 1,869	54.3	$ 1,576
1960	5,835	3,230	55.4	2,602
1970	10,236	6,279	61.3	3,957
1980	21,904	12,674	57.9	9,230
1990	36,915	21,423	58.0	15,492
2000	45,904	30,439	66.3	15,465
2006	52,423	31,969	60.9	20,454

Source: U.S. Census Bureau, *Income, Poverty, and Health Insurance Coverage in the United States 2006* (Washington DC: U.S. Government Printing Office, 2007), P60-233, Table 1.

An important social indicator is the poverty rate among blacks. After its significant drop from 48.1 percent in 1959 to 29.5 percent in 1970, it held fairly constant until dropping again in the prosperous 1990s. Today, about 1 in 4 blacks live in poverty compared to about 1 in 10 whites. Through good times and bad, the black poverty rate has consistently remained about three times that of the white rate.

One significant factor has been the **feminization of poverty**—the high percentage of impoverished families headed by women.[37] Many women lack education and job skills, and their earning potential is limited further by the unavailability or unaffordability of childcare centers, making families headed by women especially vulnerable to living in poverty. Among black female-headed households, 28 percent lived in poverty in 2004.[38] Approximately 51 percent of all black children under 18 lived in a female-headed household in 2003–2006, a matter of grave concern to African American leaders and government officials alike, even through it is a 5 percent drop from 1998.[39]

For black Americans, progress and regression have occurred simultaneously. A larger segment than ever before has better-paying positions and greater economic stability. At the same time, stagnation continues among a multigenerational poor underclass residing in urban ghettos and habitually unemployed or underemployed.

Yet, a sizable African American middle class has evolved. About 34 percent of U.S. black families have incomes of $50,000 or more, and most of these affluent individuals live in a suburban home.[40] At the same time, we have witnessed the collapse of inner city neighborhoods. Entry level urban manufacturing jobs are mostly gone, as are black middle-class role models in those areas. Instead, a welfare and underground economy exists, where the only successful people with money are drug pushers, pimps, and prostitutes. It is a world where the men often lack jobs and the women often lack husbands. A large proportion of the African Americans living in poverty make up this hard-core poor, trapped in a seemingly unending cycle of broken homes, joblessness, welfare, drugs, crime, and violence—a reality that culture-of-poverty advocates cite in support of their position.

Blauner's internal-colonialism theory (see Chapter 2) certainly applies to this trapped segment of the black population. The segregated black ghetto appears to be a more permanent phenomenon than those of European immigrants, with few individuals able to escape it. Until some large-scale improvement occurs—and none seems imminent—our urban ghettos will remain sinks of despair, decay, and fear.

Occupation

Because the nature of a person's work provides an important basis for societal esteem, the occupational distribution of an entire group serves as a comparative measure of its status in the larger society. Table 10.4 offers a statistical breakdown of this measure. Although African American representation in managerial, professional, technical, and white-collar occupations has grown slowly but steadily, significant differences remain.

In recent years black men have slowly increased their proportion working in management or professional position to 21 percent, but white men have also increased their percentage, which stood at 37 percent in 2004. Black men were also twice as likely as white men to work in service occupations (21 versus 10 percent).

TABLE 10.4   Occupational Distribution by Sex and Race, 16 Years and Over, 2004 (in percentages)

	Male		Female	
Classification	Black	White	Black	White
Managerial, professional	21.7	37.0	31.0	41.5
Technical, sales, administrative support	17.8	18.2	32.0	36.0
Service occupations	21.2	10.4	27.4	16.7
Precision production, crafts, repair	15.1	15.0	6.1	3.7
Operators, fabricators, laborers	23.7	18.7	3.3	1.9
Farming, fishing, forestry	0.6	0.8	0.1	0.2

Source: U.S. Census Bureau, "The Black Population in the United States: 2004," *Current Population Reports,* PPL-186, March 2004, Table 11.1.

These occupations include police, firefighters, food service workers, health aides, social welfare aides, and cleaning and building service workers. About 39 percent of blacks are physical laborers compared to about 34 percent of whites.[41]

Both black and white women were fairly evenly employed in sales and office support occupations (32 percent and 36 percent, respectively). Black women were more likely to work in service occupations (27 percent versus 17 percent); meanwhile, 42 percent of white women were employed in managerial and professional occupations compared to 31 percent of black women.[42]

Housing

To a large extent, the quality of one's housing reflects one's occupation and income. Moreover, because houses usually increase in value over the years, home ownership offers a means of increasing one's net worth. In 2006, 48 percent of all blacks were homeowners, compared to 76 percent of non-Hispanic whites, figures that have remained fairly constant in this decade.[43] However, racial discrimination continues to affect urban neighborhoods and population distribution. The 1968 Fair Housing Act made it "unlawful . . . to refuse to sell or rent . . . a dwelling to any person because of race, color, religion, or national origin," but more than three decades later, *de facto* segregation persists in U.S. metropolitan areas.

Redlining. One continuing problem is **redlining**—the refusal by some banks to make loans on property in lower income minority neighborhoods, which are indicated on city maps with red pencil lines. Such a practice accelerates the deterioration of older housing because owners have difficulty obtaining funds to improve buildings and potential buyers cannot secure mortgages. To overcome this problem, the Community Reinvestment Act (CRA) of 1977 stipulated that banks have an "affirmative obligation" to lend in lower income neighborhoods. When seriously applied, the CRA proved effective in helping turn neighborhoods around and enabling thousands of lower income people to become home owners.[44]

Redlining led banks to close branch offices in poor neighborhoods, thereby removing a crucial financial anchor from many communities. In 12 major U.S. cities analyzed in a 1995 study, three times as many banks per 100,000 residents

One false belief about African Americans is that most are poorly educated and live in or nearly in poverty. Slightly less than 1 in 4 do fall into that category, but with most of the remainder living working- or middle-class lives, the lifestyle revealed in this photo is far more typical of today's African Americans.

existed in white areas as in minority areas; but, in 1970, the areas had been fairly equal in their number of banks per 100,000 residents.[45] Moreover, banks are far more likely to reject mortgage applications for higher income blacks or Hispanics than lower income whites.[46]

Residential Segregation. Most African Americans now live outside central cities (Figure 10.4), continuing an outmigration to the suburbs that began over 30 years ago. Does this mean there is less black–white residential segregation? Analysts, using two measurement tools called a *dissimilarity index* and a *hypersegregation index,* reported that 2000 census data show that, although blacks remain the most segregated group, they are less segregated than they were in 1990. Hispanics, however, are more segregated than they were a decade ago. This pattern held true from coast to coast, in city and suburb, and in every region of the country.

Nationally, fewer than 4 in 10 non-Hispanic whites live in nearly all-white neighborhoods compared to more than half in 1990. Only in the Midwest do the majority of blacks live in nearly all-black neighborhoods. The lowest levels of black–white segregation are in the high-growth Sunbelt, which attracts both whites and minorities, thereby generating a growing share of Americans living in areas where the two races mix freely (Figure 10.5). Meanwhile, Hispanics are

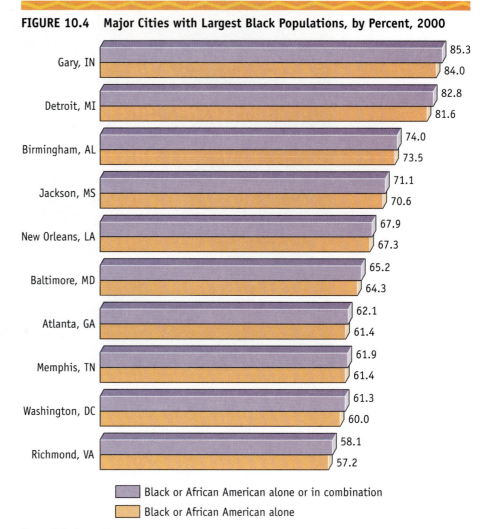

FIGURE 10.4   Major Cities with Largest Black Populations, by Percent, 2000

City	Black or African American alone or in combination	Black or African American alone
Gary, IN	85.3	84.0
Detroit, MI	82.8	81.6
Birmingham, AL	74.0	73.5
Jackson, MS	71.1	70.6
New Orleans, LA	67.9	67.3
Baltimore, MD	65.2	64.3
Atlanta, GA	62.1	61.4
Memphis, TN	61.9	61.4
Washington, DC	61.3	60.0
Richmond, VA	58.1	57.2

◼ Black or African American alone or in combination
◼ Black or African American alone

Source: U.S. Census Bureau.

increasingly living in ethnic enclaves where none existed a decade ago; Asian segregation is also increasing in numerous metropolitan areas.[47]

Racial segregation remains stubbornly rooted in the nation's older cities, where blacks and whites have always lived apart. Of the 50 metropolitan areas with the largest black populations, those with the highest levels of segregation (in descending order) are Detroit (Figure 10.6), Milwaukee, New York City, Newark, Cleveland, and Cincinnati. Such urban residential segregation limits job opportunities for youths and prevents minorities from moving closer to suburban jobs.[48] Suburbia is also becoming more integrated, although its outer rings are still mostly white. Despite the notion advanced by some that middle-class blacks are almost as segregated from whites as are poor blacks, researchers, controlling for numerous socioeconomic characteristics, found that they are not. These suburban blacks have far more white neighbors than do low-income, inner city blacks, although their white neighbors are often less affluent than they are. It

FIGURE 10.5   Percent Black or African American Alone or in Combination: 2000

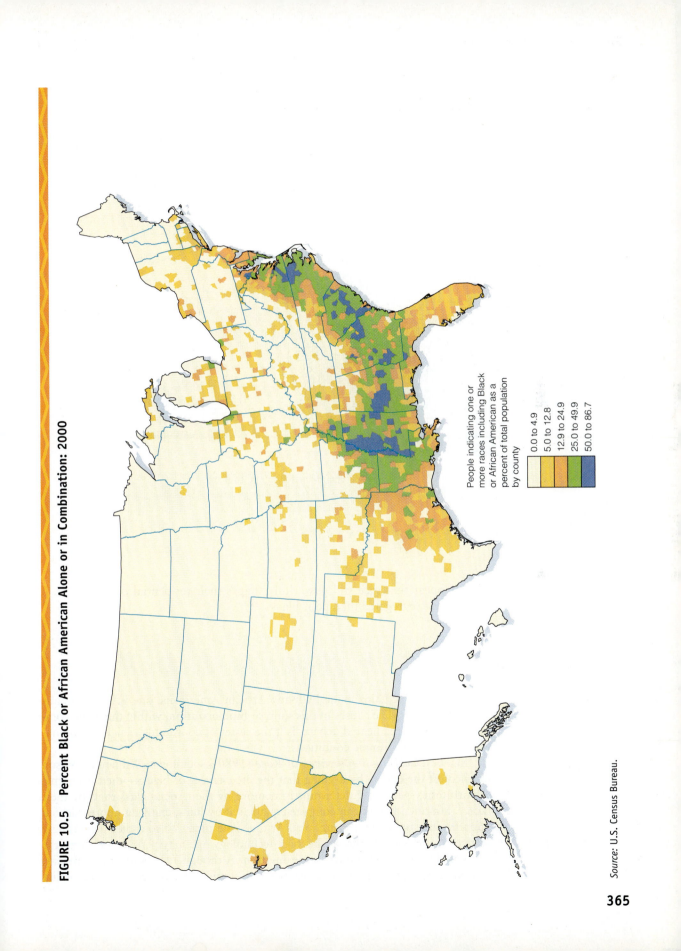

People indicating one or more races including Black or African American as a percent of total population by county

0.0 to 4.9
5.0 to 12.8
12.9 to 24.9
25.0 to 49.9
50.0 to 86.7

Source: U.S. Census Bureau.

FIGURE 10.6   Percent of Persons Who Are Black in Detroit, 2000

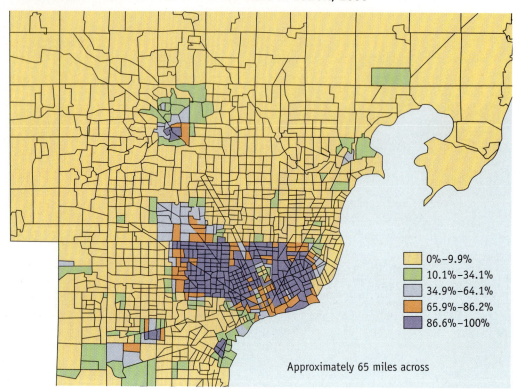

▢	0%–9.9%
▢	10.1%–34.1%
▢	34.9%–64.1%
▢	65.9%–86.2%
▢	86.6%–100%

Approximately 65 miles across

Source: U.S. Census Bureau.

would appear that race still powerfully shapes their residential options, even if they are less segregated than poor blacks.[49]

RACE OR CLASS?

Despite economic gains made by many African Americans, one in four remains mired in poverty. The causes of this split, or **bipolarization,** within the black community have stirred heated debate. Is it the result of continuing racial discrimination or of socioeconomic conditions?

In *The Declining Significance of Race* (1980), sociologist William J. Wilson touched off the debate by arguing that the life chances of blacks—their economic opportunities—are now determined far more by their social class than by their race.[50] Educated blacks can compete equally with whites, enjoying unprecedented opportunities for better-paying jobs. At the same time, Wilson said, increasingly stringent job qualifications in this high-technology age may permanently trap the black underclass in economic subordination. Although race is not insignificant, Wilson stressed that social class, not racial discrimination, denies upward mobility to the black poor. Affirmative action helps middle-class blacks, not the poor. Until we recognize the dependent nature of welfare and the need to provide skills and education to the urban poor, we cannot effectively attack the problem of inequality.

Economist Thomas Sowell echoed this view, pointing out in *Ethnic America* (1981) the parallels between blacks and other ethnic groups in social class and upward mobility as key factors in their acceptance and socioeconomic mainstreaming.[51] Similarly, Carl Gershman, a white civil rights activist and former research director of the A. Philip Randolph Institute, called the problem a class issue, suggesting that black leaders remained preoccupied with racial bias as the sole cause of ghetto poverty and ignored the reality of a bipolarization of U.S. blacks.[52]

Other black social scientists, however, disagreed with Wilson, Sowell, and Gershman. Sociologist Charles V. Willie maintained that economics is but one facet of the larger society and should therefore not be considered in isolation. White racism permeates all social institutions, controlling entry to all desirable positions in education, employment, earnings, housing, and social status. By surrendering their cultural identity, blacks may gain middle-class status, said Willie, but they become psychologically chained in a white world that permits only token entry while retaining actual power, control, and wealth.[53]

Psychologist Kenneth B. Clark called Wilson's position "wishful and premature optimism."[54] Institutionalized racism remains, said Clark, as seen in the failure of whites to resolve the problem of the urban ghettos and in the use of such racial code words as *busing, quotas, reverse discrimination, meritocracy,* and *maintaining standards,* which imply that efforts to correct racial injustice weaken the fiber of society. Three decades later, this debate continues.

One example of racism still pervading our social institutions was how the media portrayed New Orleans flood victims after Hurricane Katrina in 2007. Most of the "heart-breaker" stories were disproportionately about whites, even though most victims were blacks, but the clearest examples of bias were differing captions to photos of survivors foraging for food. One caption reads, "Two white residents wade through chest-deep water after finding bread and soda from a local grocery store." A second photo of a black reads, "A young man walks through chest deep water after looting a store."

The Black Middle Class

In a comprehensive study of the black middle class, Bart Landry tracked its three phases and its 10-fold expansion from about 3 percent of the black population in 1910. For almost 100 years after emancipation, the black middle class was mostly a mulatto elite who owned businesses in service industries (barbers, caterers, tailors), often serving a white clientele.[55] By 1960, the black middle class had grown to about 13 percent, entering the professions (accountants, doctors, lawyers, undertakers) but serving mostly a black clientele and living within the black community.[56] After the Civil Rights movement, a new black middle class emerged, employed in the predominantly white corporate world, universities, and government agencies, and with few ties to the black community. This group— with its greater economic power, suburban homes, and desire to integrate into the mainstream—prompted Wilson and others to suggest that economic, not racial, factors were now the primary constraints on African Americans.

Among those economic constraints is the reality that the average earnings of the black middle class remain lower than those of the white middle class. Also, black entrepreneurs often have limited cash resources, making their businesses riskier ventures and thus more susceptible to economic recessions and failure. Racism also remains a factor, whether in the form of a glass ceiling limiting blacks to middle-range managerial positions or in verbal epithets from strangers, harassment from police, poor restaurant service, or difficulty hailing a cab.[57]

The Black Poor

Wilson also argued that, unlike in the past, today's inner city neighborhoods face social isolation. The flight of middle- and working-class black families from inner city neighborhoods removes essential role models and undermines supportive social institutions. Furthermore, outsiders avoid these communities, which are plagued by massive unemployment, crime, and substandard schools. Consequently, area residents—women and children on welfare, school dropouts, teenage mothers, and aggressive street criminals—are cut off from mainstream society.[58] Gary Orfield effectively noted the magnitude of this isolation:

> To a considerable extent the residents of city ghettos are now living in separate and deteriorating societies, with separate economies, diverging family structures and basic institutions, and even growing linguistic separation within the core ghettos.[59]

Current social indicators about this segment of the black population do not provide any cause for optimism that significant improvement will occur in the near future. Unless some bold, innovative action addresses the multiple problems of limited education and job skills, high unemployment, and single-parent, welfare-dependent families, the situation shows every sign of perpetuating the black underclass.

The Racial Divide

Although African Americans have made significant gains since the 1960s, few sociologists would argue that racism is a thing of the past. Wilson said racism had become less prevalent, but he acknowledged that it still existed. Conservative Dinesh D'Souza, however, in *The End of Racism* (1996) held that racism originated and continues as a "rational discrimination" that is now limited to the inner cities, where the "streets are irrigated with alcohol, urine and blood."[60] Asserting that repeal of the Civil Rights Act of 1964 and of affirmative action would somehow end racism, he endorsed the need for "color blindedness" in attitudes and laws while at the same time proposing separatist solutions. (Blacks should get together and "reform their community.")

In stark contrast, Stephen Steinberg's 1996 book, *Turning Back,* attacked the so-called arrival of a color-blind society as a "spurious justification for maintaining the racial status quo."[61] His contention—in essence, the liberal position—is that programs such as affirmative action are necessary to "confront the legacy of slavery and resume the unfinished racial agenda," since part of that legacy is the continued existence of racist institutions and practices. Jill Quadagno noted that racism was a major factor both in developing policies to help those in need and in undermining the war on poverty.[62]

As these arguments rage along ideological lines among intellectuals, minority leaders, and politicians, the general public seems divided more along racial lines. Many whites believe either that a level playing field now exists—thanks to changed attitudes, majority-group enlightenment, and antidiscrimination laws—or that an uneven playing field tilted in favor of minorities exists. Many African Americans believe systemic racism against black people permeates all social institutions and everyday life.

Starkly illustrating the vastly differing racial perceptions between whites and blacks were reactions to the 1995 jury acquittal of O. J. Simpson. Public-opinion polls indicated that 83 to 87 percent of African Americans believed justice was served, so deeply ingrained was their distrust of the entire criminal justice system. Among white Americans, however, the opposite viewpoint prevailed: From 78 to 86 percent believed justice was denied, that a murderer escaped conviction because defense attorneys played the "race card" effectively. Clearly, we have a long road yet to travel before we achieve interracial understanding and cooperation.

AFRICAN AND AFRO-CARIBBEAN IMMIGRANTS

Although many nonblacks simply use Negroid racial features as the basis of group classification, much cultural diversity exists among blacks in the United States. Generalizing about them is just as inaccurate as generalizing about whites. Regional and social-class differences create distinctions among U.S. blacks, and cultural differences make Afro-Caribbean black immigrants unlike native-born blacks (Figure 10.7). Recent black immigrants from Africa are culturally distinct not only from the two former groups but also from one another when they have different countries of origin. In addition, although many native-born U.S. blacks call themselves African Americans, a wide cultural gulf separates them from the more recent African immigrants. About one-fourth of black population growth between 1990 and 2000 resulted from immigration. Such demographic changes are complicating what it means to be African American.

Afro-Caribbean Americans

The Afro-Caribbean population grew from 925,000 in 1990 to more than 1.5 million in 2000, a 67 percent increase, making them a larger U.S. ethnic group

FIGURE 10.7   Socioeconomic Profile of Black Population by Percent, 2000

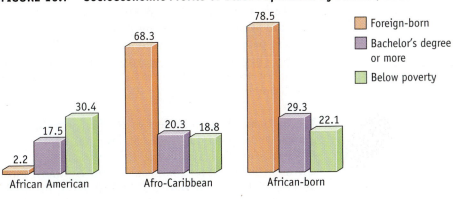

Source: U.S. Census Bureau.

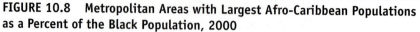

FIGURE 10.8   Metropolitan Areas with Largest Afro-Caribbean Populations as a Percent of the Black Population, 2000

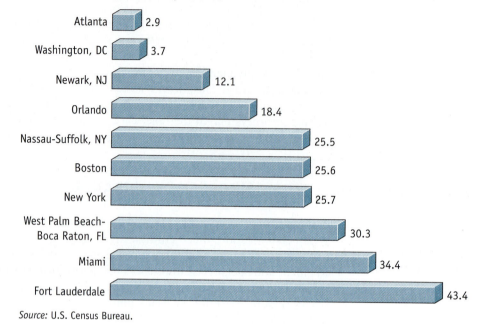

Source: U.S. Census Bureau.

than Cubans or Koreans. Primarily concentrated on the East Coast, 6 of 10 live in the New York, Miami, or Fort Lauderdale metropolitan regions. In Miami, Haitians constitute more than half of this population, while Jamaicans are the majority of this population in New York and Fort Lauderdale; both of these areas also have large Haitian populations (Figure 10.8).[63]

Residential segregation is high among Afro-Caribbean Americans in virtually all U.S. cities. Because their neighborhoods tend to overlap with African Americans, segregation from them is only moderate. However, Afro-Caribbean segregation from Africans, though still in the moderate range, is significantly higher, and their segregation from whites is the highest among all black groups.[64]

Suzanne Model and Gene Fisher found that, although fewer Afro-Caribbean men have white partners than African American men, interracial marriages are far more likely to occur among Afro-Caribbean women than African American women, particularly those who arrived as children or were born in the United States.[65] In another study, they found that, irrespective of ethnicity, blacks in England were far more likely to have a native-born white partner than were their U.S. counterparts.[66]

The Haitians. Most members of the first wave of about 4,400 Haitian immigrants, who came to the United States in the 1950s, were well-educated members of Haiti's upper class fleeing from the harsh regime of President François Duvalier. In the 1960s, almost 35,000 Haitians, mostly of the middle class, arrived in the United States. The third wave, primarily illiterate peasants and unskilled urban workers with little or no education, has been emigrating since the

Ethnicity is an everyday reality for all first-generation black Americans, who commonly take pride in their cultural roots, even as they strive to adapt to their new country. In this instance, some Haitian children wearing grass skirts and masks play drums during the Festival of Masks in Los Angeles.

mid-1970s. Since 1970, more than 464,000 Haitian immigrants entered the United States, one-fourth of them between 2001 and 2006.[67]

In the 1990s, in an action reminiscent of the Vietnamese "boat people," thousands of Haitians fled their homeland in overcrowded, flimsy boats and attempted to enter the United States. Federal policy, consistent through Republican and Democratic administrations, has been to deny refugee status to most, discourage their entry, treat them as **undocumented aliens,** and deport them. A 1992 Supreme Court ruling supported this government policy of forced repatriation, and the 1997 Nicaraguan Adjustment and Central American Relief Act failed to include Haitians among the undocumented aliens it made eligible for permanent status.

Emigration from Haiti will probably continue for a long time. In their homeland, hunger is widespread, and less than one-fourth of the population has access to clean drinking water. Rates of infant mortality, tuberculosis, and HIV are among the highest in the world. Only one-third of the land is arable, but population pressure puts 43 percent under cultivation. The struggle to eke out a living through subsistence agriculture has led to overcultivation, soil erosion, and deforestation. Haiti's forests and woodlands now only cover 1 percent of the total land area.[68]

Haiti has the highest birth rate and death rate and the highest rate of natural increase in the Western Hemisphere. With a population of 8.8 million in a land area only slightly larger than Maryland, its population density measures 824 inhabitants per square mile. Some 45 percent of all Haitians over age 15 are illiterate.[69]

Many of today's Haitian arrivals speak only Haitian Creole. French is the language of the educated elite in Haitian government, commerce, and education. Fluency in one language does not mean comprehension of the other. Nevertheless, because of the prestige attached to things French and the assumption by many U.S. residents that all Haitians speak French, Haitians often pretend to be able to speak it to enhance their status.[70]

Most Haitians are Roman Catholics, with an increasing segment attracted to evangelical Protestantism. A significant minority practice *voudou,* a religion with African roots that combines belief in the existence of a *bon Dieu,* or good God, and *lwas,* spirits who offer protection, advice, and assistance in resolving spiritual and material problems.[71]

The largest concentration of Haitians (270,000) is in South Florida. Like children of all immigrants, Haitian youth assimilate fairly easily but face a conflict as they do. Alex Stepick and his associates noted how high school students distinguish between "just come" Haitians (those whose clothing, use of Creole, and self-segregation make them visible to others and targets for derision) and "undercover" Haitians (those whose clothing, language, and interactions closely resemble native-born black Americans in their desire to "fit it"). Those with sufficient resources to live in middle-class suburbs, whether African American or ethnically mixed, encounter far less anti-Haitian prejudice and so are more likely to retain pride in their heritage and openly become Haitian Americans.[72]

In an ethnographic study conducted for the U.S. Census Bureau, Melinda Crowley found that Haitians put their trust only in family and church. Civic participation was an alien concept to her respondents, probably due to the fact that their homeland has virtually no democratic heritage. Even Haitians active in their church do not conceive of participating in a community outside of church. She also found that, on the one hand, their experiences of societal racism led Haitians to identify with African Americans, but at the same time, prejudice specifically against Haitians and some of it on the part of African Americans, impelled many to cling to a specifically Haitian identity.[73]

The Jamaicans. Jamaicans constitute the largest non-Hispanic immigrant population from the Caribbean. Of the 622,000 Jamaican Americans living in the United States in 2000, 79 percent were foreign born. Although California claimed over 18,000 Jamaican Americans by 2000, giving it by far the largest concentration west of the Appalachian Mountains, most Jamaicans settle on the East Coast in urban environments. According to the 2000 census, the leading states in Jamaican American population were New York (257,600), Florida (162,600), Connecticut (27,200), and New Jersey (26,900).[74]

Between 2000 and 2006, nearly 100,000 new Jamaican immigrants arrived, this continual large influx augmenting the Jamaicans' ethnic communities and cultural vitality. The presence of Jamaicans is perhaps most visible to other Americans through West Indian food stores and reggae music. Speech is another indicator because Jamaicans speak English but in a *patois* characterized by rapid speech patterning and a clipped accent, which sometimes causes difficulty for a first-time listener.

Jamaica itself is a pluralistic society, with three layered segments: a small white population at the top, a black segment comprising about four-fifths of the population at the bottom, and a brown population in between. Most of the immigrants who come to the United States are blacks, reflecting their homeland status as the racial group in greatest economic need. On the island, this group practices a folk culture containing numerous elements reminiscent of African societies and Caribbean slavery.[75]

Unlike the Haitians in the above-mentioned Census Bureau ethnographic study, Jamaicans come from a strongly democratic country, and so their notions of civic engagement are similar to those in the U.S. However, their sense of community in the U.S. tends to be limited to the people with whom they share a neighborhood. Many nuclear families are separated, with one partner still in Jamaica, while respondents who came to the U.S. to pursue their education commonly lived in female-headed households or with relatives whom they did not previously know very well. As a result, many recent arrivals are socially more isolated in the United States and nostalgically recall the warm families they left behind.[76]

Economic and educational opportunities are the primary motivations for immigration. Adapting quite easily to U.S. society, first-generation Jamaican Americans find their initial encounters with racism to be bitter and difficult experiences. Some become disillusioned and return home, but most remain to pursue their goals. Second-generation Jamaican Americans appear to be integrating into society as black Americans. It remains to be seen whether the present Jamaican communities will become more structured, encouraging cultural pluralism through the continued arrival of newcomers, or whether the short-term integration process will continue.[77]

African-born Americans

About 50,000 Africans arrive annually, more than in the peak years of the slave trade. In fact, since 1990 more Africans have migrated to the United States than in nearly the entire preceding two centuries.[78] Not surprisingly, the African-born population jumped 167 percent from 229,000 in 1990 to 613,000 in 2000. Unlike the Afro-Caribbean population, Africans are widely dispersed throughout the United States, with their largest numbers in Washington, DC, and New York City (see Figure 10.5). Most are from Ghana, Nigeria, and other parts of West Africa. Another large contingent hails from Ethiopia and Somalia. Because of their stronger socioeconomic status, African-born Americans tend to live in neighborhoods with higher education and income levels, as well as a greater percentage of home ownership, than African Americans and Afro-Caribbeans.[79]

A high percentage of African immigrants are well educated and possess occupational skills that enable them to achieve economic security fairly quickly. Having achieved middle-class socioeconomic status, or at worst working-class stability, these first-generation Americans usually prefer to retain their African identity rather than to blend in with the black American community. Keeping their homeland ties, they send back more than $1 billion annually to their families and friends in Africa.[80]

Cape Verdean Americans. About 400 miles off the coast of West Africa, near the equator, lie 10 islands and 5 islets known as the Cape Verde archipelago. Until 1975, these islands were a Portuguese colony. The opportune location of the Cape Verdes relative to trade winds and ocean currents made them strategically important for maritime traffic. From the early 18th to the mid-19th century, whalers from the United States often sought shelter or fresh provisions there and sometimes took on Cape Verdeans as crew members. Some remained as crew members or became harpooners, captains, and even ship owners, but most worked to pay their passage to the United States to escape the poverty and intermittent famines they faced on the islands. Once the textile mills opened in the United States in the mid-19th century, the number of Cape Verdean immigrants to New England increased from a steady trickle to hundreds, sometimes thousands, annually.

Cape Verdeans, a mixture of African and European ancestry, vary widely in their physical appearance, even within the same family. Although U.S. residents classified them as "black," they saw themselves as "Portuguese" and "white," believing that their sociocultural identity set them apart from Africans and American blacks. However, rejection by the more numerous white Portuguese in New England and simplistic racial stereotyping by other U.S. natives resulted in Cape Verdeans identifying themselves as a separate social category—as nonblack Portuguese Cape Verdeans.[81]

The pursuit of a nonblack identity, despite a physical appearance suggesting otherwise to many U.S. outsiders, encouraged continuance of such "ethnic markers" as language (Crioulo), music, and cuisine. Musical sounds come from the guitar, mandolin, and drums. Cape Verdean festivities attract friends and family who have moved away from the community clusters. Through communications and transportation technology, a strong interactional network remains. Any family crisis (childbirth, illness, death) demands social visits. Endogamy remains the norm, with marriage to a U.S. black often treated as grounds for social ostracism.[82]

Over 10,000 Cape Verdean immigrants arrived in the United States between 1997 and 2006. About 72,000 Americans claim Cape Verdean ancestry, making them the largest group of recent arrivals from sub-Saharan Africa, behind the Nigerians and Ethiopians. Massachusetts is home to over 45,000 Cape Verdean Americans, and another 16,000 live in Rhode Island. Small numbers can be found in all states except Idaho and South Dakota.[83]

Some Cape Verdeans work in the cranberry bogs of Massachusetts and Rhode Island, but most work in factory and service occupations. Many second- and third-generation Cape Verdean Americans are graduating from college and entering white-collar occupations. From their well-established communities in New England, Cape Verdean Americans are scattered throughout the United States, as well as settling in newer clusters in the Atlanta and Southern California regions.[84]

Nigerian Americans. Nigeria is Africa's most populous country and ranks ninth in the world in population, exceeding 144 million people in 2007. With 45 percent of this population under the age of 15, Nigeria's annual growth rate should continue to rise rapidly in the near future.[85]

Population pressures, economic difficulties, and political unrest are the push factors that caused immigration to the United States to increase significantly. The number of Nigerian immigrants quadrupled from about 8,800 in the 1970s to 35,400 in the 1980s. About 87,000 immigrants arrived from 1997 to 2006, making this the period of greatest Nigerian immigration.[86]

More people (165,000) claim ancestry from Nigeria than from any other African country. The primary states of residence of Nigerian Americans are Texas, California, New York, Maryland, Georgia, Illinois, and New Jersey.

About 26 percent of these immigrants enter white-collar occupations, and another 7 percent enter blue-collar and service occupations. The remainder are homemakers, children, and unemployed or retired persons.[87] Pursuing a college education to attain professional careers is the cornerstone of many Nigerian American families, while others establish small businesses as they adjust to a new life. Virtually all go through the same identity struggle as other black immigrants, caught between race and ethnicity, while maintaining relationships with family and friends in Nigeria.[88]

▲▲▲ BLACK AMERICAN ASSIMILATION

Any discussion on the subject of black American assimilation must first consider the diversity of the black population in the United States. Native-born blacks face racial issues in their social acceptance, but they grow up and live within the American culture. However, they are by no means a single entity. Socioeconomic differences affect whether they live within the mainstream or margins of society. Moreover, those raised in the Northeast are likely to differ in lifestyles and interaction patterns from those raised in the South.

Race is obviously an important factor in the U.S. experiences of Afro-Caribbeans and Africans also, but compounding theirs are the adjustment and acculturation processes all immigrants undergo. Today's first-generation black Americans thus illustrate many of the everyday ethnic realities and patterns of other immigrant groups: chain migration, residential and occupational patterning, parallel social institutions, ingroup solidarity, and endogamy.

In addition, cultural and socioeconomic differences among U.S.-born African, Afro-Caribbean, and African-born Americans result in their limited social interaction with one another. For example, African/Afro-Caribbean youths with immigrant parents place greater emphasis on family interdependence than do black youths with U.S.-born parents.[89] Because the self-selection process results in a disproportionate number of highly skilled immigrants, African-born/Afro-Caribbeans have fared better than U.S.-born African Americans.[90] This socioeconomic differential has resulted not only in significant lifestyle variations but also in some interminority tensions.[91] Recently, some black scholars complained, for instance, that increasing numbers of African-born or Afro-Caribbean immigrants are getting accepted to the nation's top colleges at the expense of U.S.-born African Americans.[92]

Yet, as Mary C. Waters details in *Black Identities: West Indian Immigrant Dreams and American Realities* (1999), ethnic heterogeneity among immigrant blacks eventually yields to racial hegemony. In what still remains a color-coded society, the dominant group views them as undifferentiated "blacks" and therefore relegates all to a separate, minority status.[93]

Black American culture remains a resilient component of U.S. society, despite the high level of cultural assimilation among most native-born blacks. Although gaps remain, secondary structural assimilation (education, income, occupation, housing) is greater than ever before, as detailed earlier. In a recent *Newsweek* poll, for example, nearly three-fourths of blacks surveyed expressed confidence that their family incomes would increase over the next 10 years, and most credited black churches and black self-help for the upturn in black conditions. Of course, not all have benefited. More black men are in prison than ever before, more young black men commit suicide, and black academic achievement still trails that of whites.[94]

Although blacks and whites interact more frequently than in the past, most of these interactions occur within secondary groups and are therefore superficial and segmented. Primary structural assimilation (friendships, primary-group memberships) remains limited, as easily witnessed on most college campuses in cafeterias or other informal settings, as well as in fraternities and sororities. We are far from an idealized racial order with black–white friendships, such as portrayed in the *Lethal Weapon* film series.[95] And as friendships are segregated, even among adolescents, it is not surprising that marital assimilation (intermarriage) remains lowest among black Americans in comparison to other racial groups.[96] My social distance findings about African Americans, discussed in Chapter 1, show both our progress and the continuing social distance between the races.

Historically, the unique experience of slavery hindered black assimilation; but, even after emancipation, the fierce refusal of many white Americans to accept black Americans as fellow citizens undermined it further. Many changes have occurred since the Civil Rights movement of the 1960s, but more are needed before skin color ceases to be a factor in social acceptance and assimilation.

SOCIOLOGICAL ANALYSIS

Blacks have been victims of slavery, restrictive laws, or racial discrimination for most of the years they have lived in the United States (see The International Scene box, below). Despite many improvements since the 1960s, problems remain. Some argue that the unique experiences of black people in the United States require separate analysis, that their situation cannot be compared to that of other ethnic groups. Others maintain that, despite certain significant dissimilarities, sufficient parallels exist to invite comparative analysis in patterns of dominant–minority relations. All three major perspectives will incorporate both views.

The Functionalist View

Inequality exists in all societies because people value certain occupational roles and social positions over others. A value consensus develops about their functional importance in meeting the needs, goals, and priorities of society. Status, esteem, and differential rewards depend on the functionalist orientation of the society and the availability of qualified personnel. As one example, slavery offered the South a practical and effective means of developing an agricultural economy based on cotton; slaves provided a cheap labor force to work long hours; and the job required only physical endurance—no unusually high level of training, skills, talent, or intelligence. The system worked, leaving slave owners free for "genteel" artistic, intellectual, and leisure pursuits while reaffirming in their minds the "inferiority" of their toiling "darkies."

This value consensus survived the social disorganization of the postbellum South. A generation later, Jim Crow laws once again formalized a system of inequality through all social institutions. A new tradition became entrenched, restricting opportunities and participation based on old values but feeding on itself for justification of the existing order. In the North, blacks filled a labor need but remained unassimilated. This lack of societal cohesion and the continued presence of blacks generated prejudice, avoidance, and reciprocal antagonism. In both the North and the South in the 20th century, these system dysfunctions—the waste of human resources and lost productivity—produced social problems of

The International Scene

The Perception of Race in Brazil

Like the United States, Brazil was colonized by Europeans (primarily the Portuguese) who subjugated the native population and imported Africans as slave laborers. In fact, Brazil today is second only to the United States in the number of its citizens of African descent outside Africa itself. Despite these similarities, race relations in Brazil have followed a very different path from that in the United States.

The United States maintains a fairly rigid biracial system, classifying people as white or nonwhite, despite its multiple-race categories in the 2000 census. This simplistic "us" and "them" categorization has long promoted racial prejudice, segregation, and hostility. Moreover, it is becoming increasingly unrealistic. The Census Bureau says there were about 2.3 million interracial married couples in 2006, up from 310,000 in 1970. According to the Population Reference Bureau, the United States is presently experiencing a boom in mixed-race babies. Biracial children now number well over 2 million, compared to a total of 460,000 reported in 1970. With such increases, how well do U.S. racial categories serve the nation's emerging multiracial society?

In Brazil, a multiracial classification system exists. In its broadest categories, the society has three population types: *pretos* (blacks), *brancos* (whites), and *pardos* (mulattos). In 2000, the racial mixture was 54 percent white, 6 percent black, 39 percent mulatto and mestizo, and 1 percent Asian or Amerindian.

Mulattos in the United States are classified with blacks, but they constitute a separate group in Brazil. Moreover, Brazilian mulattos may be further categorized into about 40 subclassifications of color variations. To identify each of these separate racial categories, Brazilians use dozens of precise terms reflecting minute distinctions in skin shading, hair, and facial features.

Since the first days of Portuguese settlement, miscegenation has been common, although usually within similar color gradients rather than between couples at opposite ends of the color line. Brazil's more fluid color continuum deters formation of a racist ideology or segregated institutions, although whites remain traditionally in a higher social class than most of the people of color.

Critical Thinking Questions: Should the United States adopt a multiracial classification system beyond just in census data? Why or why not?

---

poor education, low income, unemployment, crime and delinquency, poor housing, high disease and mortality rates, and other pathologies.

System corrections, in the form of federal judicial and legislative action, helped restore some balance to society, reorganizing social institutions and eliminating barriers to full social, political, and economic opportunities. Other dysfunctions—the Vietnam War, structural blue-collar unemployment, and sporadic economic downturns—curtailed some gains by blacks. Further adjustments are necessary to overcome the remaining problems, most especially those in the inner city.

The Conflict View

Slavery is an obvious example of past economic exploitation of blacks, but more recent practices may be less obvious. Job discrimination, labor-union discrimination—particularly in the building trades—and prejudices in educational institutions leading to low achievement and high dropout rates force many blacks into low-paying, low-status, economically vulnerable jobs. For many years, confining blacks to marginal positions preserved better-paying job opportunities for whites. Maintaining a low-cost surplus labor pool not in competition for jobs sought by whites benefited employers and the dominant society, providing domestic and sanitation workers and seasonal employees, as well as job opportunities for whites in social work, law enforcement, and welfare agencies.

Both *de jure* segregation and *de facto* segregation illustrate how successfully those with power protected their self-interests by maintaining the status quo. Control by whites of social institutions confined blacks to certain occupations and residential locations, away from participation in the political process and out of the societal mainstream. Although a black and mulatto elite did arise and some positive white actions occurred, such as President Roosevelt's 1941 executive order banning racial discrimination in defense industries, blacks mostly remained severely oppressed.

Blauner's internal-colonialism theory is appropriate here (see Chapter 2): The outside control of black segregated communities is by employers, teachers, social workers, police, and politicians who represent the establishment, making the administrative, economic, and political decisions that govern the ghetto. Unlike European groups, Blauner maintained, blacks did not gain control and ownership of their own buildings and commercial enterprises within a generation, remaining instead a subjugated and dependent colonized population.[97]

The Civil Rights movement of the 1960s, a culmination of earlier efforts and court decisions, fits the Marxist analysis of social change. Blacks developed a group cohesiveness, overcoming a false consciousness that equality was unattainable, and they formed an effective social movement. Sweeping changes through civil rights legislation, punctuated by urban violence from 1964 to 1968, brought improved life opportunities to blacks and other minorities.

The Interactionist View

Just as our attraction to strangers is based on perceived similarities, our antipathy to strangers can be based on learned prejudices. In the United States, skin color often triggers negative responses about busing, crime, housing, jobs, and poverty. Where did such attitudes originate? Earlier, we examined multigenerational stereotyping and social isolation of blacks as the legacy of racism. If beliefs about a people, culturally transmitted and reinforced by external conditions, center on their differences or alleged inferiority, then avoidance, exploitation, and subjugation can become common responses.

The opposition to integration efforts usually comes from fear of these "unlike" strangers. Although expressed reasons may include preserving neighborhoods or neighborhood schools, the real reason often is concern that blacks will "contaminate" the area or school. Beliefs that a black presence adversely affects the crime rate, school discipline, property values, and neighborhood stability often prompts whites to resist proposed integration. Similarly, unfounded beliefs that blacks are less reliable, less honest, and less intelligent than whites frequently influence hiring and acceptance decisions. The unfairness and inaccuracy of such sweeping generalizations are less significant than the fact that people act on them. Too many white people have spun a gossamer web of false reality and believe it.

Black racism works in much the same way. Black racists see all whites as the enemy and all blacks as right, and they respond with suspicion to any friendly action by whites or any white criticism of a black person. Because both sides define situations in a particular way, the interpretation they assign usually reinforces their original biases. Upward mobility—in education, occupation, and income—does much to alter people's interpretations. Eliminating residential segregation and encouraging more primary interactions will further that process.

▲▼▲ RETROSPECT

Through 200 years of slavery and 100 additional years of separate-and-unequal subjugation, blacks found society unresponsive to their needs and wants. Negatively categorized by skin color, they saw clearly that two worlds existed in this country: the white and the nonwhite. Many blacks remain trapped in poverty and isolated in urban ghettos; many who have achieved upward mobility find that they are still not accepted in white society, at least in meaningful primary relationships.

Numerous similarities exist between the black experience in the United States and the experiences of other minority peoples. Like Asians and Native Americans, blacks frequently are judged on the basis of their skin color and not their individual capabilities. They experience (as have many immigrant groups) countless instances of stereotyping, scapegoating, prejudice, discrimination, social and spatial segregation, deprivation, and violence. When they become too visible in a given area or move into economic competition with whites, the dominant group often perceives them as a threat and reacts accordingly. All this is a familiar pattern in dominant–minority relations.

More than 200 years of slavery exacted a heavy toll on U.S. blacks, and the exploitation and discrimination did not end with the abolition of slavery. As a result of generations of social conditioning, many whites preserved a master–slave mentality long after the Civil War. Two generations later, when blacks had made some progress, Jim Crow laws eliminated those gains and reestablished unequal treatment and life opportunities, thereby increasing prejudice.

A change in values and attitudes became evident with the historic Supreme Court decision of 1954 on school desegregation. Although school integration was slow, it did come about, and both blacks and whites were encouraged to seek even more changes. The resurgent Civil Rights movement peaked in the mid-1960s, with passage of a broad range of laws guaranteeing black people a more equitable life experience.

More than a half century has elapsed since the 1954 court decision, with a great many changes taking place in the land and observable improvements occurring in all aspects of life for many African Americans. Still, problems remain. A disproportionate number of nonwhite poor continue to be concentrated in the cities, frequently trapped in a cycle of perpetual poverty. *De facto* segregation remains a problem, too, with the majority of whites living in suburbs farther away from the city and the majority of blacks living in more adjacent ones.

The growing numbers of African-born and Afro-Caribbean immigrants have brought greater diversity to black America. Differing cultures and value orientations, along with a higher level of education and marketable skills among the newcomers, have created a black ethnic mosaic remindful of the white ethnic mosaic of 100 years earlier. Until assimilation reduces the social distance among U.S.-born, African-born, and Afro-Caribbean black Americans, interethnic tensions will likely continue and race-based coalitions will be less likely.

Greater interaction occurs between the two races in places of public accommodation, and this may eventually reshape white and black attitudes. That, together with improved educational opportunities, may lead to greater structural assimilation for African Americans. One element crucial to any such progress is the condition of the economy. Its ability to absorb African Americans into positions in the labor force that permit upward socioeconomic mobility will, in large measure, determine their future status in U.S. society.

KEY TERMS

Bipolarization	*De jure* segregation	Redlining
Black codes	Ebonics	Slavery reparations
Cultural drift	Feminization of poverty	Undocumented aliens
Cumulative causation	Institutionalized racism	
De facto segregation	Jim Crow laws	

DISCUSSION QUESTIONS

1. In what ways is the black experience in the United States unique?

2. What similarities exist among the experiences of blacks, Native Americans, and Asians in the United States?

3. What similarities are there between the responses of blacks and of European immigrants to prejudice and discrimination?

4. What factors have delayed African Americans in gaining economic and political power as European and Asian immigrant groups did?

5. What is the present status of African Americans in the United States, according to the leading social indicators?

6. How are the cultural orientations of African-born and Afro-Caribbean immigrants dissimilar to those of U.S.-born blacks?

7. What insights into the black experience do the three major sociological perspectives provide?

SUGGESTED READINGS

Arthur, John A. *Invisible Sojourners: African Immigrant Diaspora in the United States.* New York: Praeger, 2000.
An effective overview of the African immigrant experience, emerging ethnic consciousness, organization, and growing visibility.

Collins, Patricia Hill. *Black Feminist Thought: Knowledge, Consciousness, and the Politics of Empowerment,* 2d ed. New York: Routledge, 2000.
A classic, enlightening analysis of black feminism that provides an intellectual framework for understanding the quest for social justice.

Dent, David J. *In Search of Black America: Discovering the African American Dream*. New York: Free Press, 2001.
A rich and layered look at middle-class black Americans, showing them to be a complex group of people with a myriad of opinions, viewpoints, and beliefs.

Rogers, Reuel R. *Afro-Caribbean Immigrants and the Politics of Incorporation: Ethnicity, Exception, or Exit*. New York: Cambridge University Press, 2006.
Addresses the question of whether racism complicates or limits the political integration of racial minorities through experiences of one group in New York City.

Tatum, Beverly D. *Why Are All the Black Kids Sitting Together in the Cafeteria? And Other Conversations about Race*, 5th ed. New York: Basic Books, 2003.
A helpful book for whites and blacks in understanding racial issues and behavior, and why identity still matters to young people in a society struggling to become more color-blind.

Waters, Mary C. *Black Identities: West Indian Immigrant Dreams and American Realities*. Cambridge, MA: Harvard University Press, 2001.
Examines the wide variety of ethnicities among Afro-Caribbean immigrants and compares their experiences to Irish and Italian immigrants.

West, Cornel. *Race Matters,* rev. ed. Boston: Beacon Press, 2001.
An optimistic look at race relations that analyzes issues affecting black Americans and suggests remedies necessary to end racism.

MySocKit

Additional resources for this chapter can be found in MySocKit. If you have a subscription to MySocKit, go to www.mysockit.com to study, review, and go beyond the book to learn more about race and ethnic relations.

Hispanic Americans

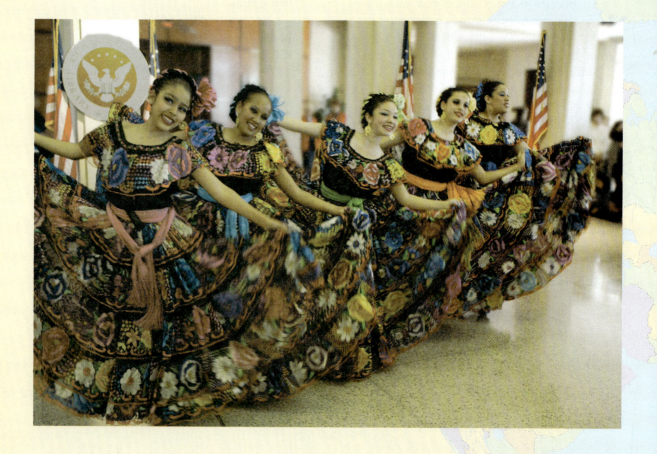

Perhaps no ethnic group attracts more public attention these days than do the Hispanic people. Their large numbers, their residential clustering, and the bilingual programs and signs associated with them make them a recognizable ethnic group. Hispanics, or Latinos, who live in poverty or are involved in gangs, drugs, or other criminal activity gain notoriety and generate negative stereotypes, but other Hispanic Americans live in the societal mainstream as working-class or middle-class citizens. Although their cultural backgrounds, social class, and length of residence in the United States differ in many ways, Hispanic Americans share a common language and heritage. Because of this commonality, outsiders often lump them all together despite their many differences.

SOCIOHISTORICAL PERSPECTIVE

Spanish influence in what is now the United States is centuries old. Long before the English settled in their colonies in the New World, Spanish explorers, missionaries and adventurers roamed through much of the Western Hemisphere, including Florida and the Southwest. In 1518, the Spanish established St. Augustine, Florida, and in the same year that the first permanent English settlement (Jamestown) was established (1609), the Spanish founded Santa Fe in what is now New Mexico. Spanish cultural influence was extensive throughout the New World in language, religion, customs, values, and town planning (e.g., locating church and institutional buildings next to a central plaza).

The nation's largest Hispanic groups—Mexicans and Puerto Ricans—became involved with the United States through two 19th-century wars 50 years apart. Through the fortunes of war, the places where they lived became part of the United States, functioning under a different set of laws of a country in which they were now a minority.

For the Mexicans, the Treaty of Guadalupe Hidalgo that ended the Mexican-American War in 1848 brought Texas, New Mexico, Arizona, and California into the United States and U.S. citizenship to about 75,000 Mexican nationals still living there one year after the treaty. Viewed as a conquered and inferior people, they soon lost title to the land where they and their ancestors had lived because they could not prove ownership in the Anglo court system. By 1892, official policy toward Mexican Americans was so biased against them that the federal government allowed anyone except them to get grazing privileges on public lands in the Southwest. Nor did the violence against them end. In fact, the interethnic violence between Anglos and Mexican Americans thereafter was so extensive that some experts believe there were more killings of Mexican Americans than lynchings of black Americans between 1850 and 1930.[1] Experienced in farming, ranching, and mining—concentrated along the fertile river valleys—the Mexican Americans proved a valuable labor pool and were incorporated within the white economy as lower-strata laborers.

Ruled by Spain for over 400 years, Puerto Ricans became U.S. nationals when the Treaty of Paris in 1898 ended the Spanish-American War and made their land U.S. territory. Until 1948, when Puerto Rico became a commonwealth with full autonomy and its people could elect their own governor, the island was a colony with appointed governors and its legislative actions subject to annulment by the U.S. Congress, which reserved the right to legislate for the island if it wished. As just one example of the island's colonial status, U.S. officials decreed that all education was to be in English. That edict remained in effect until 1991, when Puerto Ricans voted to restore Spanish as the island's official language.

Structural Conditions

The Hispanic American experience varies greatly, depending on the particular ethnic group, area of the country, and period involved (Figure 11.1). In the Southwest, agricultural needs and the presence of Mexican Americans are crucial factors in dominant–minority relations. In the East, industrial employment, urban problems, and the presence of Cubans or Puerto Ricans provide the focal points of attitudes and actions.

In the past, low-skilled immigrant groups—including Puerto Ricans and Mexicans—typically obtained jobs such as unskilled factory work that had low status, low pay, and little mobility but at least provided sufficient income to achieve some degree of economic security. Unlike past groups from less industrialized nations, however, today's Hispanic immigrants enter a postindustrial society where fewer unskilled factory jobs are available. Instead, they find work in other physical labor fields such as agriculture, construction and home improvement (demolition, flooring, framing, masonry, painting, roofing), food service, and landscaping.

Overpopulation throughout Latin America is a significant factor in the continued migration of large numbers of Hispanics to the United States (Table 11.1). High birth rates, improved sanitation, reduction of child mortality, and negative cultural and religious attitudes toward birth control have led to population booms in countries whose resources and habitable land cannot support so many people. The total population of Latin America and the Caribbean grew from over 285 million in 1970 to over 566 million in 2006. Current projections indicate that the population will reach about 700 million by 2025.[2]

Suffering from poor living conditions, inadequate schools, limited job opportunities, and economic hardship, many Latinos seek a better life in the United States—indeed, significantly more people than legal channels can accommodate. As a result, some enter illegally along the 2,000-mile border between the United

FIGURE 11.1   Central America, Caribbean, South America

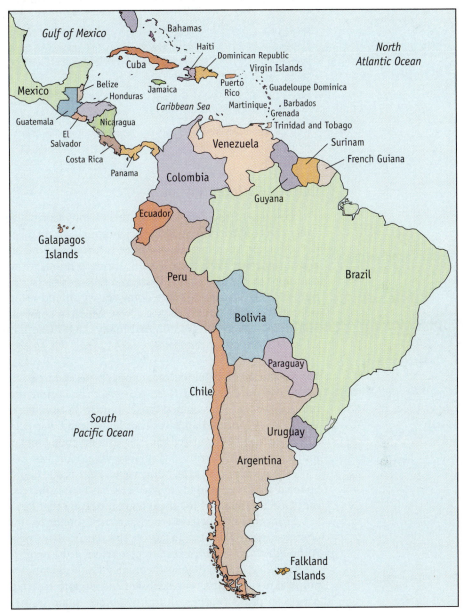

States and Mexico or into port cities by boat. Since 1990, U.S. government agents have apprehended well over 1 million **undocumented** (illegal) **aliens** annually. Most come from Mexico, with other large clusters from El Salvador, Honduras, Guatemala, and the Dominican Republic.[3] Undocumented aliens, estimated to exceed 12 million, strain local and state social services and generate dominant-group hostility, but they also make substantial economic contributions as consumers and as low-skilled workers.

TABLE 11.1   Legal Hispanic Immigration to the United States, 1961–2006

	1971–1980	1981–1990	1991–2000	2001–2006
Mexico	640,294	1,655,843	2,249,421	1,038,895
Caribbean	741,126	872,051	978,787	576,831
Central America	134,640	468,088	526,915	381,165
South America	295,741	461,847	539,656	502,247
Total	1,811,801	3,457,829	4,294,779	2,499,138

Source: U.S. Department of Homeland Security, *Yearbook of Immigration Statistics: 2006* (Washington, DC: U.S. Government Printing Office, 2007), Table 2.

Cultural Differentiation

The cultures of the peoples from the various Caribbean and Central and South American countries differ. Value orientations within a particular country also vary, depending on such factors as degree of urbanization, amount of outside contact, and social class. With these qualifications in mind, we will examine some cultural traditions that most Latinos share to a greater or lesser degree and that differ from traditional U.S. values. Before doing so, we should recognize that in areas of considerable acculturation, such as New Mexico, some of these cultural traits are muted, and Latinos have adopted many Anglo (the Latino term for mainstream white U.S.) behavior patterns.

The Cosmic Race. One cultural concept associated with Hispanics—especially Mexicans—is that of *La Raza Cosmica,* the cosmic race. The Mexican intellectual José Vasconcelos coined the term in 1925 to refer to the amalgamation of the white, black, and Indian races that he believed was occurring in Latin America.[4] In his old age, he dismissed the idea as a juvenile fantasy, but the concept evolved into a group categorization similar to what Kurt Lewin calls the recognition of an "interdependence of fate." In essence, *La Raza Cosmica* suggests that all the Spanish-speaking peoples in the Western Hemisphere share a cultural bond and that God has planned for them a great destiny that has yet to be realized.

From this mythic construct, activists sought to unify compatriots around a common political goal based on the nationalism of an imagined community. Although those cultural resources remained dormant for much of the late 20th century, *La Raza* lived on as the name of an influential newspaper and of a strong political organization representing Chicano interests. Given the growing Mexican American presence, the cultural resources found in the concept of *La Raza* may soon generate activism toward greater social and economic justice for its people.[5]

Machismo. Overstated in the Anglo stereotype, *machismo* is a basic value governing various qualities of masculinity. To Hispanic males, such attributes as inner strength in the face of adversity, personal daring, bravado, leadership, and sexual prowess are measures of one's manhood.[6] The role of the man is to be a good provider for his family, to protect its honor at all times, and to be strong, reliable, and independent. He should avoid indebtedness, accepting charity, and any kind of relationship, formal or informal, that would weaken his autonomy. The culture and family system are male dominated. The woman's role is within the family, and women are to be guarded against any onslaught on their honor. Machismo may also find expression in such forms as perceived sexual allure, fathering children, and aggressive behavior. *Marianismo* is the companion value, describing various qualities of femininity, particularly acceptance of male dominance, emphasis on family responsibilities, and the nurturing role of women.

The concept of machismo is not strictly Latin American. Such traditional sexual role orientations are common throughout most developing countries, whether African, Eastern, Middle Eastern, Western, or Pacific Island. For Latinos, machismo diminishes with increasing levels of education, assimilation, and multigenerational residence in the United States.

The result of these values can be not only a double standard of sexual morality but also a difficulty adjusting to U.S. culture, as women have more independence in the United States than in most Hispanic countries. Instead of men being the sole providers, women can also find employment, sometimes earning more money than the men of the family. The participation of Hispanic women in the labor force seems to be related to educational level. More highly educated Cuban, Central American, and South American women participate in the labor force at rates similar to those of white women in the United States, whereas Mexican and Puerto Rican women have lower rates. Overall, the participation of Hispanic women in the labor force is comparable to the national average for all women, although more are in less skilled positions.[7]

Dignidad. The cultural value of *dignidad* is the basis of social interaction; it assumes that the dignity of all humans entitles them to a measure of respect. It is primarily "a quality attributed to all, regardless of status, race, color or creed."[8] Regardless of status, each person acknowledges others' *dignidad* in a taken-for-granted reciprocal behavior pattern. Therefore, Hispanics—particularly Puerto Ricans—expect to be treated in terms of *dignidad*. Because it is an implicit measure of respect, one cannot demand it from others. Instead, one concludes that others are rude and cold if they do not acknowledge one's *dignidad*. More broadly, the concept includes a strong positive self-image.

Racial Attitudes

In most Latin American countries, skin color is less important than social class as an indicator of social status. An apparent correlation exists between darker skin color and lower social standing, but the racial line between whites and blacks that is sharply drawn in the United States is less distinct in Latin America. A great deal of color integration occurs in social interaction, intermarriage, and shared orientations to cultural values. There is also a much wider range of recognized color gradations, which helps to blunt any color prejudice. Still, in some places, such as Puerto Rico, color prejudice has increased, perhaps as a result of social and economic changes from industrialization.[9]

Color often serves as an unexpected basis of discrimination for Latinos coming to the United States. Being stereotyped, judged, and treated on the basis of one's skin color is essentially unknown to these brown-skinned peoples in their homeland, so encountering racial prejudice and discrimination is a traumatic experience for them. Before long, they realize the extent of this ugly aspect of U.S. society. Some adapt to it, others forsake it and return home, but all resent it.

Other Cultural Attributes

Hispanics generally have a more casual attitude toward time than do others in the United States, and they hold a negative attitude toward rushing, believing it robs one of dignity. Another cultural difference—one that could easily lead to misunderstanding—is their attitude about making eye contact with others. To them, not looking directly into the eyes of an authority figure such as a teacher or police officer is an act of respect, but native U.S. residents may interpret it as shyness, avoidance, or guilt. Like some Europeans, Hispanics regard physical proximity in conversation as a sign of friendliness, but Anglos are accustomed to a greater distance between conversationalists. One can envision an Anglo made uncomfortable by the seemingly unusual nearness of a Hispanic person and backing away, the latter reestablishing the physical closeness, the Anglo again backing away, and the Hispanic concluding that the Anglo is a cold or aloof individual. Each has viewed the situation from a different cultural perspective, leading to very different interpretations of the incident.[10]

Current Patterns

Hispanics are the largest ethnic group in the United States and are steadily increasing in number all the time. At 43.2 million residents in 2006 (a 93 percent increase over their 22.4 million in 1990, compared to an increase of 18 percent for the total U.S. population), they now constitute over 13 percent of the total U.S. population. As the nation's largest minority group, their proportion of the total population will increase, given their higher birth rate than other groups, a high immigration rate from Spanish-speaking countries, and a low average age of these immigrants (37 percent are under age 20).[11]

In 2000, half of all Hispanics lived in just two states: California and Texas, where they were about one-third of each state's total population (Figure 11.2). About 77 percent lived in seven states with Hispanic populations of 1 million or more (California, Texas, New York, Florida, Illinois, Arizona, and New Jersey). The Hispanic percentages of some of the nation's 10 largest cities are New York (27 percent), Los Angeles (47 percent), Chicago (26 percent), Houston (37 percent), Philadelphia (8 percent), Phoenix (34 percent), San Diego (25 percent), Dallas (36 percent), San Antonio (59 percent), and Detroit (5 percent).[12]

What do these growing numbers and extensive population clusters suggest for future dominant–minority relations? There is no simple answer because of the variance in the education, socioeconomic background, and occupational skills of the Hispanic newcomers. Despite nativist fears, however, English language mastery is a common goal of Hispanic parents for their children.[13] Concerns about ethnic tribalism or about the need to enshrine English as the "official" language of the United States seem unfounded, as we will discuss in the last chapter.

Cultural vitality, long an attribute among Mexican Americans in the Southwest, so near their homeland, will likely remain within other Latino communities, too. The dynamics of cultural pluralism are fueled by the large Hispanic presence, current migration patterns, psychological ties to the homeland, rapid transportation and communications, government policy, and societal tolerance. Acculturation and mainstreaming will no doubt occur for most Hispanics, as they have for members of other groups, but the dynamics of cultural pluralism

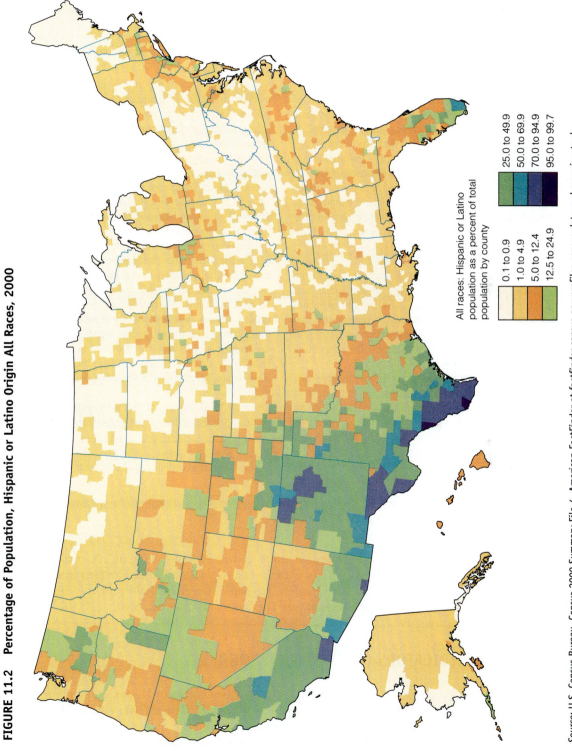

All races: Hispanic or Latino population as a percent of total population by county

0.1 to 0.9
1.0 to 4.9
5.0 to 12.4
12.5 to 24.9
25.0 to 49.9
50.0 to 69.9
70.0 to 94.9
95.0 to 99.7

Source: U.S. Census Bureau, Census 2000 Summary File 4. American FactFinder at factfinder.census.gov profiles census data and mapping tools.

The International Scene

Cultural Diffusion in Argentina

Because almost all Argentinians are descendants of relatively recent immigrants from Europe, their culture has a stronger European orientation than is found in neighboring Latin American countries. The people of Buenos Aires, the *porteños,* often call their city the Paris of South America, and with its culture and glamour, it probably earns that name. Buenos Aires is often described as Latin America's most European city. The population consists largely of the descendants of immigrants from Spain and Italy who came to Argentina in the late 19th or early 20th century. There are also significant minorities of Germans, British, Jews from central and eastern Europe, and Middle Eastern peoples, who are known collectively as *turcos.*

Since the 1930s, most immigrants to the city have come from the northern portion of Argentina, where the population is predominantly *mestizo* (mixed Indian and European). Today, the *mestizos* make up between one-fourth and one-third of the population in the metropolitan area; they tend to live in the poorest sections of the city, in the *villas miserias* and the distant suburbs. The area's black and mulatto population is of negligible size.

There are no ethnic neighborhoods, strictly speaking, but many of the smaller minorities typically settle close to one another in tightly knit communities. Villa Crespo, for example, is known as a Jewish neighborhood; the Avenida de Mayo is a center for Spaniards; and Flores is the home of many *turcos.* The assimilation of these groups has been less than complete, but the Argentinian identity has been flexible enough to allow ethnocentric mutual aid societies and

social clubs to emerge. Even the dominant Spanish language has been affected by other European cultures and has undergone changes. In the slums and waterfront districts, an Italianized dialect has emerged, and Italian cuisine is popular in the city.

Another hybrid of the Old and New Worlds is the tango, which emerged from the poor immigrant quarters of Buenos Aires toward the end of the 19th century and quickly became famous around the world as Argentina's national dance. Influenced by the Spanish tango and, possibly, by the Argentinian *milonga,* it was originally a high-spirited local dance but soon became an elegant ballroom form danced to melancholy tunes.

The combination of Old and New World cultures is also seen in the Argentinian diet. Southern European influences appear especially in the city where breakfast is often a light serving of rolls and coffee, and supper is taken, in the Spanish tradition, after nine o'clock at night. The Italian influence is seen in the popularity of pasta dishes. But the New World asserts itself in the Argentinian passion for beef, which is overwhelmingly preferred to other meats and fish. *Maté,* a native tealike beverage brewed from *yerba maté* leaves, is popular in the countryside.

Critical Thinking Question: What examples of Hispanic cultural diffusion in the United States can you name?

Source: "Argentina: The People and Cultural Life" (online) accessed at *www.britannica.com/eb/article?tocId=59303* (December 13, 2007).

suggest that the Hispanic influence will be long-lasting in U.S. society. Hispanics will not simply blend in with the rest of society. Rather, like the French who influenced the Louisiana region, Hispanic Americans will probably fundamentally affect U.S. culture itself (see The International Scene box).

SOCIAL INDICATORS OF HISPANIC PROGRESS

As Figure 11.3 shows, a much larger percentage of Hispanics than non-Hispanics are young, with proportionately more children and fewer elderly. Higher fertility, particularly among the foreign born, and the high percentage of young adult immigrants in their reproductive years create this differential. However, Hispanic groups vary in their migration and fertility patterns. For example, 20 percent of

FIGURE 11.3   Age Distribution by Sex and Hispanic Origin: 2004

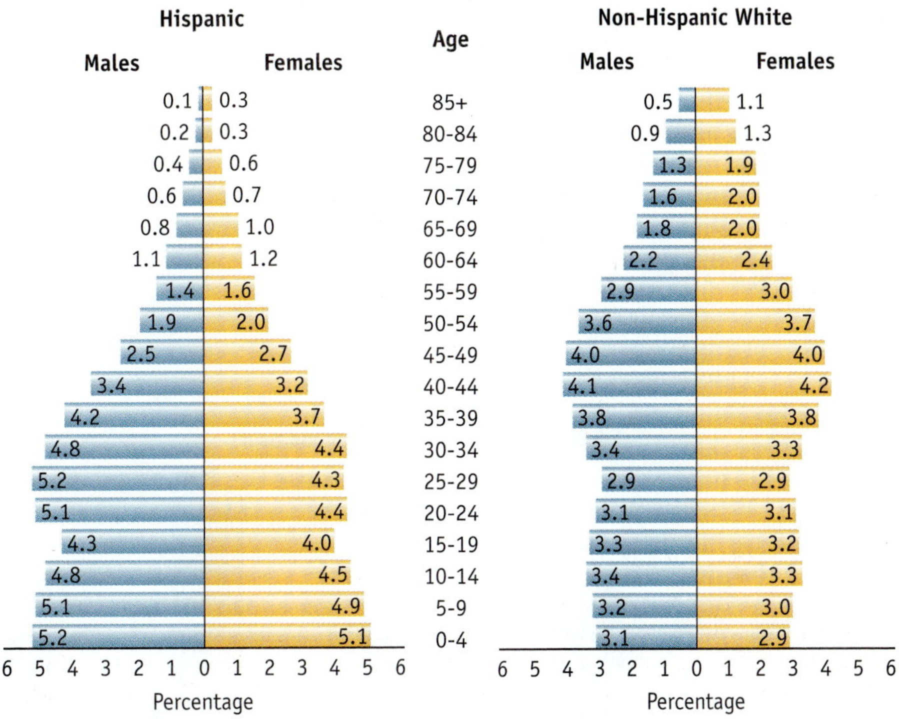

	Hispanic		Age	Non-Hispanic White		
	Males	Females		Males	Females	
	0.1	0.3	85+	0.5	1.1	
	0.2	0.3	80-84	0.9	1.3	
	0.4	0.6	75-79	1.3	1.9	
	0.6	0.7	70-74	1.6	2.0	
	0.8	1.0	65-69	1.8	2.0	
	1.1	1.2	60-64	2.2	2.4	
	1.4	1.6	55-59	2.9	3.0	
	1.9	2.0	50-54	3.6	3.7	
	2.5	2.7	45-49	4.0	4.0	
	3.4	3.2	40-44	4.1	4.2	
	4.2	3.7	35-39	3.8	3.8	
	4.8	4.4	30-34	3.4	3.3	
	5.2	4.3	25-29	2.9	2.9	
	5.1	4.4	20-24	3.1	3.1	
	4.3	4.0	15-19	3.3	3.2	
	4.8	4.5	10-14	3.4	3.3	
	5.1	4.9	5-9	3.2	3.0	
	5.2	5.1	0-4	3.1	2.9	

6 5 4 3 2 1 0 1 2 3 4 5 6   6 5 4 3 2 1 0 1 2 3 4 5 6
Percentage   Percentage

Source: U.S. Census Bureau, *Current Population Survey*, March 2004, PGP-5.

Cuban Americans are children under 15, compared to 31 percent among Mexican Americans. In contrast, children under 15 constitute 18 percent of non-Hispanic whites.[14]

Diversity among various Hispanic cultural groups also manifests itself in such social indicators as education, income, and occupation (Figure 11.4). These indicators support mixed findings on the status of Hispanic Americans and provide some cause for concern.

Education

Perhaps the most important indicator of societal mainstreaming is education, for it provides the means for greater job opportunities. Unfortunately, about 41 percent of all Latinos ages 25 or older never finished high school, compared to about 7 percent of non-Hispanic whites. The comparison for holding at least a bachelor's degree is 12 to 31 percent, respectively.[15] All Hispanic groups lag significantly behind the non-Hispanic population in producing high school graduates, with Central Americans and Mexicans having the fewest (see Figure 11.4).

Reasons cited for the education gap between Hispanics and non-Hispanics include the limited formal education of parents, less preschool experience for Hispanic children compared to whites and blacks, and cultural/linguistic differences encountered in school. Also important is the increased proportion of immigrants in the U.S. Hispanic population. Few educational differences exist

FIGURE 11.4   Social Indicators about Hispanic Subgroups in 2006 (in percentages)

Age

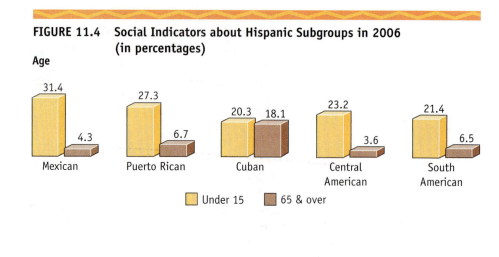

Education (of persons age 25 and over)

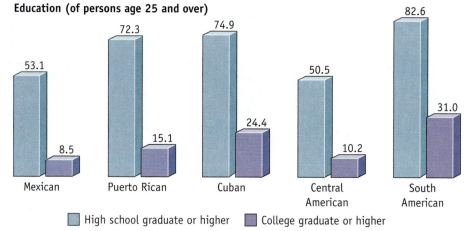

Economic Status

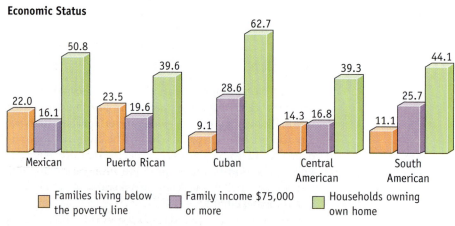

Source: U.S. Census Bureau.

between males and females. South Americans and Cuban Americans have the highest percentage of college graduates, and Mexican Americans have the lowest.

We can find two promising notes within other educational data. U.S.-born Hispanics in all ethnic groups are likelier than the foreign born to have higher percentages of high school and college graduates. About 49 percent of foreign-born Hispanic adults are high school graduates compared with 70 percent of U.S.-born Hispanic adults.[16] Further, sociologist Rubén Rumbaut—in the largest long-range survey of immigrant offspring in the nation—found that second-generation Latinos in San Diego had better grades and lower dropout rates than fellow public school students whose parents were not born in the United States.[17]

One alarming indicator is the decreasing but still high dropout rate of Hispanic high school students—in particular, Mexican and Puerto Rican teens (Table 11.2). These statistics translate into lower incomes and higher poverty rates compared to whites and blacks.

Income

The median family income for Latino families has been traditionally higher than for black families (Table 11.3). Moreover, the real income gap is growing. Despite a strong Hispanic middle class—over one in six families had incomes of $75,000 or more in 2006—one in five Hispanic families lived in poverty. Generally, Hispanics consistently have had a lower percentage of impoverished families than blacks. A higher percentage of Mexican and Puerto Rican Americans live in

TABLE 11.2   High School Dropouts by Race and Hispanic Origin, 1970, 1980, 1990, 2000, and 2005 (in percentages)

Race and Age	1970	1980	1990	2000	2005
White	10.8	11.3	10.1	9.1	7.9
16–17 years	7.3	9.2	6.4	5.8	3.3
18–21 years	14.3	14.7	13.1	12.6	10.4
22–24 years	16.3	14.0	14.0	11.7	12.8
African American	22.2	16.0	10.9	10.9	9.2
16–17 years	12.8	6.9	6.9	7.0	4.7
18–21 years	30.5	23.0	16.0	16.0	12.4
22–24 years	37.8	24.0	13.5	14.3	13.6
Hispanic	NA	29.5	26.8	23.5	18.6
16–17 years	NA	16.6	12.9	11.0	6.3
18–21 years	NA	40.3	32.9	30.0	24.5
22–24 years	NA	40.6	42.8	35.5	30.5

Note: NA = not available.

Source: U.S. Census Bureau, *Statistical Abstract of the United States 2008*, (Washington, DC: U.S. Government Printing Office, 2008), Table 265, p.172.

TABLE 11.3 Median Income of Hispanic, Black, and White Families for Selected Years, 1970–2006

	Median Family Income			Hispanic Family Income as Percentage of White Income
Year	Hispanic	Black	White	
1970	NA	$ 6,279	$10,236	NA
1980	$14,716	$12,674	$21,904	67
1990	$23,431	$21,423	$36,915	64
2000	$33,447	$30,439	$45,904	73
2006	$37,781	$31,969	$52,423	72

Note: NA = not available.

Source: U.S. Census Bureau, *Income, Poverty, and Health Insurance Coverage in the United States 2006* (Washington, DC: U.S. Government Printing Office, 2007), P60–323, Table 1.

TABLE 11.4 Persons below Poverty Level, 2006 (in percentages)

White Non-Hispanic	8.3
African American	24.9
All Hispanic	21.8
Mexican American	23.8
Puerto Rican	25.3
Cuban American	10.7
Central American	17.5
South American	12.0

Source: U.S. Census Bureau.

poverty than other Hispanic groups, whereas Cuban and South Americans are the least likely of all Hispanic subgroups to live in poverty (Table 11.4). Also, Puerto Ricans have significantly lessened their poverty numbers in recent years.

As with the education data, we must again note the impact of immigration on these income and poverty statistics. New entrants into the U.S. labor force typically earn less than those with longer residence because they often lack the education, training, experience, and seniority of other workers. Therefore, they tend to take lower-skill jobs at entry level salaries. Like past European peasant immigrants, they make economic survival their immediate goal. The United States for them is, as William Bradford described North America for the English Puritans in the early 17th century, a place "where they must learn a new language and get their livings they [know] not how."

Occupation

Occupation provides an important basis for personal esteem, and the occupational distribution of an entire ethnic group thus serves as a comparative measure of its status within the larger society. Table 11.5 addresses this aspect of Hispanic structural assimilation. As might be expected from the educational data, most Hispanic males (except Cuban and South Americans) are heavily

TABLE 11.5   Occupational Distribution, 2006

Males	Non-Hispanic	Mexican	Puerto Rican	Cuban	Central American	South American
Managerial, professional	36.6	10.5	19.8	24.9	9.9	21.8
Sales, administrative support	18.0	12.7	16.3	22.4	11.1	20.1
Service occupations	10.5	21.3	21.9	10.1	21.6	15.4
Production, transportation	16.8	22.0	22.8	20.8	20.3	20.7
Construction, extraction, maintenance	17.5	30.3	19.0	21.5	36.1	21.2
Farming, fishing, forestry	0.7	3.4	0.2	0.3	0.9	0.8
Females						
Managerial, professional	41.5	21.1	28.7	30.7	15.5	27.1
Sales, administrative support	35.5	32.7	37.2	36.3	24.3	28.2
Service occupations	17.5	30.2	27.5	23.8	42.3	31.3
Production, transportation	4.7	13.6	6.2	8.3	14.6	12.4
Construction, extraction, maintenance	0.6	1.1	0.5	0.8	2.5	1.1
Farming, fishing, forestry	0.2	1.3	–	–	0.8	–

Source: U.S. Census Bureau, "Hispanic Population in the United States: 2006," *Current Population Survey,* March 2006, Table 10.2.

underrepresented in managerial and professional occupations, and an unusually high number of Mexican and Central Americans work in unskilled blue-collar occupations. Reflecting the typical gender occupational distribution in U.S. society, Hispanic females tend to be just as likely to work in sales and administrative support positions as non-Hispanic females. Hispanic women are less likely than non-Hispanics, however, to occupy managerial and professional positions, although Cuban, Puerto Rican, and South American women are more strongly represented in these jobs than are other Hispanic women. All Hispanic women are more likely than non-Hispanics to work in service occupations as well as in unskilled blue-collar positions as operators, in transportation, and as laborers.

THE MEXICANS

Most of the 27 million Mexican Americans live in the southwestern states, accounting for more than three-fourths of all Latinos in Arizona, California, Illinois, and Texas, as well more than half of all Latinos in Colorado and New Mexico. The largest population concentrations live in Los Angeles, Chicago, Houston, San Antonio, and Phoenix.[18]

Much diversity exists within this ethnic group in degree of assimilation and socioeconomic status, ranging along a continuum from the most newly nonacculturated arrivals to the *Hispanos* of northern New Mexico and southern Colorado who trace their ancestry in that region to the days of the Spanish conquest of what is now the southwestern United States.

Throughout New Mexico—which, unlike Texas and California, has not had constant contact with Mexico through border crossings—the employment pattern is bright. In fact, Hispanic Americans there are heavily represented in civil service occupations at the local, state, and federal levels. Like many recent non-Western immigrants, they retain a cultural heritage that includes their diet, child-rearing philosophy, emphasis on the family, and extended family contacts, but they hold economically secure occupational positions.

Second-generation Mexican Americans living in large cities typically display greater structural assimilation as evidenced by separate residences for nuclear families, English-language competence, fewer children, and comparable family values, jobs, and income in border towns or agricultural regions.[19] However, most present-day Mexican Americans, whether they live in an urban setting or a rural area, lag far behind the rest of the U.S. population on every measure of socioeconomic well-being: education, income, and employment status.

Recruiting Mexicans

In the second half of the 19th century, Mexicans from south of the border helped fill U.S. labor needs for the construction of railroad lines and the expansion of cotton, fruit, and vegetable farms. Thereafter, the Chinese Exclusion Act of 1882 curtailed one source of laborers, and later the Immigration Acts of 1921 and 1924 curtailed another. However, the demand for labor—especially for agricultural workers—increased, and Mexicans left their poverty-stricken country for the economic opportunities available in the United States.

Despite U.S. government restrictions on immigration, it was easy for Mexicans to cross the largely unpatrolled border and enter the United States illegally, and many did so. The ones who crossed into Texas were known as "wetbacks" because they had crossed the Rio Grande. Some Mexican aliens also entered the United States legally as contract laborers. Under the *bracero* program, Mexican aliens entered the United States on temporary visas and then returned to Mexico after the harvest. This system provided needed workers without incurring the expenses of educating their children and of extending welfare and other social services to them during the off-season. The program lasted from 1942 until 1964, when farm mechanization, labor shortages in Mexico, and the protests of native Hispanics in the United States ended it.

Expulsion

Although cheap Mexican labor was a boon to the southwestern economy, Mexicans usually found themselves unwelcome during downturns in the U.S. economy. One such time was the 1930s, when many U.S. citizens were jobless. Some Mexicans returned home voluntarily, and others did so under pressure by local residents. Hundreds of thousands who did not leave willingly were rounded up and deported from southern California, from cities throughout the Southwest, and as far north as from Chicago and Detroit:

> In Los Angeles, official trucks would grind into the barrios—the Mexican American neighborhoods—and the occupants would be herded into them. There was little or no determination of national origin. Citizenship or noncitizenship was not considered. Families were divided; the bringing of possessions was not permitted. . . .
>
> "They pushed most of my family into one van," one of the victims, Jorge Acevedo, remembers bitterly. "We drove all day. The driver wouldn't stop for bathroom nor food nor water. Everyone knew by now we had been deported. Nobody knew why, but there was a lot of hatred and anger. . . . We had always known that we were hated. Now we had proof."[20]

Once the *bracero* program (1942–1964) provided U.S. farmers with the seasonal help they needed to harvest their crops by allowing Mexicans to enter the United States on temporary visas. Today, mostly Hispanic migrant workers, both legal and illegal immigrants, fill this need, as in this cauliflower field near Santa Cruz, California.

During the recession of the mid-1950s, the U.S. Immigration and Naturalization Service launched "Operation Wetback" to find and return all undocumented Mexican aliens. Between 1954 and 1959, concentrating on California and Texas but ranging as far north and east as Spokane, Chicago, Kansas City, and St. Louis, government officials found and expelled 3.8 million Mexicans, only 63,515 of whom ever received a formal hearing. Not all were undocumented aliens. INS agents stopped and questioned many U.S. citizens if they "looked Mexican." Those unable to prove their legal status on the spot found themselves arrested and sent "home" without any further opportunity to defend themselves.[21]

Violence

One infamous incident in which prejudices against Mexicans erupted into violence was the Zoot Suit Riot of 1943. The name came from the popularity among Mexican American youths at that time of wearing long, loose-fitting jackets with wide shoulders; high-waisted, baggy trousers with tight cuffs; and flat-topped hats with broad brims. The gamblers in the original show and the film version of *Guys and Dolls* dressed in this fashion.

On June 3, 1943, two events triggered the riot. Some Mexican boys, returning from a police-sponsored club meeting, were assaulted by a group of non-Mexican hoodlums from the neighborhood in Los Angeles. That same evening, 11 sailors on leave were attacked, and 1 sailor was badly hurt. The sailors said that their assailants were Mexican youths who outnumbered them 3 to 1. When the police, responding late, found no one to arrest in the area, about 200 sailors decided to settle the matter themselves the following evening. Cruising through the Mexican section in a caravan of 20 taxicabs, they savagely beat every Mexican they found. The police did nothing to stop them, and the press gave this event and its aftermath wide publicity:

> The stage was now set for the really serious rioting of June seventh and eighth. Having featured the preliminary rioting as an offensive launched by sailors, soldiers, and marines, the press now whipped public opinion into a frenzy by dire warnings that Mexican zoot-suiters planned a mass retaliation. To ensure a riot, the precise street corners were marked at which retaliatory action was expected and the time of the anticipated action was carefully specified. In effect these stories announced a riot and invited public participation. . . .
>
> On Monday evening, June seventh, thousands of *Angelenos,* in response to twelve hours' advance notice in the press, turned out for a mass lynching. Marching through the streets of downtown Los Angeles, a mob of several thousand soldiers, sailors, and civilians proceeded to beat up every zoot-suiter they could find. Pushing its way into the important motion picture theaters, the mob ordered the management to turn on the house lights and then ranged up and down the aisles dragging Mexicans out of their seats. Street cars were halted while Mexicans, and some Filipinos and Negroes, were jerked out of their seats, pushed into the streets, and beaten with sadistic frenzy. . . .
>
> Here is one of the numerous eyewitness accounts written by Al Waxman, editor of *The Eastside Journal:*
>
>> Four boys came out of a pool hall. They were wearing the zoot-suits that have become the symbols of a fighting flag. Police ordered them into arrest cars. One refused. He asked: "Why am I being arrested?" The police officer answered with three swift blows of the night-stick across the boy's head and he went down. As he sprawled, he was kicked in the face. Police had difficulty loading his body into the vehicle because he was one-legged and wore a wooden limb. . . .
>>
>> At the next corner a Mexican mother cried out, "Don't take my boy, he did nothing. He's only fifteen years old. Don't take him." She was struck across the jaw with a night-stick and almost dropped the two-and-a-half-year-old baby that was clinging in her arms. . . .
>>
>> A Negro defense worker, wearing a defense-plant identification badge on his work clothes, was taken from a street car and one of his eyes was gouged out with a knife. Huge half-page photographs, showing Mexican boys, stripped of their clothes, cowering on the pavements, often bleeding profusely, surrounded by jeering mobs of men and women, appeared in all of the Los Angeles newspapers. . . .
>>
>> When it finally stopped, the Eagle Rock *Advertiser* mournfully editorialized: "It is too bad the servicemen were called off before they were able to complete the job. . . . Most of the citizens of the city have been delighted with what has been going on."[22]

This bloody incident, like the Know-Nothing riots, the anti-Chinese race riots, black lynchings, and many other acts of violence, was the result of increasing societal tensions and prejudices against a minority that erupted into aggression far in excess of the triggering incident. Whatever Mexicans thought about Anglo society before this wartime incident, they would long remember this race riot waged against them with official sanction from the police, the newspapers, and city hall.

Urban Life

In some places, such as Los Angeles and New Mexico, Mexican Americans often are better integrated into the mainstream of society than their compatriots elsewhere. There they have higher intermarriage rates, nuclear instead of extended family residence patterns, and less patriarchal male roles. They enter more diverse occupations, and many attain middle-class status and move from the barrio to the suburbs and outskirts of the city. Yet in East Los Angeles and in other areas of the Southwest, particularly in smaller cities and towns, Mexican Americans reside in large ethnic enclaves, virtually isolated from participation in Anglo society. Even some *Hispano* middle-class individuals whose families have lived in the United States for generations choose to live among their own people and interact mostly with them.

Many Mexican Americans live in substandard housing under crowded conditions. In the southwestern states where most Mexican Americans live, their housing is more crowded than that of nonwhites; in Texas, twice as many Mexicans as blacks live in overcrowded housing. Segregated in the less desirable sections of town, with their children attending schools that warrant the same criticisms as inner-city schools in major cities, they experience many forms of discrimination.

The large influx of Mexican Americans and their residential clustering in urban areas have resulted in a high level of increasingly segregated schools. This trend toward isolation of schoolchildren holds for most urban Hispanics but is particularly pronounced in the Southwest. For example, the percentage of white students in Los Angeles County high schools attended by Mexican American students has dropped from 45 percent to 15 percent since 1970.[23]

Stereotyping

Negative stereotypes of Mexican Americans persist in U.S. society. Such categorizations as their being lazy, unclean, treacherous, sneaky, or thieving once appeared frequently in the mass media. Currently, the two most common stereotypes that Mexican Americans have had to combat involve being undocumented aliens and belonging to youth gangs. "Looking" Mexican often raises suspicions about legal residence or makes prospective employers wary of hiring a possible undocumented alien, even if the individual is a legal U.S. resident. In the poor urban barrios of Los Angeles, San Antonio, and El Paso, youth gangs are an integral subculture within the community. The intergang fights and killings—particularly in East Los Angeles—and the associated drug scene create a lasting, negative picture of Mexican Americans in the minds of many Anglos.

Sometimes scholarly works inadvertently contribute to the stereotype. Some people used Florence Kluckhohn's study of a remote village in New Mexico as a basis for generalizing about the values of all Mexicans. As a result, such local cultural attributes as present-time orientation, preference for intangible gratification over material rewards, and emphasis on enjoyment rather than on working hard became synonymous with being Mexican.[24] Like blacks and Puerto Ricans, Mexican Americans suffer from culture-of-poverty beliefs held by the dominant society. All too often, outsiders blame their low socioeconomic standing on their supposed cultural values.

In reality, Mexican Americans have a participation rate in the labor force comparable to all other groups—white, black, Asian, or other Hispanic.[25]

Furthermore, the percentage of Mexican Americans receiving welfare assistance is only about one-sixth that of blacks and of other Hispanic groups and about one-half that of whites. Because Mexican Americans have a large proportion of immigrant workers, the usual pattern of lower wages for the foreign-born wage earners impacts significantly on the median income reported for all Mexican Americans. Studies show that, as their length of time in the United States increases, Mexican immigrants close the earnings gap with U.S.-born Mexican Americans but not with non-Hispanic whites. The gains in earnings associated with age, time in the United States, and English proficiency differ by gender, as women do not close the gap that much.[26]

Chicano Power

Until the 1960s, the term *Chicano* was a derogatory name applied in Mexico to the "lower"-class Mexican Indian people rather than to the Mexican Spanish. Then, as an outgrowth of the Civil Rights movement and in direct contradiction to the stereotype of the passive, apathetic Mexican community, the Chicano movement emerged. Seeking to instill pride in the group's *mestizo* heritage (mixed Spanish and Indian ancestry), activists adopted the term in their efforts to promote political activism and demands for economic and educational quality. Prominent leaders emerged—César Chávez and his United Farm Workers Union, Rodolfo Gonzales and his *La Raza Unida* political third-party movement, Reies Lópes Tijerina and his Alianza group seeking to recover land lost or stolen over the years, and David Sanchez and his militant Brown Berets, who modeled themselves after the Black Panthers. These leaders have left center stage now, and a new generation of Chicanos is making its presence known, such as Janet Murguía, executive director of the National Council of La Raza. Another significant entity is the Mexican-American Legal Defense and Education Fund (MALDEF). This civil rights organization effectively uses its influence in the public arena to address such issues as bilingualism, school financing, segregation, employment practices, and immigration reform.[27]

Before this national movement dawned, rapid expansion in Sunbelt cities in the 1950s and 1960s had generated problems and tensions that led to the formation of community groups opposed to urban renewal plans threatening Mexican American neighborhoods. These organized neighborhood protests were the vanguard of what became known as the Chicano movement. In San Jose, for example, activists of diverse origins and agendas united in opposition to the effects of urban development on the barrios, and this city later became a center for the Chicano movement during its time of phenomenal growth.[28]

Older organizations, such as the League of United Latin American Citizens and the American G. I. Forum, once focused on assimilation and the Anglo world, with a primary emphasis on social functions. Newer groups—such as *La Raza Unida, Movimiento Estudiantil Chicano de Aztlan*—served as synthesizers, bringing the two cultures together. The newer groups have focused on political issues, such as the farm workers' plight, while promoting a sense of peoplehood.

Turning away from the third-party politics of the past, Chicanos are integrating into the two main political parties. In states where they are heavily concentrated, Chicanos are developing a powerful political base, electing thousands of local and state Hispanic public officials, most of whom are in Texas, California, New Mexico, Arizona, and Colorado.[29]

Current Patterns

Illinois is now the third highest state of intended residence among new Mexican arrivals, after California and Texas. The 2000 census revealed that over 1.1 million Mexican Americans live in Illinois (thanks in large measure to the lure of its meatpacking industry), making it the fourth highest in Mexican American population behind California, Texas, and Arizona. More than three times as many Mexican Americans live in Illinois as in New Mexico.[30]

Mexican immigration continues into both rural and urban areas, but most immigrants are settling in urban neighborhoods, although not necessarily in inner cities. About 92 percent live in metropolitan areas, but only 44 percent reside inside principal cities.[31] Many of the central-city residents are of a low socioeconomic status and live in areas where the school dropout rate of Mexican American youths runs as high as 45 percent, with student alienation serving as a major cause.[32]

THE PUERTO RICANS

Puerto Ricans frequently refer to their island as the "true melting pot," unlike the U.S. mainland, which has only claimed to be one. Originally inhabited by the Arawak and Caribe indigenous tribes, Puerto Rico came under Spanish domination in 1493 and remained so for 400 years. When its native population was decimated, black slaves were imported. **Miscegenation** (interracial marriage) was common, resulting in a society that deemphasized race. Reflecting the high degree of color integration is such words as *moreno, mulatto, pardo,* and *trigueño,* indicating a broad range of color gradations. Today, structural assimilation in the island's multiracial society extends to housing, social institutions, government policy, and cultural identity.[33] A high degree of intermarriage often means that people classified in one racial category have close kin relationships with people in other racial categories, either by bloodline or by adoption.

As Clara Rodriguez suggests, many Latinos—including Puerto Ricans—regard their race as primarily cultural. However, because so many are influenced by the racial categorization of mainstream U.S. society, they will—when asked about their race—answer in standard U.S. terms and identify themselves as black, white, or Indian. She adds, "Still others see themselves as Latinos, Hispanics, or members of a particular national-origin group *and* as belonging to a particular race group. For example, they may identify themselves as Afro-Latinos or white Hispanics." Rodriguez emphasizes that there is no single Latino view of race; it differs within Latin American countries, social classes, and even families.[34]

Joseph Fitzpatrick identified several cultural and historical factors that led to the more tolerant racial attitudes found in Puerto Rico (and in other Latin American countries):

1. Spain has had long experience with dark-skinned people (Moors), who often married white women.
2. In the wars of Christians against Moors and Saracens, captured whites also became slaves. Laws were developed to protect certain fundamental rights of all slaves, and this tradition carried over to the Spanish colonies.
3. Upper-class men in the Spanish colonies recognized their illegitimate children by women of color, frequently freeing the babies at their baptism.

4. Through the practice of *compadrazgo,* outstanding white members of a community became the godparents of a child of color at baptism. Even in cases where the child's real father was unknown, the *padrino,* or *compadre,* was well respected and became a significant person in the child's life.

5. A shared sense of community, by rich and poor, white and nonwhite, gave all a sense of place that was expressed in gatherings for fiestas, religious processions, and public events.[35]

Early Relations

The annexation of Puerto Rico by the United States in 1898 (after the Spanish-American War) was followed by an attempt at forced Americanization. U.S. authorities discouraged anything associated with the Spanish tradition and imposed the use of the English language. Presidents appointed governors, usually from the mainland, to rule the territory. The inhabitants received U.S. citizenship in 1917, but otherwise, the island remained a virtually ignored, undeveloped, poverty-stricken land. Citizenship brought open migration because it eliminated the need for passports, visas, and quotas, but it did not give the people the right to vote for president or to have a voting representative in Congress. By 1930, approximately 53,000 Puerto Ricans were living on the mainland. During the Depression and the war years, migration effectively stopped, but this period was followed by the mass migration of the post–World War II era.

In the 1940s, several improvements occurred. The *Partido Popular Democratico* emerged as a powerful force on the island. Puerto Rico became a commonwealth, with the people writing their own constitution and electing their own representatives. In addition, the island gained complete freedom in its internal affairs, including the right to maintain its Spanish heritage and abolition of all requirements to use English. Another party, the *Partido Nuevo Progresista,* favors statehood and enjoys substantial public support. Yet in the third voter referendum in Puerto Rico in 1998, only 46 percent voted for statehood, while 53 percent rejected any of the options presented.

To help the island develop economically, the U.S. government launched Operation Bootstrap in 1945. U.S. industries received substantial tax advantages if they made capital investments in Puerto Rico. The tax breaks and abundant supply of low-cost labor encouraged businesses to build 300 new factories by 1953 (increasing to 660 by 1960), creating over 48,000 new jobs. As a result, Puerto Rico became the most advanced industrialized land, with the highest per capita income, in the Caribbean and in most of Central and South America.

By the 1980s, however, expiring tax exemptions prompted numerous industries to leave the island in search of cheaper labor and tax exemptions elsewhere, thereby reducing available job opportunities. Puerto Rico's unemployment rate has consistently been about twice that of the mainland, rising and falling in response to mainland economic conditions. The island's unemployment rate, which peaked at 23 percent in 1983, stood at 11.2 percent in December 2007.[36]

The Push–Pull Factors

Despite the creation of thousands of factory jobs through Operation Bootstrap, the collapse of the Puerto Rican sugar industry in the 1950s triggered the beginning of *La Migracion,* one of the most dramatic voluntary exoduses in world history. One of every six Puerto Ricans migrated to the mainland, driven by the island's stagnant agrarian economy and encouraged by inexpensive plane fares and freedom of entry as U.S. citizens. Many were rural people who settled in metropolitan urban centers, drawn by the promise of jobs. The greatest period of Puerto Rican migration was 1946–1964, when about 615,000 moved to the mainland. Only the Irish migration of the mid-19th century offers a close comparison, but that was forced in part by the Potato Famine (see The Ethnic Experience box below).

After 1964, a significant drop in Puerto Rican migration occurred, aided in part by a revived Puerto Rican sugar industry after a U.S. boycott of all Cuban trade. Other factors contributed to this drop. The pull factor lost its potency, as cities such as New York City lost hundreds of thousands of manufacturing jobs and thus its promise as a job market. An island population of less than 2.4 million at that time and a declining fertility rate made sustaining the previous high exodus rate impossible. Furthermore, the earlier exodus relieved pressure on the home job market; increases in U.S. government welfare support, combined with remittances from family members on the mainland, encouraged many to stay on the island. In the 1970s, migration dropped to 65,900, before rising dramatically to 333,000 in the 1980s, prompted in large measure by the high unemployment rates mentioned earlier.

High migration rates and birth rates resulted in a 35 percent increase in the Puerto Rican population living on the mainland—from 2.7 million in 1990 to 3.7 million today.[37] Of all the Puerto Rican people living either on the island or on the mainland, about 49 percent were living on the mainland in 2006.

Like members of most ethnic groups, some Puerto Ricans return to their homeland to visit, and others to stay. Close proximity to the island is an obvious inducement, although the reasons for moving back vary. For some, the return migration stems from retirement or the desire for the more family-oriented society without discrimination and violent crime. Researchers investigating the

The Ethnic Experience

Harassment against Early Migrants

"My husband and I bought our own house in Brooklyn after the Second World War, and a few years later we bought other property on Long Island, where we moved to raise our family. In 1956 we were employed by the U.S. Military Academy, West Point, and purchased a lovely home in a so-called exclusive area not too far away. This was a quaint neighborhood where custom-built homes ranged from $40,000 up to $100,000. Shortly after we moved in, we went down to Florida on vacation. When we came back, the house was empty. We slept on the floor and the following day our attorney by telephone searched every place high and low until he found our possessions in a warehouse in Nyack. Some of our neighbors had learned we were originally from Puerto Rico, were unhappy to have us as neighbors, and had plotted this against us. The harassment continued for a long time. They threw their garbage every night on our lawn. They even sent the police to intimidate us and even tried to buy us out. We told them they couldn't afford the luxury of buying us out. We felt we had all the rights in the world to enjoy all the privileges others had. We were honest, hard-working, respectable citizens, too. So we took legal action and demanded for damages. The judge was fair and ruled for us."

Source: Puerto Rican woman who came to the mainland in 1946 in her 20s. Taped interview from the collection of Vincent N. Parrillo.

motives for this circular migration also found that economic marginality is an important factor. That is, some migrants fail to succeed economically on the mainland and return to the island. The children of these less successful returning migrants are more likely to be impoverished than the children of migrants who remain on the mainland and the children of natives who never left the island. This outcome could also be caused by migration-related disruptions in employment.[38]

The Family

In Puerto Rico, as in all Latin American countries, an individual's identity, importance, and security depend on family membership. A deep sense of family obligation extends to dating and courtship; family approval is necessary because of the emphasis on marriage as a joining of two families, not just a commitment between two individuals. An indication of family importance is the use of both the father's and mother's surnames, but in reverse order to the U.S. practice. José Garcia Rivera, whose father's last name is Garcia and whose mother's is Rivera, should be called Mr. Garcia, not Mr. Rivera. Erroneous interpretation of these names in the United States by non-Hispanics can be a source of intercultural awkwardness for Spanish-speaking people.

One common form of Puerto Rican household is the extended family residing either in the same household or in separate households with frequent visits and strong bonds. Another is the nuclear family, increasingly common among the middle class. A third type is the female-headed household, with children of one or more men but with no permanent male in the home.[39] The last type is frequently found among welfare families and is thus the target of much criticism.

Religion

The Catholic Church traditionally played an important role with immigrant groups, assisting in succession the French, Irish, Germans, Italians, Slavs, Poles, Syrians, Lebanese, and others.[40] This pattern did not at first repeat itself with the Puerto Ricans, at least in terms of representation in the church hierarchy, church leadership in the ethnic community, and immigrant involvement in the church. In 1970, Nathan Glazer and Daniel P. Moynihan observed,

> The Puerto Ricans have not created, as others did, national parishes of their own. Thus the capacities of the Church are weak in just those areas in which the needs of the migrants are great—in creating a surrounding, supporting community to replace the extended families, broken by city life, and to supply a social setting for those who feel lost and lonely in the great city. . . .
>
> Most of the Puerto Ricans in the city are Catholic, but their participation in Catholic life is small.[41]

Several factors contributed to this departure from the usual pattern. Because the island was a colony for so long, first Spanish and then U.S. priests predominated within the church hierarchy on the island. Few Puerto Ricans became priests, and the few who did rarely came to the mainland with the immigrants. The distant and alien nature of the church in Puerto Rico caused Puerto Ricans to internalize the sense of their Catholic identity without formally attending mass and receiving the sacraments. Baptisms, weddings, and funerals all became important as social occasions, and the ceremony itself was of secondary importance. Throughout Latin America, Catholicism means personal relationships with the saints and a community manifestation of faith, not the individual actions and commitments expected in the United States. Another aspect of religious life in Puerto Rico, Brazil, and other parts of Latin America is the widespread belief in spiritualism and superstition. These practices, which undoubtedly constitute remnants of old folk rites, continue to be observed by various cults as well as by many Catholics.[42]

On the mainland, a few other factors weakened any possibility that the Puerto Ricans would develop a strong ethnic church. The movement of various white Catholic ethnics out of the cities left behind clusters of old national churches with few parishioners. Church leaders decided to use these existing churches, schools, and other buildings to accommodate the newcomers. Thus, instead of having their own churches, the Puerto Ricans had the services of one or more Spanish-speaking priests, with special masses and services performed in a basement chapel, school hall, or other area of the parish. Although this practice was cost-effective for the Catholic Church, it prevented the parish from becoming the focal point for a strong, stable community because the group could not identify with it.

As the integrated parishes became more heavily Hispanic over the years, the New York archdiocese added more Spanish-speaking priests. In time, the annual *Fiesta de San Juan* each June became a widely observed religious festival in New York City. Religious/civic organizations such as the *Centro Católico Puertorriqueño* in Jersey City and the *Caballeros de San Juan* in Chicago became effective support organizations, further uniting the Puerto Rican community.

For many people in the lowest socioeconomic class, whatever their racial or ethnic background, religion serves as an emotional escape from the harsh realities of everyday life. The **Pentecostal faith,** a form of evangelical Christianity that inspires a sense of belonging through worship participation, thus offers greater attraction for some than Catholicism. Pentecostal churches represent the largest Hispanic Protestant religious movement in Puerto Rico and the U.S. mainland, as well as throughout Latin America. In the United States, storefront churches, with small and intimate congregations of about 60 to 100, offer their largely immigrant members a sense of community they cannot find elsewhere. Second-generation participation falls off sharply, however, and it remains to be seen whether Pentecostalism among Puerto Rican Americans will be more than a first-generation phenomenon of limited duration.[43]

Church estimates reveal that about 15 percent of the Puerto Rican population on the mainland belong to Protestant denominations, including Pentecostalism, and about 71 percent are Catholics.[44] It seems unlikely, then, that religious identification will be as important factor in either assimilation or cultural pluralism as it was for earlier immigrant groups.[45]

Puerto Rican Communities

New York City contains one-fourth of all Puerto Ricans living on the mainland. They comprise a larger share of the city's Hispanic population than any other group (37 percent). They are particularly concentrated in the Bronx and Brooklyn, each of which contains more people of Puerto Rican origin than any

Hispanics fuel the growth of Pentecostalism, an energetic form of evangelical Christianity less structured than traditional Christian worship. Already changing their lives by migrating, perhaps, like these worshipers in Tucson, they also seek a worship style more intimate and participatory than ritualistic Catholic masses.

other county in the nation. Puerto Ricans live in all 50 states, with the largest concentrations (more than 250,000) living in New York, Florida, New Jersey, and Pennsylvania.[46]

For many years, the continuous **shuttle migration** prevented an organized community life from fully developing. Hometown clubs—voluntary organizations based on one's place of birth—provided a place to celebrate weddings, birthdays, first communions, and confirmations. However, because they drew members from scattered New York neighborhoods, they did not serve as community centers, nor did any other social institution. Only the annual Puerto Rican Day Parade, begun in 1958, served to galvanize group identity. By 1977, however, Clara Rodriguez discerned increased ethnic neighborhood organization:

> Note, for example, the growth of what are today Puerto Rican "cuchifrito" stands, social clubs, and after-hour clubs. These and other institutions did not exist years ago or existed in a very different form. Today they are identifying symbols of a Puerto Rican neighborhood. This same phenomenon of change is also reflected in the speech of many second generation Puerto Ricans who no longer speak continuous Spanish, but whose English is decidedly "Rican."[47]

As in most ethnic communities, many social institutions have evolved. Some are informal, like the *bodega,* or local grocery store, which serves as more than a source of Hispanic foods. It is a social gathering place where social interaction, gossip, and neighborly community create an "oasis of Latin culture." Here one can obtain advice on finding a home, getting a job, or buying a car.[48] The *bodega* thus functions as an important part of the community's infrastructure.

Other community institutions are civic and social organizations. Some, born out of the War on Poverty and dependent on federal funding, have declined, but others remain strong. Most notable is *Aspira,* founded in 1961. Through guidance, encouragement, and financial assistance, *Aspira* seeks to develop cultural pride and self-confidence in youths and to encourage them to further their education and enter the professions, technical fields, and the arts. Begun in New York City, its grassroots program achieved national fame and expanded to other cities. A more direct community action group is the New York City–based Puerto Rican Community Development Project, which attempts to promote a sense of identity among Puerto Ricans and to develop community strength. Another organization begun in New York City is the Puerto Rican Family Institute, which provides professional social services to Puerto Rican families. Parent action groups, athletic leagues, cultural organizations, and social clubs also exist, providing services and fulfilling community needs. Because of their limited political involvement, Puerto Ricans have had less electoral influence than have some other groups. Although they have been U.S. citizens since 1917, island Puerto Ricans cannot vote in federal elections.

Socioeconomic Characteristics

Along with Mexican Americans, Puerto Ricans have a higher poverty rate than other Hispanic groups. However, theirs has been steadily declining in recent years while that of the Mexicans has been steadily increasing. Helping to improve their economic standing is the increased educational attainment of Puerto Ricans. Proportionately, they have twice as many college graduates as Mexican Americans and a far greater percentage of high school graduates.

About the same percentage of Puerto Rican families live in poverty as do African American families. Even though blacks have a higher educational level (81 to 72 percent high school graduates or more; 18 to 15 percent

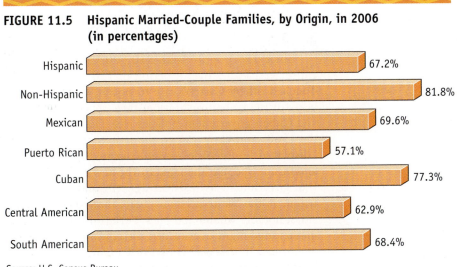

FIGURE 11.5   Hispanic Married-Couple Families, by Origin, in 2006 (in percentages)

Origin	Percentage
Hispanic	67.2%
Non-Hispanic	81.8%
Mexican	69.6%
Puerto Rican	57.1%
Cuban	77.3%
Central American	62.9%
South American	68.4%

Source: U.S. Census Bureau.

bachelor's degree or more), Puerto Ricans have a similar proportion below the poverty line.[49] One explanation for this may lie in family structure. A total of 45 percent of all African American families have a female head of household, as do 27 percent of Puerto Rican families (see Figure 11.5).[50] As discussed in Chapter 10, female-headed households are more vulnerable to living in poverty, and this is especially true for minority women who often lack sufficient education and job skills.

Although these statistics offer cause for concern, at the same time it would be a mistake to conclude that most Puerto Ricans live in poverty. In fact, many are doing quite well. In 2006, the annual income of 33 percent of Puerto Rican families (nearly two of five) exceeded $50,000, while the annual income of 17 percent (one of five families) exceeded $75,000.[51]

THE CUBANS

Although the United States granted Cuba independence after the 1898 war with Spain, it continued to exercise *de facto* control over the island. The United States pressured Cuba to relinquish the large naval base it still operates at Guantánamo Bay, and through the Platt Amendment of 1902, it reserved the right to intervene in Cuba if necessary to protect U.S. interests. The Cubans resented these infringements on their newly achieved sovereignty. Then, in the 1930s, Franklin Roosevelt's Good Neighbor Policy helped ease relations between the two countries.

Migration

Because, until 1950, the U.S. government did not differentiate Cuban immigrants from others listed as originating in the West Indies, we do not know the exact numbers of Cuban immigrants prior to that time. Almost 500,000 people came to the United States from the West Indies between 1820 and 1950, although the Cubans appear to have had little impact on the U.S. scene during that period. Still, a few legacies persisted, such as the Cuban community in northern New Jersey that dates back to 1850 and attracted many immigrants in the 1960s.

Since 1960, more than 910,000 Cubans—far more than came from the entire West Indies over a period of 130 years—have entered the United States. Touched off by Castro's rise to power, Cuban immigration surged in the first years of the Cuban revolution, then ebbed and flowed with shifts in both U.S. and Cuban government policies (see The Ethnic Experience box, page 409). In the 1960s and early 1970s, the first waves of postrevolutionary refugees were "displaced bourgeoisie"—well-educated middle- and upper-class professionals and businesspeople alienated by the new regime. Sympathetically received by the U.S. government as resisters against, and refugees from, the first communist regime in the Western Hemisphere, these Cubans concentrated in several major cities, notably Miami and New York. Initial concern in those cities that the new immigrants might overburden the educational, welfare, and social services systems quickly dissipated as the Cubans made rapid economic progress and became a part of the community.

The Ethnic Experience

Brotherhood in Talk and in Deed

"I have to tell you that the Spanish-speaking people are always talking about brotherhood and the brotherhood of the Latin American countries. They say our brother country Mexico and our brother country Venezuela, and every time they mention a Latin American country, they say the brother country. Well, in reality, it is wrong. When we needed an escape from Cuba, we only had America. America was the only country that opened the door. America is the only place where you can go for freedom and where you can live as a human being.

"I love Cuba very much but I can tell you that we never had the freedom that we have here. I can sincerely say that the opportunities in this country—America—are so great and so many, that no matter how bad they say we are as far as economics right now—they're talking about recession and everything—no matter how bad they say, it will never be as bad as it was and it is, actually, in Cuba.

"America took us in and we are grateful to America and to the Americans. And remember, when we came over, we were looking for freedom and liberty. Now we have freedom, we have liberty, and we have the chance to make money. Many Cubans are doing very well, better than me. I make enough to support my family and to live decently. I am very happy and grateful.

"Believe me, I am not only speaking for myself, but for a large group of Cubans who feel the same way I feel. We are happy here. We miss Cuba. Sometimes we get tearful when we think about the old friends and the old neighborhoods, but we are lucky. We are lucky because we still can say what we want to say, and we can move around wherever we want, and be what we want to be."

Source: Cuban refugee who came to the United States in 1960 at age 18. Taped interview from the collection of Vincent N. Parrillo.

The largest single influx of Cubans occurred in late 1980, when the Mariel boatlift brought 125,000 newcomers to the United States in just a few months. Most were urban working-class and lower-class people, but Castro also included several thousand criminals among them—which triggered an unfavorable U.S. response. By 2006, the Cuban American population exceeded 1.6 million, with about 62 percent identified as first-generation U.S. residents.[52]

Ethnic Communities

In some instances, Cubans at first found themselves treated disparagingly because non-Hispanic residents did not differentiate them from other, poorer Spanish-speaking groups such as the Puerto Ricans and Dominicans. Although the Cubans had previously looked on such other Caribbean peoples with disdain, they found that it was in their own best interests to work cooperatively with other Hispanic groups. In a pattern reminiscent of the Sephardic and Ashkenazic Jews, who first resisted and then were very helpful to the central and eastern European Jewish immigrants, the Cubans sometimes established closer relations with other Hispanic groups, particularly in New York City. These cooperative efforts helped bring greater stability and visible progress to Hispanic neighborhoods.

Cubans often settled in blighted urban areas, but their motivation, education, and entrepreneurial skills enabled them to bring color, vitality, stability, and improvement to previously declining neighborhoods. Long-time residents of areas heavily populated by Cubans often credited them with restoring or increasing the beauty and vigor of the community.

Miami offers an excellent example. Its climate and nearness to Cuba made it the ideal choice of many exiles, thereby increasing the fears of residents about so large an ethnic group being in their midst. Yet in the 1960s, the Anglos realized that the Cubans had sparked a real-estate boom, even while other major cities experienced a depressed housing market. Cuban entrepreneurs brought a new commercial vigor to the downtown area, as they created shoe, cigar, and cigarette manufacturing establishments, import houses, shopping centers, restaurants, and nightclubs. Northwest of Miami, others set up sugar plantations and mills. All this activity marked the beginning of a still-continuing boom period for Miami.[53]

In the early 1980s, however, a series of ethnic-related traumas—labor union restrictions, negative newspaper and public responses to the Marielitos, voter approval of a harsh Dade County antibilingual ordinance, and four days of anti-Cuban rioting by African Americans—prompted a Cuban reaction that quietly reshaped Miami's political, social, professional, and architectural landscape. Alejandro Portés and Alex Stepick point out that Cubans responded to discrimination by forming their own economic enclave and entering local politics. Unlike the classical assimilation model of integration and absorption within the dominant society, this movement toward economic and political empowerment enabled Cubans to assert themselves and *then* enter the societal mainstream. Significantly, studies show that Cuban entry into the labor force did *not* negatively affect the city's black population.[54]

Because two of every three Cuban Americans live in Florida, the Cuban impact on Miami, now dubbed "Little Havana," has been significant. About 52 percent of all Cuban Americans live in Miami–Dade County, where Cuban influence has transformed Miami from a resort town to a year-round commercial center with linkages throughout Latin America and has turned it into a leading bilingual cultural center. Over 57 percent of Miami–Dade County is now Hispanic, including 657,000 Cubans, 80,000 Puerto Ricans, 38,000 Mexicans, and 522,000 others from Central and South America.[55]

New Jersey has the second-largest Cuban American concentration, with 6 percent (77,000) of the U.S. total. California contains 6 percent of the Cuban American population (72,000), and New York has another 5 percent (63,000). Other Cuban Americans are scattered among the remaining states.[56]

It would be a mistake, however, to assume that there is a single Cuban American entity. The ethnocultural identity of the first generation remains embedded in Cuban culture, interested in events in Cuba, and fiercely anti-Castro. The Americanized second generation is bilingual but far less active in sociopolitical activity and more interested in the same pop culture, sports, and other matters that appeal to nonethnic young people.[57] Moreover, black Cuban Americans live between two worlds, belonging to both a successful immigrant group yet experiencing the hardships and discrimination of their race.[58]

Cultural Values

In addition to sharing a commonality of values with other Latinos, Cubans share certain subcultural values that differ from those of the dominant U.S. culture.[59] Among these are attitudes toward work, personal qualities, and the role of individuals in society.

In Miami's "Little Havana," some older Cuban American men spend the afternoon playing dominoes at a table in Maximo Gomez Park. This daily activity is an institutionalized form of ethnic solidarity and social interaction, similar to the card games once found in European clubs and coffeehouses in most U.S. cities.

Dominant-group values in the United States stress hard work as a means of achieving material well-being, whereas the Cuban orientation is that material success should be pursued for personal freedom, not physical comfort. Cubans do not consider work an end in itself, as they believe Anglos do. Instead, they think one should work to enjoy life. Intellectual pursuits are highly valued; idleness is frowned upon.

Cubans are fervent believers in generosity, in contrast to the old Anglo Puritan values of thrift and frugality. Common group traits include sharing good fortune, maintaining a warm open-house policy, and reaching out socially to others. Cubans believe that one of the worst sins is to be a *tacaño*, a cheapskate who does not readily show affection and friendship through kindnesses and hospitality.

Individualism is a value best shown through national and personal pride, which Anglos often misperceive as haughtiness. Yet Cubans believe in expressing individualism not so much through self-assertiveness as through attitudes and actions oriented toward a group, sometimes a large number of people. Hostility needs to be directed through *choteo* and *relajo*, the continuous practice of humor, jokes, and wit, and accepted by others in good part. This is because one should avoid being a *pesado*—someone unlikable, disagreeable, and without wit—which is the worst of all cultural sins. Cuban Americans thus value *personalismo* (social relations) more than their Anglo-American counterparts and so tend to spend more leisure time in social activities.

Although they remain the most metropolitan of all Hispanic American groups, Cubans today are as likely to live in such well-groomed suburbs as Coral Gables or Hialeah in Miami–Dade County, Florida—or others in California, New Jersey, or New York—as they are to live in the nearby cities. Cubans have a lower fertility rate, lower unemployment rate, higher median family income, greater education rate, and greater middle-class population composition than other Hispanic groups. As Table 11.5 on page 395 shows, 26.5 percent of males and 33.4 percent of females are in managerial or professional occupations, a significantly higher proportion than for any other Hispanic group.

CARIBBEAN, CENTRAL, AND SOUTH AMERICANS

Several push factors—overpopulation, acute shortage of farmland, economic hardship, and political turmoil—triggered a significant increase in **emigration** from several Latin American countries in recent decades. Central and South Americans now constitute 14 percent of all Hispanic Americans (Figure 11.6). After Mexico, the largest contingents come from the Dominican Republic, Cuba, Colombia, and Ecuador; they have been joined in recent years by growing numbers of refugees from El Salvador, Nicaragua, and Peru (Figure 11.7). Over 1 million Caribbean immigrants arrived in the 1990s, and another 660,000 came between 2000 and 2006. From over 430,000 Central and South American immigrants in the 1970s, their numbers leaped to about 930,000 in the 1980s and approached 1.2 million in the 1990s. An additional 997,000 arrived between 2000 and 2006.[60]

Over a half million Central Americans live in Los Angeles. Substantial numbers also reside in San Francisco; Houston; Washington, DC; New York; Chicago; New Orleans; and Miami. As the largest Central American group in the United States, Salvadorans usually constitute the majority of Central Americans in most cities, followed by Guatemalans (Table 11.6). Among Central Americans, Nicaraguans predominate in Miami, however, and Hondurans in New Orleans.

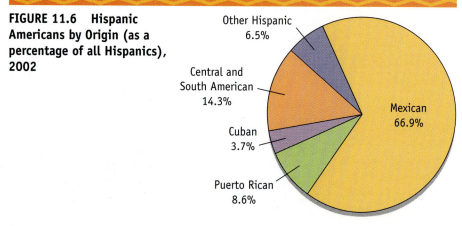

FIGURE 11.6   Hispanic Americans by Origin (as a percentage of all Hispanics), 2002

Other Hispanic 6.5%

Central and South American 14.3%

Cuban 3.7%

Puerto Rican 8.6%

Mexican 66.9%

Source: U.S. Census Bureau.

FIGURE 11.7   Leading Western Hemisphere Countries for Immigrants, 1993-2006

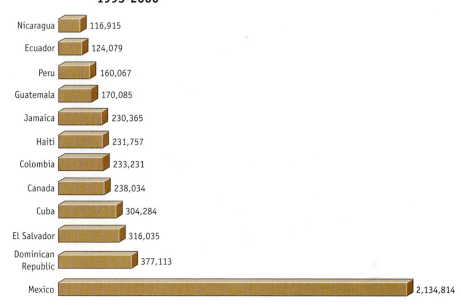

Nicaragua	116,915
Ecuador	124,079
Peru	160,067
Guatemala	170,085
Jamaica	230,365
Haiti	231,757
Colombia	233,231
Canada	238,034
Cuba	304,284
El Salvador	316,035
Dominican Republic	377,113
Mexico	2,134,814

Source: U.S. Office of Immigration Statistics.

TABLE 11.6   Number of Central and South Americans Living in the United States, 2000

Central Americans	1,686,937
Costa Ricans	68,588
Guatemalans	372,487
Hondurans	217,569
Nicaraguans	177,684
Panamanians	91,723
Salvadorans	655,165
Other Central Americans	103,721
South Americans	1,353,562
Argentineans	100,864
Bolivians	42,068
Chileans	68,849
Colombians	470,684
Ecuadorians	260,559
Paraguayans	8,769
Peruvians	233,926
Uruguayans	18,804
Venezuelans	91,507
Other South Americans	57,532

Source: U.S. Census Bureau.

A common sight in any ethnic neighborhood is stores catering to the needs of the community with familiar products and signs in the residents' native language. On East 116th Street in New York's Spanish Harlem, a Domino's national franchise outlet stands amidst the local businesses that fulfill this function.

The Dominicans

More than 903,000 Dominican immigrants have left their Caribbean homeland for the United States since 1971, in recent years averaging over 30,000 annually—which makes the Dominican Republic the second leading source of Spanish-speaking immigrants to the United States. Two of every three Dominicans live in New York State. Most live in New York City, particularly in Washington Heights in Manhattan and in the Bronx, where Dominicans are a majority in the borough. Other primary areas of residence are New Jersey, Florida, and Massachusetts.

Dominicans are more likely to live and interact within their own ethnic neighborhoods than to integrate into mixed Hispanic neighborhoods. A common pattern is to coexist alongside Puerto Ricans, each ethnic group keeping mostly to itself. As Puerto Ricans move out of ethnic neighborhoods into urban or suburban neighborhoods with a significant white or multiethnic presence, Dominicans have replaced them in the older, more segregated neighborhoods.[61]

Most Dominicans are people who have fled the poverty of their land. Because many lack specialized skills, they have a high unemployment rate and often live in poor urban neighborhoods, suffering the deprivation and family disruption so common among people with low levels of education and job skills. Racial discrimination further compounds their problems, and some find work as migrant farm laborers, away from urban troubles.

The Salvadorans

Several push factors account for the large-scale Salvadoran emigration to the United States. Agricultural modernization and expansion of property holdings by the landowning oligarchy displaced tens of thousands of rural peasants. Relocating to such urban centers as San Salvador, many of these dispossessed poor could not find work despite the growing industrialization. Conditions deteriorated when the Salvadoran government responded to protests and demonstrations with severe repression. Paramilitary death squads composed of members of the ruling elite, as well as regular security and military forces, targeted peasant leaders, union militants, and political activists. Revolutionary movements arose, and guerrilla offensives in the 1980s prompted escalating violence by the security and military forces and the death squads. Large-scale attacks against civilian populations in rural areas occurred, including massacres of entire villages believed to be sympathetic to the guerrillas.[62]

As a stream of undocumented Salvadorans fled into the United States, immigration agents sought to apprehend and return them, denying them refugee status. The Reagan-era State Department argued that, although El Salvador might be a war-torn country, none of those who left could prove that they had been specifically singled out for persecution and thus did not have the necessary "well-founded fear of persecution" to qualify for political amnesty. Out of this conflict was born the sanctuary movement in the United States: Clergy defied the government, hiding Salvadoran refugees in churches and homes. The clergy and members of their congregations provided food, shelter, and clothing and secretly helped the refugees get to safe locations. These refugees were among the 143,000 Salvadoran applicants for amnesty and permanent residence in the United States.[63]

Although the political situation improved in El Salvador in the 1990s, most Salvadorans in the United States remained, putting down roots and enjoying the support system within their evolving ethnic communities. Through chain migration, other relatives and friends join them, continuing a steady migration flow that ranks El Salvador third among Western Hemisphere countries providing immigrants to the United States in recent years. Large Salvadoran population clusters can be found in California, Texas, and the New York and Washington, DC metropolitan areas.

The Nicaraguans

Nicaraguans have entered the United States as immigrants, refugees, asylees, and undocumented aliens. A **refugee** is an alien outside the United States who is unable or unwilling to return to his or her country because of persecution or a well-founded fear of persecution. An **asylee** is identical to a refugee, except for being physically in the United States or at a port of entry when requesting refuge.

After the Sandinistas came to power in Nicaragua and the Contras undertook a guerrilla war against the new government, more than 46,000 middle-class refugees entered the United States between 1980 and 1990.[64] Simultaneously, another 79,000 Nicaraguans streamed into Texas, filing asylum applications.[65] Most of this latter group, unlike the refugees, consisted of poor, unskilled, and illiterate *campesinos* from the countryside.

Drawn by the Latin American population and the already established Nicaraguan communities in Miami and southern California, most refugees chose one of those two destinations. Miami–Dade County schools, for example, experienced almost a quadrupling of their Nicaraguan student enrollment. With no previous educational experience, most of the 13- to 15-year-olds were illiterate and had to be taught the basics of reading and arithmetic.[66] Sweetwater, a western suburb of Miami, became almost completely Nicaraguan, earning the nickname "Little Managua."

When Daniel Ortega's Sandinista regime was voted out of office in February 1990 and the Contra war fizzled out, the 11-year-long exodus of refugees subsided. Some Nicaraguans returned to their homeland, but most chose to stay in the United States.[67] All Nicaraguan refugees and asylees have since received permanent resident status. The immigrant stream in recent years is small, about 3,000 annually, but more than 230,000 now claim Nicaraguan ancestry.[68] Most live either in Florida or California. Other states with sizable population concentrations include New York, Texas, New Jersey, Maryland, and Virginia.

The Colombians

Among South American countries, Colombia supplies the most immigrants to the United States—nearly 400,000 since 1981.[69] Population pressures, the promise of better economic opportunities abroad, and chain-migration networking have increased the annual immigration totals, which are now in the tens of thousands yearly. Of the 471,000 Colombians tallied in the 2000 census, 80 percent were foreign born. Most of the remainder were children born to these first-generation Colombian Americans.

Socioeconomically, Colombians are a mixture of educated professionals and low-skilled peasants seeking a better life (see The Ethnic Experience box, page 417). Living mostly in urban neighborhoods near other Hispanics, they form their own social clubs and institutions, attempting to preserve their culture through ethnic folk-dance groups and holiday celebrations. Colombian Americans are mostly concentrated in New York, Florida, New Jersey, and California.

A minuscule percentage of Colombians are involved in the cocaine trade and in related drug-war killings. The high profile of this small number of criminals unfortunately smears the rest, just as Italian Americans have suffered from a nationality stereotype because of the Mafia. In reality, almost all Colombian Americans are decent, law-abiding people who work hard to make a life for themselves in their adopted country. Their largest residential concentrations are in South Florida, the Borough of Queens in New York City, Northern New Jersey, and the Washington, DC area.

HISPANIC AMERICAN ASSIMILATION

As with all immigrant groups, any discussion of assimilation must take into account the cultural diversity among the groups identified as "Hispanic," as well as such other variables as length of residence, place of residence, social class, family structure, and education of parents. Those differing socioeconomic characteristics among the various Latino groups, as discussed in earlier sections,

The Ethnic Experience

Cultural Traits and Adjustment

"The Colombians here are the poor people. They are the ones who had no chance for an education in Colombia. They are the ones who—because they had no education—their pay was very meager. And so over here they have a better life than they would in Colombia. So over here they really—if you can call it the American Dream—has been fulfilled in them.

"Emotionally they're very attached to their country. See, this is the thing that is very hard for people to understand. They want them to become American and to forget everything. You can't! The ties—the blood ties—are too strong! You just can't become—as I said, I cannot even become an American. I can't! Even if I wanted to. You would have to make me all over again. And I love this country and I choose to stay in this country.

"Now with these people—take some of them. They have come because of necessity—sheer necessity. We criticize them because they don't love America, but I don't think that is the fact. Also, if you notice the kind of people that come here. For instance, I had students who were the children of my father's workers on the coffee plantation. Now in my country they were tilling the soil. You know, the children of the owner go to school. The children of the worker go to till the soil. They had no chance of an education. They had huts up in the mountains where they had no running water, no electricity. Now they come here and they have all the conveniences. If they live poorly, Americans criticize them but they don't realize where they were living before. If they're not clean and spotless and they don't keep the shades the right way—but these people have been doing this for a hundred years! The people who just came in never even had a shade to talk about. They never had a venetian blind. They never even had a window to talk about! (Laughs.)

"I think we have to be careful because we often make the mistake of imposing our way to the people. Now you could say, we're not going to them, they're coming here. But if you accept them in the country, I think you also have to accept a big risk. I think the melting pot idea is not the prevalent idea. It is not a workable idea. Each one has a culture. Each people has a culture and if you want them in America, if you allow them to stay here, you have to work something by which each one is able to live. I don't mean to say that we have independent little countries, but that they are comfortable. Because you cannot remove—those are strong things that you cannot remove from a person."

Source: Colombian immigrant who came to the United States in 1952 at age 16. Taped interview from the collection of Vincent N. Parrillo.

affect integration into the societal mainstream. Because Hispanics can be of any race, we must also consider that variable in any discussion of assimilation. Consequently, Hispanic Americans can be found at all stages along the pluralism—assimilation continuum. Within the broad range of areas of assimilation, the social institutions of education and family provide valuable insights.

Education. One means of interpreting rapid assimilation to the United States is educational enrollment. Although the overwhelming majority of high school–age immigrant youths are as likely as their native-born peers to be enrolled in school, some Hispanic groups have above-average levels of school attrition. The most serious of these is among Mexican teenagers, where almost half of Mexican-born 15- to 17-year-olds are not in school. This nonenrollment pattern, though not to the same level, exists among Central American youths, especially those from El Salvador and Guatemala. However, immigrants from these countries who arrived before the start of their schooling are not more likely than native-born Americans to drop out of high school. National origin and age of entry are therefore significant variables in the effectiveness of education as an agent of assimilation.[70]

One study found that below-average rates of high school enrollment did not change with longer duration in the country for immigrants from Puerto Rico, Cuba, and the Dominican Republic. The pattern is most likely among groups concentrated in central cities and attending schools with a demoralized educational climate. In this setting, longer duration of residence in the United States may lead to greater acculturation to U.S. society but not necessarily to the middle-class ideal of high educational aspirations among these groups.

Another study gives some insight into this pattern. Ramon Grosfoguel and Chloe Ramon argue that the social position of Latino Caribbean populations in the United States today continues relationships rooted in racial hierarchies produced by centuries of European colonialism. Thus, they identify Puerto Ricans as colonial racialized subjects in the "Euro-American imaginary" and Dominicans as transformed into colonial immigrants in the New York metropolitan area. They also speak of the disassociation of pre-1980s Cuban middle-class migrants from the "Puerto Ricanization" experienced by the Dominicans. In their view, this legacy of colonialism affects the social acceptance of racially distinct Latino Americans.[71]

Family. As often stated in this book, intermarriage patterns are important indicators of assimilation. Recent studies show high rates of intermarriage with non-Hispanics among Cubans, Mexicans, Central Americans, and South Americans. A notable exception exists among Puerto Ricans and Dominicans, who have exceptionally high rates of intermarriage with each other, lower rates of intermarriage with non-Hispanics, no intergenerational increase in exogamy, and higher rates of nonmixed ancestry among the second generation.[72] Considerable intermarriage also occurs within the Hispanic population among the different national origin groups, significantly influenced—says Michael Rosenfeld—by a pan-national identity of being "Hispanic" that transcends different national origins.[73]

A related study on family and assimilation examined the relationship between acculturation and maternal teaching behaviors in Dominican and Puerto Rican mothers. One finding was that Puerto Rican mothers tended to be more acculturated than Dominican mothers. Although both groups preferred Caribbean-influenced teaching behaviors that involved giving directives, visual cues, and modeling, Puerto Rican mothers made significantly greater use of American preferences of inquiry and praise, whereas Dominican mothers employed more modeling behaviors.[74]

Language acquisition is an obvious factor in the assimilation process. As with past European immigrants, the continual influx of large numbers of new Hispanic immigrants serves to reinvigorate the use of Spanish in everyday life. Its presence has triggered English-only and Official English movements, a subject we will discuss in Chapter 15. Nevertheless, even as recently arrived adults have limited English proficiency, Hispanic children—as youngsters always do—learn the new language easily and will assimilate more readily than their parents.

Without question, cultural pluralism is an everyday reality among many Latinos and Latinas whose ethnic identity is a vibrant dynamic. A steady influx of newcomers and the presence of many first-generation Hispanic Americans mean continuance of that pattern. However, it would be a mistake either to conclude that the forces of assimilation are not at work, especially among the

Concerted voter registration campaigns have helped bolster the political power of Hispanic Americans, particularly in regions and states where they are heavily concentrated. With three Hispanics in the U.S. Senate, 26 in the House, two in the President's Cabinet, and nearly 5,000 public elected officials, Hispanics are increasingly making their presence felt.

second generation, or to ignore the assimilation of many Hispanic Americans because of their length of residence and socioeconomic status.

▲▲▲ SOCIOLOGICAL ANALYSIS

Like other immigrant groups before them, the new arrivals from Latin America are changing the face of the United States, making their distinctive contributions to the neighborhoods in which they live. But with their growing numbers, they also are encountering the hostility historically accorded to almost all newly arriving ethnic groups. Applying sociological perspectives can place their current experiences in a comparative context.

The Functionalist View

Rapid population growth has been a mixed blessing for these newcomers. They have been able to develop supportive ethnic subcommunities, providing social institutions and an interactive network that ease adjustment to a new country. Cuban settlement in deteriorated urban neighborhoods revitalized those areas and inevitably brought interethnic assistance to other Hispanic groups. Because 86 percent of all Hispanics live in nine states (California, Arizona, Colorado, New Mexico, Texas, Illinois, New York, New Jersey, and Florida), they are quickly realizing their potential political power, enabling them to improve their life situation. Concern exists that their numbers and common language may be dysfunctional, delaying assimilation and creating an "Hispanic Quebec" within the United States.

Immigrants with lower levels of educational attainment often fill the needs of industries on the periphery, such as garment factories, restaurants, and hotels, which depend on low-skilled workers, even undocumented aliens and minors. This segment of the labor market prefers to hire immigrants with less than a high school education, as discovered by Héctor Cordero-Guzmán and Ramon Grosfoguel in an ongoing study of New York City's immigrant and U.S.-born labor force. They find that immigrants with less than a high school diploma (except Dominicans, Puerto Ricans, and Russians) have higher rates of labor-force participation than U.S.-born people in the same category and that they also have slightly higher earnings. These advantages decrease with increased education, suggesting that in the less competitive, lower status jobs, Latin American immigrants have become the highest earners as they fill manual labor jobs needed by labor-intensive industries.[75]

Rapid social change is the key to functional analysis of existing problems. The influx of large numbers of immigrants in a short period and the changing occupational structure of U.S. society has prevented the social system from absorbing so many low-skilled workers right away. How can we ease Hispanic newcomers into the societal mainstream? We can either take a *laissez-faire* attitude, allowing the passage of time to produce acculturation and economic improvement, or we can seek an interventionist means of resolving the problems. Advocates of the latter approach argue that, through bilingual and other educational programs, job-training programs, and business investment incentives for more job opportunities, we can improve the system to help newcomers realize the American Dream that brought them here.

The Conflict View

Although Robert Blauner first applied the concept of internal colonialism to the black ghetto (see Chapter 2), Chicano activists found the idea appealing because it coincided with the legacy of Anglo takeover and domination of the Southwest in 1848 and continued Anglo control of the barrios in the cities of the region since that date. They readily embraced the concept of the barrio as an internal colony, dependent on Anglo investment and subservient to Anglo domination of municipal government and commerce. They criticized the concentration of the Mexican American working class in poor urban barrios and the exodus of the Anglo and Latino middle class to the suburban fringe. In these economically weakened barrios, Mexican Americans struggled against larger economic and political trends.

Analysts of internal colonialism maintain that the continued residential segregation of Hispanic Americans in ghetto areas of many U.S. cities is unlike the pattern experienced by European immigrants to the United States. In the case of Europeans, the level of segregation declined with length of residence in the United States. However, with the newer immigrants, instead of seeing a gradual acculturation or structural assimilation process, these analysts see the persistence of subordination, with Latinos confined to certain areas of rental properties controlled by absentee landlords and restricted to low-paying job opportunities, inferior schools, and many other forms of discrimination.

Economic exploitation is another dimension of conflict analysis. Mexicans, Puerto Ricans, and other Latinos work as migrant farm laborers in many places under abysmal conditions for meager pay despite repeated exposés. City sweatshops employing thousands of undocumented aliens, refugees, and low-skilled legal immigrants operate in clandestine settings, prospering from the toil of low-wage employees. The rise of an ethnic bourgeoisie—the *padrino* in urban or farm settings, the token elite among the Chicano population, or the small middle class with other Hispanic groups—only helps control the rest and does not signal an economic upgrading and assimilation of the remaining group members.

Resolving the problem of the inferior status of millions of Hispanic Americans, according to this view, will occur only through protest movements, organized resistance to exploitation, and the flexing of political muscle. New citizens need to realize more fully their commonalities, taking a lesson from the Irish and using their ballot power to create the necessary changes to benefit themselves. If they effectively wield their political clout, they will begin to overcome the power differential that exists in the social and economic spheres as well.

The Interactionist View

Anglo–Hispanic relations often are strained by inaccurate perceptions. Members of the dominant group tend to think that there is but one Spanish-speaking public, when actually a variety exists, each preferring different foods, music, and recreation and having different cultural attributes. Too many Anglos view Hispanic ethnic subcommunities, parallel social institutions, and limited command of English as detrimental to the cohesiveness of U.S. society, failing to realize that 83 percent of Hispanics are first-generation Americans repeating a resettlement pattern of earlier European immigrants. Extensive poverty among many Hispanics often invites outsiders to blame the victim or to engage in culture-of-poverty thinking. Instead of confronting the problems of poor education and lack of job skills and job opportunities, some find fault with the group itself, reacting with avoidance, indifference, or paternalistic behavior.

In our earlier discussion about eye contact, physical proximity, the notion of hurrying, and the relevance of time, we identified a few areas of potential cultural misunderstanding. Add to this Anglo impatience with language problems, African American concerns about economic competition, taxpayer resistance to welfare costs, labor union fears that wages will be undermined by cheap labor, and nativist alarm at the failure of the melting pot to "melt" the Hispanics, and you have further reasons for non-Hispanics to stereotype Latinos as an increasing social problem. Because perceptions influence interaction patterns and social policy, the potential for tensions and conflict is strong.

Witnessing extensive Spanish-language usage is no doubt the main "hot button" that triggers nativists' ire more than any other ethnic manifestation by Hispanics. Similar reactions once occurred when German and Italian newcomers concentrated in large clusters and their languages were everyday commonalities. As discussed in Chapter 2, language and culture share an interdependent relationship;

each fosters the other, with both usually ebbing through the assimilation process over the generations. In Chapter 15, we examine the issues and concerns involving language retention and English literacy.

For Hispanics, clinging to the old country's culture and ethnic identity is a matter of pride and personal commitment to a rich heritage. Some find it their only solace against discrimination, and even those who achieve economic mobility retain a strong ethnic identification. Washed afresh with new waves of Hispanic immigrants, the ethnic communities retain their vitality, prompting even successful Hispanics to hold onto their ethnic traditions. Interactionists thus point to the resilience of an ethnic self-definition, which is somewhat at odds with assimilationist views.

RETROSPECT

In many ways, recent Hispanic immigrants repeat the patterns of earlier racial and ethnic groups. Coming in large numbers from impoverished lands, many enter the lowest strata of society, cluster together in substandard housing units, and face the problems of adjustment, deprivation, frustration, and pathology (sickness and crime). Marked as strangers by their language, customs, and physical appearance, they face difficulty in gaining acceptance and achieving economic security. The Hispanic poor face the same problems and criticisms as earlier groups. They also are criticized for failing to overcome these problems immediately, even though other groups often took three generations to do so. The dominant–minority response patterns in this case are thus quite similar to those of earlier immigrant peoples.

Particularly significant for the Hispanic immigrants, in comparison to other groups, are the changed structural conditions. The restrictive immigration laws of the 1920s drastically curtailed the great influx of southern, eastern, and central Europeans. Consequently, the immigrants already here did not receive continuous cultural reinforcement from new arrivals. But among Hispanics, there is a sizable flow of new arrivals, and rapid and inexpensive communications and transportation encourage return trips to the not-so-far-away homeland. In addition, earlier European immigrants encountered sometimes heavy-handed attempts at Americanization, whereas today's immigrants live in a time when pluralism and ethnic resurgence are common among members of the dominant group.

Other crucial changes in structural conditions are in technology and the job market. When the European poor came to the United States, they could find many unskilled and semiskilled jobs. Despite many evils and abuses in industry, an immigrant could secure a little piece of the American Dream through hard physical labor. The immigrant today enters a labor market where technology has eliminated many of those types of low-skill jobs, but others remain or have taken their place: construction, installation, home maintenance, and service industries. Through hard work, they follow a path that many other immigrants pursued to gain economic security.

During the mass European migration, the fledgling labor unions successfully struggled to improve the economic condition of the immigrant workers. Nowadays, unions have limited means to help newcomers, and the federal government is less inclined to offer welfare aid than in the 1960s, when the government encouraged individuals to apply for welfare by liberalizing eligibility requirements. With structural unemployment leaving no alternative, the system maneuvers many Hispanics into a marginal existence.

Highly visible because of their numbers, language, culture, and poverty, many Latinos find themselves the objects of resentment, hostility, and overt discrimination from the dominant society. The familiar pattern of blaming the victim results in negative stereotyping, social segregation, and all shades of prejudice and discrimination against the Hispanic and Caribbean poor.

Not all are poor, of course. For those who are not, attaining economic security means a very different life experience. Other positive factors offer some promise of easing the transition to life in the United States: bilingual education, increased public awareness, a greater tolerance for cultural pluralism, and civic and government programs. Serious problems remain for a disproportionate number of Hispanic Americans, however, and it is too soon to tell whether new legislation designed to control the influx of undocumented aliens will have any positive impact on the Hispanic poor.

KEY TERMS

Asylee	*Marianismo*	Shuttle migration
Dignidad	Miscegenation	Undocumented alien
Emigration	Pentecostal faith	
Machismo	Refugee	

DISCUSSION QUESTIONS

1. What cultural value orientations do most Hispanics share to some degree?

2. What changes in structural conditions make upward mobility difficult for many of the newcomers to the United States?

3. How diverse a group are Mexican Americans? What factors influence the continued poverty status among so many of them?

4. What factors distinguish the Puerto Rican experience from that of other Hispanic groups?

5. How do Cubans differ from other Hispanics in cultural values and economic mobility?

6. What other Hispanic peoples currently migrate in significant numbers, and why are they doing so?

SUGGESTED READINGS

De Anda, Roberto M. (ed.). *Chicanas and Chicanos in Contemporary Society*, 2nd ed. Boston: Allyn & Bacon, 2004.

An anthology of essays about the roles and lives of Mexican American women and men in their families, school, and the workplace.

Pérez y González, María. *Puerto Ricans in the United States*. Westport, CT: Greenwood Press, 2000.
A thoughtful analysis of Puerto Rican culture, migrant adjustment and adaptation on the mainland, socioeconomic status, intergroup relations, and societal impact.

Perez, Gina M. *The Near Northwest Side Story: Migration, Displacement and Puerto Rican Families*. Berkeley: University of California Press, 2004.
A fascinating account of transnational migration as a survival strategy with the building of extended families and social networks.

Rodriguez, Clara E. *Changing Race: Latinos, the Census, and the History of Ethnicity in the United States*. New York: New York University Press, 2000.
Uses interviews and census data analysis to examine how Latinos define their own racial and ethnic identity in America's divided racial landscape.

Sonneborn, Liz. *Immigrants in America: The Cuban-Americans*. Farmington Hills, MI: Lucent Books, 2001.
An account of Cuban immigrants creating a vibrant community in Miami's "Little Havana" and emerging as one of America's most prosperous and politically active immigrant groups.

MYSOCKIT

Additional resources for this chapter can be found in MySocKit. If you have a subscription to MySocKit, go to www.mysockit.com to study, review, and go beyond the book to learn more about race and ethnic relations.

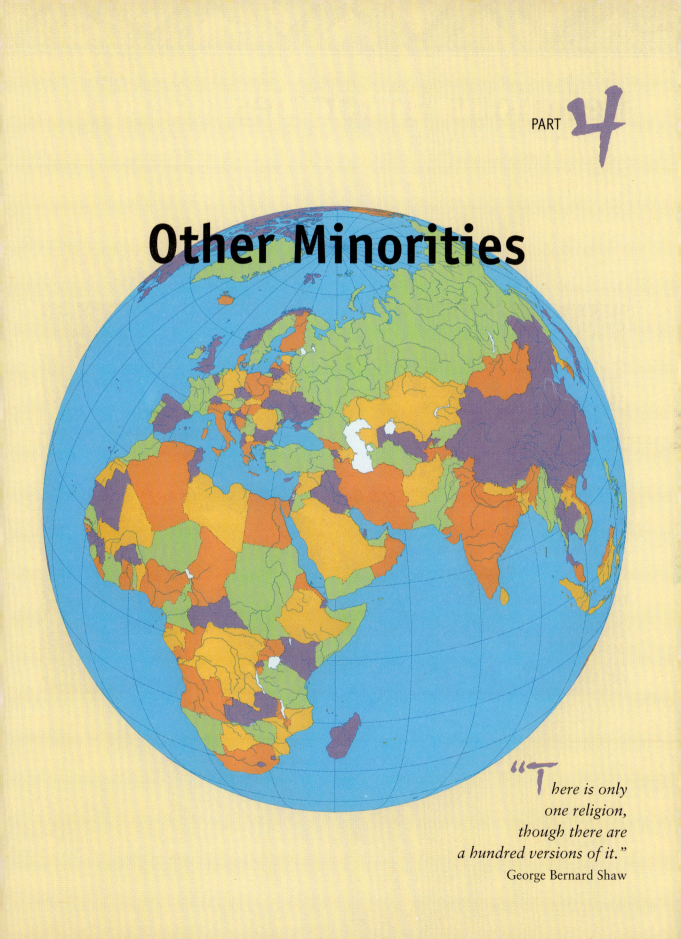

PART 4

Other Minorities

"There is only
one religion,
though there are
a hundred versions of it."
George Bernard Shaw

Religious Minorities

Any study of minority groups must include coverage of religion as well because religion can also generate ingroup–outgroup stereotyping, misunderstandings, and conflict, just as race and ethnicity sometimes do. For some immigrant groups—for instance, such earlier groups as German and Russian Jews or Irish and Italian Catholics, or such present groups as Arabic Muslims or Asian Indian Hindus—religion and ethnicity heavily intertwine, providing a basis for understanding both group solidarity and initial hostile societal reaction toward the group. Sometimes the religious group itself is an ethnic group—the Amish, for example.

Unlike most nations, in which one or a few faiths dominate, the United States has an immense diversity of faiths. Within the United States, over 1,500 religious groups exist, 200 of them conventional Christian and Jewish denominations, and 29 of these have a membership exceeding 1 million.[1] That religious pluralism has expanded so dramatically in the past 30 years that the United States, once a Christian country, is now the most religiously diverse country in the world.

Although the country remains mostly Christian (83 percent claim this faith), immigration, intermarriage, and a growing disenchantment with some of the oldest religious institutions are redefining its religious composition. For example, the United States today contains 7 times more Muslim Americans (6 million), 10 times more Buddhists (2 million), 9 times more Hindus (1 million), and 220 times more Sikhs (220,000) than it did in 1970. Religions once on the margins of mainstream Christianity are growing the most vigorously: Mormons by 90 percent, Jehovah's Witnesses by 162 percent, and the Pentecostal Assemblies of God by 267 percent. In contrast, the once dominant Episcopal, Presbyterian, and Congregational churches have declined in membership by 20 to 40 percent.[2] Furthermore, many people leaving mainstream churches in droves are joining a **nondenominational** megachurch, or what Donald E. Miller calls "new paradigm" churches that are less dogmatic and bureaucratic.[3] Yet perhaps the fastest-growing religious group in the country are those opting not to belong to any church; these "unaffiliated" exceed 49 million Americans, or

FIGURE 12.1   Ethnic and Racial Composition of Selected Religions, 2002

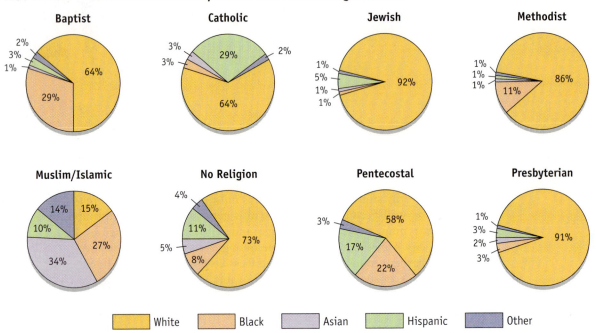

Source: Adapted from Egan Mayer, Barry A. Kosmin, and Aniela Keysar, "Race and Ethnic Make-Up of Selected Religious Groups, 2001," *American Religious Identification Survey 2001*, Graduate Center of the City University of New York.

17 percent of all Christians.[4] And in virtually all religions, we find considerable racial and ethnic diversity (Figure 12.1).

The United States today is a more secular society than ever before. Religious differences no longer fan the flames of intense bigotry and acts of mob violence. The terrorist attacks of September 11, 2001, did prompt a backlash of sporadic violence against Muslims, Sikhs, and Hindus, but most Americans did not act against members of non-Western religions. However, while this country may not be torn apart religiously as Iraq or Bosnia have been in recent years, it would be a mistake to assume that religious harmony prevails throughout the land. Religious conflicts still occur, false stereotypes still find acceptance, and religious prejudice still exists. Because of their beliefs, some religious minorities—such as the Amish, Rastafarians, and Santerians—encounter conflicts with the dominant society. In addition, issues such as abortion, birth control, and school prayer continue to bring people of varying religious beliefs into conflict with one another.

In this chapter, we examine both past and present patterns of religious tolerance and conflict in the United States. Specifically, we look at some groups that either have experienced problems similar to those confronted by racial or ethnic groups discussed in previous chapters or continue as viable religious subcultures in this pluralistic society. Because of this orientation, we do not look at other religions that do not prominently display ethnoreligious cultural marks and minority-group status, although in some cases such religions may have a larger population base.

◢◣◥ SOCIOHISTORICAL PERSPECTIVE

Since the time of the Pilgrims, this nation has been the haven for many religious groups fleeing persecution and seeking religious freedom. Even during colonial times, however, instances of religious intolerance occurred, such as when Massachusetts expelled Anne Hutchinson, Roger Williams, and their followers and when Maryland denied Catholics the right to hold political office. As the isolated settlements—many of a single religious persuasion—evolved into interactive colonies, Anglo-Saxon Protestantism dominated. Nevertheless, the Founding Fathers built into the Constitution two fundamental principles: separation of church and state and freedom of religion. Those two guarantees bestowed a unique legacy on U.S. culture that continues to the present day.

For almost all immigrant groups, religion has played a significant role. The church, synagogue, or temple typically became the central social institution of their ethnic communities, functioning both as a spiritual bond reinforcing group identity and as the social, educational, and even political base of their activities. That colonial legacy remains visible today in many older New England towns, where a church stands prominently beside the village green, in the center of the community—the place in which town meetings made participatory democracy a reality. Similarly, in the remnants of white ethnic neighborhoods in northern cities, in midwestern farming communities, in southwestern states, and in specific places such as St. Augustine, Florida, or New Orleans, still-standing religious edifices and recorded ethnic community histories and studies offer abundant testimony to the role religion played among first- and second-generation residents.

The clergy have always provided important leadership among racial and ethnic groups. In addition to spiritual guidance, they often served as a rallying force to enhance community cohesiveness as well as the economic and social welfare of their people. Frequently, priests, rabbis, and ministers have also been in the forefront of concerted efforts to ease immigrants' transition to U.S. life and their entry into the economic mainstream. Black ministers—such as Martin Luther King Jr. and Jesse Jackson—have consistently been in the vanguard of the movement for civil rights and equality. Religious leaders throughout U.S. history have played an important role not only in shaping the values and moral behavior of their congregations but in influencing public policy, encouraging charitable activities, and implementing the spirit of the Constitution.

Unfortunately, not all religious leaders have been magnanimous in promoting equality, nor have all religions experienced tolerance in the U.S. experience. Some—Catholics, Jews, and Mormons, for example—have been victims of discrimination, persecution, and even violence. Others—such as the Amish, Christian Scientists, Jehovah's Witnesses, Native Americans, and Rastafarians—have come into conflict with society over their religious beliefs. Even though the ideal culture stresses freedom of religion, in practice religious bigotry and intolerance have caused suffering and hardship to some religious minorities in the United States.

◢◣◥ CATHOLIC AMERICANS

Catholicism did not gain easy acceptance in the United States. By the mid-17th century, all the colonies had passed laws designed to thwart Catholic immigration, most of them denying Catholics citizenship, voting rights, and office-holding rights.[5] The nation remained almost exclusively a Protestant domain until 1830. Over the next 30 years, immigration had a profound political and social impact on the nation. More than 500,000 immigrants in the 1830s, 1.7 million in the 1840s, and 2.6 million in the 1850s—the great bulk of them Roman Catholics, mostly Irish and German peasants—entered the country. A feeling of alarm spread among U.S. Protestants, many of whom believed that Catholics would subvert the nation.

Societal Hostility

Samuel F. B. Morse, inventor of the telegraph and son of a militant minister, railed against an alleged papist conspiracy to take control of the U.S. government through Catholic immigration. He exhorted Protestant citizens not to be "deceived by Jesuit-controlled immigrants." Instead, they should "fly to protect the vulnerable places of your Constitution and Laws. Place your guards; you will need them, and quickly too.—And first, shut your gates."[6]

Lurid, best-selling exposés of the Catholic Church appeared. Rebecca Reed fabricated a story about her life in a convent in Charlestown, Massachusetts, that resulted in the burning of that Ursuline convent in 1834. Two years later, the most infamous of these inflammatory works appeared: *Awful Disclosures of the Hotel Dieu Nunnery of Montreal* by Maria Monk. The author claimed to be an escaped nun who had been kept prisoner in the Montreal convent and forced to have sexual relations with priests. Resisting nuns were killed, she reported, as were any babies born, their bodies then thrown into a lime pit. Although Maria Monk was later discredited as a prostitute and fraud after investigations uncovered no evidence to support her charges, many religious bigots continued to believe her story. The monograph was frequently reprinted, selling hundreds of thousands of copies and spawning a sequel and many imitators.

Throughout the 1850s, nativist hostility against Catholics intensified, with the Know-Nothing movement spearheading the agitation. Predictably, violence erupted. Mobs rioted, burning Catholic churches, schools, convents, and homes.

One particularly effective diatribe against Catholics was Josiah Strong's *Our Country* (1855), which accused Catholic immigrants of immorality, crime, corruption, and socialism. Reprinted in numerous editions, it incited public antipathy toward Catholicism for decades. The Reverend Justin H. Fulton was also an effective demagogue; his anti-Catholic books *Rome in America* (1887) and *Washington in the Lap of Rome* (1888) warned of a Catholic threat to America's liberty through the school system and through control of the government. Another Maria Monk type, Margaret Lisle Shepherd, published her autobiography, *My Life in a Convent* (1887), claiming to be an escaped nun who had fled priests' carnal lust. Her story, although false, was widely believed and added to the anti-Catholic chorus.

In 1887, a short-lived but highly successful anti-Catholic organization, the American Protective Association (APA), emerged out of Iowa to become a national force with about 500,000 members.[7] Dedicated to keeping Catholics out of office, employing only Protestants, and refusing to cooperate with Catholics in any strikes, the APA struck a responsive chord among working-class U.S. Protestants who believed Catholic immigrants were coming to take their jobs, particularly after the Panic of 1893 and the ensuing high rate of unemployment. Enjoying some success in recruiting members in the East but none in the South, the APA was strongest throughout the Midwest. Although its endorsed candidates gained control of city governments in Detroit, Kansas City, and Milwaukee—causing the firing of all Catholic officials in those cities—the APA sowed the seeds of its own destruction. Internecine fighting, charges of corruption and embezzlement of funds, and a reputation for violence combined to torpedo the APA; it had no power after 1896.[8]

Anti-Catholicism did not end with the APA's demise, however. In 1911, General Nelson Miles, former Army Chief of Staff and Congressional Medal of Honor recipient, organized the Guardians of Liberty in upstate New York. Dedicated to keeping Catholics out of office because they would supposedly take their orders from Rome, this group never wielded any real political clout. An anti-Catholic publication, *The Menace,* gained over 1.5 million readers, mostly rural. The Catholic Church sued unsuccessfully to revoke *The Menace*'s mailing privileges on the ground that the periodical's graphic depictions of the alleged immorality of the Catholic Church violated federal obscenity laws. But *The Menace* was not alone; a total of 61 anti-Catholic periodicals appeared prior to World War I.[9]

The post–World War I period saw the resurrection of the Ku Klux Klan, this time dedicated to the theme that Catholicism and Judaism were alien to Americanism. As described in Chapter 6, the KKK grew to a membership of 2 to 3 million and was partly responsible for passage of the restrictive immigration laws of 1921 and 1924. Thereafter, it declined in numbers and influence, and its final hurrah was a slanderous campaign in 1928 against Democratic presidential candidate, Al Smith, the Catholic governor of New York.

Values and Practices

Several factors help explain nativist hostility against U.S. Catholics in the 18th, 19th, and early 20th centuries. First, religion played a far greater role in people's lives in previous centuries, which made religious differences a matter of greater concern. Generations of Catholic–Protestant conflict in Europe had created a legacy of latent antagonism among European Americans. Furthermore, U.S. culture and Protestantism had evolved along parallel lines, stressing individualism and self-reliance, whether in making one's fortune or in gaining salvation through the teachings of the Bible.

Religion. Because Catholics followed Church dogma, or prescribed doctrine, and operated their local churches as part of a vast bureaucracy whose hierarchy of authority reached back to the pope in Rome, many U.S. Protestants feared that this structure would undermine their way of life. They envisioned millions of Catholic immigrants, obeying a foreign potentate (the pope), like an unthinking, indoctrinated army. If such people gained political office, some Protestants feared, control of the country would move to Rome. The physical presence of priests and nuns and the building of churches, convents, and parochial schools— all virtually nonexistent in the United States before—served to confirm the worst Protestant fears.

Other Catholic practices puzzled and disturbed many U.S. Protestants. They considered vows of **celibacy** among priests and nuns unnatural, which encouraged them to believe the lurid fabrications that were printed about sordid sexual practices within the religious orders and the priesthood. Mandatory attendance at the weekly repetition of the same mass ceremony, then spoken in Latin, seemed to them both un-American and repressive of individual thought. Use of a private confessional booth to tell one's sins to a priest, unlike the usual Protestant practice of silent confession during worship services, seemed bizarre to some. Although Catholics themselves understood and accepted the context of their own beliefs and practices, to Protestants many generations removed from familiarity with them, these outgroup differences seemed strange and threatening.

Education.   Catholic education generated perhaps the most conflict between Catholics and Protestants. Daily readings from the King James Bible in public schools constituted one of several factors prompting Catholics to establish parochial schools to provide appropriate religious training and moral guidance for their children. Efforts in the 1840s to obtain public funding for parochial schools or to substitute the Catholic version of the Bible for Catholic students in public schools generated fierce controversy in Boston, New York, Philadelphia, and Cincinnati.[10] The issue of public funding for parochial schools flared up again in the 1870s, but the opposition of President Grant and the Republican Party rendered any organized nativist opposition superfluous. Efforts in the 1880s in Massachusetts and in three midwestern states (Ohio, Illinois, and Wisconsin) to regulate parochial schools generated intense controversy.[11] Throughout this period, Protestant periodicals argued that the public school system would end the "ignorance and superstition" of Catholic children and so campaigned not only against public funding of parochial schools but in favor of eliminating them altogether.[12]

The Present Scene

Today, Roman Catholics in the United States number about 66 million, making their religion the largest single denomination in the country. Overt discrimination against them has ended; and, except for recent Filipino, Haitian, and Hispanic Catholic immigrants, most are assimilated into the economic and political mainstream. They can be found in all occupations and in many leadership roles. John F. Kennedy became the first Catholic president in 1960; in Congress, Catholics ranked first in 2008 among the denominations with 157 legislators (29 percent).

Greater dialogue occurs between Protestant and Catholic religious leaders, an outgrowth of the **ecumenical movement** initiated by Pope John XXIII four decades ago. The change from saying Mass in Latin to English in the United States helped make Catholicism seem less strange to outsiders. Also, an acute shortage of priests obliged the laity to become more active: reading scripture, leading music, distributing communion at services, and taking leadership positions in nearly every phase of the church's life, including religious instruction, family life bureaus, and financial and administrative positions. With both men and women handling these church tasks, Catholicism has in some ways become more like several Protestant denominations and thus less "different" to outsiders. Mainstream U.S. Catholic social views tend to agree with those of conservative U.S. Protestants on various subjects, including pornography, abortion, birth control, and school prayer.

Perhaps the best evidence of greater religious and ethnic tolerance, however, lies in the rise in Catholic–Protestant intermarriage. From about 18 percent in the 1920s, the Catholic intermarriage rate increased to approximately 40 percent by

1990, a level at which it presently remains.[13] Group size is an apparent factor. The larger the percentage of Catholics in a given area, the more likely that Catholics will marry within their group, but the smaller the percentage, the more like they will marry someone not of their faith.[14]

A 2007 study revealed that in recent decades non-Hispanic Catholics have been upwardly mobile in wealth distribution. Catholic values related to work and money—together with smaller nuclear families, high rates of marriage stability, and higher educational achievement—led to achievement of a wealth level comparable to that of mainline Protestants.[15]

Problem areas remain, however, including surveys showing that as many as 85 percent of Catholic Americans reject the Church's teaching on birth control and that they divide equally on the antiabortion position of the Church. At the height of the sexual abuse cases involving priests in 2002, Catholic participation in church life and satisfaction with church leadership dropped noticeably, but it has since rebounded to prescandal levels.[16]

JEWISH AMERICANS

Jewish people are a unique minority because they are not a specific religious grouping and need not even be religious. Although religion has been an important bond among Jews, it is not a cohesive force in that three main branches of Judaism exist in the United States—Orthodox, Conservative, and Reform. In addition, many agnostics and atheists also identify themselves as Jews; for these secular Jews, the emphasis is on Jewish culture and history rather than a belief in God. And with large variations in physical appearance, native languages, and cultural attributes, Jews possess that elusive quality Franklin Giddings called "consciousness of kind." In 1946, Jean-Paul Sartre wrote that a Jew is someone whom other people identify as a Jew. Perhaps then, our best informal definition of the Jewish people is that they consist of all those who think of themselves as such, with outgroup members treating them accordingly. However, conservative factions within Judaism limit Jewish identity to those who are born of a Jewish mother or who are converts.

Immigration before 1880

Although we have archeological evidence of earlier Jewish presences in New Mexico and Tennessee, the first recorded group of Jewish immigrants—4 men, 6 women, and 13 younger people—arrived in New Amsterdam in 1654 as refugees from the Portuguese takeover of previously Dutch-ruled Brazil. Benefiting from tolerant Dutch rule, Jews enjoyed open acceptance in this settlement. Later, many Jewish refugees of Spanish and Portuguese origin, fleeing the Spanish Inquisition, came to the United States by way of Holland, the Caribbean, or South America. By the end of the 18th century, about 2,000 to 3,000 Sephardic Jews were living in America.[17]

Most of the earlier discussion about nativist hostility toward Catholics applies with equal validity to Jewish immigrants. All the English colonies discouraged Jewish immigration and passed laws to keep Jews from voting or holding office. When Jews were permitted to vote in New York in 1736, a group of residents claimed the election was fraudulent on that basis. When the Know-Nothing movement reached its height in the 1850s, the Know-Nothings singled out "this peculiar race of people" for criticism and discriminatory treatment. During the Civil War, former Know-Nothing member Ulysses S. Grant, acting on unfounded charges that Jews were profiteering through smuggling and cotton speculation, issued General Order Number 11, expelling all civilian Jews from his military jurisdiction. On January 4, 1863, Lincoln revoked this order.[18]

By the mid-19th century, the second wave of Jewish migration began. In this wave came Ashkenazic Jews, mostly from the German provinces; they were more prosperous and better educated than earlier German Jewish immigrants and represented the first mass Jewish immigration—groups of entire families coming from a single locality or community. From an 1840 Jewish population of 15,000, Jewish Americans increased to 250,000 in 1880. At that point, Jewish American communities were almost exclusively German.

Newcomers and Tension

The third wave of Jewish migration was the most significant—in numbers, cultural influence, work contributions, and dominant-group reaction. From 250,000 in 1880, the U.S. Jewish population rose to almost 3 million before generally restrictive immigration laws were enacted in the 1920s. The initial impetus for this massive migration was a pogrom (organized massacre) that followed the assassination of Czar Alexander II (1881). Although no Jews were involved in the regicide, the czarist government used them as a scapegoat to divert people's attention from long-festering social, political, and economic grievances. This marked the beginning of a long series of pogroms, with many attacks, loss of lives, and extensive property damage in Jewish communities throughout the Russian Empire's Pale of Settlement region. In addition to the need to escape government-incited violence, powerful economic incentives encouraged emigration. Some people came to escape destitution. Others fled from the economic instability that resulted from government efforts to industrialize Russia.

Considerable cultural tensions developed among Jews from different areas of Europe. Sephardic Jews, the first arrivals, considered themselves superior to the 19th-century German newcomers (Ashkenazic Jews), who in turn looked with disdain on newcomers from eastern Europe. Although a few Jewish immigrants from central and eastern Europe had arrived as early as the 18th century, for some Jewish ethnics the distinctions based on place of origin and time of arrival in the United States persisted well into the mid-1940s, as this report indicates:

> The earlier arrivals scarred the later ones as crude, superstitious, and economically indigent, and the latter despised the former as snobs and religious renegades. As recently as 1925, one student of immigrant groups asserted that "intermarriage between a Sephardic Jew and a Russian Jew, for instance, is as rare, if not rarer, than intermarriage between Jew and Gentile." Even within each of these divisions of Jews there was at first aversion to marriage with some of the subdivisions. Bavarian Jews hesitated to marry with those German Jews who came from the area near the Polish border, derisively labelled "Pollacks." The Russian Jew looked down on the Polish and Galician Jews and refused to marry them or permit his children to do so. Although these intra-Jewish barriers to marriage have largely disappeared in recent times, first generation Jewish parents may still go through the motions of embarrassment when their children marry the sons and daughters of a ridiculed sub-group.[19]

Thus, ethnic prejudices, as well as cultural and class differences, led to strain between the "old" Jewish population and the "new" Jewish arrivals. German Jews, who had by this time supplanted the Sephardic Jews as an ethnic elite, were embarrassed by their lowly co-religionists with their "strange" appearance, Yiddish language, and orthodox religious practices. At first, many rejected the new arrivals, partly out of fear that growing anti-Semitic feeling would place all Jews—old and new—into one negative category. Soon, however, these Americanized Jews created community organizations to help the newcomers adjust to their new country. In addition, they attempted, with limited success, to settle the newcomers in widely dispersed farm communities, away from congested urban centers.[20]

Anti-Semitism

Anti-Jewish stereotyping spread in the arts and the media as it had for other immigrant groups, such as the Irish and Asians. On stage, Jews were sometimes depicted either as scoundrels or as comic characters. Newspapers and magazines at times ran cartoons and editorials that were openly anti-Semitic. One example was *Life* magazine, published in New York City, where the Jewish population rose from 4 percent in 1880 to 25 percent in 1910. The magazine called the city "Jew York" and attacked supposed Jewish clannishness, pushiness, and domination of the theater. In the early 20th century, about half of the actors, songwriters, publishers, and entrepreneurs in New York City were Jewish; this included those who worked in the flourishing Yiddish-language theater that served the immigrant community. *Life*'s editors launched a 10-year attack on the "Jewish Theatrical Trust," accusing it of poisoning U.S. values and of lowering the moral tone of the theater by running lascivious plays for profit. The accusations were false or distorted. By catering to a specific ethnic group, the Yiddish theater was "different," but the plays were not lewd or lascivious.

Two notorious incidents emphasize the heights anti-Semitic feelings reached in the late 19th and early 20th centuries. In the first instance, Joseph Seligman, an eminent banker and frequent guest of President Grant at the White House (who declined an offer to become secretary of the treasury), was denied accommodations in 1877 at a fashionable resort hotel in Saratoga Springs, New York. Although he and his family had stayed there several times before, the hotel's new policy of "not accepting Israelites" made headlines across the country. This incident brought latent anti-Jewish attitudes into the open, and many other establishments quickly followed suit.

The second incident concerned Leo Frank, the manager of an Atlanta pencil factory, who in 1913 was hastily convicted on flimsy evidence of murdering a young factory girl. Many felt he was convicted because he was a Jew, and his case spurred the formation of the B'nai B'rith's Anti-Defamation League. With prominent Georgia newspapers and clergymen calling for a new trial and many Jews contributing money to Frank's legal appeal, the state's governor commuted Frank's execution to life imprisonment, an act praised by the Georgia press. However, some of the dead young woman's friends and neighbors abducted Frank from the state prison, transported him 175 miles to her hometown, and lynched him. It was more than a local episode. Nationwide press coverage of the incident included comments about the "Parasite Race," helping fan the flames of prejudice.

Anti-Semitism of varying intensity has continued to the present day. The Silver Shirts, led by William Pelley, and the National Union for Social Justice, headed by the "radio priest," Father Charles Coughlin, were two of the most active movements against the Jews in the late 1930s. Anti-Semitic behavior declined after World War II, however, partly because of revulsion against Nazi genocide and partly because pluralism became more generally accepted. Still, isolated incidents occur, mostly acts of vandalism or desecration. Some analysts suggest that the roots of anti-Semitism can be found in the teachings of Christianity (now renounced in the Catholic Church by Vatican II), which for centuries blamed the Jews for the death of Christ.[21] Latent anti-Semitism may also manifest itself for other reasons, including status and economic rivalries.

Although the number of anti-Semitic incidents in the United States are no longer as high as in 1994 (with nearly 2,100 anti-Semitic incidents, including 143 on college campuses), they still occur with frequency. In 2006, there were a total of 1,554 such incidents, including 81 on college campuses. States with the most anti-Semitic incidents were New York (284), New Jersey (244), California (204), Florida (179), Massachusetts (96), and Pennsylvania (94).[22] One encouraging note is increasing community activism against such incidents. For example, a few years ago when a Jewish family's home in Billings, Montana, was vandalized after displaying a menorah in the window, the entire neighborhood—Jews and Christians alike—quickly displayed menorahs in all homes.

Upward Mobility

Like many other immigrants, most East European Jews who came to the United States were poor. Most, therefore, settled in or near the large cities that were ports of entry (Boston, New York, and Philadelphia). Many went to work in the garment industry, while others became street peddlers until they saved enough capital to open their own stores. Because two-thirds of the Jewish male immigrants were skilled workers, compared to an average of one-fifth of the males from other immigrant groups, their absorption into the U.S. economy proceeded relatively smoothly.[23] As a result, they climbed the socioeconomic ladder more quickly and in larger proportions than most other groups, except into middle-management positions in much of the corporate world.[24]

Several cultural factors contributed to the success of some first- and many second-generation Jewish Americans. First, because of generations of discrimination in Europe, they had been relegated to such self-sustaining occupations as merchant, scholar, and self-employed artisan. Thus, they brought with them skills and knowledge useful in an industrial society, together with values that encouraged deferred gratification, seriousness of purpose, patience, and perseverance—precisely the virtues stressed by the U.S. middle class and the Protestant ethic (see The Ethnic Experience box, page 437).

Second, during the period of great immigration, 1880 to 1920, most Jews came with their entire families; in many other ethnic groups, males usually came first and then either returned to the old country or sent for their families.[25] Having the entire family unit together from the outset gave Jewish newcomers greater emotional stability against the psychological strain of the immigrant experience and an advantage in cooperative economic efforts.

A third factor was the Jewish people's traditional emphasis on learning—especially for boys. Even if the children were illiterate in the language of their

The Ethnic Experience

My American Dream

"I heard a lot about the streets in America being paved with gold but I knew one thing, because I came in contact with GI's and I saw they came from different backgrounds in different parts of the country, and I knew one thing—that I was going to have to work in the United States. People didn't actually still say the streets were paved with gold, but this was still the belief in Europe because, you know, the dollar was the Almighty. In Europe you could buy five, six times with the dollar what you could buy in the United States. So this was why people still believed the streets were paved with gold. All what you needed was a shovel. But I knew. I was prepared. I never was disappointed in coming here to the United States.

"What is to me the American Dream? To some people maybe it's a bigger car or a bigger house. This is their dream. Take more vacations. Sure, we need vacations, but I think our way of life should be to practice just what we preach, just what we have in our Constitution. I mean, not to discriminate against people of all kinds, because this country—if it really is a melting pot—for this one reason, because it is so great this country, because from so many countries, the idea can be put together."

Source: Polish Jewish immigrant who came to the United States in 1948 at age 35. Taped interview from the collection of Vincent N. Parrillo.

country of origin—and this was less often true for Jews than for many other immigrant groups—they had learned Hebrew and, as a result, the discipline of study. By the time he was 13, a Jewish boy, if raised in a religious family, was prepared to read from the Torah for his bar mitzvah. Today, a large number of Jewish girls also participate in this ceremony (then called a bat mitzvah). In Jewish culture, this positive orientation toward learning carried over to public education and secular studies. Although parents toiled in low-status factory jobs, they encouraged their children to further their education and then enter the professions. The high percentage of Jewish youths attending public and private colleges in the first few decades of the 20th century is all the more remarkable because of their limited residence in the United States and because most U.S. citizens placed less emphasis on a college education in those times.[26]

Gordon reported that, by the 1940s, the occupational distribution of Jews was comparable to that of members of high-status Protestant denominations.[27] Yet Jews have been significantly underrepresented in some industries, such as steel, oil, banking, and insurance. Not all experienced upward mobility. Thousands of Jewish poor, especially among the aged, exist on a level far from the stereotyped portrait of successful Jews.

Social Interaction

Social ostracism often accompanied their economic successes. Higher economic status did not necessarily mean a comparable increase in social prestige. Even when Jews gained positions with higher levels of income, they still found themselves excluded from social and recreational clubs and had to establish parallel social and recreational organizations for themselves. They also encountered restrictions in housing; admissions quotas for colleges, universities, and professional schools; and other obstacles designed to keep them at a social, economic, and educational distance from white Protestants.

Although many Jewish middle-class families moved to the suburbs after World War II, they continued to be socially segregated in the 1950s and early 1960s. Gerhard Lenski found that the frequency of close associations between Jews and non-Jews in Detroit declined after adolescence, particularly at the time of choosing a mate.[28] In Elmira, New York, John P. Dean found that approximately 75 percent of his Jewish sample socialized occasionally with their closest non-Jewish friends but that few participated regularly in a mixed social clique.[29] Herbert J. Gans reported that the Jewish suburban housewives of Park Forest, outside Chicago, took part in daytime social activities of the entire neighborhood but that in the evening and on weekends their social relationships were confined to other Jews.[30] Albert Gordon suggested that this pattern of relative isolation in suburban evening or weekend social gatherings was fairly common and not necessarily voluntary.[31] Milton Gordon, echoing the concept of the triple melting pot (discussed in Chapter 4), suggested that Catholics, Protestants, and Jews all tend to interact in meaningful primary relationships with members of their own religioethnic group.[32]

These observations seem less true today. A major study commissioned by the Council of Jewish Federations (CJF) revealed that interfaith marriages among Jews in the United States increased from 9 percent in 1964 to 52 percent by 1990.[33] Other studies uncovered wide variations from one community to the next, but there is general agreement that intermarriage rates are at an all-time high, ranging somewhere between 43 and 52 percent.[34] Recently, the New York–based Jewish Outreach Institute issued a report pointing to a future when more intermarried households will exist in the U.S. Jewish community than "in-married" households.[35] Although some experts argue that religious intermarriage does not reflect values emphasizing assimilation, others agree with Gordon that increased intermarriage is one of the final stages of assimilation.[36] At the very least, such a pattern reveals a significant increase in meaningful primary relationships between Jews and non-Jews.

Another significant finding from the CJF study was that only 28 percent of the children of mixed marriages are brought up as Jews, 31 percent are reared in no religion at all, and 41 percent are reared in another faith or in an amalgam of Judaism and other beliefs.[37] This finding, coupled with a low birth rate and a low immigration rate, has led Jewish traditionalists to be fearful about the future of Judaism in the United States, including predictions that the Jewish American population will drop by over 1 million from its present 5.7 million.[38] Others lament that intermarriage will bring more divorces, alcoholism, and family violence than existed in past all-Jewish families.[39] Jewish sociologists and modernists are more optimistic, seeing the Jewish community in the United States as a cohesive and dynamic source of networks and resources maintained by the forces of social structure, which will ensure its continued vitality.[40]

Jewish Identity

For the large numbers of Jewish immigrants in the late 19th and early 20th centuries, the synagogue played a significant role in the community structure. At the same time, it competed with various cultural, ideological, and self-help organizations supported by many Jews. Classes offered by such organizations as the Educational Alliance on New York City's Lower East Side provided opportunities for acculturation. Together, the synagogues and organizations provided cohesive

This interfaith marriage between an Episcopalian bride and a Jewish groom, performed by a rabbi and a priest, shows a continuing trend in marital assimilation along ethnic and religious lines. Recent studies show many children from these marriages are not raised in the Jewish faith, suggesting a further decline of the U.S. Jewish population.

bonds, laying the foundation for community organization, social activities, and a feeling of belonging.[41]

As Jews became more highly educated and assimilated, the ethnicity that had closely secured European immigrants to their religious traditions lost its hold. New focal points of Jewish identity became building and supporting the nation of Israel, as well as politics and social concerns within the United States. In 2008, Jewish legislators in Congress totaled 43, or 8 percent.

Many Jewish Americans today see religion less as an inherited ethnic identity and more as a personal choice of belief and practice.[42] Jewish survey data show that only 20 percent of Jews in the United States (half of them Orthodox) are seriously religious.[43] Affixed to their Jewishness culturally but secular in their beliefs, such people are more likely to intermarry and assimilate. It is to them that rabbis and leaders in the Reform branch of Judaism have been reaching out in an effort to maintain the Jewish community. Yet rabbis and leaders in the more traditional Conservative and Orthodox branches view welcoming interfaith couples into the religion as diluting Judaism. This emotional issue continues as all these groups struggle to ensure the survival of American Jewry and somehow maintain the integrity of Jewish thought, values, and institutions.

Since 1981, nearly 100,000 Israelis have migrated to the United States. Eight percent of today's Jewish adults are immigrants, and two-thirds of these emigrated from one of the republics of the former Soviet Union.[44] The most favored settlement areas have been the New York and Los Angeles metropolitan regions. (For information on religious diversity in Israel, see The International Scene box, page 440.)

The International Scene

Religious Diversity in Israel

Religious diversity is not a concept most people associate with Israel, a nation founded in the mid-20th century as the Jewish state. To many outsiders, Israel seems monolithic and homogeneous, consisting mostly of Jewish inhabitants with a small Palestinian minority. This, however, is far from the reality. In 2005, Jews constituted 76 percent of the total population, with Muslims (mostly Sunni) next at 16 percent, Christians at 2 percent, Druze at 1.6 percent, and other faiths at 4 percent. With its population becoming even more diverse from a continuing influx of immigrants and a growing Arabic population, Israel faces a growing challenge of inclusion.

Despite popular belief that most of Israel's Arab population lives on the West Bank, 60 percent live in the Sea of Galilee and northern regions. Still others live in the inland area and in seven mixed-religion cities throughout the country. Since the 1967 reunification of Jerusalem, for example, that city's Arab Muslim population has increased faster than its Jewish population.

The Druze—a relatively small Middle Eastern sect centered in Lebanon, with a turbulent near-1,000-year-old history—cloak their religion in secrecy and maintain a close-knit identity and loyalty. Their prohibitions against intermarriage and conversion, either away from or into their religion, make their survival and continuity across almost a millennium all the more remarkable.

In the city of Haifa is a small community of Baha'i, whose religion was founded in the mid-19th century by Baha' Ullah. The Baha'i—with houses of worship in Africa, Australia, Central America, Europe, and the United States—believe in a universal faith. No preaching occurs in their temples; instead, services consist of the recitation of scriptures of all religions.

The mostly Jewish population itself is hardly a single entity. The majority are secular but retain some loyalty to religious traditions, particularly during Yom Kippur and Passover. About 25 percent would classify themselves as devoutly Orthodox. Not only does Israel's Jewish population range from ultra-Orthodox to secular, but it also contains great diversity because of immigration. Gaps between second- and third-generation Jews of European descent (Ashkenazim) and those of North African and Middle Eastern descent (Mizrahim), who each comprise approximately half the Jewish population, have narrowed over the years but still remain. The Ashkenazi are the dominant elite and tend to be more affluent, secular, and Westernized, while the Mizrahi are more traditional, conservative, and religious. Occasionally, tensions between the two groups spill over into violence.

Critical Thinking Question: What do you know of religious diversity among Jews in the United States?

THE MORMONS

The Church of Jesus Christ of Latter-Day Saints offers a fascinating portrait of a religious group evolving from a despised and persecuted people into a highly successful and respected church. This group is unique as a minority group because its principal migration was to leave what was then the United States. Its series of relocations westward, ultimately ending with permanent settlement in the Rocky Mountains during the 1840s, gave it an enduring sense of territoriality and shared tradition.[45]

The Early Years

At age 18, by his own account, Joseph Smith received the first of several visitations from the angel Moroni, who guided him to a hidden stack of golden plates, each eight inches square.[46] Aided by two stones called the Urim and Thummin, Joseph Smith translated the hieroglyphics into the *Book of Mormon*, a massive and controversial work. Mormons consider it the true word of God, providing one of the foundations of their faith along with the Bible. In 1830, two years after completing his translation of the book, Joseph Smith—now 25 years old—founded the Mormon faith in the western New York State region where he then lived. Within a year, the church had over 1,000 members.

As the church continued to grow rapidly under Smith's charismatic leadership, it attracted enemies. Fleeing harassment in New York and then Ohio, the Mormons resettled in Missouri, incurring further hostility because of their anti-slavery views, growing political power, and cooperative communities, which their more individualistically oriented neighbors found threatening on the sparsely settled frontier. Expelled by the governor in 1838 following officially sanctioned killings, the Mormons moved to Illinois, where they faced their worst clashes as the church's encouragement of polygamy, together with the Mormons' growing numbers and strength, inflamed societal hostility into frequent acts of violence. In 1844, Joseph Smith and his brother, Hyrum, were lynched by a mob storming the jail in which they had been incarcerated. Thereafter, raids, pitched battles, burned homes and temples, the rape of Mormon women, and even the use of artillery pieces by both sides brought Mormon existence to a crisis stage.[47]

Faced with extermination or forced assimilation, most of the Mormons (about 30,000), under the leadership of Brigham Young, migrated westward until they reached the Great Salt Lake Valley in 1847. Intergroup conflict had strengthened their group identity and cohesiveness, and now the Mormons experienced steady and rapid growth in the isolated Salt Lake region. Part of this growth was due to the arrival throughout the 19th century of tens of thousands of converts from England and Scandinavia. The discovery of gold in California ended Mormon isolation, however, because their settlement was located along the best route to the California gold fields.

Bruce Campbell and Eugene Campbell suggest that Mormon theocratic political power threatened federal control of the Utah territory and thus control of the route to California, generating several decades of government attempts to alter Mormon economic, political, and social institutions.[48] In one instance of this, President Buchanan sent troops to Utah in 1857 in an unsuccessful attempt to impose a non-Mormon as territorial governor in place of Brigham Young.

Government efforts next shifted to an attack on **polygyny,** the Mormon practice of men having more than one wife. Although permitted by church doctrine, polygyny occurred among only 20 percent of the eligible males, two-thirds of whom had one additional wife.[49] Lurid newspaper stories about alleged Mormon depravity inflamed public opinion and created a stereotype of Mormon males as evil, seductive, promiscuous, sexually virile libertines. Non-Mormon opportunists produced such products as Brigham Young Tablets and Mormon Bishop Pills that were supposedly able to increase a man's sexual desire or ability.[50] In 1862, Lincoln signed the Morrill Act, forbidding bigamy in U.S. territories. Continually harassed by federal agents after the Civil War, the Mormons challenged the law as an infringement on their religious freedom, but in 1878, the U.S. Supreme Court ruled in *Reynolds v. United States* that the law was constitutional.

Unable to gain access to church records to prove the multiple marriages, the government passed a new law in 1882 forbidding anyone from living in "lewd cohabitation," which resulted in the jailing of hundreds of Mormon polygamists. In 1887, the Edmunds–Tucker Act dissolved the Mormon Church as a legal entity and provided for the confiscation of church property. When this law was upheld by the Supreme Court in 1890 as constitutional, church president Wilford Woodruff issued a manifesto ending the open practice of plural marriage.

President Benjamin Harrison then granted pardons to all imprisoned polygamists. In 1896, Utah became a state, beginning a new era of relations between Christians and Mormons.

Values and Practices

Following the behavioral code established by Joseph Smith, whom they believe was a prophet of God, Mormons typically do not smoke or drink any form of alcoholic beverages, coffee, tea, or caffeinated soda beverages. Emphasis is on group rather than individual activities, promoting group identification. Especially encouraged are the performing arts, team sports, and organized recreational activities. Other aspects of the Mormon faith, described in the following sections, are deeply embedded in the group's social institutions.

Family. Mormons place heavy emphasis on the family, both as the primary agent for socializing people into the Mormon belief system and as the basic social organization in the eternal Kingdom of God. Anything undermining family growth or stability is discouraged—for example, premarital and extramarital sex, indecent language, immodest behavior, abortion, birth control, intermarriage, and divorce. These problems occur far less often among active, observing Mormons than among those who are less religiously involved. Drugs and premarital sex are a problem among Mormon teenagers and young adults, although to a smaller degree than the national average.[51]

Unlike typical U.S. families, in which each person pursues individual interests and activities, Mormon families do many things together. Monday is set aside as Family Home Evening. At other times, families attend social and sporting events together, with the emphasis on the intermingling of different age groups. Among older Mormon families of pioneer stock, the kinship network manifests itself in annual summer reunions. All families engage in the genealogical search for ancestors to secure for them a proxy baptism or sealing ceremony in a Mormon temple to enter God's presence in the Celestial World. Through the Mormon Genealogical Society, more than 10 billion names have been preserved on microfilm—obtained from vital statistics, census materials, church records, and other official records. Each year, this extensive collection increases, and it is available to Mormons and non-Mormons alike for genealogical investigation.

Education. Because of Joseph Smith's revelation in 1833 that intelligence reflects the glory of God, Mormons place great stress on education. Mormons founded both the University of Utah (the oldest university west of the Mississippi) and Brigham Young University (the nation's largest church-related university, with over 35,000 students enrolled in 2007–2008). Utah leads the nation in literacy and in the percentage of enrolled college students and college graduates.[52]

Religion. A vigorous and systematic missionary program involves about 53,000 young missionaries, aged 19 to 26, in the field at any given time, fulfilling a cherished two-year assignment.[53] With 5.7 million U.S. members, the Church of Jesus Christ of Latter-Day Saints is the eighth-largest religious body in the United States, more than the combined membership of the Episcopal and Lutheran churches—two pillars of the U.S. religious establishment.[54] Another significant factor in the spectacular growth of the church is its members' practice of tithing—giving 10 percent of their gross income to the church. Income from tithing supports meeting house construction and maintenance, its educational system, religious institutes for students, missionary work, curriculum materials, and world relief efforts. Worldwide, Mormon membership is now over 13 million, and such remarkable growth means that U.S. residents account for less than half of this worldwide major faith.

Economics. Mormons take care of their own poor, without public-welfare assistance. Through a national exchange program to bishops' storehouses (resembling small supermarkets), the Mormon poor receive their needed foodstuffs. Other items—clothing, toiletries, and household items—are also available there, provided through monthly cash donations by other Mormons.

The Mormon Church, with assets exceeding $25 billion, generates an annual gross income of $5.9 billion from its investments and tithes from church members. That income goes toward massive foreign construction projects, charitable spending, and investments. Most of its investments go not into stocks or bonds but directly into church-run agribusiness, insurance, media, real estate, and retail-store companies. Deseret Management Corporation—the company through which the church holds almost all its commercial assets—has vast real estate holdings both in the United States and abroad, including skyscrapers in Salt Lake City and New York City. The church's Polynesian Cultural Center is Hawaii's foremost paid visitor attraction, with annual revenues of at least $40 million. In addition to 49 other farms and ranches, it owns and operates the top-grossing beef ranch in the world—the 312,000-acre Deseret Cattle & Citrus Ranch in Florida, with an estimated real-estate value of $858 million. Other commercial ventures include a television station, a chain of 30 bookstores in Utah, the Beneficial Life Insurance Company, AgReserves, Inc. (the largest producer of nuts in the United States), and Bonneville International Corporation (the country's 14th largest radio chain).[55]

Current Problem Areas

Although the Mormons incurred the wrath of many whites for their opposition to slavery in the 1840s, by the 1960s they were under attack for "racist" church doctrine. Blacks could become church members (as indeed some did throughout the 19th century), but they could not join the priesthood. Then, in June 1978, church president Spencer W. Kimball announced a divine revelation that blacks could become priests. Four other revelations—Brigham Young's guidance to Utah, Wilford Woodruff's instruction to end plural marriage, and two concerning life after death—have been reported since Joseph Smith's death. Widespread acceptance and adaptation quickly followed.

Although the church championed women's suffrage in the 19th century, it came under fire in recent years for being sexist. The church has always encouraged higher education for women and never prohibited them from working, but it did not permit them to become elders in the church leadership or to espouse feminist causes. Supporters maintain that women fill numerous positions in the church, such as the efforts of the Relief Society, teaching doctrinal study classes, directing choirs and dramatic productions, officiating in temple ceremonies, and serving at all levels on welfare committees. They also argue that the doctrine of the Church of Jesus Christ of Latter-Day Saints converges in some areas with ideals of feminism (e.g., as equality between men and women), but it is at odds

This peaceful setting of the Salt Lake City Temple reflected in the pool of Temple Square belies the controversy swirling over LDS church expansion to include Main Street Plaza between North and South Temple Streets. The Unitarian Church and American Civil Liberties Union are suing over free speech issues for public access and non-LDS use.

with versions of feminism that emphasize female sufficiency apart from men and the radical feminist critique of the family as an institution for the repression of women. Although some individual families may be repressive and dysfunctional, most Latter-Day Saints believe that the defect is not inherent in the structure. Indeed, they consider the family the source of both men's and women's greatest work and joy.[56]

Under the leadership of Gordon B. Hinckley, the church's president—and its current prophet—the Mormons have been downplaying their differences with mainstream Christianity. Beginning in 1982, editions of the *Book of Mormon* began carrying the subtitle "Another Testament of Jesus Christ." The official letterhead and Web site for the Church of Jesus Christ of Latter-Day Saints now have "Jesus Christ" in much larger letters. Officials now ask the media to use the term "the Church of Jesus Christ" instead of "the Mormon Church." As it continues to attract new members and achieve more mainstream acceptance, the Church of Jesus Christ also serves as a conservative repository of old-fashioned values and as a homegrown religion success story.

MUSLIM AMERICANS

Although Westerners may think of Islam (the religious faith of Muslims) as an Arab religion, most Muslims throughout the world are not Arabs. Indonesia contains the largest Muslim population (about 170 million). Other non-Arab countries with large Muslim populations include India (about 133 million), China (about 20 million), Malaysia (about 16 million), and Kazakhstan (about 7 million). Throughout the

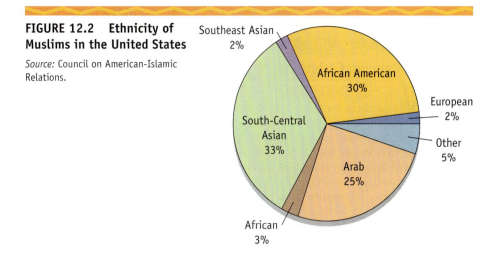

FIGURE 12.2   Ethnicity of Muslims in the United States

Source: Council on American-Islamic Relations.

many black African countries, Islam has millions of adherents. Worldwide, Islam embraces about 1.3 billion people, making it second only to Christianity in membership (see Figure 12.2 on the ethnicity of U.S. Muslims).

About 10 percent of the early Syrian immigrants to the United States were Muslims and Druze. After 1908, the Ottoman government began drafting Muslim Arabs into the Turkish army, and several thousand immigrated to the United States to escape military service. In 1916, a large group of Muslim Arabs settled in Dearborn, Michigan, to work at the nearby Ford Motor Company plant. That legacy continues today, as Dearborn still boasts the largest Muslim community in the United States.[57]

Because their numbers were relatively few and because few Muslim women came to the United States before World War II, only four mosques were built until that time. Without women, stable communities and institutions had little chance to develop.[58]

Since World War II, however (and especially after 1965) many Muslim immigrants from all parts of the world have come to the United States (see The Ethnic Experience box below). Over 1,200 mosques now dot the U.S. landscape, two-thirds of them built since 1981. Today, Muslim Americans number about 4.7 million, of whom about 1.8 million are black.[59]

Values and Practices

In Islamic belief, Muhammad was the greatest prophet, completing a line of prophets from Adam through Moses to Jesus. Islam, which translates to "submission to one all-powerful God," incorporates many of the beliefs and practices of the Jewish and Christian faiths. Muslims subscribe to a rigorous Holy Law, or Shari'ah, based on teachings from the *Quran* (Koran). They keep the Sabbath on Friday and do not eat pork or drink alcoholic beverages:

> The Shari'ah also requires all Muslims to fulfill the "five pillars of faith." The first pillar, the profession of faith, involves stating and believing the words "There is no God but the One God and Muhammed is His Messenger." The second pillar directs believers to bow in prayer toward the holy city of Mecca five

The Ethnic Experience

A Muslim among Christians

"When I was in high school, I was interested to know about the United States. There was an American Cultural Center in Kabul that offered a lot of books, magazines, and journals for the people of Afghanistan to study and learn about the United States. Also there had been shown films about the United States. I studied them and learned and knew about how the people lived and how they improved their country. I wished and I prayed that I could go there for my education and see this great country. But it was not to be for many years later when my family and I escaped from the communists and the United States took us in. . . .

"The culture is so very different in this country. When we first came here there were hardly any Muslims in Paterson and virtually no Afghans. We did not then have a mosque for worshiping or an Islamic religious community to offer us any spiritual support. As we struggled to improve our English and make some money not just for the basics of food, clothes, and rent, but also for a set of dishes, lamps, tables, and other housing needs, we had to sustain ourselves spiritually by ourselves, praying alone. Fortunately,

my brother and his family lived nearby (he was my sponsor), and our families got together once a week to pray.

"I must tell you, though, how wonderful this country is for people of different religions. Two Salesian Sisters befriended me just a few days after I arrived here. When they heard that I had a science background but had no job, they helped me find one teaching science in a Catholic school even though my English then was not as good as now. Here I was a new Muslim immigrant, teaching in an American Catholic school! The religious freedom and acceptance is one of the beautiful things I love about this country.

"There are many more Muslims here now and a half-dozen mosques in this area. I don't feel so alone any more in my faith; but you know, I was so accepted by the Christian people around me, I never found any negative attitudes. My new American friends helped me find a better life for myself and my wife and children, so we may have once been alone in our faith, but we never felt isolated from the Americans."

Source: Afghan refugee who came to the United States in 1980 at age 40. Taped interview from the collection of Vincent N. Parrillo.

times a day. According to the third, Muslims must give alms to the poor and needy. The fourth pillar requires fasting during the daylight hours throughout the holy month of Ramadan, the ninth month of the Muslim calendar, during which Muhammed received his first revelation from God. To fulfill the fifth pillar, Muslims must make a pilgrimage to Mecca at least once in their lifetime.[60]

To Muslims, religious beliefs and the social mores of public conduct and private experience are inseparable. Submission to the will of Allah means observing a prescribed code of conduct in every facet of life, including personal hygiene, similar in concept and practice to the Bengali, Gujarati, and Hindus. Muslims, for example, eat their food only with the right hand and clean their body after defecating only with the left hand. Thus, a reprehensible sight to them is to witness Westerners using their left hand to place food in their mouths.

Conservative in their values and attitudes, Muslims also reject the dominant U.S. group's preoccupation with materialism and their self-indulgent pleasures at the expense of obligations to family and community. Female immodesty, societal sexual permissiveness, pornography, high rates of alcohol and drug abuse, illegitimate births, abortions, and divorce all concern U.S. Muslims who are attempting to maintain the integrity of their way of life.

Muslims, of course, are but one of many conservative religious groups in the United States who nonetheless identify themselves as loyal Americans and as part of U.S. society. No one should confuse them with radical Muslims who pervert the teachings of the *Quran* to justify violence and killing.

Just as the past influx of Catholic and Jewish immigrants resulted in construction of many new churches and temples, so too has the arrival of hundreds of thousands of Muslims prompted the building of mosques in or near the new ethnic communities. This mosque in Toledo, Ohio, is one of over 2,000 non-Western temples and mosques throughout the United States.

Confronting Prejudice and Discrimination

You will recall from earlier chapters how French Americans in 1798 and German Americans during World War I faced overt prejudice, even violent acts of discrimination under the guise of patriotism. Following the terrorist attacks of September 11, 2001, Muslim Americans similarly faced hostility that unfortunately still continues. In 2007, the Center for American-Islamic Relations (CAIR) reported that the number of total reported incidents and experiences of anti-Muslim bias, discrimination, harassment, threats, physical attacks, and vandalism increased 25 percent from 1,972 cases in 2005 to 2,467 in 2006. The 167 Anti-Muslim hate crimes in 2006 was a nine percent increase from 2005.[61]

A 2007 Princeton Survey Research Associates public opinion poll revealed that 63 percent of Americans thought U.S. Muslims did not condone violence, while 19 percent thought they did, and 18 percent said they did not know. Respondents with a negative view were typically older, less educated, and conservative.[62] U.S. public views of Islam, despite the war in Iraq and the ongoing threat of terrorism at home, remains sharply divided. National polls consistently show about two in five Americans saying they have a favorable view of Islam, while another two in five Americans say they have an unfavorable view. Generally, those under age 30 tend to have a more favorable view, as do college students and graduates, while among religious groups, seculars express a favorable opinion by a 2-to-1 margin, in almost direct proportion to the opposite view held by white, evangelical Protestants.[63]

Several Muslim American nonprofit organizations actively work to promote understanding and counter the negative stereotyping, prejudice, and discrimination. Besides the aforementioned Council on American-Islamic Relations, the American Muslim Alliance is a political organization dedicated to involving Muslim Americans in the mainstream political process through such political empowerment efforts as coalition building, fielding Muslim candidates, and generating voter turnout.

THE AMISH

The Amish—like the Mennonites and the Hutterites—are a sect descended from the Swiss Anabaptists, who believe in voluntary adult baptism only, as practiced by the early Christians. Their founder, a Mennonite bishop named Jakob Ammann, began a sectarian movement when a schism arose in 1693 over enforcement of the still-practiced *Meidung,* or **shunning**—a powerful social control mechanism that enables the Amish to maintain their way of life.

When a bishop, acting on the near-unanimous vote of the congregation, imposes the *Meidung* on an errant member, others, including family members, cannot look upon, talk to, or associate with that person without also being placed under the ban. Informal sanctions such as ridicule and group disapproval, followed by a formal admonition from a clergy member, if necessary, precede such an action. Unusual but not altogether rare, the *Meidung* can also be revoked if the transgressor admits the error and personally asks the congregation for forgiveness.[64]

Although some Amish may have come earlier, their first documented arrival in America is 1727, when a few families left Switzerland and settled in Pennsylvania. Migration continued from this region and from Germany between 1727 and 1780, with large numbers of Alsatian and Bavarian Amish migrating between 1815 and 1840 and establishing communities in Ontario (Canada), Illinois, and Ohio.[65] With an intensive agricultural orientation, the Amish found the unlimited availability of land in the New World so attractive an inducement that they completely transplanted themselves to North America. Their subculture became extinct in Europe, as the Amish who remained there were absorbed into the dominant society.

Values, Symbols, and Practices

Forming *gemeinschaft* communities—intimate, homogeneous, and characterized by strong religious tradition—the Amish have remained remarkably constant in a continually modernizing dominant society. Their communities are highly integrated because their social institutions—family, school, church, and economic endeavors—are complementary and consistent in values and expectations. Young and old live similar lives. The entire group shares the same lifestyle and restrictions, accepting them as the will of God.

Pride is a major sin, so wearing jewelry—even wedding bands—and making other efforts at promoting physical attraction are forbidden; boasting is rare, and seeking a leadership role is frowned on. No Amish seeks political office and many do not register to vote. Here we must distinguish between the more conservative Old Order Amish—highly concentrated in Indiana, Ohio, and Pennsylvania—and the somewhat less conservative communities of the midwestern states. The latter tend to vote Republican and adamantly oppose farm subsidies, believing they would undermine their self-help social system.

Clothing is an important symbol of group identity that helps maintain separatism from outgroups and continuity within the community. In an unchanged, three-centuries-old tradition, the men wear low-crowned wide-brim hats; coats without collars, lapels, and pockets; and trousers with suspenders but without cuffs or creases. Belts and gloves are not permitted, even in cold weather. Women wear solid-color one-piece dresses, with long skirts and aprons, and keep their heads covered at all times, whether indoors or outdoors. Clothing thus expresses a common understanding among those sharing similar traditions and expectations. Other aspects of appearance—beards, but not mustaches, for all married men and a special braided hairstyle for females—further reinforce this orientation.

Language serves as another symbolic attribute of the *unser Satt Leit* (our sort of people). Pennsylvania Dutch is a German dialect resembling Palatine German folk speech and is common to all Amish, regardless of where they live. English is the group's second language, usually introduced to children when they enter school and learned without difficulty. High German is used exclusively for the preaching service and formal ceremonies; the families teach High German to their children so all can understand it when it is used in sermons and hymns.[66]

Amish farmers use teams of horses instead of tractors and gain an additional benefit from the natural supply of fertilizer. Amish homes may be lacking in modern conveniences, but they are clean, solid, kept in good repair, and, like the farms, well run:

> Newer Amish houses differ from the traditional variety in a number of ways. They tend to be smaller, and many do not have a "farmhouse" appearance at all. In fact, except for such items as no electrical wiring and the lack of curtains, they often look much like non-Amish houses. In the matter of modern appliances and equipment, the differences between "traditional" and "new" are even more significant.
>
> The Amish have never permitted their members to use electricity furnished by public power lines. The church has been unyielding on this point, and the prohibition has served to restrict the kinds of devices and appliances available to members. Over the years, however, the followers of Jacob Ammann have come up with some rather interesting alternatives: bottled gas, batteries, small generators, air pressure, gasoline motors, hydraulic power. The net result has been a variety of modern devices that have become available to the Amish, not only in their homes, but in their barns, workshops, stores, and offices. . . .
>
> Amish homes in the Lancaster area, furthermore, though surprisingly modern in certain respects, are without electricity. There are no light bulbs, illumination being provided by oil lamps or gas-pressured lanterns. And the list of prohibitions remains long: dishwashers, clothes dryers, microwaves, blenders, freezers, central heating, vacuum cleaners, air conditioning, power mowers, bicycles, toasters, hair dryers, radios, television—all are taboo.[67]

Several Amish congregations have accepted some elements of modern life. The Beachy Amish, founded by Amish bishop Moses M. Beachy in 1927, permit ownership of automobiles and certain other modern conveniences, and the

"New Amish" allow telephones, electricity, and tractors.[68] Even for some of the Old Order Amish, however, the modern world forces compromises. A combination of growing population and limited land availability oblige some to enter occupations other than farming. A half century ago, virtually all the Amish were farmers, but now less than half of them are. As they become business **entrepreneurs,** they adapt as they must yet strive to maintain their way of life.[69]

The Amish consider adolescence the most dangerous period of an individual's life. Because of physical and emotional changes and peer-group influence exceeding family control, adolescents strain for independence, to be free of Amish restraints. Interestingly, the Amish keep most of their young people willing to adopt the Amish way of life by first experiencing *rumspringa* ("running around"). They allow their youth to experiment with the larger world and its temptations: regular clothing, cell phones, movies, drinking, smoking, cruising in cars, dancing, flirting, drugs, and wild parties. The teens may "go away" on a Friday night and not return until Sunday evening. *Rumspringa* takes place while the youngsters live at home and carry on their ordinary work activities, on family farms or in factories. It is limited to their free times, in the evenings and weekends away from the Amish homes.[70]

However, exposure to high school worldliness is forbidden; formal education ends with the eighth grade, and teens receive vocational training at home thereafter. Because baptism does not occur until a person's late teens or early twenties, adults are more tolerant of discreet adolescent *rumspringa* activities, hoping that their teenagers will learn enough to give up worldly ways forever and become baptized in the Amish church or else remain in the outside world.

Clinging to their traditional values and lifestyle as a persistent subculture, the Amish continue to thrive both culturally and economically. One obvious sign of their contrast to modern society is a horse and buggy traveling down a roadway surrounded by diesel- and gas-driven vehicles, as here in Shipshewana, Indiana.

Most young people do return to Amish ways, get baptized, and assume adult responsibilities. About 20 percent of Amish youths may leave, often joining a more liberal Mennonite group, but only a very small percentage of baptized Amish ever leave.[71]

If an individual wishes to remain part of the community, the Amish insist on an endogamous marriage. The Amish do not practice birth control and so have a high birth rate, with average family of six to eight children. They have grown from 59,000 in 1970 to about 200,000 today.[72] Social class has no meaning to the Amish, and all share a strong sense of social obligation to one another. This includes helping others when disaster or tragedy strikes and providing home care rather than institutionalization for the aged.

Conflicts with Society

The Amish oppose social security and all other forms of insurance, believing the Christian brotherhood is responsible for its own people. Besides rejecting social security payments from the government, they refused to pay the mandatory self-employment social security tax. During years of conflict with the government over this issue, the government confiscated some Amish farms and horses to collect owed taxes. Finally, Amish leaders went to Washington, astounding the legislators by their request to be exempted from government benefits. Consequently, a law was passed, exempting them from both payments and benefits.

State laws making school attendance compulsory until age 16 provided another arena of conflict for the Amish with society. Because the Amish refused to send their children to high school, some were harassed and arrested by state officials. A Wisconsin case ultimately reached the U.S. Supreme Court, resulting in a ruling in favor of the Amish. For them, an eighth-grade education is sufficient, with farm vocational training occurring thereafter.

Under Amish tradition, youngsters work as apprentices after the eighth grade. For years, that didn't conflict with federal law because the Amish community's livelihood was rooted in agriculture, and farms are exempt from child-labor laws. With the growing costs of farming and land in the past decade, many families turned to woodworking and other trades, bringing them into conflict with these laws. Some businesses were fined thousands of dollars for employing youths, usually their own children. Claiming the laws threaten their religious and work values, the Amish sought an exemption. Finally, in 2004, President Bush signed legislation exempting the Amish from child-labor laws.[73]

Tourism annoys the Amish, especially in Lancaster County, Pennsylvania. About 5 million tourists visit Lancaster County each year, 350 visitors for every Amish individual. Ignoring Amish religious beliefs against having their pictures taken, camera-wielding tourists routinely take such pictures. Guided bus tours (as many as 50 a day) clog the narrow roads, block Amish vehicles, and park in front of the Amish schools and farms. Motels, restaurants, antiques, handicraft, and souvenir outlets, and many other commercial enterprises cover the region, generating hundreds of millions of dollars from tourists, of which only a small portion actually goes to the Amish.[74]

Despite these problems, the Amish thrive. Non-Amish neighbors and leaders praise their integrity, work ethic, and neighborliness. Their birth rate, ingroup solidarity, and resistance to outside influences suggest they will continue as a persistent subculture for many more years.

⬩ THE RASTAFARIANS

Rastafarians provide a contemporary example of a misunderstood religious minority group that frequently experiences prejudice and harassment. They fulfill the characteristics of a minority group: unequal treatment, easy identification, self-conscious identity, real or assumed common ancestry, and **endogamy**. Factors that direct attention to them are their skin color, distinctive hairstyling, and use of *ganja* (marijuana) for religious purposes, much as Navajos and Huicholes use peyote in their religion.

The Early Years

Marcus Garvey, Jamaican-born founder of the Back to Africa movement of the early 20th century, was influential in Jamaica before leaving the island for the United States in 1916. On his departure, he is supposed to have said, "Look to Africa, [where] a black king shall be crowned, for the day of deliverance is near." When Ras Tafari was crowned as Emperor Haile Selassie in 1930, in Ethiopia, he added the titles "King of Kings" and "Lion of the Tribe of Judah," placing himself in the legendary line of King Solomon. The coronation of the young Ethiopian emperor reminded Garvey's followers of his words and seemed to fulfill the biblical prophecy of Revelation 5:2–5:

> And I saw a mighty angel, who announced in a loud voice, "Who is worthy to break the seals and open the scroll?" But there was no one in heaven or on earth or in the world below who could open the scroll or look inside it. Then one of the elders said to me, "Don't cry. Look! The Lion from Judah's tribe, the great descendant of David, has won the victory, and he can break the seven seals and open the scroll."

Finding other corroborating scriptural passages (Revelation 19:16, Psalm 68:4, and Daniel 7:9 describing the king's hair as being "like pure wool"), the Rastas believed themselves to be the black Israelites of the Diaspora. Four ministers—Leonard Howell, Joseph Hibbert, Archibald Dunkley, and Robert Hinds—spread the message, attracting many followers. To black Jamaicans experiencing both economic frustration at the time of a worldwide depression and white colonial rule, the movement offered hope and the promise of a better day coming.[75]

Three major themes dominated the early phase of the Rastafarian movement: the innate wickedness of whites, the racial superiority of blacks, and the eventual revenge of blacks against whites by means of enslavement. Living at the bottom of the ladder in a highly stratified society, Jamaican blacks thus protested against white racism and economic exploitation through the Rastafarian movement. Since then, most Rastafarians have taken a more conciliatory stance toward whites, no longer condemning them en masse.[76]

Believing the colonial social institutions enchained them, the Rastas flouted the laws, denying the jurisdiction of the rulers. Since working for taxpayers or social institutions implied recognition and thus tacit approval of the existing social structure, the Rastas refused to do so. Instead, they eked out an existence off the land, living as squatters in temporary shacks. Because the Rastas were poor, these attitudes provided them with coping mechanisms while they awaited the end of their exile from Africa.

From Outcasts to Social Acceptance

The Rastas' rebelliousness, although passive, brought quick condemnation in the early years of the movement. Jamaican newspapers called the Rastas unpatriotic, despicable, *ganja*-smoking criminals. Some schools refused to admit their children, and the government disrupted their meetings, arrested members, and raided and burned their homes. Dominant-group persecution served only to unify the Rastafarians further. Finally, the Rastas invited the University of the West Indies (UWI) to conduct an impartial investigation of their movement. The UWI report rehabilitated their public image, and a new period of reciprocal cooperation began between the Rastas and the dominant society. A high point was reached on April 21, 1966, when Haile Selassie visited Jamaica and some Rastas were invited to the residence of the governor general for the first time to meet with the emperor in private. Each year, on that date, Rastafarians in Jamaica and the United States celebrate the event.

In the past few decades, Rastas have become more assimilated into the sociocultural milieu of the island society. Their expressive art forms have been featured in public exhibitions and at the annual National Festival; their imprint on Jamaican music, from ska to reggae, has been significant. Their widened appeal now includes numerous groups among the U.S. public as well in Jamaica. As a socially recognized group, Rastafarians in Jamaica also attract members from the middle and upper classes as well.

Dreadlocks hairstyling among Rastafarian men helps establish social distance, setting them apart from outgroup members while creating a recognizable ingroup bond. In contrast, their unique reggae music has attracted a large following among various age groups throughout most of U.S. society and other countries as well.

Values, Symbols, and Practices

Although some Rastafarians do not wear their hair long, most do so as a symbol of unity, power, freedom, and defiance to outgroups and in accordance with biblical custom.[77] Because they reject almost all chemically processed goods, Rastafarians do not use soap, shampoo, or combs. They are far from unsanitary, however, washing their hair and body in water and herbs very frequently. The hair grows long and is braided into dreadlocks.

Food is another symbol of religious identification. Rastafarians rarely eat meat, abhorring pork and favoring small fish and vegetables. They will not drink liquor, milk, or coffee, preferring instead herbal tea. No manufactured foods, salt, or processed shortening is used; natural foods and oil from dried coconut are the staples in *I-tal* food and cooking, the name signifying the Rastafarian diet.

Smoking *ganja* originally gave the Rastas *communitas*—a sense of cohesive unity. By producing an altered state of consciousness, they could gain temporary escape from their lives of hardship. Gradually, smoking *ganja* became identified with seeking communion with the supernatural, experiencing the self as God.[78]

The Rastafarians' language also symbolizes their philosophy and perception of reality. A form of Creole English, Rastafarian speech is almost devoid of subject–object opposition; *you* and *me* are almost never used, an *I and I* primary combination being used instead, even to outgroup members. Shedding the cognitive shell and asserting a new self-concept and worldview that they believe to be their natural, African state, Rastafarians use *I and I* to identify soulfully with others at a higher level than I–Thou or I–It relationships. *I and I* is a special communal term meaning "I and myself," "I and my brothers," or "I and God."[79]

Rastafarian Americans

Rastafarianism survives because of its adaptive capabilities. An existential interpretation of their doctrines has enabled the Rastas to adjust to industrialism and to U.S. society without sacrificing their naturist ethic. When increased numbers of Jamaicans migrated to the United States (over 485,000 since 1980), many Rastafarians were among them.

Mostly poor, unskilled workers, the Rastafarians tend to live in low-rent urban neighborhoods. Their cultural orientations isolate them from both white and black Americans, the social distance forging a small, cohesive subculture. Rastafarians frequently encounter problems with the police, their appearance and regular use of marijuana inviting harassment. Their ingroup solidarity, adaptability, and social distance from the dominant society make the Rastafarians likely to remain a persistent subculture, much as the Gypsies have been.

THE SANTERÍANS[80]

A fairly new religion in the United States is Santería or La Regla Lucumí, which originated in the region of West Africa now divided between Nigeria and Benin. Because it evolved from preliterate communal experiences of the Yoruba people into a traditional religion, the belief structure of Santería flows from an oral tradition. There is no written scripture or body of sacred texts.[81]

Santeros believe in one god known as Olorun or Olodumare. Olorun is the source of *ashé,* the spiritual energy that makes up the universe, all life, and all things material. Olorun interacts with the world and humankind through emissaries called *orishas.* The *orishas* rule over every force of nature (e.g., wind, water, storms, and forests) and every aspect of human life (e.g., love, illness, maternity, and fate). Fans of popular Latin jazz musicians Tito Puente, Celia Cruz, and Eddie Palureri know that some of their music mentions the *orishas.* Communication between *orishas* and humankind occurs through ritual, prayer, divination, and *ebó* or offerings (including sacrificial offerings). Song, rhythms, and trance possession are other means of interacting with the *orishas* and of learning how to develop deeper and fuller lives during one's stay in this world.[82]

From 1511 until the mid-19th century, about 702,000 African slaves were brought to Cuba, compared to about 427,000 African slaves brought to the United States.[83] Prohibited from practicing their religion openly in Cuba, the Yoruba hid much of their religion beneath a façade of their captors' and owners' Catholicism. Yoruba spirits, or *orishas,* received devotion through the iconography of Catholicism by being accorded dual identity with Catholic saints. The *orisha* Shangó (or Changó), for example—who represents the natural/cosmic forces of fire, thunder, and lightning and whose functions/power are passion, virility, and strength—became associated with St. Barbara, patron saint of artillery. Thus, the Yoruba people began to practice "Santería"—"the way of the saints." The memory of this subterfuge period of their religion's history is why many practitioners today consider the term *Santería* derogatory.[84]

Santería flourishes in Cuba today. Experts estimate that 70 percent of all Cubans practice Santería, whether through an occasional offering or rigorous practice. Critics say Castro quietly promoted the emergence of Santería by funding Santerían museums and trips for priests abroad to counter the Catholic Church's influence in Cuba. That helps build tourism even as it undercuts the Church's authority as the most powerful institution outside the state.[85]

Values, Symbols, and Practices

Santeros (male priests) and santeras (female priests) fiercely preserve the traditions of Santería; full knowledge of the rites, songs, and language are prerequisites to any deep involvement in the religion. Since *orishas* each have a distinctive *ashé* that humans need, a believer must give an *ebó* for that specific *orisha* to take and, through its magical powers, transform into the type of *ashé* necessary to achieve what the petitioner wants.[86] Specific colors, numbers, and natural objects are symbols associated with *orishas.* For example, red and white, the numbers 4 and 6, apples, bananas, roosters, and rams are attributes for Shangó.

Animal sacrifice is just one of many categories of *ebó* in the religion. Offerings such as *addimú* include candles, fruits, candy, or any number of items or actions that may be appreciated by the *orishas* in the religion. In divination (a basic Santería ritual), the *orishas* may ask (through the santero or santera) for a favorite fruit or dish, or they may call for the person to heed advice given. At times, they may demand that a person give up drinking or other practices that are unwise for that individual. They may request that a person wear certain jewelry, receive initiations, or perform any number of other actions. Or they may request sacrifice of an animal—usually a chicken or a dove—before coming to that person's aid. As a rule, animal sacrifice is called for only in major situations such as sickness or serious misfortune. And to critics who complain about these animal sacrifices, the santeros answer that the U.S. poultry industry kills more animals in one day than the religion has sacrificed worldwide in the last several hundred years.[87]

Trance possession is an important aspect of Santería. During a *bembé* or drumming party for the *orishas*, an *orisha* may be persuaded to join the party by entering the body of one of the participants. This is referred to as being "mounted" by the *orisha*, or the *orisha* is described as having "come down" from heaven to be with humans. When the songs, rhythms, and dances—deliberately calculated to entreat the *orishas* to come down—result in a trance possession, it is a time of great joy, as believers feel blessed by the spirits' counsel, cleansings, and sheer presence.

Santería in the United States

Because of the secrecy associated with Santería, no one knows exactly how many practitioners live in the United States, although estimates run as high as 500,000. The largest concentration, perhaps 300,000, lives in New York City. Another 70,000 may live in South Florida.[88] Their presence is partly evidenced by the many store-front *botanicas* in Miami and the Northeast providing Santería figures, incense, and herbs for the faithful. About a dozen Web sites also spread the word.

As Santería evolves from a black folk religion to an alternative type of Latin postmodernity, it is becoming more widespread across the United States, attracting many non-Cubans, both blacks and whites, and people from various social classes. This wider appeal and a declining reliance on the use of Spanish reduce the "ethnocentric, cliquish character" of this imported religion.[89] As it attracts more U.S. converts, its beliefs, rituals, and structure are changing. Santería is moving away from a mythological structure to a belief system incorporating some principles of psychology and Christian ethics. Initiation rituals now involve shorter periods of time (three months instead of three years), are open to all (not just to a select few who have been touched by an *orisha*), and consecrated bata drums are no longer necessary, either because of their unavailability or to avoid complaints from neighbors.[90] In urban areas with large Puerto Rican populations—such as New York City and northern New Jersey—Santería is blending with Puerto Rican spiritism to take on yet another new form.[91]

As Santería became more visible, local officials sought to ban its animal sacrifices. Animal-rights activists received a setback in 1993, however, when the U.S. Supreme Court ruled in *Lukumi Babalu Aye v. City of Hialeah* that a Florida city could not outlaw the ritual animal sacrifices of Santería. Although the basis for the decision was that the ordinances prohibiting animal sacrifice specifically targeted religion in a constitutionally impermissible manner, the Court left open the possibility that a neutrally framed, generally applicable local or state statute forbidding cruelty toward animals might pass constitutional muster and be applied to prevent the ritual sacrifices of chickens, goats, and other animals to the Santería *orisha*. Since that ruling, local challenges to the ritual sacrifices have continued, including in Dallas, Texas, and Coral Gables, Florida suburbs in 2007.[92]

HINDU AMERICANS

Most people outside India think of Hinduism as a religion, but more accurately, it reflects a whole set of practices and a range of philosophical and metaphilosophical concepts called *Santana Dharma* (which roughly translates to "everlasting religion"). Unlike most Western religions, Hinduism does not have a single founder, a specific theological system, a single system of morality, or a religious organization. Its roots are traceable to the Indus Valley civilization circa 4000 to 2200 BCE.[93] Over thousands of years, numerous cultural and military invasions shaped its development. Most influential was the arrival in northern India (circa 1500 to 500 BCE) of Indo-Europeans from the steppes of Russia and Central Asia, who brought with them the religion of Vedism. These beliefs became mixed with the indigenous Indian native beliefs. Since then, Hinduism has grown to become the world's third largest religion, claiming over 837 million believers, or 13 percent of the world's population.[94] It is the dominant religion in India and has many adherents in Malaysia and Sri Lanka.

The most important of all Hindu texts is the *Bhagavad Gita,* a poem describing a conversation between a warrior Arjuna and his charioteer Krishna. Vedism survives in the *Rigveda,* a collection of more than 1,000 hymns. Other sacred texts include the *Brahmanas,* the *Sutras,* and the *Aranyakas.*[95] Because Hinduism is not a religion in the strict sense, it does not have converts; one can be a Catholic, Jew, Muslim, or Protestant and still practice Hinduism.

Values, Symbols, and Practices

At the heart of Hinduism is the monotheistic principle of Brahman, that all reality is a unity; the entire universe is one divine entity. Hindus visualize that deity as a triad consisting of Brahman, the Creator, who continually creates new realities; Vishnu, the Preserver, who sustains these new creations by traveling from heaven to earth in 1 of 10 incarnations whenever dharma (eternal order, righteousness, religion, law, and duty) is threatened; and Shiva, the Destroyer, who is at times compassionate, erotic, and destructive.

Cattle slaughter is a sacrilege, as Hindus revere the cow as a mother to all humankind for the nourishing milk it provides. The origins of this value orientation probably rest on a largely agrarian Indian society that depended on the cow for milk, for carting, and even for the practical use of cow dung as a fertilizer, a disinfectant, and a fuel. Hindus are not necessarily vegetarians, however; most, in fact, eat meat other than beef.

The *Rigveda* defined five social castes. Normally, people were assigned to the same caste as their parents, and marriages occurred within the same caste. Caste determined the range of possible jobs or professional choices a person could decide among. In decreasing status, the five castes are Brahmins (the priests and academics), Kshatriyas (the military), Vaishyas (farmers and merchants), Sudras (peasants and servants), and Harijan (the outcasts, commonly known as the untouchables). Although India formally abolished the caste system in 1949, it remains a significant force, particularly in southern India.

Hindus believe in transmigration of the soul, resulting in reincarnation. They perceive humans as being trapped in *samsara,* a meaningless cycle of birth, life, death, and rebirth. *Karma* is the accumulated sum of one's good and bad deeds, which determines how you will live your next life. Through dedication to pure acts, thoughts, and devotion, one can be reborn at a higher level. Eventually, one can escape *samsara* and achieve enlightenment. Conversely, bad deeds can cause a person to be reborn at a lower level or even as an animal. Hindus thus accept society's unequal distribution of wealth, prestige, and suffering as natural and just consequences for people's previous acts, both in this life and in previous lives. Meditation, particularly yoga, is a common practice. Other activities may include daily devotions, public rituals, and the ceremonial dinner, *puja.*

Just as wearing a cross (for Christians) or a Star of David (for Jews) is an identifying symbol of one's faith, wearing a *pottu* (a dot on the forehead) is an ethnoreligious symbol for Hindus. An unmarried female wears a black dot, and a married woman a red one. The *pottu,* also called a *bindi,* symbolizes the third eye mentioned in Hindu scriptures. These teach that the ultimate end of human life is liberation (*moksha*) from the finite human consciousness in which we see all things as separate from one another and not as part of a whole. When a higher consciousness dawns on us, we see the individual parts of the universe as deriving their true significance from the central unity of spirit. The Hindu scriptures call the beginning of this experience the second birth, or the opening of the third eye or the eye of wisdom.[96]

About 80 percent of Hindus are Vaishnavites, who worship Lord Vishnu. Others follow various reform movements or neo-Hindu sects. Various sects of Hinduism have evolved into separate religious movements, including Hare Krishna, Sikhism, Jainism, and Theosophy. Two recent popular variations in the Western world—Transcendental Meditation and the New Age movement—both use Hindu techniques and concepts.[97]

Hinduism in the United States

Over 1.1 million Hindu Americans live in the United States.[98] Most of that number consists of Asian Indian immigrants arriving since 1965 and their descendants. Their greatest concentrations are in the New York–New Jersey metropolitan area, California, Illinois, Texas, Pennsylvania, Michigan, Maryland, and Ohio.

In a recent study of first- and second-generation Hindu Americans, Amber Oliver found that all the parents—who immigrated between 1965 and 1981—wanted their children to learn about Hinduism for its values and beliefs. Only 25 percent, however, felt strongly about their children performing traditional Hindu rituals, and most were receptive to the idea of their children marrying a non-Hindu. Three-fourths of their children, whose average age was 22, said they were raised in a traditional Hindu way but had moved away from those traditional aspects of Hinduism, instead placing more emphasis on Hindu values in their day-to-day lives, independently of whether their parents strictly observed Hindu practices. Even though 60 percent of the children said they would willingly marry a non-Hindu for love, all said that they wanted their children to learn about Hinduism—either to continue the tradition or to have a basis for deciding about incorporating Hinduism into their daily lives.[99]

Oliver also found that many of the children believed that their parents had not "vigorously" incorporated Hinduism into their lives because they had chosen to reside in the United States and not in India. She suggests that this contention may account for the widespread view among second-generation Hindu Americans of Hinduism as a social religion and not a religion requiring rituals and practices. About 80 percent of the children envisioned Hinduism undergoing great change in the next 50 years, including a decline in its prevalence among future generations. However, children who do incorporate some aspect of traditional Hinduism in their lives appear less pessimistic about the future of Hinduism in the United States. Similarly, the practicing parents view Hinduism as a progressing and living religion, which will change but not be lost. In fact, the parents almost unanimously spoke of Hinduism as becoming more attractive as a religion to future generations through its various changes.[100]

RELIGION AND U.S. SOCIETY

Religion is an important aspect of U.S. culture. In a 2007 Gallup poll, 86 percent of U.S. residents said they believe in God; 59 percent said religion was "very important" in their lives in a CBS News Poll. Such responses have been fairly consistent for decades and are two to three times higher than in other Western nations.[101] About half of the population of the United States belongs to a church or synagogue (Figure 12.3). Although 42 percent attendance at weekly worship

FIGURE 12.3   Vital Signs of Religion in the United States, 2007

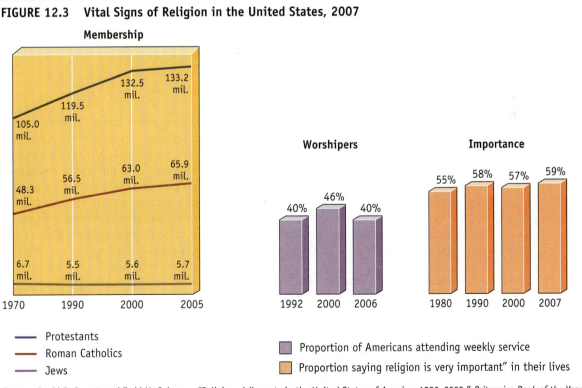

Sources: David B. Barrett and Todd M. Johnson, "Religious Adherents in the United States of America, 1900–2005," *Britannica Book of the Year 2007* (Chicago: Encyclopaedia Britannica, 2007); CBS News Polls, "For Almost All Americans, There Is God," Accessed at www.cbsnews.com/stories/2006/04/13/opinion/polls/main1498219.shtml, July 27, 2007.

service may appear low, it is by far the highest of all developed countries; for example, only 20 percent of Canadians and 7.5 percent of the British attend church weekly.[102]

Undoubtedly, some Americans use religion for social rather than religious purposes, finding in their church a source of community and a reaffirmation of the values of humanitarianism, work, individualism, and group conformity. Nevertheless, religiosity is an important element in society. In a national comparative study, George Yancey found that religiosity was highest among African Americans in comparison to Asian Americans, Hispanic Americans, and European Americans. This higher religiosity was not merely the result of cross-racial economic differences or racial oppression, but also due to specific cultural elements within the African-American community.[103]

As we mentioned earlier, much religious diversity exists in the United States. Even Catholicism and Protestantism have great diversity within their churches; they are not the monolithic entities some assume them to be. The ethnic diversity of subgroups of the Catholic Church—French, German, Haitian, Hispanic, Irish, Italian, and Polish, to name but a few—promotes varying forms of religious behavior among these subgroups.[104] The Irish—as ethnic Italians and Poles have long recognized—dominate Catholicism in the United States. At present, Irish Americans represent less than 15 percent of the Catholic population but about half of the U.S. bishops. Protestants range from the more liberal Congregationalists and Episcopalians with their formal religious ceremonies to the more conservative American Lutherans and American Baptists with their less elaborate worship services. The Assemblies of God and Jehovah's Witnesses are but two of the many different Protestant faiths, as are such fundamentalists as the Missouri Synod Lutherans and Southern Baptists, with their strict interpretations of the Bible.

Civil Religion

Sociologist Robert Bellah suggested that the United States has a **"civil religion,"** a shared belief system incorporating all religious elements into a sanctification and celebration of the American way of life.[105] Since the 1950s, our Pledge of Allegiance has identified us as a nation "under God." All our coins and paper money declare "In God We Trust." Congress begins each session with a prayer; presidents regularly schedule prayer breakfasts with government leaders, and they mention God in almost all their state of the union and inaugural addresses. Religion is an important element in oaths of office, in courtroom procedures, and on most formal public occasions. The Boy Scouts and Girl Scouts both emphasize "God and Country" in their philosophies and oaths/promises and in various awards and badges. The list is virtually endless.

Current Controversies

The U.S. Supreme Court often issues controversial decisions interpreting the First Amendment's stipulation about the separation of church and state. In its efforts to avoid any appearance of an "establishment of religion," the court has sometimes outraged religious advocates of particular moral issues. From a religious perspective, its most controversial decisions have been those banning prayer in public schools and permitting abortion in the first two trimesters of pregnancy. Other decisions—for example, upholding the Amish exemption from compulsory-education laws and allowing certain forms of federal assistance to parochial schools (lunches, books)—encourage certain religious activities while striving to maintain First Amendment principles.

School prayer and abortion continue to be controversial issues. Proposed constitutional amendments have lacked sufficient support for adoption, but religious groups persist in their efforts. Catholics, Mormons, Lutherans, Baptists, and other conservative sects and denominations have combined their efforts to overturn the abortion ruling through lobbying and support of sympathetic legislators. School prayer does not generate the same degree of emotion, but it too unites people of different faiths to effect a change. Opposing them are strict constitutionalists, secularists, and people of more liberal religious persuasions.

Creationists' support for a literal interpretation of the Bible puts them in conflict with an array of scientific theories with implications of a non-Biblical origin of the world. These include Big Bang theory, the red shift, isotope decay and carbon dating, plate tectonics, stratigraphy, and evolutionary theory. In recent years, creationists have been crusading for "balanced treatment" about the origins of life. Objecting in particular to textbooks and curriculums on the subject of evolution, Christian fundamentalists insist that the book of Genesis be included as well. Arkansas, Louisiana, and Mississippi passed legislation requiring such an approach, and 18 other states were considering similar laws when a federal district court in early 1982 struck down the Arkansas law as a violation of the First Amendment. Since then, creationists have continued their battle against the orthodox sciences and the courts continue to rule that mandated creationist teaching in the schools is unconstitutional.

RELIGIOUS ASSIMILATION

The assimilation of religious minority groups in the United States depends heavily on prevailing societal attitudes, degree of dissimilarity, and length of residence. For example, in the 17th and 18th centuries, this was mostly a Protestant land. Even so, the social distance among the various sects and denominations was significant. The religious intolerance of the 17th century, for example, continued persecution of Baptists in New England and then yielded by the 18th century to greater tolerance among the various Protestant faiths. However, most continued to look on one another with disdain. One common ground did unite them: their dislike of Catholics, whose assimilation was then considered impossible.

Extensive Catholic immigration in the 19th century, as discussed earlier, sounded alarm bells in Protestant America. Jewish immigration, particularly in the second half of the century, added to nativist concerns. As the multigenerational assimilation process brought the once-contentious Protestant sects and denominations into a shared mainstream, Catholic and Jewish Americans remained on the periphery well into the 20th century. As white ethnics, the ethnolinguistic cultural marks of these white ethnics disappeared and so too did the social distance between them and Protestant Americans. Today, some religious bias still remains with pockets of bigotry and sporadic bias incidents, but few would argue that Catholic and Jewish Americans continue to live outside the societal mainstream. Similarly, Mormons easily function within the societal mainstream and Amish traditions may keep them a persistent subculture, but others nevertheless accept them fully as a distinct part of U.S. society.

On the edge of the mainstream today are other religious minorities, primarily consisting of first- and second-generation Americans of non-Western faiths. They therefore face more than just the difficulties of adjustment and acceptance all foreigners face. Representing cultures and faiths outside the Judeo-Christian mainstream of most black and white Americans, they will probably not experience complete assimilation for at least several generations.

For that to occur, three steps are necessary. First (and easiest through the generations), Americanization must significantly reduce the ethnolinguistic marks that make them a visible minority. As with past religious minorities in other convergent subcultures, this is a normal process. Second, just as the United States went from a single melting pot for Protestants into a triple melting pot to absorb Catholics and Jews before changing again into a single melting pot, we will again need to expand our melting-pot concept into a society of more than three major faiths. Third, because many of these religious adherents are people of color, we need to eliminate the racial barrier in our melting-pot concept.

Perhaps one aftermath of the 9/11 terrorist attacks and subsequent terrorist actions by radical Muslims may be an accelerated assimilation process among Muslim Americans. That's what happened following the tragic, wrongful internment of 110,000 Japanese Americans in 1942 and with German Americans during World War I. So too may the desire of Muslim Americans to dissociate from Islamic terrorists and be identified as "Americans" speed up their social integration into the fabric of U.S. society. Even as they struggle for full integration into U.S. society, Muslim Americans are already a socioeconomic success story. They are the "most affluent, integrated, politically engaged Muslim community in the Western world."[106] A major 2007 study by the Pew Research Center revealed that their income and educational levels are about the same as native-born Americans and that an overwhelming number (71 percent) believed that one can get ahead in America with hard work.[107]

SOCIOLOGICAL ANALYSIS

Each of our three theoretical frameworks provides a means of understanding the significance of religion in intergroup relations and within the activities of convergent and persistent subcultures. Although different in emphasis, these perspectives offer unifying themes about religious pluralism in the United States.

The Functionalist View

In *The Elementary Forms of Religious Life* (1912), Émile Durkheim identified religion as an integrative bond for society, a theme elaborated on by modern functionalists. Religion, they maintain, serves as social "cement," uniting people with shared values and beliefs to celebrate harvests and life-cycle events. Religion gives meaning and purpose to people's lives, offering emotional and psychological support to individuals in both good and bad times. Religious teachings also help maintain social control, reinforcing important values and norms and providing moral standards.

Each of the groups discussed in this chapter—Catholics, Jews, Muslims, Mormons, Amish, Rastafarians, Santeríans, and Hindus—used their religious bonds as a means of strengthening their resolve and identity in a pluralistic and sometimes harsh society. Catholic and Jewish immigrants usually lived in ethnic neighborhoods with their church or synagogue as the focal point of their community activities, easing their transition to the U.S. lifestyle. Experiencing acts of hostility, Mormons and Rastafarians (and often Catholics and Jews) drew closer to other ingroup members and sustained hope through their faith. Mormons, Muslims, and Rastafarians, in particular, function in the secular world but maintain their sense of identity and purpose through adherence to specific religious tenets. Because of their strong religious convictions, the Amish and the Hasidic Jews remain constant in their ways despite the changing world around them.

As separatist minorities, the Amish and Hasidim developed economic and social interaction patterns that intensified their values and beliefs. All aspects of their daily lives have functioned together in harmony, eliminating stress and conflict between religion and daily living. Amish institutionalization of adolescent rebelliousness operates as a safety release for otherwise strict communes. The socialization efforts by Amish, Catholics, Hindus, Jews, Mormons, and Muslims of children and youths, although varying greatly in approach and intensity, serve to transmit and sustain over generations a continuing social system organized around specific religious beliefs and practices. Language, symbols, and rituals further instill a shared religious identity and social bond.

The Conflict View

Karl Marx and later conflict theorists considered religion a social control mechanism designed to protect the interests of those in power. The dominant religion of a society represents the ruling economic and political class, and it legitimizes the existing social structure, blunting people's frustration, anger, and pain with the promise of an afterlife reward. Religion can be a divisive factor, breeding dissension and violence, though conflict theorists suggest that the real reasons behind such upheavals are economic and political. What appears to be religious bigotry or fanaticism is usually a struggle for power and control disguised as a religious matter. Even the participants may be unaware of the reality of the situation, caught up as they are in the religious justification given for the conflict.

Notice how nativist alarm over mid-19th-century Catholic immigrants centered on their perceived growing political strength; fears of papal rule of the United States were very real then. Loss of political control still haunted Protestant Americans 30 years later. The American Protective Association even dedicated itself to keeping Catholics out of office. Problems arose for Rastafarians in Jamaica because they challenged the political status quo, and the Mormons in Illinois and Missouri made enemies because of their political strength in those states. The Amish, on the other hand, sought no political leadership or economic dominance and so encountered little hostility for those reasons.

Economic competition did create religious antagonism against Catholics and Jews. The rebelliousness of striking Irish laborers against mine and factory owners sparked anti-Catholic reactions, as did the recessions in the 1870s and 1890s, causing workers to fear that Catholics would take away their jobs. Similarly, rapid upward mobility among Jewish Americans ignited fears of their dominance, resulting in unflattering Shylock stereotyping and exclusion from organizations and establishments of affluent Christians. Such actions support conflict-theory argument that the roots of religious confrontation, whether peaceful or violent, actually lie in political and economic distributions of resources.

The Interactionist View

Appearance is a key element in perceptions of those of different religions. Away from their worship services, most U.S. residents offer few clues about their religious preference; some do, however. When an outsider sees a physically distinct believer—a Hasidic Jew, a Hare Krishna follower, an Amish person, a Rastafarian, or a devout Muslim, for instance—the dissimilarities announce a social distance and tend to reduce the chances of close interactions. Those physical clues may even foster negative responses. Conversely, outward appearance becomes a source of comfort and reinforced religious identity to a fellow believer. The wearing of religious symbols—perhaps ashes or a dot on one's forehead or a cross or a Star of David on a necklace—also may induce positive or negative reactions.

Self-identity emerges out of the orderliness of day-to-day accomplishments of individuals interacting face to face, interpreting and reinterpreting their ways of doing things. Under insulated conditions, these shared definitions become more solidified, and the group members grow into a more cohesive unit. Amish and Hasidic Jews living in their separate communities, and the Mormons in the Utah Territory succeeded in developing their own social systems encompassing all aspects of daily life, thereby reinforcing the precepts of their religious beliefs. Rastafarians, in rejecting the dominant economic system and language syntax, created a symbolic world so differentiated from the dominant society that their everyday interrelationships with one another reinforced their group solidarity. Even Catholics and Jews, as well as the Mormons of modern times, benefit from such cooperative interpretation with one another because studies show each tends to interact in primary-group relations outside religious settings with members of the same faith.[108] For members of all faiths, the religious bond serves both to unite and insulate; it is preserved and maintained through daily interactions with like-minded individuals.

Societal labeling of dissimilar religious minorities often results in negative attitudes and actions toward them, with an avoidance response promoting subcultural insularity. If Catholics are attacked as "docile and superstitious," Jews as "mercenary," Mormons as "chauvinistic," Amish as "backward," Rastafarians as "potheads," and Santeríans as "weird," group members are likely to turn inward to achieve the sense of personal worth denied them in the outside world.

RETROSPECT

Founded on the principle of religious freedom, the United States became a place of refuge for people of many faiths. Yet religious tolerance has not always prevailed; some groups have been harassed both verbally and physically as they have sought the right to follow their beliefs.

Throughout much of the nation's history, Catholics have been vilified and abused. Anti-Catholic actions included colonial statutes against their political participation, vicious pamphlets and books, hostile political party platforms, Know-Nothing and Ku Klux Klan demonstrations and violence, and American Protective Association activities. Proposed aid to parochial schools remains controversial, as do Catholic positions on abortion, birth control, and nuclear arms. Catholics today are the largest single religious denomination in the country.

Jewish Americans encountered many of the same problems as Catholics, often from the same nativist groups. Overt anti-Semitic stereotyping and actions continued well into the 20th century. Upward mobility occurred more quickly for Jews than for most other immigrants because more of them entered the United States as skilled workers with families intact, and their religious emphasis on learning encouraged secular education and entry into better-paying jobs. A high intermarriage rate—a cause for concern among many Jewish leaders—is seen by others as irrelevant to continued vitality in the Jewish community.

The Latter-Day Saints (Mormons), a persecuted minority expelled from several states, grew into a large, successful, and respectable church. Their emphasis on family and education earns the Mormons high praise, as do their economic investments and assistance to their poor. Although criticisms directed toward plural marriages and perceived racism have ended through changes in church doctrine, charges of sexism remain, though most Mormon women appear satisfied with their role in the church.

U.S. Muslims are growing in number, and mosques are now common throughout the United States. Many of their conservative views parallel those of members of the Catholic and Mormon faiths, and they face enormous difficulty in dissociating themselves from Islamic terrorists. The Amish are a good example of a persistent subculture, and they remain a vibrant and growing community. Rastafarians, Santeríans, and Hindus are becoming more numerous in the United States because of immigration, and each group's religious practices have brought the nation greater cultural diversity.

Today, religion remains an important aspect of culture in the United States, as indicated by public-opinion polls and church attendance. A civil religion arguably exists, and religion-based controversies over abortion, school prayer, and the teaching of evolutionary theory continue.

Functionalists stress the integrative aspects of religion, while conflict theorists focus on economic and political power struggles as the basis for religious conflict. Interactionists examine how social interpretations foster ingroup solidarity and outgroup acceptance or hostility.

KEY TERMS

Celibacy	Endogamy	Polygyny
Civil religion	Entrepreneurs	Shunning
Ecumenical movement	Nondenominational	Social ostracism

DISCUSSION QUESTIONS

1. How did the past experience of Catholic Americans match the experiences of members of many immigrant nationality groups?

2. Apply the concepts of prejudice, stereotyping, marginality, and xenophobia to the Jewish experience in the United States.

3. Discuss the similarity–attraction bond in the societal response to the Mormons.

4. What similarities and differences can be found between Islam and other major religions in the United States?

5. How do the Amish illustrate a persistent subculture?

6. Discuss the similarity–attraction bond in the societal response to the Rastafarians.

7. What unique features of the Santería religion attract followers and upset municipal officials?

8. What unique features of Hinduism allow its followers to adapt to U.S. society?

9. Discuss the role of religion in present-day U.S. culture.

10. How do the three sociological perspectives help us to understand religion?

SUGGESTED READINGS

Diner, Hasia R. *A New Promised Land: A History of Jews in America*. New York: Oxford University Press, 2004.
Offers an excellent insight into the history and evolution of Jewish American immigration, institutions, and contemporary issues.

Gaustad, Edwin S., Philip L. Barlow, and Richard W. Dishno. *New Historical Atlas of Religion in America*, 3rd ed. New York: Oxford University Press, 2000.
Excellent maps and eloquent text make this one of the best resources on the growth or shrinkage and clustering of all religions in America.

Jenkins, Philip. *The New Anti-Catholicism: The Last Acceptable Prejudice*. New York: Oxford University Press, 2003.
Recaps the history of American anti-Catholicism, then draws attention to prevalent bias today in academia, the media, and pubic discourse.

Miller, Donald E. *Reinventing American Protestantism: Christianity in the New Millennium*. Berkeley: University of California Press, 2000.
An engaging, insightful discussion of the recent trend toward nondenominational churches, leading to what the author calls a "second Reformation."

Prell, Riv-Ellen. *Fighting to Become Americans: Jews, Gender, and the Anxiety of Assimilation*. Boston: Beacon Press, 2000.
A sociohistorical analysis of the evolution of gender stereotypes among Jews, and their relevance as to how men and women, Jews and gentiles, perceive one another.

Shachtman, Tom. *Rumspringa: To Be or Not Be Amish*. New York: North Point Press, 2007.
A fascinating look at the Amish youth culture, with vivid portraits of teens and their parents as they work through experimentation to make a life decision.

Schaefer, Richard T. and William W. Zellman. *Extraordinary Groups: An Examination of Unconventional Life-Styles*, 8th ed. New York: Worth, 2008.
A fine sociological portrait of the Amish, Christian Scientists, Hasidim, Mormons, Jehovah's Witnesses, and other groups.

Viswanathan, Ed. *Am I a Hindu?/The Hinduism Primer*. Columbia, MO: South Asia Books, 1996.
A comprehensive profile of Hinduism within the broader context of other world religions, offering clear insights into Hindu beliefs, ideals, and values.

MySocKit

Additional resources for this chapter can be found in MySocKit. If you have a subscription to MySocKit, go to www.mysockit.com to study, review, and go beyond the book to learn more about race and ethnic relations.

Women as a Minority Group

Sexism is an ideology, or set of generalized beliefs, that one gender is superior to the other. For centuries, the presumption of male superiority led to patterns of prejudice and discrimination against women, and many of those patterns persist. Only in recent decades has the problem of sexism become widely understood and treated as a matter of public concern. Previously, women had been subordinate to men in virtually all societies throughout history. Aristotle, for example, thought men were active by nature and women passive, making women intellectually and morally inferior to men.[1] In 1879, Gustav LeBon, a founder of social psychology, made the following observation:

> In the most intelligent races, as among the Parisians, there are a large number of women whose brains are closer in size to those of gorillas than to the most developed male brains. This inferiority is so obvious that no one can contest it for a moment; only its degree is worth discussion. All psychologists who have studied the intelligence of women, as well as poets and novelists, recognize today that they represent the most inferior forms of human evolution and that they are closer to children and savages than to an adult, civilized man. They excel in fickleness, inconstancy, absence of thought and logic, and incapacity to reason. Without doubt there exist some distinguished women, very superior to an average man, but they are as exceptional as the birth of any monstrosity, as, for example, of a gorilla with two heads; consequently, we may neglect them entirely.[2]

In the 20th century, Sigmund Freud advanced notions that sexual differences affected behavior. He believed that the fact that males have a penis made them more aggressive, whereas "penis envy" made females feel shame and a sense of inferiority. Erik Erikson suggested that male genitalia influenced boys to be questing, aggressive, and outward-thrusting and that female genitalia directed girls to be concerned about boundaries, limits, and "interiors." Subsequent cross-cultural studies disproved such claims, instead demonstrating how the socialization process and societal expectations of men and women produce variances in gender-role norms and behavior.

Not everyone had been blind to the effects of male domination. In an appendix to his classic and influential analysis of black–white relations, *An American Dilemma* (1944), Gunnar Myrdal noted a parallel between the position of women and blacks in U.S. society.[3] In fact, he observed, the legal position of women and children as falling under the control of the male head of the household had supplied the basis for the legal position of black servants in the 17th century. In 1951, sociologist Helen Hacker identified major areas of sexual discrimination in U.S. society and described women as marginal in a masculine society.[4] Not until the 1960s, however, did the feminist movement make any headway, launched in part by Betty Friedan's consciousness-raising book *The Feminine Mystique* (1963).[5]

As public awareness of women as an oppressed group increased, the parallels of their status to that of racial and ethnic groups became more obvious. For example, the minority-group characteristics discussed in Chapter 1 clearly apply to women, too. Women are born into their sexual identity (**ascribed status**), and most are easily identifiable by physical and cultural characteristics. In addition, women now recognize their commonality with one another as victims of an ideology (sexism) that, like racism, attempted to justify their unequal treatment.

Yet another characteristic, the minority-group practice of **endogamy**, may seem inapplicable, but in marriage, the domination–subordination lines are also manifest. Traditional marriage ceremonies provide for the man to cherish his wife while she promises to obey her husband, and when the traditional ceremony ends, they are pronounced not "husband and wife," but "man and wife," grafting the woman's identity and maiden name onto her relationship to her husband. For many decades, property laws, credit regulations, social security benefits, divorce laws, and even telephone listings reinforced this less than equal status until recent changes occurred in most of these areas.

SOCIOHISTORICAL PERSPECTIVE

Early colonists in the New World, re-creating in miniature the social systems of their homelands, continued male-dominance patterns. In settlements and on the advancing frontier, women were valuable "commodities," both for their skills and labor in the battle for survival and as sexual property in a region with a shortage of women. Although some instances of female independence in land ownership, inheritance, and voting rights did arise in those early years, for the most part, women remained subordinate to men, with few legal rights except as appendages to their husbands (see The Gender Experience box, page 471). The U.S. Constitution did not give voting rights to women until ratification of the Nineteenth Amendment in 1920, and the courts did not interpret its other provisions regarding full and equal participation as applying to women until many decades later.[6]

The status and power of Native American women varied considerably from one tribe to another, depending on cultural orientations and patrilineal or matrilineal structure. In **matrilineal** and **matrilocal** societies, women had considerable power because property (housing, land, tools) belonged to them and passed from mother to daughter. Because the husband joined his wife's family, he was more of a stranger, yielding authority to his wife's eldest brother, and thus was unlikely to become an authoritative, domineering figure. Among such peoples as the Cherokee, Iroquois, Pueblo, and Navajo, a disgruntled wife could divorce

The Gender Experience

An Early Plea for Equal Rights

"I long to hear that you have declared an independency—and by the way in the new Code of Laws which I suppose it will be necessary for you to make I desire you would Remember the Ladies, and be more generous and favorable to them than your ancestors. Do not put such unlimited power into the hands of the Husbands. Remember all men would be tyrants if they could. If particular care and attention is not paid to the Ladies we are determined to foment a Rebellion, and will not hold ourselves bound by any Laws in which we have no voice, or Representation.

"That your Sex are Naturally Tyrannical is a Truth so thoroughly established as to admit of no dispute, but such of you as wish to be happy willingly give up the harsh title of Master for the more tender and endearing one of Friend. Why then, not put it out of the power of the vicious and the Lawless to use us with cruelty and indignity with impunity. Men of Sense in all Ages abhor those customs which treat us only as the vassals of your Sex. Regard us then as Beings placed by Providence under your protection and in imitation of the Supreme Being make use of that power only for our happiness."

Source: Letter from Abigail Adams to John Adams, March 31, 1776. Retrieved December 15, 2007. [www.teachingamericanhistory.org/library/index.asp?document=63]

her husband simply by tossing his belongings out of their residence. Also, in matrilineal societies such as the Iroquois, women were influential in tribal governance because principal civil and religious offices were kept within matrilineal lineages. If the actions of a tribal delegate displeased the women, they removed him from office.[7]

Restrictions on Women

As the United States grew and prospered—and as the Industrial Revolution changed the very nature of society—a dichotomy emerged in the roles of women. Poor women, mostly from immigrant families, went to work in factories at low-skill jobs for wages lower than men's. Middle- and upper-class women (usually native born) from families of prosperous merchants and industrialists were elevated to a pedestal as towers of moral strength, refinement, and soothing comfort to their world-weary males. Prevailing values in the 19th and early 20th centuries held that the nature of women was to please and the nature of men was to achieve.[8]

Legal restrictions denied U.S. women any right to self-determination. They could not vote, own property in their own name, testify in court, make a legal contract, spend their own wages without their husband's permission, or even retain guardianship over their own children if their husband died or deserted them. Because men were supposedly active and women passive, only men were thought to enjoy sex; any woman who also enjoyed it was considered deviant and degenerate. A double standard in sexual conduct thus emerged. In a similar vein, public speaking by women was taboo because a passive, refined lady would not behave so crudely.

Did everyone think and act this way in the 19th century? Certainly not, but these were the prevailing norms. Still, the abolitionist movement attracted female activists to fight against the continuance or expansion of slavery. The New York

State legislature in 1848 acted to protect the property rights of married women; and, in 1869, Wyoming Territory gave women the right to vote, continuing that practice after it became a state in 1890—the first state to do so.

The Suffrage Movement

Efforts to give all women the right to vote met with fierce resistance. As the suffragists held rallies, protest marches, and demonstrations, they were ridiculed, insulted, and abused—slapped, tripped, and pelted with overripe fruits and vegetables and burning cigar stubs. Chaining themselves to the posts, fences, and grillwork of public buildings, these early feminists endured arrest and jail. In 1913, in Washington, DC, federal troops were brought in to quell the unrest. In 1916, six months of picketing at the White House ended with mass arrests and imprisonment when the women refused to pay what they labeled "unjust" fines. Hostility against such challenges to the male establishment is indicated by this account of how the prison guards maltreated the demonstrators:

> I saw Miss Lincoln, a slight young girl, thrown to the floor. Mrs. Nolan, a delicate old lady of seventy-three, was mastered by two men. . . . Whittaker [the prison superintendent] in the center of the room directed the whole attack, inciting the guards to every brutality. Two men brought in Dorothy Day, twisting her arms above her head. Suddenly they lifted her and brought her body down twice over the back of an iron bench. . . . The bed broke Mrs. Nolan's fall, but Mrs. Cosu hit the wall. They had been there a few minutes when Mrs. Lewis, all doubled over like a sack of flour, was thrown in. Her head struck the iron bed and she fell to the floor senseless. As for Lucy Burns, they handcuffed her wrists and fastened the handcuffs over her head to the cell door.[9]

Finally, in 1919, Congress passed the Nineteenth Amendment, giving women the right to vote. Ratified a year later, it became the law of the land. Yet other feminist reforms did not follow. Women did not use their newly gained political power much, and few won elective office despite their numbers among the electorate. About 90 percent of the suffragists ceased further activist measures as the feminist movement faded—until it was resurrected some 40 years later. Antisuffrage groups remained active, though, campaigning against local laws to prevent women from serving on juries, holding elected office, or getting jobs competitive with those of men.

Following passage of the Nineteenth Amendment, labor force participation by women increased to about 25 percent, although job discrimination continued. Women rarely held decision-making positions and were the first fired during the Great Depression. Society still frowned on the career woman, tolerating only women who worked for needed supplemental income. The approved female role was still as the good wife and mother, the woman's primary responsibility being to the home.[10]

World War II changed all that—temporarily. Now women were needed in all work areas to contribute to the war effort while the men went overseas to fight the enemy. The percentage of women working increased to 36 percent, with training programs and childcare centers often available to them. A postwar recession and the return of GIs to their former jobs resulted in the firing of 2 million women within 15 months after the war ended. As childcare centers were dismantled, propaganda encouraged women to leave their jobs and return to their home

A common suffragist tactic, prior to passage of the Nineteenth Amendment in 1919, was to march in major U.S. cities—in this case, New York City in 1912—to urge the passage of legislation giving women the right to vote. These first feminists incurred the wrath of many men and the disdain of numerous women for challenging existing norms. After 1919, the women's movement lay dormant until reactivated in the 1960s.

responsibilities full time. Nevertheless, the proportion of women working gradually increased: by the 1980s, it exceeded 50 percent.

The Women's Liberation Movement

The 1960s was a decade of social activism inspired by many factors, including President Kennedy's appointment of a Presidential Commission on the Status of Women, which documented extensive sexual discrimination in the country. When Congress failed to act on the commission's recommendations, a number of feminist advocates formed the National Organization for Women (NOW) in 1966, and a new phase of the feminist movement began. Resisted at first by most other women's groups, the New Left, and even civil rights groups, the women's liberation movement eventually gained acceptance, succeeding in its efforts to end many forms of sexual discrimination, particularly economic ones.

THE REALITY OF GENDER DIFFERENCES

Men and women differ biologically, but do they differ in other ways, too? Are women naturally more tender, loving, nurturing, and passive? Are men more aggressive, intelligent, and dominant? When Freud argued that biology was destiny, he was simply restating a prevailing belief that had existed for centuries. Abundant evidence almost everywhere demonstrated the lower socioeconomic status for women, suggesting that their inferiority rested on biological differences. Yet how many of these "natural" differences actually result from sociocultural factors and how many are truly innate? We still do not know completely because of the difficulty in untangling the impact of cultural molding from inherent capabilities. Still, we do have some clues from research investigations.

Biological Explanations

Aside from physical and reproductive differences, males and females are biologically distinct in other ways. Females tend to have a lower infant mortality rate, a higher tolerance for pain, and greater longevity. Males tend to have greater physical strength. Scientists studying newborn infants, however, have not detected any significant differences in personality traits between the sexes.

In *Brain Sex: The Real Difference between Men and Women* (1992), British geneticist Anne Moir cites numerous studies showing gender-specific differences in brain function.[11] For example, men have fewer fibers connecting the verbal and emotional areas of the brain, making it more difficult for them to express emotions. Because they have more fibers in the reasoning area of the brain, however, they demonstrate a superior ability to understand abstract relationships, which may make them more naturally suited to disciplines such as mathematics and engineering.

By the time a man reaches his 40s, his previously larger brain shrinks to the size of a woman's, and men experience reduced performance in verbal and spatial memory, general spatial abilities, and ability to pay attention. No significant changes occur in a woman's brain as she ages.[12] Brain–gender researchers continue to examine the differences in male and female abilities. Some of these gender-specific differences may be due to differing structures and activities in the brain's lobes and to the exposure of fetuses to hormones in the womb.[13]

Thought processes are not the same as differences in behavior and social status, however. In fact, cross-cultural comparisons show the weakness of the biological argument. Why, for example, are women often physical laborers in Russia, as well as accounting for about one-third of the engineers and three-fourths of the physicians? The answer lies in society's definitions of gender identity and of the appropriate behavioral roles within that identity.

Socialization and Gender Roles

Although gender identity is an ascribed status, society shapes that identity through socialization. In the process of learning traits and activities that are desirable and correct, individuals internalize approved gender-role behavior as a real part of themselves. These cultural dictates of appropriate male–female conduct sometimes vary from one society to another. Anthropologist Margaret Mead found, for example, the following variations among three tribes in New Guinea: The Arapesh culture produced both men and women with decidedly feminine traits, whereas the Mundugamor produced both men and women with pronounced masculine traits. Among the Tchambuli, meanwhile, the usual gender-role behavior of Western society was completely reversed.[14] Mead's findings emphasized the influential role of culture and socialization in developing sexual differentiation.

In much of the world, male dominance has long existed, reinforced by the writings of male philosophers and religious leaders. Even the sacred books of the world's three major religions promote sexist ideology, evoking supernatural justification for male supremacy. Islam's Koran states, "Men are superior to women on account of qualities in which God has given them preeminence." In the New Testament, Saint Paul proclaims, "Let the woman learn in silence with all subjection. But I suffer not a woman to teach, nor to usurp authority over the man, but to be in silence . . . she shall be saved in childbearing, if they continue in faith and charity and holiness with sobriety." Finally, the morning prayer of male Orthodox Jews includes the line, "Blessed art Thou, oh Lord our God, King of the Universe, that I was not born a woman."

Childhood Socialization. Influenced by value pronouncements such as those described in the preceding section, but even more so by their own upbringing, parents convey their expectations to children in thousands of ways. Studies show mothers and fathers touch, handle, speak to, play with, and discipline children differently depending on the child's gender. Children learn to play differently, girls more often in exclusive dyadic relationships and boys more often in larger groups.[15] Boys usually grow up experiencing more expansive territory on their bikes or hikes, requiring numerous adaptive decisions, while girls generally experience a more structured, narrower world, which limits their opportunities to develop self-reliance. Children also learn from parents and other adult role models, assuming their attitudes and evaluations.

The impact of parents, family, friends, school, and the media in shaping differences in sexual behavior extends to personalities as well. Through their childhood experiences, boys tend to become inquisitive, self-assured, and convinced that they can control things, whereas girls tend to become passive, timid, and fearful of new situations. Although individuals vary in personality and temperament, this pattern emerges through the socialization process to match self-evaluations with the unequal rewards of the system, thereby completing the vicious circle of justification (see The Gender Experience box, page 476).[16]

The **gender-role expectations** set by society impact heavily on the development of males and females. Conformity to them serves as a basis for status and popularity, even in elementary school.[17] Culturally influenced behavioral differences between boys and girls become the social norm as a child grows older. Studies typically show that, in the passage of time between preschool years and second grade, girls usually demonstrate a higher frequency of domestic and gender-role exploring behaviors, in contrast to boys, who tend to engage in explorative acting and information-seeking behaviors.[18]

Socialization is a lifelong process; throughout one's childhood, adolescence, and adulthood, a continuous array of experiences reinforces early influences.[19] Toys, games, textbooks, teachers' attitudes and actions, and peer influence all help maintain gender stereotypes. Most influential is the role of the media, particularly television commercials and programming. If we are to believe television, only men live life with gusto, buy cars, and have group fun, whereas women use the right shampoo to avoid the "frizzies," wear a seductive perfume, or get their floors to shine brightly.[20] A content analysis of the lyrics of many of today's hit songs and the images conveyed in many music videos reveal the continuance of gender stereotyping.[21]

The Gender Experience

A Feminist's List of "Barbarous Rituals"

Woman is:

- kicking strongly in your mother's womb, upon which she is told, "It must be a boy, if it's so active!"
- being confined to the Doll Corner in nursery school when you are really fascinated by Tinker Toys.
- being labeled a tomboy when all you wanted to do was climb that tree to look out and see a distance.
- seeing grownups chuckle when you say you want to be an engineer or doctor when you grow up—and learning to say you want to be a mommy or nurse, instead.
- dreading summertime because more of your body with its imperfections will be seen—and judged.
- liking math or history and getting hints that boys are turned off by smart girls.
- discovering that what seems like everything worthwhile doing in life "isn't feminine," and learning to just delight in being feminine and "nice"—and feeling somehow guilty.
- swinging down the street feeling good and smiling at people and being hassled like a piece of meat in return.
- brooding about "how far" you should go with the guy you really like. Will he no longer respect you? Will you get—oh God—a "reputation"? Or, if not, are you a square? Being pissed off because you can't just do what you feel like doing.
- finding that the career you've chosen exacts more than just study or hard work—an emotional price of being made to feel "less a woman."
- being bugged by men in the office who assume that you're a virginal prude if you don't flirt, and that you're an easy mark if you are halfway relaxed and pleasant.
- wanting to go back to school, to read, to join something, do something. Why isn't home enough for you? What's wrong with you?
- feeling a need to say "thank you" when your guy actually fixes himself a meal now that you're dying with the flu.
- being widowed, or divorced, and trying to get a "good" job—at your age.
- getting older, getting lonelier, getting ready to die—and knowing it wouldn't have had to be this way after all.

Source: From Robin Morgan, *Going Too Far: The Personal Chronicle of a Feminist* (New York: Vintage Books, 1978), pp. 107–13.

Advertising. The impact of advertising in reinforcing traditional gender roles and stereotypes is very pervasive. Jean Kilbourne argues,

> There is no doubt that flagrant sexism and sex role stereotyping abound in all forms of the media. There is abundant evidence about this. It is far more difficult to document the effects of these stereotypes and images on the individuals and institutions exposed to them because, as I've said, it is difficult to separate media effects from other aspects of the socialization process and almost impossible to find a comparison group (just about everyone in America has been exposed to massive doses of advertising).
>
> But, at the very least, advertising helps to create a climate in which certain attitudes and values flourish, such as the attitude that women are valuable only as objects of men's desire, that real men are always sexually aggressive, that violence is erotic, and that women who are victims of sexual assault "asked for it."[22]

Research on television advertising reveals four significant patterns: Men do most of the commercial voiceovers; women tend to perform typical family activities, usually in the home and benefiting men, but men carry out a wide variety of activities; women are younger than men; and fewer girls and women appear than

Advertisers long ago discovered the effectiveness of using women as sex objects to get the viewers' attention and to sell a product, as here in New York City. In the past few years, billboards and advertisings in public spaces have increased in numbers, prompting public advocate groups to protest the sexual nature of many ads.

boys and men.[23] Moreover, as Erving Goffman observed, subtle forms of sexism are common in print advertising as well:

> (1) Overwhelmingly, a woman is taller than a man only when the man is her social inferior; (2) a woman's hands are seen just barely touching, holding or caressing—never grasping, manipulating or shaping; (3) when a photograph of men and women illustrates an instruction of some sort the man is always instructing the woman—even if the men and women are actually children (that is, a male child will be instructing a female child); (4) when an advertisement requires someone to sit or lie on a bed or a floor that someone is almost always a child or a woman, hardly ever a man; (5) when the head or eye of a man is averted it is only in relation to a social, political, or intellectual superior, but when the eye or head of a woman is averted it is always in relation to whatever man is pictured with her; (6) women are repeatedly shown mentally drifting from the scene while in close physical touch with a male, their faces lost and dreamy, "as though his aliveness to the surroundings and his readiness to cope were enough for both of them"; (7) concomitantly, women, much more than men, are pictured at the kind of psychological loss or remove from a social situation that leaves one unoriented for action (e.g., something terrible has happened and a woman is shown with her hands over her mouth and her eyes helpless with horror).[24]

In today's world, women continue to make gains in all areas. Yet we remain in a transitional stage, and socialization inequities continue. Sometimes advertisers emphasize the strengths of emancipated women to sell their products, but more often, they contribute to **role entrapment** by depicting women in stereotypical or sex-object ways. Many writers and educators at all grade levels emphasize women's rights and the ideals of gender equality, and many parents seek to maximize their daughters' future possibilities, but gender differentiation remains deep-rooted in all our social institutions, including the family and education. During the 2005–2006 prime-time television season, women accounted for 40 percent of all characters and, among the major news networks (ABC, CBS, NBC), women correspondents reported just 25 percent of the news stories.[25]

IMMIGRANT AND MINORITY WOMEN

Almost all immigrants, past and present, have come from traditional societies with clearly defined gender-role models of behavior and responsibility. Those internalized self-concepts and expectations were not only part of everyday life in their homeland but a source of continuing norms within their ethnic communities after immigration. In culturally insulated neighborhoods with parallel social institutions, women seldom worked outside the home, performing instead their traditional roles for their families within the home, a pattern still evident in many immigrant communities today.

Vestiges of White Ethnic Orientations

In many northeastern U.S. cities, numerous elderly immigrant poor live on meager fixed incomes, struggling to survive in decaying neighborhoods that are no longer cohesive or homogeneous. Most of these elderly are female, with a limited command of English, because their traditional role in the old ethnic community did not necessitate fluency in English and because most arrived in the United States long before the advent of the feminist movement. Lacking job skills and much formal education, and unfamiliar with the workings of a bureaucratic society or reluctant to seek public assistance, they cling to the remnants of their familiar world. For them, being women who are advanced in years and unprepared for independence, life presents daily challenges. Among many first-generation white U.S. women today, the traditional view of gender identity—with women primarily in a subservient, nurturing role—manifests itself in everyday life.

Often overlooked in discussions of ethnicity are second-generation adult Americans. Yet their primary socialization revolves around homeland value orientations and traditional gender-role models, which shape their perceptions of the world somewhat differently from those of children of native-born parents. Studies of working-class Americans—many of them second-generation U.S. residents of central, southern, and eastern European heritage—revealed some of these continuing values. In her classic work, *Worlds of Pain* (1976), Lillian Rubin offered a portrait of working-class women who defined themselves as wives and mothers, even if they worked, and who rejected the notion of work as liberating and considered the issues of the feminist movement as irrelevant to them.[26]

By the 1990s, Rubin's field research revealed how two decades of economic transformation (disappearing jobs, declining incomes, and the need for wives to work) had brought the struggle to reorder gender roles into the consciousness of women at all class levels. White ethnic working-class women no longer thought that women's issues had nothing to do with them. Yet even as they strived for emotional reciprocity and division of family labor in their marital relationships, the old gender roles and rules remained deeply internalized, often resulting in confusing and contradictory remarks and feelings.[27]

Their traditional gender roles apparently affect minority women's employment prospects in that they limit their social interactions with the outside world. One team of researchers found that a lack of bridging social networks is a greater obstacle to employment among minority women in Los Angeles than the cultural forces stressed by conservative policymakers, such as a decrease in family values and individual responsibility. Because such networks link individuals to information, resources, and opportunities, they are more important among African American, Hispanic, and white women than other forms of cultural capital.[28]

Today's Minority Women

Machismo, the pervasive value orientation of the male as provider and dominant force in the family, has a major effect on the daily lives of lower-income Hispanic women. Problems arise among low-income Hispanic Americans when only the woman is able to find work or when she earns more than her spouse. This situation creates family strain and gender self-identity stability as economic reality collides with the internalized male self-image and culturally prescribed role behavior.

The status and roles of Asian American women vary with their place of birth and that of their husbands, as well as with their educational levels. Generally, these foreign-born women maintain traditional family and gender roles. The higher their education and the more Americanized the women are, the higher their status. Although more Asian women are combining career and family roles, Morrison Wong reports that the Chinese wife tends to assume the role of helper to her husband rather than equal partner.[29] Kerrily J. Kitano suggests that the personal dissatisfaction among second-generation Japanese American women in their expected female roles may be a primary reason that their acculturation was more rapid and their outgroup marriage rate greater than those of other Asian American women.[30]

The dichotomy among African Americans, discussed in Chapter 10, relates directly to the status and role of African American women in U.S. society. College-educated African American women are more likely to benefit from the feminist movement in employment, income, and egalitarian marriages, although their greater numbers compared to African American male college graduates can be a disadvantage in finding a spouse of the same social class and race.[31] In contrast, low-income African American women at first did not identify with the feminist movement because many of its demands then seemed irrelevant to their needs. Their focus was on economic stability, a better future for their children, and racial discrimination; sexism did not then seem a high priority.[32]

Two basic themes emerge from a consideration of women in various racial and ethnic groups: cultural attributes and intensified subordinate status. Not only do immigrant groups re-create in miniature their old familiar worlds to establish a secure place in an alien country, but their evolving ethnic self-consciousness and community organization encourage them to maintain accompanying male dominance patterns as well. These traditional gender roles have either reflected sexism within the entire society or resisted recent advances in sexual equality. Moreover, as both a woman and a minority-group member, an individual is at a double disadvantage, encountering prejudice and discrimination on two fronts—because of her sex and because of her race or ethnicity.

Special concerns of minority women include monolingual education and services, high infant and maternal mortality rates, poor housing, unsuitable psychological and employment testing, reduced enforcement of affirmative action, deportation of Hispanic mothers of U.S.-born children, special-admission quality education programs, unemployment, declining welfare programs, and family stability.

Feminist scholars now speak of a "third wave" in examining intergenerational feminist activism.[33] Ula Taylor noted, however, that contemporary African American women reject the term *black feminism* in favor of the term *womanism*, although she believes the terms are interchangeable. The only difference, she contends, is that this new empowerment theory has not yet undergone a thorough scholarly examination. Because it remains a cornerstone of African American women's commitment to self-empowerment, black activists continue to embrace their feminist identities.[34]

Marilyn J. Davidson reminds us that issues of gender, race, and class also combine in complex ways to produce numerous role conflicts among professional black and ethnic-minority women. The dual burden of career and family affects their experiences and career development, just as it does with their white counterparts. However, they also live in a bicultural world that produces unique experiences and stresses as black or ethnic-minority women defy both organizational stereotypes and the traditional gender roles of their own communities, which appear to be more resilient than in the Anglo community. Furthermore, there is little room for their own ethnic or cultural identity within the organizations in which they work. Indeed, black and ethnic-minority women face stereotypical and prejudicial perceptions about such identities in organizations where there are few or no role models. The need to balance their organizational and cultural identity is a conscious activity that can create self-doubt and self-criticism.[35]

SOCIAL INDICATORS OF WOMEN'S STATUS

The justification for considering women as a minority group and for speaking of the existence of sexism becomes readily understandable through scrutiny of leading social indicators. As with racial minorities in earlier chapters, we now examine the comparative status of women in terms of education, employment, and income. In addition, we look at sexual harassment, law, and politics (see also The International Scene box, page 481).

Education

For many generations, education was segregated by gender. Males and females often attended different schools or were physically and academically separated in "coeducational" schools. For example, the still-standing Henry Street grammar school on New York's Lower East Side—a well-known white ethnic area for over a century—contains the word *Boys* engraved over one of its two opposite-end entrances and the word *Girls* over the other. Women were once taught only the social graces and morals. Teaching academic subjects to females was considered a

The International Scene

Women's Status in Canada

In many ways, the social indicators on Canadian women reveal comparable socioeconomic circumstances to U.S. women, although a few differences exist. In 1929, less than 4 percent of women worked outside the home, but now 62 percent are in the labor force, and they make up 35 percent of all self-employed persons. While most families have dual-income-earner couples, only 16 percent of families have the father as the sole breadwinner.

For more than a decade, Canadian law has mandated equal pay for equal work ("comparable worth"). These laws seek to create pay equity through job evaluations that take into account the skill, effort, and responsibility required to do a job and the conditions under which the work is performed. Nevertheless, a wage gap persists between men and women. On average, women working in full-time, full-year jobs earn 78 percent of what men earn.

Canada also has a problem with the feminization of poverty. About 16 percent of all families in the nation are headed by women. Women who head single-parent families are among Canada's poorest; 47 percent of such families live in poverty.

Education data offer hopeful signs. Women make up more than 55 percent of full-time undergraduates at Canadian universities. Currently, 40 percent of all women ages 15 and over have a high school diploma or better, and over 10 percent hold a university degree.

In the Canadian House of Commons, 64 of the 308 members of Parliament (21 percent) in 2007 were women. In the Senate, 35 of 100 seats (35 percent) were held by women. For the first time, a woman is the Chief Justice of the Supreme Court.

All jurisdictions in Canada give women a statutory right to take maternity leave without penalty, usually for a period of 17 weeks. An additional 24 weeks of parental leave, which may be taken by either parent, is available to certain workers, mostly employees of the federal government, banks, and transportation and communications companies. While these rights are for unpaid leave, the Employment Insurance Program also provides 15 weeks of maternity benefits for mothers and 10 weeks of parental benefits for natural or adoptive parents. Families with children under age 13 are eligible for tax deductions and allowances for childcare support while the parents work.

Critical Thinking Question: In what ways does Canada differ from the United States in various statistics and in addressing women's issues relating to family and work?

Source: Data are from *Statistics Canada* (online) accessed at www. statcan.ca [January 26,2008].

waste of time; a Harvard professor in 1911 even proclaimed that such an attempt would "weaken the intellect of the teacher."[36]

Even after females overcame these prejudices and took academic subjects alongside males, the educational system maintained sexism in both obvious and subtle ways. Teachers and counselors with traditional gender-role expectations fostered gender-linked aspirations and career choices. Children's books and textbooks reinforced sexual stereotypes, with male characters heavily outnumbering female characters and males portrayed as active and adventuresome in contrast to the more passive females. Stereotypical activities—boys creating things or earning money and girls shopping, cooking, and sewing—existed in all texts, even in mathematics books. In standard English usage, male pronouns identified a nongender-specific individual, further biasing children's education and the culture in general. Although many of these stereotypical depictions no longer exist through pressure on publishers to adopt gender-neutral language, problems still remain.

Despite many changes in recent decades, gender bias in the schools remains, according to a report issued by the American Association of University Women Educational Foundation.[37] Girls enter the first grade with the same skills and ambitions as boys, or even higher ones, but classroom sexist conditioning results

Americans have long relied on education as one of the best means of achieving greater equality in our society. With increasing percentages of women earning bachelor's degrees in a wider range of majors, as well as their greater representation in advanced degrees in professional fields, further progress in gender equality looks promising.

in lower self-confidence and aspirations by the time they graduate from high school. Two-thirds of the nation's teachers may be women, but they tend to favor sexual stereotypes, recalling more positively the assertive male students while liking least the assertive females. Teachers call on boys more often, give them more detailed criticism, and praise the intellectual content of boys' work more than girls' work, while more likely praising girls for their neatness.[38] Teachers also allow boys to shout out answers and take risks, but they reprimand girls who do the same thing for rudeness. In addition, few educators encourage girls to pursue careers in math or science. Single-sex classrooms evolved as an answer to these problems, but although research indicates that they tend to produce girls with more self-confidence and higher grades, critics charge that they are a "bogus" solution that sets back the cause of gender equity and true coeducation.[39] Perhaps the inclusion of gender studies in teacher preparation courses would help resolve these forms of school bias.

As Table 13.1 shows, the number of school years males and females complete is very close when controlled for race. Despite parity in the level of educational attainment, however, the choice of academic fields of study still reflects significant sexual differentiation (Table 13.2). Women continue to be underrepresented in such male-dominated majors as computer and information technology, engineering, and the physical sciences; and they are overrepresented in the traditional female career areas of education, home economics, health services, and psychology. Advanced degrees conferred in medicine, dentistry, law, and theology show a steady lessening of the sex-ratio imbalance (Table 13.3).

TABLE 13.1   Educational Attainment by Race, Ethnicity, and Sex, Aged 25 and Older, 2006 (in percentages)

	Completed 4 Years of High School or More	Completed 4 Years of College or More
All Races		
Male	85.0	29.2
Female	85.9	26.9
African American		
Male	80.1	17.2
Female	81.2	19.4
Asian and Pacific Islander		
Male	89.6	52.5
Female	85.5	47.1
Hispanic		
Male	58.5	11.9
Female	60.1	12.9
Non-Hispanic White		
Male	90.2	32.8
Female	90.8	29.3

Source: U.S. Census Bureau, "Educational Attainment in the United States," *Current Population Survey* (March 2007), Table 1a.

TABLE 13.2   Female-Earned Bachelor's Degrees by Field of Study (in percentages)

	1980	2006
Business management	33.6	36.7
Communications	52.1	50.3
Computer and information sciences	30.4	30.2
Education	73.2	75.3
Engineering	9.3	10.1
Foreign languages	75.7	69.9
Health sciences	82.8	79.1
Mathematics	42.1	41.7
Natural sciences	23.6	39.6
Psychology	63.3	68.2
Social sciences	43.6	57.9

Source: Adapted from U.S. National Center for Education Statistics, *Digest of Education Staticstics,* 2006, Table 10.

Since 1991, the proportion of women enrolled in college has exceeded that for men, and that gap is steadily widening. In 2005, about 43 percent of women ages 18 to 24 were enrolled in college, compared to 35 percent of men in that age range. At the college level, the gender gap is widest among African Americans. In 2005, 28 percent of black men were enrolled in college compared to 37 percent of black women. Only among Asian Americans did the male enrollment rate exceed that for women.

TABLE 13.3   Degrees Conferred in Selected Professions (in percentages)

Type of Degree	1960	1970	1980	1990	2000	2005
Medicine (MD)						
Men	94.5	91.6	76.6	65.8	56.7	52.7
Women	5.5	8.4	23.4	34.2	43.3	47.3
Dentistry (DDS, DMD)						
Men	99.2	99.1	86.7	69.1	61.4	56.2
Women	0.8	0.9	13.3	30.9	38.6	43.8
Law (LLB, JD)						
Men	97.5	94.6	69.8	57.8	52.7	51.3
Women	2.5	5.4	30.2	42.2	47.3	48.7
Theology (BD, MDV, MHL)						
Men	NA	97.7	86.2	75.2	67.0	64.4
Women	NA	2.3	13.8	24.8	32.0	35.6

Note: NA = not available.

Source: U.S. National Center for Education Statistics, *Digest of Education Statistics,* annual.

Employment

About 69 percent of all women are employed, up from 46 percent in 1980.[40] The greatest increase in working women has been among wives with school-age children. In 2005, about 73 percent of mothers with children ages 6 to 13 were employed, up from 52 percent in 1975. About 60 percent of all women with children under age 6 were employed, up from 37 percent in 1975.[41] In all categories, the percentages of African American working mothers were higher than the national averages and the percentages of whites (Figure 13.1; Table 13.4).

FIGURE 13.1   Labor Force Participation Rates for the Population Ages 20 to 64, 2005

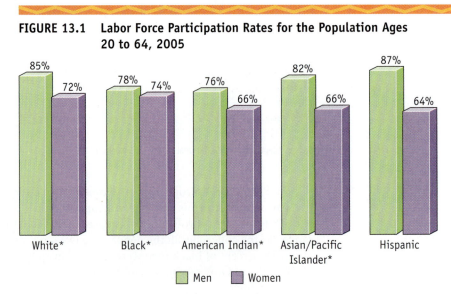

| White* | Black* | American Indian* | Asian/Pacific Islander* | Hispanic |

Men / Women

*Non-Hispanic

Source: Population Reference Bureau analysis of the 2005 ACS microdata files.

TABLE 13.4   Labor-Force Participation by Wives (Husbands Present), by Age of Children, 1975 and 2005 (in percentages)

	Total		African American		White	
	1975	2005	1975	2005	1975	2005
No children under 18	43.8	53.8	47.6	57.0	43.6	53.5
With children under 18	44.9	68.1	58.4	76.4	43.6	67.8
Children under 6	36.7	59.8	54.9	72.8	34.7	59.3
Children 6 to 13	51.8	73.0	65.7	78.7	50.7	72.8
Children 14 to 17	53.5	79.6	52.3	80.4	53.4	80.1

Source: U.S. Bureau of the Census, *Statistical Abstract of the United States* 2007, Table 585 (Washington DC: U.S. Government Printing Office, 2008), p. 380.

Despite the increase in the rate of women's participation in the labor force and in women's proportional representation in previously male-dominated occupations, significant differences in male–female career categories remain. First, a female occupational ghetto exists, with many women in traditional low-paying, low-status jobs. Such "pink-collar" jobs include those of bank tellers, bookkeepers, cashiers, health technicians, librarians, sales clerks, secretaries, and telephone operators. About 60 percent of all working women are mired in lower-paying clerical and sales jobs. Male-dominated occupations, on the other hand, tend to be the higher-paying, higher-status positions (Table 13.5 and Figure 13.2).

Another problem is the **glass ceiling,** a real but unseen discriminatory policy among companies that limits the upward mobility of women, keeping them out of top management positions, high-profile transfers, and key assignments. A 1995 report from the Glass Ceiling Commission, a bipartisan panel created

TABLE 13.5   Women and Men Employed in Selected Occupations, 2006 (in percentages)

Female		Male	
Dental hygienists	98.6	Electricians	98.1
Secretaries	96.9	Airplane pilots, navigators	97.8
Receptionists	92.7	Carpenters	97.6
Data-entry keyers	91.6	Truck drivers	92.8
Registered nurses	91.3	Automobile mechanics	88.4
Bookkeepers	90.3	Civil engineers	88.1
Nursing aides, orderlies	88.9	Police & sheriff's patrol officers	87.2
Speech pathologists	85.3	Barbers	82.3
Bank tellers	84.8	Architects except naval	77.8
Social workers	82.6	Dentists	77.4
Elementary schoolteachers	82.2	Physicians and surgeons	67.8
Travel agents	77.3	Lawyers	67.4
Waiters	71.5	Mail carriers	64.3
File clerks	71.2	Financial analysts	61.6

Source: U.S. Bureau of Labor Statistics, *Employment and Earnings* (Washington, DC: U.S. Government Printing Office, January 2008).

FIGURE 13.2   Female Professional and Technical Workers, by Percentage of Total Workers in Each Field, 2005

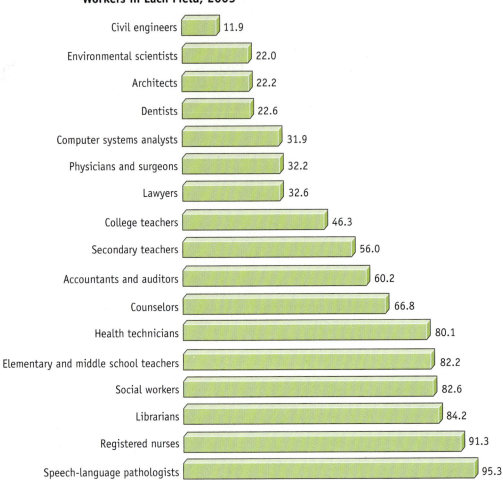

Civil engineers	11.9
Environmental scientists	22.0
Architects	22.2
Dentists	22.6
Computer systems analysts	31.9
Physicians and surgeons	32.2
Lawyers	32.6
College teachers	46.3
Secondary teachers	56.0
Accountants and auditors	60.2
Counselors	66.8
Health technicians	80.1
Elementary and middle school teachers	82.2
Social workers	82.6
Librarians	84.2
Registered nurses	91.3
Speech-language pathologists	95.3

Source: U.S. Bureau of Labor Statistics.

by Congress, concluded that women remain blocked from top management positions, defined as those of vice president and above. Constituting only 29 percent of the work force, white men hold 95 of every 100 senior management positions in industries across the nation. Women had greater success moving into the ranks of middle management, which included assistant vice presidents and office managers; white women held close to 40 percent of those jobs, African American women about 5 percent, and African American men about 4 percent.[42]

Since 1995, though, the picture has been improving. In 2006, women were chief executive officers (CEOs) of 10 of the Fortune 500 companies and of 20 of the Fortune 1000 companies. The percentage of female CEOs is small, but it is the highest ever. With women constituting about half of all managers below the top 20 people in most major companies, the possibilities loom large that many women will soon be breaking through to the top positions.[43] Moreover, a rising and significant portion of Fortune 500 companies—10 percent at this writing and including Citigroup, General Electric, and NBC—promoted women into their top financial post: the chief financial officer (CFO).[44]

Working women face an additional burden at home. Their husbands typically spend no more time on household chores than do husbands of full-time homemakers. According to the University of Michigan Institute for Social Research, married women in dual-career families average 18 hours per week of housework to their husbands' 7 hours, although for men that is double what they did in 1968.[45] This imbalance of women doing about two-thirds of all housework constitutes what sociologist Arlie Hochschild called a "second shift."[46] Her study of married couples over an eight-year period found the women feeling constantly fatigued, emotionally drained, and torn by the conflicting demands of their multiple roles. In an analysis of the division of household labor in 22 countries, Jeanne Batalova and Philip Cohen found that, in countries with higher levels of overall gender equality, married couples that cohabited before marriage have a more equal division of housework.[47] Feminists argue that household labor divisions provide an excellent measure of power relationships in the home.

Childcare centers enable working mothers to provide supervised quality time for their children while also pursuing a career and generating family income. Still, they must juggle both roles, for when they return home, women face a "second shift" of work in food shopping, cooking, cleaning, and other childcare tasks.

Income

Ever since pay equity became a civil rights goal in the 1970s, minorities and women have made some progress toward it, but a significant gap remains. Among year-round, full-time workers ages 18 and older, for example, women earn 77 cents for every dollar earned by men. The picture is a bit brighter for weekly earnings; in June 2007, women earned about 81 cents.[48] Occupational distribution by gender into lower-paying and higher-paying fields of work partially explains the remaining income disparity. However, women still earn less than men in almost every field, including those dominated by women. A portion of this difference may be caused by variations in qualifications and seniority, but even when these variables are controlled for, the disparity still exists.[49]

Generally, the median earnings across all educational categories of year-round, full-time workers are higher for men than for women and higher for whites than for African Americans. African American men earn about 75 percent of the income of white men with a comparable education, whereas African American women earn 93 percent of that of white women with similar educational levels. Moreover, black female college graduates earn 84 cents for every dollar earned by a black male college graduate, a pay inequity suggesting that sexual discrimination compounds the problems of racial discrimination in the workplace.[50]

Part of the pay inequity no doubt reflects the choice corporate women must make between the **fast track** and the **mommy track.** Those opting for the fast track to earn promotions over other candidates must make a full commitment to the management. Often, this entails 60-hour-plus workweeks, frequent travel, weekend meetings, and "drop everything" crises to resolve. To meet such demands, some women delay childbearing or forgo motherhood entirely. Even then, executives may assume that a woman's familial responsibilities will interfere with her productivity and that the company will incur additional expenses for maternity leaves.

Choosing motherhood usually forces women to lower their occupational goals and to delay, if not eliminate, their readiness for promotions. Soon, women with children fall behind childless women in earnings, as the latter group ascends the corporate ladder faster. Women thus risk their career mobility by having children. Although nine of ten male executives ages 40 and older are fathers, only one of three female executives ages 40 and older is a mother.[51]

Opting for the mommy track places the additional strain on women of juggling both family and work to find reliable **child care.** Although some companies provide on-site daycare centers or **flex-time** work schedules (allowing workers to set, within limits, their own working hours), most do not. This need usually gets fulfilled through a relative or neighbor, or else through some nearby childcare center. The cost of child care is a major reason many women quit their jobs or delay entry into the workforce.[52]

When we consider the growing number of households headed by women (Figure 13.3), childcare needs and women's typically lower earnings take on alarming significance. About one in five Hispanic families and two in five black families are headed by women, whose greater probability of unavailable childcare facilities and limited earning power have a negative impact on the family's economic health. Thus, the number of female-headed minority households is an important factor in the **feminization of poverty** among blacks and Hispanics. In 2006, 31 percent of families headed by women lived in poverty, an increase from 3 million families in 1980 to nearly 4 million.[53]

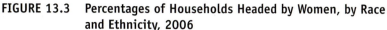

FIGURE 13.3   Percentages of Households Headed by Women, by Race and Ethnicity, 2006

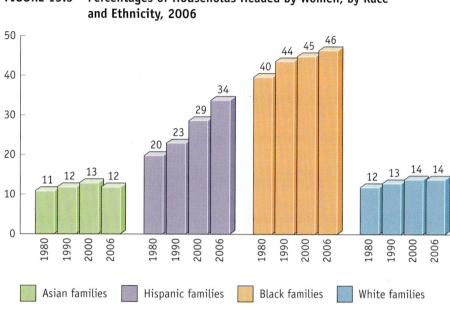

Source: U.S. Census Bureau.

SEXUAL HARASSMENT

For years, U.S. society ignored the issue of sexual harassment, dismissing it as an individual, personal problem. Conventional wisdom then viewed such situations simply as "natural" and unobjectionable: A man, attracted to a particular woman, made sexual advances and received a positive, negative, or "maybe" response. Until 1976, women tended to keep silent, thinking the experience an isolated encounter and not recognizing it as part of a larger pattern connected to their subordination and vulnerability in the occupational structure.

Redbook magazine's 1976 survey of 9,000 women defined the extent of the problem: 90 percent reported having experienced sexual harassment at work. Soon the feminist movement raised awareness of the group basis of this problem. Then, in a 1978–1980 study, the federal government's Merit System Protection Board reported a $189 million cost in hiring, training, absenteeism, and job-turnover expenses caused by harassment and suggested that the figure probably ran into billions of dollars if private industry's costs were included. The government survey also estimated that 1 percent, or about 9,000, female federal employees had been victims of attempted rape by supervisors or coworkers.

In 1979, Catharine A. MacKinnon wrote the first book on this subject, *Sexual Harassment of Working Women: A Case of Sex Discrimination*. She identified sexual harassment as either a single occurrence at work or a series of incidents ranging along a continuum of varying intensity, including

> verbal sexual suggestions or jokes, constant leering or ogling, brushing against your body "accidentally," a friendly pat, squeeze or pinch or arm against you, catching you alone for a quick kiss, the indecent proposition backed by the threat of losing your job, or forced sexual relations.[54]

Since 1980, the courts have generally used 31 pages of guidelines from the federal Equal Employment Opportunity Commission to protect employees from conduct considered illegal under Title VII of the Civil Rights Act of 1964. These guidelines define sexual harassment as

> unwelcome sexual advances, requests for sexual favors, and other verbal or physical conduct of a sexual nature . . . when submission is made a condition of employment, or rejection of the advance is used as the basis for future employment decision, or interfering with the individual's performance or creating an intimidating, hostile, or offensive working environment.

Other obnoxious and questionable behaviors, however, escape this definition. California's Fair Employment and Housing Department established broader guidelines: unsolicited written, verbal, or physical contacts; suggestive or obscene notes; continual leering; obscene gestures; display of obscene objects or pictures; blocking movements by physical touching; and forced involvement in obscene joking. Although these forms of sexual harassment are not specifically mentioned in Title VII, recent court decisions have declared them as such, thereby establishing judicial precedent for future cases.[55] For men uncertain about what constitutes acceptable behavior with women, a good "rough measure" of sexual harassment would be to ask yourself, "Would you be embarrassed to have your remarks displayed in the newspaper or actions described to your family?"

The Hill–Thomas Hearings

Telecasts of the 1991 Senate Judiciary Committee hearings into sexual-harassment charges by Anita Hill against U.S. Supreme Court nominee Clarence Thomas stunned the nation. Three days of testimony enlightened the public about how lewd and crude remarks constitute sexual harassment. Ultimately, however, the charges were never resolved to anyone's satisfaction. Anita Hill became a folk hero, received numerous offers of speaking engagements, and was honored in 1992 by the American Bar Association. Clarence Thomas became a Supreme Court Justice, one of the most important and influential legal posts in the United States.

Public opinion polls taken right after the confirmation hearings showed the public believing Thomas by a 3 to 1 margin. A year later, a new poll showed a dramatic shift to an evenly divided public and an increase from 8 to 39 percent of those who thought the committee treated Hill unfairly.[56] Even though the Senate confirmed the nomination of Justice Thomas, the hearings galvanized public awareness, and formal complaints filed with the Equal Employment Opportunity Commission (EEOC) charging sexual harassment nearly doubled.[57] Without question, this controversy redefined the rules for social interaction between the sexes in the workplace, guidelines still in place today.

Complaints and Actions

Sexual harassment in the military continually attracted media attention during the 1990s. Since the 1991 Tailhook scandal, involving U.S. Navy combat aviators molesting female officers at a convention, all branches of the military faced serious accusations and embarrassments. Sexual harassment of females—including assault or rape complaints by recruits against platoon sergeants, by cadets against classmates, by pilots against male pilots, and by aides against superiors—revealed serious problems in the military in gender relations. Although the Department of Defense has a "zero tolerance" policy on acts of sexual harassment in all branches of the military and acts quickly on complaints, such incidents remain a problem.

The military is not alone, of course, in experiencing sexual harassment charges. In recent years, numerous litigants have filed lawsuits against companies (e.g., Ford, W. R. Grace Corporation, and Mitsubishi Motors), against politicians (e.g., former Senator Robert Packwood of Oregon and former President William Clinton), and against universities (e.g., Brown and Stanford). Part of the increase in litigation is due to greater sensitivity by workers as to the definition of sexual harassment.[58]

Although men or women can be victims of sexual harassment, the vast majority of victims are women. Two social realities contribute to this situation: (1) a culture that encourages male sexual assertiveness and female sexual responsiveness and (2) a workplace in which power is distributed unequally and where men tend to supervise the work of women. Part of the solution to sexual harassment might occur when women achieve gender equality in status and power and are treated as persons rather than as sex objects. Not to be overlooked is the fact that sexual harassment in educational institutions is the chief mechanism of sexism and subordination in this crucial crucible of socialization.

SEXISM AND THE LAW

Stereotyping women as passive and in need of protection became institutionalized in the common law of England from which U.S. law arose. Many labor laws, originally intended to prevent the exploitation of women, became a means of restricting their job opportunities and income potential. A vast array of state laws assuming certain inabilities of women ran counter to reality. As sociologist Rosalind J. Dworkin wryly commented:

> A mother can carry her 40-pound child, move furniture in her home, and finish her housekeeping chores late at night. But the same woman, working outside the home, legally could not carry more than 30 pounds of weight or work overtime in some states. . . . [T]hese protective laws . . . degrade women to a childlike status by assuming they are unable, or not wise enough, to protect themselves, individually or collectively, from exploitation.[59]

Although many of these laws have since changed, compliance does not necessarily follow. Many women do not know their legal rights, or they find the difficulties involved in securing them are likely to outweigh the rewards. Because changing hundreds of state laws is a long, arduous process—and because legal principles enacted by a simple majority vote can be repealed by a similar simple majority—Congress approved the Equal Rights Amendment (ERA) in 1972, intending it to extend full and equal legal rights to women. The proposed constitutional amendment's wording was brief: "Equality of rights under the law shall not be denied or abridged by the United States or by any state on account of sex." Requiring separate ratification by three-fourths of the states (a total of 38), it gained approval from only 35. The failure of the ERA resulted from the opposition of numerous groups, including many women, labor leaders, conservatives, religious groups, and insurance companies.

In 1986, the U.S. Supreme Court ruled in *Meritor Savings Bank v. Vinson* that sexual harassment by a supervisor violates the 1964 Civil Rights Act prohibiting sex discrimination in the workplace. Women's groups hailed the court's identification of harassment as a form of discrimination. In 1993, the Supreme Court further ruled that a complainant need not prove that the offending behavior caused severe psychological damage or impaired the victim's ability to perform expected work. Instead, drawing from the EEOC guidelines (quoted earlier), it defined actionable harassment as (among other things) a working atmosphere so sexually tainted by abuse that any reasonable person would find it too hostile to continue. Although this decision gave lower courts more freedom to decide for plaintiffs who bring charges of abuse without evidence of medical or psychological injury, it did not offer detailed guidance about what a hostile environment exactly involves, nor did the 1998 court decisions that set more stringent guidelines on employer accountability. As a result, local officials have wide scope in interpreting an offensive, hostile environment compared to other abuses of power in the workplace, leading critics to complain that clearer standards of conduct are necessary.[60]

WOMEN AND POLITICS

When women first secured voting rights, they did not immediately use their political power to improve their lives or to win a proportional share of elected offices. A combination of prevailing norms and the burden of household chores not yet lightened by machines contributed to this political inaction. For decades, women's representation in national, state, and local elected office was disproportionately low. In 1990, for example, only 2 of 100 U.S. senators (2 percent) were female, 27 of 435 congressional representatives (6 percent), 3 of 50 governors (6 percent), and 17 percent of all state legislators. In 2008, women accounted for 16 senators (16 percent), 86 congressional representatives (16 percent), 9 governors (18 percent), and 24 percent of all state legislators (Figure 13.4).[61] These gains reduce the imbalance somewhat, but a significant gender imbalance remains, with the U.S. Congress about 81 percent male (see The International Scene box, page 494).

What accounted for the lack of political involvement by women for so many years prior to 1992? The question intrigued both sociologists and political scientists, and their explanations are many and varied. Most political careers evolve out of training, experience, and leadership in law or business, areas in which women have participated only slightly until the last decade or so. Men control the political parties and often resist placing women in positions of organizational power or as viable candidates for "serious" offices. Politics has been a male bastion for so many generations that male politicians long viewed female politicians as strangers whose feminine values and way of life were incompatible with the world of politics. Both men and women tend to prefer male leaders, placing more confidence in them. Finally, women do not form a voting bloc because they are not residentially segregated and they do not tend to vote along socioeconomic lines.[62]

Even when women enter political contests, differential media coverage had a negative effect on their campaigns. An analysis of general election coverage of mixed-gender gubernatorial or U.S. Senate races in 2000 revealed that, although

FIGURE 13.4   Percentage of Women in State Legislatures, 2006

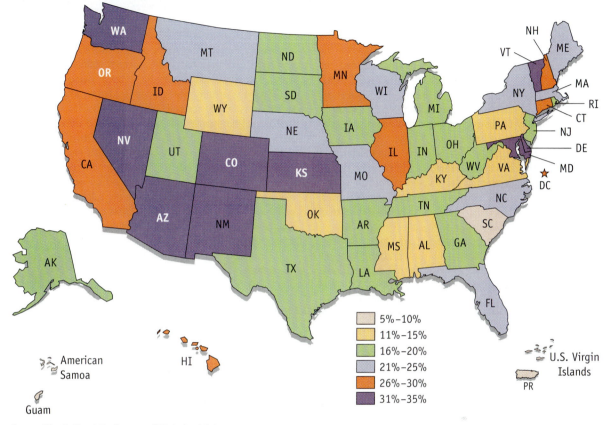

	5%–10%
	11%–15%
	16%–20%
	21%–25%
	26%–30%
	31%–35%

Source: The National Conference of State Legislatures.

the coverage from the primaries to the general election was relatively consistent across most categories of analysis, female candidates nevertheless still faced some stereotypical biases in the news coverage of their campaigns.[63] The precedent-setting presidential campaign of Hillary Clinton in 2007–2008 also prompted sexist coverage in the media.[64]

SOCIOLOGICAL ANALYSIS

Every society has had a gender-based division of labor, but this has not always meant sexual inequality. Why has the male role been considered superior in many societies? Functionalists, conflict theorists, and interactionists differ both in explaining the reasons for male dominance and in advocating steps to eliminate it.

The Functionalist View

In preindustrial societies, from which most immigrants to the United States have come, assigning work tasks by sex effectively created a smoothly functioning society. Such was also the case in the United States in the early 19th century, when

The International Scene

Women's Changing Status in Japan

Traditionally, Japanese men and women had clearly defined roles: the man was employed, and the woman stayed home with the children. In recent years, however, a battle of the sexes has been quietly escalating. National surveys reveal that most Japanese men look upon married family life as part of adulthood and seek a wife who will be a good housekeeper. Women, on the other hand, are rebelling. Educated, employed, and independent minded, many no longer feel compelled to marry by age 25. The Ministry of Health and Welfare predicts that 14 percent of women born after 1980 will stay single all their lives, which would reduce the country's already low birth rate of 1.3 children per women.

Even though Japanese women are among the best educated and most prosperous in the world, in 2007 only 9 percent of the members of the country's most powerful legislative body, the lower house of parliament (45 of 480), were women. Japanese women argue that their nation would be a different place if they had a louder political voice. Rather than endless parliamentary debates on highways and history, women might urge discussion of job discrimination against them, Japan's ban on oral contraceptives, and national labor laws that identify them as the "weaker" sex. One such law limits women's overtime hours, but not men's, and another entitles women to stay at home during their menstrual periods, giving male bosses an excuse to inquire into their female employees' private lives.

Sexual harassment (*seku hara*) is a serious problem in the workplace. In a 1998 survey of female government workers, almost 94 percent of respondents said they had experienced some form of sexual harassment, ranging from a display of nude posters in the office to forced sex. About 6 percent said they had been raped or almost raped at work. Although complaints have been rising, sexual harassment is a fairly new concept in Japan, where such conduct was largely accepted until the 1980s. The nation's first sexual-harassment lawsuit wasn't filed until 1992, and in 1997, the parliament adopted a law that requires corporations to take steps to prevent sexual harassment. Since then significant progress has occurred in combating this problem, but glass ceilings preventing women from reaching high positions still exist in most Japanese companies. Interestingly, no word for "glass ceiling" exists in Japanese, making it a difficult problem to confront, as many people do not even know the concept.

Japanese women feel bias in every aspect of life. For example, Japanese law requires a married couple to choose one name. If a husband wants to keep his name, the wife cannot keep her name after marriage. Legislators argued that allowing husbands and wives to use different names would be a dangerous step toward weakening the Japanese family.

Critical Thinking Question: How does the status of women in Japan compare to that in the United States, and what steps should be taken to improve conditions in both countries?

Sources: "Discrimination in Japan." Accessed at www.jref.com/society/discrimination_in_japan.shtml [January 26, 2008]; Howard W. French, "Fighting Sex Harassment and Stigma in Japan," *New York Times* (July 15, 2004, p. 41.)

---

distinct sex roles facilitated social stability, with women and men mostly accepting gender-specific roles in society. Sociologists Talcott Parsons and Robert Bales maintained that the efficient functioning of a society—indeed its very survival—depends on satisfying both instrumental and expressive needs.[65] Traditionally, men performed the instrumental tasks—goal-oriented activities necessary for family survival, such as earning a living and finding food to supplement what the female agriculturalists and herbalists grew or found. Women handled the expressive tasks—providing harmony, love, emotional support, and stability within the family. Today, many are questioning why these necessary tasks should be gender-linked and not shared—or reversed, if desired.

As mentioned in the section about biological explanations, the tendency of men to be larger, stronger, and more aggressive may explain their emergence as

In 2007, female representation in Congress was at an all-time high, with 16 senators and 71 representatives. However, with women constituting 51 percent of U.S. society, these numbers in the House and Senate are still disproportionate. In the Senate, eleven are Democrats and five are Republicans; in the House, 51 are Democrats and 20 are Republicans. At the state level, 24 percent of legislators are female.

dominant in the social order. As male dominance continued over the generations, a sexist ideology evolved to justify the existing order as "natural"; gender role and status became institutionalized through socialization and practice. As long as society remained relatively unchanged, gender-role differentiation did not emerge as a concern to most people or generate among women a group consciousness and desire for change.

Social changes caused by the Industrial Revolution threw the gender-based social structure out of balance. Machines curtailed the men's advantage of greater strength for work tasks. Reductions in the infant-mortality rate and in family size—together with labor-saving home appliances—freed women from spending most of their adult lives doing chores and raising small children. Values, attitudes, and expectations about women's proper role did not change as rapidly as social and economic conditions. This cultural lag caused strain among individuals, in families, and in society itself.

Among immigrants, both past and present, family and traditions have offered two vital means of preserving identity and stability in a new country. Persons with traditional gender-role value orientations experience problems adapting to a more egalitarian society. Working Hispanic women present a conflict to the *machismo* concept of the male as the sole provider. Social activities and dating practices among teenagers challenge traditional homeland norms about adolescent male–female interaction. Higher education for women runs counter to traditional notions that women should just marry and bear children.

Achieving sexual equality, functionalists stress, requires restoration of a balance between expectations and conditions. To some, changes have been too extensive, and system harmony requires a return to the past, with clearly defined gender roles restoring a stable family life and an efficient division of labor. Most functionalists, however, call for redefined gender roles and adjustments in the family system and other social institutions to eliminate sexual discrimination. Changes in societal conditions and expectations require system adjustments if the dysfunctions are to be overcome.

The Conflict View

For conflict theorists, male dominance, the subordination of women, sexual inequality, and gender discrimination illustrate the universal human problems of exploitation and oppression. Substituting the words *men* and *women* for the names of dominant and minority groups, or *sex* or *gender* for *class*, enables us to incorporate women as a group in Marxist concepts of false consciousness, exploitation, awakened awareness, and organized challenges to the social order. In fact, Friedrich Engels observed that the first class oppression in history was of "the female sex by the male."[66]

When the economic contributions of the two sexes were fairly even, as in hunting-and-gathering societies, sexual equality existed to a high degree. Women in those societies gathered a good share of edible foods and the men were not always successful in their hunting expeditions, thus making the activities of both important. Agrarian and pastoral societies drew on male strength for needed labor in plowing, irrigation, construction, crafts, and military defense. Sexual inequality then became more marked as disparities in economic contributions—a pattern continuing into early industrial societies, with women working only in low-paying positions.[67]

In industrial societies, their role as child bearers kept females dependent on male breadwinners and thus in an inferior position. The situation continued unchallenged until increasing numbers of women entered the labor force. The fairly recent demands for sexual equality correlate with women's growing economic contributions. In other words, women's economic position determines the degree of equality in relations between men and women in society.[68] As they achieved greater economic independence, women developed a heightened awareness of their shared bond of exploitation, and the feminist movement gained momentum and many successes in eliminating sexual discrimination.

A society's gender-based cultural characteristics, which are the product of generations of thought and reinforced patterns of behavior, live on through social institutions that perpetuate the sexist ideology that women are childlike, passive, and inferior. For centuries, the social structure of most societies placed men in controlling positions of political, economic, and social power. The subordinate role of women in society and in the family clearly benefited men, giving them little incentive to change the gender-role patterns. A prevailing male value system conferred superior status on men and an inferior one on women, defining the female role as supportive to the more highly valued male activities. In classic Marxist theory, only the social action of the subordinate group in challenging this arrangement can effect a change.

Who benefits from sexual inequality? Men do, in higher status, better jobs, higher pay, greater life satisfaction, and more leisure time at home while their wives fulfill domestic and childcare chores. Business and industry reap higher profits by employing women at lower rates than men through a process that sociologists Robert Nelson and William Bridges call "organizational inequity" (i.e., not free-market driven).[69] This oppression of women exacts a toll from members of both sexes: denial of full human development and full use of one's talents, loss to the society of much human creativity and leadership, and individual suffering in economic deprivation and in emotional and psychological strain.

The Interactionist View

Through social interaction and the internalization of others' expectations, the self emerges. From birth through adulthood, children go through a socialization process that shapes their sense of identity on the basis of cultural value orientations about gender roles. All the socialization agents—family, school, peers, church, media—promote gender-role identity and norms in various ways, including example and reinforcement. Social definitions of appropriate behavior, emotions, and goals for boys and girls become internalized as desirable attributes for acceptance and praise. Because these social definitions begin early, are pervasive, and are accepted by those so defined, they appear to be "natural," explaining how "nature" or "God" intended us to be.

In this socially constructed reality of shared expectations about the capabilities and proper behavior of men and women, people interact with one another on the basis of their cultural conditioning. Men do not, however, consciously and deliberately subjugate women, and women do not passively submit to their masters. For the most part, both sexes have long interacted with each other in a taken-for-granted manner as to their "place" in the social structure. William I. Thomas's famous statement (made in 1911) indicates both the consequences of social definitions (including sexism) and the "male reality" of his time: "If men define a situation as real, it is real in its consequences."

Technological changes have altered our social structure and life expectations. As a result, traditional gender roles no longer find acceptance among many women. Yet a consensus does not exist about what it means to be male or female, a fact that creates an ambiguous situation. Gender roles may be blurring, but strongly held concepts of masculinity and femininity remain popular and influential. We live in a transitional period, during which society is redefining gender roles even while many aspects of traditional gender-role attitudes and practices continue. How long and difficult will this transitional period be? No one knows, although evidence from surveys on gender-role attitudes shows increased acceptance of women in nontraditional roles among both men and women.[70] As new patterns of male–female interaction become institutionalized in various social arenas, we may find greater acceptance of sexual equality.

Because the socialization process is so critical, interactionists stress the need to change its content and approach. Thus, parents can be made more aware of existing sexual biases in behavioral expectations of their children, encouraging them to develop fully all aspects of their personalities. Through education and the media, a more enlightened approach—eliminating sexual stereotypes and providing varied role models for both sexes—could do much to promote change and sexual equality. The media and the academic world could also do much to resocialize women to overcome their past conditioning and to resocialize all adults to adopt a more egalitarian value system. This perspective holds that ideas tend to have a life of their own and that, by concentrating on how we interpret the world, we can create a new social reality.

◆◆◆ RETROSPECT

U.S. society has only recently recognized sexism as a social problem, although it has existed for centuries. Minority-group characteristics—ascribed status, physical and cultural visibility, unequal treatment, and shared-group awareness—apply to women just as they do to various racial and ethnic groups, even though they are not a numeric minority. The practice of endogamy does not apply, but in marriage, the dominant–subordinate roles are often quite obvious. Females who accept their minority status are thus predisposed not to challenge it.

Throughout much of U.S. history, male-dominance patterns prevailed. Women lacked voting, contract, and property rights and were even denied the right to enjoy sex without being thought deviant. After a long struggle, women gained the right to vote nationally in 1919 but for a long time did not elect many women to office. During World War II, many women were employed, but peacetime brought a renewed emphasis on the home as a "woman's proper place." In the 1960s, the feminist movement began anew, fostering social awareness and still unfolding social change.

Despite some biological differences between the sexes in size, strength, and longevity, socialization primarily shapes gender identity and gender-role behavior. Entrenched value orientations result in a conditioning process that produces differential behavior patterns and life goals. The resulting sexual inequality is evident throughout society and doubly so among minority women. In education, employment, income, legal status, and political power, women's status has improved but remains far from parity with men.

Functionalists contend that a gender-based division of labor was an efficient means of achieving a smoothly functioning society in the past, but they argue that technology has since thrown the social system out of balance, requiring some form of adjustment. Conflict theorists stress the oppression of women as economically based and beneficial to male status and power. Interactionists focus on the social interpretation of reality through socialization and interaction patterns, suggesting that changing the content of the socialization process will eliminate sexual inequality.

KEY TERMS

Ascribed status	Flex-time	Mommy track
Child care	Gender-role expectations	Role entrapment
Endogamy	Glass ceiling	Sexism
Fast track	Matrilineal	
Feminization of poverty	Matrilocal	

DISCUSSION QUESTIONS

1. How can we consider women a minority group?
2. What are some examples of past male discrimination against women?
3. Discuss the biological and sociological explanations of gender-role behavior.

4. Give some examples of the problems of sexism among first- and second-generation U.S. residents.

5. Give examples of sexual discrimination in education, work, income, and law.

6. What are some consequences, both in and out of academia, of accepting the classification of women as a minority?

7. How do the three major sociological perspectives explain sexism?

SUGGESTED READINGS

Andersen, Margaret L. *Thinking about Women: Sociological Perspectives on Sex and Gender*, 7th ed. New York: Macmillan, 2006.
A thorough analysis of women's lives, covering such issues as culture, biology, family life, work, and social change.

Carroll, Susan J. (ed.). *Women and American Politics: New Questions, New Directions*. New York: Oxford University Press, 2003. Leading scholars in this area discuss recent developments and challenges for women in different aspects of the political arena.

Ferree, Myra Marx, and Beth B. Hess. *Controversy and Coalition: The New Feminist Movement across Three Decades of Change*, rev. ed. New York: Routledge, 2000. A solid, sociological examination of the women's movement, from Betty Friedan's groundbreaking book in 1963 through the early 1990s.

Hochschild, Arlie R. *The Time Bind: When Work Becomes Home and Home Becomes Work*. New York: Owl Books, Holt, 2001. Persuasively describes a growing chasm between family and work as parents jockey for more time at the office, leaving children to longer shifts in daycare or after-school activities.

Kimmel, Michael S. *The Gendered Society*, 3rd ed. New York: Oxford University Press, 2007. Examines current thinking about gender relations today, demolishes myths and misunderstandings, and explores how gender convergence—not androgyny—is the promise of the future.

Reskin, Barbara F., and Irene Padavic. *Women and Men at Work*, 2nd ed. Thousand Oaks, CA: Pine Forge Press, 2002. A lucid analysis of such issues as gender-segregated work, wage differentials, the work–family dilemma, and male–female work interactions.

Richardson, Laurel, Verta Taylor, and Nancy Whittier (eds.). *Feminist Frontiers*, 6th ed. New York: McGraw-Hill, 2003. An excellent anthology covering a wide range of women's issues, including diversity, the social construction of gender, work, family, health, violence, and the feminist movement.

MYSOCKIT

Additional resources for this chapter can be found in MySocKit. If you have a subscription to MySocKit, go to www.mysockit.com to study, review, and go beyond the book to learn more about race and ethnic relations.

Gays, People with Disabilities, and the Elderly

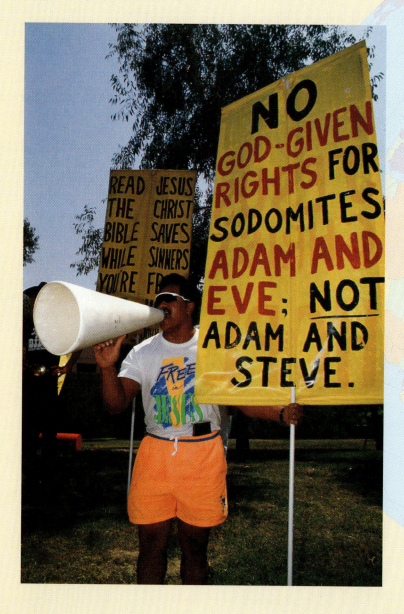

People can be members of minority groups because of race, ethnicity, and gender as discussed in earlier chapters, or they may struggle against prejudice and discrimination to gain equal rights and full integration into society. Despite significant progress in improving their quality of life, the unequal treatment and life experiences of gays and lesbians, the disabled, and the elderly reveal that much more remains to be done for them to achieve equal rights the same as other citizens in a democracy.

As with the other minorities we have studied, to varying degrees these three groups share the minority-group characteristics discussed in Chapter 1. This is particularly true in their receiving unequal treatment as a group and feeling a sense of group solidarity. The disabled and elderly share distinguishing physical characteristics, the elderly are typically married to others of a comparable age, and membership in their group is, for the most part, involuntary. Moreover, in keeping with the theme and title of this book, in a very real sense they are "strangers" when it comes to being inclusive members of society. Our discussion in Chapter 1 about similarity and attraction, social distance, categoric knowing, Simmel's duality of remoteness and nearness, and Schutz's "intersubjective understanding" are all helpful in understanding more completely how these three groups compare to other minority groups in attempting to overcome their marginalization and also to learn what current issues remain to be addressed.

SEXUAL ORIENTATION

History has recorded descriptive evidence of the existence of homosexuality for millennia. Most of our knowledge of the sexual behaviors and norms of past historical periods, however, comes by inference from the literature and public writings of the times. We do not really know how most people were behaving.

▲▲▲ SOCIOHISTORICAL PERSPECTIVE

Homosexuality existed without sanctions among the ancient Babylonians, Chinese, Egyptians, and Romans. The ancient Greeks not only accepted it as a natural expression of sexual instinct, but praised it as more genuine and tender than heterosexual love. The word *pederasty* literally means the love of boys, and most homosexuality in ancient Greece was between men and adolescents—often between a well-born teacher or mentor and his student or apprentice—not between adult males. Less well documented is homosexuality among nonaristocratic ancient Greeks. About the only evidence we have is the mention of freeborn male prostitutes.

> To the bisexual Greek, women and boys were both defined as submissive non-males. Many non-Western societies have similar attitudes and behavior patterns, and one finds this in highly diluted form in much of the Mediterranean world today. A man can have boys as well as women as long as he takes a clearly dominant role and "womanizes" partners of both genders.[1]

Such practices extend beyond the Mediterranean world. For example, the Bedamini people of New Guinea believe that the sharing of semen between older and younger males is a natural means of enhancing masculinity and strength.[2]

Throughout the Middle Ages and the Renaissance, European society viewed homosexuality and heterosexual sodomy as sins and crimes. Governments in most of Europe, from Sweden to England to Italy, executed individuals found guilty of such acts. In 1492, for example, Venetian officials ordered a nobleman and a priest to be publicly beheaded and burned for committing homosexual acts. In France, authorities in 1586 burned at the stake a former provost of the University of Paris for injuring a boy in the act of anal rape.[3] Such events indicate the stance of the Church and of society toward homosexuality but not how prevalent such forbidden conduct was.

For many years, social science researchers—influenced by societal norms that included religion-based condemnation and psychiatric labeling of homosexuality as an aberration signaling mental illness—focused on homosexuality as a social problem. In fact, much of what was written through the late 1980s came from a psychiatric or psychoanalytical perspective that assumed homosexuality was pathological and that homosexuals were "sick" or "perverted."[4] In 1973, the American Psychiatric Association deleted homosexuality from its list of psychiatric disorders and began efforts to end discrimination against homosexuals. Nowadays—with homosexuality no longer labeled an illness, with an increasing body of research suggesting that sexual preference is a function of biology not choice, with growing public acceptance, and with sexual preference protected under civil rights legislation—researchers emphasize discriminatory practices against homosexuals as a social problem instead.

▲▲▲ GAY GENETICS

Although many people long insisted on a biological explanation for homosexuality, it was not until the 1990s that several studies claimed the discovery of such proof. One scientist, Simon LeVay, conducted postmortem examination of brain tissues of nineteen homosexual males, sixteen heterosexual males, and six heterosexual females. In the anterior hypothalamus (a part of the brain scientists believe plays a part in sexual behavior), he found significant differences. In the homosexual males this region was about the same size as those found in women's brains, whereas those of the heterosexual males were three times larger.[5] Another study disclosed size differences in a structure inside the anterior commissure (a band of nerve fibers scientists believe facilitates communication between the left and right hemispheres of the brain). This part of the brain was larger in homosexual men than in women or heterosexual men.[6]

Other geneticists studied forty-four sets of gay male twins and found that 75 percent of them shared a unique part of the X chromosome, which is far greater than would occur by chance alone. Furthermore, they found that these men were significantly more likely to have gay male relatives on their mother's side. Since men receive the X chromosome from their mothers only, this finding would suggest a genetic link to sexual orientation.[7] However, no other scientist has been able to replicate this finding.[8] Numerous recent studies have found significant physiological and cognitive differences between gays and straights, suggesting biology does play some role. However, the American Academy of Pediatrics maintains that sexual orientation probably is not determined by any one factor but by a combination of genetic, hormonal, and environmental influences.[9]

These studies, sometimes contradictory, remain controversial, partly because of sample size and partly because they only show a biological component to homosexuality, not a cause and effect. Expression of a biological trait, such as left-handedness or temperament, depends not only on a great many social factors but also can be altered by them. At best, these studies on homosexuality suggest a partial biological explanation.

HOMOSEXUALITY IN THE UNITED STATES

Openness about being homosexual was uncommon in the United States prior to the 1960s, except in major cities, where strong subcultures thrived. For example, George Chauncey described New York City's gay community from 1890 to 1940 as having its own traditions, gathering places, and cultural and social events that sustained and enhanced gay men's communal ties and group identity.[10] Although existing laws criminalized gay men's sexual behavior and even their nonsexual association with each other, these laws were indifferently enforced. As a result, gay men formed a wide world of overlapping social networks with excellent support systems: emotional, social, and commercial. By the 1930s, popular fascination with gay culture led thousands of people to attend the city's drag balls, and newspapers published sketches of the most sensational gowns.

Stigma and Sanctions

A shift in public attitude about lifestyle experimentation—prompted perhaps by a coalescing of the conservative currents that underlay religious fundamentalism and Prohibition and augmented by fears of social disintegration raised by the Depression, labor unrest, and the specter of Bolshevism—resulted in more stringent enforcement of all laws during the 1930s and 1940s, including the previously ignored ones against homosexuality, which society now labeled as deviant sexual behavior. During the Cold War of the 1950s, Communist hunter U.S. Senator Joseph McCarthy warned that homosexuals in the State Department were threatening national security. At that time, discovery or even suspicion as a homosexual could severely disrupt a person's life in any occupation. Getting fired was quite possible; getting taunted was probable. Going into an area known to be frequented by homosexual men or lesbians and beating them up was a popular teenage pastime. To most homosexuals, "passing," or carrying out their lives in such a way as to appear heterosexual, was crucial. As Chauncey observes, "The State built the closet and forced the homosexuals into it."[11]

Though not as severe as the laws in Britain (where, until 1861, anal intercourse was punishable by death), U.S. laws were still quite harsh toward homosexual men. Until recently, many sexual acts commonly practiced in the United States, such as oral–genital sex and anal sex, were considered "crimes against nature" and were illegal. Municipalities invoked these laws, usually lumped under sodomy statues, primarily to prosecute homosexual men.

Tolerance and Backlash

The **homophobia** (an irrational fear of gay people) of the 1950s and the resulting stigma and harm that could result from openness about their sexual preference led many homosexuals to adopt a low profile despite the efforts of activist organizers in several cities. To avoid exposure, many gays hid their true selves from the straight world and quietly sought companionship in their bathhouses and bars.[12] In 1969, at one such gay bar, the Stonewall Inn in New York City, an event occurred that marked a shift in the gay community from passive adaptive goals to active militancy. The police had routinely raided the bars in the past, but on this occasion, the customers fought back rather than retreating. The event galvanized the gay community to become more assertive and to publicly acknowledge their sexual identity. As other minorities had done earlier in the 1960s, gays and lesbians joined organizations and struggled to secure equal rights and opportunities.[13]

The 1970s and 1980s saw major gains in public tolerance, including the addition of "sexual orientation" to antidiscrimination policies and statutes at local, state, and national levels. Tolerance of gay people increased as the gay rights movement gained strength. More gays "came out of the closet" and annual Gay Pride parades became part of large city celebrations. Then the AIDS epidemic of the 1980s devastated the gay community, bringing enormous personal loss and grief, but also a renewed outburst of prejudice, discrimination, and violence against homosexuals.[14] A dramatic increase in cases of arson, assault, and murder against homosexuals marked the 1990s.[15]

Religious and political conservatives launched campaigns in the 1990s to pass local ordinances condemning homosexuality and to prevent the inclusion of sexual orientation under the protection of state antidiscrimination laws.[16] They also objected, along with military leaders, when President Bill Clinton attempted in 1993 to repeal the official ban on gays in the armed forces. The "don't ask, don't tell" compromise sidesteps the issue of equal rights for people of all sexual orientations, but it does allow gay men and women to serve in the military without surveillance or persecution, provided they do not make their sexual preference known.[17] Such a policy, however, exacts a heavy toll. With a shortage of Arabic linguists to handle military intelligence, as of mid-2007, more than 58 have been kicked out of the military for being gay, and 11,000 other service members have been involuntarily discharged.[18]

A 1986 U.S. Supreme Court decision (*Bowers v. Hardwick*) said people do not have a constitutional protection to engage in private homosexual conduct. In other cases, the Court has ruled in favor of gays, such as its 1996 negation of a Colorado referendum that banned all measures protecting homosexuals from discrimination. Perhaps most important was its 2003 decision, *Lawrence v. Texas*, which over-turned *Bowers* and ruled that intimate consensual sexual conduct was one of the liberties protected under due process by the Fourteenth Amendment. In effect, this decision invalidated all state laws that criminalized private homosexual activity between consenting adults, leading gay rights activists to call the decision historic, the equivalent of the 1954 *Brown v. Board of Education* desegregation ruling.

How Many Gays Are There?

How common is homosexuality in the United States? The exact population of homosexuals has always been difficult to determine. Until the late twentieth century, the source most often cited was the 1948 research of Alfred Kinsey, which estimated that 10 percent of all Americans were homosexuals. However, although Kinsey used a large sample, it was not a **random sample,** an objective process that allows everyone the same chance of being selected. Instead, Kinsey settled for a **convenience sample,** relying largely on college student volunteers who had attended his lectures on sexuality. Convenience samples may thus overestimate prevalence because they sample the dependent variable, in this case young, sexu-ally active people more likely to have diverse experiences. A truly representative cross-section of the public is a more likely probability sample and so most social scientists feel uncomfortable using a convenience sample to make generalizations. In Kinsey's case, subsequent studies showed his findings were inflated estimations.

Recent studies from Britain, Canada, Denmark, France, and Norway have identified the number of homosexuals in these countries to be in the 1 to 4 percent range, significantly below Kinsey's findings of 10 percent in the United States. Gay rights activists argued that the European findings were flawed because sexual orientation is not just actual behavior but also feelings—how a person falls in love—which is not measurable. This issue of proportion has political overtones, since the accepted number could strengthen or weaken the impact of gays as a recognized constituency on lawmakers and other government officials.[19]

In 1994, a more definitive, scientific answer came from Robert T. Michael, John H. Gagnon, Edward O. Laumann, and Gina Kolata, who reported their find-ings from the largest study of sexual behavior ever conducted in the United States using a random sample.[20] The researchers used computers to select addresses at random; then they chose which members of households to interview, again at ran-dom. From interviewer training to question development, they conducted this study according to strict rules of scientific data collection. They found that 2.7 percent of the males and 1.3 percent of the females reported having had sex with someone of the same gender within the past year. The findings were higher when the time frame extended back to puberty: 7.3 percent for males and 3.8 percent for females. When asked if they were sexually attracted to others of the same gender, 6.2 percent of the males and 4.4 percent of the females said they were (Figure 14.1).

The varying percentages suggest an important element about sexual behavior that Kinsey discovered in 1948. Sexual orientation is a continuum, not a simple

FIGURE 14.1   Homosexuality in the United States

Have you had sex with someone of the same gender?

In the past year?

Men — 2.7%
Women — 1.3%

Since puberty?

Men — 7.3%
Women — 3.8%

Are you sexually attracted to people of the same gender?

Men — 6.2%
Women — 4.4%

Source: Robert T. Michael, John H. Gagnon, Edward O. Laumann, and Gina Kolata, *Sex in America: A Definitive Survey* (Boston: Little, Brown, 1994).

classification of people into one of two distinct categories. Kinsey created a seven-point rating scale with exclusive homosexuality at one end and exclusive heterosexuality at the other—with desires, actions, and their frequency determining the five in-between stages. Whatever the criteria, however, the 1994 study suggested that the actively homosexual population is considerably smaller than Kinsey had estimated.

Public Attitudes about Homosexuality

Public opinion about homosexuality, including civil unions and gay adoptions, is steadily becoming more tolerant.[21] For example, a 2004 Gallup poll revealed that 54 percent of Americans considered homosexuality an acceptable alternative lifestyle, compared to 35 percent in 1989. However, Americans were equally divided between those approving (43 percent) and those disapproving of gay rights (42 percent), with the rest uncertain. On the questions of whether the effort to protect gay rights has been about right, not enough, or gone too far, Americans answered 22 percent, 25 percent, and 45 percent respectively. Thus, a plurality said efforts had gone too far.[22]

In a 2004 Gallup poll, a majority of Americans (58 percent) reported that they personally knew someone who was gay (a friend, relative, or coworker). This is a dramatic increase from 1983, when pollsters routinely found that only 24 percent knew a homosexual. In a 2004 *Los Angeles Times* poll, 69 percent said they knew someone who was gay or lesbian, while 62 percent said so in a 2004 NBC/*Wall Street Journal* poll. These increasing percentages augur well. The **intergroup contact hypothesis** maintains that, when social interaction is marked by equal status (as with coworkers) or affective ties (as with friends and relatives), individuals will have more positive attitudes (e.g., less antigay prejudice) and behaviors (e.g., making fewer anti-gay comments or jokes).[23] Indeed, this is the case. Persons who know a homosexual are more likely to have generally supportive attitudes toward gay rights—73 percent, as compared to 55 percent among respondents who do not know gay people.[24] Furthermore, 70 percent of all persons surveyed think society should allow gays and straights (nonhomosexuals) equal workplace opportunities.[25]

CURRENT ISSUES

Although antidiscrimination laws, affirmative action guidelines establishing sexual orientation as a protected category, and a growing level of tolerance in society have improved conditions for gays and lesbians, it would be foolish to suggest they no longer encounter problems (see The Ethnic Experience below). In a recent poll, half of all Americans said things had "gotten better" when it comes to treating gay people with respect and courtesy, but 24 percent thought things remained about the same and 15 percent thought the situation was worse. Eleven percent said they didn't know.[26] Contentious issues heightening emotions and no doubt affecting such mixed feelings are hate crimes, same-sex marriages, and gay parenting.

Hate Crimes

Although they have declined somewhat in recent years, hate crimes remain a serious concern. The FBI reported that in 2006, 15.5 percent of all hate crimes were due to sexual orientation bias, claiming over 1,500 victims. Although

The Ethnic Experience

Double Marginality

I hated being me practically my entire life. I hated being Italian American practically my entire life. I hated the negative stereotypes associated with being Italian American; I did not want to admit that I was American of Italian descent because of such negative stereotypes and images. As a young child, I wanted to change my last name to "Carson," or something else "non-Italian." I was embarrassed and ashamed of who I was and where I came from. My identity was in a crisis, and it would not be until many years later—in my adulthood—after reading much about Italian Americans, written by Italian Americans, that my identity crisis would come to an end. Literature has amazing powers that can change the lives of the readers; literature saved my life.

When I was a young child in elementary school—I cannot remember the exact age—I had a difficult time relating to the other students. I knew that I did not "fit in." I was not the only American of Italian descent, but

I was one of the few in a school with mostly Jewish American and Irish American children. And, of course, I befriended the other three to five children who were also Italian American. We formed a close bond.

Later in life, I would come to realize that my ethnicity was not the only aspect of my life that marginalized me, and made me not "fit in." As a homosexual male, my sexual orientation also marginalized me, and made me feel like an outcast, made me feel less than human. And it must be stated, and known, that with its conservative and traditional ways of thinking, the Italian American community—my own community—has not always been accepting and understanding of my sexual orientation. Ironically, one marginalized community marginalizes—even minimizes and oppresses—another marginalized community.

Source: Michael Carosone, New York City, 2007. Recorded commentary from the collection of Vincent N. Parrillo.

homosexuals get protection under hate crime and civil rights laws, their protection under the Constitution rests on a case-by-case judicial decision.

Even though it happened in 1998, the murder of University of Wyoming student Matthew Shepard remains the national centerpiece of hate crimes against gays. In a bar shortly after midnight on October 7th, 21-year-old Shepard met Russell McKinney and Aaron Henderson, who, according to their girlfriends, had gone there to rob a gay man. Shepard asked them for a ride home. Subsequently, they took him to a remote rural area, robbed him, and pistol whipped him so severely that they fractured his skull from the front to the right ear, causing severe brain stem damage. They then tied him to a fence, where he was discovered by a cyclist 18 hours later. Brought to a hospital where doctors determined his injuries were too severe for them to operate, he lay unconscious and on full life support for four days, his case prompting candlelight vigils around the world. After his death, the two murderers were found, arrested, convicted and sentenced to life terms in prison. In the aftermath, then-President Bill Clinton renewed attempts to extend federal hate crime legislation to include gay and lesbian individuals, women, and people with disabilities. After various setbacks, the Matthew Shepard Act passed the House of Representatives in March 2007; but in December 2007 Congress dropped this legislation, as it was attached as a rider to a defense spending bill. As of this writing, its fate remains uncertain as President Bush has threatened to veto the bill if it passes the Senate.

Same-Sex Marriages

As of 2007, same-sex marriages were legally permissible in Belgium, Canada, the Netherlands, Spain, and in the state of Massachusetts. The states of California, Connecticut, Hawaii, New Jersey, and Vermont—as well as fifteen other European countries—allowed gays and lesbians to enter into civil unions or domestic partnerships, entitling them to receive all benefits, rights, privileges, and obligations as heterosexual couples.[27] However, in the United States, same-sex couples are presently denied any and all federal benefits.

Although national public opinion polls show that the majority of Americans oppose same-sex marriage (SSM), over the years the surveys show a fairly constant trend toward greater acceptance. A March 2006 poll by the Pew Center found 39 percent supportive of SSM, but an April 2006 poll by Peter D. Hart Research Associates found only 27 percent giving a positive response. Major opposition comes from Evangelical Christians (83 percent opposed in 2003) and African Americans (64 percent opposed). Interestingly, in several national polls of high school seniors in 2001 and 2005, about twice as many respondents favored SSM as did adults in national polls taken at the same time.[28]

Gay Parenting

The controversy swirling around the issue of gay parenting comes from deep-seated religious beliefs about the morality of homosexuality and possible negative child development consequences (gender role confusion, biased sexual orientation) for children raised by same-sex adoptive parents. However, research findings indicate that, when comparing children of same-sex parents with opposite-sex parents, no differences occur "on measures of popularity, social adjustment, gender role behavior, gender identity, intelligence, self-concept,

Four of five children living with gay parents are adopted and the remaining ones have foster parents. Because of religious beliefs, some states, such as Florida, do not permit gay adoptions. In comparing straight and gay families, research shows children are equally well-adjusted in gender identity and behavior.

emotional problems, interest in marriage and parenting, locus of control, moral development, independence, ego functions, object relations, or self-esteem."[29]

States vary greatly in their laws about adoption. Gays and lesbians, as individuals, can adopt in almost every state. Florida prohibits adoption by homosexuals, although they may be foster parents. Mississippi bans adoption by same-sex couples but gay singles may adopt. Utah prohibits any unmarried couple, whether heterosexual or homosexual, from adoption. In the past few years, at least 16 other state legislatures seriously considered banning gay adoptions but, as of this writing, none did so.

A 2007 report from the nonpartisan Urban Institute estimated that 65,500 adopted children (four percent of all adoptees) and another 14,100 foster children (three percent of the total) are living with gay or lesbian parents. California is home to the most gay parents (about 16,000). Same-sex couples raising adopted children are older, more educated, and have more economic resources than other adoptive parents. More than half of gay men and 41 percent of lesbians want to have a child. An estimated two million gay and lesbian people are interested in adopting.[30]

PEOPLE WITH DISABILITIES

People with disabilities have been members of all societies for thousands of years. For example, the *Rig-Veda*, an ancient sacred poem of India written between 3500 and 1800 BCE, tells of a warrior queen, Vishpla, who—after losing a leg in warfare—was fitted with a iron artificial limb and returned to battle. Despite such exceptional amputee battle heroes—Roman General Marcus Sergius (against Carthage in 218 BCE) and German mercenary knight Gotz von Berlichingen (Battle of Landshut in 1508 CE) are two others—most people with disabilities throughout recorded history lived ordinary lives but often struggled to overcome indifference, maltreatment, or pity, receiving little to nothing in the way of societal assistance.

The term *disability*, of course, refers to far more than only those who suffer loss of a limb. Definitions vary greatly, but U.S. federal law defines a "disability" as any physical or mental impairment that substantially limits one or more major life activities, such as breathing, hearing, learning, seeing, speaking, taking care of oneself, walking, or working. Such a disability may be partial or total, temporary or permanent.

Given the varying definitions and subjective nature of reporting among countries, the exact number of people with disabilities is difficult to determine. The highest estimate comes from the United Nations, which places the figure at 650 million, while the World Health Organization estimates the total at about 600 million.[31] In the United States, 56 million people have some type of disability; 2.5 million use wheelchairs, 1.7 million are legally blind, and 11 million use sign language as their primary means of communication (see Figure 14.2 and The Minority Experience, pages 511 and 512). These are only the visible disabilities; tens of millions more have AIDS, cancer, diabetes, epilepsy, hypertension, mental retardation, some forms of multiple sclerosis, psychiatric disorders, and traumatic brain injury.[32] This makes people with disabilities the third largest U.S. minority group, behind African and Hispanic Americans.

These numbers will continue to increase, from casualties in the fighting in Afghanistan and Iraq, and from people living longer and thus becoming more susceptible to debilitating ailments. In addition, thanks to continuing advances in medicine, people who previously would have died from life-threatening illnesses or accidents now survive but do so with less than fully functioning capabilities.

◆◆◆ SOCIOHISTORICAL PERSPECTIVE

Until about the mid-nineteenth century, the prevailing view in most cultures was those with disabilities were "bad people" under punishment from God. Accordingly, families with someone with a disability typically felt embarrassment and shame and so would hide disabled family members away from school and other societal interactions, thereby excluding them from any meaningful role in society. The public, when aware of individuals with disabilities, might feel sympathy for them and a moral obligation to offer them some assistance and support as charity cases. Essentially though, this one-time prevalent viewpoint often resulted in both a negative self-image (even self-hatred) among the disabled and social ostracism.

With the evolution of modern medicine in the mid-19th century, doctors sought to treat, if not cure, the problems associated with disability. The placement of individuals with disabilities into a "sick role" under the care of a medical professional meant institutionalization or confinement (exclusion) for some and a state of dependency for others. This latter social construct occurred because, when people are classified as "sick," a common assumption arises that they cannot do the things others do—learn in a regular classroom, engage in

FIGURE 14.2 Disability Status, 2000

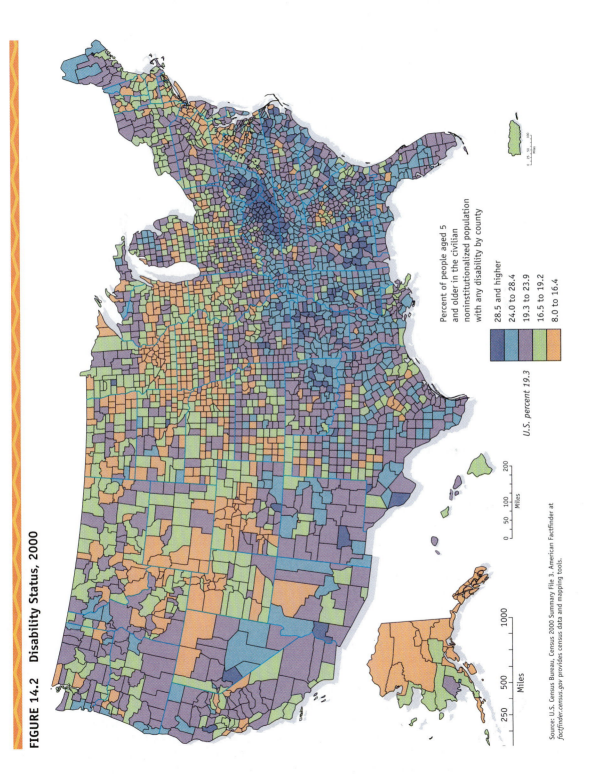

Percent of people aged 5 and older in the civilian noninstitutionalized population with any disability by county

28.5 and higher
24.0 to 28.4
19.3 to 23.9
16.5 to 19.2
8.0 to 16.4

U.S. percent 19.3

Source: U.S. Census Bureau, Census 2000 Summary File 3. American Factfinder at *factfinder.census.gov* provides census data and mapping tools.

The Minority Experience

Deafness in a Hearing World

A regretful irony of the telephone is that it sprang out of Alexander Graham Bell's efforts to devise speech communication instruments for deaf people. Instead, by premising human speech and hearing as the isolated means of telecommunication, the telephone served as the greatest technology disenfranchisement that deaf people ever experienced.

Due to the inaccessibility of the telephone to us, my deaf family had to depend on the kindness of our neighbors in making only those calls deemed absolutely essential. We compensated for the lack of an inclusive design by devising the teletypewriter (TTY) as an assistive technology to enable telecommunications through telephones. Still, for more than two decades, those with TTYs were limited to calling others who also had TTYs.

As a fledgling lawyer in the late 1980s, the only means available to me to telecommunicate with other attorneys was through a volunteer operated relay system where I would use my TTY to call someone who would assist in my call by voicing my typewritten message to the telephone user and vice versa. I cannot begin to say how many times I was hung up on or treated rudely as a result of a telephone user irritated with the slowness of my typed and relayed conversation. Adding injury to insult were the limitations on the charitable-based relay service, including allowance of only 3 calls at a time, with busy numbers counted, and queues often stretching up to an hour before my gaining access to the next available individual to relay my call.

Fast forward to nearly two decades after enactment of the 1990 Americans with Disabilities Act (ADA). Title IV of the ADA requires common carriers (telephone companies) to establish interstate and intrastate telecommunications relay services (TRS) 24 hours a day, 7 days a week. TRS enables callers with hearing and speech disabilities who use telecommunications devices for the deaf (TDDs or updated teletypewriters, the TTYs), and callers who use voice telephones to communicate with each other through a third party communications assistant. However, there is a significant disparity between the rates of typing speech versus the speed one could sign or receive someone's interpreted oral communications. In 2002, the Federal Communications Commission (FCC) recognized that a visual telecommunications medium was needed for people whose native language was American Sign Language (ASL) and permitted the inclusion of video phones as part of the relay system, whereby deaf people can telecommunicate through a video interpreter. As a result, more than a dozen Video Relay Service (VRS) providers now provide sign language interpreting services for millions of deaf people, ushering in a new era of functional equivalency in telecommunications well more than a century after Bell patented the telephone.

Significantly, VRS providers employ a disproportionately higher percentage of deaf and hard of hearing people in every level of the industry. The VRS model serves as a powerful example of how a civil right (Title IV of the ADA) can be leveraged by a publicly-funded, market-based approach to bring about technology that is inclusive of people with disabilities rather than us chasing technology through separate and stand alone devices such as the TTY/TDD.

Source: Jeff Rosen is a third generation deaf person and the General Counsel and Vice President of Governmental Affairs for a company that provides a video relay service for deaf and hard of hearing people.

physical activities, work, or otherwise engage in normal social activities—until they get "fixed." Until then, they "need" someone to take care of them. Such an approach places individuals under the control of others. If they try to be independent and go to work, they could lose their disability status and all related benefits (including health care coverage).[33]

Another problem with this **medical model** is its implication that, since the disabled supposedly cannot function independently, society has no responsibility to integrate them, be it wheelchair access to buildings, sign language interpreters at important gatherings, or access to public transportation. The emphasis is that the individual is the problem and must adapt to the world as it is or else be placed in an institution or isolated at home.

Paralyzed in both legs to the hips by polio at age 39 in 1921, Franklin Delano Roosevelt, not wishing to be stigmatized, hid his disability from public view. In private moments, such as here at his Hyde Park retreat in New York where he is talking to the caretaker's daughter, Ruthie Bie, he would sit in a wheelchair.

Beginning in the 1960s, a new approach evolved that took note of the "differently abled," people whose physical or mental impairments may not lead to disability if society adapts to accommodate them rather than the other way around (Figure 14.3). This **social model** sought to eliminate the prejudice, exclusion, and barriers in society—whether deliberate or unintentional—that resulted in the disabled as a socially marginalized group. Efforts thus focused on changing attitudes and physical structures, on mainstreaming children in schools, and other societal restructuring that provides empowerment and equality to the disabled so that they can live lives to the fullest extent possible.

Impetus for many of these changes came from Ed Roberts—a polio victim and "father of the independent living movement"—who, together with other young adults with disabilities at Cowell (UC Berkeley Health Center), formed a group in 1970 called the Rolling Quads and the Disabled Students' Program on the campus and then in 1971 created a Center for Independent Living (CIL). Originally the CIL was a two-bedroom, roach-infested apartment, until the group received a $50,000 grant from the Rehabilitation Administration a year later. It became a model for hundreds of other similar centers throughout the United States.[34]

In the latter part of the 20th century, a disability rights movement (led by persons with disabilities) and precedent-setting legislation (to be discussed shortly) began a sea change in attitudes and behaviors, a process still unfolding. As these changes take root, they are unraveling decades of social prejudice and institutional discrimination.

FIGURE 14.3 Disability Models

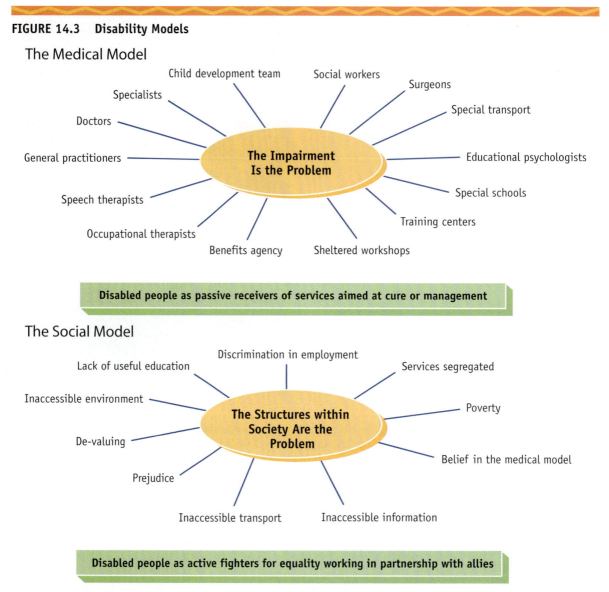

The Medical Model

Child development team
Social workers
Surgeons
Specialists
Special transport
Doctors
General practitioners — **The Impairment Is the Problem** — Educational psychologists
Speech therapists
Special schools
Occupational therapists
Training centers
Benefits agency
Sheltered workshops

Disabled people as passive receivers of services aimed at cure or management

The Social Model

Discrimination in employment
Lack of useful education
Services segregated
Inaccessible environment
The Structures within Society Are the Problem
Poverty
De-valuing
Belief in the medical model
Prejudice
Inaccessible transport
Inaccessible information

Disabled people as active fighters for equality working in partnership with allies

Source: Disability Equality & Education.

AMERICANS WITH DISABILITIES

In the 2000 census, about one in five persons, aged five and older in the civilian noninstitutionalized population, reported a disability. Within this population, Census 2000 found: 9.3 million (3.6 percent) with a sensory disability involving sight or hearing; 12.4 million (4.8 percent) with a physical, mental, or emotional condition causing difficulty in learning, remembering, or concentrating; 21.2 million (8.2 percent) with a condition limiting basic physical activities, such as walking, climbing stairs, reaching, lifting, or carrying; and 6.8 million (2.6 percent) with a physical, mental, or emotional condition causing difficulty in dressing, bathing, or getting around inside the home. (Respondents could select more than one type of disability.)

Disability rates rose with age, with persons 65 or older twice as likely to report a sensory, physical, mental, or self-care disability causing difficulty going outside the home. These disability rates varied among the major racial and ethnic groups. The overall disability rate was higher for Hispanics than for non-Hispanic whites (despite the latter having the highest median age), while Asians had the lowest disability rate (Figure 14.4).

FIGURE 14.4   Disability Rate, by Racial and Ethnic Group, 2000

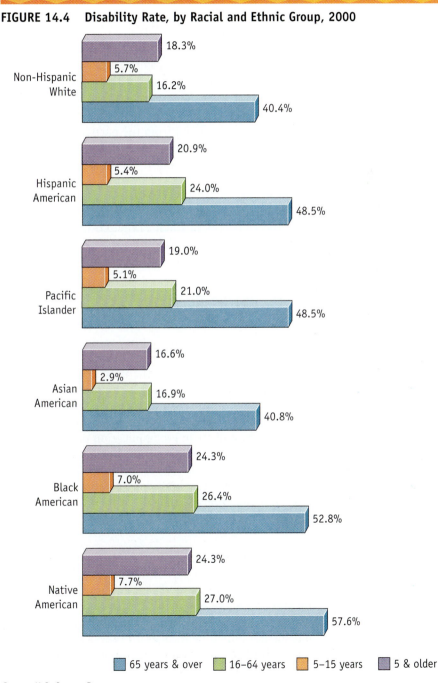

Source: U.S. Census Bureau.

LEGISLATIVE ACTIONS

No doubt inspired by the civil rights and feminist movements of the 1960s, numerous advocacy groups and organizations in the 1970s combined forces to launch a powerful social movement for disability rights. Aiding their cause was the presence of 75,000 severely disabled veterans from the Vietnam War (1959–1975).

Rehabilitation Act of 1973

As the first civil rights legislation in the world for people with disabilities, the Rehabilitation Act of 1973 marked a turning point in societal treatment of this minority group and prompted similar legislation in other developed countries. Of particular importance was Section 504, which stipulated that "any program or activity receiving federal financial assistance" cannot allow anyone to "be excluded from the participation in, be denied the benefits of, or be subjected to, discrimination." This meant, for instance, that airports, colleges and universities, and public libraries had to make their facilities barrier-free.

However, when the U.S. Department of Health, Education and Welfare began watering down the regulations in 1977, a group of disabled people took over the Department's San Francisco office to protest. Their historic action, which became the nation's longest sit-in of a federal building, was successful, and the 504 regulations were finally signed and enacted.

Americans with Disabilities Act of 1990

The next significant legislation, after years of extensive lobbying, occurred in 1990. "Let the shameful wall of exclusion finally come tumbling down," said President George H. W. Bush, as he signed the Americans with Disabilities Act of 1990.[35] This legislation, the most comprehensive antidiscrimination action since the 1964 Civil Rights Act, took effect in 1992. Title I prohibits private employers with more than 25 employees, state and local governments, employment agencies, and labor unions from discriminating against qualified individuals with disabilities in job application procedures, hiring, firing, advancement, compensation, job training, and other terms, conditions, and privileges of employment. The Act also covers public services and public transportation (Title II), public accommodations and commercial facilities (Title III), and telecommunications (Title IV).

MYTHS AND STEREOTYPES

One of the prevailing myths about disabled people is that they are helpless victims, requiring a dependency status, so they need someone to take care of them. This paternalistic view, while it may be justified toward those who have a serious mental impairment, does a disservice to all other disabled individuals. Too many people make simplistic assumptions about that one physical characteristic (e.g., blindness, deafness, paralysis, loss of limb) and ignore the totality of each complex human being. Focusing on just one characteristic of a person and disregarding all others is a typical element of prejudice that leads to various behaviors that reinforce this attitude. Limitation in one area does not mean limitation in others. Some people foolishly assume, for example, that individuals with physical disabilities also have mental disabilities as well, leading them to talk to them in a condescending manner or even talk about them in their presence.

Such a social construct can lead even well-intentioned people to create other uncomfortable situations for the disabled. Whether it takes such forms as staring, continual questions, inane comments about some noteworthy disabled individual, or simply awkward silences in conversations, the result is to remind disabled people that they are "different," whether they are children or adults.[36] Sometimes, then, the *reaction* of society becomes as great a difficulty to overcome as the *actual* disability.

Before passage of the Americans with Disabilities Act, these reactions included job discrimination, institutional discrimination in the form of access to buildings and public transportation, and media portrayals of disabled as overachievers or pitiful and/or childlike objects, as well as social exclusion from all kinds of activities. Although media portrayals are still problematic (particularly with otherwise well-meaning charity telethons), significant improvements have occurred in the other areas, but progress is slow and wide gaps still remain, as we discuss in the next section.

Today, people in wheelchairs may still encounter stares and stairs as obstacles but legislation has allowed for much progress in their becoming full participants in society. Jesse Horn, shown here graduating in 2007 from Colorado College, was born without legs but became a national champion disabled snowboarder.

CURRENT ISSUES

A 2004 National Organization on Disability/Harris national poll revealed findings consistent with previous studies in 1986, 1994, 1998, and 2000, that Americans with disabilities remain at a critical disadvantage compared to other Americans. Among the findings were:

- Only 35 percent of people with disabilities reported being employed full or part time, compared to 78 percent of those who do not have disabilities.
- Three times as many live in poverty, with annual household incomes below $15,000 (26 percent versus 9 percent).
- People with disabilities remain twice as likely to drop out of high school (21 percent versus 10 percent).
- They are twice as likely to have inadequate transportation (31 percent versus 13 percent), and a much higher percentage go without needed health care (18 percent versus 7 percent).
- People with disabilities are less likely to socialize, eat out, or attend religious services than are their nondisabled counterparts.

Not surprisingly given the persistence of these gaps, life satisfaction for people with disabilities also lags, with only 34 percent saying they are very satisfied compared to 61 percent of those without disabilities.[37]

Clearly, much remains to be done in all of these areas. Unlike the United Kingdom and other European countries with government policies that treat the disabled as automatically eligible for entitlement benefits, the United States takes a civil rights approach to advocate inclusion and equality to address these concerns. Between July 1992 and September 2006, the Equal Employment Opportunity Commission (EEOC) resolved over 251,000 complaints, resulting in more than $622.7 million in payment to people with disabilities whose rights had been violated.[38]

Closely related to the U.S. viewpoint is the insistence of disability rights activists that they not only wish to challenge negative societal views and to promote full integration into mainstream society, but they also want the disabled to have a voice in all policy decisions that affect them. Accordingly, they make a distinction between organizations *for* the disabled (charitable organizations, parents' groups, and service providers) and self-help organizations *of* disabled people in which they can be their own advocates for independence.[39]

OLD AGE

One unique aspect about the elderly is that, assuming a normal life span, everyone eventually becomes a member of this minority group. For most readers of this book, that time is in the distant future. Until then, more immediate needs and concerns require one's attention. Even so, unlike most other minority groups, the problems of the elderly have an interconnectiveness that affects in many ways the lives of nongroup members. For example, the economic reality of increasing payroll deductions for social security and Medicare impact on everyone's earning power. Also, many families experience severe strain over the time demands and costs of caring for aged parents. And, unless we improve the quality of life for the elderly when we have the power and influence to do so, their present situation becomes ours in old age when we no longer can be an agent for change.

SOCIOHISTORICAL PERSPECTIVE

Rapid social change in industrial societies generated a shift in value orientations toward the aged. Preindustrial societies (including colonial America), rooted in tradition, usually looked to old people as the source of wisdom and experience, deferring to their judgment on any problems facing the family or community. With a large **extended family** (two or more kinship families sharing economic and social responsibilities) and with property ownership generally passed on to the oldest male (primogeniture), older people were typically the more powerful and affluent. Industrialization and technology revolutionized the existing social order, bringing about the preeminence of the **nuclear family,** a unit of parents and their children living apart from other relatives. Land ownership was no longer the only main source of wealth. Increased mobility was possible, and one had to keep abreast constantly of new discoveries and developments to remain competitive.

Before the industrial age, the aged still worked, had clearly defined roles, were held in high esteem, and continued to make valuable contributions to the family and community. In an industrial society where work determines one's status or worth, people tend to view the aged as outmoded or obsolete, no longer productive, necessary, or important. This "Detroit Syndrome" whereby people, like cars, are assigned a limited useful life to be replaced by newer models (younger workers) is an unfortunate by-product of an industrial society coming to believe that "new" means "better." As a result, age prejudice became institutionalized in our society in laws, employment practices, advertising, media portrayals, and intergenerational interaction.[40]

Long a neglected segment of U.S. society, problems of senior citizens have drawn increased public attention in recent years. Several factors explain this heightened awareness, including demographic changes in the population composition, increased group cohesiveness, and political clout among older citizens. Senior citizens have powerful advocacy groups, such as the American Association of Retired Persons (AARP), and they have the highest voter registration and voter turnout rates of any age group, making them a voice that politicians heed.

THE GRAYING OF AMERICA

In 1900, 3 million persons (4 percent of the total population) were 65 or older; in 2007, this age group numbered 37.8 million (12.6 percent of the total). The number of senior citizens will increase even more dramatically as the first baby boomers turn 65 in 2011, initiating a "senior boom" that by 2030 will be double the older population in 2000, growing from 35 million to 72 million. At that point, one in five Americans will be 65 years or older.[41]

The AARP is a powerful special interest group with considerable political clout. Claiming more than 38 million members, it directs its efforts towards quality of life issues, including financial security and health care, as in this demonstration to change the law to enable senior citizens to import cheaper drugs from Canada.

Every day nearly 6,000 Americans reach the age of 65. Three-fourths of the population reaching that age live, on average, for another 16.8 years to age 81. Because of the increasing proportion of older citizens in our society, social scientists now utilize three subcategories for this group: those 65–74, those 75–84, and those 85 or older. In 2007, the 65–74 age group numbered about 19.4 million; those 75 or older totaled about 18.5 million. By 2030, 47 percent of the elderly will be 75 or older; with well over half this group over 80. The oldest-old, those 85 or older, will double from 4.7 million in 2003 to almost 10 million in 2030, and then double again to 21 million in 2050 (see The International Scene for worldwide comparisons).[42]

The importance of all these statistics is the responsibility placed upon the **sandwich generation,** the elderly's adult children still providing for their own dependent children (including those in college) and also for aging parents who are slowly deteriorating and becoming less and less independent, particularly after age 75.

Growing Diversity of the Older Population

As the older population grows larger, it will also grow more diverse, reflecting the demographic changes in the U.S. population as a whole over the last several decades. In 2003, non-Hispanic whites accounted for nearly 83 percent of the U.S. older population; followed by blacks (8 percent); Hispanics, who may be any race (6 percent); and Asians (3 percent). Projections suggest that

FIGURE 14.5   Population Aged 65 and Older, by Race and Hispanic Origin, 2003, 2030, and 2050 (in percent of total population aged 65 and over)

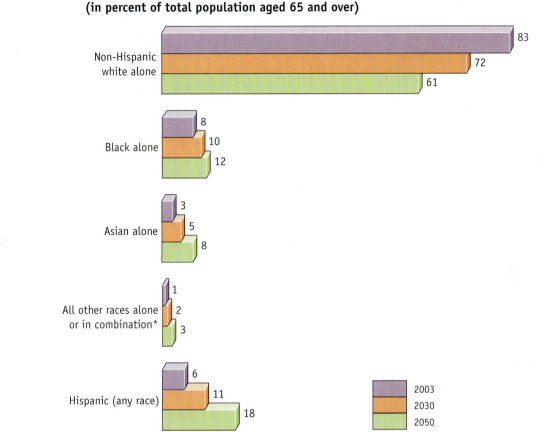

*The race group "All other races alone or in combination" includes American Indian and Alaska Native alone, Native Hawaiian and Other Pacific Islander alone, and all people who reported two or more races.

Note: The reference population for these data is the resident population.

Source: U.S. Census Bureau, 2004.

by 2030 the composition of the older population will be 72 percent non-Hispanic white, 11 percent Hispanic, 10 percent black, and 5 percent Asian (Figure 14.5).[43]

All these groups will experience growth in their older populations. Both Asian and Hispanic American older populations will increase fourfold by 2030. The older Asian population will grow from nearly 1 million in 2003 to about 4 million, while projections show the older Hispanic population growing from just over 2 million to nearly 8 million. By 2030, the Hispanic older population will be larger than the older African American population.[44]

The geographic distribution of the U.S. elderly varies by race and ethnicity. The 2000 Census revealed that almost three-fourths of all older Hispanics (1.4 million) live in just four states: California, Florida, Texas, and New York. About two-thirds of all older Asians (514,000) live in the western states. More than half of older blacks (1.5 million) live in the South. More than one-third of non-Hispanic white

The International Scene

The age structure of societies—their distribution of people into various age categories—varies according to birth and longevity rates. A higher birth rate results in smaller proportions of an elderly age cohort, but as the birth rate drops, the aged population proportion increases. In less developed countries, the **total fertility rate** (the average number of children born per woman in her lifetime) was 2.83 in 2007, compared to a TFR of 1.61 in more developed countries (see Table 14.1). As a result, individuals aged 65 and older in less developed countries in 2007 constituted 5.7 percent of the total population, compared to 15.7 percent in more developed countries (see more details in the chart below). Demographers project those percentages to increase by 2030 to 10.1 percent and 22.8 percent, respectively. Table 14.2 shows the current and projected proportions of elderly people by selected countries. In many developed countries, the proportion of the elderly citizenry will increase from one in six or seven to one in four or five, further increasing the pressures and problems about their needs in relation to other groups.

Percent of the Population Aged 65 and Over for Regions of the World, 2000 and 2030

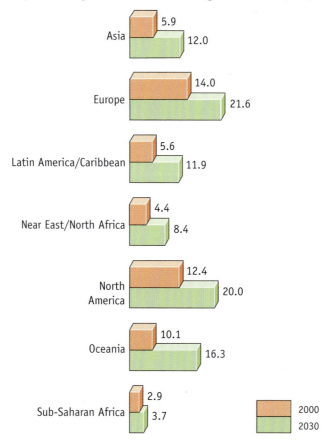

Region	2000	2030
Asia	5.9	12.0
Europe	14.0	21.6
Latin America/Caribbean	5.6	11.9
Near East/North Africa	4.4	8.4
North America	12.4	20.0
Oceania	10.1	16.3
Sub-Saharan Africa	2.9	3.7

Source: U.S. Census Bureau, 2004.

Countries with greater proportions of older adults face funding problems for their social security and medical coverage because they have a smaller labor force to pay taxes or contribute to pension plans. Many European nations have sought foreign workers to meet labor shortages, creating problems in multicultural relations in what had been mostly homogeneous countries. Even so, many countries below a TFR of 2.1—the minimum rate to maintain population stability—will shrink in total population size within the next few years.

TABLE 14.1   Total Fertility Rate in More Developed Countries, 2007

Belgium	1.64	Japan	1.40
Bulgaria	1.39	Latvia	1.28
Canada	1.61	Lithuania	1.21
Cyprus	1.80	Netherlands	1.66
Czech Republic	1.22	Norway	1.78
Denmark	1.74	Poland	1.26
Estonia	1.41	Romania	1.38
Finland	1.73	Russia	1.39
France	1.84	Slovakia	1.33
Georgia	1.42	Slovenia	1.26
Germany	1.40	Spain	1.29
Greece	1.35	Sweden	1.66
Hungary	1.33	Switzerland	1.44
Iceland	1.91	Ukraine	1.24
Ireland	1.86	United Kingdom	1.66
Italy	1.29	United States	2.09

Source: U.S. Census Bureau, International Data Base. Accessed at www.census.gov/ipc/www/idb/. [December 15, 2007].

TABLE 14.2   Population Age 65 and Older, 2007 and 2030 (by percent)

Country	2007	2030	Country	2007	2030
Australia	13.2	21.1	Italy	19.9	27.2
Belgium	17.4	25.0	Japan	20.6	28.8
Canada	13.5	22.9	Mexico	5.9	11.5
China	7.9	16.4	Netherlands	14.4	23.5
Czech Republic	14.7	24.3	Norway	14.8	22.4
Denmark	15.4	22.7	Philippines	4.1	7.7
Finland	16.4	26.0	Poland	13.3	23.1
France	16.4	23.7	Romania	14.7	19.6
Germany	19.8	27.5	Russia	14.4	28.9
Greece	19.0	24.9	Spain	17.8	25.3
Hong Kong, S.A.R.	12.9	29.3	Sweden	17.9	24.4
Hungary	15.4	21.9	Switzerland	15.8	24.7
India	5.1	9.7	Ukraine	16.3	22.1
Israel	9.8	14.9	United Kingdom	15.8	22.5
Ireland	11.7	18.4	United States	12.6	19.6

Source: U.S. Census Bureau, International Data Base. Accessed at www.census.gov/ipc/www/idb/ [December 15, 2007].

elderly (10 million) live in the South, with the remainder distributed fairly evenly throughout the rest of the country.[45]

Demographic Factors

Two major reasons for the growing proportion of older people are the increasing life expectancy (average number of years a newborn can expect to live) and the declining birth rate. Reductions in infant mortality, improved nutrition, and advances in healthcare, particularly for heart disease, have significantly increased life expectancy. Boys born today can expect to live to be 75, and girls to be 80, although African Americans average five years less than whites.[46] Increased life expectancy for all has emerged through the medical profession's success in reducing major causes of death for those over 55 (open-heart surgery, coronary bypass operations, kidney transplants, etc.).

Since industrialization began in the 19th century, the U.S. birth rate has been dropping, interrupted only in the 1940s and 1950s by the baby boom. Since 1972, we have experienced a 2.1 or lower birth rate which, if sustained for five decades, will result in zero population growth, a stable population size. This means a continued rise in the median age of the population, with fewer young people and a greater proportion of older people. To illustrate, the median age rose from 22.9 in 1900 to 36.4 in 2005, and it is projected to be 39 by 2030.[47]

Some states—like Florida, Arizona, Nevada, New Mexico, and Hawaii—are rapidly increasing their proportion of senior citizens, who are attracted by the climate and recreational opportunities. However, fewer than five percent of the retired elderly move away to such locales, either because they cannot afford to do so or because they prefer to remain near family and friends. Three-fourths of Americans 65 or older actually live in metropolitan areas. Senior citizens also constitute the highest proportion of small town and rural populations but are least represented in suburbs. Many of the snowbelt states have the greatest percentages of the nation's older and poorer senior citizens, which places even greater demand in these economically depressed areas for economic, health, and social assistance for the aged.[48]

VALUES ABOUT AGE

We can better understand the position of the aged in U.S. society if we examine how the social construction of reality affects the perception of old people by others, as well as their own self-perceptions. Americans are products of a youth-oriented culture in which physical attraction, productivity, sexuality, usefulness, and worth are rarely attributed to the old. So pervasive is this orientation that it has resulted in **ageism,** the manifestation of prejudice, aversion, or even hatred toward the old.[49] Like the ideologies of racism and sexism, this generalized set of beliefs abounds in negative stereotypes, ignores individual differences, and assumes the subordinate status of the aged lies in a biological rather than social explanation.

Advertisers, in order to sell their products, subtly reinforce people's uneasiness about growing older. Cosmetics, lotions, creams, baby oil, and even dishwashing liquid are marketed as products to smooth and soften skin and keep mothers looking as young as their teenage daughters. Hair coloring, cosmetics, and cosmetic surgery promise to help any who wish to defy at least the appearance of growing old. However, when we are "past our prime," other commercials alert us to the supposed preoccupations of old age: constipation irregularity, hemorrhoids, loose dentures, baldness, and "tired" blood.

Many of us also greatly limit our interaction with the healthy elderly, perhaps because they are living testimony to a part of the life cycle we don't want to think about. For those living alone—the 30 percent of those aged 65 to 74, the

Many elderly people—especially those in their 60s and 70s—lead energetic, imaginative, and active lives, thereby giving countless daily examples to refute the false stereotypes about them. Also, most old people experience little overall decline in mental ability, despite the common ageist assumption that they do.

48 percent aged 75 to 84, and the 57 percent aged 85 or older—this limited interaction means isolation and loneliness are distinct possibilities.[50] No doubt this is a partial reason, in addition to physical debilitation, for the high suicide rates among the elderly. In 2004, the average suicide rate for all ages was 10.9 per 100,000; but for those aged 65 to 74, it was 12.3; for those aged 75 to 84, it was 16.3; and for those 85 and older, it was 16.4. Older blacks have the lowest suicide rates while older whites have the highest, three times greater than blacks (Figure 14.6).[51]

MYTHS AND STEREOTYPES

Closely interrelated to the prevalence of ageism in our society are the myths and stereotypes that are all too commonly believed. Because society tends to address a social problem in terms of the generally accepted definition of the situation, examining both the false and accurate portrayals of the U.S. elderly is important.

Mental Capacities

One of the most commonly held beliefs and, in large measure, the one responsible for much ageist prejudice and discrimination, is that advancing age occasions a decline in one's mental faculties. Many people believe that intelligence, memory, and learning ability become less than in earlier years. "You can't teach an old dog new tricks" is the traditional folk saying. Old people are often thought of as senile,

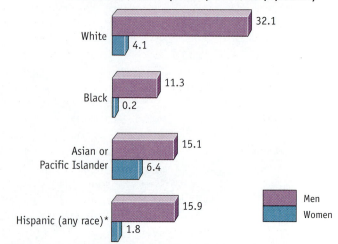

FIGURE 14.6 Death Rates for Suicide among People Aged 65 and Over, by Race and Gender, 2004 (Deaths per 100,000 population)

White: 32.1 / 4.1
Black: 11.3 / 0.2
Asian or Pacific Islander: 15.1 / 6.4
Hispanic (any race)*: 15.9 / 1.8

Men
Women

*Since there were fewer than 20 deaths for Hispanic women, data are not shown.

Note: The reference population for these data is the resident population.

Source: National Center for Health Statistics, 2007, Table 46.

childlike, and out of touch with reality.[52] Such beliefs often result in discriminatory practices in hiring or promotions or in a reluctance to train or educate older people in new areas. Despite such popular notions, research studies—including longitudinal studies of the same persons over many years—show little overall decline in mental ability with age. Certain physiological changes may occur in one's outward appearance and reflexes and responses may slow down a little, but intellectual capabilities remain constant or increase with age even into and past the seventies.[53]

The view that many seniors are senile and/or childlike is just not true. About five percent of those over age 65 may become senile, with most progressive organic brain impairment caused by Alzheimer's disease, which strikes one in five people by age 80. Still, that means the vast majority of 80 year olds don't have the disease nor do they experience any significant mental decline. While the average 80 year old may receive and process information more slowly than the average 30 year old, the differences are modest and can be offset by an older person's experience and wisdom. Furthermore, the age-linked memory decline appears limited to the storing of new information, with virtually no decline in the ability to recall, recognize, or perform things previously seen, heard, or learned.[54]

However, approximately 100 treatable and reversible disorders can mimic Alzheimer-type disease, and, tragically, many of these are attributed to old age and are neglected. Also, what passes for senile behavior can actually result from misuse or overuse of prescription drugs or even vitamin deficiencies, since old people may react quite differently than young people to certain drugs. The reality is that over 80 percent of the elderly do not experience any significant mental impairment.

Sexuality

Another misconception about older people is that they are sexually inactive because of a lack of interest and/or ability. Considering our youth-oriented society, it is not surprising that people mistakenly view the aged as asexual.

Supposedly, romance is for the young, sexual attraction means good-looking bodies, and sex is a young person's "thing." Old people should "act their age;" if they don't, they're "dirty old men" or "horny old women." All forms of media reinforce this thinking through emphasis on young people in love. Older people, either because of their more conservative sexual values or societal disapproval, tend to avoid public displays of sexual interest in another person.

Research findings, however, present a different reality about sexual interest and capacity among old people. Masters and Johnson observed that men and women well into their eighties and beyond were physiologically capable of having a pleasurable sex life.[55] Other studies have also found no end point in sexual fulfillment for people in good general health in their later years. Availability of a partner is a major factor, however, so those living alone are far less likely to engage in sexual activity than those living with someone.[56]

Sexuality among the aged is more a matter of attitude than of physiology. Susan Sontag suggests a double standard of aging hypothesis, that society allows men to age more gracefully than women, who become "sexually disqualified" with the calendar as "final arbiter."[57] Although both men and women may suffer lowered self-esteem if their sexual function physiologically begins to fail, society tends to assume increased aging in women *must* be accompanied by diminished sexual capacity, and this societal perception in turn tends to diminish the older woman's sense of self-worth. Because the older man's sexual capacity is not necessarily expected to diminish, it is easier for him to maintain a higher level of self-esteem.

CURRENT ISSUES

The elderly are by no means a homogeneous group. They vary greatly among themselves in educational levels, income, living arrangements, health, and quality of life. Three areas of concern to all members of this diverse group, however, are age discrimination, economic security, and healthcare.

Age Discrimination

Even before retirement age, older workers are often victims of job discrimination. Companies prefer to hire people under 40, and unemployed workers above that age may encounter great difficulty finding new jobs. The 1967 Age Discrimination in Employment Act (ADEA) was intended to protect workers aged 40 to 65, making it illegal to advertise positions with age restrictions or to deny employment for reasons of age. In practice, however, employers can easily circumvent the law by stating older workers are "over qualified" because of their extensive experience or "under qualified" because of their educational background. This legislation also protected older workers from being fired as a cost-saving practice in order to hire younger workers at lower salaries. In 1996, the Supreme Court reduced the burden of legal proof, ruling that a claimant need not prove replacement by someone under 40 years of age. As a result, legal experts believe employers may find it more difficult to defend themselves against age discrimination claims.

Prior to passage of this legislation, discrimination against older workers in hiring, training, promotions, and other areas was common.[58] Since then, the number of older workers in the work force has steadily increased.[59] Age discrimination continues nonetheless, although exact statistics are difficult to obtain. Analysts identify its continued existence through the longer period of time that it takes for older men and women to find employment, the lower income many receive on reemployment, and the size of court awards to age discrimination victims.[60]

Another area of past age discrimination was mandatory retirement at age 65, which was the norm in U.S. society until 1978, when Congress raised the age limit to 70. In 1986, with passage of the Age Discrimination Act, Congress abolished mandatory retirement altogether in most occupations. Among the exceptions were police and firefighters, airline pilots, and air traffic controllers.

Even though mandatory retirement is no longer permitted in business, companies often force their older workers to retire by other means. They do so because of assumptions that older workers are less productive and more costly to retrain, are more accident prone, and are more likely to be absent for health reasons. Also, older workers earn higher salaries and affect coverage costs for company health care plans.[61] Older workers may indeed cost companies more money in salaries and healthcare plans, but otherwise their value is significant. They offer experience and insights younger workers lack, actually have lower absenteeism, greater job loyalty, a more positive job attitude than younger workers, and can relate well to older customers.[62]

As a cost-cutting device on both salaries and retirement plans, companies often terminate employees before they reach retirement age by eliminating positions through layoffs, restructuring, or other means. Since the courts have upheld an employer's right to lay off older workers for economic reasons, abuses of this tactic with the subsequent hiring of younger, cheaper workers have not been unusual. Another employer approach is to offer bonus pension incentives or attractive early retirement programs to older workers so that younger workers can be brought in or the company can downsize, as all the major U.S. automobile manufacturers did in 2007. Such incentives are effective; usually about one-third of all workers aged 55 to 64 take early retirement.[63]

Economic Security

Generally, the economic picture for the U.S. elderly has significantly improved. During the 1960s and 1970s, they had the highest poverty rate of all age groups. In 1959, for example, 35.2 percent of older people lived in poverty; in 1966, their poverty rate had decreased to 28.5 percent, still an unusually high percentage. Since then, various government programs designed to ease the financial burdens of the older population have led to a downward trend, with minor fluctuations, so that the poverty rate for those 65 and older in 2006 was 10.1 percent, lower than for any other age group.[64]

Another economic indicator is **net worth,** the difference between assets and liabilities that a person or household has at any given time. In 2000, the median net worth of U.S. households was $55,000 and that of households with householders 65 and older was $108,885. Home equity often represented a major portion of that net worth. Excluding that element, the median net worth of households maintained by people 65 and older in 2000 was $23,369, compared to $3,300 for households maintained by people under age 35.[65]

Such statistics can be misleading, however. Many older Americans squeak by on fixed incomes just to meet normal living expenses. One-third of them entirely depend on Social Security benefits, while another third rely on Social Security for anywhere from 50 to 89 percent of their income. Constituting 12.6 percent of the population, Americans 65 or older receive 51 percent of all government expenditures for social services, from education to pensions. And, without Social Security and its cost-of-living increases, another 48 percent, or 17 million elderly, would fall below the poverty line.[66]

Although one in ten people over age 65 live in poverty, women and minorities are heavily overrepresented. Among all races, 11.3 percent of older women were in poverty in 2006, compared to 6.6 percent of older men. Another 7.7 percent of older women lived in near poverty compared to 5.0 percent of older men. Poverty rates also varied by race and Hispanic origin, with non-Hispanic whites living in poverty at 7.0 percent, blacks at 22.7 percent, and Hispanics at 12.8 percent.[67] Differences in poverty rates become even more pronounced when factoring in living arrangements. As Figure 14.7 shows, older householders living alone are at

FIGURE 14.7   Percent of People Aged 65 and Over in Poverty, by Living Arrangement, Race, and Hispanic Origin, 2006[1]

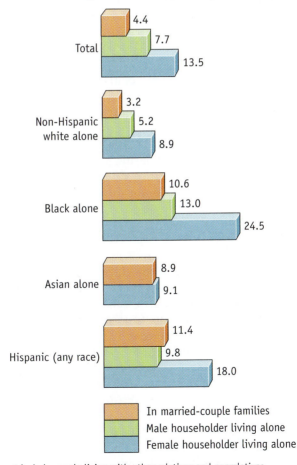

Total
4.4
7.7
13.5

Non-Hispanic white alone
3.2
5.2
8.9

Black alone
10.6
13.0
24.5

Asian alone
8.9
9.1

Hispanic (any race)
11.4
9.8
18.0

■ In married-couple families
■ Male householder living alone
■ Female householder living alone

[1]Does not include people living with other relatives and nonrelatives.
[2]Derived measure is not shown when the base is less than 75,000.

Note: The reference population for these data is the civilian noninstitutionalized population.

Source: U.S. Census Bureau, 2007, Table POV2.

greater risk of living in poverty, women far more so than men, and minorities at least twice as likely as non-Hispanic whites.

In 2006, 10.7 million older Americans lived alone, three-fourths of them women. This is not surprising for, as age increases, so does widowhood, with women living longer than men. However, an important cultural factor comes into play, as older Asian, black, and Hispanic women are far more likely than older, non-Hispanic white women to live with relatives. This pattern also holds true among immigrant families.[68] Although the potential for social isolation certainly exists, particularly for the 29 percent who have no living children, government studies reveal that most of those living alone are in good health and live close to family with whom they have frequent contact. The paradox is that, although older, unmarried people living alone (most of them widowed) are generally in better health than those who do not live alone, they are also more likely to live in poverty than those who live with their spouses.[69]

Concentrated primarily in the north central and southern regions, the rural elderly (almost 30 percent of the total elderly population) experience perhaps the greatest deprivation.[70] They most likely lack health services and live in older substandard, poorly insulated, poorly heated dwellings. Because of low population density, the rural elderly also tend to live isolated, lonely, and limited lives.

Seventy-seven percent of Americans aged 65 and older live in metropolitan areas.[71] Although more facilities and services are available than in rural areas, the elderly do not necessarily live near them. Their reduced income and mobility, and also their vulnerability to street crime, make them less likely to enjoy available urban opportunities. Often living in deteriorating neighborhoods, urban life for many elderly is a combination of insecurity and subsistence. For the suburban elderly, housing problems usually center on meeting rising property taxes, fire insurance rates, and maintenance costs, as well as getting around, since many do not drive and public transportation is quite limited in the suburbs.[72]

Healthcare

A primary concern of the elderly is healthcare, since they experience greater health problems than other age groups. Most people aged 65 to 74 are healthy, active, and have a positive self-image, but serious physical decline and illness becomes a greater reality from age 75 onward. Illustrative of this point is the fact that only about one percent of those aged 65 to 74 are in nursing homes, compared to 21 percent of those aged 85 and older.[73]

In the area of healthcare, of greatest concern to older persons is access and cost. Although they constitute about 13 percent of the total U.S. population, the elderly represent one-third of the hospital population and use one-fourth of the prescribed drugs. Their medical expenses are three times greater than those of middle-aged adults and six times greater than for young adults, yet the income of the elderly is usually far less than that of young and middle-aged adults. Medicare, Medicaid, and prescription drug programs have greatly reduced the personal health costs to the elderly; but, since they do not cover all expenses, the elderly average twice the personal health costs of those under 65.[74]

With increased age, older people also become less mobile, driving themselves less because of high automobile costs, including insurance, fuel, and maintenance, as well as the infirmities of old age. Many therefore become more dependent on others to travel to clinics, doctor's offices, and hospitals. Many physicians tend to take less interest in treating elderly patients because of ageist biases, their preference for specialization instead of primary care and, among many, their lack of preparation in geriatrics. Although geriatric medicine programs now exist at most U.S. medical schools and osteopathic schools for future practitioners, this remarkable growth over the past three decades is still not enough to provide the projected needed numbers of geriatricians.[75]

SOCIOLOGICAL ANALYSIS

Instead of simply examining the statistics and data about homosexuals, the disabled, and the aged and the problems they face, social scientists attempt to formulate a theoretical framework in which to understand the causes and possible solutions to the social situation. Our three theoretical viewpoints once again offer different approaches to these insights.

The Functionalist View

For centuries, most societies placed sexuality primarily within the context of marriage and so viewed some form of social control of sexuality as necessary for preservation of the family and for a stable society. Consequently, traditional family values, religious teachings, and cultural norms all emphasized heterosexuality as "correct," and homosexuality as "deviant." Deviation was not socially acceptable. Instead, it was seen as a symptom of social disorganization and the breakdown of society's institutions, resulting in the stigmatization and social ostracism of gays and the implementation of many forms of discrimination. Society is presently in the midst of social change, with government policies, laws, and activists promoting equal rights for all, regardless of sexual orientation. Because traditionalists consider some of these areas—such as same-sex marriage and gay parenting—as dysfunctional to the family and a violation of social mores, they condemn such alternate lifestyles and strive to stop them.

Similarly, activism for disability rights means fighting entrenched attitudes and behaviors. However, these patterns are not wrapped in moral values and so change is not as contentious an issue, although critics do maintain disability criteria and access stipulations "go too far." On the other hand, efforts to fully integrate the disabled into society to fully participate is seen as a functional approach, whether it be doorway and elevator access, curb ramps, traffic lights with sound signals, or other access amenities.

Rapid social change has created social disorganization and dysfunctions in society concerning the elderly. The lower birth rate and longer life span have resulted in a greater proportion of older people than ever before, but they have fewer functions to perform in an industrial society. Gone are their respected roles as senior members of the extended family, and as we have seen, societal attitudes and social policy have built in an obsolescence to their occupational roles. Within this context we may consider two major conflicting theories in social gerontology: activity and disengagement.

Activity Theory. The dominant theoretical perspective known as **activity theory** holds that people of all ages require adequate levels of social activity to remain well adjusted. In the 1940s the writings of Ernest Burgess, one of the first social gerontologists, identified a lack of social functions as the reason for the needless exclusion of the aged from socially meaningful activity, resulting in their having a "roleless role."[76] Activity theorists maintain that if new activities replace those an aging individual is forced to give up, that person is more likely to be better adjusted mentally, physically, and socially. However, the new activities need not be at the same level of action as in middle age to maintain the same high degree of life satisfaction, as studies show that older Americans do prefer a somewhat more relaxed lifestyle.[77]

Disengagement Theory. In contrast, this school of thought argues that the usual and even inevitable pattern is for people to become more passive and decrease their activity as they reach old age. To maintain optimal functioning, a modern society requires persons with new skills and energy. So a mutual withdrawal occurs, its times and form dependent on the individual. Social interaction and social ties weaken as society seeks out "new blood" and aging individuals recognize their own diminishing capacity and seek escape from the stress of daily life encounters.

Heavily criticized, **disengagement theory** stimulated much research, some of which supports the theory whereas most does not. Some aged do disengage, but studies demonstrate that disengagement is not inevitable with old age.[78] Society is more likely to withdraw roles from the aged than they themselves are likely to relinquish them. Perhaps Robert Atchley most effectively made this point in his comment, "Disengagement is not what most older people want. It is, however, what older people get."[79]

The Conflict View

Conflict theorists focus on gays, the disabled, and elderly as disadvantaged minority groups suffering at the hands of the rest of society. Whether treated with hostility or indifference, members of all three groups—once extensively denied fair treatment and equal opportunity—still struggle to gain full acceptance despite the significant progress achieved by each group.

For gays and lesbians, the struggle—through the gay rights movement and advocacy groups—includes challenges to laws about same-sex marriage, benefits to same-sex couples, and gay adoptions and parenting. For the disabled, the struggle includes the right to work without loss of benefit and wider access to all buildings and activities. For older Americans the struggle includes elimination of the remnants of age discrimination and greater economic security.

In the struggle for more resources and wider acceptance, conflict is inevitable. Organized social movements challenge the status quo to correct the inequality. For more than a quarter of a century, these groups have formed organizations, hired lobbyists, and used their political clout to pressure elected officials. Their heightened group consciousness and cohesiveness influenced the passage of laws to protect their interests and advance their causes. In turn, their actions sparked backlashes from various quarters, depending on the group and its goals. Religious advocates challenge the morality of homosexuality, determined not to allow any form of official recognition of this minority group's demands. Numerous local public officials, business leaders, and organizations claim the Americans with Disabilities Act is being too broadly interpreted, creating extensive expenses for compliance in building and program access. Younger workers chafe under the sizable payroll deductions for Social Security and Medicare for retired workers and wonder if such programs will even be available for them when they themselves retire.

The Interactionist View

Social scientists draw heavily on the idea of socially determined **sexual scripts** for explaining both heterosexual and homosexual development.[80] Since our sexual urges find expression in socially determined ways, whether heterosexual or homosexual, the process by which one choice becomes "normal" and the other "deviant" can be more readily understood through **labeling theory**, which explains how conformity and deviance result from the responses of others.

If, for example, a person who is a conformist in the rest of his or her life commits a random and isolated homosexual act that becomes known and the person is thus labeled as a homosexual, a process may begin that changes the original deviance from primary deviance, to secondary deviance, a persistent pattern of behavior that leads to deviant status and eventually membership in a deviant subculture with its own norms and patterns.[81] Often, stigmatized individuals reject the negative views others hold of them, create a new in-group ethic which affirms their worth as equal members of society, and hence reject accommodative strategies of stigma management.

The positive aspects of homosexual identity are often found in the group's most prestigious publications. A content analysis of articles and stories published in the *Ladder,* a well-known lesbian publication, shows a change from secondary to tertiary deviance. For example, during its early years, the *Ladder* advocated an accommodative stance. Lesbians were urged to fit in as well as possible, to conceal any outward differences between themselves and straight women. The change to tertiary deviance began when the *Ladder* changed from a lesbian periodical to a feminist magazine openly supportive of lesbians. Increasingly, lesbianism was defined as a choice made by women in response to a sexist society. It was defined as a sensible choice, and a radical political statement, not a deviation for which a person was labeled and rejected.

People learn social behavior in interactions with other people and through these interactions they form self-concepts about being gay, disabled, or old. Western society stigmatizes gays, pities the disabled, and dismisses the old. Members of each of these groups increasingly depend on external cues because of diminished ego strength, uncertain identity, lack of role models, and specific norms. Told they are deviant, incompetent, or obsolete, they internalize these negative societal attitudes and adopt the role assigned to them. In this role they learn new appropriate behaviors and skills, which undermine their sense of self-worth and self-confidence. This negative cycle of events then intensifies as they become even more susceptible to feelings of uselessness, which society or even other family members help reinforce.

In other words, the societal definition of the situation results in the social reconstruction of reality, causing negative changes in the individual's self-concept. To break this cycle of events, intervention needs to focus on changing societal attitudes, especially in terms of work determining personal worth. Another possibility is helping these minority group members develop greater self-confidence and coping mechanisms through their own self-determination.

RETROSPECT

Homosexuality existed in ancient civilizations without sanctions and was institutionalized among ancient Greeks and Asians as a natural expression of sexual instinct. During the Middle Ages and Renaissance, European society viewed homosexuality and heterosexual sodomy as sinful and criminal, with the guilty often executed. Twentieth-century social scientists changed from viewing homosexuality as a mental illness and social problem to emphasizing instead the discrimination against homosexuals as the problem.

A 1994 U.S. study identified three percent of males and one percent of females as active homosexuals. Although the public has grown more tolerant toward sexual orientation than in the past, and although antidiscrimination laws now exist, Americans remain divided over the morality of homosexuality, which in turn affects their attitudes about same-sex marriage and gay parenting.

About one in five Americans reported some disability in the 2000 Census, and about 21 million have a condition that limits their daily physical activities. The Americans with Disabilities Act has provisions requiring their inclusion in public activities and easier access to buildings. Its underpinning motivation is to focus on what the disabled *can* do, instead of what they cannot do. Too often society reacts to the disabled as one-dimensional, focusing only on the limitation and not on the many other capabilities of each human being. Despite recent gains, national surveys continue to show disabled persons at a critical disadvantage to other Americans in virtually every aspect of life.

The majority of people eventually become part of the elderly minority group. More developed countries, including the United States, have low birth rates, and their elderly populations are growing in proportion to the rest of their populations. Despite significant gains in economic security for the U.S. elderly, problems still remain in this area, particularly for racial and ethnic minorities. False stereotypes about ability, mental capacity, and sexuality are all factors in the still-continuing age discrimination many elderly face. Healthcare and medical expenses—despite Medicare, Medicaid, and prescription drug programs—remain a major concern for many.

Various theoretical approaches are valuable for analyzing the minority group status of homosexuals, the disabled, and the aged. The functionalist viewpoint offers helpful insights, particularly through utilization of activity or disengagement theory. Issues of exploitation, organized social movements, and intergroup tensions are best examined through conflict theory. The interactionists' employment of labeling theory furthers our understanding of the challenges faced by all three groups.

KEY TERMS

Activity theory
Ageism
Convenience sample
Disengagement
  theory
Extended family

Homophobia
Intergroup contact
  hypothesis
Labeling theory
Medical model
Net worth

Nuclear family
Random sample
Sandwich generation
Sexual scripts
Social model
Total fertility rate

DISCUSSION QUESTIONS

1. How do members of groups categorized as gay or lesbian, disabled, or elderly fit the sociological concept of the stranger as a social phenomenon?

2. What dominant and minority response patterns, discussed in Chapter 4, can offer some sociological insights into the experiences of gays, the disabled, and the aged in comparison to the other groups we studied?

3. How do conflicting values about equality and morality impact on the issue of homosexuality?

4. On the subject of the disabled, what are the differences between entitlement programs and civil rights issues, and how might they differently affect societal attitudes?

5. What are the stereotypes about older Americans, and why do they persist?

6. If age discrimination is illegal, why does it continue?

7. What theoretical perspective do you find most helpful for analyzing the experiences of each group in this chapter? Is it the same one or different ones? Why?

SUGGESTED READINGS

Boesser, Sara L. *Silent Lives: How High a Price?* Lanham, MD: Hamilton Books, 2004.
An effective, well-written book about sexual orientation from multiple viewpoints, showing how homophobia and exclusion exact a heavy price on everyone, gay or straight.

Crompton, Louis. *Homosexuality and Civilization.* Cambridge, MA: Belknap Press, 2006.
Probably the best chronicling in scope and readability of the history of homosexuality in Europe and Asia from ancient times through the 18th century.

Gullette, Margaret Morganroth. *Aged by Culture.* Chicago: University of Chicago Press, 2004.
A highly informative book about how cultural norms and practices foster fears and anxieties and how we might revise our place in the life cycle.

Labonte, Alan. *A Million Reasons: Why I Fought for the Rights of the Disabled.* Cohasset, MA: Hot House Books, 2006.
An inspiring and gripping account of one man's successful fight against his former employer that became a precedent-shattering case defending the rights of the disabled.

The Ever-Changing
U.S. Mosaic

As a nation of immigrants, the United States has seen many different groups of strangers arrive and interact with its people. The strangers perceived a different world that the native population took for granted, and their reactions ranged from wonder to bewilderment to dismay, from fulfilled expectations to culture shock. Because their language, appearance, and cultural background often made them conspicuous, the newcomers were categorically identified and judged as a group rather than individually. Native-born U.S. residents' responses ranged from receptive to impatient and intolerant, while their actions ranged from indifferent to helpful to exploitative.

Throughout the nation's history, then, varied patterns of majority–minority relations existed. Ethnocentric values prompted the natural development of ingroup loyalty and outgroup hostility among both indigenous and migrant groups. Competition for scarce resources, colonialism, and political dominance by the Anglo-Saxon core groups also provided a basis for conflict. However, the resulting prejudicial attitudes and discriminatory actions varied greatly in intensity. In addition, attitudes and social and economic conditions in this country changed over the years, affecting the newcomers' experiences.

Not all groups came for the same reasons or from the same backgrounds. Because of variations in social class, education, and occupational skills, not all immigrants began at the bottom of the socioeconomic ladder. Some came as sojourners, intending to stay only long enough to earn enough money for a better life back in their homeland. Some came with the desire to become U.S. citizens in every sense of the word; others insisted on retaining their own culture.

Dominant attitudes, as well as sociological analyses, tend to focus on either assimilation or pluralism as the preferred minority adaptation. Which process the public considers more acceptable greatly influences dominant–minority relations. For example, if assimilation is held to be the "proper" goal, then evidence of pluralism will probably draw negative reaction, even though pluralism is a normal manifestation among first- and second-generation Americans. In recent years, the growing presence in U.S. cities and suburbs of Spanish-speaking peoples and of people of color from non-Western cultures has led many other U.S. residents to question the country's immigration policies. Although race and economics are undoubtedly influencing factors, so, too, are genuine concerns about widespread pluralism overwhelming the "melting-pot" capabilities of the United States.

Stir in words such as *affirmative action, illegal aliens,* and *multiculturalism,* and the debate reaches "white heat" temperatures. These aspects of intergroup relations suggest to many that the majority group and the dominant culture are seriously threatened. In many quarters, the level of intolerance for any manifestation of pluralism has risen to alarming proportions.

How important is ethnicity today? Are immigration and assimilation concerns justified? What is the future of race and ethnicity in the United States? In this chapter, we attempt to answer these questions as we examine concepts of ethnic consciousness; evolutionary changes in ethnicity; and issues of legal and illegal immigration, bilingual education, and multiculturalism.

ETHNIC CONSCIOUSNESS

Sociologists have long been interested in the attitudinal and behavioral patterns that emerge when people migrate into a society with a different culture. For example, what factors encourage or discourage ethnic self-awareness or culture preservation? If succeeding generations supposedly identify less with their country of origin, how do we explain the resurgence of ethnicity among white ethnics in recent years? Are there ethnic differences in social mobility, social change, and behavior patterns even among third-generation U.S. citizens? Sociologists frequently raise these questions and offer a number of sociological explanations in an effort to describe scientifically the diversity of ethnic experience.

Country of Origin as a Factor

Focusing on the relationship between the migrant and the country of origin will produce a better understanding of the degree of assimilation.[1] Assuming that a migrant group today is affected primarily by factors in the receiving country is incorrect, although this may have been truer of groups that came to the United States before World War I, when transportation and communication were limited. Furthermore, immigration restrictions in the 1920s sharply curtailed the number of new immigrants, thereby aiding the assimilation process, because fewer newcomers arrived to reinforce the language and customs of the old country.

In today's world, however, an immigrant group can maintain instant and continuous contact with the country of origin through telecommunications, rapid transportation, and the continued arrival of newcomers. Mexican and Caribbean immigrant communities benefit from geographic proximity, and the homeland can exert more influence over its emigrants than in years past. Where greater social contact occurs, cultural transmission is greater, too.

Such contact with one's country of origin also affects politics. In an analysis of the political activities of Asian Americans, I identified three general and overlapping phases of acculturation in their political activities. These were (1) the *alien phase,* when the political locus remains with the country of origin; (2) the *reactionary phase,* when they form political organizations to protect their interests and fight discrimination; and (3) the *acceptance phase,* when they display a greater degree of cultural and structural assimilation.[2]

In examining the political activities of immigrants from the Dominican Republic, Haiti, and El Salvador, José Itzigsohn found manifestations of that first phase. Immigrants' transnational politics rested heavily on the government structure and political parties in the country of origin. The rise of a pattern of transnational politics, he states, is contingent on the home country's need for a steady flow of remittances, migrant organizations in the country of reception, and consolidation of competitive politics in democratic regimes.[3]

Sheila E. Henry finds a connection between country of origin and recent levels of ethnic and racial inequality in the United States. Focusing on Chinese, Japanese, and African Americans, she suggests that the U.S. stratification system closely reflects global economic stratification systems. Because Japan ranks among the leading capitalist nations, its immigrants enjoy a status of "honorary whites," something she suggests Chinese immigrants may soon enjoy, given their country's current economic boom. However, because no African country is likely to achieve economic global success in the near future, she thinks it is unlikely that the ethnic-group status of African Americans will change.[4]

The degree of stability or social change in the homeland, suggests Mary Sengstock, has a profound effect on the migrant community's sociocultural patterns and lifestyle:

> Where the country of origin has experienced a relatively stable or gradually changing culture, the effect on the immigrant community will most likely be to encourage retention of the ethnic culture. This is much the same case as has occurred with Puerto Ricans and Mexican-Americans.
>
> Some societies, however, have experienced drastic changes in recent years. When groups of immigrants from such areas experience constant immigration and other types of contact with the mother country, one might expect such contact to produce profound effects on the immigrant community as well.[5]

To illustrate her position, Sengstock used a study of Chaldean immigrants from Iraq who settled in Detroit both before and after World War II. Iraq is no longer a colonial land of different tribes; it replaced centuries-old tribal rivalries with the unity of nationalism, and these changes reached the Detroit community through visitors and immigrants. More recent immigrants, who had more education and more experience with urban settings and bureaucracies, were more likely to interact with others. Thus, willingness to extend one's social contacts to members of other groups could, suggests Sengstock, produce a more assimilable group. The social structure of an immigrant group's country of origin, then, may help to explain both nationalistic sentiment and social interaction with others in the adopted country.[6]

The Three-Generation Hypothesis

Pulitzer-Prize winner and historian Marcus Hansen conceptualized a normal pattern of ethnic revival in what he called the "Law of the Return of the Third Generation."[7] The third generation, more secure in its U.S. identity and socioeconomic status through **intergenerational mobility**, becomes interested in the ethnic heritage that the second generation neglected in its efforts to overcome discrimination and marginality. Simply stated, "What the child wishes to forget, the grandchild wishes to remember." Hansen, who based his conclusions mainly on midwestern Swedish Americans, reaffirmed his position several years later:

> Whenever any immigrant group reaches the third-generation stage in its development a spontaneous and almost irresistible impulse arises which forces the thoughts of many people of different professions, different positions in life and different points of view to interest themselves in that one factor which they have in common: heritage—the heritage of blood.[8]

Hansen suggested a pattern in the fall and rise of ethnic identity in succeeding generations of Americans. His hypothesis generated extensive discussion in the academic community, resulting in studies and commentaries that both supported and criticized his views.

Hansen's law assumes that the second generation perceives its ethnicity as a disadvantage in being accepted in U.S. society. However, Peter Skerry sees a different pattern in the reawakening of one's ethnic identity on college campuses as well as in group competition and conflict. In relating the complexities of the assimilation process to Hansen's hypothesis, Skerry states, "However flawed as a precise predictor of generational differences within specific ethnic groups, Hansen's basic insight remains valid: the process of assimilation is a dialectical one."[9] By this he means that assimilation is not simply a linear progression but instead a process that moves back and forth across the generations. Assimilation is not irreversible. Subsequent generations, even those who are the product of intermarriages, may emphasize their ethnic identity and learn the language of their cultural heritage.

In contrast, a study by Neil Sandberg found that Polish Americans in the Los Angeles area tended to become less ethnic over several generations.[10] In a similar study of Italian Americans in two suburbs of Providence, Rhode Island, John P. Roche also found increased assimilation and lower levels of attitudinal ethnicity over several generations.[11]

Studies of more recently arrived groups also find a similar decline in ethnicity among second-generation Asian and Hispanic Americans as they seek to assimilate. In fact, Sean Valentine found a negative relationship between cultural assimilation and Hispanic identity; the acculturation process functioned as a trade-off between traditional Latino tendencies and mainstream Anglo-American practices.[12] Similarly, Alejandro Portes and Dag MacLeod, in a survey of immigrant children from south Florida and southern California, reported that children who adopt the "Hispanic" label are the least well assimilated; these children had poorer English skills, lower self-esteem, and higher rates of poverty than those who identified themselves as Americans or as hyphenated Americans.[13]

Among Asian Americans, Nazli Kibria found that second-generation East Asian Americans (those whose ancestry was from China, Japan, or Korea) developed a sense of a shared Asian American culture in their socialization into the Asian values of education, family, hard work, and respect for elders. In this instance, the "backlash" in the construction of a common cultural background was an attempt to distinguish it from the homogeneously conceived white mainstream culture.[14]

Although most Asian and Hispanic Americans are too recently part of U.S. society to apply the three-generation hypothesis, the experience of Japanese Americans, among whom many are third-, fourth-, and even fifth-generation Americans, may offer an insight. With above-average educational, occupational, and income levels, as well as high intermarriage rates, they are arguably the most assimilated of all Asian Americans. Still, they retain symbolic vestiges of their heritage and cling to the aforementioned values as part of their sense of self and group identity.[15] Perhaps a similar future awaits our newest groups, although undoubtedly their racial experiences will mediate their identity formation.

Harold Abramson dismissed the three-generation hypothesis, arguing that the many dimensions of ethnic diversity preclude any macrosocial theory about ethnic consciousness.[16] Besides differences in time period—which may have influenced the experience, adjustment, and intergenerational conflict or consensus of ethnic groups—diversity exists within the groups themselves. Possibly, only the better educated among each ethnic group, being in wider contact with the outside world and more ambivalent about their identity, experience an ethnic resurgence, while the majority quietly progress in some steady fashion. In addition, the enormous variability in the U.S. social structure affects what happens to the grandchildren of all ethnic groups:

> Here I am talking about the diversity of region, of social stratification, of urban and rural settlement. In other words, the immigrants of Old and New and continuing migrations, the blacks of the North and of the South, the native American Indians, all experience their encounters with America under vastly different conditions. The French-Canadians in depressed mill towns of New England, the Hungarians and Czechs in company coal towns of Pennsylvania, and the Chicanos in migrant labor fields of California, do not experience the social mobility or social change of the Irish in Boston politics, the Jews in the garment industry of New York, or the Japanese in the professions of Hawaii. Not only are there traditional cultural factors to explain these phenomena, but there are structural reasons of settlement, region, and the local composition of the ethnic mosaic as well.[17]

Furthermore, the responses of different cultural groups to the host society vary. Conservative social scientists such as Thomas Sowell argue that cultural characteristics that either mesh or clash with the dominant cultural values determine a group's upward mobility.[18] Liberal social scientists such as Stephen Steinberg downplay cultural characteristics and emphasize social-structural variables instead. Steinberg maintains that pluralism appeals only to groups that benefit from maintaining ethnic boundaries, whereas disadvantaged groups willingly compromise their ethnicity to gain economic security and social acceptance.[19] More likely the interplay of culture and social structure enables groups to achieve economic success or prevents them from doing so.

Another dimension to examining both intergenerational assimilation and mobility lies in a fairly new social science concept, the **1.5 generation,** which is a term that refers to immigrants who arrive before or in their early teens. The term recognizes that their socialization began in the home country inculcating them with certain cultural characteristics, but their socialization continues in the host country, resulting in a blended cultural identity of the old and new. Although many factors will affect their sense of group identity, generally their bilingualism and biculturalism serve as a bridge for their parents in their own acculturation.

THE CHANGING FACE OF ETHNICITY

We can gain helpful insights into the complex, varied experiences and adjustments of different racial and ethnic groups by considering three important concepts: transnationalism, social capital, and segmented assimilation.

Transnationalism

We have long recognized the fact that immigrants, even when intent on blending into the societal mainstream of the host country, nevertheless retain much of their "cultural baggage" that affects not only their adjustment to their new land but also serves as a stabilizing link to their homeland and sense of self.[20] Despite that "old world" influence, the traditional view of social scientists was that the political and social behavior of the newcomers occurred within the cultural/structural framework of the host society. However, an expanding global economy, together with rapid communications and travel, has led scholars in recent years to revise traditional migration theory in recognition of a changed interaction pattern between immigrants and the host society.[21]

This new orientation recognizes that recent global transformations have led to the creation of social ties and support networks no longer restricted by national boundaries. **Transnationalism** thus refers to sustained ties of persons, networks, and organizations across national borders that result from the current international migration patterns and refugee flows.[22] The easy flow of people and their ideas back and forth between two countries has given many people the ability to maintain dual identities, with strong cultural ties and the capacity to make contributions to both places.[23] Instant transactions and communications have compressed time and space, allowing populations to be culturally and socially anchored at multiple sites. Instead of a permanent move from one country to another, today's immigrant retains more intense, interconnected, even legitimized links (cultural, economic, familial, and political) than ever before (see The Ethnic Experience box). Some scholars therefore argue that transnationalism makes obsolete the traditional terms of assimilation, integration, or segregation, in which states have dealt with immigration.[24]

Social Capital

The term **social capital** refers to actual or virtual resources available to an individual or group through a "durable network" of "institutionalized relationships of mutual acquaintance and recognition." Social capital thus refers to the potential value of information, social support, and personal connections inherent in social network relationships that are indispensable for achieving social, economic, and political goals.[25]

When we examine ethnic communities in terms of social capital, we can determine how community-based support systems and cultural orientations do or do not assist first- and second-generation Americans in their quest to share in the American Dream. Social capital is not a fixed object but rather a constantly changing means that facilitates access to benefits and resources that best suit the goals of specific immigrant groups.[26]

Essentially, social capital offers resources to racial or ethnic minorities that are beyond their individual reach by creating connections and support. The presence of these networks cultivates hope, trust, communication, mutual assistance, and problem solving through cooperative, collective action. Although the presence of strong social capital does not guarantee a minority group's successful integration into the economic and political mainstream, it certainly makes life easier than in a community lacking it.

Ethnic communities with strong social capital can offer help to new arrivals in securing informal sources of credit, insurance, child support, English language

The Ethnic Experience

Transnationalism on a Personal Level

I am a child of immigrants, as both my parents are from Ghana in West Africa. Transnationalism is a reality in my family. My father is a businessman and he runs his business both in Ghana and America, and so in a year, he makes about six trips from the States to Ghana back and forth. I keep asking him to move here and just take care of his business here in the States, but he insists that he cannot leave his other business at home and come here to stay.

Because plane tickets are very expensive, my siblings and I do not travel back and forth. As a matter of fact, ever since I left Ghana when I was 15 years old, I have never visited there although I plan to do so next year. I was in the U.K. for four years and then moved here to the U.S. Even though the U.K. is not my country, since I came to America I have traveled there several times.

Transnationalism is not something new. Most immigrants have dual identities, and they do this in order to be able to travel back forth. And I think that is really good because you enjoy both cultures, and it does not make you forget about your culture or your language because when you are in America you have to speak English and when you go back to your country you speak the language spoken there. The only thing is that is not all countries permit you to have dual identities. In some African countries, once you become a citizen of another country, you have to give up your citizenship in your native country. But even with that, people still steel themselves to have dual identities.

And if you're a permanent resident and you are a Green Card holder, which means you are not yet a citizen of the U.S., you have no choice but to the stay in country for at least the first six months before you can travel. If you want to travel back and forth, what you have to do is at least every year you have to come to the U.S. for three months in order to keep your Green Card. That is only if you want to be traveling back forth, but if you have decided to stay in America forever, then you can stay in the States, but you cannot stay in native country for a year without visiting the states, or else your Green Card will [be] collected from you. I know this because my mother is going through that right now with the immigration.

Source: Ghanian immigrant who came to the United States in 2003 at age 15. Taped interview from the collection of Vincent N. Parrillo.

---

training, and job referrals. Less successful communities display a short-term commitment to their host country and are less able to provide their members with important services. Thus, Koreans in Los Angeles and Chinese in San Francisco can better assist new immigrants than can Dominicans in New York or Mexicans in San Diego.[27]

Segmented Assimilation

Building on the concept that immigrant groups possess different levels of social capital, Alejandro Portés and Min Zhou advanced their theory of **segmented assimilation.** As its name implies, this hypothesis suggests a variety of outcomes among, and even within, contemporary immigrant streams. Instead of a uniform adaptation process that becomes more successful with longer residence in the United States, new immigrant groups may follow different assimilation paths than did previous immigrants. Besides the variants in available social capital, such factors as country of origin, settlement area, social class, race, and education also play an important role.[28]

In a positive scenario, those groups that are received favorably and possess high levels of human capital may quickly move up the socioeconomic ladder and integrate into the societal mainstream. In contrast, a second scenario depicts groups with limited resources as unable to find stable employment to earn enough income to support their children's education. Moreover, longer residence in an inner-city environment may result in their children's acculturation to other minority peers, leading to lower educational aspirations and downward mobility, somewhat of a "new rainbow underclass."[29] Yet a third scenario is limited assimilation, in which immigrant parents support their children's educational success but reinforce traditional cultural values and thus limit their acculturation into the U.S. youth subculture.[30]

The segmented-assimilation hypothesis provides a lens for understanding the discrepancy in research findings on the educational enrollment of recent immigrants and the children of immigrants in the United States. Reynolds Farley and Richard Alba, for example, saw significant intergenerational progress in educational attainment for many second-generation groups. Indeed, some surpassed those of third-generation or higher whites and African Americans. However, those of Mexican and Puerto Rican heritage languished behind the other groups.[31] Charles Herschman found that a downward mobility pattern for Hispanic Caribbean youths was consistent with the second possible outcome of the segmented-assimilation hypothesis, whereas Afro-Caribbean youths appeared to illustrate the third type of outcome.[32] Similarly, in their study of the Vietnamese community in New Orleans, Min Zhou and Carl Bankston reported that those more successful in school were those who were able to retain their mother tongue and traditional values.[33] In another study, Mary Waters found that Caribbean immigrants often pass along to their children an immigrant or ethnic identity that retards acculturation into the African American community.[34]

If, therefore, we are to understand more completely the acculturation patterns among today's immigrants, the segmented-assimilation hypothesis informs us that one model does not fit all groups or even all members of any group. Groups differ in their incorporation into the U.S. stratification system, and this theory attempts to explain how and why they do.

Naturalization

After five years of continuous legal residence in the United States, immigrants are eligible to become naturalized citizens, provided they are of good moral character and demonstrate a command of English and knowledge of U.S. history and government. It is a reasonable assumption that those who become U.S. citizens are demonstrating a desire to join fully in U.S. society through this formal process.

As Figure 15.1 shows, the longer the residence in the United States, the higher the percentage of naturalized citizens. Those who arrived in the 1970s, for example, have a greater proportion of naturalized citizens than those who arrived in the 1980s, who in turn exceed those who arrived in the 1990s. Moreover, Asian immigrants lead all other groups in all time periods in the percentage of those who became U.S. citizens. How much of a role transnationalism or segmented assimilation play in the level of naturalization among groups is a matter of great interest to social scientists.

We must be careful in analyzing the citizenship data. At first glance, the smaller proportion of newer arrivals compared to earlier immigrants in becoming naturalized citizens would seem to support the argument that newcomers are less likely to "become Americans." However, the correlation between length of U.S. residence and the proportion of those becoming citizens has been fairly constant

FIGURE 15.1   Percentage of Naturalized Citizens by Period of Entry, 2000

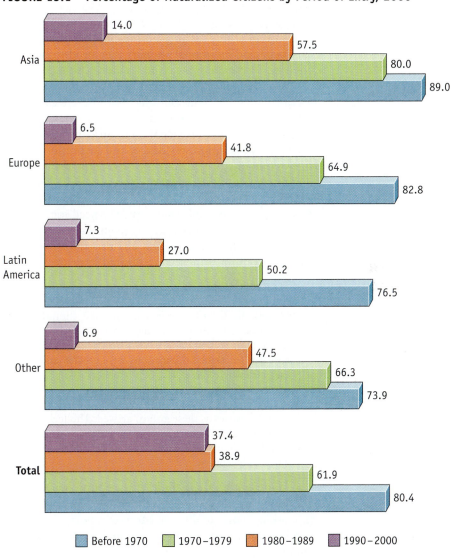

Source: U.S. Census Bureau.

for a great many decades. For example, although seven in ten of all immigrants who arrived in the 1970s are now citizens, less than half of them were citizens in the early 1990s.

In recent years the number of naturalized citizens has steadily grown, increasing from 463,000 in 2003 to about 703,000 in 2006. In the first half of 2007, applications surged further, prompted by fees increasing on July 30 to $675 (up 69 percent from $400) and by a desire to gain greater security for the family and for employment.[35]

Ethnicity as a Social Process

Ethnicity is a creation of a pluralistic U.S. society. Usually, culture shock and an emerging self-consciousness lead immigrant groups to think of themselves in terms of an ethnic identity and to become part of an ethnic community to gain the social and emotional support they need to begin a new life in their adopted country. That community is revitalized with a continual influx of new arrivals.

Some sociologists have argued that ethnicity should be regarded not as an ascribed attribute, with only the two discrete categories of assimilation and pluralism, but as a continuous variable. In a review of the literature, William Yancey, Eugene Ericksen, and Richard Juliani concluded that ethnic behavior is conditioned by occupation, residence, and institutional affiliation—that is, the structural situations in which groups have found themselves.[36] The old immigrants, migrating before the Industrial Revolution, had a more dispersed residential pattern than did later immigrants, who bunched together because of concentrated large-scale urban employment and the need for low-cost housing near their place of employment. Furthermore, these immigrants were drawn to areas of economic expansion, and the migration chains—the subsequent arrival of relatives and friends—continued their concentrated settlement pattern (Figure 15.2):

> The Germans and Irish, who were earlier immigrants, concentrated in the older cities such as Philadelphia and St. Louis. By contrast, the new immigrants from Poland, Italy and Russia concentrated in Buffalo, Cleveland, Detroit and Milwaukee, as well as in some of the older cities with expanding opportunities. Different migration patterns occurred for immigrants with and without skills. . . . Rewards for skilled occupations were greater, and the skilled immigrant went to the cities where there were opportunities to practice his trade. Less highly skilled workers went to the cities with expanding opportunities. Thus, the Italian concentration in construction and the Polish in steel were related to the expansion of these industries as these groups arrived. The Jewish concentration in the garment industry may have been a function of their previous experience as tailors, but it is also dependent upon the emergence of the mass production of clothing in the late nineteenth century.[37]

These authors conclude that group consciousness arises and crystallizes within the work relationships, common residential areas, interests, and lifestyles of working-class conditions. Moreover, normal communication and participation in ethnic organizations on a cosmopolitan level can reinforce ethnic identity even among residentially dispersed groups.[38]

Migration Patterns

Stanley Lieberson and Mary C. Waters examined the location of ethnic and racial groups in the United States on the basis and patterns of internal migration. They found that the longer a group had been in the United States, the less geographically concentrated it was (Figure 15.3). This was hardly a surprising finding, but their analysis of internal migration patterns revealed that ethnicity still affected the changing spatial patterns:

> We have concluded that although current patterns of internal migration are tending to reduce some of the distinctive geographic concentrations in the nation, this will still not fully eliminate distinctive ethnic concentrations. This is because

groups differ in their propensity to leave and in their propensity to enter each area in a way that reflects the existing ethnic compositions of the areas. Thus, even with the massive level of internal migration in the United States, there is no evidence that the ethnic linkage to region is disappearing.[39]

Lieberson and Waters observed that a numerically small group, if highly concentrated in a small number of localities, possesses greater political and social influence than one dispersed more uniformly. Thus, the linkage between demographic size and location influences visibility, occupational patterns, interaction patterns, intermarriage, and assimilation.

In 2006, 64 percent of the nearly 1.3 million immigrants who came to the United States entered through just six states.[40] At the same time, three of these gateway states—California, New York, and Texas—had considerable net outmigration of their foreign-born populations to other states. As the leading destination for migrants from abroad, California and New York were also the leaders in their internal migration, sending 237,000 and 205,000, respectively, to other states over a five-year period.[41]

Just as chain migration is an important factor in migration from abroad, so too does it appear to play an important role in this population redistribution of the foreign born to other states (Figure 15.4). As a result, the ethnic dimension in internal migration patterns that Lieberson and Waters found 20 years earlier is still significant. By far, the greatest numbers of interstate movers were Asians (667,000), followed by Mexicans (472,000) and other Latin Americans (438,000). States where this internal migration had the most dramatic impact on population composition were Nevada, North Carolina, Georgia, Arkansas, Minnesota, Nebraska, and Indiana.[42]

Focusing on ethnic and racial settlement patterns is helpful in understanding part of the assimilation process. In his ecological model of Chicago's growth and development, Robert Park noted the linkage between social and spatial mobility. Where one lives is as valid an indicator of upward mobility as are income, education, and occupation.[43] Housing markets are segmented along class and racial lines, and since the most desirable neighborhoods tend to be inhabited by non-Hispanic whites, the relocation by minority members typically involves a process of integration.[44] Because such spatial mobility implies greater access to cultural, economic, physical, and social resources and is indicative of social and economic assimilation, the term **spatial assimilation** is often used to identify this process.

Symbolic Ethnicity

Among first-generation U.S. immigrants, ethnicity is an everyday reality that everyone takes for granted. For most immigrants living within an ethnic community, shared communal interactions make ethnic identity a major factor in daily life. Not yet structurally assimilated, these immigrants find that their ethnicity provides the link to virtually everything they say or do, what they join, and whom they befriend or marry.

What happens to the ethnicity of subsequent generations depends on the immediate environment. As Richard Alba reaffirmed in a 1990 study in Albany, New York, the presence of ethnic neighborhoods or organizations in the vicinity helps sustain a strong sense of ethnic identity.[45] For most whites of European origin, living away from visible ethnic links and becoming part of the societal mainstream

FIGURE 15.2 Where We Settled

Go west, go east

At first they came to New England, the Carolinas and what are now the mid-Atlantic states. Then they crossed the Appalachians and headed west. Now, the destination for many immigrants is California, and most are reaching it by going east or north—from Asia or Latin America. In 2006, 21 percent of new immigrants settled in California, compared to 14 percent settling in New York, which until 1976 was the first choice of new arrivals.

These maps show the biggest concentration of ethnic groups—500,000 or more in a state—as identified in the 2000 census. California is the top choice for immigrants from China, El Salvador, Guatemala, Hong Kong, India, Iran, Korea, Mexico, the Philippines, and Vietnam. New York has the most from Bangladesh, Colombia, the Dominican Republic, Ecuador, Guyana, Jamaica, Pakistan, and the former Soviet Union.

Captions below the maps show where specific ethnic groups make up the biggest shares of the state's population, such as South Dakota with its large percentage of people of German descent.

☐ States in color are those with at least 500,000 persons of the indicated ethnic groups in the latest census.

German

Highest densities: North Dakota 46%, South Dakota 46%, Nebraska 43%, Wisconsin 43%, Minnesota 38%, Iowa 37%, Kansas 33%, Ohio 30%, Indiana 27%.

Irish

Highest densities: Massachusetts 23%, New Hampshire 21%, Rhode Island 20%, Delaware 19%, Connecticut 18%, New Jersey 17%, Missouri 14%, New York 14%, West Virginia 14%.

English

States with the highest densities of English: Utah 30%, Maine 25%, Idaho 22%, New Hampshire 21%, Wyoming 19%, Vermont 18%, Oregon 15%, Delaware 14%.

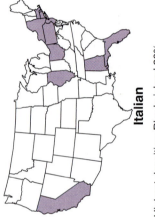

Italian

Highest densities: Rhode island 20%, Connecticut 20%, New Jersey 18%, New York 15%, Massachusetts 14%, Alabama 11%, New Mexico 8%.

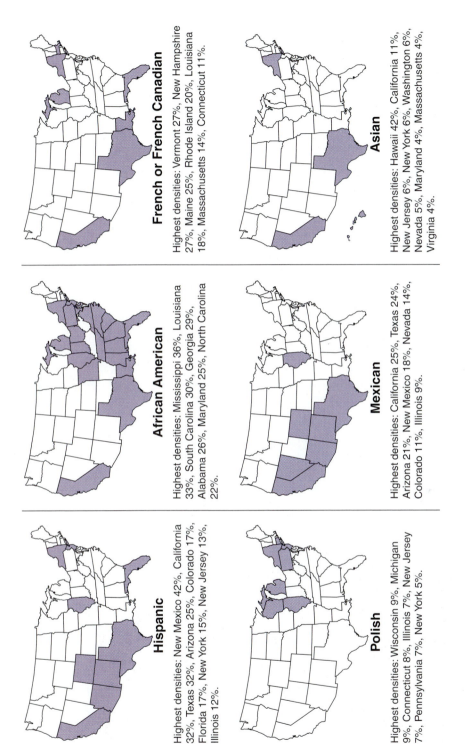

French or French Canadian

Highest densities: Vermont 27%, New Hampshire 27%, Maine 25%, Rhode Island 20%, Louisiana 18%, Massachusetts 14%, Connecticut 11%.

Asian

Highest densities: Hawaii 42%, California 11%, New Jersey 6%, New York 6%, Washington 6%, Nevada 5%, Maryland 4%, Massachusetts 4%, Virginia 4%.

African American

Highest densities: Mississippi 36%, Louisiana 33%, South Carolina 30%, Georgia 29%, Alabama 26%, Maryland 25%, North Carolina 22%.

Mexican

Highest densities: California 25%, Texas 24%, Arizona 21%, New Mexico 18%, Nevada 14%, Colorado 11%, Illinois 9%.

Hispanic

Highest densities: New Mexico 42%, California 32%, Texas 32%, Arizona 25%, Colorado 17%, Florida 17%, New York 15%, New Jersey 13%, Illinois 12%.

Polish

Highest densities: Wisconsin 9%, Michigan 9%, Connecticut 8%, Illinois 7%, New Jersey 7%, Pennsylvania 7%, New York 5%.

Source: Basic data from U.S. Census Bureau.

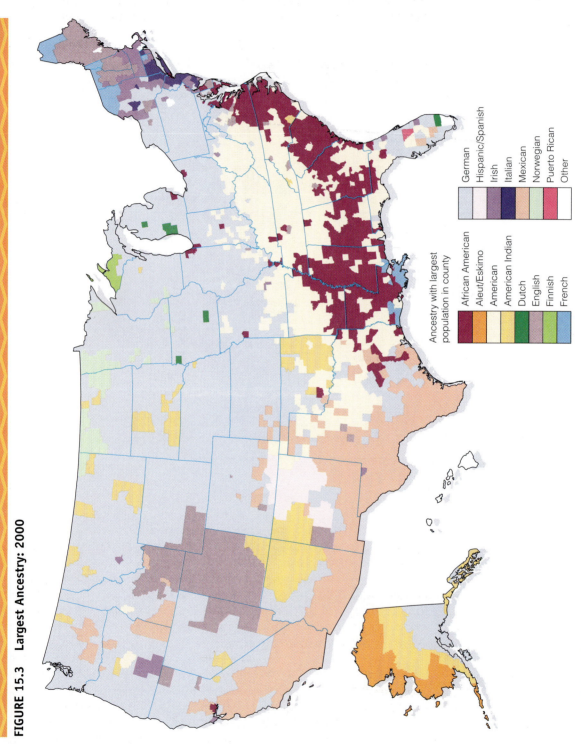

FIGURE 15.3 Largest Ancestry: 2000

Ancestry with largest
population in county

African American	
Aleut/Eskimo	
American	
American Indian	
Dutch	
English	
Finnish	
French	

German
Hispanic/Spanish
Irish
Italian
Mexican
Norwegian
Puerto Rican
Other

Source: U.S. Census Bureau, *Ancestry: 2000* (June 2004), Figure 3.

FIGURE 15.4   Percentage of Foreign-Born in Largest U.S. Cities, 2000

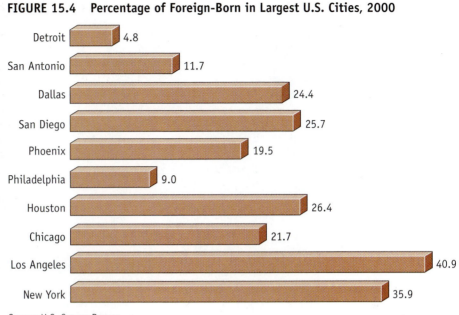

Source: U.S. Census Bureau.

reduce the importance of their ethnic identity in comparison to their occupational and social identity. At this point, ethnicity rests on acknowledging ancestry through attachment to a few ethnic symbols not pertinent to everyday life.[46]

Alba speaks of a twilight stage of ethnicity among white ethnics. High intermarriage rates not only have reduced the intergenerational transmission of distinctive cultural traits but also have diversified the ethnic ancestry of third- and fourth-generation European Americans. A coalesced new ethnic group, European Americans, has emerged. Its ethnicity is muted and symbolic, a personal and voluntary identity that finds expression in such activities as "church and synagogue attendance, marching in a St. Patrick's or Columbus Day parade, [or] voting for a political candidate of a similar ethnicity."[47] It also includes supporting a political cause associated with the country of origin, such as statehood for Palestine or the return of democracy to Cuba.

Although socially assimilated and integrated into middle-class society, third- and fourth-generation European Americans maintain this quiet link to their origins. As Herbert Gans suggests, it can find form in small details, such as objects in the home with an ethnic meaning, occasional participation in an old-country ritual, or a fondness for ethnic cuisine, even the use of religious symbols without regular participation in a religious culture or organization.[48] Individuals may remain interested in the immigrant experience, participate in ethnic political and social activities, or even visit the ancestral homeland. All these private, leisure-time activities help preserve ethnicity in symbolic ways, giving people a special sense of self in the homogenized world of white U.S. culture.

African Americans express symbolic ethnicity through such elements as musical styles, fashion and dress styles (Afros, braids, dreadlocks, tribal symbols cut into the hair, bandanna headbands, Kufi hats, harem pants, African beads), cuisine (soul

Symbolic ethnicity is an occasional means for native-born U.S. residents to reaffirm their cultural heritage. Sometimes these activities are carryovers from the old country, but sometimes they are of U.S. origin, as with Kwanzaa, a fairly recently developed observance based on traditional African harvest celebrations.

food), and festivals (such as Kwanzaa, a week-long festival honoring African-American heritage that is celebrated primarily in the United States). Sometimes called *manifestations of cultural nationalism*—a movement toward African American solidarity based on encouraging African culture and values—these activities resemble those of the descendants of other ethnic groups proudly recalling their heritage.

CURRENT ETHNIC ISSUES

Two highly controversial issues punctuate race and ethnic relations in the United States: immigration and bilingual education. Although the latter is a fairly new issue, arguments against both repeat objections that were hotly asserted in the late 19th and early 20th centuries. Nativist fears of being overrun by too many "non-American types" and losing societal cohesion as a result of their cultural pluralism are quite similar to concerns raised by dominant-group members of past generations. Closely related to these two issues is a third one: multiculturalism. This subject causes ongoing debates between its advocates and those insisting on assimilation.

Immigration Fears

The ebb and flow of immigrant waves have an impact on the host nation in many ways. Their cultural impact can enrich the society—in architecture, art, foods,

TABLE 15.1   Leading Suppliers of Immigrants to the United States, 1820–2006

1. Germany	7,260,729
2. Mexico	7,177,045
3. Italy	5,453,028
4. United Kingdom	5,379,171
5. Ireland	4,791,701
6. Canada and Newfoundland	4,637,911
7. Austria/Hungary[1]	4,387,428
8. Soviet Union[2]	4,212,820
9. Philippines	1,856,841
10. China	1,676,509
11. Sweden	1,269,188
12. Cuba	1,060,631
13. Dominican Republic	1,010,700
14. Korea	928,553
15. France	836,367

[1]Data for Austria/Hungary were not reported until 1861. Austria and Hungary have been reported separately since 1905. From 1938 to 1945, Austria was included in figures for Germany.

[2]Soviet Union is no longer a political entity. Data include immigrants from republics formerly part of the Soviet Union.

Source: U.S. Department of Homeland Security, *Yearbook of Immigration Statistics: 2006* (Washington, DC: U.S. Government Printing Office, 2007), Table 2.

and music, to name just a few—but some fear language retention and nonassimilation will undermine societal cohesion. Immigrant labor can be a boon to the economy, but critics express concern about the lowering of wages and loss of jobs for native workers. Because most immigrants are now people of color and have a higher birth rate than native-born Americans, some worry about the changing racial demographics. Moreover, with developing countries now the primary sending areas, the interests of the newly naturalized citizens—and in turn, U.S. foreign policy—become increasingly involved in developments in those parts of the world (Table 15.1).

Many immigrants still come from European countries, but they now account for less than 16 percent annually of the total number, due to the large increase in Asian and Hispanic immigrants. Given the ongoing processes of chain migration and family reunification—and contrasting birth rates in Europe as opposed to Asia and Latin America—we can safely assume the continued dominance of developing nations in sending new strangers to these shores (Table 15.2).

About 9.1 million legal immigrants (including undocumented aliens who were subsequently granted amnesty) came to the United States between 1991 and 2000, exceeding the previous record set in 1901–1910, when 8.8 million arrived. Current trends suggest this decade will set an even higher record number of legal immigrants. Add in the millions of undocumented immigrants, now thought to exceed 12 million, and the issue of immigration becomes a fiercely debated one.

Some opposition to current immigration results from concern about the ability of the United States to absorb so many immigrants. Echoing xenophobic fears of earlier generations, immigration opponents worry that U.S. citizens will lose control of the country to foreigners. This time, instead of fears about the religiously different Catholics and Jews or the physically different Mediterranean

TABLE 15.2 Major Sources of Newcomers to the United States, 1965 versus 2006

1965		2006	
1. Canada	38,327	1. Mexico	170,046
2. Mexico	37,969	2. China, People's Republic	83,628
3. United Kingdom	27,358	3. Philippines	71,134
4. Germany	24,045	4. Russia	59,760
5. Cuba	19,760	5. India	58,072
6. Colombia	10,885	6. Cuba	44,248
7. Italy	10,821	7. Colombia	42,024
8. Dominican Republic	9,504	8. Dominican Republic	37,997
9. Poland	8,465	9. El Salvador	31,259
10. Argentina	6,124	10. Vietnam	29,705
11. Ireland	5,463	11. Jamaica	24,538
12. Ecuador	4,392	12. Korea	24,472
13. China and Taiwan	4,057	13. Canada	23,913
14. France	4,039	14. Guatemala	23,687
15. Haiti	3,609	15. Haiti	21,628

Source: U.S. Department of Homeland Security, *Yearbook of Immigration Stastistics: 2006* (Washington, DC: U.S. Government Printing Office, 2006), Table 2.

whites who were dark-complexioned, the new anti-immigration groups fear the significantly growing presence of religiously and physically different immigrants of color. Visible differences, together with the prevalence of languages other than English, constantly remind native-born Americans about the strangers in their midst, whom they may perceive as a threat to U.S. society as they know it. This is especially true for Arabs and Muslim Americans, whom anti-immigration advocates point to as illustrating too liberal an immigration policy that allowed terrorists into our midst. The reality that virtually all Arab and Muslim Americans denounce terrorism does little to reduce public fears.

It is not just the increasing visibility of so many "strangers" in neighborhoods, schools, and workplaces that encourages this backlash. The nation's stable birth rate means that the migration and birth rates of immigrants account for a larger share of population growth than in previous years (Figure 15.5). According to the Population Reference Bureau, immigration contributed at least a third to the total population increase between 1990 and 2000.[49] Consequently, the Census Bureau projects that the racial composition of the United States will change dramatically in the next two generations, a prospect that displeases some people.

Another concern about immigration is economic. The public worries that immigrants take away jobs, drive down wages, and use too many government services at taxpayers' expense while not contributing sufficiently to the cost. How real are these fears?

Jobs. Do immigrants take jobs away from Americans? In a May 2007 CBS News/*New York Times* national poll, 30 percent of respondents thought so, but 59 percent thought that they mostly took jobs Americans don't want.[50] On the one hand, immigrants create many new jobs by starting new businesses (about

FIGURE 15.5   Native and Foreign-Born Populations by Age and Sex: 2003 (in percent)

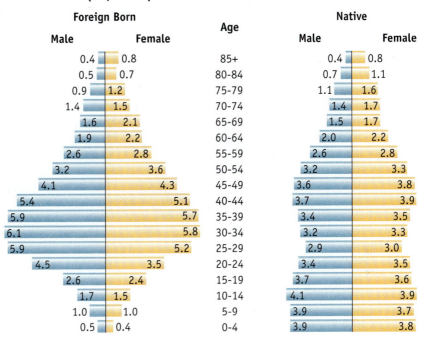

	Foreign Born		Age	Native		
	Male	Female			Male	Female
	0.4	0.8	85+		0.4	0.8
	0.5	0.7	80-84		0.7	1.1
	0.9	1.2	75-79		1.1	1.6
	1.4	1.5	70-74		1.4	1.7
	1.6	2.1	65-69		1.5	1.7
	1.9	2.2	60-64		2.0	2.2
	2.6	2.8	55-59		2.6	2.8
	3.2	3.6	50-54		3.2	3.3
	4.1	4.3	45-49		3.6	3.8
	5.4	5.1	40-44		3.7	3.9
	5.9	5.7	35-39		3.4	3.5
	6.1	5.8	30-34		3.2	3.3
	5.9	5.2	25-29		2.9	3.0
	4.5	3.5	20-24		3.4	3.5
	2.6	2.4	15-19		3.7	3.6
	1.7	1.5	10-14		4.1	3.9
	1.0	1.0	5-9		3.9	3.7
	0.5	0.4	0-4		3.9	3.8

Source: U.S. Census Bureau, Current Population Survey, 2003 Annual Social and Economic Supplement.

18 percent of the total). The explosion of lawn-care businesses and manicure parlors are just two examples. Or, consider that immigrants from Russia, Taiwan, and India founded Google, Yahoo!, and Sun Microsystems, respectively. Furthermore, immigrants increase the demand for goods and services that still others fill through these new jobs. At the same time, between 2000 and 2004, the decline in native-born employment was most pronounced in states where immigrants increased their share of workers the most. Immigration has its biggest impact on the lower part of the labor market—particularly building maintenance, construction, and food services—where native-born unemployment numbers closely match the increase in immigrant employment increases. In other labor sectors, there appears to be far less impact.[51]

Wages. The debate over immigrants lowering wages typically does not deal with skilled workers, as near-unanimous agreement exists that they give a big lift to the U.S. economy. Instead, the debate centers on the continuing arrival of millions of unskilled laborers, whom some fear take away jobs and lower wages. George Borjas and Leonard Katz, in a study of Mexican immigration, concluded that it reduced the wages of high school dropouts by 7 percent between 1980 and 2000.[52] However, even the most pessimistic economists think such downward pressure on wages affects no more than 10 percent of the labor force or that the drop has been more than five percent over the past 20 years.

THE IMMIGRANT.

This political cartoon was published in *Judge* in 1903, during a decade of a then un-precedented high influx of immigrants, most of whom were culturally and physically different. Then, as now, a debate raged about immigration and this cartoon asked the still-pertinent question: Is the immigrant an acquisition or a detriment? (*Source:* © Library of Congress [LC-US ZC4-3659])

David Card, in studying patterns in different U.S. cities, concluded that immigration did not lower wages for U.S. workers because not only has the percentage of native-born high school dropouts fallen sharply in the past few decades, but also immigrants and low-skilled U.S. workers fill rather different roles in the economy. To give just two examples of many, 54 percent of tailors in the U.S. are foreign-born, compared with less than 1 percent of crane operators, and 44 percent of plaster-stucco masons are immigrants, while less than 1 percent of sewer-pipe cleaners are foreign-born. With different skills, inclinations, and ideas, immigrants do not simply copy the behavior of U.S. workers.[53]

Costs and Contributions. At the local and state levels, immigrants typically use more in services than they pay in local taxes. Those with low levels of education and job skills cost the most, particularly in healthcare and use of schools. In some states with large concentrations of immigrants, such as California, the newcomers consume far more in government benefits (education, healthcare, social services) than they contribute in taxes (a cost of $1,178 per native-born household in the mid-1990s). However, in most states the cost per native-born household is one or two hundred dollars a year, but this is offset in their contributions to the states' economies in consumer spending and sales and property taxes paid.[54] A helpful insight comes to us from North Carolina, which has one of the fastest-growing foreign-born populations in the country. Over the past decade, while filling one-third of the state's new jobs, their consumer spending totaled $9.2 billion. Add in the $1.9 billion they placed in savings, and North Carolina experienced a total growth dividend of $11 billion, which far exceeded the $61 million that the newcomers cost the state (or $102 per native-born taxpayer) in the difference between taxes paid and services required.[55]

In an oft-cited 1997 study, the National Research Council reported that immigrants may add as much as $10 billion to the economy each year.[56] Even Borjas, the favorite economist of immigration restrictionists, admits the net gain to the U.S. from immigration is about $7 billion annually.[57]

Immigrant labor allows many goods and services to be produced more cheaply and provides the work force for some businesses that otherwise could not exist. These include U.S. textile and agricultural industries, as well as restaurants and domestic household services. In addition, economists say, immigrants and their children bring long-term benefits for most U.S. taxpayers because—like most U.S. residents—they and their descendants will add more to government coffers than they receive over their lifetimes.

Public-Opinion Polls. Statistics notwithstanding, Americans have mixed opinions about immigration. For example, in a May 2007 CBS News/*New York Times* national poll, 57 percent of respondents said they felt that the most recent immigrants contribute to the country while 28 percent thought they caused problems. Yet in a June 2007 NBC News/*Wall Street Journal* national poll, a more even split occurred, with 46 percent saying immigration helps more than it hurts the U.S. and 44 percent saying the opposite.[58]

These and other differing poll findings are likely reflecting the public blurring of legal and illegal immigration, as most Americans—63 percent—think the majority of immigrants came here illegally.[59] When specifically asked in the above-mentioned CBS News/*New York Times* poll how serious a problem they thought illegal immigration was, 61 percent viewed it as "very serious," and another 30 percent said it was "somewhat serious."[60]

Undocumented Aliens

In the aftermath of the terrorist attacks on September 11, 2001, amid concerns about insufficient screening of aliens coming to the United States and the growing presence of undocumented aliens, the government reorganized in 2003. Services once provided by the much-criticized Immigration and Naturalization Service now occur within the Department of Homeland Security under the U.S. Citizenship and Immigration Services (USCIS). With 15,000 federal employees working in 250 offices around the world, this office adjudicates immigrant visa petitions, naturalization petitions, and asylum and refugee applications.[61]

What fuels public debate about immigration is the rising number of unauthorized foreign-born people in the United States, now estimated to be over 12 million. Jeffrey Passel estimates that 1.3 million undocumented immigrants arrived in the 1980s, 5.8 million in the 1990s, and 3.1 million between 2000 and 2004. About two-thirds have been in the United States for less than ten years.[62]

Mexicans comprise the largest segment of undocumented migrants (estimated to be 57 percent of the total), a proportion that has remained steady for a decade. Another 24 percent are from elsewhere in Latin America. About 9 percent come from Asia, 6 percent from Europe and Canada, and 4 percent from other parts of the world.[63] A large number of people from foreign lands continue to slip across U.S. borders, but others (about 165,000 annually) first arrive legally as visitors (tourists, students, or businesspeople) but do not leave—and so then become visa violators.

Entering the country easily and then disappearing within it, these undocumented aliens usually escape detection by the Department of Homeland Security, which spends millions to patrol the borders of the United States. In the Southwest, the problem draws the greatest amount of public attention and generates the most apprehensions of undocumented aliens (about 1.2 million in 2006). Mexicans dominated the list of those apprehended, at 88 percent of the total. Other major source countries of those apprehended were El Salvador, Honduras, Guatemala, Cuba, Dominican Republic, Brazil, and China.[64]

Public pressure mounted in 2006–2007 to do something about securing our borders and dealing with those undocumented migrants already here. Political debates, opposing legislative proposals for amnesty or a crackdown on illegals, calls for a 700-mile wall along the border, Congressional hearings, and mass demonstrations in many U.S. cities all illustrated the fundamental disagreements about how to deal with the situation. In mid-2007, however, a divided Congress was unable to pass any immigration reform bill and, as of this writing, any resolution remains elusive.

Calls for reform come at a time when parts of the U.S. economy are dependent on the labor of undocumented migrants. Mostly Latinos, these unskilled workers have spread to a wide range of industries (Figure 15.6). Moreover, about 10 percent of the labor force of Mexico—as well as several other Central American and Caribbean countries—are now working in the United States, and their sending monies to their families back home is a major source of financial support there.[65]

Language Retention

One of the most divisive issues in majority–minority relations is language retention. For many native-born Americans, the presence of groups not speaking English goes to the heart of their assumptions that the newcomers aren't even trying to assimilate. The large-scale presence of an immigrant group—whether on a national level such as the Hispanics or in a local area such as the Vietnamese in California—intensifies this perception. On a personal level, witnessing foreign-

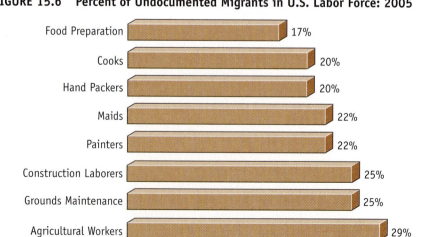

FIGURE 15.6   Percent of Undocumented Migrants in U.S. Labor Force: 2005

Food Preparation — 17%
Cooks — 20%
Hand Packers — 20%
Maids — 22%
Painters — 22%
Construction Laborers — 25%
Grounds Maintenance — 25%
Agricultural Workers — 29%

Source: Jeffrey Passel, "The Size and Characteristics of the Unauthorized Migrant Population in the United States," *Pew Hispanic Center Research Report* 61 (2006).

born parents speaking in public to their children in the language of their homeland or seeing signs or television programs in languages other than English also deepens an individual's concern about societal cohesion.

However, if we examine language retention concerns about past immigrants, we find similar patterns. Remember Benjamin Franklin's concern about the Germans' meager command of English and need for interpreters given in Chapter 5? Similarly, as millions of Italian immigrants in the first two decades of the twentieth century settled in the "Little Italys" of many U.S. cities, the prevalence of Italian language usage, signs, newspapers, and radio programs led many Americans to denounce these "inassimilable" Italians and to seek restrictive legislation to stop any more from coming here.

Although Spanish is now the second most frequent language spoken at home (about 31 million do so), other languages have also been increasing significantly. Foremost among these are Chinese, French, German, Tagalog (a language spoken in the Philippines), Vietnamese, Italian, Korean, Russian, Polish, and Arabic. In 1990, French was the third most spoken language; today it is Chinese (Figure 15.7).

With a million or more immigrants entering the United States each year, the extensive use of other languages alarms many nativists. Of course, many Asian and other non-English-speaking immigrants add to nativists' concerns. The Census Bureau estimates that nearly one in five Americans does not speak English at home. In fact, more than 10.5 million said they speak little or no English, up from 6.5 million in 1990. According to experts, some of the rise is due to the fast growth of the new-immigrant population, which included millions of people who came here illegally. The share of people who speak little English is highest among those in their working years, aged 18 to 64.[66]

FIGURE 15.7   Ten Languages Most Frequently Spoken at Home Other Than English and Spanish, Age 5 Years and Older, in Millions: 2000

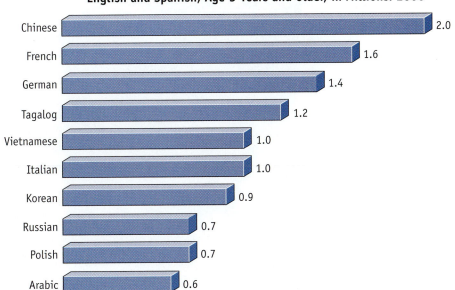

Language	Millions
Chinese	2.0
French	1.6
German	1.4
Tagalog	1.2
Vietnamese	1.0
Italian	1.0
Korean	0.9
Russian	0.7
Polish	0.7
Arabic	0.6

Source: U.S. Census Bureau, Census 2000 Summary File 3.

Bilingual Education

Offering **bilingual education**—teaching subjects in both English and the student's native language—can take the form of a transitional program (gradually phasing in English completely over several years) or a maintenance program (continued native-language teaching to sustain the students' heritage with a simultaneous but relatively limited emphasis on English proficiency). For the many U.S. residents who assume that English-speaking schools provide the heat for the melting pot, the popularity of bilingual education—particularly maintenance programs—is a sore point. Some see such efforts as counterproductive because they tend to reduce assimilation in, and the cohesiveness of, U.S. society, while simultaneously isolating ethnic groups from one another. Advocates of bilingual programs emphasize that they are developing **bilingualism**—fluency in both English and the students' native tongue—and that many youngsters are illiterate in both when they begin school.

Public funding for bilingual education began in 1968, when Congress passed the Bilingual Education Act, designed for low-income families only. Two years later, the Department of Health, Education, and Welfare specified that school districts in which any national-origin group constituted more than 5 percent of the student population had a legal obligation to provide bilingual programs for low-income families.

In 1974, two laws significantly expanded bilingual programs. The Bilingual Act eliminated the low-income requirement and urged that children receive various courses that provided appreciation of their cultural heritage. The Equal Opportunity Act identified failure to take "appropriate action" to

Bilingual education continues to stir controversy over cost, effectiveness, and its alleged "threat" to societal cohesiveness, provoking some demands for its elimination. Several recent studies indicate that immersion programs have success rates comparable to bilingual programs, but contradictory findings in other studies keep the issue in dispute.

overcome language barriers impeding equal participation in school as a form of illegal denial of equal educational opportunity. **English-as-a-second-language** (ESL) programs have since expanded to function in about 125 languages, including 20 Native American languages. With nearly 11 million immigrant children now enrolled in the public schools—both urban and suburban—schools must overcome cultural, language, and literacy barriers to provide for their education.

Schools thus face an enormous challenge in overcoming the language barrier so many students face. Between 1979 and 2004, the number of school-age children (ages 5–17) who spoke a language other than English at home increased from 9 to 19 percent (from 3.8 to 9.9 million). If current trends continue, by 2010, children of immigrants may constitute 25 percent of the total K–12 student population.[67]

Because 95 percent of all immigrant children attend urban schools, this challenge falls primarily to urban areas and most especially to those in the six states where immigrants are most concentrated (California, New York, Florida, Texas, New Jersey, and Illinois). For example, almost half of all school-age children in California are children of immigrants. However, new immigrant patterns are doubling, even tripling the enrollment of immigrant children in such states as Nevada, North Carolina, Georgia, and Nebraska.[68]

Three-fourths of all limited-English-proficient (LEP) students receive English-as-a-second-language instruction, and only one-fourth have this instruction paired with native-language academic instruction, more commonly known as bilingual programs. Together, the programs enable educators to teach 10 million school-age students in the United States whose first language is not English, as well as 3.4 million other students whose English proficiency is limited.[69]

The practical value of ESL programs over native-language instruction is readily apparent since it is practically impossible to offer native-tongue classes in so many languages. As it is, urban and suburban schools struggle for funds, space, and qualified teachers for their various bilingual programs (Figure 15.8).

Older naturalized U.S. citizens often cite difficulty with the English language while they were students as one of the most difficult aspects of adjusting to the United States and gaining acceptance. Bilingual proponents argue that their programs ease that adjustment and accelerate the learning process. Since the 1970s, the National Education Association has supported an **English-plus program** to promote the integration of language-minority students into the U.S. mainstream and to develop foreign-language competence in native-born U.S. students to function in a global economy.[70]

How effective is bilingual education in helping children learn English? Christine H. Rossell and Keith Baker examined 300 studies pursuing this question and found that in only 22 percent of methodologically acceptable studies was transitional bilingual education better than regular classroom instruction when the outcome is reading; for math, it was only 9 percent.[71] Most recent studies are inconclusive, showing neither bilingual education nor English immersion to be superior to the other. Some concluded that it's not the model of instruction that matters, but the quality. Other researchers completed a synthesis of all available research on literacy, including that of the U.S. Department of Education, and found that children did somewhat better if they received some instruction in their home language, in addition to that in English, but it was unclear how much or what kind of home language instruction was best.[72]

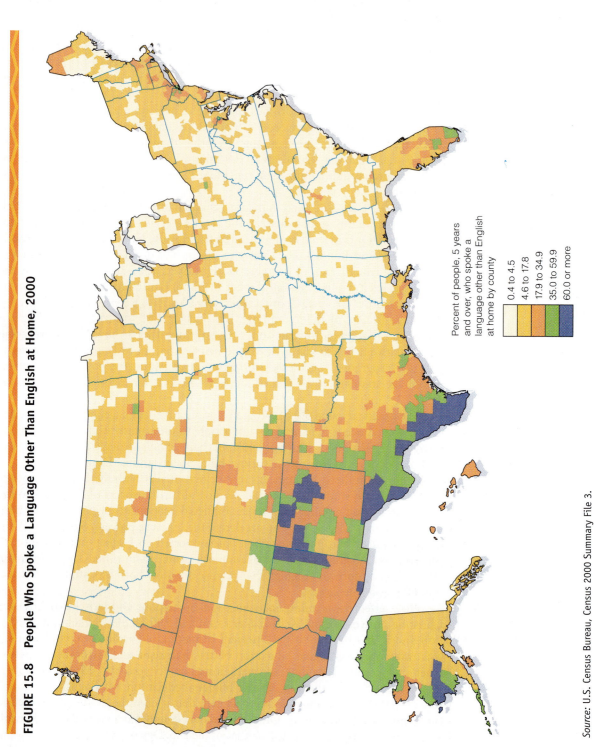

FIGURE 15.8 People Who Spoke a Language Other Than English at Home, 2000

Percent of people, 5 years and over, who spoke a language other than English at home by county

- 0.4 to 4.5
- 4.6 to 17.8
- 17.9 to 34.9
- 35.0 to 59.9
- 60.0 or more

Source: U.S. Census Bureau, Census 2000 Summary File 3.

Since bilingual programs vary so widely in approach and quality, it is difficult to assess their overall effectiveness. However, studies show that students who are given enough time in well-taught bilingual programs to gain English proficiency test better in the eleventh grade than do those with no prior preparation in any bilingual program.[73]

The English-Only Movement

Opponents of bilingual education argue that the program encourages "ethnic tribalism," fostering separation instead of a cohesive society. Their objections come in response to Hispanic leaders in such groups as the National Council of La Raza and the League of United Latin American Citizens (LULAC), who claim that "language rights" entitle Hispanic people to have their language and culture maintained at public expense, both in the schools and in the workplace. The oldest Hispanic civil rights group still in existence, LULAC was founded in 1929. Ironically, it began as an assimilationist organization, accepting only U.S. citizens as members, conducting its official proceedings in English, and declaring one of its goals to be "to foster the acquisition and facile use of the official language of our country."[74]

In reaction, the nativists have pressed to make English the official language for all public business. The largest national lobbying group, U.S. English, was cofounded by Japanese immigrant S. I. Hayakawa, a former U.S. senator from California and former president of and linguistics professor at San Francisco State University. By 2007, the group claimed 1.8 million members, and its success prompted critics to attack it as being anti-immigrant, racist, divisive, and dangerous.[75] The group's goals are to reduce or eliminate bilingual education, to abolish multilingual ballots, and to prevent state and local expenditures on translating road signs and government documents and translating to assist non-English-speaking patients at public hospitals.

By 2007, 30 states had passed official English laws, with several other states poised to pass similar legislation. Public opinion polls strongly support making English the official language. A 2006 Rasmussen Reports poll, for example, found 85 percent of Americans saying so.[76] Since 1981, over 50 bills have been introduced in Congress to make English the nation's official language. Six of these bills passed in one chamber but not in the other; the U.S. Senate passed such legislation in 2006 and 2007. As this book goes to press, proponents continue to lobby for passage in both houses.

Although proponents of English-only legislation claim that such action is essential to preserve a common language and provide a necessary bridge across a widening language barrier within the country, numerous polls and studies demonstrate that the action is unnecessary. For more than 25 years, public opinion polls have consistently shown that the large majority of foreign-born Americans believe learning English is important to become a part of U.S. society and to find a job.[77]

That attitude manifests itself in action. Today, first- and second-generation Americans are becoming fluent in English at a faster pace than did past immigrants. In the largest longitudinal study of second-generation Americans (5,200 immigrant children in Miami and San Diego), Rubén Rumbaut and Alejandro Portés found that 99 percent spoke fluent English and less than one-third maintained fluency in their parents' tongues by age 17.[78] Similarly, another study by

Rumbaut revealed the preference by 73 percent of second-generation immigrants in Southern California with two foreign-born parents to speak English at home instead of their native tongue. By the third generation, more than 97 percent of these immigrants—Chinese, Filipino, Guatemalan, Korean, Mexican, Salvadoran, and Vietnamese—preferred to speak only English at home.[79]

On a broader scale, the U.S. Census Bureau reports that, of those U.S. residents aged 18 to 64 who spoke an Asian or Pacific Islander language in 2000, 78 percent also spoke English "very well" or "well." Of the same age cohort who spoke Spanish in 2000, 68 percent also spoke English "very well" or "well."[80] Rubén Rumbaut reports that those who do not yet speak English well or at all are disproportionately the elderly (especially those in dense ethnic enclaves, such as among the Cubans in Miami), the most recently arrived, the undocumented, and the least educated.[81]

Multiculturalism

In its early phase, during the 1970s, **multiculturalism** meant including material in the school curriculum that related the contributions of non-European peoples to U.S. history. Next followed efforts to change all areas of the curriculum in elementary and secondary schools and colleges to reflect the diversity of U.S. society and to develop students' awareness of and appreciation for the impact of non-European civilizations on U.S. culture. The intent of this movement was to promote an expanded U.S. identity that recognized previously excluded groups as integral components of the whole, both in heritage and in present actuality (see The International Scene box).

Some multiculturalists subsequently moved away from an assimilationist or integrative approach, rejecting a common bond of identity among the distinct minority groups. These multiculturalists advocate "minority nationalism" and "separatist pluralism," with a goal not of a collective national identity but of specific, separate group identities.[82] To create a positive group identity, they go beyond advocacy for teaching and maintaining a group's own cultural customs, history, values, and festivals. They also deny the validity of the dominant culture's customs, history, values, and festivals. Two examples are Native Americans who object to Columbus Day parades and Afrocentrists who assert that Western culture was merely derived from Afro-Egyptian culture. Another striking example is the argument that only groups with power can be racist. This view holds that because whites have power, they are intrinsically racist, whereas people of color lack power and so cannot be racist.[83]

Opponents counter that racism can and does exist within any group, regardless of how much power that group has. John Miller, a long-time pro-immigration advocate, argues that multiculturalism undermines the assimilation ethic and that the weaker our assimilation efforts, the fewer immigrants we can accept. His 10-point "Americanization Manifesto" includes ending ethnic-group preferences, bilingual education, and multilingual voting, strengthening the naturalization process, and reducing illegal immigration.[84]

Another battleground for multiculturalists involves offering or eliminating courses in Western civilization. Some institutions, such as Providence College in Rhode Island, expanded such course requirements and made them interdisciplinary; other institutions, such as Stanford University, questioned their inclusion at all. At many institutions, the proposals for curriculum change ranged from

The International Scene

Multiculturalism in France

For many generations, the French saw themselves as a seamless population bloc whose culture was directly descended from that of the tribes of ancient Gaul. Those who lived in the provinces—Alsatians, Bretons, Gascons, Provençals, and Savoyards, for example—were trained in school to become "French." Physically punished if they spoke their provincial dialects during recess, all were homogenized into the dominant culture, with the brightest students finishing their education in Paris. Even today, the French government attempts to stop the incursion of any non-French words into the language, such as its 2003 ban on the use of "e-mail" in all government ministries, documents, publications or Web sites, demanding instead use of the term *courier electronique* (electronic mail).

Not surprisingly, the millions of Italian, Polish, and Spanish immigrants who entered France did not join the mainstream easily, despite their common Catholic faith and European heritage. At the turn of the 20th century in southern France, for instance, a massacre of Italians occurred. Just before World War II, the French government imposed a ban against the establishment of any organizations by foreigners—a stricture that remained in effect until 1981. Assimilation, or Franco-conformity, was the allowable choice—not pluralism.

France has over 4.9 million legal immigrants (6 percent of the total population) and perhaps another million *clandestines* (illegal aliens), most coming from Muslim North Africa. Many French became concerned that their nation was losing its cultural identity because of the large influx of immigrants whose appearance, language, religion, and values were so different. Indeed, after winning a record 15 percent of the vote in 1998, the far-right, anti-immigrant National Front Party finished second in the 2002 election, with a 17 percent total. Spearheaded by left-wing parties and human rights groups, both elections sparked protest demonstrations by tens of thousands of people across France. In the streets of Paris, people chanted, "We're all immigrants."

That public chanting echoed former Prime Minister Michel Rocard's call for a new recognition of French diversity. It also recalled the encouragement of a multiculturalist viewpoint by President François Mitterrand, who, several years earlier, had observed: "We are French. Our ancestors are the Gauls, and we are also a little Roman, a little German, a little Jewish, a little Italian, a small bit Spanish, more and more Portuguese, who knows, maybe Polish, too. And I wonder whether we aren't already a bit Arab."

In the 2007 presidential election with an impressive 85 percent voter turnout, the National Front Party garnered only 10 percent of the vote. The son of Hungarian immigrants, Nicolas Sarkozy, became president, opening a new chapter in French political history. Still, the French do not encourage cultural diversity. Instead, they stress a uniform, secularized French identity as the best guarantor of national unity and the separation of church and state. In 2004, for example, the government enacted a ban on religious symbols in schools, including Muslim dress (notably the *hijab,* or women's headscarf that covers the hair and neck), Jewish *yarmulke* (skullcaps), and large crosses. The move is primarily part of French efforts to cope with the influx of North African Muslims and the challenge they present to the unofficial French creed of secularism.

Critical Thinking Question: How do you think France and the United States compare in public attitudes about immigration and diversity?

making all students take non-Western and women's studies courses as part of their degree requirements to excluding all Western history and culture courses from requirements.

Regardless of their orientation, most multiculturalists are pluralists waging war with assimilationists. Neither side will vanquish the other, though, for both forces remain integral parts of U.S. society. The United States continues to offer a beacon of hope to immigrants everywhere, keeping the rich tradition of pluralism alive and well. And yet, as has been consistently demonstrated for centuries, assimilationist forces will remain strong, particularly for immigrant children and their descendants. Multiculturalism will no more weaken that process than did the many past manifestations of ethnic-ingroup solidarity.

Following the 9/11 terrorist attacks, interfaith actions across America showed that most would not condemn an entire group for the actions of a few. Symbolizing that attitude, people from Jewish, Christian, and Muslim faiths linked arms in front of a Detroit mosque that had been spray painted "Go home 911 murderers."

People who cite the Afrocentrist movement as divisive need to consider the reality of separate racial worlds within the United States, from colonial times to the revelations generated by the 1995 O. J. Simpson verdict. These separate worlds result not from multiculturalist teachings but from systemic racism. Only by breaking down the remaining racial barriers, eliminating institutional discrimination, and opening up paths to a good education and job opportunities for everyone can society improve racial integration. Afrocentrist schools do not undermine a cohesive U.S. society any more than Catholic schools, yeshivas, or other religious schools do.

RACIAL AND ETHNIC DIVERSITY IN THE FUTURE

The Census Bureau—working from current demographic patterns and making certain assumptions about future births, deaths, and international migration—projects a dramatic change in the composition of U.S. society by the mid-21st century. It reports that the cumulative effects of immigration will be more important than births to people already living in the United States. By the mid-21st century, 21 percent of the population (an estimated 82 million) will be either immigrants who arrived after 1991 or children of those immigrants.[85]

The rapid growth of the Hispanic population, says the Census Bureau, enabled Hispanics of all races to surpass the African American population in 2000, when there were 35.3 million Hispanics and 34.7 million African Americans in the United States. By 2050, Hispanics will number about 102.6 million, or 24 percent

FIGURE 15.9   America's Growing Diversity

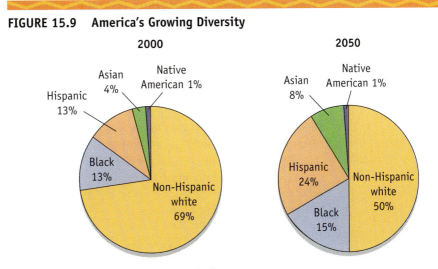

Source: U.S. Census Bureau middle-range projections, 2004.

of the total population. The Census Bureau projects that African Americans will then number about 61.4 million, or 15 percent (Figure 15.9). All data reflect midrange projections, not high or low estimates.

The nation's Asian population will grow to about 33.4 million, or 8 percent, by 2050. Native Americans will increase to about 3.2 million by then, slightly less than 1 percent of the total. The number of non-Hispanic whites will be 210 million by 2050, or 50 percent of the population.[86]

Some observers have reacted to these projections with alarm, using them to argue for immigration restrictions. Others relish the thought of U.S. society becoming more diverse. These projections, however, have some limitations, not the least of which is their assumption that conditions worldwide will remain constant several decades into the future. Certainly, four or five decades ago, no one would have predicted the current birth, death, and migration patterns that currently affect the United States. A forecast about the year 2050, then, is anything but certain.

Even more significant is the high probability that these Census Bureau projections will fall victim to the **Dillingham Flaw.** Who is to say that today's group categories will have the same meaning in the mid-21st century? Fifty years ago, Italian, Polish, and Slavic Americans were still members of distinct minority groups that lacked economic, political, and social power. They displayed all the classic characteristics of minority groups: ascribed status, endogamy, unequal treatment, and visibility. Today, they are mostly in the mainstream, displaying traits of civic, marital, and structural assimilation. Like European Americans who intermarried earlier, those whose ancestry is Italian, Polish, and Slavic are now mostly a blend of other nationalities. Fifty years from now, the same may be true of other groups, such as Hispanics. Two generations from now, Americans will likely view one another very differently from how we do now.

Indicators of Ethnoreligious Change

Although the demographic patterns of fertility, mortality, and migration are helpful in making projections, other patterns give reason for caution in predicting the future.

Interethnic Marriages. Our expectation that Hispanic Americans will marry outside their ethnic group, as have European Americans, finds support in the process that is already under way. In 2006, nearly 2.2 million Hispanic Americans were married to someone of non-Hispanic origin, up 250 percent from 891,000 in 1980. That is approximately 5 percent of the adult Hispanic American population, still a small proportion but an ever-growing one.[87] The children born from these exogamous marriages are obviously of mixed ethnic heritage, and if this trend continues, one day "Hispanic American" may be no more a separate ethnic category than Italian, Polish, or Slavic now is.

Interracial Marriages. For generations we have failed to eliminate the racial barrier, so by mid-century that barrier may still exist. Nevertheless, one present-day trend suggests that our current simplistic racial categories are already obsolete. In 2006, 3.8 percent of all marriages in the continental United States were interracial, compared to 1.3 percent in 1980. By 2006, interracially married couples numbered about 2.3 million, almost one-fifth of them (403,000) black–white couples, six times more than the 65,000 in 1970. Whites married to a nonwhite spouse of a race other than black (most often, Asian) grew from 233,000 to 1.8 million. Couples consisting of blacks married to a nonblack spouse of a race other than white increased from 12,000 to 145,000.[88]

Researchers are developing some interesting findings about interracial relationships. George and Sherelyn Yancey report that biracial relationships seem to form along the same lines as same-race relationships—that race is only an aesthetic factor, similar to others' preference of hair color or eye color.[89] They also suggested that, because interracial dating brings together individuals from different cultures, such relationships may increase appreciation for the partner's culture and promote healthy racial relations through marital assimilation.[90] Richard Lewis Jr., George Yancey, and Siri S. Bletzer found that people with a premarital history of biracial dating said cross-racial personal and sexual attractiveness, along with ease of talking, were important spouse selection factors.[91] An intriguing study by Adam Troy, Jamie Lewis-Smith, and Jean-Philippe Laurenceau found partners in interracial relationships reported significantly higher relationship satisfaction compared to those in intraracial relationships.[92]

Racial and interracial marriage patterns vary if we control for ethnicity. For example, Suzanne Model and Gene Fisher found that West Indian men of any generation have lower exogamy rates than African American men, while exogamy rates are higher among West Indian women who arrived as children or were born in the United States than among African American women.[93] In this study, both gender and racial differences in interracial marriages occurred because of ethnicity.

As George Yancey suggests, interracial romantic relationships are a useful barometer of race relations and structural assimilation in U.S. society. In a study that separately analyzed African, Asian, European, and Hispanic Americans, he found similar demographic and social factors that predicted outdating across racial groups. Men were more likely to date interracially than women, particularly if they attended interracial schools. Neither religious preference nor geographic region were significant factors, nor did his findings support the notion that majority-groups members use interracial dating relationships to "trade up" by dating racial minorities with higher economic and educational attainment.[94] It would appear, as also suggested by my social distance study discussed in Chapter 1, that the racial barrier is lowering when it comes to intimate social relations.

Over 3 million biracial children now live in the United States, and many adult blacks and whites also claim mixed racial ancestry. If we add Hispanics, Filipinos, Native Americans, and Hawaiians with multiracial ancestry to the biracial offspring from these marriages, we can readily understand why past Census Bureau single-race classifications were inadequate. Fortunately, the census in 2000 for the first time enabled people to identify themselves as members of more than one racial group, allowing the bureau to report more accurately the multiracial reality that contributes to U.S. diversity and aiding demographers in making projections in this area. As a result, 6.8 million Americans said they belonged to more than one race in that census. As Kathleen Korgen reports,

> Biracial Americans today face choices in racial identity never available to preceding generations. Now the nation must adjust to their growing resolve to identify with both sides of their racial heritage.[95]

An excellent example of a multiracial American illustrating Korgen's point is golf champion Tiger Woods, who is one-fourth Chinese, one-fourth Thai, one-fourth

A biological blend of four races—African American, Asian, Caucasian, and Native American, golf champion Tiger Woods is one of the most visible of the more than 7 million multiracial Americans. With interracial marriages increasing each year, their numbers will continue to grow.

African American, one-eighth Native American, and one eighth Dutch. He calls himself a "Cablinasian," a word fusion that he created of **Ca**ucasian, **Bl**ack, American **In**dian, and **Asian**.

Religion and Migration. Earlier immigration waves transformed the United States from an almost exclusively Protestant country into a land of three major faiths: Catholic, Jewish, and Protestant. Because religion is often closely intertwined with ethnicity, current migration patterns offer clues about the religious preferences of future Americans, if current trends continue.

Hispanic and Filipino migration may increase the U.S. Catholic population from the current 22 percent to perhaps 30 percent by 2050. Migration from Africa, Asia, and the Middle East may increase the Muslim population from 1 percent of the total to 5 percent. Given current patterns, the Jewish population may decline from 2 percent to 1 percent and the Protestant population from 56 percent to 49 percent; the populations of other religions—including Buddhism, Hinduism, and Sikhism—may slightly increase from 4 percent to 5 percent. Even if these predictions turn out to be somewhat inaccurate, the future will show even greater religious diversity than the present does.

Caution is needed in accepting these predictions, of course, because the Dillingham Flaw of oversimplified generalizations and the imposition of present-day sensibilities may lead to a misreading of the eventual reality. Religious intermarriage is now increasing among followers of all faiths, and the nonreligious segment of society is also growing, so we may find a very different future with respect to religion than we can accurately project.

Beyond Tomorrow

Diversity is the word that best describes the past, present, and future of the United States. United by a core culture and shared beliefs in certain ideals, the nation's peoples have not always understood their common bond or openly accepted one another as equals. As the dual realities of assimilation and pluralism continue to pull people seemingly in two directions at once, few people recognize that they are witnessing a recurring set of historical patterns. Instead, some voices cry out again against immigration, brand the newcomers as "unassimilable," and express fear for the character and cohesiveness of society. Yet immigrants have always been important to the growth of U.S. society, and their presence has continually strengthened the country.

Despite some progress, the United States has never fully resolved its race-relations problems. As it becomes a more multiracial society than ever before, it may see a worsening of race relations. We've seen some indicators here: black–Asian and black–Latino conflicts in addition to black–white conflicts and polar-opposite perceptions between blacks and whites of the O. J. Simpson trial and verdict. Perhaps, though, the situation will improve with deconstruction of the rigid racial categories that presently promote greater social distance and with more sharing of power through the increased presence of people of color in elective offices and other policymaking positions. Perhaps, too, the unity of diverse peoples that occurred after the 2001 terrorist attacks will serve as another catalyst for improved race relations in the years to come. Gender equality—as well as inclusiveness and protection of rights for the aged, disabled, and homosexuals—are other areas in which some gains have occurred but in which additional concerted efforts are necessary for all to achieve their fullest potential.

As we approach the future, we do so with the educational attainment of all Americans rising. If knowledge is power, perhaps that reality will lead us to greater appreciation and tolerance for one another. This book has been an attempt to enhance that understanding. We need to comprehend the larger context and patterns within which the dynamics of intergroup relations exist. We need to realize that pluralism has always been part of the U.S. experience and does not threaten either the assimilation process or the cohesiveness of society. We need to recognize that race and ethnicity are simply other people's humanity. When we reach that level of understanding, we will be able to acknowledge that diversity is the nation's strength, not its weakness, and when that happens, our society will be even stronger.

KEY TERMS

Bilingual education
Bilingualism
Dillingham Flaw
English-as-a-second-
  language (ESL)

English-plus programs
Hansen's law
Intergenerational
  mobility
Multiculturalism

1.5 generation
Segmented assimilation
Social capital
Spatial assimilation
Transnationalism

DISCUSSION QUESTIONS

1. What are some of the explanations for ethnic consciousness? Which seems most plausible? Why?
2. Discuss ethnicity as a social process, applying the concepts of assimilation and pluralism to your discussion.
3. What do current immigration patterns indicate? Is immigration a problem for native-born U.S. residents? Explain.
4. What are the pros and cons of bilingual education?
5. Describe the varying viewpoints and complexities about multiculturalism.
6. What is the future of ethnicity in the United States?

SUGGESTED READINGS

Bean, Frank D. *America's Newcomers and the Dynamics of Diversity*. New York: Russell Sage Foundation, 2005.
A social scientific assessment of the impact of immigration on the United States and the country's transformation into a multiethnic and multiracial society.

Graham, Otis L, Jr. *Unguarded Gates: A History of America's Immigration Crisis*. Rowman & Littlefield, 2006.

A provocative examination of past restrictive immigration as a framework for addressing the current immigration crisis.

Lind, Michael. *Next American Nation: The New Nationalism and the Fourth American Revolution*, reprint ed. New York: Free Press, 1996.
A wide-ranging, thought-provoking proposal for a coherent, unified national identity based on recognition that the forces of nationalism

and the ideal of a transracial melting pot need not conflict with one another.

Miller, John J. *The Unmaking of Americans: How Multiculturalism Has Undermined America's Assimilationist Ethic*. New York: Simon & Schuster, 1998.
A history of Americanization from its organized beginnings around 1907 to the current controversy on multiculturalism and a call for renewed Americanization efforts to sustain higher immigration.

Moen, Phyllis, Donna Dempster-McClain, and Henry A. Walker (eds.). *A Nation Divided: Diversity, Inequality, and Community in American Society*. Ithaca, NY: Cornell University Press, 1999.
Leading social scientists explore persisting tensions and new sources of strain involving sexual and gender minorities, white and non-white immigrants, rich and poor.

Ngai, Mae M. *Impossible Subjects: Illegal Aliens and the Making of Modern America*. Princeton, NJ: Princeton University Press, 2005.
A thought-provoking analysis of 20th-century U.S. immigration and the emergence of the sociolegal category of "illegal immigrant."

Parrillo, Vincent N. *Diversity in America*, 3rd ed. Thousand Oaks, CA: Pine Forge Press, 2008.
A brief look at our past, present, and future, with emphasis on immigration, multiculturalism, assimilation versus pluralism, and national identity. Includes a full discussion of the Dillingham Flaw.

Tichenor, Daniel J. *Dividing Lines: The Politics of Immigration Control in America*. Princeton, NJ: Princeton University Press, 2002.
An excellent narrative history of U.S. immigration policy and reform and the changing politics and social institutions shaping those decisions.

MySocKit

Additional resources for this chapter can be found in MySocKit. If you have a subscription to MySocKit, go to www.mysockit.com to study, review, and go beyond the book to learn more about race and ethnic relations.

Immigration by Region and Selected Country of Last Residence: Fiscal Years 1820–2006

Region and country of last residence[1]	1820 to 1829	1830 to 1839	1840 to 1849	1850 to 1859	1860 to 1869	1870 to 1879	1880 to 1889	1890 to 1899
Total	**128,502**	**538,381**	**1,427,337**	**2,814,554**	**2,081,261**	**2,742,137**	**5,248,568**	**3,694,294**
Europe	99,272	422,771	1,369,259	2,619,680	1,877,726	2,251,878	4,638,677	3,576,411
Austria-Hungary[2,3,4]	-	-	-	-	3,375	60,127	314,787	534,059
Austria[2,4]	-	-	-	-	2,700	54,529	204,805	268,218
Hungary[2]	-	-	-	-	483	5,598	109,982	203,350
Belgium	28	20	3,996	5,765	5,785	6,991	18,738	19,642
Bulgaria[5]	-	-	-	-	-	-	-	52
Denmark	173	927	671	3,227	13,553	29,278	85,342	56,671
France[7]	7,694	39,330	75,300	81,778	35,938	71,901	48,193	35,616
Germany[3,4]	5,753	124,726	385,434	976,072	723,734	751,769	1,445,181	579,072
Greece	17	49	17	32	51	209	1,807	12,732
Ireland[8]	51,617	170,672	656,145	1,029,486	427,419	422,264	674,061	405,710
Italy	430	2,225	1,476	8,643	9,853	46,296	267,660	603,761
Netherlands	1,105	1,377	7,624	11,122	8,387	14,267	52,715	29,349
Norway-Sweden[9]	91	1,149	12,389	22,202	82,937	178,823	586,441	334,058
Norway[9]	-	-	-	-	16,068	88,644	185,111	96,810
Sweden[9]	-	-	-	-	24,224	90,179	401,330	237,248
Poland[3]	19	366	105	1,087	1,886	11,016	42,910	107,793
Portugal[10]	177	820	196	1,299	2,083	13,971	15,186	25,874
Romania	-	-	-	-	-	-	5,842	6,808
Russia[3,11]	86	280	520	423	1,670	35,177	182,698	450,101
Spain[12]	2,595	2,010	1,916	8,795	6,966	5,540	3,995	9,189
Switzerland	3,148	4,430	4,819	24,423	21,124	25,212	81,151	37,020
United Kingdom[8,13]	26,336	74,350	218,572	445,322	532,956	578,447	810,900	328,759
Other Europe	3	40	79	4	9	590	1,070	145
Asia	34	55	121	36,080	54,408	134,128	71,151	61,285
China	3	8	32	35,933	54,028	133,139	65,797	15,268
India	9	38	33	42	50	166	247	102
Japan	-	-	-	-	138	193	1,583	13,998
Turkey	19	8	45	94	129	382	2,478	27,510
Other Asia	3	1	11	11	63	248	1,046	4,407
America	9,655	31,905	50,516	84,145	130,292	345,010	524,826	37,350
Canada and Newfoundland[15,16]	2,297	11,875	34,285	64,171	117,978	324,310	492,865	3,098
Mexico[16,17]	3,835	7,187	3,069	3,446	1,957	5,133	2,405	734
Caribbean	3,061	11,792	11,803	12,447	8,751	14,285	27,323	31,480
Central America	57	94	297	512	70	173	279	649
South America	405	957	1,062	3,569	1,536	1,109	1,954	1,389
Other America[20]	-	-	-	-	-	-	-	-
Africa	15	50	61	84	407	371	763	432
Egypt	-	-	-	-	4	29	145	51
Liberia	1	8	5	7	43	52	21	9
South Africa	-	-	-	-	35	48	23	9
Other Africa	14	42	56	77	325	242	574	363

See footnotes at end of table.

Immigration by Region and Selected Country of Last Residence: Fiscal Years 1820–2006 *(Continued)*

Region and country of last residence[1]	1820 to 1829	1830 to 1839	1840 to 1849	1850 to 1859	1860 to 1869	1870 to 1879	1880 to 1889	1890 to 1899
Total	**128,502**	**538,381**	**1,427,337**	**2,814,554**	**2,081,261**	**2,742,137**	**5,248,568**	**3,694,294**
Oceania	3	7	14	166	187	9,996	12,361	4,704
Australia	2	1	2	15	-	8,930	7,250	3,098
New Zealand	-	-	-	-	-	39	21	12
Other Oceania	1	6	12	151	187	1,027	5,090	1,594
Not Specified[20, 21]	19,523	83,593	7,366	74,399	18,241	754	790	14,112

Region and country of last residence[1]	1900 to 1909	1910 to 1919	1920 to 1929	1930 to 1939	1940 to 1949	1950 to 1959	1960 to 1969	1970 to 1979
Total	**8,202,388**	**6,347,380**	**4,295,510**	**699,375**	**856,608**	**2,499,268**	**3,213,749**	**4,248,203**
Europe	7,572,569	4,985,411	2,560,340	444,399	472,524	1,404,973	1,133,443	825,590
Austria-Hungary[2, 3, 4]	2,001,376	1,154,727	60,891	12,531	13,574	113,015	27,590	20,387
Austria[2, 4]	532,416	589,174	31,392	5,307	8,393	81,354	17,571	14,239
Hungary[2]	685,567	565,553	29,499	7,224	5,181	31,661	10,019	6,148
Belgium	37,429	32,574	21,511	4,013	12,473	18,885	9,647	5,413
Bulgaria[5]	34,651	27,180	2,824	1,062	449	97	598	1,011
Czechoslovakia[6]	-	-	101,182	17,757	8,475	1,624	2,758	5,654
Denmark	61,227	45,830	34,406	3,470	4,549	10,918	9,797	4,405
Finland	-	-	16,922	2,438	2,230	4,923	4,310	2,829
France[7]	67,735	60,335	54,842	13,761	36,954	50,113	46,975	26,281
Germany[3, 4]	328,722	174,227	386,634	119,107	119,506	576,905	209,616	77,142
Greece	145,402	198,108	60,774	10,599	8,605	45,153	74,173	102,370
Ireland[8]	344,940	166,445	202,854	28,195	15,701	47,189	37,788	11,461
Italy	1,930,475	1,229,916	528,133	85,053	50,509	184,576	200,111	150,031
Netherlands	42,463	46,065	29,397	7,791	13,877	46,703	37,918	10,373
Norway-Sweden[9]	426,981	192,445	170,329	13,452	17,326	44,224	36,150	10,298
Norway[9]	182,542	79,488	70,327	6,901	8,326	22,806	17,371	3,927
Sweden[9]	244,439	112,957	100,002	6,551	9,000	21,418	18,779	6,371
Poland[3]	-	-	223,316	25,555	7,577	6,465	55,742	33,696
Portugal[10]	65,154	82,489	44,829	3,518	6,765	13,928	70,568	104,754
Romania	57,322	13,566	67,810	5,264	1,254	914	2,339	10,774
Russia[3, 11]	1,501,301	1,106,998	61,604	2,463	605	453	2,329	28,132
Spain[12]	24,818	53,262	47,109	3,669	2,774	6,880	40,793	41,718
Switzerland	32,541	22,839	31,772	5,990	9,904	17,577	19,193	8,536
United Kingdom[8, 13]	469,518	371,878	341,552	61,813	131,794	195,709	220,213	133,218
Yugoslavia[14]	-	-	49,215	6,920	2,039	6,966	17,990	31,862
Other Europe	514	6,527	22,434	9,978	5,584	11,756	6,845	5,245
Asia	299,836	269,736	126,740	19,231	34,532	135,844	358,605	1,406,544
China	19,884	20,916	30,648	5,874	16,072	8,836	14,060	17,627
Hong Kong	-	-	-	-	-	13,781	67,047	117,350
India	3,026	3,478	2,076	554	1,692	1,850	18,638	147,997
Iran	-	-	208	198	1,144	3,195	9,059	33,763
Israel	-	-	-	-	98	21,376	30,911	36,306
Japan	139,712	77,125	42,057	2,683	1,557	40,651	40,956	49,392
Jordan	-	-	-	-	-	4,899	9,230	25,541
Korea	-	-	-	-	83	4,845	27,048	241,192
Philippines	-	-	-	391	4,099	17,245	70,660	337,726
Syria	-	-	5,307	2,188	1,179	1,091	2,432	8,086
Taiwan	-	-	-	-	-	721	15,657	83,155
Turkey	127,999	160,717	40,450	1,327	754	2,980	9,464	12,209
Vietnam	-	-	-	-	-	290	2,949	121,716
Other Asia	9,215	7,500	5,994	6,016	7,854	14,084	40,494	174,484

Region and country of last residence[1]	1900 to 1909	1910 to 1919	1920 to 1929	1930 to 1939	1940 to 1949	1950 to 1959	1960 to 1969	1970 to 1979
Total	**8,202,388**	**6,347,380**	**4,295,510**	**699,375**	**856,608**	**2,499,268**	**3,213,749**	**4,248,203**
America	277,809	1,070,539	1,591,278	230,319	328,435	921,610	1,674,172	1,904,355
Canada and Newfoundland[15, 16]	123,067	708,715	949,286	162,703	160,911	353,169	433,128	179,267
Mexico[16, 17]	31,188	185,334	498,945	32,709	56,158	273,847	441,824	621,218
Caribbean	100,960	120,860	83,482	18,052	46,194	115,661	427,235	708,850
Cuba	-	-	12,769	10,641	25,976	73,221	202,030	256,497
Dominican Republic	-	-	-	1,026	4,802	10,219	83,552	139,249
Haiti	-	-	-	156	823	3,787	28,992	55,166
Jamaica[18]	-	-	-	-	-	7,397	62,218	130,226
Other Caribbean[18]	100,960	120,860	70,713	6,229	14,593	21,037	50,443	127,712
Central America	7,341	15,692	16,511	6,840	20,135	40,201	98,560	120,374
Belize	77	40	285	193	433	1,133	4,185	6,747
Costa Rica	-	-	-	431	1,965	4,044	17,975	12,405
El Salvador	-	-	-	597	4,885	5,094	14,405	29,428
Guatemala	-	-	-	423	1,303	4,197	14,357	23,837
Honduras	-	-	-	679	1,874	5,320	15,078	15,651
Nicaragua	-	-	-	405	4,393	7,812	10,383	10,911
Panama[19]	-	-	-	1,452	5,282	12,601	22,177	21,395
Other Central America	7,264	15,652	16,226	2,660	-	-	-	-
South America	15,253	39,938	43,025	9,990	19,662	78,418	250,754	273,608
Argentina	-	-	-	1,067	3,108	16,346	49,384	30,303
Bolivia	-	-	-	50	893	2,759	6,205	5,635
Brazil	-	-	4,627	1,468	3,653	11,547	29,238	18,600
Chile	-	-	-	347	1,320	4,669	12,384	15,032
Colombia	-	-	-	1,027	3,454	15,567	68,371	71,265
Ecuador	-	-	-	244	2,207	8,574	34,107	47,464
Guyana	-	-	-	131	596	1,131	4,546	38,278
Paraguay	-	-	-	33	85	576	1,249	1,486
Peru	-	-	-	321	1,273	5,980	19,783	25,311
Suriname	-	-	-	25	130	299	612	714
Uruguay	-	-	-	112	754	1,026	4,089	8,416
Venezuela	-	-	-	1,155	2,182	9,927	20,758	11,007
Other South America	15,253	39,938	38,398	4,010	7	17	28	97
Other America[20]	-	-	29	25	25,375	60,314	22,671	1,038
Africa	6,326	8,867	6,362	2,120	6,720	13,016	23,780	71,408
Egypt	-	-	1,063	781	1,613	1,996	5,581	23,543
Ethiopia	-	-	-	10	28	302	804	2,588
Liberia	-	-	-	35	37	289	841	2,391
Morocco	-	-	-	73	879	2,703	2,880	1,967
South Africa	-	-	-	312	1,022	2,278	4,360	10,002
Other Africa	6,326	8,867	5,299	909	3,141	5,448	9,314	30,917
Oceania	12,355	12,339	9,860	3,306	14,262	11,353	23,630	39,980
Australia	11,191	11,280	8,404	2,260	11,201	8,275	14,986	18,708
New Zealand	-	-	935	790	2,351	1,799	3,775	5,018
Other Oceania	1,164	1,059	521	256	710	1,279	4,869	16,254
Not Specified[20, 21]	33,493	488	930	-	135	12,472	119	326

Immigration by Region and Selected Country of Last Residence: Fiscal Years 1820–2006 *(Continued)*

Region and country of last residence[1]	1980 to 1989	1990 to 1999	2000	2001	2002	2003	2004	2005	2006
Total	**6,244,379**	**9,775,398**	**841,002**	**1,058,902**	**1,059,356**	**703,542**	**957,883**	**1,122,373**	**1,266,264**
Europe	668,866	1,348,612	131,920	176,892	177,059	102,546	135,663	180,449	169,197
Austria-Hungary[2,3,4]	20,437	27,529	2,009	2,303	4,004	2,176	3,689	4,569	2,991
Austria[2,4]	15,374	18,234	986	996	2,650	1,160	2,442	3,002	1,301
Hungary[2]	5,063	9,295	1,023	1,307	1,354	1,016	1,247	1,567	1,690
Belgium	7,028	7,077	817	997	834	515	746	1,031	891
Bulgaria[5]	1,124	16,948	4,779	4,273	3,476	3,706	4,042	5,451	4,690
Czechoslovakia[6]	5,678	8,970	1,407	1,911	1,854	1,472	1,871	2,182	2,844
Denmark	4,847	6,189	549	732	651	435	568	714	738
Finland	2,569	3,970	377	497	365	230	346	549	513
France[7]	32,066	35,945	4,063	5,379	4,567	2,926	4,209	5,035	4,945
Germany[3,4]	85,752	92,207	12,230	21,992	20,977	8,061	10,270	12,864	10,271
Greece	37,729	25,403	5,113	1,941	1,486	900	1,213	1,473	1,544
Ireland[8]	22,210	65,384	1,264	1,531	1,400	1,002	1,518	2,083	2,038
Italy	55,562	75,992	2,652	3,332	2,812	1,890	2,495	3,179	3,406
Netherlands	11,234	13,345	1,455	1,888	2,296	1,321	1,713	2,150	1,928
Norway-Sweden[9]	13,941	17,825	1,967	2,544	2,082	1,516	2,011	2,264	2,111
Norway[9]	3,835	5,211	508	582	460	385	457	472	532
Sweden[9]	10,106	12,614	1,459	1,962	1,622	1,131	1,554	1,792	1,579
Poland[3]	63,483	172,249	9,750	12,308	13,274	11,004	14,048	14,837	16,705
Portugal[10]	42,685	25,497	1,373	1,611	1,301	808	1,062	1,084	1,439
Romania	24,753	48,136	6,506	6,206	4,515	3,305	4,078	6,431	6,753
Russia[3,11]	33,311	433,427	43,156	54,838	55,370	33,513	41,959	60,395	59,760
Spain[12]	22,783	18,443	1,390	1,875	1,588	1,102	1,453	2,002	2,387
Switzerland	8,316	11,768	1,339	1,786	1,493	862	1,193	1,465	1,199
United Kingdom[8,13]	153,644	156,182	14,427	20,118	17,940	11,155	16,680	21,956	19,984
Yugoslavia[14]	16,267	57,039	11,960	21,854	28,051	8,270	13,213	19,249	11,066
Other Europe	3,447	29,087	3,337	6,976	6,723	6,377	7,286	9,486	10,994
Asia	2,391,356	2,859,899	254,932	336,112	325,749	235,339	319,025	382,744	411,795
China	170,897	342,058	41,804	50,677	55,901	37,342	50,280	64,921	83,628
Hong Kong	112,132	116,894	7,181	10,282	7,938	5,015	5,421	5,004	4,514
India	231,649	352,528	38,938	65,673	66,644	47,032	65,507	79,140	58,072
Iran	98,141	76,899	6,481	8,003	7,684	4,696	5,898	7,306	9,829
Israel	43,669	41,340	3,871	4,892	4,907	3,686	5,206	6,963	6,667
Japan	44,150	66,582	7,688	10,424	9,106	6,702	8,655	9,929	9,107
Jordan	28,928	42,755	4,476	5,106	4,774	4,008	5,186	5,430	5,512
Korea	322,708	179,770	15,107	19,728	19,917	12,076	19,441	26,002	24,472
Philippines	502,056	534,338	40,465	50,644	48,493	43,133	54,651	57,656	71,134
Syria	14,534	22,906	2,255	3,542	3,350	2,046	2,549	3,350	3,080
Taiwan	119,051	132,647	9,457	12,457	9,932	7,168	9,314	9,389	8,546
Turkey	19,208	38,687	2,702	3,463	3,914	3,318	4,491	6,449	6,433
Vietnam	200,632	275,379	25,159	34,537	32,372	21,227	30,074	30,832	29,705
Other Asia	483,601	637,116	49,348	56,684	50,817	37,890	52,352	70,373	91,096
America	2,695,329	5,137,743	392,461	470,794	477,363	305,936	408,972	432,748	548,848
Canada and Newfoundland[15,16]	156,313	194,788	21,289	29,991	27,142	16,447	22,439	29,930	23,913
Mexico[16,17]	1,009,586	2,757,418	171,445	204,032	216,924	114,758	173,711	157,992	170,046
Caribbean	790,109	1,004,687	84,250	96,384	93,914	67,498	82,116	91,378	144,480
Cuba	132,552	159,037	17,897	25,832	27,435	8,685	15,385	20,651	44,248
Dominican Republic	221,552	359,818	17,373	21,139	22,386	26,112	30,063	27,366	37,997
Haiti	121,406	177,446	21,977	22,470	19,151	11,924	13,695	13,496	21,628
Jamaica[18]	193,874	177,143	15,603	15,031	14,507	13,045	13,581	17,775	24,538
Other Caribbean[18]	120,725	131,243	11,400	11,912	10,435	7,732	9,392	12,090	16,069

Region and country of last residence[1]	1980 to 1989	1990 to 1999	2000	2001	2002	2003	2004	2005	2006
Total	**6,244,379**	**9,775,398**	**841,002**	**1,058,902**	**1,059,356**	**703,542**	**957,883**	**1,122,373**	**1,266,264**
Central America	339,376	610,189	60,331	72,504	66,298	53,283	61,253	52,636	74,258
Belize	14,964	12,600	774	982	983	616	888	901	1,263
Costa Rica	25,017	17,054	1,390	1,863	1,686	1,322	1,811	2,479	3,459
El Salvador	137,418	273,017	22,301	30,876	30,472	27,854	29,297	20,891	31,259
Guatemala	58,847	126,043	9,861	13,399	15,870	14,195	18,655	16,475	23,687
Honduras	39,071	72,880	5,851	6,546	6,355	4,582	5,339	6,825	8,036
Nicaragua	31,102	80,446	18,258	16,908	9,171	3,503	3,842	3,196	4,035
Panama[19]	32,957	28,149	1,896	1,930	1,761	1,211	1,421	1,869	2,519
South America	399,862	570,624	55,143	67,880	73,082	53,946	69,452	100,811	136,149
Argentina	23,442	30,065	2,472	3,426	3,791	3,193	4,672	6,945	7,239
Bolivia	9,798	18,111	1,744	1,804	1,660	1,365	1,719	2,164	4,000
Brazil	22,944	50,744	6,767	9,391	9,034	6,108	10,247	16,331	17,748
Chile	19,749	18,200	1,660	1,881	1,766	1,255	1,719	2,354	2,727
Colombia	105,494	137,985	14,125	16,234	18,409	14,400	18,055	24,710	42,024
Ecuador	48,015	81,358	7,624	9,654	10,524	7,022	8,366	11,528	17,625
Guyana	85,886	74,407	5,255	7,835	9,492	6,373	5,721	8,772	9,010
Paraguay	3,518	6,082	394	464	413	222	324	523	725
Peru	49,958	110,117	9,361	10,838	11,737	9,169	11,369	15,205	21,300
Suriname	1,357	2,285	281	254	223	175	170	287	341
Uruguay	7,235	6,062	396	516	499	470	750	1,110	1,639
Venezuela	22,405	35,180	5,052	5,576	5,529	4,190	6,335	10,870	11,758
Other South America	61	28	12	7	5	4	5	12	13
Other America[20]	83	37	3	3	3	4	1	1	2
Africa	141,990	346,416	40,790	50,009	56,002	45,559	62,623	79,701	112,108
Egypt	26,744	44,604	4,323	5,333	6,215	3,928	6,590	10,296	13,163
Ethiopia	12,927	40,097	3,645	4,620	6,308	5,969	7,180	8,380	13,395
Liberia	6,420	13,587	1,225	1,477	1,467	1,081	1,540	1,846	3,736
Morocco	3,471	15,768	3,423	4,752	3,188	2,969	3,910	4,165	4,704
South Africa	15,505	21,964	2,814	4,046	3,685	2,088	3,335	4,425	3,173
Other Africa	76,923	210,396	25,360	29,781	35,139	29,524	40,068	50,589	73,937
Oceania	41,432	56,800	5,928	7,201	6,495	5,076	6,954	7,432	8,001
Australia	16,901	24,288	2,694	3,714	3,420	2,488	3,397	4,090	3,770
New Zealand	6,129	8,600	1,080	1,347	1,364	1,030	1,420	1,457	1,344
Other Oceania	18,402	23,912	2,154	2,140	1,711	1,558	2,137	1,885	2,887
Not Specified[20, 21]	305,406	25,928	14,971	17,894	16,688	9,086	24,646	39,299	16,315

- Represents zero or not available.

[1] Data for years prior to 1906 refers to country of origin; data from 1906 to 2006 refer to country of last residence.

[2] Data for Austria and Hungary not reported separately for all years during 1860 to 1869, 1890 to 1899, 1900 to 1909.

[3] From 1899 to 1919, data for Poland included in Austria-Hungary, Germany, and the Soviet Union.

[4] From 1938 to 1945, data for Austria included in Germany.

[5] From 1899 to 1910, included Serbia and Montenegro.

[6] Currently includes Czech Republic and Slovak Republic.

[7] From 1820 to 1910, included Corsica.

[8] Prior to 1926, data for Northern Ireland included in Ireland.

[9] Data for Norway and Sweden not reported separately until 1869.

[10] From 1820 to 1910, included Cape Verde and Azores Islands.

Immigration by Region and Selected Country of Last Residence, Fiscal Years 1820–2006 *(Continued)*

[11] From 1820 to 1920, data refer to the Russian Empire. Between 1920 and 1990 data refer to the Soviet Union. From 1991 to present, the data refer to the Russian federation, Armenia, Azerbaijan, Belarus, Georgia, Kazakhstan, Kyrgyzstan, Moldova, Russia, Tajikistan, Ukraine, and Uzbekistan.

[12] From 1820 to 1910, included the Canary Islands and Balearic Islands.

[13] Since 1925, data for United Kingdom refer to England, Scotland, Wales and Northern Ireland.

[14] Currently includes Bosnia-Herzegovina, Croatia, Macedonia, Slovenia, Serbia, and Montenegro.

[15] Prior to 1911, data refer to British North America. From 1911, data includes Newfoundland.

[16] Land arrivals not completely enumerated until 1908.

[17] No data available for Mexico from 1886 to 1893.

[18] Data for Jamaica not reported separately until 1953. Prior to 1953, Jamaica was included in British West Indies.

[19] From 1932 to 1972, data for the Panama Canal Zone included in Panama.

[20] Included in 'Not Specified' until 1925.

[21] Includes 32,897 persons returning in 1906 to their homes in the United States.

Note: From 1820 to 1867, figures represent alien passenger arrivals at seaports; from 1868 to 1891 and 1895 to 1897, immigrant alien arrivals; from 1892 to 1894 and 1898 to 2006, immigrant aliens admitted for permanent residence; from 1892 to 1903, aliens entering by cabin class were not counted as immigrants. Land arrivals were not completely enumerated until 1908. For this table, fiscal year 1843 covers 9 months ending September, 1843; fiscal years 1832 and 1850 cover 15 months ending December 31 of the respective years; and fiscal year 1868 covers 6 months ending June 30, 1868.

Source: U.S. Department of Homeland Security

Glossary

Abstract typification The generalization of people or things into broad categories.

Acceptance A minority response to prejudice and discrimination; based on powerlessness, fear for personal safety, desire for economic security, or split-labor-market theory fatalism.

Accommodation (pluralistic) theory A tendency to accept the situation as it exists, without seeking to change it or make others conform; pluralism.

Acculturation The process by which a group changes its distinctive cultural traits to conform with those of the host society.

Action-orientation level of prejudice A positive or negative predisposition to engage in discriminatory behavior toward members of a particular group.

Activity theory A theoretical perspective that people of all ages require adequate levels of social activity to remain well adjusted.

Affirmative action Deliberate efforts to improve minority representation, as well as their economic and educational opportunities.

Afrocentrism A viewpoint emphasizing African culture and its influence on Western civilization and U.S. black behavior.

Ageism The manifestation of prejudice, aversion, or even hatred toward the old.

Amalgamation (melting-pot) theory The biological and cultural blending of two or more groups of people into a distinct new type; the melting-pot theory. A synonym is marital assimilation.

Americanization movement The effort to have ethnic groups quickly give up their cultural traits and adopt those of the dominant U.S. group.

Anglo-conformity A behavioral adherence to the established white Anglo-Saxon Protestant prototype; what many ethnocentric U.S. residents mean by assimilation.

Annihilation The extermination of a specific group of people.

Ascribed status One's socially defined, unchangeable position in a society based on such arbitrary factors as age, sex, race, or family background.

Assimilation (majority-conformity) theory The process by which members of racial or ethnic minorities are able to function within a society without indicating any marked cultural, social, or personal differences from the people of the majority group.

Asylee An alien found in a country or port of entry who is unable or unwilling to return to his or her country of origin, or to seek the protection of that country, because of persecution or a well-founded fear of persecution.

Avoidance A minority-group response to prejudice and discrimination by migrating or withdrawing to escape further problems; a majority-group attempt to minimize contact with specific minority groups through social or spatial segregation.

Bilingual education Teaching subjects in both English and the student's native language to develop fluency in both.

Bilingualism Fluency in two languages.

Bipolarization Two opposite trends occurring simultaneously.

Black codes Southern state laws enacted during Reconstruction to keep blacks in a condition close to slavery.

Brain drain Emigration of large numbers of skilled workers, professionals, or scientists who are badly needed by their home country.

Categoric knowing A stereotype of others based merely on information obtained visually and perhaps verbally.

Celibacy Refraining from any form of sexual intimacy.

Chain migration A sequential flow of immigrants to a locality previously settled by friends, relatives, or other compatriots.

Child care Supervised, quality care for preschool youngsters while one or both parents work.

Civil religion A shared, nondenominational belief system incorporated into the culture.

Cognitive level of prejudice Beliefs and perceptions about other racial or ethnic groups.

Conflict theory A macrolevel sociological perspective emphasizing conflict as an important influence and permanent feature of life.

Convenience sample A selection of individuals or cases on the basis of feasibility or ease of access, which can be biased and nonrepresentative of the entire population.

Convergent subculture A subgroup gradually becoming completely integrated into the dominant culture.

Cultural assimilation (acculturation) Changing cultural patterns of behavior to those of the host society; acculturation.

Cultural determinism A theory that a group's culture explains its position in society and its achievements or lack thereof.

Cultural differentiation Differences between cultures that make one group distinguishable from another.

Cultural diffusion The spread of ideas, inventions, and practices from one culture to another.

Cultural drift A gradual change in the values, attitudes, customs, and beliefs of the members of a society.

Cultural pluralism Two or more culturally distinct groups coexisting in relative harmony.

Cultural relativism A view of the customs and beliefs of other peoples within the context of their culture rather than one's own.

Cultural transmission The passing of a society's culture from one generation to another.

Culture The values, attitudes, customs, beliefs, and habits shared by members of a society.

Culture of poverty A controversial viewpoint arguing that the disorganization and pathology of lower-class culture are self-perpetuating through cultural transmission.

Culture shock Feelings of disorientation, anxiety, and a sense of being threatened when unpreparedly brought into contact with another culture.

Cumulative causation Gunnar Myrdal's term for the vicious-circle process in which prejudice and discrimination mutually "cause" each other, thereby continuing and intensifying the cycle.

De facto segregation Physical separation of a group that is entrenched in customs and practices.

Defiance A peaceful or violent action to challenge openly what a group considers a discriminatory practice.

De jure segregation Physical separation of a group that is established by law.

Deviance Characteristics or behavior violating social norms and therefore negatively valued by many people in that society.

Dichotomy A division into two, possibly contrasting, parts.

Dignidad Hispanic cultural value that the dignity of all humans entitles them to a measure of respect.

Dillingham Flaw Any inaccurate comparison based on simplistic categorizations and anachronistic judgments.

Discrimination Differential and unequal treatment of other groups of people, usually along racial, religious, or ethnic lines.

Disengagement theory A perspective that asserts that people inevitably become more passive and decrease their activity as they reach old age.

Displaced aggression Hostility directed against a powerless group rather than against the more powerful cause of the feelings of hostility.

Dominant group Any culturally or physically distinctive social grouping possessing economic, political, and social power and discriminating against a subordinate minority group.

Ebonics An African American systematic language dialect with its own grammar, pronunciation, and vocabulary.

Economic determinism A theory that a society's economic base establishes its culture and general characteristics.

Ecumenical movement An effort to find universality among all faiths.

Emigration Act of leaving one's country or region to settle in another.

Emotional level of prejudice The feelings aroused in a group by another racial or ethnic group.

Endogamy The tendency for people to marry only within their own social group.

English-as-a-second-language (ESL) programs Teaching children English competence as one would teach English speakers another language.

English-plus programs A dual approach under which foreign-language students learn English and native-born U.S. students develop foreign-language competence.

Entrepreneurs People who set about to carry out any enterprise.

Ethclass A social-group classification based on a combination of race, religion, social class, and regional residence.

Ethnicity A cultural concept in which a large number of people who share learned or acquired traits and close social interaction regard themselves and are regarded by others as constituting a single group on that basis.

Ethnic stratification Structured inequality of different groups with different access to social rewards as a result of their status in the social hierarchy.

Ethnic subcultures Ongoing lifestyles and interaction patterns separate from the larger society that are based on religious or other cultural group memberships.

Ethnocentrism A tendency to judge other cultures or subcultures by the standards of one's own culture.

Ethnogenesis A process in which immigrants hold onto some homeland values, adapt others, and adopt some values of the host country.

Ethnophaulism A derogatory word or expression used to describe or refer to a racial or ethnic group.

Ethnoviolence Behavior ranging from verbal harassment and threats to murder against people targeted solely because of their race, religion, ethnicity, or sexual orientation.

Eurocentrism A viewpoint emphasizing Western civilization, history, literature, and other humanities.

Exploitation The selfish use of the labor of others for profit at their expense.

Expulsion The forced removal of a group of people from an area.

Extended family A family unit that includes other kin in addition to parents and children.

Exurbs Newest ring of settlement beyond the old suburbs.

False consciousness Holding attitudes that do not accurately reflect the objective facts of a situation.

Fast track When women delay childbearing or forgo motherhood entirely to give full commitment to management to earn promotions over other candidates.

Feminization of poverty A term describing female-headed households living in poverty.

First-generation American Someone born in another country who immigrated to the United States.

Flex time An arrangement that allows workers, within predetermined limits, to set their own working hours.

Functional theory A macrolevel sociological perspective emphasizing societal order and stability, with harmonious interdependent parts.

Gemeinschaft A small, tradition-dominated community characterized by intimate primary relationships and strong feelings of group loyalty.

Gender-role expectations Anticipated behaviors because of one's gender.

Glass ceiling A real but unseen discriminatory policy that limits female upward mobility into top management positions.

Group A collectivity of people closely interacting with one another on the basis of shared expectations about behavior.

Hansen's law A theory that what the child of an immigrant wishes to forget, the grandchild wishes to remember; also called the three-generation hypothesis.

Homophobia The fear or hatred of homosexuals and homosexual behavior.

Ideology A generalized set of beliefs that collectively explains and justifies the interests of those who hold them.

Immigration Movement of people into a new country to become permanent residents.

Indigenous Person, plant, or animal in its natural, native habitat.

Ingroup The group to which an individual belongs and feels loyal.

Institutional discrimination Unequal treatment of subordinate groups inherent in the ongoing operations of society's institutions.

Institutionalized racism Unequal treatment of a racial group inherent in the ongoing operations of society's institutions.

Interactionist theory A microlevel sociological perspective emphasizing the shared interpretations and interaction patterns in everyday life.

Intergenerational mobility The change in social status within a family from one generation to the next.

Intergroup contact hypothesis A perspective that holds attitudes and behaviors in social interactions depend on the comparative status and affective ties of the participants.

Internal-colonialism theory A concept explaining the experiences of blacks, Hispanics, and Native Americans in terms of economic exploitation and rigid stratification.

Invasion-succession The ecological process in which one group displaces another group in a residential area or business activity.

Jigsaw method A teaching technique that creates interdependent cooperative learning groups.

Jim Crow laws Southern-state segregation laws, passed in the 1890s and early 1900s; covered use of all public facilities, including schools, restaurants, transportation, waiting rooms, rest rooms, drinking fountains, and parks.

Kye A rotating credit fund enabling Korean Americans to start or expand their businesses.

Labeling theory A perspective addressing how others' categorizations affect one's self-identity and behavior.

Latent functions Hidden, unexpected results within a social structure.

Linguistic relativity The recognition that different languages dissect and present reality differently.

Machismo Value orientation defining masculinity in varying terms of virility, honor, and providing for one's family.

Macrosocial theories Any theory that examines the empirical world from the societal level.

Manifest functions Obvious and intended results within a social structure.

Marginality The situation of individuals who are the product of one culture but are attempting to live within another, and therefore are not fully a part of either one.

Marianismo Value orientation defining feminine virtue as accepting male dominance and emphasizing family responsibilities.

Marital assimilation (amalgamation) A pattern of intermarriage of minority-group members with dominant-group members. A synonym is melting-pot theory.

Material culture All physical objects created by members of a society and the meanings/significance attached to them.

Matrilineal When descent and inheritance pass through the female side of the family.

Matrilocal The custom of married partners settling in or near the household of the wife's family.

Medical model A concept that emphasizes the individual's physical situation and not societal elements that may be affecting it.

Melting-pot theory *See* Amalgamation (melting-pot) theory and marital assimilation.

Microsocial theory Any theory that looks at the empirical view from a close, individual level.

Middleman minority A minority group occupying an intermediate occupational position in trade or commerce between the top and bottom strata.

Migration Movement of people into and out of a specified area, either within a country or from one country to another.

Minority group A culturally and physically distinctive group that experiences unequal treatment, an ascribed status, and a sense of shared identity and that practices endogamy.

Minority–minority relations A focus on interaction patterns between different minority groups.

Miscegenation Mixture of races by sexual union.

Mommy track When women try to juggle both family and work, which often slows or halts their upward mobility within the company.

Mortality rate Number of deaths per 1,000 people in a given year.

Multiculturalism Ranges from efforts for an all-inclusive curriculum to an emphasis on separatist pluralism.

Nativist One who advocates a policy of protecting the interests of native inhabitants against those of immigrants.

Negative self-image The result of social conditioning, differential treatment, or both, causing people or groups to believe themselves inferior.

Net worth The difference between assets and liabilities that an individual or household has at any given time.

Nondenominational Interchurch; not pertaining to any particular faith.

Nonmaterial culture Abstract human creations and their meanings/significance in life.

Norms The internalized rules of conduct that embody the fundamental expectations of society.

Nuclear family A unit of parents and their children living apart from other relatives.

Occupational mobility Ability to change one's job position with regard to status and economic reward.

1.5 generation Any immigrant arriving before or during early teens and socialized in both countries.

Outgroup Any group to which an individual does not belong or feel loyal.

Pan-Indianism Social movement in which tribes not united by kinship join together in a common cause.

Paralinguistic signals Use of sounds but not words to convey distinct meanings.

Parallel social institutions A subcultural replication of institutions of the larger society, such as churches, schools, and organizations.

Paternalism A condescending treatment of adults, managing and regulating their affairs as a father would handle his children's affairs.

Pentecostal faith A form of evangelical Christianity that inspires a sense of belonging through worship participation.

Persistent subculture A subgroup adhering to its own way of life and resisting absorption into the dominant culture.

Pluralism A state in which minorities can maintain their distinctive subcultures and simultaneously interact with relative equality in the larger society.

Polygyny A form of marriage joining one male with two or more females.

Power-differential theory The theory that intergroup relations depend on the relative power of the migrant group and the indigenous group.

Prejudice A system of negative beliefs, feelings, and action orientations regarding a certain group or groups of people.

Primary structural assimilation Integration in which dominant- and minority-group members share close, personal interactions in churches, families, social clubs, or gatherings.

Primogeniture Inheritance or succession by the eldest son.

Push–pull factors A combination of negative elements at home and positive inducements elsewhere that encourage migration from one place to another.

Race A categorization in which a large number of people sharing visible physical characteristics regard themselves or are regarded by others as a single group on that basis.

Racial profiling Action initiated on the erroneous presumption that individuals of a particular group are more likely to engage in illegal activity than individuals of other groups.

Racism False linkage between biology and sociocultural behavior to assert the superiority of one race.

Random sample A sample of a population where each member of the population has an equal chance of being in the sample.

Redlining Unwillingness of some banks to make loans in lower-income minority neighborhoods.

Reference group A group to which people may or may not belong but to which they refer when evaluating themselves and their behavior.

Refugee Any person outside his or her country of origin who is unable or unwilling to return because of persecution or a well-founded fear of persecution.

Relative deprivation A lack of resources or rewards in one's standard of living in comparison with others in the society.

Reputational method A technique for measuring social class by questioning people about others' social standing.

Role entrapment The culturally defined need to be "feminine" that prevents many women from doing things that would help them achieve success and self-realization.

Sandwich generation The generation of people who care for their aging parents while raising their own children.

Scapegoating Placing blame on others for something that is not their fault.

Scientific method A process involving repeated observation, precise measurement, careful description, theory formulation, and gathering further information based on questions that followed from those theories.

Secondary group A collectivity of people who interact on an impersonal or limited emotional basis for some practical or specific purpose.

Secondary structural assimilation Integration in which dominant- and minority-group members share the more impersonal public sphere of civic, school, recreational, or work settings.

Second-generation American A child born in the United States of immigrant parents; can also refer to a child born elsewhere but raised from a young age in the United States by immigrant parents.

Segmented assimilation Refers to a variety of outcomes among or within the contemporary immigrant streams.

Selective perception A tendency to see or accept only information that agrees with one's value orientations or that is consistent with one's attitudes about other groups.

Self-justification A defense mechanism whereby people denigrate another person or group to justify maltreating them.

Separatist pluralism Effort to seek specific, separate group identity rather than a collective U.S. national identity.

Sexism Institutionalized prejudice and discrimination based on gender.

Sexual script Enactments of complex sets of cultural meanings, the normative cultural contexts that give sex its meaning.

Shunning An Amish social-control practice of complete avoidance, including even eye contact.

Shuttle migration Large-scale movement back and forth between two countries.

Slavery reparations Cash or land compensation to descendants of slaves to rectify past injustices.

Social capital Actual or virtual resources available through a network of institutionalized relationships.

Social class A categorization designating people's places in the stratification hierarchy on the basis of similarities in income, property, power, status, and lifestyle.

Social construction of reality The process by which definitions of reality are socially created, objectified, internalized, and then taken for granted.

Social discrimination Exclusion of outgroup members from close relationships with ingroup members.

Social distance The degree of closeness or remoteness one desires in interaction with members of a particular group.

Social identity theory Holds that ingroup members enhance their self-image by considering their group better than others.

Socialization process The process of social interaction by which people acquire personality and learn the culture or subculture of their group.

Social model The way in which society adapts to accommodate people with disabilities.

Social norms Generally shared rules or expectations of what is and is not proper behavior.

Social ostracism Excluding a person or persons from social privileges and interaction.

Social segregation A situation in which participation in social, fraternal, service, and other types of activities is confined to members of the ingroup.

Social stratification The hierarchy within a society based on the unequal distribution of resources, power, or prestige.

Social structure The organized patterns of behavior in a social system governing people's interrelationships.

Sojourners Those who stay temporarily.

Sovereign Having independent power or authority.

Spatial assimilation The process of minority groups integrating into housing markets inhabited by non-Hispanic whites.

Spatial segregation The physical separation of a minority group from the rest of society, such as in housing or education.

Split-labor-market theory A concept explaining ethnic antagonism on the basis of conflict between higher-paid and lower-paid labor.

Status positions Places a person holds in society as determined by class structure, gender, and occupational roles.

Stereotype An oversimplified generalization attributing certain traits or characteristics to any person in a group without regard to individual differences.

Structural assimilation Large-scale entrance of minority-group members into primary-group relationships with the host society in its social organizations and institutions.

Structural differentiation Status distinctions for different racial and ethnic groups entrenched within the social system.

Structural pluralism Coexistence of racial and ethnic groups in separate subsocieties; also may be divided along social class and regional boundaries.

Subculture A group that shares in the overall culture of a society while retaining its own distinctive traditions and lifestyle.

Symbolic ethnicity Identifying with one's heritage through ethnic foods, holidays, and political and social activities.

Symbolic interaction The use of symbols—such as signs, gestures, and language—through which people interact with one another.

Third-generation American Someone born in the United States whose grandparents immigrated to the United States.

Thomas theorem An observation that if people define situations as real, the situations become real in their consequences.

Three-generation hypothesis *See* Hansen's law.

Total fertility rate The average number of children born per woman in her lifetime

Transnationalism Sustained ties of persons, networks, and organizations across national borders.

Triple-melting-pot theory The concept that intermarriage is occurring among various nationalities within the three major religious groupings.

Undocumented alien Illegal immigrant without a green card or visa authorizing entry.

Upward mobility An improvement in one's socio-economic position.

Value neutrality An ideal state, never fully possible, in which the observer eliminates all personal bias in order to be completely objective.

Values Socially shared conceptions of what is good, desirable, and proper or bad, undesirable, and improper.

Vicious-circle phenomenon Dynamics of intergroup relations where prejudice and discrimination serve as reciprocal stimuli and responses to reinforce one another.

Xenophobia The irrational fear of or contempt for strangers or foreigners.

Notes

CHAPTER 1

1. Aristotle, *The Rhetoric* (New York: Appleton, 1932), Book I, Chapter 11.
2. See, for example, Theodore Newcomb, "The Acquaintance Process: Looking Mainly Backward," *Journal of Personality and Social Psychology* 36 (1978): 1075–83.
3. Donn Byrne et al., "The Ubiquitous Relationship: Attitude Similarity and Attraction. A Cross-Cultural Study," *Human Relations* 24 (1971): 201–07.
4. Emory S. Bogardus, "Comparing Racial Distances in Ethiopia, South Africa, and the United States," *Sociology and Social Research* 52 (1968): 149–56.
5. See Tom W. Smith and Glenn R. Dempsey, "The Polls: Ethnic Social Distance and Prejudice," *Public Opinion Quarterly* 47 (1983): 584–600.
6. Milton Kleg and Kaoru Yamamoto, "As the World Turns: Ethno-Racial Distances after 70 Years," *Social Science Journal* 35 (April 1998): 183–90.
7. Vincent N. Parrillo and Christopher Donoghue, "Updating the Bogardus Social Distance Studies: A New National Survey," *Social Science Journal* 42:2 (2005): 257–71.
8. James Dyer, Arnold Vedlitz, and Stephen Worchel, "Social Distance among Racial and Ethnic Groups in Texas: Some Demographic Correlates," *Social Science Quarterly* 70 (1989): 607–16.
9. Patricia Odell, Kathleen Korgen, and Gabe Wang, "Cross-Racial Friendships and Social Distance Between Racial Groups on a College Campus," *Innovative Higher Education* 29:4 (2005): 291–305.
10. Michael J. White, Ann H. Kim, and Jennifer E. Glick, "Mapping Social Distance: Ethnic Residential Segregation in a Multiethnic Metro," *Sociological Methods & Research* 34:2 (2005): 173–203.
11. Mark Fossett, "Ethnic Preferences, Social Distance Dynamics, and Residential Segregation: Theoretical Explorations Using Simulation Analysis," *Journal of Mathematical Sociology* 30 (2006): 185–273.
12. Lyn H. Lofland, *A World of Strangers* (New York: Basic Books, 1973), p. 16.
13. Georg Simmel, "The Stranger," in Kurt H. Wolff (ed.), *The Sociology of Georg Simmel* (New York: Free Press, 1950).
14. Alfred Schutz, "The Stranger," *American Sociological Review* 69 (May 1944): 449–507.
15. Ta-Nehisi Paul Coates, "Is Obama Black Enough?" *Time* (February 1, 2007). Accessed online at www.time.com/time/nation/article/0,8599,1584736,00.html [July 19, 2007]; Richard Carter, "Once Again, Is Obama Really Black Enough for Black Voters?" *New York Amsterdam News* (May 3, 2007), pp. 10, 41.
16. Donald Young, *American Minority Peoples* (New York: Harper, 1932), p. viii.
17. Louis Wirth, "The Problem of Minority Groups," in Ralph Linton (ed.), *The Science of Man in the World Crisis* (New York: Columbia University Press, 1945), pp. 347–72.
18. Richard Schermerhorn, *Comparative Ethnic Relations* (New York: Random House, 1970), p. 8.
19. Tamotsu Shibutani and Kian M. Kwan, *Ethnic Stratification* (New York: Macmillan, 1965).
20. Charles Wagley and Marvin Harris, *Minorities in the New World* (New York: Columbia University Press, 1964).
21. See Ashley Montagu, *Man's Most Dangerous Myth: The Fallacy of Race,* 5th ed. (New York: Oxford University Press, 1974).
22. Michael J. Bamshad and Steve E. Olson,

"Does Race Exist?" *Scientific American* 289 (December 2003): 78–85.

23. See Maria P. P. Root (ed.), *Racially Mixed People in America* (Newbury Park, CA: Sage, 1992). See also J. C. Brigham and L. W. Biesbrecht, "All in the Family: Racial Attitudes," *Journal of Communication* 26 (1976): 69–74.

24. See Winthop D. Jordan, *White over Black: American Attitudes toward the Negro, 1550–1812,* reissue ed. (Williamsburg, VA: Omohundro Institute, 1995), p. 217; Pierre van den Berghe, *Race and Racism: A Comparative Perspective* (New York: Wiley, 1967), p. 11; Peter I. Rose, *The Subject Is Race* (New York: Oxford University Press, 1968), pp. 32–33.

25. Arab American Institute, "Arab Americans: Demographics." Accessed online at www. aaiusa.org/arab-americans/22/demographics [June 16, 2007].

26. Brewton Berry and Henry L. Tischler, *Race and Ethnic Relations,* 4th ed. (Boston: Houghton Mifflin, 1978), pp. 30–32.

27. Milton Gordon, *Assimilation in American Life* (New York: Oxford University Press, 1964), p. 27; Shibutani and Kwan, *Ethnic Stratification,* p. 47; Jerry D. Rose, *Peoples: The Ethnic Dimension in Human Relations* (Chicago: Rand McNally, 1976), pp. 8–12.

28. William Graham Sumner, *Folkways* (Boston: Ginn, 1906), p. 13.

29. See Henri Taifel, *Human Groups and Social Categories* (Cambridge, England: Cambridge University Press, 1981).

30. See Marc J. Schwartz, "Negative Ethnocentrism," *Journal of Conflict Resolution* 5 (March 1961): 75–81.

31. Robin M. Williams Jr., *Strangers Next Door* (Englewood Cliffs, NJ: Prentice Hall, 1964), p. 23.

32. Robert A. Levine and Donald T. Campbell, *Ethnocentrism: Theories of Conflict, Ethnic Attitudes, and Group Behavior* (New York: Wiley, 1972), pp. 68, 202.

33. Kenneth E. Boulding, *Conflict and Defense: A General Theory* (New York: Harper, 1962), pp. 162–63; Lewis A. Coser (ed.), *Sociological Theory: A Book of Readings* (New York: Macmillan, 1957), pp. 87–110; P. C.

Rosenblatt, "Origins and Effects of Group Ethnocentrism and Nationalism," *Journal of Conflict Resolution* 8 (1964): 131–46; M. Sherif and C. W. Sherif, *Groups in Harmony and Tension* (New York: Harper, 1953), p. 196.

34. Brewton Berry, *Race and Ethnic Relations,* 3rd ed. (Boston: Houghton Mifflin, 1965), p. 55.

35. Morton Klass and Hal Hellman, *The Kinds of Mankind* (New York: Lippincott, 1971), p. 61.

36 Molefi Kete Asante, *The Afrocentric Idea* (Philadelphia: Temple University Press, 1987).

37. Martin E. Spencer, "Multiculturalism, 'Political Correctness,' and the Politics of Identity," *Sociological Forum* 9 (1994): 547–67.

38. Vincent N. Parrillo, "Diversity in America: A Sociohistorical Analysis," *Sociological Forum* 9 (1994): 523–35.

39. Vincent N. Parrillo, *Diversity in America* (Thousand Oaks, CA: Pine Forge Press, 1996), p. 14.

40. C. Wright Mills, *The Sociological Imagination* (New York: Oxford University Press, 1959), p. 8.

41. Ibid., p. 9.

42. Ibid., p. 146.

43. John Solomos and Les Back, "Marxism, Racism, and Ethnicity," *American Behavioral Scientist* 38 (1995): 407–20.

44. See Albert Szymanski, "Racial Discrimination and White Gain," *American Sociological Review* 41 (1976): 403–14; Sidney M. Willhelm, "Can Marxism Explain America's Racism?" *Social Problems* 28 (1980): 98–112.

45. Erving Goffman, *The Presentation of Self in Everyday Life* (Garden City, NY: Doubleday 1959).

46. Barbara Ballis Lal, "Symbolic Interaction Theories," *American Behavioral Scientist* 38 (1995): 421–41.

47. Peter L. Berger and Thomas Luckmann, *The Social Construction of Reality* (Garden City, NY: Doubleday, 1963).

CHAPTER 2

1. See, for example, Lee Cronk, *The Complex Whole: Culture and the Evolution of Human Behavior* (Boulder, CO: Westview Press, 1999).

2. The importance of symbols to social interaction has drawn much attention in sociology.

See Benjamin Lee Whorf, *Language, Thought and Reality* (New York: Wiley, 1956); Gertrude Jaeger and Philip Selznick, "A Normative Theory of Culture," *American Sociological Review* 29 (1964): 653–59; Herbert Blumer, *Symbolic Interaction: Perspective and Method* (Englewood Cliffs, NJ: Prentice Hall, 1969).

3. Institute for Diversity and Ethics in Sport, *The Racial and Gender Report Card.* Accessed online at www.tidesport.org/racialgender reportcard.html [June 14, 2007].

4. Ibid.

5. Harry C. Bredemeier and Richard M. Stephenson, *The Analysis of Social Systems* (New York: Holt, Rinehart & Winston, 1962), p. 3.

6. Bear climbing a tree as seen from opposite side. Giraffe going past a second-story window. Hot dog on a hamburger roll. Partial aerial view of four elephants at a watering trough.

7. This connection between Lippmann's comments, the Droodles, and human response to definitions of stimuli was originally made by Bredemeier and Stephenson, *The Analysis of Social Systems,* pp. 2–3.

8. Edward O. Wilson, *Sociobiology,* reprint ed. (Cambridge, MA: Belknap Press, 2000), p. 550.

9. Desmond Morris, *Manwatching: A Field Guide to Human Behavior* (New York: Abrams, 1977).

10. William I. Thomas, "The Relation of Research to the Social Process," in *Essays on Research in the Social Sciences* (Washington, DC: Brookings Institution, 1931), p. 189.

11. See the discussion on p. 100.

12. Gregory Razran, "Ethnic Dislike and Stereotypes: A Laboratory Study," *Journal of Abnormal and Social Psychology* 45 (1950): 7–27.

13. Copyright (c)1949 by Richard Rodgers and Oscar Hammerstein II. Copyright renewed. Williamson Music, Inc., owner of publication and allied rights for the Western Hemisphere and Japan. International copyright secured. All rights reserved. Used by permission.

14. John Gillis, *The Ways of Men* (New York: Appleton-Century-Crofts, 1948), p. 556.

15. For a case study of England from 1000 to 1899, see Margaret T. Hodgen, *Change and History* (New York: Wenner-Gren Foundation for Anthropological Research, 1952).

16. Stanley Lieberson, "A Societal Theory of Race and Ethnic Relations," *American Sociological Review* 26 (December 1961): 902–10.

17. See Andrew M. Greeley, *The American Catholic: A Social Portrait* (New York: Basic Books, 1977), chap. 1; see also Richard D. Alba, *Italian Americans: Into the Twilight of Ethnicity* (Englewood Cliffs, NJ: Prentice Hall, 1985), pp. 9–12.

18. Mary C. Sengstock, "Social Change in the Country of Origin as a Factor in Immigrant Conceptions of Nationality," *Ethnicity* 4 (March 1977): 54–69.

19. W. Lloyd Warner and Paul S. Lunt, *The Social Life of a Modern Community,* Yankee City Series, Vol. 1 (New Haven, CT: Yale University Press, 1941).

20. Stephan Thernstrom, "'Yankee City' Revisited: The Perils of Historical Naïveté," *American Sociological Review* 30 (1965): 234–42.

21. W. Lloyd Warner and Leo Srole, *The Social System of American Ethnic Groups,* Yankee City Series, Vol. 3 (New Haven, CT: Yale University Press, 1945).

22. Alan C. Kerckhoff, *Socialization and Social Class* (Englewood Cliffs, NJ: Prentice Hall, 1972), pp. 126–28.

23. John C. Leggett, "Economic Insecurity and Working Class Consciousness," *American Sociological Review* 29 (1964): 226–47.

24. Richard Centers, *The Psychology of Social Classes: A Study of Class Consciousness* (Princeton, NJ: Princeton University Press, 1949); Oscar Glantz, "Class Consciousness and Political Solidarity," *American Sociological Review* 23 (August 1958): 375–82; Robert W. Hodge and Donald J. Treiman, "Class Identification in the U.S.," *American Journal of Sociology* 73 (March 1968): 535–47; Werner S. Landecker, "Class Crystallization and Class Consciousness," *American Sociological Review* 28 (April 1963): 219–29; Robert T. Morris and Raymond J. Murphy, "A Paradigm for the Study of Class Consciousness," *Sociology and Social Research* 50 (April 1966): 298–313.

25. Stephen Steinberg, *The Ethnic Myth: Race, Ethnicity, and Class in America,* 3rd ed. (Boston: Beacon Press, 2001).

26. Thomas Sowell, *Ethnic America: A History* (New York: Basic Books, 1981).

27. Colin Greer (ed.), *Divided Society* (New York: Basic Books, 1974), p. 34.

28. Milton M. Gordon, *Assimilation in American Life* (New York: Oxford University Press, 1964).

29. William M. Newman, *American Pluralism* (New York: Harper & Row, 1973), p. 84.

30. Gordon, *Assimilation in American Life,* p. 47.

31. See Patricia L. McCall and Karen F. Parker, "A Dynamic Model of Racial Competition, Racial Inequality, and Interracial Violence," *Sociological Inquiry* 75 (2005): 273–93; Leo Kuper, *Race, Class, and Power: Ideology and Revolutionary Change* (Los Angeles: Aldine Transaction, 2005); Clair J. Kim, "Imagining Race and Nation in Multiculturalist America," *Ethnic and Racial Studies* 27:6 (2004): 977–1005.

32. Thomas M. Pettigrew, "The Changing but Not Declining Significance of Race," *Michigan Law Review* 77 (January-March 1979): 917–24; Charles V. Willie, "The Inclining Significance of Race," *Society* 15 (July–August 1978): 10–15.

33. E. Franklin Frazier, *The Negro Family in Chicago* (Chicago: University of Chicago Press, 1932); see also *The Negro Family in the United States,* rev. ed. (Chicago: University of Chicago Press, 1932).

34. Daniel P. Moynihan, *The Negro Family: The Case for National Action* (Washington, DC: U.S. Department of Labor, 1965).

35. Ibid., p. 5.

36. Ibid., p. 6.

37. Ibid., pp. 30, 47.

38. Daniel P. Moynihan, "Families Falling Apart," *Society* (July-August 1990): 21–22.

39. Originally in Daniel Patrick Moynihan, "A Family Policy for the Nation," *America* 113 (September 18, 1965): 280–83. See also Moynihan, "Families Falling Apart," p. 21; David Gergen, "A Few Candles in the Darkness," *U.S. News & World Report* (May 25, 1992), p. 44.

40. Oscar Lewis, *The Children of Sanchez* (New York: Random House, 1961); Oscar Lewis, *La Vida,* (New York: Vintage, 1966), pp. xlii–lii.

41. Ibid., p. xlv.

42. See David L. Harvey and Michael H. Reed, "The Culture of Poverty: An Ideological Analysis," *Sociological Perspectives* 39 (Winter 1996): 465–95.

43. Edward C. Banfield, *The Unheavenly City: The Nature and Future of Our Urban Crisis* (Boston: Little, Brown, 1970), pp. 210–11.

44. See, for example, William F. Spriggs, "Poverty in America: The Poor *Are* Getting Poorer," *Crisis* 113 (2006): 14–19.

45. William Ryan, *Blaming the Victim,* rev. ed. (New York: Vintage, 1976).

46. Charles A. Valentine, *Culture and Poverty* (Chicago: University of Chicago Press, 1968).

47. Ibid., p. 129.

48. Harvey and Reed, "The Culture of Poverty."

49. Michael Harrington, *The Other America: Poverty in the United States* (Baltimore: Penguin, 1963).

50. Ibid., p. 21.

51. Lola M. Irelan, Oliver C. Moles, and Robert M. O'Shea, "Ethnicity, Poverty, and Selected Attitudes: A Test of the 'Culture of Poverty' Hypothesis," *Social Forces* 47 (1969): 405–13.

52. Eliot Liebow, *Tally's Corner: A Study of Negro Streetcorner Men* (Boston: Little, Brown, 1967), pp. 222–23. See also Ulf Hannerz, *Soulside: Inquiries into Ghetto Culture and Community* (New York: Columbia University Press, 1969).

53. See Jemima Pierre, "Black Immigrants in the United States and the 'Cultural Narratives' of Ethnicity," *Identities: Global Studies in Culture and Power* 11 (2004): 141–70; David Steigerwald, "Our New Cultural Determinism," *Society* 42 (January/ February 2005): 71–75; Richard C. Bagall, "Lifelong Learning and the Limitations of Economic Determinism," *International Journal of Lifelong Education* 19 (2000): 20–35.

54. Robert E. Park, *Race and Culture* (Glencoe, IL: Free Press, 1949), p. 150.

55. Seymour M. Lipset, "Changing Social Status and Prejudice: The Race Theories of a Pioneering American Sociologist," *Commentary* 9 (May 1950): 479.

56. Stanford M. Lyman, *The Black American in Sociological Thought: A Failure of Perspective* (New York: Putnam, 1972), pp. 49–50.

57. Warner and Srole, *The Social System of American Ethnic Groups,* pp. 285–86.

58. Michael A. Zarate, Berenice Garcia, and Azenett A. Garza, "Cultural Threat and Perceived Realistic Group Conflict as Dual Predictors of Prejudice," *Journal of Experimental Social Psychology* 40 (2004): 99–105.

59. Peter Burns and James G. Gimpel, "Economic Insecurity, Prejudicial Stereotypes, and Public Opinion on Immigration Policy," *Political Science Quarterly* 115 (2000): 201–25.

60. Ashley W. Doane Jr., "Dominant Group Ethnic Identity in the United States: The Role of 'Hidden' Ethnicity in Intergroup Relations." *The Sociological Quarterly* 38 (Summer 1997): 375–97.

61. Lieberson, "A Societal Theory of Race and Ethnic Relations," pp. 902–10.

62. William J. Wilson, *Power, Racism, and Privilege* (New York: Free Press, 1973), pp. 47–65.

63. Robert Blauner, "Internal Colonialism and Ghetto Revolt," *Social Problems* 16 (Spring 1969): 393–406.

64. Ibid., p. 397.

65. Donald L. Noel, "A Theory of the Origin of Ethnic Stratification," *Social Problems* 16 (Fall 1968): 157–72.

66. Lewis A. Coser, "Conflict: Social Aspects," in David Sills (ed.), *International Encyclopedia of the Social Sciences* (New York: Macmillan, 1968), pp. 234–35.

67. Ralf Dahrendorf, *Class and Class Conflict in Industrial Society* (Stanford, CA: Stanford University Press, 1959), pp. 215–18.

68. Max Weber, "Class, Status, Party," 1922, in Hans Gerth and C. Wright Mills (trans. and ed.), *From Max Weber* (New York: Oxford University Press, 1946), pp. 193–94.

69. See Hubert M. Blalock Jr., *Toward a Theory of Minority-Group Relations* (New York: Wiley, 1967), pp. 199–203.

70. James M. O'Kane, "Ethnic Mobility and the Lower-Income Negro: A Socio-Historical Perspective," *Social Problems* 16 (1969): 309–11; see also Leonard Reissman and Michael N. Halstead, "The Subject Is Class," *Sociology and Social Research* 54 (1970): 301–04.

71. O'Kane, "Ethnic Mobility and the Lower-Income Negro, pp. 303–11.

72. See Blauner, "Internal Colonialism and Ghetto Revolt," p. 397; Stuart L. Hills, "Negroes and Immigrants in America," *Sociological Focus* 3 (Summer 1970): 85–96; Nathan Glazer, "Blacks and Ethnic Groups," *Social Problems* 18 (1971): 444–61.

73. Jeff Hitchcock, *Lifting the White Veil* (Roselle, NJ: Crandall, Dustie & Douglass Books, 2002), pp. 115–16.

CHAPTER 3

1. See Hortense Powdermaker, *Probing Our Prejudices* (New York: Harper, 1941), p. 1.

2. Louis Wirth, "Race and Public Policy," *Scientific Monthly* 58 (1944): 303.

3. Ralph L. Rosnow, "Poultry and Prejudice," *Psychology Today* (March 1972): 53.

4. Reported by Daniel Wilner, Rosabelle Price Walkley, and Stuart W. Cook, "Residential Proximity and Intergroup Relations in Public Housing Projects," *Journal of Social Issues* 8(1) (1952): 45. See also James W. Vander Zanden, *American Minority Relations*, 3rd ed. (New York: Ronald Press, 1972), p. 21.

5. Gordon W. Allport, "Prejudice: Is It Societal or Personal?" *Journal of Social Issues* 18 (1962): 129–30.

6. Bernard M. Kramer, "Dimensions of Prejudice," *Journal of Psychology* 27 (April 1949): 389–451.

7. L. Perry Curtis Jr., *Apes and Angels: The Irishman in Victorian Caricature* (Washington, DC: Smithsonian Press, 1971).

8. See Marvin B. Scott and Stanford M. Lyman, "Accounts," *American Sociological Review* 33 (February 1968): 40–62.

9. Philip Mason, *Patterns of Dominance* (New York: Oxford University Press, 1970), p. 7. See also Philip Mason, *Race Relations* (New York: Oxford University Press, 1970), pp. 17–29.

10. T. W. Adorno, Else Frankel-Brunswik, Daniel J. Levinson, and R. Nevitt Sanford, *The Authoritarian Personality* (New York: Harper & Row, 1950).

11. H. H. Hyman and P. B. Sheatsley, "The Authoritarian Personality: A Methodological Critique," in R. Christie and M. Jahoda (eds.), *Studies in the Scope and Method of "The Authoritarian Personality"* (Glencoe, IL: Free Press, 1954).

12. Solomon E. Asch, *Social Psychology* (Englewood Cliffs, NJ: Prentice Hall, 1952), p. 545.

13. E. A. Shils, "Authoritarianism: Right and Left," in *Studies in the Scope and Method of "The Authoritarian Personality."*

14. D. Stewart and T. Hoult, "A Social-Psychological Theory of 'The Authoritarian Personality,'" *American Journal of Sociology* 65 (1959): 274.

15. H. C. Kelman and Janet Barclay, "The F Scale as a Measure of Breadth of Perspective," *Journal of Abnormal and Social Psychology* 67 (1963): 608–15.

16. For an excellent summary of authoritarian studies and literature, see John P. Kirscht and Ronald C. Dillehay, *Dimensions of Authoritarianism: A Review of Research and Theory* (Lexington, KY: University of Kentucky Press, 1967).

17. George E. Simpson and J. Milton Yinger, *Racial and Cultural Minorities: An Analysis of Prejudice and Discrimination* (New York: Harper & Row, 1953), p. 91.

18. See, for example, Thomas F. Pettigrew, "Intergroup Contact Theory," *Annual Review of Psychology* 49 (1998): 65–85.

19. See Adam D. Galinsky and Gillian Ku, "The Effects of Perspective-Taking on Prejudice: The Moderating Role of Self-Evaluation," *Personality and Social Psychology Bulletin* 30 (May 2004): 594–604.

20. Brenda Major, Cheryl R. Kaiser, and Shannon K. McCoy, "It's Not My Fault: When and Why Attributions to Prejudice Protect Self-Esteem," *Personality and Social Psychology Bulletin* 29 (June 2003): 772–81.

21. See Russell G. Geen, *Human Aggression*, 2nd ed. (Berkshire, England: Open University Press, 2001).

22. Leviticus 16:5–22.

23. Gordon W. Allport, *The Nature of Prejudice* (Cambridge, MA: Addison-Wesley, 1954), pp. 13–14.

24. Carl I. Hovland and Robert R. Sears, "Minor Studies of Aggression: Correlation of Lynchings with Economic Indices," *Journal of Psychology* 9 (Winter 1940): 301–10.

25. See Leonard Berkowitz, "Whatever Happened to the Frustration-Aggression Hypothesis?" *American Behavioral Scientist* 21 (1978): 691–708; L. Berkowitz, *Aggression: A Social Psychological Analysis* (New York: McGraw-Hill, 1962).

26. D. Zillman, *Hostility and Aggression* (Hillsdale, NJ: Erlbaum, 1979); R. A. Baron, *Human Aggression* (New York: Plenum Press, 1977); N. Pastore, "The Role of Arbitrariness in the Frustration-Aggression Hypothesis," *Journal of Abnormal and Social Psychology* 47 (1952): 728–31.

27. A. H. Buss, "Instrumentality of Aggression, Feedback, and Frustration as Determinants of Physical Aggression," *Journal of Personality and Social Psychology* 3 (1966): 153–62.

28. J. R. Averill, "Studies on Anger and Aggression: Implications for Theories of Emotion," *American Psychologist* 38 (1983): 1145–60.

29. Talcott Parsons, "Certain Primary Sources and Patterns of Aggression in the Social Structure of the Western World," in *Essays in Sociological Theory* (New York: Free Press, 1964), pp. 298–322.

30. For an excellent review of Parsonian theory in this area, see Stanford M. Lyman, *The Black American in Sociological Thought: A Failure of Perspective* (New York: Putnam, 1972), pp. 145–69.

31. Herbert Blumer, "Race Prejudice as a Sense of Group Position," *Pacific Sociological Review* 1 (1958): 3–7.

32. John Dollard, "Hostility and Fear in Social Life," *Social Forces* 17 (1938): 15–26.

33. Muzafer Sherif, O. J. Harvey, B. Jack White, William Hood, and Carolyn Sherif, *Intergroup Conflict and Cooperation: The Robbers Cave Experiment* (Norman: University of Oklahoma Institute of Intergroup Relations, 1961). See also M. Sherif, "Experiments in Group Conflict," *Scientific American* 195 (1956): 54–58.

34. Donald Young, *Research Memorandum on Minority Peoples in the Depression* (New York: Social Science Research Council, 1937), pp. 133–41.

35. Andrew Greeley and Paul Sheatsley, "The Acceptance of Desegregation Continues to Advance," *Scientific American* 210 (1971): 13–19; T. F. Pettigrew, "Three Issues in Ethnicity: Boundaries, Deprivations, and Perceptions," in M. Yinger and S. J. Cutler (eds.), *Major Social Issues: A Multidisciplinary View*

(New York: Free Press, 1978); R. D. Vanneman and T. F. Pettigrew, "Race and Relative Deprivation in the United States," *Race* 13 (1972): 461–86.

36. See Harry H. L. Kitano, "Passive Discrimination in the Normal Person," *Journal of Social Psychology* 70 (1966): 23–31.

37. Thomas Pettigrew, "Regional Differences in Anti-Negro Prejudice," *Journal of Abnormal and Social Psychology* 59 (1959): 28–36.

38. Jeanne Watson, "Some Social and Psychological Situations Related to Change in Attitude," *Human Relations* 3 (1950): 15–56.

39. John Dollard, *Caste and Class in a Southern Town*, 3rd ed. (Garden City, NY: Doubleday Anchor Books, 1957).

40. Joachim Krueger and Russell W. Clement, "The Truly False Consensus Effect: An Ineradicable and Egocentric Bias in Social Perception," *Journal of Personality and Social Psychology* 67 (1994): 596–610.

41. Michael R. Leippe and Donna Eisenstadt, "Generalization of Dissonance Reduction: Decreasing Prejudice through Induced Compliance," *Journal of Personality and Social Psychology* 67 (1994): 395–414.

42. William M. Newman, *American Pluralism* (New York: Harper & Row, 1973), p. 197.

43. Eliot Aronson, *The Social Animal*, 9th ed. (San Francisco: Worth, 2003), p. 197.

44. David Katz and Kenneth Braly, "Racial Stereotypes of One Hundred College Students," *Journal of Abnormal and Social Psychology* 28 (1933): 280–90; G. M. Gilbert, "Stereotype Persistence and Change among College Students," *Journal of Abnormal and Social Psychology* 46 (1951): 245–54; Marvin Karlins, Thomas L. Coffman, and Gary Walters, "On the Fading of Social Stereotypes: Studies in Three Generations of College Students," *Journal of Personality and Social Psychology* 13 (1969): 1–16.

45. See, for example, Lee Jussim, Melvin Manis, Thomas E. Nelson, and Sonia Soffin, "Prejudice, Stereotypes, and Labeling Effects: Sources of Bias in Person Perception," *Journal of Personality and Social Psychology* 68 (1995): 228–46; Leonard Gordon, "College Student Stereotypes of Blacks and Jews on Two Campuses: Four Studies Spanning 50 Years," *Sociology and Social Research* 70 (1986): 200–01.

46. Howard J. Ehrlich, *The Social Psychology of Prejudice* (New York: Wiley & Sons, 1973), p. 22.

47. Erdman Palmore, "Ethnophaulisms and Ethnocentrism," *American Journal of Sociology* 67 (1962): 442–45.

48. Brian Mullen, "Ethnophaulisms for Ethnic Immigrant Groups," *Journal of Social Issues* 57 (2001): 457–75.

49. See, for example, Mahadev L. Apte, "Ethnic Humor Versus Sense of Humor," *American Behavioral Scientist* 30 (1987): 26–40.

50. Lois Leveen, "Only When I Laugh: Textual Dynamics of Ethnic Humor," *MELUS* 21 (1996): 29–55.

51. U.S. Commission on Civil Rights, *Window Dressing on the Set: Women and Minorities in Television* (Washington, DC: U.S. Government Printing Office, 1977); *Window Dressing on the Set: An Update*, 1979.

52. George Gerbner, quoted in "Life According to TV," *Newsweek* (December 6, 1982), p. 136.

53. Ibid.

54. Dennis J. Ganahl, Thomas J. Prinsen, and Sara Baker Netzley, "A Content Analysis of Prime Time Commercials: A Contextual Framework of Gender Representation," *Sex Roles* 49 (2003): 545–51.

55. Shannon N. Davis, "Sex Stereotypes in Commercials Targeted toward Children: A Content Analysis," *Sociological Spectrum* 23 (2003): 407–25.

56. Jennifer J. Henderson and Gerald J. Baldasty, "Race, Advertising, and Prime-Time Television," *Howard Journal of Communications* 14 (2003): 97–112.

57. Children Now, "Why It Matters: Diversity on Television," Media News. Accessed online at www.childrennow.org/assets/pdf/issues_media_medianow_2002.pdf [June 17, 2007].

58. Ed Palmer, K. Taylor Smith, and Kim S. Strawser, "Rubik's Tube: Developing a Child's Television World View," pp. 143–54 in Gordon L. Berry and Joy K. Asamen (eds.), *Children and Television in a Changing Socio-Cultural World* (Newbury Park, CA: Sage Publications, 1993).

59. Nina Huntemann and Michael Morgan, "Mass Media and Identity Develoment," Chapter 15, in Dorothy G. Singer and Jerome L. Singer (eds.), *Handbook of Children and the Media* (Thousand Oaks, CA: Sage Publications, 2001).

60. For an overview of research on this program, see Stuart H. Surlin, "Five Years of *All in the Family:* A Summary of Empirical Research Generated by the Program," *Mass Communication Review* 3 (1976): 2–6. See also J. C. Brigham and L. W. Biesbrecht, "*All in the Family:* Racial Attitudes," *Journal of Communication* 26 (1976): 69–74.

61. Neil Vidmar and Milton Rokeach, "Archie Bunker's Bigotry," *Journal of Communication* 24 (1974): 36–47.

62. Scott Coltrane and Melinda Messineo, "The Perpetuation of Subtle Prejudice: Race and Gender Imagery in 1990s Television Advertising," *Sex Roles* 42 (2000): 363–89.

63. Dana E. Mastro and Susannah R. Stern, "Representations of Race in Television Commercials: A Content Analysis of Prime-Time Advertising," *Journal of Broadcasting & Electronic Media* 47 (2003): 638–47.

64. Jean Kilbourne, *Can't Buy My Love* (New York: Touchstone Books, 2000).

65. Gina M. Wingood, Ralph J. DiClemente, Jay M. Bernhardt, Kathy Harrington, Susan L. Davies, Allysa Robillard, and Edward W. Hook, III, "A Prospective Study of Exposure to Rap Music Videos and African American Female Adolescents' Health," *American Journal of Public Health* 93 (2003): 437–39.

66. See Gordon W. Allport, *The Nature of Prejudice,* p. 251; Robin M. Williams Jr., *Strangers Next Door* (Englewood Cliffs, NJ: Prentice Hall, 1964), p. 150; James W. Vander Zanden, *American Minority Relations,* 3rd ed. (New York: Ronald Press, 1972), pp. 460–69.

67. Brewton Berry and Henry L. Tischler, *Race and Ethnic Relations,* 4th ed. (Boston: Houghton Mifflin, 1978), p. 250. See also David G. Myers, *Social Psychology,* 2nd ed. (New York: McGraw-Hill, 1987), pp. 55–56.

68. Elliot Aronson and Neal Osherow, "Cooperation, Prosocial Behavior, and Academic Performance: Experiments in the Desegregated Classroom," *Applied Social Psychology Annual* 1 (1980): 163–96.

69. Iain Walker and Mary Crogan, "Academic Performance, Prejudice, and the Jigsaw Classroom: New Pieces to the Puzzle," *Journal of Community and Applied Social Psychology* 8 (1998): 381–93.

70. See the nine articles in the special issue, "Tolerance and Education: Can Schooling Promote Tolerance for Social and Political Diversity?" *Review of Education/Pedagogy/Cultural Studies* 16 (1994): 273–463.

71. Charles H. Stember, *Education and Attitude Change* (New York: Institute of Human Relations Press, 1961).

72. Blumer, "Race Prejudice as a Sense of Group Position," pp. 3–7.

73. Vincent N. Parrillo, *Diversity in America*, 2nd ed. (Thousand Oaks, CA: Pine Forge Press, 2005), pp. 139–42.

74. U.S. Department of Defense, *2004 Demographics: Profile of the Military Community* (Arlington, VA: Military Family Resource Center, 2004), p. v.

75. See Mark E. Engberg, "Improving Intergroup Relations in Higher Education: A Critical Examination of the Influence of Educational Interventions on Racial Bias," *Review of Educational Research* 74:4 (2004): 473–524.

76. See Elizabeth L. Paluck, "Diversity Training and Intergroup Contact: A Call to Action Research," *Journal of Social Issues* 62:3 (2006): 577–95.

77. Allport, *The Nature of Prejudice*.

78. The Prejudice Institute, "What Is Ethnoviolence?" Accessed online at www.prejudiceinstitute.org/ethnoviolenceFS.html [June 17, 2007].

79. Williams, *Strangers Next Door*, pp. 124–25.

80. Robert K. Merton, "Discrimination and the American Creed," in Robert M. MacIver (ed.), *Discrimination and National Welfare* (New York: Harper, 1949), pp. 99–126.

81. Stokely Carmichael and Charles Hamilton, *Black Power* (New York: Vintage Books, 1967). This book has been reissued as Stokely Carmichael, Kwame Ture, and Charles Hamilton, *Black Power: The Politics of Liberation* (New York: Vintage Books, 1992).

82. Hubert M. Blalock Jr., *Toward a Theory of Minority Group Relationships* (New York: Capricorn Books, 1970), pp. 204–07. For

insight into the origin of this argument, see Stanford M. Lyman, "Cherished Values and Civil Rights," *The Crisis* 71 (December 1964): 645–54, 695.

83. John Rawls, *A Theory of Justice*, new ed. (Cambridge, MA: Belknap Press, 2005).

84. Joseph Tussman and Jacobus tenBroek, "The Equal Protection of the Laws," *California Law Review* 37 (September 1949): 341–81.

85. Ibid., p. 381.

86. Stanford M. Lyman, "Asians, Blacks, Hispanics: Confronting Vestiges of Slavery," paper presented at Eastern Sociological Society meeting, Boston, May 1, 1987.

87. John Leo, "Endgame for Affirmative Action," *U.S. News & World Report* (March 13, 1995), p. 18.

88. Gertrude Ezorsky, *Racism and Justice: The Case for Affirmative Action* (Ithaca, NY: Cornell University Press, 1991).

89. Michael Wines, "How Affirmative Action Got So Hard to Sell," *New York Times* (July 23, 1995), p. E3.

90. Justice Harry A. Blackmun, 1978.

91. Linda Greenhouse, "Justices Back Affirmative Action by 5 to 4, but Wider Vote Bans a Racial Point System," *New York Times* (June 24, 2003), p. A1.

92. Steven Greenhouse and Jonathan D. Glater, "Companies See Law School Ruling as a Way to Help Keep the Diversity Pipeline Open," *New York Times* (June 24, 2003), p. A25.

93. John Gpuhl and Susan Welch, "The Impact of the Bakke Decision on Black and Hispanic Enrollment in Medical and Law Schools," *Social Science Quarterly* 71 (1990): 458–73.

94. Cited in Evan Thomas and Bob Cohn, "Rethinking the Dream," *Newsweek* (June 26, 1995), p. 20.

95. See, for example, Troy Duster, "Individual Fairness, Group Preferences, and the California Strategy," pp. 111–34, in Robert Post and Michael Ragin (eds.), *Race and Representation: Affirmative Action* (Cambridge, MA: Zone Books, 1998).

96. Tim J. Wise, *Affirmative Action: Racial Preference in Black and White* (New York: Routledge, 2003), p. 164.

97. Linda Chavez, "Court Abandons Colorblind Society," *Human Events* 59 (June 30, 2003):

1–2; Thomas Sowell, "How Affirmative Action Hurts Blacks," *Forbes* 160 (October 6, 1997): 64.

98. Wines, "How Affirmative Action Got So Hard to Sell."

99. CBS News (January 5–8, 2006). Accessed online at www.pollingreport.com/race.htm [June 17, 2007].

100. Sam Howe Verhovek, "In Poll, Americans Reject Means but Not Ends of Racial Diversity," *New York Times* (December 14, 1997), p. A1.

101. Associated Press, "Races Split on Achieving School Diversity" (March 10, 2003).

102. Department of Health and Human Services, *National Survey on Drug Use and Health: 2005* (Rockville, MD: U.S. Government Printing Office, 2006), Table 1.28A.

103. Department of Justice, *Racial Profiling Fact Sheet* (June 17, 2003). Accessed online at www.usdoj.gov/opa/pr/2003/June/racial_profiling_fact_sheet.pdf [June 17, 2007].

104. American Civil Liberties Union, "ACLU Report Documents Continued Racial Profiling Problems in Rhode Island; Calls for Changes in Police Practices." Accessed online at www.aclu.org/racialjustice/racialprofiling/27849res20070105.html [July 22, 2007].

CHAPTER 4

1. See Brent Simpson and Michael W. Macy, "Power, Identity, and Collective Action in Social Exchange," *Social Forces* 82 (2004): 1373–1409; Laura S. Billings et al., "Race-Based Social Judgment by Minority Perceivers," *Journal of Applied Social Psychology* 30 (2000): 221–40; Connie M. Kane, "Differences in Family of Origin Perceptions among African American, Asian American, and Hispanic American College Students," *Journal of Black Studies* 29 (1998): 93–105.

2. See, for example, A.E. Taslitz (ed.), "The New Data: Over-Representation of Minorities in the Criminal Justice System," *Law and Contemporary Problems* 66 (2003): 1–298; Rebecca A. Anderson and Amy L. Otto, "Perceptions of Fairness in the Justice System: A Cross-Cultural Comparison," *Social Behavior and Personality* 31 (2003): 557–63;

Marvin D. Free Jr., "Race and Presentencing Decisions in the United States: A Summary and Critique of the Research," *Criminal Justice Review* 27 (2002): 203–32; Jody Clay-Warner, "Perceiving Procedural Injustice: The Effects of Group Membership and Status," *Social Psychology Quarterly* 64 (2001): 224–38; Saundra D. Westervelt and John A. Humphrey (eds.), *Wrongly Convicted: Perspectives on Failed Justice* (New Brunswick, NJ: Rutgers University Press, 2001).

3. Clifford R. Shaw and Henry D. McKay, *Juvenile Delinquency and Urban Areas* (Chicago: University of Chicago Press, 1942).

4. J. Philippe Ruston et al., "Cross-National Variation in Violent Crime Rates: Race, R-K Theory, and Income," *Population and Environment* 23 (2002): 501–11; Per-Olof H. Wikstrom et al., "Do Disadvantaged Neighborhoods Cause Well-Adjusted Children to Become Adolescent Delinquents?" *Criminology* 38 (2000): 1109–42; Matthew R. Lee, "Community Cohesion and Violent Predatory Victimization," *Social Forces* 79 (2000): 683–706.

5. Ronald L. Simons and Phyllis A Gray, "Perceived Blocked Opportunity as an Explanation of Delinquency among Lower-Class Black Males: A Research Note," *Journal of Research in Crime and Delinquency* 26 (1989): 90–101.

6. Paul R. Vowell and David C. May, "Another Look at Classic Strain Theory: Poverty Status, Perceived Blocked Opportunity, and Gang Membership as Predictors of Adolescent Violent Behavior," *Sociological Inquiry* 70 (2000): 42–60. See also Scott Cummings and Daniel J. Monti, *Gangs: The Origin and Impact of Contemporary Youth Gangs in the United States* (Albany, NY: State University of New York Press, 1993).

7. Patricia H. Jenkins, "School Delinquency and School Commitment," *Sociology of Education* 68 (1995): 221–39.

8. See Donna K. Nagata and Yuzuru J. Takeshita, "Psychological Reactions to Redress: Diversity among Japanese Americans Interned during World War II," *Cultural Diversity & Ethnic Minority Psychology* 8 (2002): 41–59, for a study on acceptance by ex-internees decades later after government redress.

9. Travis Hirschi, "Procedural Rules and the Study of Deviant Behavior," *Social Problems* 2 (1973): 159–73.

10. Kurt Lewin, *Resolving Social Conflicts* (New York: Harper & Row, 1948), pp. 186–200.

11. Gordon W. Allport, *The Nature of Prejudice* (Reading, MA: Addison-Wesley, 1954), pp. 152–53.

12. Jennifer Crocker, Kristin Voelkl, Maria Testa, and Brenda Major, "Social Stigma: The Affective Consequences of Attributional Ambiguity," *Journal of Personality and Social Psychology* 60 (1991): 218–28; Frances E. Aboud, "The Development of Ethnic Self-Identification and Attitudes," in Jean S. Phinney and Mary Jane Rotheram (eds.), *Children's Ethnic Socialization* (Newbury Park, CA: Sage, 1987), pp. 32–55; Margaret Beale Spencer, "Black Children's Ethnic Identity Formation: Risk and Resilience of Castelike Minorities," in ibid., pp. 103–16.

13. Gunnar Myrdal, *An American Dilemma* (New York: McGraw-Hill, 1964), pp. 25–28; first published by Harper, 1944.

14. Gordon W. Allport, "The Role of Expectancy," in H. Cantril (ed.), *Tensions That Cause Wars* (Urbana, IL: University of Illinois Press, 1950), chap. 2.

15. Allport, *The Nature of Prejudice*, p. 160.

16. Robert E. Park, "Human Migration and the Marginal Man," *American Journal of Sociology* 33 (May 1928): 891; see also Everett V. Stonequist, *The Marginal Man* (New York: Scribner, 1937).

17. See Debra Harley, Kristine Jolivette, and Katherine McCormick, "Race, Class, and Gender: A Constellation of Positionalities with Implications for Counseling," *Journal of Multicultural Counseling and Development* 30 (2002): 216–38.

18. See Adam Weisberger, "Marginality and Its Directions," *Sociological Forum* 7 (1992): 425–46.

19. Hubert M. Blalock Jr, *Toward a Theory of Minority Group Relations* (New York: Wiley, 1967), pp. 79–84.

20. Edna Bonacich, "A Theory of Middleman Minorities," *American Sociological Review* 38 (1973): 583–94.

21. Edna Bonacich and John Modell, *The Economic Basis of Ethnic Solidarity*

(Berkeley: University of California Press, 1980), p. 30.

22. See Lyn H. Lofland, *A World of Strangers* (Long Grove, IL: Waveland Press, 1985); Gideon Sjoberg, *The Preindustrial City: Past and Present* (New York: Free Press, 1965).

23. See John J. Macionis and Vincent N. Parrillo, *Cities and Urban Life,* 4th ed. (Upper Saddle River, NJ: Prentice Hall, 2007), pp. 43–46.

24. See Allport, *The Nature of Prejudice,* pp. 53–54.

25. Deuteronomy 2:32–35; 3:1, 3–4, 6–7 (King James Version).

26. Arnold J. Toynbee, *A Study of History* (London: Oxford University Press, 1934), p. 465.

27. See James Morris, "The Final Solution, Down Under," in Frank Chalk (ed.), *The History and Sociology of Genocide: Analyses and Case Studies* (New Haven, CT: Yale University Press, 1990), pp. 204–22.

28. See Winthrop D. Jordan, *White over Black: American Attitudes toward the Negro, 1550–1812,* reissue ed. (Chapel Hill, NC: University of North Carolina Press, 1995).

29. See Joseph A. Page, *The Brazilians* (Boston: Addison-Wesley, 1996), p. 95.

30. For a discussion of black lynchings, see Stewart E. Tolnay, E. M. Beck, and James L. Massey, "Black Lynchings: The Power Threat Hypothesis Revisited," *Social Forces* 67 (March 1989): 605–33.

31. See Colin M. Tatz, *With Intent to Destroy: Reflections on Genocide* (New York: Norton, 2003).

32. Southern Poverty Law Center. Accessed online at www.splcenter.org/intel/map/hate.jsp [June 18, 2007].

33. Federal Bureau of Investigation, "Hate Crime Statistics 2005," *Uniform Crime Reports.* Accessed online at www.fbi.gov/ucr/hc2005/incidentsoffenses.htm [June 18, 2007].

34. Edna Bonacich, "A Theory of Ethnic Antagonism: The Split Labor Market," *American Sociological Review* 37 (1972): 554.

35. Ibid.

36. Ibid., p. 550.

37. Cliff Brown, "The Role of Employers in Split Labor Markets: An Event-Structure Analysis of Racial Conflict and AFL Organizing, 1917–1919," *Social Forces* 79 (2000): 653–81.

38. Kathleen Auerhahn, "The Split Labor Market and the Origins of Antidrug Legislation in the United States," *Law and Social Inquiry* 24 (1999): 436.

39. RainbowPUSH Coalition, "About RPC." Accessed online at www.rainbowpush.org/about/history.html [July 22, 2007].

40. See Mindiola Tatcho, Jr., Yolanda F. Niemann, and Nest Rodriguez, *Black-Brown Relations and Stereotypes* (Austin: University of Texas Press, 2003).

41. William M. Newman, *American Pluralism* (New York: Harper & Row, 1973), p. 53.

42. Barbara Solomon, *Ancestors and Immigrants* (Chicago: University of Chicago Press, 1956), pp. 59–61.

43. John Higham, *Strangers in the Land* (New Brunswick, NJ: Rutgers University Press, 1955), p. 247.

44. George R. Stewart, *American Ways of Life* (Garden City, NY: Doubleday, 1954), pp. 23, 28.

45. Milton Gordon, *Assimilation in American Life* (New York: Oxford University Press, 1964), pp. 70–71.

46. Ibid., p. 81.

47. See Gerhard Lenski, *The Religious Factor* (Garden City, NY: Doubleday, 1961), pp. 326–30; Will Herberg, *Protestant-Catholic-Jew* (Garden City, NY: Doubleday, 1955); William M. Dobriner, *Class in Suburbia* (Englewood Cliffs, NJ: Prentice Hall, 1963); Bennett M. Berger, *Working Class Suburbs,* 2nd ed. (Berkeley, CA: University of California Press, 1960).

48. Louis Wirth, "The Problem of Minority Groups," in Ralph Linton (ed.), *The Science of Man in the World Crisis* (New York: Columbia University Press, 1945), pp. 347–72.

49. Solomon, *Ancestors and Immigrants,* pp. 59–81.

50. Newman, *American Pluralism,* p. 63.

51. J. Hector St. John de Crèvecoeur, *Letters from an American Farmer* (New York: Albert & Charles Boni, 1925), pp. 54–55. First published 1782.

52. Frederick Jackson Turner, *The Frontier in American History* (New York: Holt, 1920), p. 351.

53. Israel Zangwill, *The Melting-Pot: Drama in Four Acts* (New York: Macmillan, 1921), p. 33.

54. Actually, any student of Western civilizations would point out that centuries of invasions, conquests, boundary changes, and so on often resulted in cross-breeding and that truly distinct or pure ethnic types were virtually non-existent long before the 18th century.

55. Gordon, *Assimilation in American Life,* pp. 109–10.

56. Ruby Jo Reeves Kennedy, "Single or Triple Melting Pot? Intermarriage Trends in New Haven, 1870–1940," *American Journal of Sociology* 49 (January 1944): 331–39; see also her follow-up study in *American Journal of Sociology* 58 (July 1952): 52–59.

57. See Herberg, *Protestant-Catholic-Jew.*

58. Henry Pratt Fairchild, *Immigration* (New York: Macmillan, 1925), p. 396.

59. Herberg, *Protestant-Catholic-Jew,* pp. 33–34.

60. Newman, *American Pluralism,* p. 67.

61. Horace M. Kallen, "Democracy versus the Melting Pot," *The Nation* (February 18, 1915), pp. 190–94; (February 25, 1915), pp. 217–20.

62. Gordon, *Assimilation in American Life,* p. 135.

63. Richard D. Alba, "Assimilation's Quiet Tide," *Public Interest* (Spring 1995): 3–4.

64. Herbert J. Gans, "Toward a Reconciliation of 'Assimilation' and 'Pluralism': The Interplay of Acculturation and Ethnic Retention," *International Migration Review* 31 (Winter 1997): 875–92.

65. Richard D. Alba and Victor Nee, "Rethinking Assimilation Theory for a New Era of Immigration," *International Migration Review* 31 (Winter 1997): 826–74.

CHAPTER 5

1. Nathan Glazer and Daniel P. Moynihan, *Beyond the Melting Pot,* 2nd ed. (Cambridge, MA: MIT Press, 1970), p. 1.

2. Gary B. Nash, *Class and Society in Early America* (Englewood Cliffs, NJ: Prentice Hall, 1970), p. 19.

3. Lawrence H. Fuchs, *The American Kaleidoscope: Race, Ethnicity, and the Civic Culture* (Hanover, NH: Wesleyan University Press, 1990).

4. Quoted in *American Observer* 50 (November 29, 1971): 4.

5. Quotations and commentary taken from John C. Miller, *Crisis in Freedom* (Boston: Little, Brown, 1951), pp. 41–42.

6. W. S. Shaw to Abigail Adams, May 20, 1798, *Adams Papers,* Vol. 8, No. 48, Massachusetts Historical Society, Cambridge, MA.

7. R. Ernst, "The Living Conditions of the Immigrant," in A. M. Wakestein (ed.), *The Urbanization of America* (Boston: Houghton Mifflin, 1949), p. 266.

8. Carleton Beals, *Brass Knuckle Crusade* (New York: Hastings House, 1960), p. 5.

9. Ibid.

10. Ray Allen Billington, *The Protestant Crusade, 1800–1860* (New York: Macmillan, 1938), p. 388.

11. John Higham, *Strangers in the Land* (New York: Atheneum, 1973), p. 7.

12. Harriet Martineau, *Society in America,* 1837 quoted in *American Observer* 50 (November 29, 1971): 4.

13. Ralph H. Orth and Alfred K. Ferguson (eds.), *The Journals and Miscellaneous Notebooks of Ralph Waldo Emerson,* Vol. 9 (Cambridge, MA: Belknap Press, 1971), pp. 299–300.

14. William Bradford, *Of Plymouth Plantation,* Harvey Wish (ed.). (New York: Capricorn Books, 1962), p. 29.

15. Ibid., p. 33.

16. Ibid., pp. 16–17, 184.

17. Rowland Berthoff, *British Immigrants in Industrial America, 1790–1950* (Cambridge, MA: Harvard University Press, 1953), pp. 30–56.

18. Ibid., pp. 125–31.

19. Ilja M. Dijour, "A Seminar on the Integration of Immigrants," 1960, p. 6, quoted in Wilbur S. Shepperson, *Emigration and Disenchantment: Portraits of Englishmen Repatriated from the United States* (Norman, OK: University of Oklahoma Press, 1965), p. 182.

20. Shepperson, *Emigration and Disenchantment,* pp. 16–17, 184.

21. A Report of the Commissioner of Immigration upon the Causes Which Incite Immigration to the U.S., 52nd Congress, 1st session (1891–1892), *House Executive Document 235,* Part I, pp. 260, 282.

22. Berthoff, *British Immigrants in Industrial America, 1790–1950,* pp. 103–04.

23. U.S. Office of Immigration Statistics, *2005 Yearbook of Immigration Statistics* (Washington, DC: U.S. Government Printing Office, 2006), Table 2, p. 10.

24. Suzanne Levy and David Strick, "While the Monarchy Falls Apart . . . Thousands of Brits Are Building Sand Castles in Santa Monica," *New York Times Magazine* (November 27, 1994), pp. 64–67.

25. U.S. Office of Immigration Statistics, *2005 Yearbook of Immigration Statistics*, Table 2, p. 10.

26. Hans Koningsberger, *Holland and the United States* (New York: Netherlands Information Service, 1968), p. 20.

27. Donald B. Cole, *Martin Van Buren and the American Political System* (Princeton, NJ: Princeton University Press, 1984), p. 14.

28. See John C. Fitzpatrick (ed.), *The Autobiography of Martin Van Buren* (New York: DaCapo, 1973), p. 9; John Niven, *Martin Van Buren: The Romantic Age of American Politics* (New York: Oxford University Press, 1983).

29. U.S. Department of Agriculture, National Agricultural Statistics Service, *Milk: Production* (April 18, 2007). Accessed online at www.nass.usda.gov/Publications/Todays _Reports/reports/mkpr0407.pdf [June 19, 2007].

30. Arthur Henry Hirsch, *The Huguenots of Colonial South Carolina* (Hamden, CT: Shoe String Press, 1962), p. 95.

31. Miller, *Crisis in Freedom*, pp. 13, 42–43.

32. T. Lynn Smith and Vernon J. Parenton, "Acculturation among the Louisiana French," *American Journal of Sociology* 44 (November 1938): 357.

33. Vernon J. Parenton, "Socio-Psychological Integration in a Rural French-Speaking Section of Louisiana," *Southwestern Social Science Quarterly* 30 (December 1949): 195.

34. Carl A. Brasseaux, "Four Hundred Years of Acadian Life in North America," *Journal of Popular Culture* 23 (Summer 1989): 13–17.

35. Wayne Curtis, "Cajun Country," *Smithsonian* 38 (May 2007): 62–65.

36. Rick Bragg, "Reported to Be Vanishing, Cajuns Give a Sharp 'Non'," *New York Times* (August 16, 2001), pp. A1, A20.

37. Angela Brittingham and G. Patricia de la Cruz, *Ancestry: 2000*, Census 2000 Brief (June 2004), Table 3, p. 6.

38. Marcus L. Hansen and J. B. Prebner, *The Mingling of the Canadian and American Peoples* (New Haven, CT: Yale University Press, 1940), pp. 123–68.

39. Quoted in W. C. Smith, *Americans in the Making* (New York: Appleton-Century, 1939), p. 394.

40. Maurice R. Davie, *World Immigration* (New York: Macmillan, 1936), p. 36.

41. Carl Wittke, *We Who Build America*, rev. ed. (Cleveland, OH: Case Western Reserve University Press, 1967), pp. 196–99; James S. Olson, *The Ethnic Dimension in American History* (New York: St. Martin's Press, 1979), pp. 103–06.

42. Georg Simmel, *Conflict and the Web of Group Affiliations* (New York: Free Press, 1955); Kathleen Neils Conzen, "Germans," in Stephan Thernstrom, Ann Orlov, and Oscar Handlin (eds.), *Harvard Encyclopedia of American Ethnic Groups* (Cambridge, MA: Belknap Press, 1980), p. 423.

43. Maldwyn Allen Jones, *American Immigration* (Chicago: University of Chicago Press, 1960), pp. 45–46.

44. Maldwyn Allen Jones, "Scotch-Irish," in Stephen Thernstrom, Ann Orlov, and Oscar Handlin (eds.), *Harvard Encyclopedia of American Ethnic Groups*, pp. 899–900.

45. Quoted in James M. Smith, *Freedom's Fetters* (Ithaca, NY: Cornell University Press, 1956), p. 25.

46. Charles F. Marden and Gladys Meyer, *Minorities in American Society*, 5th ed. (New York: Van Nostrand Reinhold, 1978), p. 77.

47. Edward Everett, "Letters on Irish Emigration," in Edith Abbott (ed.), *Historical Aspects of the Immigration Problem, Select Documents* (Chicago: University of Chicago Press, 1926), pp. 462–63.

48. Peter I. Rose, *They and We*, 2nd ed. (New York: Random House, 1974), p. 39.

49. Hasia R. Diner, *Erin's Daughters in America: Irish Immigrant Women in the Nineteenth Century* (Baltimore: Johns Hopkins University Press, 1983), pp. 73–74.

50. Patrick J. Blessing, "Irish," in Stephen Thernstrom, Ann Orlov, and Oscar Handlin (eds.), *Harvard Encyclopedia of American Ethnic Groups*, p. 531.

51. For information about middleman minorities, see Hubert M. Blalock Jr, *Toward a Theory of Minority Group Relations* (New York: Wiley, 1967), pp. 79–84; Edna Bonacich, "A Theory of Middleman Minorities," *American Sociological Review* 38 (October 1973): 583–94.

52. Oscar Handlin, *Boston's Immigrants*, rev. ed. (Cambridge, MA: Harvard University Press, 1959), p. 176.

53. Ellen Horgan Biddle, "The American Catholic Irish Family," in Charles H. Mindel and Robert W. Habenstein (eds.), *Ethnic Families in America: Patterns and Variations*, 2nd ed. (New York: Elsevier, 1981), p. 96.

54. Alfred J. Kutzik, "American Social Provision for the Aged: An Historical Perspective," in Donald E. Gelfand and Alfred J. Kutzik (eds.), *Ethnicity and Aging: Theory, Research, and Policy* (New York: Springer, 1979), pp. 32–65.

55. Arnold Shrier, *Ireland and the American Emigration 1850–1900* (Minneapolis: University of Minnesota Press, 1958), p. 34.

56. Carl Wittke, *The Irish in America* (New York: Russell & Russell, 1970), pp. 191–92.

57. Robert Kelley, *The Cultural Pattern in American Politics: The First Century* (New York: Knopf, 1979), pp. 195, 237.

58. Joel T. Headley, *The Great Riots of New York, 1712–1873* (Indianapolis, IN: Bobbs-Merrill, 1970); James McCague, *The Second Rebellion* (New York: Dial Press, 1968).

59. Joseph P. O'Grady, *How the Irish Became Americans* (New York: Twayne, 1973); Edgar Litt, *Beyond Pluralism: Ethnic Politics in America* (Glencoe, IL: Scott, Foresman, 1970), chap. 8.

60. Richard Krickus, *Pursuing the American Dream: White Ethnics and the New Populism* (Bloomington, IN: Indiana University Press, 1976), chap. 4; D. W. Brogan, *Politics in America*, (New York: Harper, 1954).

61. Judith Waldrop, "Irish Eyes on America," *American Demographics* (March 1989): 6.

62. U.S. Office of Immigration Statistics, *2005 Yearbook of Immigration Statistics*, Table 2, p. 10.

63. Kevin Cullen, "Boom Times, Crackdown Slow Emerald Wave," *The Boston Globe*, March 18, 2007. Accessed online at www.boston.com/news/local/massachusetts/articles/2007/03/18/boom_times_crackdown_slow_emerald_wave/ [January 25, 2008].

64. Rose, *They and We*, p. 68.

65. Ole E. Rölvaag, *Giants in the Earth* (New York: Harper, 1927), p. 425.

66. Peter Kivisto, *Immigrant Socialists in the United States* (Madison, NJ: Fairleigh Dickinson University Press, 1984), pp. 72–74.

67. Peter Kivisto, "Form and Content of Immigrant Socialist Ideology: The Case of the Finnish-American Left," *Siirtolaisuus* 3 (1983): 12–13.

68. Peter Kivisto, "The Decline of the Finnish American Left, 1925–1945," *International Migration Review* 17 (1983): 65–94.

69. Paul C. Nyholm, *The Americanization of the Danish Lutheran Churches in America* (Minneapolis, MN: Augsburg Publishing, 1963), pp. 249–91.

70. Merle Curti, *The Making of an American Community: A Case Study of Democracy in a Frontier County* (Stanford, CA: Stanford University Press 1959), pp. 84, 96, 101, 104, 112.

71. Carl Chrislock, *Ethnicity Challenged: The Upper Midwest Norwegian American Experience in World War* (Northfield, MN: Norwegian-American Historical Association, 1981), pp. 40, 44.

72. Kendric C. Babcock, *The Scandinavian Element in the United States* (New York: Arno Press, 1969), pp. 15–16. First published 1914.

73. See Gary B. Nash, *Class and Society in Early America* (Englewood Cliffs, NJ: Prentice Hall, 1970).

74. U.S. Census Bureau, *Historical Statistics of the United States, Part II*, Series Z 20–132 (Washington, DC: U.S. Government Printing Office, 1976).

75. Vincent N. Parrillo, *Diversity in America*, 2d ed. (Thousand Oaks, CA: Pine Forge Press, 2005), p. 140.

76. Ibid.

77. J. Hector St. John de Crèvecoeur, *Letters from an American Farmer* (New York: Albert and Charles Boni, 1925), pp. 54–55. First published 1782.

CHAPTER 6

1. "From Farm to Factory: Immigrant Adjustment to American Industry," *Spectrum* 1 (May 1975): 1.
2. Milton M. Gordon, *Assimilation in American Life* (New York: Oxford University Press, 1964), p. 136.
3. Madison Grant, *The Passing of the Great Race* (New York: Arno Press, 1970), p. 91. First published 1916.
4. Gordon, *Assimilation in American Life*, p. 97.
5. Ronald M. Pavalko, "Racism and the New Immigration: Toward a Reinterpretation of the Experiences of White Ethnics in American Society," *Sociology and Social Research* 65 (1981): 56–77.
6. Isaac A. Hourwich, *Immigrants and Labor* (New York: Huebach, 1922), quoted in ibid., p. 8.
7. Pavalko, "Racism and the New Immigration," p. 22.
8. Ibid., p. 24.
9. See the discussion on negative self-image in Chapter 4; see also Gordon, *Assimilation in American Life*, pp. 137–38.
10. Ellwood P. Cubberly, *Changing Conceptions of Education* (Boston: Houghton Mifflin, 1909), pp. 15–16.
11. *Public Opinion* I (1886): 82–86.
12. "The Age of Steel," quoted in *Public Opinion* I (1886): 355.
13. Henry Pratt Fairchild, *The Melting Pot Mistake* (Boston: Little, Brown, 1926), quoted in *American Observer* 50 (November 29, 1971): 5.
14. Victor R. Greene, *The Slavic Community on Strike* (South Bend, IN: University of Notre Dame Press, 1968), pp. 40–41.
15. Ibid., pp. 49–50.
16. See Charles B. Nam, "Nationality Groups and Social Stratification in America," *Social Forces* 37 (1959): 328–33.
17. U.S. Department of State, *Refugees Admissions Program for Europe and Central Asia Fact Sheet* (May 9, 2006). Accessed online at www.state.gov/g/prm/rls/fs/2006/66015.htm [July 23, 2007].
18. Henryk Sienkiewicz, *Portrait of America, Letters of Henryk Sienkiewicz*, ed. and trans. Charles Morley (New York: Columbia University Press, 1959), pp. 272–73.
19. Ibid., p. 279.
20. William I. Thomas and Florian Znaniecki, *The Polish Peasant in Europe and America*, 5 vols. (Boston: Badger, 1918–1920).
21. "Immigrants and Religion: The Persistence of Ethnic Diversity," *Spectrum* 1 (September 1975): 2.
22. Helena Znaniecki Lopata, *Polish Americans: Status Competition in an Ethnic Community* (Englewood Cliffs, NJ: Prentice Hall, 1976), p. 92.
23. Ibid., p. 145.
24. Beverly Duncan and Otis Dudley Duncan, "Minorities and the Process of Stratification," *American Sociological Review* 33 (June 1968): 356–64; Stanley Lieberson, *Ethnic Patterns in American Cities* (New York: Free Press, 1963), p. 189.
25. Lopata, *Polish Americans*, p. 95.
26. James S. Pula, "Image, Status, Mobility and Integration in American Society," *Journal of American Ethnic History* 16 (1996): 74–94.
27. Neil C. Sandberg, *Ethnic Identity and Assimilation: The Polish-American Community* (New York: Praeger, 1974).
28. See the discussion on ethnicity and social class in Chapter 2.
29. "St. Stanislaus Kostka Church." Accessed online at www.ststansk.com/whoweare.html [June 21, 2007].
30. U.S. Office of Immigration Statistics, *Yearbook of Immigration Statistics: 2006* (Washington, DC: U.S. Government Printing Office), Table 2.
31. Based on data from Mark Wischnitzer, *Visas to Freedom*, prepared by Hebrew Immigration Assistance Society (Cleveland, OH: World Publishing, 1956); U.S. Immigration and Naturalization Service, *Annual Report* (Washington, DC: U.S. Government Printing Office, 1981), Table 13, p. 63.
32. Jerome Davis, *The Russian Immigrant* (New York: Arno Press, 1970), p. 98. First published 1922.
33. Edward T. Devine, "Family and Social Work," in Jerome Davis (ed.), *The Russians and Ruthenians in America* (New York: Arno Press, 1970), p. 32. First published 1922.

34. Davis, *The Russian Immigrant*, pp. 173–74.

35. John Higham, *Strangers in the Land: Patterns of American Nativism, 1860–1925* (New Brunswick, NJ: Rutgers University Press, 1955), pp. 230–31; see also Frederick R. Barkley, "Jailing Radicals in Detroit," *Nation* 110 (1920): 136.

36. U.S. Office of Immigration Statistics, *Yearbook of Immigration Statistics: 2006*, Table 3.

37. "The Russian Orthodox Church Outside of Russia." Accessed online at www.russian orthodoxchurch.ws/synod/indexeng.htm [June 22, 2007].

38. Wasyl Halich, *Ukrainians in the United States* (New York: Arno Press, 1970), pp. 28–29. First published 1937.

39. U.S. Office of Immigration Statistics, *Yearbook of Immigration Statistics: 2006* (Washington, DC: U.S. Government Printing Office), Table 3.

40. Emil Lengyel, *Americans from Hungary* (New York: Lippincott, 1948), p. 128.

41. *New York Tribune* (September 11–12, 1897), pp. 1, 3.

42. Irving Lewis Allen, *Unkind Words* (New York: Bergin & Garvey, 1990), pp. 31, 62.

43. John Korosfoy (ed.), *Hungarians in America* (Cleveland, OH: Szabadsag, 1941), pp. 15–28.

44. "Gypsies in America: From Open Road to Internet," *The Economist* (March 28, 1998), p. 29.

45. Werner Cohn, "Some Comparison between Gypsy (North American Rom) and American English Kinship Terms," *American Anthropologist* 71 (June 1969): 477–78.

46. Glen W. Davidson, "'Gypsies': People with a Hidden History," in Sally TeSelle (ed.), *The Rediscovery of Ethnicity* (New York: Harper & Row, 1973), p. 84.

47. Allan Pinkerton, *The Gypsies and the Detectives* (New York: Carleton 1879), pp. 68–69.

48. Rena C. Gropper, *Gypsies in the City* (Princeton, NJ: Darwin, 1987), pp. 60–66.

49. Gulbun Coker, "Romany Rye in Philadelphia: A Sequel," *Southwestern Journal of Anthropology* 22 (1966): 85–100.

50. Jean-Paul Clebert, *The Gypsies* (London: Vista, 1963), p. 96.

51. Jan Yoors, *The Gypsies* (New York: Simon & Schuster, 1967), p. 7.

52. Anne Sutherland, *Gypsies: The Hidden Americans*, reprint ed. (New York: Waveland, 1986), p. 232.

53. Gropper, *Gypsies in the City*, p. 162.

54. Sutherland, *Gypsies: The Hidden Americans*, p. 248.

55. Carol Miller, "American Rom and the Ideology of Defilement," in Farnham Rehfisch (ed.), *Gypsies, Tinkers, and Other Travelers* (New York: Academic Press, 1975), p. 41.

56. Ronald Lee, *Goddam Gypsy: An Autobiographical Novel* (Montreal: Tundra, 1984), pp. 29–30.

57. Sutherland, *Gypsies: The Hidden Americans*, p. 264.

58. Gropper, *Gypsies in the City*, pp. 92–93.

59. Miller, "American Rom and the Ideology of Defilement," pp. 45–46.

60. Peter Maas, *King of the Gypsies* (New York: Viking, 1975), p. 29.

61. Sutherland, *Gypsies: The Hidden Americans*, p. 98.

62. Carol Silverman, "Everyday Drama: Impression Management of Urban Gypsies," *Urban Anthropology* 11 (Fall-Winter 1982): 382.

63. Ian Hancock, "Gypsies," in Stephen Thernstrom (ed.), *Harvard Encyclopedia of American Ethnic Groups* (Cambridge, MA: Harvard University Press, 1980), p. 441.

64. Marion D. Frankfurter and Gardner Jackson (eds.), *The Letters of Sacco and Vanzetti* (New York: Viking, 1928), p. 377.

65. Higham reports, for example, that under the heading "Italians" in the 1902 *New York Tribune Index*, 55 of the 74 entries were clear accounts of crime and violence (*Strangers in the Land*, p. 363).

66. For excellent insight into the Italian community of Chicago's West Side, see Gerald D. Suttles, *The Social Order of the Slum* (Chicago: University of Chicago Press, 1968).

67. See Rudolph Vecoli, *The Peoples of New Jersey* (Princeton, NJ: Van Nostrand, 1965), pp. 221–36.

68. Herbert J. Gans, *The Urban Villagers* (New York: Free Press, 1962), pp. 204–05.

69. William Foote Whyte, *Street Corner Society* (Chicago: University of Chicago Press, 1943), p. 274.

70. Richard D. Alba, "The Twilight of Ethnicity

among Americans of European Ancestry: The Case of the Italians," *Ethnic and Racial Studies* 8 (January 1985): 141.

71. Richard D. Alba, *Italian Americans: Into the Twilight of Ethnicity* (Englewood Cliffs, NJ: Prentice Hall, 1985), p. 159.

72. Stefano Luconi, "Mafia-Related Prejudice and the Rise of Italian Americans in the United States," *Patterns of Prejudice* 33 (January 1999): 43–57.

73. Leonard Dinnerstein and David M. Reimers, *Ethnic Americans* (New York: Harper & Row, 1975), p. 43.

74. In 1972, a Boston city survey—the Omnibus Survey—revealed that its sizable Greek immigrant population had a zero unemployment rate, no one on welfare, and a median income $4,000 above the Boston average.

75. Theodore Saloutos, *The Greeks in the United States* (Cambridge, MA: Harvard University Press, 1964), pp. 78–79.

76. Henry Pratt Fairchild, *Greek Immigration* (New Haven, CT: Yale University Press, 1911), pp. 239, 241–42.

77. John Tierney, "The Coffee Shop, Cornered," *New York Times Magazine* (June 5, 1994), p. 26.

78. Gerald A. Estep, "Portuguese Assimilation in Hawaii and California," *Sociology and Social Research* 26 (September 1941): 64.

79. Donald R. Taft, *Two Portuguese Communities in New England,* reprint ed. (New York: Arno Press, 1969), p. 79.

80. Ibid., p. 348.

81. See Louis Adamic, *A Nation of Nations* (New York: Harper, 1945), pp. 287–88.

82. Marjorie Housepian, *The Unremembered Genocide* (New York: American Jewish Committee, 1965), p. 31.

83. Frank A. Stone, *Armenian Studies for Secondary Students* (Storrs, CT: Parousia Press, 1975), p. 8.

84. Emory S. Bogardus, "Comparing Racial Distance in Ethiopia, South Africa, and the United States," *Sociology and Social Research* 52 (1968): 149–56.

85. Gary A. Kulhanjian, *The Historical and Sociological Aspects of Armenian Immigration to the United States, 1890 to 1930* (San Francisco: R. & E. Research Associates, 1975), p. 25.

86. Ibid., p. 29.

87. "Armenians in California," *The Economist* (January 19, 1991), p. 28.

88. Nicole E. Vartanian, "A Fruitful Legacy," *Cobblestone* 21 (2000): 10.

89. Vincent N. Parrillo, *Diversity in America*, 2nd ed. (Thousand Oaks, CA: Pine Forge Press, 2005), p. 96.

90. See Alice Kestler-Harris, *Out to Work* (New York; Oxford University Press, 1982); Leslie Woodcock Tentler, *Wage-Earning Women: Industrial Work and Family Life, 1900–1930* (New York: Oxford University Press, 1979).

91. Parrillo, *Diversity in America,* p. 97.

92. Ibid.

93. Grant, *The Passing of the Great Race.*

94. Michael Novak, *The Rise of the Unmeltable Ethnics* (New York: Macmillan, 1971).

CHAPTER 7

1. See Lee E. Huddleston, *Origins of the American Indians: European Concepts, 1492–1729* (Austin: University of Texas Press, 1967).

2. Bureau of Indian Affairs, *Performance and Accountability Report: Fiscal Year 2005.* Accessed online at www.doi.gov/bia/BIA _PAR_2005_ FINAL_02242006_web.pdf [June 22, 2007].

3. John Boyd Thacher (ed.), *Christopher Columbus,* Vol. 1 (New York: AMS Press, 1967), p. 533.

4. See Lewis Hanke, *The First Social Experiments in America: A Study in the Development of Spanish Indian Policy in the Sixteenth Century* (Gloucester, MA: Peter Smith, 1964).

5. Douglas Edward Leach, *Flintlock and Tomahawk, New England in King Philip's War* (New York: Norton, 1958), pp. 20–22.

6. Chester E. Jorgenson and Luther Frank Mott (eds.), *Benjamin Franklin* (New York: Hill & Wang, 1962).

7. George Catlin, *Letters and Notes of the Manners, Customs and Conditions of the North American Indians* (New York: Dover, 1973), Vol. 1, pp. 102–03. First published in 1841.

8. Bruce E. Johansen, *Forgotten Founders: How the American Indian Helped Shape Democracy* (New York: Gambit, 1987). See also Jack

Weatherford, *Indian Givers: How the Indians of the Americas Transformed the World* (New York: Crown, 1988).

9. Wilcomb E. Washburn, *The Indian in America* (New York: Harper & Row, 1975), p. 32.

10. Ibid., pp. 39–40.

11. See D'Arcy McNickle, *They Came Here First: The Epic of the American Indian* (Philadelphia: Lippincott, 1949), p. 128.

12. Anthony F. C. Wallace, *The Death and Rebirth of the Seneca* (New York: Knopf, 1970), p. 28; John Axtell, "The Scholastic Philosophy of the Wilderness," *William and Mary Quarterly* 29 (1972): 359.

13. Albert Britt, *Indian Chiefs* (Freeport, NY: Books for Libraries Press, 1969), pp. 8–26.

14. Peter Farb, *Man's Rise to Civilization as Shown by the Indians of North America from Primeval Times to the Coming of the Industrial State* (New York: Dutton, 1968), p. 158.

15. See Keith H. Basso, "'To Give Up on Words': Silence in Western Apache Culture," *Southwestern Journal of Anthropology* 26 (1970): 213–20.

16. William Lang, "The Fundamental Dilemma: Conflict between the European and Native American World Views." Paper presented at the Fourth Annual Polish Association for American Studies Conference, Pulawy, Poland, October 28, 1994.

17. Edward H. Spicer, "American Indians," in Stephen Thernstrom, Ann Orlov, and Oscar Handlin (eds.), *Harvard Encyclopedia of American Ethnic Groups* (Cambridge, MA: Belknap Press, 1980), pp. 85–86.

18. Alvin M. Josephy Jr., *The Indian Heritage of America* (New York: Knopf, 1968), p. 324.

19. Dale Van Every, *Disinherited: The Lost Birthright of the American Indian* (New York: Discus Avon Books, 1966), p. 163.

20. James Mooney, *Myths of the Cherokee*, 19th Annual Report, Bureau of American Ethnology (Washington, DC: U.S. Government Printing Office, 1900), p. 130.

21. James D. Richardson, *Messages and Papers of the President*, Vol. 3 (Washington, DC: U.S. Government Printing Office, 1897), p. 497.

22. Farb, *Man's Rise to Civilization*, p. 310.

23. Ibid., p. 309.

24. Ibid.

25. Elizabeth S. Grobsmith and Beth R. Ritter, "The Ponca Tribe: The Process of Restoration of a Federally Terminated Tribe," *Human Organization* 51 (Spring 1992): 2.

26. See Theodore Stern, *The Klamath Tribe* (Seattle: University of Washington Press, 1966).

27. Josephy, *The Indian Heritage of America*, p. 354.

28. U.S. Census Bureau, "The American Community—American Indians and Alaska Natives: 2004," *American Community Survey Reports* (May 2007), pp. 1, 9.

29. American Indian Policy Review Committee, "Report on Indian Education" (Washington, DC: U.S. Government Printing Office, 1976), p. 245.

30. American Indian Policy Review Commission, "Report on Urban and Rural Non-Reservation Indians" (Washington, DC: U.S. Government Printing Office, 1976), p. 25.

31. U.S. Census Bureau, "The American Community—American Indians and Alaska Natives: 2004," p. 13.

32. Schafer, Shaun, "Tribal Colleges Filling Growing Need," *Houston Chronicle* (June 25, 2006), p. A9.

33. Timothy J. Nichols and Diane Kayonogo-Male, "The Dynamics of Tribal College–State University Collaboration," *Journal of American Indian Education* 42 (2003): 1–24.

34. "Demographics," *Rosebud Sioux Tribe*. Accessed online at www.rosebudsioux tribe-nsn.gov/demographics/index.htm [June 23, 2007].

35. U.S. Census Bureau, "The American Community—American Indians and Alaska Natives: 2004," p. 14.

36. "Overview of Tribal Business," *Choctaw Vision*. Accessed online at www.choctaw.org/ economics/tribal_business_overview.htm [June 23, 2007].

37. J. M. Hirsch, "Blueberries Equal Big Business in Maine," Associated Press State & Local Wire (August 11, 2006).

38. Donald L. Barlett and James B. Steele, "Wheel of Misfortune," *Time* (December 8, 2002), pp. 44–49.

39. Indian Health Service, "Facts on Indian Health Disparities," Accessed at http://info.

ihs.gov/Files/DisparitiesFacts-Jan2007.doc [June 23, 2007].

40. Ibid.

41. U.S. Commission on Civil Rights, *Broken Promises: Evaluating the Native American Health Care System* (Washington, DC: U.S. Government Printing Office, 2004), p. 6.

42. National Center for Health Statistics, *Health, United States: 2006* (Washington, DC: U.S. Government Printing Office, 2006), Table 46, pp. 230–31.

43. Faye A. Gary, "Perspectives on Suicide Prevention among American Indian and Alaska Native Children and Adolescents: A Call for Help," *Online Journal of Issues in Nursing* 10 (2005): 170–211; Melissa L. Walls, Constance L. Chapple, and Kurt D. Johnson, "Strain, Emotion, and Suicide among American Indian Youth," *Deviant Behavior* 28 (May/June 2007): 219–46.

44. Lawrence A. Greenfeld and Stephen K. Smith, *American Indians and Crime*, Bureau of Justice Statistics, NJC 173386 (February 1999).

45. National Center for Health Statistics, *Health, United States: 2006* (Hyattsville, MD: NCHS, 2006) Table 29, pp. 179–80.

46. Greenfeld and Smith, *American Indians and Crime*, p. 9.

47. Philip A. May, "The Epidemiology of Alcohol Abuse among American Indians: The Mythical and Real Properties," *American Indian Culture & Research Journal* 18 (1994): 124.

48. Michael T. Garrett and Jane J. Carroll, "Mending the Broken Circle: Treatment of Substance Dependence among Native Americans," *Journal of Counseling & Development* 78 (2000): 380.

49. James Moran and Marian Bussey, "Results of an Alcohol Prevention Program with Urban Native American Youth," *Child & Adolescent Social Work Journal* 24 (February 2007): 1–21.

50. Stephen Kulis, Maria Napoli, and Flavio F. Marsiglia, "Ethnic Pride, Biculturalism, and Drug Use Norms of Urban American Indian Adolescents," *Social Work Research* 26 (June 2002): 101–12.

51. See James R. Moran et al., "Measuring Bicultural Ethnic Identity among American Indian Adolescents: A Factor Analytic Study," *Journal of Adolescent Research* 14 (1999): 405–26.

52. Housing Assistance Council, "Housing on Native American Lands," September 2006; National American Indian Housing Council, "Fact Sheet: Native Americans and Housing," April 22, 2004.

53. Robert C. Holman, Aaron T. Curns, James E. Cheek, Joseph S. Bresee, Rosalyn J. Singleton, Karen Carver, and Larry J. Anderson, "Respiratory Syncytial Virus Hospitalizations among American Indian and Alaska Native Infants and the General United States Infant Population," *Pediatrics* 114 (2004): 437–44.

54. John Files, "Indian Fund Investigator Angrily Quits," *New York Times* (April 7, 2004), p. A15.

55. Katherine M. Peters, "Trail of Trouble," *Government Executive* 33 (April 2001): 95–103. See also Peter Maas, "The Broken Promise," *Parade* (September 9, 2001), pp. 4–6.

56. John J. Fialka, "Judge Holds Interior Secretary in Contempt Over Indian Trust." *Wall Street Journal* (September 18, 2002), p. A6; Fialka, "Panel Removes Federal Judge from Indian Trust-Fund Case," *Wall Street Journal* (July 12, 2006), p. A6.

57. See the home page of the Sweet Hills Protective Association. Accessed online at http://comus.msun.edu/Hon290/HillsHome.html [October 2, 2004].

58. "The Landless Landed," *Economist* (June 8, 1991), p. 32.

59. Sandra D. Atchison, "The Navajos May Generate Juice—and Even Power," *Business Week* (November 11, 1991), p. 162P.

60. "UN Investigates U.S. Human Rights," *Earth Island Journal* 13 (Summer 1998): 22.

61. Alexander Cockburn, "The Shame Continues at Big Mountain," *Los Angeles Times* (April 27, 1997), p. M5.

62. Jenny Kammer, "Navajos' Eviction by U.S. Not Likely," *The Arizona Republic* (January 29, 2001), p. 1.

63. Felicity Barringer, "Navajos and Environmentalists Split on Power Plant," *New York Times* (July 27, 2007), p. A14; "Navajo Coal Fear," *Ecologist* 37 (May 2007), p. 11.

64. Susan Moran, "The Tribe That Earned a Triple-A Bond Rating," *New York Times* (July 24, 2007), pp. C1, C4.

65. Council of Energy Resource Tribes, "CERT Member Tribes." Accessed online at www.certredearth.com/members.php [June 24, 2007].

66. "Wastes," Environmental Protection Agency. Accessed online at www.epa.gov/ebtpages/wastes.html [June 24, 2007].

67. See Daniel Brook, "Environmental Genocide: Native Americans and Toxic Waste," *American Journal of Economics and Sociology* 57 (1998): 105–13; Mary Hager, "Dances with Garbage," *Newsweek* (April 19, 1991), p. 36.

68. David R. Lewis, "Native Americans and the Environment: A Survey of Twentieth-Century Issues," *American Indian Quarterly* (Berkeley) 19 (1995): 423–25.

69. Michael Satchell, "Dances with Nuclear Waste," *U.S. News & World Report* (January 8, 1996), pp. 29–30.

70. Serban Negoita et al., "Chronic Diseases Surveillance of St. Regis Mohawk Health Service Patients," *Journal of Public Health Management and Practice* 7 (2001): 84–90.

71. Somini Sengupta, "A Sick Tribe and a Dump as a Neighbor," *New York Times* (April 7, 2001), p. B1.

72. Aric Press et al. "The Indian Water Wars," *Newsweek* (June 13, 1983), pp. 80–81.

73. "Water Rights Create Legal Disputes," *Utility Business* (July 2001), p. 12.

74. Suzi Parker, "Suburban Sprawl Spurs Fights over Sacred Indian Sites across the U.S.," *Christian Science Monitor* (August 16, 2001), p. 2.

75. Josephy, *Red Power*, p. 4.

76. Quoted in Morris Freedman and Carolyn Banks, *American Mix* (Philadelphia: Lippincott, 1972), pp. 46–47.

77. See Dee Brown, *Bury My Heart at Wounded Knee* (New York: Holt Paperbacks, 2007).

78. "Wounded Knee: The Media Coup d'État," *Nation* 216 (June 25, 1973): 807.

79. "Sioux Chiefs Urged to Reject U.S. Offer," *New York Times* (September 2, 1979), p. 22.

80. "Dances with Lawyers," *Economist* (August 10, 1991), p. A18.

81. Glen Coin, "Judge to Oneida: No Taking Back the Land," *The Post-Standard* (May 22, 2007), p. A1.

82. "Audit Raises Concerns on Special Education in BIA-Funded Schools," *Education Week* (April 18, 2007), p. 11.

83. Katherine M. Peters, "Trail of Trouble," pp. 95–96, 103.

84. Matthew B. Krepps and Richard E. Caves, "Bureaucrats and Indians: Principal-Agent Relations and Efficient Management of Tribal Forest Resources," *Journal of Economic Behavior and Organization* (July 1994): 133–51.

85. "Urban Challenge," *Government Executive* (December 2000), p. 27.

86. U.S. Census Bureau, "The American Indian and Alaska Native Population: 2000," *Census 2000 Brief*, February 2002, p. 8.

87. Sarah Staveteig and Alyssa Wigton, "Racial and Ethnic Disparities: Key Findings from the National Survey of America's Families," Urban Institute. Accessed online at www.urban.org [June 25, 2007].

88. See Donald L. Fixico, *The Urban Indian Experience in America.* (Albuquerque, NM: University of New Mexico Press, 2000).

89. See "The Scope of the Problem," *Alchohol Research & Health* 28 (2004/2005): 111–20; Paul Spicer, Douglas K. Novins, Christina M. Mitchell, and Janette Beals, "Aboriginal Social Organization, Contemporary Experience and American Indian Adolescent Alcohol Use," *Journal of Studies on Alcohol* 64 (2003): 450–57.

90. Mei L. Castor, Maile M. Taualii, Alice N. Park, and Ralph A. Forquera, "A Nationwide Population-Based Study Identifying Health Disparities Between American Indians/Alaska Natives and the General Populations Living in Select Urban Counties," *American Journal of Public Health* 96 (August 2006): 1416–22.

91. Fixico, *The Urban Indian Experience in America*, pp. 161–70.

92. Josephy, *The Indian Heritage of America*, p. 32.

93. Ibid.

94. Ibid., p. 34.

95. R. K. Heinrich, I. L. Corbine, and K. R. Thomas, "Counseling Native Americans," *Journal of Counseling and Development* 69 (1990): 128–33.

96. Vine Deloria Jr., *Custer Died for Your Sins: An Indian Manifesto* (Norman, OK: University of Oklahoma Press, 1988).

97. Mei E. Castor et al., "A Nationwide Population-Based Study Identifying Health Disparities Between American Indians/Alaska Natives and the General Populations Living in Select Urban Counties"; J. T. Garrett and Michael T. Garrett, *Medicine of the Cherokee: The Way of Right Relationship* (Santa Fe, NM: Bear & Company, 1996).

98. Michael T. Garrett and Eugene F. Pichette, "Red as an Apple: Native American Acculturation and Counseling with or without Reservation," *Journal of Counseling and Development* 78 (2000): 3–13.

99. D. Deyhle, "Constructing Failure and Maintaining Cultural Identity: Navajo and Ute School Leavers," *Journal of American Indian Education* 31 (1992): 24–47.

100. Craig D. Freed and Mary Samson, "Native Alaskan Dropouts in Western Alaska: Systemic Failure in Native Alaskan Schools," *Journal of American Indian Education* 43 (2004): 33–45.

101. Greenfeld and Smith, *American Indians and Crime.*

CHAPTER 8

1. U.S. Census Bureau, *The Asian Alone Population in the United States: March 2004,* Table 1.1.

2. U.S. Census Bureau, *The Asian Population: 2000,* Census 2000 Brief (February 2002), Tables 2, 3.

3. "China," *Encyclopaedia Britannica,* 7th ed. (1842), Vol. 6.

4. Otis Gibson, *The Chinese in America* (Cincinnati, OH: Hitchcock & Walden, 1877), pp. 51–52.

5. Ibid.

6. Alexander Saxton, *The Indispensable Enemy: Labor and the Anti-Chinese Movement in California* (Berkeley: University of California Press, 1971), p. 63.

7. Ibid.

8. Hinton Helper, *The Land of Gold: Reality versus Fiction* (Baltimore, 1855), pp. 94–96, quoted in Saxton, *The Indispensable Enemy,* p. 19.

9. "The Growth of the U.S. through Emigration—The Chinese," *New York Times* (September 3, 1865).

10. *New York Times* (June 7, 1868).

11. Senator James G. Blaine, *Congressional Record* (February 14, 1879), p. 1301.

12. U.S. Immigration and Naturalization Service, *Annual Report* (Washington, DC: U.S. Government Printing Office, 1926), pp. 170–81.

13. Ibid.

14. American Federation of Labor, *Proceedings,* 1893, p. 73.

15. D. Y. Yuan, "New York Chinatown," in Arnold M. Rose and Caroline B. Rose (eds.), *Minority Problems* (New York: Harper & Row, 1965), pp. 277–84.

16. Albert W. Palmer, *Orientals in American Life* (New York: Friendship Press, 1934), pp. 1–2, 7.

17. Stanford M. Lyman, "Conflict and the Web of Group Affiliation in San Francisco's Chinatown, 1850–1910," *Pacific Historical Review* 43 (1974): 473–99. This work is an application of ideas developed by Georg Simmel in two theoretical essays, "Conflict" and "The Web of Group Affiliation."

18. Ibid., pp. 494–99.

19. S. W. Kung, *Chinese in American Life* (Seattle, WA: University of Washington Press, 1962), p. 89.

20. Stanford M. Lyman, "Marriage and the Family among Chinese Immigrants to America," *Phylon* 29 (Winter 1968): 324.

21. U.S. Immigration and Naturalization Service, *1990 Statistical Yearbook* (Washington, DC: U.S. Government Printing Office, 1991), Table 12, pp. 71–73.

22. Lyman, "Marriage and the Family among Chinese Immigrants to America," p. 327.

23. Ibid., p. 330.

24. Ibid., p. 328.

25. *Congressional Record* (October 21, 1943), p. 8626.

26. Mark Abrahamson, *Urban Enclaves: Identity and Place in America* (New York: St. Martin's Press, 1996), pp. 67–84.

27. See Miriam Ching Yoon Louie, *Immigrant Warriors: Immigrant Women Workers Take On the Global Factory* (Cambridge, MA: South End Press, 2001).

28. Ming-Jung Ho, "Migratory Journeys and Tuberculosis Risk," *Medical Anthropology Quarterly* 17 (2003): 442–58.

29. See Peter Kwong, *Forbidden Workers: Immigrants and American Labor* (New York: New Press, 1999).

30. Peter Kwong, *The New Chinatown*, rev. ed. (New York: Hill & Wang, 1996), p. 41.

31. Ko-Lin Chin, *Chinatown Gangs: Extortion, Enterprise, and Ethnicity*, New Ed. (New York: Oxford University Press, 2000).

32. U.S. Census Bureau, *2000 Census*, Summary Tape 3A.

33. Stanford M. Lyman, "Generation & Character: The Case of the Japanese-Americans," in Hilary Conroy and T. Scott Miyakawa (eds.), *East across the Pacific: Historical and Sociological Studies of Japanese Immigration and Assimilation* (Santa Barbara, CA: American Bibliographical Center—Clio Press, 1972), p. 279. Also in S. Lyman, *The Asian in North America* (Santa Barbara, CA: Clio Press, 1977), pp. 151–76.

34. Morton Grodzins, *Americans Betrayed* (Chicago: University of Chicago Press, 1949).

35. Lyman, "Generation & Character: The Case of the Japanese-Americans," pp. 279–80.

36. Eugene V. Rostow, "Our Worst Wartime Mistake," *Harper's Magazine* (September 1945): 193–201.

37. See Michi Weglyn, *Years of Infamy: The Untold Story of America's Concentration Camps* (New York: Morrow, 1976).

38. Esther B. Rhoads, "My Experience with the Wartime Relocation of Japanese," in Hilary Conroy and T. Scott Miyakawa (eds.), *East across the Pacific: Historical and Sociological Studies of Japanese Immigration and Assimilation* (Santa Barbara, CA: American Bibliographical Center—Clio Press, 1972), pp. 131–32.

39. Ted Nakashima, "Concentration Camp, U.S. Style," *New Republic* (June 15, 1942), pp. 822–23.

40. Justice Robert H. Jackson, dissenting opinion, *Korematsu v. United States of America*, 65, *Supreme Court Reporter* (1944): 206–08.

41. Bill Hosokawa, *Nisei: The Quiet Americans*, reprint ed (Boulder, CO: University Press of Colorado, 1992), pp. 439–46.

42. John Leo, "An Apology to Japanese Americans," *Time* (May 2, 1988), p. 70.

43. Harry H. L. Kitano, *Japanese Americans: The Evolution of a Subculture*, 2nd ed. (Englewood Cliffs, NJ: Prentice Hall, 1976), p. 132.

44. See ibid., pp. 23–24, 107–08.

45. U.S. Census Bureau, *2000 Census*, Summary Tapes 1A and 2A.

46. Zhenchao Qian, Sampson L. Blair, and Stacey D. Ruf, "Asian American Interracial and Interethnic Marriages," *International Migration Review* 35 (2001): 557–86.

47. U.S. Office of Immigration Statistics, *Yearbook of Immigration Statistics: 2006* (Washington, DC: U.S. Government Printing Office, 2007), Table 2.

48. Jeremy Schlosberg, "Turning Japanese," *American Demographics* (May 1990): 48.

49. *Morrison et al. v. California* (1934), 291 U.S. Supreme Court Reports (1934) 85–86.

50. Davis McEntire, *The Labor Force in California: A Study of Characteristics and Trends in Labor Force, Employment and Occupations in California, 1900–1950* (Berkeley: University of California Press, 1952), p. 62.

51. Carey McWilliams, *Brothers under the Skin* (Boston: Little, Brown, 1951), p. 239.

52. Sylvain Lazarus, San Francisco Municipal Court, January 1936, quoted in Manuel Braken, *I Have Lived with the American People* (Caldwell, CA: Caxton, 1948), pp. 136–38.

53. Letter from Sylvester Saturday, in *Time* (May 11, 1936), p. 4.

54. Letter from Ernest D. Ilustre, in *Time* (April 27, 1936), p. 3.

55. McWilliams, *Brothers under the Skin*, p. 244.

56. Bernicio T. Catapusan, "Filipino Intermarriage Problems in the United States," *Sociology and Social Research* 22 (1938): 265–72.

57. For an excellent sociological study of Filipinos in dance halls, see Paul G. Cressey, *The Taxi-Dance Hall* (New York: Routledge, 2003).

58. R. T. Feria, "War and the Status of the Filipino Immigrants," *Sociology and Social Research* 31 (1946): 50.

59. See Linus Yamane, "Native-Born Filipana/o Americans and Labor Market Discrimination," *Feminist Economics* 8 (2002): 125–44.

60. Yen Le Espiritu, *Home Bound: Filipino Lives Across Cultures, Communities, and Countries* (Berkeley, CA: University of California Press, 2003), pp. 190–92.

61. Pyong Gap Min, *Asian Americans: Contemporary Trends and Issues*, 2nd ed. (Thousand Oaks, CA: Sage, 2005), pp. 180–203.

62. U.S. Census Bureau, *The Asian Population: 2000*, Table 4 (2002), p. 9; U.S. Office of Immigration Statistics, *Yearbook of Immigration Statistics: 2006* (Washington, DC: U.S. Government Printing Office), Table 2.

63. Harold H. Sunoo and Sonia S. Sunoo, "The Heritage of the First Korean Women Immigrants in the United States: 1903–1924," *Korean Christian Journal* 2 (1977): 144, 146, 165; Bernice H. Kim, "The Koreans in Hawaii," *Social Science* 9 (1934): 409.

64. Lee Houchins and Chang-su Houchins, "The Korean Experience in America, 1903–1924," *Pacific Historical Review* 43 (1974): 560.

65. See Jennifer Lee, Esther S. Chang, and Lisa Miller, "Ethnic-Religious Status and Identity Formation: A Qualitative Study of Korean American Christian Youth," *Journal of Youth Ministry* 5 (2006): 9–40; Young Lee Hertig, *Cultural Tug of War: Korean Immigrant Family and Church in Transition* (Nashville, TN: Abingdon Press, 2002).

66. Kelly H. Chong, "What It Means to Be Christian: The Role of Religion in the Construction of Ethnic Identity and Boundary among Second-Generation Korean Americans," *Sociology of Religion* 59 (1998): 259–86.

67. Rebeca Raijman and Marta Tienda, "Immigrants' Pathways to Business Ownership: A Comparative Ethnic Perspective," *International Migration Review* 24 (2000): 682–706.

68. Miriam Jordan, "In Los Angeles, You Say 'Hola!' I Say, 'Ahn-nyung'" *Wall Street Journal* (June 2–3, 2007), pp. A1, A7; Dae Young Kim, "Beyond co-ethnic solidarity: Mexican and Ecuadorean employment in Korean-owned businesses in New York City, *Ethnic and Racial Studies* 22 (1999): 581–605.

69. Emory S. Bogardus, "Comparing Racial Distance in Ethiopia, South Africa, and the United States," *Sociology and Social Research* 52 (1968): 149–56. Vincent N. Parrillo and Christopher Donoghue, "Updating the Bogardus Social Distance Studies: A New National Survey," *Social Science Journal* 42:2 (2005): 257–71.

70. "Future of Refugees: The Furor and the Facts," *U.S. News & World Report* (May 19, 1975), p. 16.

71. The author wishes to thank Walter H. Slote, Ph.D., and Stephen Young, J.D., for sharing their expertise about the Vietnamese and Vietnamese Americans.

72. Walter H. Slote, "Adaption of Recent Vietnamese Immigrés to the American Experience: A Psycho-Cultural Approach," paper presented at the 29th annual meeting of the Association for Asian Studies, March 1977, p. 9.

73. Ibid., p. 11.

74. Bayard Webster, "Studies Report Refugees Plagued by Persistent Stress," *New York Times* (September 11, 1979), p. C1.

75. Jean S. Phinney and Anthony D. Ong, "Adolescent–Parent Disagreements and Life Satisfaction in Families from Vietnamese- and European-American Backgrounds," *International Journal of Behavioral Development* 26 (2002): 556–61.

76. Yu Xie and Kimberly Goyette, "A Demographic Portrait of Asian Americans," *Population Bulletin* (2004) 53, 25–35.

77. Betty Rairdan and Zana Roe Higgs, "When Your Patient Is a Hmong Refugee," *American Journal of Nursing* 92 (1992): 52–55.

78. U.S. Census Bureau, Ethnic and Hispanic Branch, 2000 Census Special Tabulations.

79. See, for example, Majorie Valbrun, "Laotians Teach U.S. How Not to Resettle Refugees," *Wall Street Journal* (April 4, 2000), p. B1; David W. Haines (ed.), *Refugees in America in the 1990s: A Reference Handbook* (Westport, CT: Greenwood Press, 1996).

80. See Stacey J. Lee, "More Than 'Model Minorities' or 'Delinquents': A Look at Hmong American High School Students," *Harvard Educational Review* 71 (2001): 505–29.

81. Asian American Justice Center, *2002 Audit of Violence against Asian Pacific Islanders.* Accessed online at www.advancingequality. org/files/2002_Audit.pdf [June 27, 2007].

82. Pauline Yoshihashi and Sarah Lubman, "American Dreams," *Wall Street Journal* (June 16, 1992), p. A6.

83. See In-Jin Yoon, *On My Own: Korean Businesses and Race Relations in America* (Chicago: University of Chicago Press, 1997).

84. Louis Winnick, "America's 'Model Minority,'" *Commentary* 90 (1990): 23.

85. Hye Jin Paek and Hemant Shah, "Racial Ideology, Model Minorities, and the 'Not-So-Silent Partner': Stereotyping of Asian Americans in U.S. Magazine Advertising," *The Howard Journal of Communication* 14 (2003): 225–43.

86. Miranda Oshige McGowan and James Lingren, "Testing the 'Model Minority Myth'" *Northwestern University Law Review* 100 (2006): 331–77.

87. David Budge, "Model Minority Tag Hides Dropout Problem," *Times Educational Supplement* (May 7, 2004), p. 16.

88. U.S. Census Bureau, "Income, Poverty, and Health Insurance Coverage in the United States: 2005," *Current Population Reports* P60–231 (August 2006).

89. U.S. Census Bureau, *Educational Attainment in the United States: 2006* (March 2007).

90. U.S. Census Bureau, *The Foreign-Born Population in the United States: 2003*, P20–551 (August 2004).

91. U.S. Census Bureau, "The Asian and Pacific Islander Population in the United States: March 2002," *Current Population Reports*, P20–540 (May 2003).

92. Vincent Kang Fu, "Racial Intermarriage Pairings," *Demography* 38 (May 2001), 147–59.

93. Lee, "Asian Americans: Diverse and Growing," p. 23.

94. Kyeyoung Park, *The Korean American Dream: Immigrants and Small Business in New York City* (Ithaca, NY: Cornell University Press, 1997).

CHAPTER 9

1. U.S. Office of Immigration Statistics, *Yearbook of Immigration Statistics: 2006* (Washington, DC: U.S. Government Printing Office, 2007), Table 2.

2. U.S. Census Bureau, *Profile of Selected Social Characteristics: 2000*, Supplemental Survey Summary Tables: United States.

3. U.S. Office of Immigration Statistics, *Yearbook of Immigration Statistics: 2005*, Table 29.

4. Ibid., Table 21.

5. See Chapter 1, pp. 6–7.

6. U.S. Office of Immigration Statistics, *Yearbook of Immigration Statistics: 2006*, Table 10.

7. Gurdial Singh, "East Indians in the United States," *Sociology and Social Research* 30 (1946): 210–11.

8. Joan M. Jensen, "Apartheid: Pacific Coast Style," *Pacific Historical Review* 38 (1969): 335–40.

9. Gary R. Hess, "The Forgotten Asian Americans: The East Indian Community in the United States," *Pacific Historical Review* 43 (1974): 580.

10. Singh, "East Indians in the United States," pp. 210–11.

11. "Hindu Invasion," *Collier's* 45 (March 26, 1910): 15.

12. Hess, "The Forgotten Asian Americans," pp. 583–84.

13. Juan L. Gonzales Jr., "Asian Indian Immigration Patterns: The Origins of the Sikh Community in California," *International Migration Review* 20 (Spring 1986): 46.

14. Hess, "The Forgotten Asian Americans," p. 590.

15. Ibid., p. 593.

16. Ibid., pp. 593–94.

17. U.S. Office of Immigration Statistics, *Yearbook of Immigration Statistics: 2006*, Table 2.

18. U.S. Census Bureau, *The American Community—Asians: 2004*, American Community Survey Reports (February 2007), pp. 2, 8–9.

19. Susumu Awanohara, "Political Indian Summer," *Far Eastern Economic Review* 151 (May 23, 1991): 35.

20. Carl Haub and O. P. Sharma, "India's Population Reality: Reconciling Change and Traditions," *Population Bulletin* 61:3 (2006): 4–5.

21. Ibid., pp. 8, 13.

22. See Arpana G. Inman, Erin E. Howard, and Jessica A. Walker, "Cultural Transmission: Influence of Contextual Factors in Asian Indian Immigrant Parents' Experiences,"

Journal of Counseling Psychology 54:1 (2007): 93–100.

23. U.S. Office of Immigration Statistics, *Yearbook of Immigration Statistics: 2006*, Table 21.

24. Jim Hopkins, "Asian Business Owners Gaining Clout," *USA Today* (February 27, 2002), p. 1.

25. Jonathan Brooks, "American Owned: Gujarati Indians in the Lodging Industry," *Dissertation Abstracts International: The Humanities and Social Sciences* 64 (10) (April 2004): 3855–A.

26. U.S. Census Bureau, *The Arab Population: 2000*, C2KBR–23 (December 2003).

27. Nabeel Abraham and Andrew Shyrock (eds.), *Arab Detroit: From Margin to Mainstream* (Two Rivers, WI: Great Lakes Books, 2000).

28. See Nadine Naber, "Ambiguous Insiders: An Investigation of Arab American Invisibility," *Ethnic and Racial Studies* 23 (2000): 37–61.

29. Mona H. Faragallah, Walter R. Schumm, and Farrell J. Webb, "Acculturation of Arab-American Immigrants: An Exploratory Study," *Journal of Comparative Family Studies* 28 (Autumn 1997): 182–203; Andrzej Kulczycki and Arun Peter Lobo, "Patterns, Determinants, and Implications of Intermarriage among Arab Americans," *Journal of Marriage and Family* 64 (2002): 202–10.

30. Arab American Institute, *Arab American Demographics*. Accessed online at www.aaiusa.org/arab-americans/22/demographics [June 28, 2007].

31. Vincent N. Parrillo, "Arab American Residential Segregation: Differences in Patterns," *Resources in Education*, ERIC ED 243 991, 1984.

32. See Jonathan K. Stubbs, "The Bottom Rung of America's Race Ladder: After the September 11th Catastrophe, Are American Muslims Becoming America's New N . . . s?" *Journal of Law and Religion* 19 (2003/2004): 115–31; Matthew Purdy, "For Muslims, Flag-Flying and Fear," *New York Times* (September 14, 2001), p. A9.

33. Philip M. Kayal and Joseph M. Kayal, *The Syrian-Lebanese in America* (New York: Twayne, 1975), pp. 50, 61.

34. Elizabeth Boosahda, *Arab-American Faces and Voices: The Origins of an Immigrant Community* (Austin: University of Texas Press, 2003).

35. Alixa Naff, *The Arab Americans* (New York: Chelsea House, 1998), pp. 59, 72.

36. Cyril Anid, *I Grew with Them* (Jounieh, Lebanon: Paulist Press, 1967), p. 18.

37. Morris Berger, "America's Syrian Community," *Commentary* 25(4) (1958): 316.

38. Ibid., 311.

39. Kayal and Kayal, *The Syrian-Lebanese in America*, p. 108.

40. See Michael W. Suleiman (ed.), *Arabs in America: Building a New Future* (Philadelphia: Temple University Press, 2000).

41. Milton M. Gordon, *Assimilation in American Life* (New York: Oxford University Press, 1964).

42. U.S. Census Bureau, *The Arab Population: 2000*, Census 2000 Brief (December 2003), p. 3; Mariam Shahin, "A 50 Year Oppression," *Middle East* (May 1998): 8–10.

43. Michele Chabin, "Palestinians Look to Home for Brides," *USA Today* (August 3, 1998). Accessed online at www.usatoday.com/life/lds002.htm [June 28, 2007].

44. Maboud Ansari, *Iranian Immigrants in the United States: A Case Study of Dual Marginality* (New York: Associated Faculty Press, 1988), pp. 65–67.

45. Ibid., p. 73.

46. Ibid., pp. 46–62.

47. U.S. Office of Immigration Statistics, *Yearbook of Immigration Statistics: 2006*, Table 2.

48. Ansari, *Iranian Immigrants in the United States*, p. 106.

49. Nilou Mostofi, "Who We Are: The Perplexity of Iranian-American Identity," *The Sociological Quarterly* 44 (2003): 681–703.

50. Mary C. Sengstock, "Social Change in the Country of Origin as a Factor in Immigrant Conceptions of Nationality," *Ethnicity* 4 (March 1977): 54–69.

51. Ibid., p. 61.

52. U.S. Office of Immigration Statistics, *Yearbook of Immigration Statistics: 2006*, Supplemental Table 1.

53. John J. Grabowski, "Prospects and Challenges: The Study of Early Turkish Immigration to the United States," *Journal of American Ethnic History* 25 (Fall 2005): 85–86, 88.

54. Emory S. Bogardus, "Comparing Racial Distances in Ethiopia, South Africa, and the

United States," *Sociology and Social Research* 52 (1968): 152.

55. U.S. Census Bureau. 2003. *Census of Population and Housing, 2000.* Summary Files 3(SF3) and 4 (SF4). Accessed online at http://factfinder.census.gov.

56. Ilhan Kaya, "Identity and Space: The Case of Turkish Americans," *The Geographical Review* 95 (2005): 431.

57. U.S. Office of Immigration Statistics, *Yearbook of Immigration Statistics: 2006*, Table 3; U.S. Census Bureau, *Ancestry: 2000*, Census 2000 Brief (June 2004), Table 2, pp. 4–5.

58. Michael Luo, "Study of Taxi Drivers Finds More Immigrants at the Wheel," *New York Times* (July 7, 2004), p. B3.

59. Sarah Kershaw, "The 99 Cent American Dream," *New York Times* (January 23, 1997), p. B1.

60. Caroline B. Brettell, "The Spatial, Social, and Political Incorporation of Asian Indian Immigrants in Dallas, Texas," *Urban Anthropology* 34 (2005): 247–80.

61. Adriana J. Umana-Taylor, Ruchi Bhanot, and Nana Shin, "Ethnic Identity Formation among Adolescents: The Critical Role of Families," *Journal of Family Issues* 27 (2006): 390–414.

62. Mona H. Faragallah, Walter R. Schumm, and Farrell J. Webb, "Acculturation of Arab-American Immigrants," *Journal of Comparative Family Studies* 28 (1997): 182–203.

CHAPTER 10

1. Ira De Augustine Reid, *The Negro Immigrant*, reprint ed. (New York: Arno Press 1969), p. 32. First published 1939.

2. See James O. Buswell III, *Slavery, Segregation and Scripture* (Grand Rapids, MI: Eerdmans, 1964); George D. Kelsey, *Racism and the Christian Understanding of Man* (New York: Scribner's, 1965); W. E. B. DuBois, *The World and Africa* (New York: International Publishers, 1965); Keith Irvine, *The Rise of the Colored Races* (New York: Norton, 1970).

3. Irvine, *The Rise of the Colored Races*, p. 13.

4. DuBois, *The World and Africa*, pp. 19–20.

5. See the discussion on p. 100.

6. See the discussion on pp. 96–97.

7. See the discussion on pp. 34–37.

8. C. Vann Woodward, *The Strange Career of Jim Crow*, 3rd ed. (New York: Oxford University Press, 2001).

9. Gunnar Myrdal, *An American Dilemma* (New York: McGraw-Hill, 1964).

10. Ibid., pp. 25–38.

11. Dewey H. Palmer, "Moving North: Migration of Negroes during World War I," *Phylon* 27 (Spring 1967): 52–62.

12. W. E. B. DuBois, *Dusk of Dawn* (New York: Harcourt, Brace, 1940), p. 264.

13. The Supreme Court specifically cited Kenneth B. Clark's study on negative self-image among black schoolchildren. For detailed information on the social scientist's role in the decision, see Kenneth B. Clark, *Prejudice and Your Child*, 2nd ed. (Boston: Beacon Press, 1963).

14. Jerome H. Skolnick, *The Politics of Protest: Violent Aspects of Protest and Confrontation* (Washington, DC: National Commission on the Causes and Prevention of Violence, 1969), pp. 101–02.

15. U.S. Census Bureau, *Statistical Abstract of the United States: 2007* (Washington, DC: U.S. Government Printing Office, 2007), Table 403, p. 255.

16. Lewis M. Killian, *The Impossible Revolution, Phase II* (New York: Random House, 1975), p. 70.

17. Charles Silberman, *Crises in Black and White* (New York: Random House, 1964), p. 8.

18. See Robin M. Williams Jr., "Social Change and Social Conflict: Race Relations in the United States, 1944–1964," *Sociological Inquiry* 35 (Winter 1965): 20–24. See also Stanley Lieberson and Arnold R. Silverman, "The Precipitants and Underlying Conditions of Race Riots," *American Sociological Review* 30 (1965): 887–98.

19. From the *Report of the National Advisory Commission on Civil Disorders* (Washington, DC: U.S. Government Printing Office, 1968).

20. "Major U.S. Racial Disturbances since 1965," *Facts on File* 52 (May 7, 1992): 328.

21. Ibid.

22. See Brian Duffy, "Days of Rage," *U.S. News & World Report* (May 11, 1992), pp. 21–26.

23. Robert L. Boyd, "Black and Asian Self-Employment in Large Metropolitan Areas: A Comparative Analysis," *Social Problems* 37 (May 1990): 268.

24. Ibid., p. 269.

25. See Duffy, "Days of Rage."

26. Richard J. Herrnstein and Charles Murray, *The Bell Curve: The Reshaping of American Life by Differences in Intelligence* (New York: Free Press, 1994).

27. See Tom Morganthus, "IQ: Is It Destiny?" *Newsweek* (October 24, 1994), pp. 50–51.

28. Charles Willie and Howard Taylor, "The Bell Curve Debate," papers presented at Eastern Sociological Society annual meeting, Philadelphia, PA, March 31, 1995.

29. See Thomas Sowell, "New Light on Black I.Q.," *New York Times Magazine* (March 27, 1977), p. 57.

30. Audrey Shuey, *The Testing of Negro Intelligence* (Lynchburg, VA: Bell, 1958), p. 318.

31. Arthur R. Jensen, "How Much Can We Boost I.Q. and Scholastic Achievement?" *Harvard Educational Review* 39 (1969): 1–123. In December 1979, Jensen reexamined this issue, claiming that assumptions about biased tests were inaccurate because mean differences remained despite attempts to raise black test scores; see Arthur R. Jensen, *Bias in Mental Testing* (New York: Free Press, 1980).

32. Sowell, "New Light on Black I.Q.," p. 57.

33. Ossie Davis, "The English Language Is My Enemy," *IRCD Bulletin* 5 (Summer 1969): 13.

34. "African American Vernacular English," Center for Applied Linguistics. Accessed online at www.cal.org/topics/dialects/aae.html [July 23, 2007].

35. College Entrance Examination Board, *National Report: College Bound Seniors, 2006* (New York: CEEB, 2006), Table 7 and Graph 10.

36. U.S. Census Bureau, "Income, Poverty, and Health Insurance Coverage in the United States 2005," *Current Population Reports,* P60–231, August 2006.

37. Diane Pierce, *The Feminization of Poverty: A Second Look* (Washington, DC: Institute for Women's Policy Research, 1989).

38. U.S. Census Bureau, "The Black Population in the United States: March 2004," *Current Population Survey,* PPL–186, Table 17.

39. U.S. Census Bureau, *America's Families and Living Arrangements: 2006,* Table C2.

40. U.S. Census Bureau, "Black Population in the United States: 2002," pp. 5–6.

41. U.S. Census Bureau, "The Black Population in the United States: March 2004," Table 11.2.

42. Ibid., Table 11.3.

43. U.S. Census Bureau, "Annual Statistics: 2006," *Housing Vacancies and Ownership,* Table 20.

44. See Peter Dreier, "The Future of Community Reinvestment," *Journal of the American Planning Association* 69 (2003): 341–53.

45. Penny Loeb, Warren Cohen, and Constance Johnson, "The New Redlining," *U.S. News & World Report* (April 17, 1995), pp. 51–58.

46. "Widespread Redlining Exposed," *New York Amsterdam News* (August 20, 1998), pp. 30–31.

47. See John R. Logan, *Separate and Unequal: The Neighborhood Gap for Blacks and Hispanics in Metropolitan America,* Lewis Mumford Center, October 15, 2004.

48. Tom Larson and Madhu Mohanyt, "Youth Employment, Residential Location, and Neighborhood Jobs: A Study of Los Angeles County," *Review of Black Political Economy* 27 (1999), 33–62; Ted Mouw, "Job Relocation and the Racial Gap in Unemployment in Detroit and Chicago," *American Sociological Review* 65 (2000), 730–53.

49. Richard D. Alba, John R. Logan, and Brian J. Stults, "How Segregated Are Middle-Class African Americans?" *Social Problems* 27 (2000), 543–58.

50. William J. Wilson, *The Declining Significance of Race* (Chicago: University of Chicago Press, 1978).

51. Thomas Sowell, *Ethnic America* (New York: Basic Books, 1981).

52. Carl Gershman, "A Matter of Class," *New York Times Magazine* (October 5, 1980), p. 24.

53. Charles V. Willie, *Caste and Class Controversy,* 2nd ed. (New York: Rowan & Littlefield, 1989).

54. Kenneth B. Clark, "The Role of Race," *New York Times Magazine* (October 5, 1980), p. 25.

55. Bart Landry, *The New Black Middle Class* (Berkeley CA: University of California Press, 1987).

56. See E. Franklin Frazier, *The Black Bourgeoisie: The Rise of a New Middle Class in the United States* (New York: Free Press, 1957) for a critical analysis of this group.

57. Ellis Cose, *The Rage of a Privileged Class: Why Do Prosperous Blacks Still Have the Blues?* reprint ed. (New York: Perennial, 1995).

58. William J. Wilson, *The Truly Disadvantaged: The Inner City, the Underclass, and Public Policy,* reprint ed. (Chicago: University of Chicago Press, 1997). First published 1987.

59. Gary Orfield, "Ghettoization and Its Alternatives," in Paul E. Peterson (ed.), *The New Urban Reality* (Washington, DC: Brookings Institution, 1988), p. 103.

60. Dinesh D'Souza, *The End of Racism* (New York: Free Press, 1996).

61. Stephen Steinberg, *Turning Back* (Boston: Beacon Press, 1996).

62. Jill Quadagno, *The Color of Welfare: How Racism Undermined the War on Poverty* (New York: Oxford University Press, 1996).

63. John R. Logan and Glenn Deane, *Black Diversity in Urban America* (Albany, NY: Lewis Mumford Center for Comparative Urban and Regional Research, 2003).

64. Ibid., Table 6.

65. Suzanne Model and Gene Fisher, "Black–White Unions: West Indians and African Americans Compared," *Demography* 38 (2001): 177–85.

66. Suzanne Model and Gene Fisher, "Unions between Blacks and Whites: England and the U.S. Compared," *Ethnic & Racial Studies* 25 (2002): 728–54.

67. U.S. Office of Immigration Statistics, *Yearbook of Immigration Statistics: 2006* (Washington, DC: U.S. Government Printing Office), Table 2.

68. Jane Regan, "Forest Land in Haiti Fading Fast; Natural Resource Nudged to the Brink," *Miami Herald* (August 5, 2003), p. A1.

69. "Haiti," *Britannica Book of the Year 2007* (Chicago: Encyclopedia Britannica, 2007), p. 594.

70. See Flore Zephir, *The Haitian Americans* (Westport, CT: Greenwood Press, 2004); C. R. Foster, "Creole in Conflict," *Migration Today* 8 (1990): 5–13.

71. See Ken Gelder, "Postcolonial Voodoo," *Postcolonial Studies* 3 (2000): 89–98.

72. Alex Stepick, Guillermo Grenier, Max Castro, and Marvin Dunn, *This Land Is Our Land: Immigrants and Power in Miami* (Berkeley: University of California Press, 2003), pp. 118–122.

73. Melinda Crowley, "Generation X Speaks Out on Civic Engagement and the Decennial Census: An Ethnographic Approach," *Census 2000 Ethnographic Study* (Washington, DC: U.S. Census Bureau, 2003), p. 24.

74. U.S. Census Bureau, Census 2000 Supplemental Survey Summary Tables, PCTO24: Ancestry-First Reported.

75. Milton Vickerman, *Crosscurrents: West Indians and Race* (New York: Oxford University Press, 1998).

76. Crowley, "Generation X Speaks Out," pp. 24–25.

77. See Sherri Grasmuck and Ramon Grosfoguel, "Geopolitics, Economic Niches, and Gendered Social Capital among Recent Caribbean Immigrants in New York City," *Sociological Perspectives* 40 (1997): 339–63.

78. Sam Roberts, "More Africans Enter U.S. than in Days of Slavery," *New York Times* (February 21, 2005), pp. A1, B4.

79. Logan and Deane, *Black Diversity in Urban America,* p. 2.

80. Roberts, "More Africans Enter U.S. than in Days of Slavery," p. A1.

81. Marilyn Halter, *Between Race and Ethnicity: Cape Verdean American Immigrants: 1860–1965* (Champaign: University of Illinois Press, 1993), pp. 120–124.

82. Ibid., p. 88.

83. U.S. Census Bureau, *Census 2000,* Summary File 3.

84. Jane E. Spear, "Cape Verdean Americans." Accessed online at www.everyculture.com/multi/Bu-Dr/Cape-Verdean-Americans.html [July 1, 2007].

85. Population Reference Bureau, *2006 World Population Data Sheet.* Accessed online at www.prb.org [July 1, 2007].

86. U.S. Office of Immigration Statistics, *Yearbook of Immigration Statistics: 2006,* Table 3.

87. U.S. Immigration and Naturalization Service, *Statistical Yearbook 2001* (Washington, DC: U.S. Government Printing Office), Table 20, pp. 76, 79.

88. Kalu Ogbaa, *The Nigerian Americans* (Westport, CT: Greenwood Press, 2003).

89. Vivian Txeng, "Family Interdependence and Academic Adjustment in College: Youth from Immigrant and U.S.-Born Families," *Child Development* 75 (2004): 966–83.

90. Winston James, "Explaining Afro-Caribbean

Social Mobility in the United States: Beyond the Sowell Thesis," *Comparative Studies in Society and History* 44 (2002): 218–62.

91. Reuel R. Robers, "Race-Based Coalitions among Minority Groups: Afro-Caribbean Immigrants and African-Americans in New York City," *Urban Affairs Review* 39 (2004): 283–317.

92. Sara Rimer and Karen W. Arenson, "Top Colleges Take More Blacks, but Which Ones?" *New York Times* (June 24, 2004), pp. A1, A18.

93. Mary C. Waters, *Black Identities: West Indian Immigrant Dreams and American Realities* (Cambridge, MA: Harvard University Press, 1999).

94. Ellis Cose, "The Good News about Black America," *Newsweek* (June 7, 1999), pp. 28–32.

95. Norman K. Denzin, "Lethal Weapons in the Hood," *Perspectives on Social Problems* 12 (2000): 149–79.

96. U.S. Census Bureau, Table MS-3. Interracial Married Couples: 1980 to 2002; published 15 September 2004; available online at www.census.gov/population/www/socdemo/hh-fam.html; and unpublished data.

97. Robert Blauner, "Internal Colonialism and Ghetto Revolt," *Social Problems* 16 (1969): 393–408.

CHAPTER 11

1. Wayne Moquin, *Documentary History of the Mexican Americans* (New York: Bantam Books, 2000).

2. Population Reference Bureau, *2006 World Population Data Sheet.* Accessed online at www.prb.org [July 1, 2007].

3. U.S. Office of Immigration Statistics, *Yearbook of Immigration Statistics: 2006* (Washington, DC: U.S. Government Printing Office), 2006, Table 35, p. 92.

4. José Vasconcelos and Didier T. Jaen, *The Cosmic Race: A Bilingual Edition* (Baltimore: Johns Hopkins University Press, 1997).

5. Lisa A. Flores and Marouf A. Hasian Jr., "Returning to Aztlan and La Raza: Political Communication and the Vernacular Construction of Chicano/a Nationalism," in Alberto González and Dolores Tanno, *Politics,*

Communication, and Culture (Thousand Oaks, CA: Sage, 1997), pp. 186–203.

6. See Rafael L. Ramirez, Rosa E. Casper, and Peter J. Guarnaccia, *What It Means to Be a Man: Reflections of Puerto Rican Masculinity* (New Brunswick, NJ: Rutgers University Press, 1999); Ray Gonzalez (ed.), *Muy Macho: Latino Men Confront Their Manhood* (New York: Anchor, 1996).

7. U.S. Census Bureau, "The Hispanic Population in the United States: March 2004," *Current Population Reports,* Table 9.1.

8. See Ismael Garcia, *Dignidad: Ethnics through Hispanic Eyes* (Nashville, TN: Abingdon Press, 1997).

9. See, for example, Clara Rodriguez, *Changing Race: Latinos, the Census, and the History of Ethnicity* (New York: New York University Press, 2000).

10. For some excellent cross-cultural analyses of attitudes regarding distance between people, see Edward T. Hall, *The Hidden Dimension,* reprint ed. (Mangolia, MA: Smith Publishing, 1992), and *The Silent Language,* reprint ed. (Westport, CT: Greenwood Press, 1980).

11. U.S. Census Bureau, "The Hispanic Population in the United States: March 2004," Table 1.1.

12. U.S. Census Bureau, *Census 2000,* Summary File 1.

13. See Rubén G. Rumbaut, "Origins and Destinies: Immigration to the United States since World War II," *Sociological Forum* 9 (December 1994): 615.

14. U.S. Census Bureau, "The Hispanic Population in the United States: March 2004," Tables 1.1 and 1.2.

15. Ibid., Table 6.1.

16. Kelvin M. Pollard and William P. O'Hare, "America's Racial and Ethnic Minorities," *Population Bulletin* 54 (September 1999): 30.

17. Rubén G. Rumbaut, *Passages to Adulthood: The Adaptation of Children of Immigrants in Southern California* (East Lansing, MI: Michigan State University, 1997).

18. U.S. Census Bureau, *Census 2000 Brief: The Hispanic Population,* pp. 4, 8.

19. See Roberto M. De Anda, *Chicanas and Chicanos in Contemporary Society,* 2nd ed. (Lanham, MD: Rowan & Littlefield, 2004), chaps. 5 and 7.

20. See James Diego Vigil, *From Indians to Chicanos: The Dynamics of Mexican-American Culture*, 2nd ed. (Prospect Heights, IL: Waveland Press, 1997).

21. See David G. Gutierrez, *Walls and Mirrors: Mexican Americans, Mexican Immigrants, and the Politics of Ethnicity* (Berkeley, CA: University of California Press, 1995).

22. Carey McWilliams, with an update by Matt S. Meier (ed.), *North from Mexico* (New York: Praeger, 1990), pp. 247–50.

23. See Rubén Donato, *The Other Struggle for Equal Schools: Mexican Americans during the Civil Rights Era* (Albany, NY: State University of New York Press, 1997).

24. Florence Kluckhohn, *Variations in Value Orientations* (Westport, CT: Greenwood Press, 1973).

25. U.S. Census Bureau, *The Hispanic Population: March 2004*, Tables 9.

26. Elaine M. Allensworth, "Earnings Mobility of First and '1.5' Generation Mexican-Origin Women and Men: A Comparison with U.S.-born Mexican Americans and Non-Hispanic Whites," *International Migration Review* 31 (1997): 386–410.

27. See Peter Skerry, "Racial Politics in the Administrative State," *Society* 42 (2005): 36–45.

28. Joseph A. Rodriguez, "Ethnicity and the Horizontal City: Mexican Americans and the Chicano Movement in San Jose," *Journal of Urban History* 21 (1995), 597–621.

29. National Association of Latino Elected and Appointed Officials, *National Roster of Hispanic Officials*. Accessed online at www.naleo.org/ataglance.html [July 2, 2007].

30. U.S. Census Bureau, *Census 2000 Brief: The Hispanic Population*, p. 4.

31. U.S. Census Bureau, "The Hispanic Population in the United States: 2002," Table 18.2.

32. See, for example, Mira Mayer, "The Dropout Rates of Mexican American Students in Two California Cities," *Research for Educational Reform* 9 (2004): 14–24; Jeffrey C. Wayman, "Student Perceptions of Teacher Ethnic Bias: A Comparison of Mexican American and Non-Latino White Dropouts and Students," *High School Journal* 85 (2002): 27–37.

33. See Clara Rodriguez, *Changing Race: Latinos, the Census, and the History of Ethnicity in the United States*.

34. Ibid., p. 6.

35. Joseph P. Fitzpatrick, *Puerto Rican Americans*, 2nd ed. (Englewood Cliffs, NJ: Prentice Hall, 1987), pp. 106–07.

36. U.S. Bureau of Labor Statistics, *Puerto Rico: State at a Glance.* Accessed online at http://stats.bls.gov/ eag/eag.pr.htm [July 3, 2007].

37. U.S. Census Bureau, *The Hispanic Population: March 2004*, Table 1.2.

38. R. S. Oropesa and Nancy S. Landale, "From Austerity to Prosperity: Migration and Child Poverty among Mainland and Island Puerto Ricans," *Demography* 37 (August 2000): 323–38.

39. Gina M. Prez, *The Near Northwest Side Story: Migration, Displacement, and Puerto Rican Families* (Berkeley: University of California Press, 2004).

40. See Oscar Handlin, *The Uprooted*, 2nd ed. (Philadelphia: University of Pennsylvania Press, 2002), pp. 105–128.

41. Nathan Glazer and Daniel P. Moynihan, *Beyond the Melting Pot*, 2nd ed. (Cambridge, MA: MIT, 1970), pp. 103–04.

42. Andrés I. Pérez y Mena, "Cuban Santería, Haitian Vodun, Puerto Rican Spiritualism," *Journal for Scientific Study of Religion* 32 (1998): 15–27.

43. Larry L. Hunt, "Hispanic Protestantism in the United States: Trends by Decade and Generation," *Social Forces* 77 (1999): 1601–24.

44. Larry L. Hunt, "Race, Gender, and the Hispanic Experience in the United States: Catholic/Protestant Differences in Religious Involvement, Social Status, and Gender-Role Identities," *Review of Religious Research* 43 (2001): 139–60.

45. See H. B. Cavalcanti and Debra Schleef, "The Case for Secular Assimilation: The Latino Experience in Richmond, Virginia," *Journal for the Scientific Study of Religion* 44 (2005): 473–83.

46. U.S. Census Bureau, *Census 2000 Brief: The Hispanic Population*, p. 3.

47. Clara Rodriguez, "Assimilation in the Puerto Rican Communities of the U.S.: A New Focus," paper presented at the 72nd annual meeting of the American Sociological Association, 1977, p. 8.

48. Carol J. Kaufman and Sigfredo A. Hernandez, "The Role of the Bodega in a U.S. Puerto

Rican Community," *Journal of Retailing* 67 (Winter 1991): 378.

49. U.S. Census Bureau, "The Hispanic Population in the United States: March 2004," Table 3.2.

50. Ibid., Tables 4 and 7.

51. Ibid., Table 12.2.

52. U.S. Census Bureaus, "The Hispanic Population in the United States," Table 1.2.

53. Tom Alexander, "Those Amazing Cuban Emigrés," *Fortune Magazine* 74 (October 1966): 144–46.

54. Alejandro Portés and Alex Stepick, *City on the Edge: The Transformation of Miami* (Berkeley: University of California Press, 1993).

55. U.S. Census Bureau, *General Demographic Characteristics: 2000*, p. 44.

56. U.S. Census Bureau, *Census Brief: 2000, The Hispanic Population*, Table 2, p. 4.

57. Marta Diaz Fernandez, "Intergenerational Dynamics in the Cuban Community in Southern Florida: Identity and Politics in the Second Generation," *Cuban Studies* 31 (2001): 76–101.

58. Mireya Navarro, "Black and Cuban-American: Bias in Two Worlds," *New York Times* (September 13, 1997), p. 8.

59. Alejandro Brice, *An Introduction to Cuban Culture for Rehabilitation Service Providers* (Buffalo, NY: Center for International Rehabilitation Research Information & Exchange, 2002), pp. 8–10.

60. U.S. Department of Homeland Security, *Yearbook of Immigration Statistics: 2003*, Table 2, p. 14.

61. Arun P. Lobo, Ronald J. O. Flores, and Joseph J. Salvo, "The Impact of Hispanic Growth on the Racial/Ethnic Composition of New York City Neighborhoods," *Urban Affairs Review* 37 (2002): 703–27.

62. See Nora Hamilton and Norma Stoltz Chinchilla, "Central American Migration: A Framework for Analysis," *Latin American Research Review* 26 (Winter 1991): 75–110.

63. See Cecilia Mejivar, "Family Reorganization in a Context of Legal Uncertainty: Guatemalan and Salvadoran Immigrants in the United States," *International Journal of Sociology of the Family* 32 (2006): 223–45.

64. U.S. Immigration and Naturalization Service, *Statistical Yearbook 1990* (Washington, DC: U.S. Government Printing Office), Table 3, p. 53.

65. Ibid., Table G, p. 101.

66. See Dorothy Norris-Tirrell, "Immigrant Needs and Local Government Services: Implications for Policymakers," *Policy Studies Journal* 30 (2002): 58–69.

67. Mireya Navarro, "After Year in Exile in South Florida, Nicaraguans Feel the Tug of 2 Homes," *New York Times* (March 21, 1995).

68. U.S. Office of Immigration Statistics, *Yearbook of Immigration Statistics: 2006*, Table 2.

69. U.S. Department of Homeland Security, *Yearbook of Immigration Statistics: 2003*, Table 2, p. 14.

70. Charles Hirschman, "The Educational Enrollment of Immigrant Youth: A Test of the Segmented-Assimilation Hypothesis," *Demography* 38 (August 2001): 317–36.

71. Ramon Grosfoguel and Chloe S. Ramon, "'Coloniality of Power' and Racial Dynamics: Notes toward a Reinterpretation of Latino Caribbeans in New York City," *Identities* 7 (March 2000): 85–125.

72. See, for example, Greta A. Gilbertson, Joseph P. Fitzpatrick, and Lijun Yang, "Hispanic Intermarriage in New York City: New Evidence from 1991," *International Migration Review* 30 (Summer 1996): 445–59.

73. Michael J. Rosenfeld, "The Salience of Pan-National Hispanic and Asian Identities in U.S. Marriage Markets," *Demography* 38 (May 2001): 161–75.

74. Ruth Planos, Luis H. Zayas, and Nancy A. Busch-Rossnagel, "Acculturation and Teaching Behaviors of Dominican and Puerto Rican Mothers," *Hispanic Journal of Behavioral Sciences* 17 (May 1995): 225–36.

75. Héctor Cordero-Guzmán and Ramon Grosfoguel, "The Demographic and Socio-Economic Characteristics of Post-1965 Immigrants to New York City: A Comparative Analysis by National Origin," *International Migration* 38 (2000): 41–77.

CHAPTER 12

1. Eileen W. Linder (ed.), *2007 Yearbook of American and Canadian Churches* (Nashville, TN: Abingdon Press, 2007).

2. Mary Rourke, "Redefining Religion in America," *Los Angeles Times* (June 21, 1998), p. 1.

3. Donald E. Miller, *Reinventing American Protestantism: Christianity in the New Millennium* (Berkeley: University of California Press, 1999).

4. David B. Barrett, Todd M. Johnson, and Peter F. Crossing, "Religious Adherents in the United States of America, 1900–2005," *Britannica Book of the Year 2007* (Chicago: Encyclopedia Britannica, 2007), p. 293.

5. Thomas J. Curran, *Xenophobia and Immigration, 1820–1930* (Boston: Twayne, 1975), pp. 12–13.

6. Samuel F. B. Morse, *Imminent Dangers to the Free Institutions of the United States through Foreign Immigration and the Present State of the Naturalization Laws: A Series of Numbers Originally Published in the New York Journal of Commerce Revised and Corrected with Additions*, New York, 1835.

7. Curran, *Xenophobia and Immigration, 1820–1930*, pp. 99–108.

8. Ibid., p. 107.

9. Ibid., pp. 130–31.

10. Ibid., pp. 32–35.

11. John Higham, *Strangers in the Land* (New Brunswick, NJ: Rutgers University Press, 2002), p. 59.

12. Curran, *Xenophobia and Immigration, 1820–1930*, p. 78.

13. See Evelyn L. Lehrer, "Religious Intermarriage in the United States: Determinants and Trends," *Social Science Research* 27 (1998): 245–63; Fran Schumer, "Star-Crossed," *New York* (August 2, 1990), p. 34.

14. James D. Davidson and Tracy Widman, "The Effect of Group Size on Interfaith Marriage among Catholics," *Journal for the Scientific Study of Religion* 41 (2002): 397–404.

15. Lisa A. Keister, "Upward Wealth Mobility: Exploring the Roman Catholic Advantage," *Social Forces* 85 (March 2007): 1195–225.

16. Laurie Goodstein, "Study Sees Church Rebounding from Scandal," *New York Times* (May 18, 2006), p. A16.

17. Oscar Reiss, *The Jews in Colonial America* (Jefferson, NC: McFarland & Company, 2004).

18. Curran, *Xenophobia and Immigration, 1820–1930*, pp. 13, 76–77.

19. Milton L. Barron, "The Incidence of Jewish Intermarriage in Europe and America," *American Sociological Review* 1 (February 1946): 11.

20. See Joseph Brandes, *Immigrants to Freedom* (Philadelphia: University of Pennsylvania Press, 1971); Fred Rosenbaum, *Free to Choose: The Making of a Jewish Community in the American West* (Berkeley: Judah I. Magnes Memorial Museum, 1976).

21. See John Kaufman, *Jew Hatred: Anti-Semitism, Anti-Sexuality, and Mythology in Christianity* (Pomona, CA: Arts Colony Publishers, 2001).

22. Anti-Defamation League, *Audit of Anti-Semitic Incidents*. Accessed online at www.adl.org/PresRele/ASUS_12/4993-12.htm [July 5, 2007].

23. Leonard Dinnerstein and David Reimers, *Ethnic Americans*, 4th ed. (New York: Columbia University Press, 1999).

24. See Bernard C. Rosen, "Evaluation of Occupations: A Reflection of Jewish and Italian Mobility Differences," *American Sociological Review* 22 (1957): 546–53; Thomas Sowell, *Ethnic America*, reprint ed. (New York: Basic Books, 1983), chap. 4.

25. "Distribution of Immigrants," *Senate Documents* 20 (61st Congress, 3rd Session): 47ff.

26. Dinnerstein and Reimers, *Ethnic Americans*, p. 53: "By 1915 Jews comprised 85 percent of the student body at New York's free but renowned City College, one fifth of those attending New York University and one sixth of the students at Columbia."

27. Milton M. Gordon, *Assimilation in American Life* (New York: Oxford University Press, 1964), p. 185.

28. Gerhard Lenski, *The Religious Factor* (New York: Doubleday, 1961), pp. 33–34.

29. John P. Dean, "Patterns of Socialization and Association between Jews and Non-Jews," *Jewish Social Studies* 17 (July 1955): 252–54.

30. Herbert J. Gans, "The Origin and Growth of a Jewish Community in the Suburbs: A Study of the Jews of Park Forest," in Marshall Sklare (ed.), *The Jews: Social Patterns of an American Group* (Glencoe, IL: Free Press, 1958), p. 227.

31. Albert I. Gordon, *Jews in Suburbia* (Boston: Beacon Press, 1956).

32. Milton M. Gordon, *Assimilation in American Life,* pp. 173–224.

33. Two informative articles on more recent Jewish assimilation are Seymour Martin Lipset, "A Unique People in an Exceptional Country," *Society* 28 (November–December 1990): 4–13, and Shmuel A. Eisenstadt, "The Jewish Experience with Pluralism," *Society* 28 (November–December 1990): 21–25.

34. Jack Wertheimer, "Surrendering to Inter-marriage," *Commentary* 111 (March 2001): 25–32.

35. "Intermarriage Rate among U.S. Jews Increases," *Society* 40 (2003): 6.

36. See Chaim I. Waxman, "Whither American Jewry?" *Society* 28 (November–December 1990): 34–41.

37. See Peter Steinfels, "Debating Intermarriage and Jewish Survival," *New York Times* (October 18, 1992), pp. 1, 40.

38. David B. Barrett, Todd M. Johnson, and Peter F. Crossing "Religious Adherents in the United States of America, 1900–2005," p. 293.

39. Sylvia Barack Fishman, "The Changing American Jewish Family," *USA Today* (May 1991), p. 54.

40. See Waxman, "Whither American Jewry?" pp. 40–41.

41. See Hutchins Hapgood, *The Spirit of the Ghetto* (Cambridge, MA: Belknap Press, 1983).

42. See Robert P. Amyot and Lee Seman, "Jews without Judaism? Assimilation and Jewish Identity in the United States," *Social Science Quarterly* 77 (1996): 177–89.

43. See Uzi Rebhun, "Jewish Identification in Contemporary America: Gans' Symbolic Ethnicity and Religiosity Theory Revisited," *Social Compass* 51 (2004): 349–66; Kenneth L. Woodward, "The Intermarrying Kind," *Newsweek* (July 22, 1991), p. 49.

44. Jonathan Ament, *Jewish Immigrants in the United States* (New York: United Jewish Committee, 2004), pp. 3–4.

45. Dean L. May, "Mormons," in Stephan Thernstrom (ed.), *Harvard Encyclopedia of American Ethnic Groups* (Cambridge, MA: Harvard University Press, 1980), pp. 720–21.

46. Joseph Smith, *Pearl of Great Price* (Whitefish, MT: Kessinger Publishing, 2003), pp. 50–51.

47. See Leonard J. Arrington and Davis Bitton, *The Mormon Experience: A History of the Latter-Day Saints,* 2nd ed. (Champaign, IL: University of Illinois Press, 1992).

48. Bruce L. Campbell and Eugene E. Campbell, "The Mormon Family," in Charles H. Mindel, Robert W. Habenstein, and Roosevelt Wright Jr. (eds.), *Ethnic Families in America,* 4th ed. (Upper Saddle River, NJ: Prentice Hall, 1998), p. 484.

49. Sarah Barringer Gordon, *The Mormon Question: Polygamy and Constitutional Conflict in Nineteenth-Century America* (Chapel Hill, NC: University of North Carolina Press, 2001), p. 211.

50. Lester E. Bush, "Mormon Elder's Wafers: Images of Mormon Virility in Patent Medicine Ads," *Dialogue: A Journal of Mormon Thought* 10 (1976): 89–93.

51. Jeffery L. Sheler, "The Mormon Movement," *U.S. News & World Report* (November 11, 2000), pp. 58–65.

52. National Institute for Literacy, *The State of Literacy in America.* Accessed online at www.nifl.gov/reders/reder.htm [July 5, 2007].

53. Church of Jesus Christ of Latter-Day Saints, *The Missionary Program.* Accessed online at www.lds.org/ [July 5, 2007].

54. U.S. Census Bureau, *Statistical Abstract of the United States: 2007,* (Washington, DC: U.S. Government Printing Office, 2007), Table 74, p. 60.

55. Kenneth L. Woodward, "A Mormon Moment," *Newsweek* (September 10, 2001) pp. 44–49; David Van Biema, "Kingdom Come," *Time* (August 4, 1997), pp. 50–57.

56. See Daniel H. Ludlow (ed.), *Encyclopedia of Mormonism,* Vol. 2, "Feminism" (New York: Macmillan, 1992).

57. Alixa Naff, *The Arab Americans* (New York: Chelsea House, 1998), pp. 33, 45.

58. Ibid., p. 73.

59. David B. Barrett, Todd M. Johnson, and Peter F. Crossing, "Religious Adherents in the United States of America, 1900–2005," p. 293. See also "Muslim Life in America," U.S. Department of State. Accessed online at http://usinfo.state.gov/products/pubs/muslimlife/ [July 5, 2007].

60. Naff, *The Arab Americans,* p. 21.

61. Council on American-Islamic Relations, *The Status of Muslim Civil Rights in the United States: 2007*, p. 5. Accessed online at www.cair-net.org/pdf/2007-Civil-Rights-Report.pdf [July 24, 2007].

62. Lisa Miller, "Islam in America: A Success Story," *Newsweek* (July 30, 2007), p. 27.

63. Pew Research Center, "Views of Islam Remain Sharply Divided." Accessed online at http://people-press.org/commentary/display.php3?AnalysisID=96 [July 24, 2007].

64. John A. Hostetler, *Amish Society*, 4th ed. (Baltimore: Johns Hopkins University Press, 1993), pp. 62–65.

65. Ibid., p. 38, 40.

66. Ibid., pp. 138–44.

67. William H. Kephart, *Extraordinary Groups*, 7th ed. (New York: Worth Publishers, 2001), pp. 18–19.

68. Hostetler, *Amish Society*, pp. 276–77.

69. Joshua Kurlantzick, "Goodbye to Amish Country," *Washingtonian* 39 (September 2004): 137–9; Gene Burd, "Amish Enterprise," *Utopian Studies* 2 (2004): 246–50.

70. Tom Shachtman, *Rumspringa: To Be or Not Be Amish* (New York: North Point Press, 2007), pp. 4–9.

71. Ibid. See also Denise M. Reiling, "The 'Simmie' Side of Life: Old Order Amish Youths' Affective Response to Culturally Prescribed Deviance," *Youth and Society* 34 (2002): 146–71.

72. Donald B. Kraybill, *The Riddle of Amish Culture* (Baltimore: Johns Hopkins University Press, 2001), p. 14.

73. "An Amish Exception," *Economist* (February 7, 2004), p. 33.

74. Kephart, *Extraordinary Groups*, p. 46.

75. See Nathaniel S. Murrell, William D. Spencer, and Adrian A. McFarlane, *Chanting Down Babylon: The Rastafari Reader* (Philadelphia: Temple University Press, 1998).

76. Barry Chevannes, *Rastafari: Roots and Ideology* (Syracuse, NY: Syracuse University Press, 1995).

77. Ennis B. Edmonds, *Rastafari: From Outcasts to Culture Bearers* (New York: Oxford University Press, 2003), p. 59.

78. Ibid., p. 61.

79. Ibid., p. 141.

80. The author wishes to thank James Mahon for providing much of this information on Santería.

81. Lewis M. Hopfe, *Religions of the World*, 10th ed. (Upper Saddle River, NJ: Prentice Hall, 2006).

82. *What Is Santería?* Accessed online at www.orishanet.org/santeria.html [July 6, 2007].

83. Albert J. Raboteau, *Slave Religion: The "Invisible Institution" in the Antebellum South*, 2nd ed. (New York: Oxford University Press, 2004), pp. 89–90.

84. *What Is Santería?* (online).

85. Tom Masland and Brook Larmer, "Cuba's Real Religion," *Newsweek* (January 19, 1998), p. 42; Tom Masland, "Learning to Keep the Faith (Religious Revival in Cuba)," *Newsweek* (March 13, 1995), p. 30.

86. Migene Gonzalez-Wippler, *Powers of the Orishas: Santería and the Worship of Saints* (Plainview, NY: Original Publications, 1992), pp. 321–22.

87. "Ebó (Sacrifice)." Accessed online at www.africawithin.com/religion/ebo.html [July 6, 2007].

88. Harry G. Lefever, "When the Saints Go Riding In: Santería in Cuba and the United States," *Journal for the Scientific Study of Religion* 35 (1996): 318–30. See also George A. Mather and Larry A. Nichols, *Dictionary of Cults, Sects, Religions and the Occult* (Grand Rapids, MI: Zondervan, HarperCollins, 1993), p. 240.

89. See Johan Wedel, *Santería Healing: A Journey into the Afro-Cuban World of Divinities, Spirits, and Sorcery* (Gainesville, FL: University Press of Florida, 2003).

90. Raul Canizares, *Walking with the Night: The Afro-Cuban World of Santería,* (Rochester, VT: Destiny Books, 1993), p. 33.

91. A. I. Perez y Mena, *Speaking with the Dead: Development of Afro-Latin Religion among Puerto Ricans in the United States* (New York: AMS Press, 1991); George Brandon, *Santería from Africa to the New World: The Dead Sell Memories* (Bloomington: Indiana University Press, 1993).

92. Elaine De Valle, "Santería Priests Accuse Police of Force," *Miami Herald* (June 28, 2007), p. 1; Anabelle Garay, "Santería Priest's

Suit Highlights Religious, Cultural Clashes," *Associated Press State & Local Wire* (March 24, 2007).

93. Because the Western world's use of AD (Anno Domini, or "Year of Our Lord") and BC (Before Christ) have a Christian orientation, the use of CE (Common Era) and BCE (Before the Common Era) are often used instead, particularly when discussing other religions.

94. *Early History of Hinduism.* Accessed online at www.religioustolerance.org/hinduism.htm [July 6, 2007].

95. *Sacred Texts.* Accessed online at www.religious tolerance.org/hinduism2.htm [July 6, 2007].

96. *Nine Questions about Hinduism.* Accessed online at www.himalayanacademy.com/ resources/books/hbh/hbh_ch-10.html [July 6, 2007].

97. *Hindu Sects and Denominations.* Accessed online at www.religioustolerance.org/ hinduism3.htm [July 6, 2007].

98. Barrett, Johnson, and Crossing, "Religious Adherents in the United States of America, 1900–2005," p. 293.

99. Amber Oliver, "Hinduism in America," Brown University. Accessed online at www.brown.edu/ Departments/AmCiv/Studentprojects/apurva/ index.htm [July 6, 2007].

100. Ibid.

101. The Gallup Organization, *Religion.* Accessed online at www.pollingreport.com/religion.htm [July 27, 2007]; CBS News Poll, "For Almost All Americans, There Is God." Accessed online at www.cbsnews.com/stories/2006/04/ 13/opinion/polls/main1498219.shtml.

102. Charles Moore, "Is Christianity 'Almost Vanquished'?" *Western Catholic Reporter* (October 15, 2001), p. 1.

103. George Yancey, "A Comparison of Religiosity Between European-Americans, African-Americans, Hispanic-Americans, and Asian Americans," *Research in the Social Scientific Study of Religion* 16 (2005): 83–104.

104. See Pamela Schaeffer, "Catholics Show Their Diversity," *National Catholic Reporter* (July 28, 2000), pp. 16–17.

105. See Robert Bellah, "Religion and Legitimation in the American Republic," *Society* 35 (1998): 193–201.

106. Lisa Miller, "Islam in America: A Success Story," p. 26.

107. Ibid.

108. Robert Wuthnow, "The *Religious Factor* Revisited," *Sociological Theory* 22 (2004): 205–18.

CHAPTER 13

1. See Carol Tavris, *Mismeasure of Woman* (Gloucester, MA: Peter Smith Publisher, 1999), pp. 43–54.

2. Gustav LeBon, *Revue d'Anthropologie* (1879), pp. 60–61, quoted in Stephan Jay Gould, *The Mismeasure of Man*, Rev. Exp. ed. (New York: Norton, 1996), p. 1045.

3. Gunnar Myrdal, *An American Dilemma: The Negro Problem and Modern Democracy* (New York: Harper, 1944), pp. 1073–78.

4. Helen M. Hacker, "Women as a Minority Group," *Social Forces* 30 (1951): 60–69.

5. Betty Friedan, *The Feminine Mystique* (New York: W. W. Norton & Company, [1963] 2001.

6. See Carol Berkin, *First Generations: Women in Colonial America* (New York: Hill and Wang, 1997).

7. Vincent N. Parrillo, *Diversity in America*, 2nd ed. (Thousand Oaks, CA: Pine Forge Press, 2005), pp. 21–22.

8. See Mary Kelly, *Private Woman, Public Stage* (Chapel Hill, NC: University of North Carolina Press, 2002).

9. Joyce Cowley, *Pioneers of Women's Liberation* (New York: Merit, 1969), p. 13.

10. Jo Freeman, *The Politics of Women's Liberation* (Lincoln, NE: Universe, 2000), pp. 19–25.

11. Anne Moir, *Brain Sex: The Real Difference between Men and Women* (New York: Carol Publishing, 1992).

12. Tabitha M. Powledge, "Ever Different: Brain Sex Differences, Research Update," *BioScience* 46 (June 1996): 39–95.

13. See Doreen Kimura, *Sex and Cognition* (Cambridge, MA: Bradford Books, 2000).

14. Margaret Mead, *Sex and Temperament in Three Primitive Societies* (New York: Harper Perennial, 2001).

15. See JoNell Strough and Cynthia A. Berg, "Goals as a Mediator of Gender Differences in

High-Affiliation Dyadic Conversations," *Developmental Psychology* 36 (2000): 117–25; Ronald L. Mullis and Ann K. Mullis, "The Effects of Context on Parent-Child Interactions," *Journal of Genetic Psychology* 151 (1990): 341–413.

16. Susan Douglas, *Where the Girls Are* (New York: Random House, 1995); Richard Della Fave, "Sex Differences in Children's Friendships," *American Sociological Review* 43 (1980): 955–70; Erving Goffman, *Gender Advertisements,* rev. ed. (New York: HarperColophon, 1988).

17. Patricia A. Adler, Steven J. Kess, and Peter Adler, "Socialization in Gender Role: Popularity among Elementary School Boys and Girls," *Sociology of Education* 65 (1992): 169–87.

18. See, for example, N. Kenneth Sandnabba, Pekka Santtila, Malin Wannas, and Katja Krook, "Age and Gender Specific Behaviors in Children," *Child Abuse & Neglect* 27 (2003): 579–605.

19. See Estelle Disch, *Reconstructing Gender: A Multicultural Anthology*, 4th ed. (New York: McGraw-Hill, 2005).

20. See Scott Coltrane and Melinda Messineo, "The Perpetuation of Subtle Prejudice: Race and Gender Imagery in 1990s Television Advertising," *Sex Roles* 42 (2000): 363–89.

21. See, for example, Douglas, *Where the Girls Are,* p. 303.

22. Jean Kilbourne, *Can't Buy My Love: How Advertising Changes the Way We Think and Feel* (New York: Free Press, 2000), pp. 290–91.

23. See, for example, Martha M. Lauzen and David M. Dozier, "Recognition and Respect Revisited: Portrayals of Age and Gender in Prime-Time Television," *Mass Communication and Society* 8 (2005): 241–56.

24. Erving Goffman, *Gender Advertisements* (New York: HarperColophon, 1979), p. viii.

25. Media Report to Women, *Industry Statistics.* Accessed online at www.mediareporttowomen.com/statistics.htm [July 6, 2007].

26. Lillian B. Rubin, *Worlds of Pain: Life in the Working-Class Family,* reprint ed. (New York: Basic Books, 1992).

27. Lillian B. Rubin, *Families on the Fault Line* (New York: HarperCollins, 1995), pp. 71–75; see also Patricia R. Pessar, "On the Homefront and in the Workplace: Integrating Immigrant Women into Feminist Discourse," *Anthropological Quarterly* 68 (1995): 37–47.

28. James H. Johnson Jr., Elisa J. Bienenstock, Walter C. Farrell, and Jennifer L. Walter, "Bridging Social Networks and Female Labor Force Participation in a Multiethnic Metropolis," in Lawrence D. Bobo et al. (eds.), *Prismatic Metropolis: Inequality in Los Angeles* (New York: Russell Sage Foundation, 2000), pp. 383–416.

29. Morrison G. Wong, "The Chinese American Family," in Charles H. Mindel, Robert W. Habenstein, and Roosevelt Wright, Jr. (eds.), *Ethnic Families in America,* 4th ed. (New York: Elsevier, 1998), p. 301.

30. Harry H. L. Kitano, "The Japanese American Family," in ibid., p. 319.

31. See Margaret M. Porter and Arline M. Bronzaft, "Do the Future Plans of Educated Black Women Include Black Mates?" *Journal of Negro Education* 64 (1995): 162–70.

32. bell hooks, *Ain't I a Woman: Black Women and Feminism* (Boston: South End Press, 1981), p. 195.

33. Kimberly Springer, "Third Wave Black Feminism," *Signs* 27 (2002): 1059–82.

34. Ula Y. Taylor, "Making Waves: The Theory and Practice of Black Feminism," *Black Scholar* 28 (1998), 18–28.

35. Marilyn J. Davidson, *The Black and Ethnic Minority Woman Manager: Cracking the Concrete Ceiling* (London: Paul Chapman Publishing, 1997).

36. C. P. Gilman, *Women and Education* (1911) in Nancy Reeves (ed.), *Womankind: Beyond the Stereotypes,* 2nd ed. (Chicago: Aldine, 1983), p. 301.

37. See Debra Viadero, "AAUW Study Finds Girls Making Some Progress, but Gaps Remain," *Education Week* (October 14, 1998), p. 9.

38. Myra P. Sadker and David M. Sadker, *Teachers, Schools, and Society,* 7th ed. (New York: McGraw-Hill, 2004).

39. See Teresa Méndez, "A Bid to Boost Single-Sex Classrooms," *Christian Science Monitor* (May 25, 2004), p. 11.

40. Population Reference Bureau, *2007 U.S. Population Data Sheet* (Washington, DC: Population Reference Bureau, 2007).

41. Ibid., Table 585, p. 380.

42. Peter T. Kilborn, "For Many in Work Force, 'Glass Ceiling' Still Exists," *New York Times* (March 16, 1995), p. A22.

43. "Women CEOs for FORTUNE 500 Companies." Accessed at http://money.cnn.com/magazines/fortune/fortune500/womenceos/ [July 8, 2007].

44. Alix Stuart, "What Women Want," *CFO* Magazine (June 1, 2006). Accessed December 15, 2007. [www.cfo.com/article.cfm/6970016?f=search].

45. Elizabeth Kelleher, "In Dual-Earner Couples, Family Roles Are Changing in U.S." (March 21, 2007). Accessed online at usinfo.state.gov [July 16, 2007].

46. Arlie Russell Hochschild, with Anne Machung, *Second Shift: Working Parents and the Revolution at Home*, reissue ed. (New York: Viking Penguin, 2003).

47. Jeanne A. Batalova and Philip N. Cohen, "Premarital Cohabitation and Housework: Couples in Cross-National Perspective," *Journal of Marriage & Family* 64 (2002): 743–55.

48. U.S. Department of Labor, *Employment & Earnings*, June 2007, Table 39.

49. Linda Wirth, *Breaking Through the Glass Ceiling: Women in Management* (London: International Labour Office, 2001).

50. Computed from U.S. Census Bureau, *Income, Poverty, and Health Insurance Coverage in the United States: 2005* (August 2006), PINC-04.

51. See Carol Hymowitz, "While Some Women Choose to Stay Home, Others Gain Flexibility," *Wall Street Journal* (March 30, 2004), p. B1.

52. Marcia K. Meyers, Theresa Heintze, and Douglas A. Wolf, "Child Care Subsidies and the Employment of Welfare Recipients," *Demography* 39 (2002): 165–79.

53. U.S. Census Bureau, *Current Population Survey: 2006*, Table POV02.

54. Quoted in Linda Lemoncheck and James P. Sterba, *Sexual Harassment: Issues and Answers* (New York: Oxford University Press, 2001), pp. 198–99.

55. See, for example, Pamela P. Stokes and Sue Stewart-Belle, "The Supreme Court Holds Class on Sexual Harassment: How to Avoid a Failing Grade," *Employee Responsibilities & Rights Journal* 12 (June 2000): 79–91.

56. Gloria Borger and Ted Gest, "The Untold Story," *U.S. News & World Report* (October 12, 1992), pp. 28–37.

57. Michele Ingrassia, "Abused and Confused," *Newsweek* (October 25, 1993), p. 57.

58. See Heather Antecol and Deborah Cobb-Clark, "The Changing Nature of Employment-Related Sexual Harassment," *Industrial and Labor Relations Review* 57 (2004): 443–61.

59. Rosalind J. Dworkin, "A Woman's Report," in Anthony G. Dworkin and Rosalind J. Dworkin (eds.), *The Minority Report,* 3rd ed. (Belmont, CA: Wadsworth, 1999).

60. Debbie R. Sandler, "Sexual Harassment Rulings Less Than Meets the Eye," *HRMagazine* 43 (October 1998): 136–38; Lloyd R. Cohen, "Sexual Harassment and the Law," *Society* 28 (1991): 8–13.

61. "Women in Elective Office 2007," Center for American Women and Politics. Accessed online at www.cawp.rutgers.edu/Facts/html [July 16, 2007].

62. See Amy H. Handlin, *Whatever Happened to the Year of the Woman? Why Women Still Aren't Making It to the Top in Politics* (Philadelphia: Arden Press, 1998).

63. Mary C. Banwart, Dianne G. Bystrom, and Terry Robertson, "From the Primary to the General Election," *American Behavioral Scientist* 46 (2003): 658–76.

64. See Katha Pollitt, "HRC: Can't Get No Respect," *The Nation* 283 (November 20, 2006): 12.

65. Talcott Parsons and Robert Bales, *Family, Socialization, and Interaction Process* (Glencoe, IL: Free Press, 1955).

66. Friedrich Engels, *The Origin of the Family, Private Property, and the State* (New York: International Publishers, 1993).

67. See Leonore Davidoff, *Worlds Between: Historical Perspectives on Gender and Class* (New York: Routledge, 1995).

68. See Malcolm Waters (ed.), *Modernity: Critical Concepts,* vol. 2. *Cultural Modernity* (New York: Routledge, 1999).

69. Robert L. Nelson and William P. Bridges, *Legalizing Gender Inequality: Courts, Markets, and Unequal Pay for Women* (Portchester, NY: Cambridge University Press, 1999).

70. See, for example, David W. Wright and Robert Young, "The Effects of Family Structure and Maternal Employment on the Development of Gender-Related Attitudes among Men and Women," *Journal of Family Issues* 19 (1998): 300–14.

CHAPTER 14

1. Ann Karlen, *Sexuality and Homosexuality* (New York: W.W. Norton, 1971), p. 34.
2. Gilbert H. Herdt, ed., *Ritualized Homosexuality in Melanesia* (Berkeley: University of California Press, 1984.
3. Laud Humphries, *Tearoom Trade: Impersonal Sex in Public Places* (New York: Aldine de Gruyter, 1970), p. 121.
4. S. Krieger, "Lesbian Identity and Community: Recent Social Science Literature," *Signs* 8 (1982): 91–108.
5. Simon LeVay, "A Difference in Hypothalamic Structure between Heterosexual and Homosexual Men," *Science* 253 (1991): 1034–1037.
6. Laura S. Allen and Roger A. Gorski, "Sexual Orientation and the Size of the Anterior Commissure in the Human Brain, "*Proceedings of the National Academy of Science 9* (1992): 7199–202.
7. Dean Hamer and Peter Copeland, *The Science of Desire: The Search for the Gay Gene and the Biology of Behavior* (New York: Simon & Schuster, 1994).
8. George Rice, Carol Anderson, Neil Risch, and George Ebers, "Male Homosexuality: Absence of Linkage to Microsatellite Markers at Xq28: *Science* 284 (1999): 665–67.
9. Barbara L. Frankowski, "Sexual Orientation and Adolescents," *Pediatrics* 113 (June 2004): 1827–832.
10. George Chauncey, *Gay in New York: Gender, Urban Culture, and the Making of the Gay Male World: 1890–1940* (New York: Basic Books, 1994).
11. Ibid., p. 9.
12. Eric Marcus, *Making History: The Struggle for Gay and Lesbian Equal Rights* (New York: HarperCollins, 1992).
13. Martin B. Duberman, *Stonewall* (New York: Dutton, 1993).

14. Gregory M. Herek and Kevin T. Berrill, *Hate Crimes: Confronting Violence Against Lesbians and Gay Men* (Newbury Park, CA: Sage, 1992); John Gagnon, Cathy Greenblat, and Michael Kimmel, *Human Sexualities*, 2nd ed. (Boston: Allyn & Bacon, 1995); W.R. Greer, "Violence Against Homosexuals Rising, Groups Seeking Wider Protection Say," *New York Times* (November 23, 1986), p. A36.
15. Valerie Jenness, "Social Movement Growth, Domain Expansion, and Framing Processes," *Social Problems* 42 (1995): 145–70.
16. Steven A. Holmes, "Gay Rights Advocates Brace for Ballot Fights," *New York Times* (January 12, 1994): p. A17.
17. Wilbur J. Scott and Sandra Carson Stanley (eds.), *Gays and Lesbians in the Military: Issues, Concerns, and Contrasts* (New York: Aldine de Gruyter, 1994).
18. Stephen Benjamin, "Don't Ask, Don't Translate," *New York Times* (June 8, 2007).
19. Priscilla Painton, "The Shrinking Ten Percent," *Time* (April 26, 1993), pp. 27–29.
20. Robert T. Michael, John H. Gagnon, Edward O. Laumann, and Gina Kolata, *Sex in America: A Definitive Survey* (Boston: Little, Brown, 1994).
21. Gary R. Hicks and Tien-tsung Lee, "Public Attitudes Toward Gays and Lesbians: Trends and Predictors," *Journal of Homosexuality* 51 (2006): 57–77.
22. "Gay Rights: People's Chief Concerns," PublicAgenda. Accessed online at www.pubicagenda.com/issues [June 9, 2007].
23. Thomas F. Pettigrew, "Intergroup Contact Theory," *Annual Review of Psychology* 49 (1998): 65–85.
24. "Straight Talk about Gays," *U.S. News & World Report* (July 5, 1993): p. 46.
25. NORC, *General Social Surveys, 1972–2006: Cumulative Casebook* (Chicago: National Opinion Research Center, 2007).
26. "Gay Rights: People's Chief Concerns," Public Agenda. Accessed online at www.pubicagenda.com/issues [June 9, 2007].
27. Noelle Knox, "European Gay Union Trends Influence U.S. Debate," *USA Today* (July 14, 2004), p. 5A.

28. "Longitudinal U.S. Public Opinion Polls: Same-Sex Marriage (SSM)." Accessed online at www.religioustolerance.org/hom_poll5.htm [June 9, 2007].

29. Cheryl L. Meyer, "Legal, Psychological, and Medical Considerations in Lesbian Parenting," *Law & Sexuality* 2 (1992): 239–40.

30. Gary Gates, Lee M.V. Badgett, Jennifer Ehrle Macomber, and Kate Chambers, *Adoption and Foster Care by Lesbian and Gay Parents in the United States*, Urban Institute (March 27, 2007). Accessed online at www.urban.org/url.cfm?ID= 411437 [June 10, 2007].

31. United Nations, *Human Functioning and Disability*. Accessed online at http://unstats.un.org/unsd/demographic/sconcerns/disability/default.htm [June 6, 2007]; World Health Organization, *Disability and Rehabilitation Team*. Accessed online at www.who.int/disabilities/en/ [June 5, 2007].

32. Jim Dickson, "People with Disabilities: The Sleeping Giant of American Politics," *Civil Rights Journal* 6 (2002): 44–45.

33. Deborah Kaplan, *The Definition of Disability*, The Center for an Accessible Society. Accessed online at www.accessiblesociety.org/topics/demographics-identity/dkaplanpaper.htm [June 4, 2007].

34. "Disability History Timeline," Disability Social History Project. Accessed online at www.disabilityhistory.org/timeline_new.html [June 11, 2007].

35. George H.W. Bush, *Remarks of President George Bush at the Signing of the Americans with Disabilities Act*. Accessed online at www.eeoc.gov/ada/bushspeech.html [June 6, 2007].

36. M.V. Castañeto and E.W. Willemsen, "Social Perception of the Development of Disabled Children," *Child: Care, Health & Development* 33 (May 2007): 308–18; Dawn Stanton, "Less Than Human," *Psychology Today* 40 (January/February 2007): 18; Joan Fleitas, "Sticks, Stones, and the Stigmata of Childhood Illness and Disability," *Reclaiming Children and Youth* 9 (2000): 146–50.

37. National Organization on Disability, *Landmark Disability Survey Finds Pervasive Disadvantages (June 25, 2004)*. Accessed online at www.nod.org [June 11, 2007].

38. U.S. Equal Employment Opportunity Commission, *Americans with Disabilities Act of 1990 (ADA) Charges*. Accessed online at www.eeoc.gov/stats/ada-charges.html [June 11, 2007].

39. See Richard K. Scotch, *From Good Will to Civil Rights: Transforming Federal Disability Policy*, 2nd ed. (Philadelphia: Temple University Press, 2001).

40. Alex Comfort, "Age Prejudice in America," *Social Policy* 17 (1976): 3–8.

41. Wan He, Manisha Sengupta, Victoria A. Velkoff , and Kimberly A. De Barros, U.S. Census Bureau, Current Population Reports, P23–209, *65+ in the United States: 2005* (Washington, DC: U.S. Government Printing Office, 2005), p. 12.

42. Ibid., p. 13.

43. Ibid., pp. 6–7.

44. Ibid., p. 3.

45. Wan He, et al., *65+ in the Untied States: 2005*, pp. 127–30.

46. National Center for Health Statistics, *Health, United States, 2006*, Table 27, p. 176.

47. Wan He, et al., *65+ in the United States: 2005*, p. 14.

48. U.S. Census Bureau, "Age and Sex for States and for Puerto Rico: April 1, 2000 to July 1, 2005," published August 4, 2006. Accessed online at www.census.gov/popest/states/asrh/SC-EST2005-02.html [June 6, 2007].

49. See, for example, Michael Butler, *Why Survive? Being Old in America*. Baltimore: Johns Hopkins University Press, 2002.

50. Wan He, et al., *65+ in the United States: 2005*, p. 151.

51. National Center for Health Statistics, *Health, United States, 2006*, Table 46, pp. 230–32.

52. See Susan M. Hillier and Georgia M. Barrow, *Aging, the Individual, and Society* 8th ed. (New York: Wadsworth, 2006), pp. 27–28.

53. S.A.H. van Hooren, A.M. Valentin, H. Bosma, R.W. Ponds, M.P. van Boxtel, and J. Jolles, "Cognitive Functioning in Healthy Older Adults Aged 64–81: A Cohort Study into the Effects of Age, Sex, and Education," *Aging, Neuropsychology & Cognition* 14 (January 2007): 40–54.

54. "Live Longer, Feel Younger," *Consumer Reports on Health* 11 (March 1999): 1, 3.

55. William Masters and Virginia Johnson, *Human Sexual Inadequacy* (Boston: Little, Brown, 1970).

56. Terrie Beth Ginsberg, Sherry C. Pomerantz, and Veronika Kramer-Feeley, "Sexuality in Older Adults: Behaviours and Preferences," *Age & Ageing* 34 (September 2005): 475–480; S. Umidi, M. Pini, M. Ferretti, C. Vergani, and G. Annoni, "Affectivity and Sexuality in the Elderly: Often Neglected Aspects," *Archives of Gerontology & Geriatrics* 44 (May 2007): 413–17.

57. Susan Sontag, The Double Standard of Aging" pp. 19–24 in *The Other Within Us: Feminist Explorations of Women and Aging*, edited by Marilyn Pearsall (Boulder, CO: Westview Press, 1997).

58. Wan He, et al., *65+ in the United States, 2005*, p. 92.

59. David Neumark, "Age Discrimination Legislation in the United States," NBER Working Paper No. 8152 (Cambridge, MA: National Bureau of Economic Research).

60. Sara E. Rix, "Update on the Older Worker: 2002," Public Policy Institute, American Association of Retired Persons.

61. Jill Quadragno and M. Hardy, "Regulating Retirement Through the Age Discrimination in Employment Act," *Research on Aging* 13 (1991): 470–75.

62. James M. Pethokoukis, "The Economy May Face Shortage of Qualified Workers," *U.S. News & World Report* (June 12, 2006), pp. 46–47.

63. "At Chrysler Unit, Buyouts for Older Workers," *New York Times* (February 24, 2007), p. C2.

64. Wan He, et al., *65+ in the United States, 2005*, pp. 101–04.

65. Ibid., pp. 108–09.

66. Kathryn H. Porter, Kathy Larin, and Wendell Primus, *Social Security and Poverty among the Elderly: A National and State Perspective* (Washington, DC: Center of Budget and Policy Priorities, 1999); Robert Haveman, Karen Holden, Kathryn Wilson, and Barbara Wolfe, "Social Security, Age of Retirement, and Economic Well-Being: Intertemporal and Demographic Patterns among Retired-Worker Beneficiaries," *Demography* 40 (2003): 369–94.

67. Kathryn H. Porter, Kathy Larin, and Wendell Primus, *Social Security and Poverty among the Elderly: A National and State Perspective* (Washington, DC: Center of Budget and Policy Priorities, 1999); Robert Haveman, Karen Holden, Kathryn Wilson, and Barbara Wolfe, "Social Security, Age of Retirement, and Economic Well-Being: Intertemporal and Demographic Patterns among Retired-Worker Beneficiaries," *Demography* 40 (2003): 369–94.

68. Janet M. Wilmoth, "Living Arrangements among Older Immigrants in the United States," *The Gerontologist* 41 (2001): 228–38.

69. National Center for Health Statistics, *Health, United States, 1999, with Health and Aging Chartbook* (Hyattsville, MD: U.S. Government Printing Office, 1999); Joseph Dalaker, *Poverty in the United States: 1998*, Current Population Reports, P60–207, U.S. Census Bureau (Washington, DC: U.S. Government Printing Office, 1999).

70. "More Resources for Rural Elderly," *Aging* 366 (1994): 69–70.

71. Wan He, et al., *65+ in the United States, 2005*, p. 138.

72. Iver Peterson, "As Taxes Rise, Suburbs Work to Keep Elderly," *New York Times* (February 27, 2001), p. A1.

73. Robyn I. Stone, "Long-Term Care for the Elderly with Disabilities: Current Policy, Emerging Trends, and Implications for the 21st Century," *Milbank Memorial Fund*, 2000.

74. See, for example, Dana Goldman, *Health Status and Medical Treatment of the Future Elderly: Final Report* (Washington, DC: RAND Corporation, 2004).

75. Gregg A. Warshaw and Elizabeth J. Bragg, "The Training of Geriatricians in the United States: Three Decades of Progress," *Journal of the American Geriatrics Society* 51 (2003): S338-S345.

76. Ernest M. Burgess, *Aging in Western Societies* (Chicago: University of Chicago Press, 1978).

77. Robert J. Havighurst, "Successful Aging," *Gerontologist* 1 (1981): 8–13.

78. Chaonan Chen, "Revisiting the Disengagement Theory with Differentials in the Determinations of Life Satisfaction," *Social Indicators Research* 64 (2003): 209–24; Michael Butler, *Why Survive? Being Old in America*.

79. Robert C. Atchley and Amanda Barusch, *Social Forces and Aging*, 10th ed. (Belmont, CA: Wadsworth, 2003).

80. See Alison P. Lenton and Angela Bryan, "An Affair to Remember: The Role of Sexual Scripts in Perception of Sexual Intent," *Personal Relationships* 12 (2005): 483–98.

81. For a fuller discussion, see Edwin Lemert, *Social Pathology: A Systematic Approach to the Theory of Sociopathic Behavior* (New York: McGraw-Hill, 1951).

CHAPTER 15

1. Mary C. Sengstock, "Social Change in the Country of Origin as a Factor in Immigrant Conceptions of Nationality," *Ethnicity* 4 (1977): 54–69.

2. Vincent N. Parrillo, "Asian Americans in American Politics," in Joseph S. Roucek and Bernard Eisenberg (eds.), *America's Ethnic Politics* (Westport, CT: Greenwood Press, 1982), pp. 89–112.

3. José Itzigsohn, "Immigration and the Boundaries of Citizenship: The Institutions of Immigrants' Political Transnationalism," *International Migration Review* 34 (2000): 1126–54.

4. Sheila E. Henry, "Ethnic Identity, Nationalism, and International Stratification: The Case of the African American," *Journal of Black Studies* 29 (1999): 438–54.

5. Sengstock, "Social Change in the Country of Origin as a Factor in Immigrant Conceptions of Nationality," pp. 56–57.

6. Ibid., pp. 61, 64.

7. Marcus L. Hansen, "The Third Generation in America," *Commentary* 14 (1952): 492–500.

8. Marcus L. Hansen, "The Third Generation," in Oscar Handlin (ed.), *Children of the Uprooted* (New York: Harper & Row, 1966).

9. Peter Skerry, "Do We Really Want Immigrants to Assimilate?" *Society* 37 (2000): 57–62.

10. Neil C. Sandberg, *Ethnic Identity and Assimilation: The Polish-American Community* (New York: Praeger, 1974).

11. John P. Roche, "Suburban Ethnicity: Ethnic Attitudes and Behavior among Italian Americans in Two Suburban Communities," *Social Science Quarterly* 63 (1982): 145–53.

12. Sean Valentine, "Self-Esteem, Cultural Identity, and Generation Status as Determinants of Hispanic Acculturation," *Hispanic Journal of Behavioral Sciences* 23 (2001): 459–68.

13. Alejandro Portés and Dag MacLeod, "What Shall I Call Myself? Hispanic Identity Formation in the Second Generation," *Ethnic and Racial Studies* 19 (1996): 523–47.

14. Nazli Kibria, "The Construction of 'Asian American': Reflections on Intermarriage and Ethnic Identity among Second-Generation Chinese and Korean Americans," *Ethnic and Racial Studies* 30 (1997): 523–44.

15. See Reed Ueda, "American National Identity and Race in Immigrant Generations: Reconsidering Hansen's 'Law'" *Journal of Interdisciplinary History* 22 (1992): 483–91.

16. Harold J. Abramson, "The Religioethnic Factor and the American Experience: Another Look at the Three-Generation Hypothesis," *Ethnicity* 2 (1975): 163–77.

17. Ibid., p. 173.

18. Thomas Sowell, *Ethnic America: A History* (New York: Basic Books, 1983).

19. Stephen Steinberg, *The Ethnic Myth: Race, Ethnicity, and Class in America* (New York: Atheneum, 1982).

20. See, for example, Vincent N. Parrillo, "Asian Americans in American Politics."

21. Nina Glick Schiller, Linda Basch, and Cristina Blanc-Szanton, "Transnationalism: A New Analytic Framework for Understanding Migration," in N. Glick Schiller, L. Basch, and C. Blanc-Szanton (eds.), *Towards a Transnational Perspective on Migration: Race, Class, Ethnicity, and Nationalism Reconsidered* (New York: New York Academy of Sciences, 1992), pp. 1–24.

22. Thomas Faist, "Transnationalization in International Migration: Implications for the Study of Citizenship and Culture," *Ethnic & Racial Studies* 23 (2000): 189–222.

23. "Immigrant Temporalities: Transnationalism, the Diaspora, Exiles, and Refugees," *National*

Center for English Language Acquisition. Accessed online at www.ncela.gwu.edu/pathways/immigration/transnationalism.htm [October 31, 2004].

24. Glick Schiller et al., chaps. 1 and 8.

25. Pierre Bourdieu and Loïc Wacquant, *An Invitation to Reflexive Sociology* (Chicago: University of Chicago Press, 1992), p. 119.

26. Patricia M. Fernández-Kelly, "Social Capital and Cultural Capital in the Urban Ghetto: Implications for the Economic Sociology of Immigration," in Alejandro Portés (ed.), *Economic Sociology of Immigration* (New York: Russell Sage Foundation, 1995).

27. Alejandro Portés (ed.), *The Economic Sociology of Immigration* (New York: Russell Sage Foundation, 1999); Ivan Light and Stavros Karageorgis, "The Ethnic Economy," in Neil Smelser and Richard Swedberg (eds.), *Handbook of Economic Sociology* (Princeton, NJ: Princeton University Press, 1994).

28. Alejandro Portés and Min Zhou, "The New Second Generation: Segmented Assimilation and Its Variants," *Annals of the American Political and Social Sciences* 530 (1993): 74–96.

29. Roger Waldinger and Cynthia Feliciano, "Will the New Second Generation Experience 'Downward Assimilation'? Segmented Assimilation Re-Assessed," *Ethnic & Racial Studies* 27 (2004): 376–402.

30. Charles Herschman, "The Educational Enrollment of Immigrant Youth: A Test of the Segmented-Assimilation Hypothesis," *Demography* 38 (2001): 317–36.

31. Reynolds Farley and Richard Alba, "The New Second Generation in the United States," *International Migration Review* 36 (2002): 669–90.

32. Herschman, "The Educational Enrollment of Immigrant Youth."

33. Min Zhou and Carl L. Bankston, "The Social Adjustment of Vietnamese American Adolescents: Evidence of a Segmented-Assimilation Approach," *Social Science Quarterly* 78 (1997): 508–13.

34. Mary C. Waters, *Black Identities: West Indian Immigrant Dreams and American Realities* (Cambridge, MA: Harvard University Press, 1999).

35. Julia Preston, "Surge Seen in Applications for Citizenship," *New York Times* (July 5, 2007), p. A1.

36. William L. Yancey, Eugene P. Ericksen, and Richard N. Juliani, "Emergent Ethnicity: A Review and Reformulation," *American Sociological Review* 41 (June 1976): 391–403.

37. Ibid., p. 393.

38. See Itzigsohn, "Immigration and the Boundaries of Citizenship."

39. Stanley Lieberson and Mary C. Waters, "The Location of Ethnic and Racial Groups in the United States," *Sociological Forum* 2 (1987): 780–810.

40. U.S. Office of Immigration Statistics, *Yearbook of Immigration Statistics: 2006* (Washington, DC: U.S. Government Printing Office), Table 4.

41. Marc J. Perry and Jason P. Schachter, "Migration of Natives and the Foreign Born: 1995 to 2000," *Census 2000 Special Reports* (August 2003).

42. Ibid., Table 1, p. 3.

43. Robert E. Park, "The Urban Community as a Spatial Pattern and a Moral Order," in Ernest W. Burgess (ed.), *The Urban Community* (Chicago: University of Chicago Press, 1926), pp. 3–18.

44. Douglas S. Massey and Nancy A. Denton, "Spatial Assimilation as a Socioeconomic Outcome," *American Sociological Review* 50 (1985): 94–105.

45. Richard D. Alba, *Ethnic Identity: The Transformation of White America* (New Haven, CT: Yale University Press, 1990).

46. Richard D. Alba, *Italian Americans: Into the Twilight of Ethnicity* (Englewood Cliffs, NJ: Prentice Hall, 1985), pp. 159–75.

47. Yancey, Ericksen, and Juliani, "Emergent Ethnicity," p. 399.

48. See Herbert J. Gans, "Symbolic Ethnicity and Symbolic Religiosity: Towards a Comparison of Ethnic and Religious Acculturation," *Ethnic and Racial Studies* 17 (1994): 577–92.

49. Philip Martin and Elizabeth Midgley, "Immigration: Shaping and Reshaping America," *Population Bulletin* 61(4) (December 2006): 19.

50. Steven A. Camarota, "Immigrant Job Gains and Native Job Losses 2000 to 2004," Center for Immigration Studies. Accessed online at

www.cis.org/articles/2005/sactestimony 050405.html [July 10, 2007]; David Card, "Is the New Immigration Really So Bad?" *The Economic Journal* 115 (2005): 300–23.

51. "Immigration." Accessed online at www.pollingreport.com/immigration.htm [July 17, 2007].

52. George J. Borjas and Leonard F. Katz, "The Evolution of the Mexican-American Workforce in the United States," National Bureau of Economic Research, NBER Working Paper No. 11281 (April 2005).

53. Tyler Cowen and Daniel M. Rothschild, "Don't Bad-Mouth Unskilled Immigrants," *Reason* 38:4 (2006): 42–44.

54. Tamar Jacoby, "Immigration Nation," *Foreign Affairs* 85:6 (2006): 50–65.

55. Ibid.

56. Martin and Midgley, "Immigration: Shaping and Reshaping America," pp. 26–27.

57. Cowen and Rothschild, "Don't Bad-Mouth Unskilled Immigrants."

58. "Immigration." Accessed online at www.pollingreport.com/immigration.htm [July 17, 2007].

59. "Immigration: Overview." Accessed online at www.publicagenda.com/issues [July 17, 2007].

60. "Immigration." Accessed online at www.pollingreport.com/immigration.htm [July 17, 2007].

61. U.S. Citizenship and Immigration Services, *About Us*. Accessed online at www.uscis.gov/portal/site/uscis [July 18, 2007].

62. Jeffrey Passel, "The Size and Characteristics of the Unauthorized Migrant Population in the United States," Pew Hispanic Center Research Center (June 14, 2005), p. 5.

63. Ibid., p. 6.

64. Mary Dougherty, Denise Wilson, and Amy Wu, "Immigration Enforcement Actions: 2005" (Washington, DC: Office of Immigration Statistics, 2006), Table 3.

65. Philip Martin, "The Battle over Unauthorized Immigration to the United States," Population Reference Bureau (April 11, 2006): 1.

66. Hyon B. Shin and Rosalind Bruno, "Language Use and English-Speaking Ability: 2000," *Census 2000 Brief* (October 2003).

67. U.S. Department of Education, National Center for Education Statistics, *The Condition of Education: 2006* (Washington, DC: U.S. Government Printing Office, 2006), p. 34.

68. Michael Fix, "Immigrant Children, Urban Schools, and the No Child Left Behind Act," Migration Policy Institute (November 2005).

69. Marnie Shaul, "Four Overlapping Programs Could Be Consolidated," *FDCH Government Account Reports* (May 14, 2001).

70. See Vickie W. Lewelling, "Official English and English Plus: An Update," *ERIC Digest*. Accessed online at www.cal.org/resources/digest/lewell01.html [July 18, 2007].

71. Christine H. Rossell and Keith Baker, "The Educational Effectiveness of Bilingual Education," *Research in the Teaching of English* 30 (1996): 7–74.

72. Kendra Hamilton, "Bilingual or Immersion?" *Diverse Issues in Higher Education* 23 (2006): 23–26.

73. Alejandro Portés and Richard Schauffler, "Language and the Second Generation: Bilingualism Yesterday and Today," in Alejandro Portés (ed.), *The New Second Generation* (New York: Russell Sage Foundation, 1996), pp. 8–29.

74. Linda Chavez, "Hispanics vs. Their Leaders," *Commentary* (October 1991), pp. 47–49.

75. U.S. English. Accessed online at www.us-english.org/foundation/ [July 18, 2007].

76. Rasmussen Reports, "85% Support English as Official Language of U.S." Accessed online at www.rasmussenreports.com/2006/June%20Dailies/EnglishAsNationalLanguage.htm [July 18, 2007].

77. See Pew Hispanic Center, "Hispanic Attitudes Toward Learning English (2006). Accessed online at http://pewhispanic.org/files/factsheets/20.pdf [July 18, 2007]; Public Agenda, "Immigration: People's Chief Concerns." Accessed online at www.publicagenda.org/issues [July 18, 2007].

78. Rubén G. Rumbaut and Alejandro Portés, *Ethnicities: Children of Immigrants in America* (Berkeley: University of California Press, 2001).

79. Rubén G. Rumbaut, "A Language Graveyard? Immigration, Generation, and Linguistic Acculturation in the United States," paper presented to the International Conference on The Integration of Immigrants: Language and

Educational Achievement, Social Science Research Center, Berlin, Germany, June 30-July 1, 2005.

80. U.S. Census Bureau, *Census 2000 Supplementary Survey,* Table PO35.

81. Rubén G. Rumbaut, "Origins and Destinies: Immigration to the United States since World War II," *Sociological Forum* 9 (1994): 615.

82. Martin E. Spencer, "Multiculturalism, Political Correctness and the Politics of Identity," *Sociological Forum* 9 (December 1994): 547–67.

83. Jacob Weisbergm, "Thin Skins," *New Republic* (February 18, 1991): 23.

84. John J. Miller, *The Unmaking of Americans: How Multiculturalism Has Undermined America's Assimilation Ethic* (New York: Simon & Schuster, 1998).

85. U.S. Census Bureau, "U.S. Interim Projections by Age, Race, and Hispanic Origin," (Washington, DC: U.S. Government Printing Office, 2004).

86. Ibid.

87. U.S. Census Bureau, *Statistical Abstract of the United States: 2007*, Table 58, p. 52

88. Ibid.

89. George A. Yancey and Sherelyn W. Yancey, "Black–White Differences in the Use of Personal Advertisements for Individuals Seeking Interracial Relationships," *Journal of Black Studies* 27 (May 1997): 650–67.

90. George A. Yancey and Sherelyn W. Yancey, "Interracial Dating: Evidence from Personal Advertisement," *Journal of Family Issues* 19 (May 1998): 334–48.

91. Richard Lewis Jr., George Yancey, and Siri S. Bletzer, "Racial and Nonracial Factors That Influence Spouse Choice in Black/White Marriages," *Journal of Black Studies* 28 (September 1997): 60–78.

92. Adam B. Troy, Jamie Lewis-Smith, and Philippe Laurenceau, "Interracial and Intra-racial Romantic Relationships: The Search for Differences in Satisfaction, Conflict, and Attachment Style," *Journal of Social and Personal Relationships* 23 (2006): 665–80.

93. Suzanne Model and Gene Fisher, "Black–White Unions: West Indians and African Americans Compared," *Demography* 38 (2001): 177–85.

94. George Yancey, "Who Interracially Dates: An Examination of the Characteristics of Those Who Have Interracially Dated," *Journal of Comparative Family Studies* 33 (2002): 179–90.

95. New America Media, *California Dreamers: A Public Opinion Portrait of the Most Diverse Generation the Nation Has Ever Known.* Accessed online at http://news.newamericamedia.org/news/view_custom.html?custom_page_id=340 [July 31, 2007].

96. Kathleen Odell Korgen, *From Black to Biracial: Transforming Racial Identity among Americans* (Westport, CT: Praeger, 1998).

Index

of Jews, 100
in mass media, 72, 74–77, 475, 476
model-minority, 295–296
of Mormons, 441
of Native Americans, 211–212,
221–222
negative self-image and, 99
of people with disabilities, 516–517
racial profiling, 89
of religious groups, 435
of strangers, 8
of terrorists, 332
Stonewall Inn, New York City, 504
Strangers, 4–10, 539, 556
Stratification. *See also* Social class
ethnic, 53–57
social, 43–44
U.S. system, 541, 546
Strip mining, 239, 240
Structural assimilation
defined, 46, 116
of Hispanic Americans, 394, 396, 401
of Italians, 195
of Japanese Americans, 279
of Koreans, 287
of Middle Eastern Americans, 329
Structural conditions
culture and, 43
for the Dutch, 139–140
for European immigrants, 169–170
for Hispanic Americans, 384–385
for Middle East immigrants, 304–306
in pre-Civil War period, 133–135
Structural differentiation, 44, 52–53,
219–221
Structural pluralism, 120–121
Student Nonviolent Coordinating
Committee (SNCC), 347, 348,
351
Subcultures, 40–42
Amish, 448–452
Cajuns, 143–144
convergent, 41
French Canadians, 144–145
Gypsies, 189–191
persistent, 41–42, 94, 189
of poverty, 48–49
religious minorities, 448–452, 454
Subordinate group, 53
Suburban sprawl, 243–244
Suffrage movement, 472–473
Sugar industry, 402, 403
Suicide, 237, 525, 526
Superordinate group, 53
Supreme Court rulings
affirmative action, 86–87
on age-related job discrimination, 527
Amish education, 451
on animal sacrifice, 456
desegregation, 342, 346

forced repatriation, 371
on gay rights, 505
on Japanese issues, 274, 278
on Native American issues, 225, 243,
246–247
on polygyny, 441
religious freedom, 460–461
on segregation, 342
on sexual harassment, 492
"white persons" defined, 280, 308
Sweatshops, 110, 112, 421
Sweden, 220
Swedish Americans, 157, 158, 542
Sweet Grass Hills, Montana, 239
Swiss Anabaptists, 448
Symbolic ethnicity, 549, 553–554
Symbolic interaction, 25–26
Symbols, 25, 34–36
Syrian Christians, 201
Syrian immigrants, 309, 314, 318–322,
328, 332, 445

Tagalogs, 280
Tai Dam, 291
Tailhook military scandal, 490
Taiping Rebellion, 262
Taiwanese immigrants, 272
Tammany Hall, New York, 153
Taos Pueblo, 243, 246
Technology
communication for deaf people, 512
structural conditions and, 43
Television. *See also* Advertising; Media
and ethnogenesis, 143
and prejudice, 72, 74–75, 76
views of lifestyles, 346
Telkeffes, 327
Termination Act (1953), 229–230
Terrorism, 306, 317, 323, 348, 428, 447,
462, 556
Texas, Hopwood v., 86
Texas, Lawrence v., 505
Thailand, 291
Thais, 271, 276
Thatcher, Margaret, 139
Thayer, Webster, 192, 199
Theosophy, 458
Thomas, Clarence, 490
Thomas, William I., 36, 180, 181, 497
Thomas theorem, 36–37
Three-generation hypothesis, 541–543
Time, cultural attitude toward, 388
Total fertility rate, 522, 523
Toxic Substance Control Act, 243
Toxic-waste dumping, 242–243
Trail of Tears, 105, 227
Transcendental Meditation, 458
Transnationalism, 544, 545
Treaties with Native Americans, 218,
223, 225, 226, 246, 247

Treaty of Guadalupe Hidalgo, 383
Treaty of Paris (1898), 384
Tribal Colleges Executive Order, 233
Tribal enterprise, 235
Tribal relationships, 220–221, 253
Triple melting pot theory, 119, 438, 462,
572
Tuberculosis, 271, 296
Tule Lake, California, 277
Turkey, 42, 201, 319
Turkish immigrants, 318, 327–329
Tuscarora tribe, 219, 247
Tuskegee Institute, 107
Tyding-McDuffie Act (1935), 282

Ukrainian immigrants, 185–186, 187
Undocumented aliens
as current ethnic issue, 555, 559–560
Haitians, 371
Hispanic, 385, 397, 399, 415, 420,
421
in Italy, 171
Mexicans, 559–560
Union of Russian Workers, 184
Unitarian Church, 444
United Farm Workers Union, 400
United Nations
estimate of disabled population, 510
Navajo appeal to, 241
United States
colonial period, 129–130
early national period, 130–132
immigration controls, 103
Native American policy compared to
Latin American, 217
pre-Civil War period, 132–135
settlement patterns, 550–552
stratification system, 541, 546
United States, Endo v., 278
United States, Korematsu v., 278
United States, Reynolds v., 441
Unity syndrome, 6
Universal Declaration of Human Rights,
241
University of Alabama, 348, 349
University of the West Indies (UWI), 453
Upward mobility
of black Americans, 342, 366, 367
of Catholics, 433
in conflict theory, 205
IQ testing and, 355–356
of Irish Americans, 153–154
of Italian Americans, 195
of Jewish Americans, 436–437, 464
of Polish Americans, 181–182
of Slavic immigrants, 179
structural conditions and economy, 43
of Syrian Americans, 321–322
of women, 485
Urban Institute, 509

Credits

People Who Spoke a Language Other Than English at Home, 2000

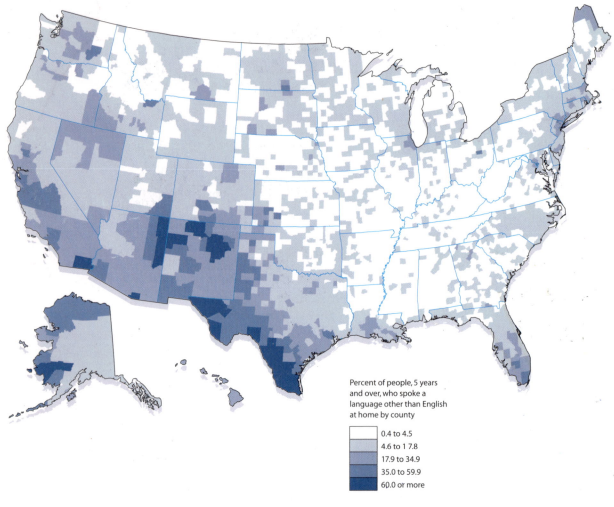

Percent of people, 5 years
and over, who spoke a
language other than English
at home by county

- 0.4 to 4.5
- 4.6 to 1 7.8
- 17.9 to 34.9
- 35.0 to 59.9
- 60.0 or more

Source: U.S. Census Bureau, Census 2000 Summary File 3.

Total Immigration to the United States from 1820 to 2000, by Decade

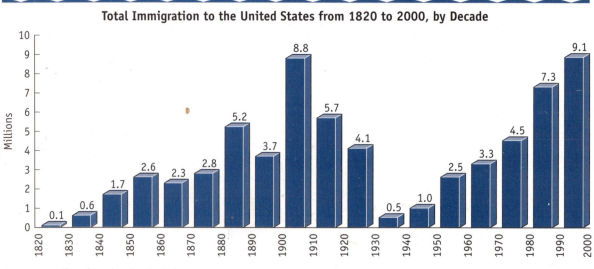

Source: U.S. Office of Immigration Statistics.